Understanding the Biological Basis of Behavior

Rik Carl D'Amato • Andrew S. Davis
Elizabeth M. Power • Eleazar Cruz Eusebio
Editors

Understanding the Biological Basis of Behavior

Developing Evidence-Based Interventions for Clinical, Counseling and School Psychologists

Springer

Editors
Rik Carl D'Amato
Department of School Psychology
The Chicago School of Professional
Psychology and Presence Learning
Chicago, IL, USA

Andrew S. Davis
Neuropsychology Laboratory, Department
of Educational Psychology
Ball State University
Muncie, IN, USA

Elizabeth M. Power
Department of School Psychology
The College of Saint Rose
Albany, NY, USA

Eleazar Cruz Eusebio
School Psychology
Prince George's County Public Schools
Adelphi, MA, USA

ISBN 978-3-030-59161-8 ISBN 978-3-030-59162-5 (eBook)
https://doi.org/10.1007/978-3-030-59162-5

This Springer imprint is published by the registered company Springer Nature Switzerland AG
The registered company address is: Gewerbestrasse 11, 6330 Cham, Switzerland

This book is dedicated to my sons and their families, Michael and Charissa, and David and Lizzie. Thank you for demonstrating the power of love in your lives. It is the most important emotion that can positively change the world. Each day of your lives you make me proud.

–Rik Carl D'Amato

This book is dedicated to my friend and mentor, Dr. Rik Carl D'Amato, who helped me realize that I had the potential to become a scholar.

–Andrew S. Davis

To my parents, Sue and Tom, and my siblings, Tom, Kate, and Maureen. This book is also dedicated to my closest friends, especially my strong female warriors.

–Elizabeth M. Power

To my beautiful sons, Asher and Bodhi. You are my life's greatest inspiration.

–Eleazar Cruz Eusebio

Foreword

For too long, clinical neuropsychology has been thought of as a set of tests or intervention techniques. It is not, and this work demonstrates this fact clearly. Neuropsychology is the study of brain-behavior relationships, and clinical neuropsychology is the application of this knowledge base to the clinical problems of individuals. What this means is that clinical neuropsychology is a way of thinking about and conceptualizing behavior and related clinical presentations. In this sense, all tests are neuropsychological tests if interpreted from this framework—just as all interventions are neuropsychological if conceptualized from the same framework. As my colleague Dr. Erin Bigler is fond of reminding us all, *every behavior has an anatomy*. Not all schools of thought in psychology would agree, but neuropsychology would, and as our study of neurobiology of behavior advances, we see more and more evidence that this is so.

This work captures the fundamental conceptual basis as well as the evidentiary basis that underlies neuropsychological practice. Clinical neuropsychology is presented not as a set of techniques, but as a way of understanding behavior and how to be a more effective change agent where a brain-behavior perspective is the best avenue of thought. It is then appropriate that the foundations part of the book focuses on neurobiology, both normal and abnormal in its development and how we currently study it, emphasizing advances in neuroimaging, an area that is moving remarkably quickly and at times astounding in what it promises to reveal in the near future. Each chapter in this part does a good job of staying focused on why this is important to conceptualizing our practice.

This is not a book for the journeyman neuropsychologist – rather it is a work focused on the original clinical specialties of psychology (clinical, counseling, and school) and how to conceptualize and understand the neurobiology of behavior and apply it to everyday problems of practice, using science as the basis for our work as opposed to faddish adoption of the newest catchphrase related to the brain and improving its function. Links to practice in each of these areas of specialization are emphasized throughout the work generally and then tied together in the concluding part of the work. I do think if read early enough in one's career, it will inspire more clinicians, established and in training, to move to neuropsychology as a field of study and practice.

This is also an optimistic work – it not only gives us a foundation of thinking but links it to science and to practice – and takes the position that we can have a positive impact on patient outcomes in all spheres of our practice, whether as a treatment provider or consultant to other healthcare providers, if we understand the impact of the patient's neurobiology on their behavior and stay close to our science. I agree.

Kudos to all involved in this work–well accomplished.

Cecil R. Reynolds
Austin, TX, USA
September 2020

Preface

The field of clinical neuropsychology has given greater focus to the influence of biological variables in research and in the clinical practice of psychology. Along with several professional organizations, the field has supported the study of our biological aspects of behavior. In fact, all doctoral psychology programs approved by the American Psychological Association (APA) must include a course concerning the biological aspects of behavior. This book has been developed to meet the need as an introductory neuroscience, neurobiology, and neuropsychology text for health service psychologists, including clinical, counseling, and school psychologists-in-training, as well as for related health service practitioners.

Within the last several decades, clinical neuropsychology has gained wide recognition with relevance to family medicine, behavioral neurology, psychiatry, as well as clinical, counseling, and school psychology. Although the history of neuropsychological practice is rooted in its efforts to develop techniques to assist in differential diagnosis comparing functional to organic causes of behavior, contemporary neuropsychology has begun to redefine its role, seeking the scientific knowledge and tools to be able to answer more practical questions related to positive psychology and health as well as pathology and evidence-based behavioral change. The growth of neuropsychology has led to the development of new subspecialties including pediatric neuropsychology, school neuropsychology, geriatric neuropsychology, forensic neuropsychology, pediatric psychology, and rehabilitation neuropsychology. Many texts focus on a single subject such as forensic neuropsychology or a *single* age group such as pediatric or school neuropsychology. One goal of this book is to evaluate and offer information for clinical psychologists, counseling psychologists, and school psychologists who serve clients of **all ages** in a variety of professional **settings**, such as schools, hospitals, colleges/universities, business/organizations, and clinics. The application of neuroscientific findings must be our focus in all human service practice areas including psychology.

Current approaches to neuropsychological services focus on rehabilitation where the most commonly used intervention strategies generally target environmental modifications, compensatory strategies, mental health behaviors, or restorative counseling approaches. Because brain injuries often affect multiple systems, intervention typically includes a variety of these approaches. In all situations, engaging the client and their support system (i.e., family) in a collaborative relationship to develop meaningful measurable functional goals is critical. Environmental modifications are used to address elements of the client environment to reduce the impact of the impairment.

Several influences will likely continue to shape the future of clinical neuropsychology. Specific advances in neuroimaging, psychopharmacology, and neurofeedback have dramatically affected the scope of neuropsychological practice. In addition, rehabilitation neuropsychologists are faced with increasing pressure to demonstrate empirically based practice that is ecologically valid for unique populations. With this understanding of the neurological aspects of many behaviors, current intervention options have significantly expanded. In addition to shaping the role of clinical neuropsychologists, scientific advancements have provided researchers and practitioners with new techniques to study developmental changes in the brain to understand neuroplasticity and neuroreorganization. The critical ability to evaluate the complex interactions between cognitive, emotional, social, and situational influences will be required for psychologists to make predictions regarding client abilities related to life enhancement and neurobiological understanding.

Today, clinical neuropsychologists are expected to demonstrate proficiency in choosing their assessment tools and methodology when addressing more complex questions such as predicting a client's ability to function in a particular context given an increasingly diverse population. In addition, neuropsychologists must address whether particular techniques are valid for individuals from different cultural and linguistic backgrounds and in various contexts. Moreover, the field must consider the recent dual pandemic, referring to the simultaneous COVID-19 pandemic and social unrest due to racial inequity, when completing comprehensive evaluations and offering appropriate services. The future of applied human service psychology will depend on the ability to accurately assess neuropsychological impairment in addition to reliably identifying appropriate, effective, and innovative interventions that are scientifically valid. As neuropsychology is grounded in a rich history of empiricism that is constantly influenced by advancements in related fields, psychologists who understand the interactions between physical and psychological processes and individual social environments are uniquely positioned to integrate information across disciplines in an effort to understand each client's central nervous system functioning – subsequently, they must develop and monitor the effectiveness of individually tailored and functionally related treatment plans. With each bit of new knowledge the boundry between behavior and biology continues to merge and one day these two disciplines may evolve into an integrated human service practitioner.

We believe the composition of the authors of our book, who are some of the leading scientists the neurosciences (including psychology), is noteworthy. These authors call for the advancement of our practice, and we want to thank them for their innovative and timely contributions. The enduring contribution of neuroscience in modern times will likely remain contingent upon each psychology practitioner's commitment to socially just, ethically based, empirically focused practice, continuing education, and scientific discovery. The challenge to health service psychologists will be in meeting the needs of an increasingly diverse population by providing quality evidence-based ecologically valid neuropsychological interventions currently not abundant or available in the field.

Chicago, IL, USA — Rik Carl D'Amato
Muncie, IN, USA — Andrew S. Davis
Albany, NY, USA — Elizabeth M. Power
Adelphi, MA, USA — Eleazar Cruz Eusebio

Contents

Contributors

Christopher Anzalone Department of Psychology, University of South Carolina, Columbia, SC, USA

Cortney Bindrich Private Practice, Chicago, IL, USA

Rachel M. Bridges Department of Psychology, University of South Carolina, Columbia, SC, USA

Elise M. Chalus Department of School Psychology, The Chicago School of Professional Psychology, Chicago, IL, USA

Jacob Yuichung Chan Department of Counseling, Psychology & Guidance Services, Ball State University, Muncie, IN, USA

Mary (Rina) M. Chittooran Educational Policy and Equity Program, Saint Louis University, Saint Louis, MO, USA

Caitlin Cox Treffert Department of School Psychology, The Chicago School of Professional Psychology, Chicago, IL, USA

Rik Carl D'Amato Department of School Psychology, The Chicago School of Professional Psychology and PresenceLearning, Chicago, IL, USA

Andrew S. Davis Department of Educational Psychology, Ball State University, Muncie, IN, USA

Scott L. Decker Department of Psychology, University of South Carolina, Columbia, SC, USA

Eleazar Cruz Eusebio School Psychology, Prince George's County Public School, Adelphi, MD, USA

Stephanie Forness Canvas Health, Forest Lake, MN, USA

Whitney Gibson Department of School Psychology, The Chicago School of Professional Psychology, Chicago, IL, USA

Alyssa Gonzalez Department of Educational Psychology, Texas A&M University, College Station, TX, USA

Jaclyn Hoffmeister Department of School Psychology, The Chicago School of Professional Psychology, Chicago, IL, USA

Tiffany Keller Department of School Psychology, The Chicago School of Professional Psychology, Chicago, IL, USA

Jessica C. Luedke Department of Psychology, University of South Carolina, Columbia, SC, USA

Richard McNulty Department of Psychology, The University of Memphis, Memphis, TX, USA

Erica McConnell Department of School Psychology, University of Northern Colorado, Greeley, CO, USA

Sydney Mitchell Department of School Psychology, The College of Saint Rose, Albany, NY, USA

Chad A. Noggle School of Medicine, Southern Illinois University, Carbondale, IL, USA

Kristin Perrone-McGovern Department of Counseling, Social Psychology, and Counseling, Ball State University, Muncie, IN, USA

Anna Pignatiello Department of School Psychology, The Chicago School of Professional Psychology, Chicago, IL, USA

Elizabeth M. Power Department of School Psychology, The College of Saint Rose, Albany, NY, USA

Cynthia A. Riccio Department of Educational Psychology, Texas A&M University, College Station, TX, USA

Christy Roman Department of School Psychology, The Chicago School of Professional Psychology, Chicago, IL, USA

Walter R. Schamber Clinical Psychology, Fairview, PA, USA

Ashley Schoener Department of Counseling, Social Psychology, and Counseling, Ball State University, Muncie, IN, USA

Bethany M. Schwandt Department of Educational Psychology, Ball State University, Muncie, IN, USA

Margaret Semrud-Clikeman University of Minnesota Medical School, Minneapolis, MN, USA

Cathrine M. Short Department of Educational Psychology, Ball State University, Muncie, IN, USA

Amanda Skierkiewicz Clinical Neuropsychology, Landstrom Center, Schaumburg, IL, USA

Amanda R. Slonaker Indianapolis Neurobehavioral Health Center, Muncie, IN, USA

Linda Huilin Sun Department of Educational Psychology, Texas A&M University, College Station, TX, USA

Michael J. Tincup Rowland Unified School District, Rowland Heights, CA, USA

Jonathan E. Titley Rocklin Unified School District, Rocklin, CA, USA

Catherine Van Damme Department of School Psychology, The Chicago School of Professional Psychology, Chicago, IL, USA

Gertina Van Schalkwyk Department of Psychology, University of Macau, Zhuhai, China

Fan Wu Office of the Provost, University of Houston, Houston, TX, USA

Christina Zafiris Department of Neuropsychology, University of Miami/Jackson Memorial Hospital, West Palm Beach, FL, USA

Part I
Introduction and Foundations of Clinical Practice

Chapter 1
Understanding the Past, Present, and Future of Clinical Neuropsychology from a Health Service Provider Perspective

Catherine Van Damme and Rik Carl D'Amato

Learning Objectives

- To understand the basic concepts of clinical neuropsychology.
- To understand how clinical neuropsychology fits within a health service psychology framework.
- To understand the major health service provider specialties in psychology and when is post-doctoral training required.
- To understand information on training and licensing for clinical neuropsychologists.
- To understand the services that a clinical neuropsychologist provides.
- To understand the highest level of expertise needed in clinical neuropsychology.

Understanding the History of Clinical Neuropsychology

The science of psychology is linked to current medical advances which have culminated in improved living. Clinical neuropsychology is the study of the relationship between the human brain and behavior (MacNeil et al., 2008; Meier, 1974; Smith & Moulin, 2012). Our brain is the basic and complex foundation for which all human interactions originate including simple to complex behaviors and thoughts. Today,

C. Van Damme
Department of School Psychology, The Chicago School of Professional Psychology, Chicago, IL, USA

R. C. D'Amato (✉)
Department of School Psychology, The Chicago School of Professional Psychology, Chicago, IL, USA

School Psychcology, Presence Learning, New York, NY, USA
e-mail: rdamato@thechicagoschool.edu; rik.damato@presencelearning.com

R. C. D'Amato et al. (eds.), *Understanding the Biological Basis of Behavior*,
https://doi.org/10.1007/978-3-030-59162-5_1

researchers understand the brain because of historical knowledge from dozens of real-life cases. The study of psychology became a cornerstone for advancing areas of science, understanding, improving life, and helping humankind lead to societal change (Schultz & Schultz, 2015). The focus of this chapter is on understanding the importance of our biological basis of behavior and how it interacts to shape individuals, society, and the world. This chapter will integrate where clinical neuropsychology has been, where clinical neuropsychology is now, and where clinical neuropsychology will be going in the future. A special focus will be on relating clinical, counseling, and school psychology to the practice of clinical neuropsychology. The chapter will conclude with a focus on how one may become a clinical neuropsychologist and what current standards of training would need to be followed.

Most practicing psychologists know the famous case of Phineas Gage, the man who survived the metal rod and was arguably one of the first neuroscience cases (Larner & Leach, 2002). Phineas was a railroad worker, and an explosion thrusted a metal rod through his skull destroying most of his frontal lobe. Detailed accounts showed that after the rod pierced his skull, he was talking and aware of his surroundings in only a few minutes. Early on, practitioners believed that any significant damage to the brain would cause complete dysfunction in the individual such as resulting in a irreparable brain damage and total dysfunction (D'Amato & Hartlage, 2008). What happened in the nineteenth century helped to clarify that there are distinct structures with unique functions in the human brain. Moreover, this case demonstrated that the brain has a significant impact on each individual's personality; in the example of Mr. Gage's, he experienced a serious personality shift from a competent adult to an erratic and often angry man. This case example was one of many such studies that have demonstrated the impact of localized brain injuries on human behavior (Dean & Reynolds, 1997; Pankseep & Biven, 2012). Today we understand the brain more than ever and can apply treatment to a localized injury area. Neuropsychological practices can be implemented in the assessment and diagnosis of patients, as well as to determine the most effective treatment for patients. The American Psychological Association (APA), the largest group of psychologists in the world, oversees professional development, training, and credentialing with model licensure acts and professional associations found in every state encompassing the diverse field of psychology. The APA is organized according to more than 50 divisions that relate to specialty areas with Division 40 labeled as the Society for Clinical Neuropsychology which is most related to this text. Other professional associations such as the National Academy of Neuropsychology, the International Neuropsychological Society, and the American Board of Professional Psychology also are leading organizations which help to define, articulate, and advocate for understanding and training related to our biological basis of behavior, affective, social, and cognitive functioning. Through a neuropsychological perspective, researchers and clinicians alike can use what neuropsychology has to offer by developing treatments based on patient cognitive strengths and weaknesses to implement treatments that best match the cognitive capabilities of those patients (Power & D'Amato, 2018).

Altogether, neuropsychology was a major transition for the field of psychology from the work of Reitan who indicated at the beginning of his career his focus on neuropsychology which was seen as aberrant to the times (Reitan & Wolfson, 1985). Most departments and universities abandoned their historical focus on psychoanalysis and now focused on behavior. Over Reitan's life, he saw a complete change as journals who initially rejected his articles were then seeking his research which focused on neuropsychology and brain-behavior relations. The zeitgeist of the times had changed from psychoanalysis to behaviorism and now to clinical neuropsychology and behavioral neuroscience.

The Past: Foundations of Clinical Neuropsychology

Origins of Neuropsychology

Neuropsychology is the combination of several mental and physical sciences combined to create a field focused on brain and behavior relationships. While all science has advanced, so has neuropsychology which absorbed new information and applied it within a clinical framework. Specifically, as researchers continue to understand the brain through localized injury, they are able to better understand the behavioral outcomes related to each specific deficit, and study brain damage. Witsken, D'Amato, and Hartlage (2008), p. 5 defined clinical neuropsychology as "the scientific application of psychological and psychometric measurement procedures to assess and understand behaviors related to the central nervous system."

History of Rehabilitation

Rehabilitation focuses on developing a lost skill or teaching a new skill. One of the first rehabilitation programs was focused on developing and/or restoring reading skills (Boake, 2003). Later rehabilitation focused on treating brain injury, specifically New York University developed one of the first traumatic brain injury programs (Rothlisberg et al., 2003). This program revolutionized the way we currently treat brain injury, focusing on preparing the individual for the future through teaching skills and supporting family engagement. The program developed a six-stage growth model for individuals who had brain injuries (see Table 1.1).

The World Wars

As the wars took place over the twentieth century, there was an increased demand for psychologists based on evaluation and treatment needs (Kennedy & Moore, 2010; Schultz & Schultz, 2015). Both World War I and World War II created a large number of veterans who required psychological support after the stress and damage

Table 1.1 Clinical/cognitive stages of growth

Stage 1	Improve alertness, attention, and concentration
Stage 2	Develop self-awareness of the brain injury and adjust to the change
Stage 3	Master cognitive tasks
Stage 4	Control compensatory strategies
Stage 5	Accept the limits due to brain injury
Stage 6	Establish an identity

Note: Six stages are taken from Rothlisberg et al. (2003)

inflicted by combat. In addition, many of the most prominent psychologists fled to the United States during World War II which brought with a great body of research and interest to the scientific community (Schultz & Schultz, 2015). Prior to the World Wars, there were two types of clinical psychologists: the first were those who conducted psychotherapy and mental health counseling, and the latter focused on psychometrics and took a more analytical approach focused on assessment (D'Amato et al. & Dean, 2011). After the wars, many clinicians trained in both models to allow assessment to *drive* intervention rather than having two distinct entities.

Early Neuropsychologists

Early neuropsychology developed as both a clinical and research specialty which was focused on understanding areas of damage to the brain. For example, Marshall Hall learned that damaging and decapitated animals lead to specific behavioral outcomes (Schultz & Schultz, 2015). Pierre Flourens destroyed parts of the brain in pigeons hoping to understand the human brain. Marc Dax in 1836 wrote a paper on damage to the left hemisphere and the impact on an individual's behavior (Benton, 2000; Schultz & Schultz, 2015). Later, Paul Broca, the well-known surgeon, found supporting evidence that language is impacted when damange to the left hemisphere of the brain occurs (Broca, 1960/1865). Researchers then took on the challenge to start mapping out the human brain, which in part is correct because specific areas have been found to correlate with behaviors (Benton, 2000; Parks, Levine & Long, 1998). However, this was a misled endevour due to the wrong singular application approach, today we understand that each area has a number of purposes and functions (Dean & Noggle, 2013a; 2013b; MacNeil et al, 2008; Smith & Moulin, 2012).

The Present: Current Practice of Clinical Neuropsychologist

Modern medicine and technological advances have revolutionized the role of the clinical neuropsychologist. In the past, the neuropsychologist used assessments to identify brain damage in patients. Then as technology advanced with scanning, we were able to see where the brain damage was through brain imaging (Papanicolaou,

2017). Now, we understand the brain-behavior relationship and that assessments can be used to inform treatment interventions. Neuropsychology has been argued as a way of thinking rather than simply a battery of tests (Davis & D'Amato, 2005; D'Amato, 1990; Power & D'Amato, 2018). It is true that neuropsychologists use a range of diverse tests to assess individuals; however, a patient who achieves a specific score can be viewed differently by health service provider psychologists. One train of thought could indicate a behavioral impairment, while the other may indicate cerebral dysfunction requiring specific rehabilitation. Thus, the same data may be interpreted differently from practitioners with distinct theoretical training (D'Amato & Rothlisberg, 1992/1997). Throughout the rigorous training regimen to becoming a neuropsychologist—this distinct perception and understanding of human behavior and cognitive capabilities was established. Clinical neuropsychologists are skilled in the assessment, interpretation, and treatment of comprehensive psychological disorders. Essential skills include neuropsychological assessment techniques, intervention techniques, research design and analysis, professional issues and ethics, culturally competent approaches, and understanding of implications of conditions for behavior and adjustment (Davis & D'Amato, 2014; Lezak et al., 2012; Zaroff & D'Amato, 2015). Competence in clinical neuropsychology requires the ability to integrate findings with medical knowledge, psychosocial and behavioral data, as well as the experise from from the neurosciences, to interpret findings in light of an appreciation of ecological and ethical issues (APA, 2017; D'Amato et al., 2005). Progress monitoring data can also be collected via neuropsychological assessment with a focus on cognitive or social-emotional processing. For example, a child with attention deficit/hyperactivity disorder (ADHD) can benefit from regular progress monitoring when a teacher completes a daily sheet based on both positive and negative work completion. In this example, progress monitoring consists of an analysis of the child's data and developing a report to provide feedback to the child and the family. A related concept is the topic of self-monitoring which is often used with individuals who have experienced a traumatic brain injury, such as setting a timer before turning on the stove to help manage a potentially dangerous living situation or using biofeedback to help regulate physiological symptoms related to anxiety.

The Health Service Provider and Clinical Practice

To be an effective psychologist, the clinician must be trained in the comprehensive basics of professional practice. In students' first years of training, they are given opportunities to develop both practical skills and theoretical underpinnings. Clinicians must attain competency in a variety of psychological domains including the biological and cognitive aspects and the affective basis of behavior. The purpose of this text is to teach the biological aspects of behavior but also to achieve an understanding of the neuroscientific systems of psychology and the cognitive aspects of behavior. Health service psychology covers the initial, middle, and end of both the developing human lifespan as well as advancing public health and university training programs. For example, learning about neurodevelopment will help a patient understand why they present in a certain fashion with a type of problem. For advanced practicum, it will help diagnose and recommend future and appropriate services, knowing the outcome of the client given the unique neurodiversity of the individual. In addition, professional and personal development is achieved through the training stages of practicum, advanced practicum, and internship training.

"Health Service Psychology: *is defined as the integration of psychological science and practice in order to facilitate human development and functioning. Health service psychology includes the generation and provision of knowledge and practices that encompass a wide range of professional activities relevant to health promotion, prevention, consultation, assessment, and treatment for psychological and other health-related disorders. Programs that are accredited to provide training in health service psychology prepare individuals to work in diverse settings with diverse populations. Individuals who engage in health service psychology have been appropriately trained to be eligible for licensure as doctoral-level psychologists."* (American Psychological Association, 2017, p. 2)

Understanding Medicine as It Relates to Psychology

The human body is a complex system that requires training specialties to treat and support a healthy person. Figure 1.1 demonstrates the variety of focus areas a practicing doctor can specialize in according to the American Medical Association (2014).

As health service psychologists, we are trained to support the overall health of human beings. To do this, the psychologist must not only be able to understand psychological symptoms but also help to connect patients with related services. For instance, an individual might suffer from depression and clearly demonstrate symptoms, but their hearing might be declining which presents as a reduction in the amount of social interactions. Having a trained psychologist recommending yearly doctor visits to get general testing can help to reduce and remove missed areas that support healthy human development. Alternatively, an individual might suffer from a lifelong disorder such as congenital anomalies which present as anxiety related to the outcomes. Together psychologists, physicians, and patients can increase positive outcomes through consultation and collaboration. Table 1.2 demonstrates the areas of specialty across the world according to the *International Classification of Diseases, Tenth Edition* (ICD-10).

The application of neuropsychological research for professionals has broadened and reached out to an array of fields (e.g., forensic neuropsychology, school psychology) and is not only used by researchers but also hospitals, prisons, and other vocational settings. Clinical neuropsychology is now very much valued as involving the assessment of cognitive pathology and playing a major role in the rehabilitation

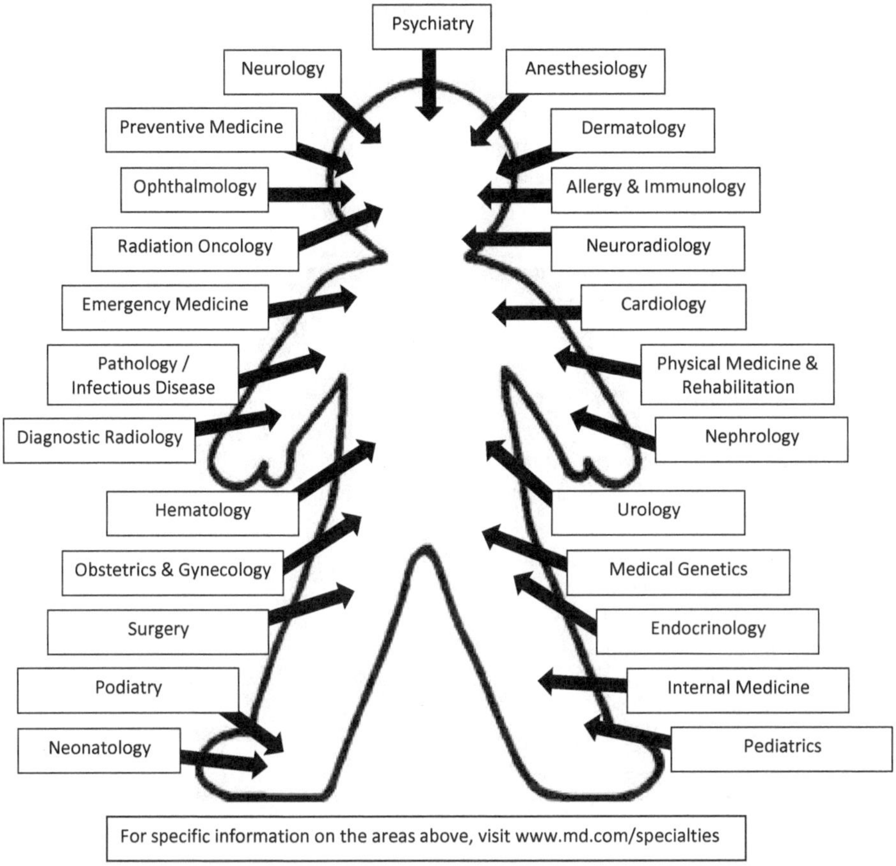

Fig. 1.1 Graphic Display of Medical Podiatry Nephrology Specialty Areas Podiatry

of patients (Goldstein & McNeil, 2012). Neuropsychologists conduct comprehensive evaluations to determine appropriate supports for patients who may have difficulty learning or functioning in daily life (Power & D'Amato, 2018). For example, the ability to live alone, drive a car, or take care of others is often critical to living independently. It is important to delineate the difference between brain scanning techniques which reveal the presence of abnormalities and how such neurological abnormalities impact life functioning. Indeed, brain damage alone does not reveal clear behavioral outcomes until considered within the context of rehabilitation and a full comprehensive neuropsychological evaluation. Medical technology alone is not sufficient for understanding behavioral outcomes – clinical neuropsychology should offer recommendations for understanding behavioral results related to everyday living. In general, brain impairment can take the form of degenerative diseases, traumatic injury, infections, and environmental toxins. All of these challenges create the need for comprehensively trained psychologists to work as health service providers.

Table 1.2 International Classification of Diseases, Tenth Edition (ICD-10) – areas of focus

1: Infectious and Parasitic Diseases
2: Neoplasms
3: Endocrine, Nutritional and Metabolic Diseases, and Immunity Disorders
4: Diseases of the Blood and Blood-Forming Organs
5: Mental, Behavioral, and Neurodevelopmental Disorders
6: Diseases of the Nervous System
7: Diseases of the Eye and Adnexa
8: Diseases of the Ear and Mastoid Process
9: Diseases of the Circulatory System
10: Diseases of the Respiratory System
11: Diseases of the Digestive System
12: Diseases of the Skin and Subcutaneous Tissue
13: Complications of Pregnancy
14: Diseases of the Genitourinary System
15: Diseases of the Musculoskeletal System and Connective Tissue
16: Congenital Anomalies
17: Certain Conditions Originating in the Perinatal Period
18: Symptoms, Signs, Ill-Defined Conditions
19: Injury, Poisoning, External Causes
20: Factors Influencing Health
21: External Causes of Morbidity

Note: The classifications above are from the American Medical Association (2014)

Practice of Clinical Neuropsychology

One of the largest growth areas in the field of psychology has been the practice of clinical neuropsychology (Davis & D'Amato, 2005; Davis, 2011). In fact, researchers have analyzed job openings and found that a large number of positions required neuropsychological skills (D'Amato et al., 1987). As time goes on, the number of open positions only increase due to technology and transportation (Witsken et al., 2008). Advances in transportation and communications have revolutionized the amount of time it takes to provide emergency medical services to individuals in need. The 911 emergency system has allowed bystanders with cell phones to dispatch emergency services such as ambulances and helicopters in seconds. These technological advances reach more individuals than ever before and have drastically improved emergency medicine allowing experts to save individuals who even 10-years ago would have been lost. Concomitantly, advances in medical technology such as scanning techniques allow medical practitioners to diagnose and intervene with life-saving medicine (Dean & Noggle, 2013a; 2013b; Kennedy & Moore, 2010; Lee 2010). Figure 1.2 demonstrates the variety of populations health service psychologists can work with, along with the services provided and the setting in which they are located.

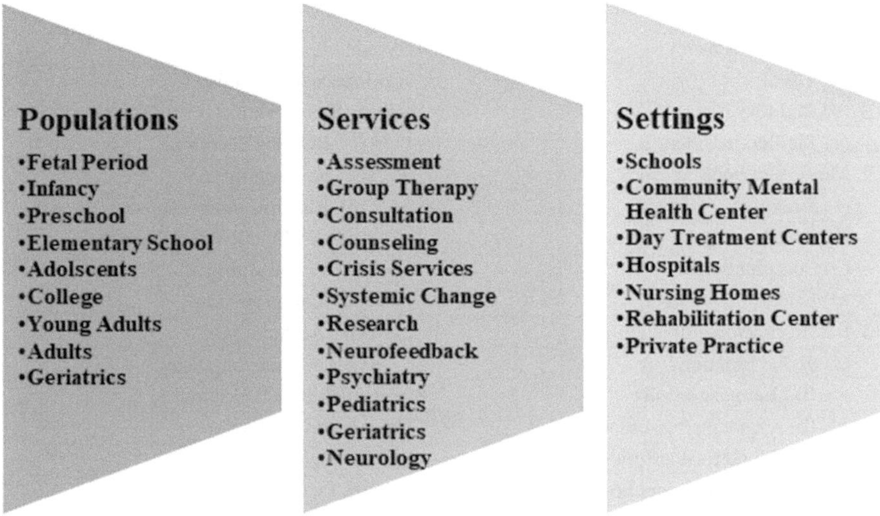

Fig. 1.2 Major areas of specialization by population, services, and settings

Since survival from a major accident or illness has dramatically increased, enduring aftercare treatment has also seen substantial growth with few psychological providers available. Moreover, advances in neonatal care and evidence-based practices greatly increased the survival rates of babies saved each year (Darmstadt et al., 2005, The Apgar score, 2006). Medical advances have created numerous populations (e.g., infant, toddler, children, adults, geriatrics) where providers are limited and these areas (i.e., geriatric neuropsychologists) will need workforce growth in the future. Prevention and intervention have created a need for services such as neurofeedback. Clinical hypnosis has provided opportunities to increase life satisfaction or, even more, to generally maintain physical health through regular exercise and healthy eating habits to increase overall life satisfaction. Today there is a focus on the importance of positive psychology groups and care groups focusing on grief, dieting, and smoking cessation. Most hospitals now provide preventative care to help support and enrich an individual's overall life. What society has now realized is that they need both psychological wellness and physical health to live a long life (Thornicroft & Tansella, 2004; Webb, 2011). This opens doors to the practice of psychology at every life stage to provide an abundance of services. The practice of psychology in medical settings is a growing and lucrative area of psychology starting with a comprehensive clinical interview including a medical, family, and environmental history. Appendix A provides a sample neuropsychological questionnaire developed by D'Amato et al. (2021). The questionnaire focuses on the presenting problem or reason for referral, living conditions, home environment, pregnancy, birth, development, medical history, socialization, current functioning, pathology, personality organization, and behavior. Table 1.3 demonstrates the areas a health

Table 1.3 What areas should be assessed from a neuropsychological assessment?

1. Perceptual/sensory	7. Academic achievement
(a) Visual	(a) Preacademic skills
(b) Auditory	(b) Academic skills
(c) Tactile/kinesthetic	(i) Reading decoding
2. Motor functions	(ii) Reading fluency
(a) Strength	(iii) Reading comprehension
(b) Speed	(iv) Arithmetic facts/calculation
(c) Coordination	(v) Social studies
(d) Lateral preference	(vi) Language arts
3. Intelligence/cognitive abilities	(vii) Science
(a) Verbal functions	(viii) Written language
(i) Language skills	8. Personality/behavior/family
(ii) Concepts/reasoning	(a) Adaptive behavior
(iii) Numerical abilities	(i) Daily living
(iv) Integrative functions	(ii) Development
4. Executive functioning/attention	(iii) Play/leisure
(a) Sustained attention	(b) Environmental/social
(b) Inhibition	(i) Parental/family
(c) Shifting set	(ii) School environment
(d) Problem-solving	(iii) Peers
5. Memory	(iv) Community
(a) Short-term memory	(c) Student coping/tolerance
(b) Long-term memory	(d) Family interpersonal style
(c) Working memory	9. Educational classroom environment
6. Communication/language skills	(a) Learning environment fit
(a) Phonological processing	(b) Peer reactions
(b) Listening comprehension	(c) Community reactions
(c) Expressive vocabulary	(d) Teacher/staff reactions
(d) Receptive vocabulary	(e) Classroom descriptions
(e) Speech/articulation	
(f) Pragmatics	

Note: Adapted from Power and D'Amato (2018)

service psychologist may have to investigate when working with an individual patient.

Above are the general areas a clinician should know to ask during an evaulation. This highlights the vast range of possible interventions that should accompany any outcome results related to the individual's deficits. A clinical neuropsychologist goes one step further in this process to work to understand the underlying biological functioning that might be impacting assessment results, which makes it even more important that intervention is tied to the assessment results to provide strong services for some of the highest needs population.

Screening Measures Used in Medicine Within the medical setting, there are numerous opportunities for neuropsychologists to assess the physical status of patients. One of the first steps in understanding the abilities in a presenting patient should be an introduction and review of the patient's complaints. Many examinations begin with an analysis of understanding the client's orientation (e.g., knowing who they are, where they are, current time, and presenting reason). Widely used screening measures such as the Glasgow Coma Scale and the Rancho Los Amigos have been used to help psychologists understand severe concussions (Reswick & Rogers, 1976; Rowley & Fielding, 1991). The Glasgow Coma Scale offers insight into the functioning of eyes, motor, and verbal skills, while the Rancho Los Amigos has allowed a tiered rating system to help identify the current level of performance with a rating at ten different levels. For example, a Level I is someone who has no response and requires total support, while a middle-level Level V is seen as confused, having inappropriate behaviors given the individual's personality and requiring maximal assistance, ending with Level X which requires very minimal support. A neurological and psychiatric screener such as the Minnesota Multiphasic Personality Inventory, Second Edition (MMPI-2), would be a useful tool for a psychiatric hospital. Another area individuals may focus on is perinatal neurodevelopment is the universally used APGAR score is generated when children are born (American Academy of Pediatrics, 2006). Utilizing these scales allow professionals to communicate efficiently and demonstrate focused and well understood medical terminology.

Neuropsychology developed as a psychological concentration which has depended on the innovative theoretical models and the growth of a rigorous scientific base (Goldstein & McNeil, 2013). In the East, many would advocate that Luria conceived the neuropsychological case study approach to understanding individuals with unique profiles (Semrud-Clikeman et al., 2005). In the West, many would see Halstead as establishing a standardized neuropsychological approach to evaluating and understanding brain damage with individuals using his newly developed test (Davis et al., 2005). Initially, the role of clinical neuropsychology was to help practitioners understand the *what* meaning what was wrong with a patient and how to help. Since then, the specialty field of clinical neuropsychology has expanded the delineation of the brain-behavior relationship and the necessary concentrations for successful interventions for treatments of neuropsychological pathology to help address the *why*. Practitioners now focus more on understanding the uniqueness of patients and seek to understand the strengths as well as the deficits when interpreting data and in providing services and recommendations. Practitioners and researchers also use the advances in computer technology to improve assessment and treatment procedures. While working in the hospital, there was a football player who had a severe concussion. This young adult, with raging hormones, was attractive and fit. The nurses reported that he was in a coma (drug-induced to help his brain heal). When he awoke from his coma, he was cognitively cloudy, which is a common experience. Often the first few days after a brain injury are groggy, and he had no memory of the injury. The nurses reported to the neuropsychologists that he was flirting with them, and mom reported this behavior was unusual. The neuropsychologist were professional and ignored his flirting; a few days later while still in the hospital, the football player really liked one nurse in particular. He requested water and the nurse left to get the water; then a few moments later, his mom came into his hospital room, so he, not knowing his mother was coming, decided to pull his gown up to his neck, and he pulled the sheet off and said "Oh hello, there" to his mother. Horrified by his actions, his mom was both embarrassed and confused by the behaviors. Once he realized it was his mother, he quickly covered himself. While this instance is not a common side effect, it highlights a common theme with brain injury; an individual may have reduced impulse control and may have poor memory then forgetting that the incident occurred. It also emphaizes that a brain injury can present in a range of behavioral outcomes both expected and unexpected.

Who Are Clinical Neuropsychologists?

As the medical field continues to advance, the need for clinical neuropsychologists becomes more urgent. Clinical neuropsychology is a specialty in professional psychology that applies the principles of assessment and intervention to patients based upon the scientific study of human behavior as it relates to normal and abnormal functioning of the central nervous system. As science progresses, so does the average life expectancy for humans, bringing with it more complex neurological disorders. An emphasis, experience, and exposure within the pre-doctoral and post-doctoral internship help to prove the structure for knowledge on brain-behavior relationships (APA, 2017). There are a number of specialties which cover populations and techniques similar to those in neuropsychology, and an individual might want to consider related specialties like rehabilitation psychology, school psychology, pediatric and adolescent psychology, forensic psychology, or clinical child psychology. Most of these areas require pre-doctoral training and/or post-doctoral training.

Roles and Duties

Neuropsychology plays an integral role in the research and practice of many professional fields. Neurologists and neurosurgeons request behavioral evaluations to aid in diagnosis and to document the course of brain disorders or the effects of treatment. Rehabilitation specialists request neuropsychological assessments to assist in rehabilitation planning and management of a neurological condition. School psychologists have also applied the neuropsychological perspective in testing and providing intervention services for students (Root et al., 2005). A clinical neuropsychologist may assess a defendant when there is a reason to suspect that brain dysfunction contributed to the misbehavior or when there is a question about the mental capacity to stand trial (Lezak et al., 2012). Pediatric neuropsychologists provide clinical services to children and adolescents (and their families). More specifically the APA designates clinical neuropsychologists as a specialty. The APA describes the roles as the assessment and treatment of brain disorders. The most important aspects include understanding and applying a neuropsychological battery of assessments and interpretation of the findings related to brain-behavior relationships. A neuropsychologist is responsible for taking in large amounts of complex data and interpreting how the results and injury are impacting their daily functioning. In addition, a clinical neuropsychologist needs to be well established in understanding cutting-edge research, making adjustments related to cultural competency, and the interventions that support the individual with a deficit in functioning.

Where Do Clinical Neuropsychologists Work?

Traditionally, the area of psychiatry is where many neuropsychologists have worked. The major questions psychiatrists have are the behaviors functional (environmental) or organic in origin (neurobiology). Exploring the disorders origin helps to direct pharmacological intervention and understanding of the behavioral outcome for a patient. Psychiatry is less about the uniqueness of the case but about how available you are as a practitioner to provide immediate support to clients with significant mental health needs. Psychologists can also work within neurology departments to help highlight appropriate interventions when neurological deficits are presented. D'Amato and Dean (1988) acknowledged the unique situation of a psychologist's understanding of both cognitive psychology and emotional development and connecting that understanding within a medical treatment plan. Neurologists can "pinpoint" where the neurological issues are located, and clinical neuropsychologists can evaluate the behavioral outcomes and provide long-term services (D'Amato & Dean, 1988).

As noted earlier, as the medical field advances, so do survival rates for infants born with neurological deficits and genetic disorders (D'Amato & Dean, 1988). Science has advanced over the last few decades to increase the survival rate for babies born early and for enduring complications. Clinical neuropsychologists should be an integral part of the child's treatment team and can often consult with physicians on what the future outcomes are while recommending treatment options. One of the earliest indicators of biological-neurological deficits is diagnosed after birth. Neuropsychologists provide a secondary understanding of the current neurological data that inform outcomes and early interventions. Some pediatric neuropsychologists are trained in perinatal development and intervention. Clinical neuropsychologists may work alongside pediatricians in the hospital setting to support families and the child during their initial stages of understanding biological components to their deficits. As with the example of the young boy with a concussion, traumatic brain injury is another area where clinical neuropsychologists can facilitate long-term treatment planning and interventions. Specifically, when an individual has a significant brain injury, they are likely to lose the ability to do the things that they had prior to the injury. Clinical neuropsychologists are able to help the individual retain or create new interpersonal connections, teach skill training, and complete psychotherapy if needed (Rothlisberg et al., 2003). In fact, the first program developed was in 1977 at New York University Head Trauma Rehabilitation Program focused on a holistic program which helped patients develop self-care routines, functional skills, and social skills (Rothlisberg et al., 2003). Today we understand even more about outcomes for traumatic brain injuries and can provide additional support throughout the recovery process.

Soon there will be a large call for geriatric services due to the shift in birthrates. The baby boomers are aging, retiring, and requiring additional supportive services. There will be a call for psychologists who can perform mental status exams and full neuropsychological evaluations to determine the level of need for an individual. This growth in our aging population coupled with the decline in current childbirth rates in the United States sets up a high demand for these services in the health psychology field. There is also significant work clinical neuropsychologists can do with the geriatric population. As individuals take place in the natural aging process, there are cognitive changes that the individual will likely experience, and neuropsychologists can complete baseline data as well as monitor the progression of some neurodegenerative disorders (Albert & Moss, 1988). As an individual ages, there is an increased chance of presenting as confused, developing dementia, and cerebrovascular disease all which impact the mental functioning of older individuals (Albert & Moss, 1988). Altogether clinical neuropsychologists can play an important role in helping to manage the stages of dementia and can provide families with psychoeducation about what to expect in terms of treatment. One case example was a 75- and a 78-year-old married couple of 60 years who had never spent a night apart. At the intake, the thought was that the woman might have had a heart attack and her husband was emotionally distraught over having to spend his first night apart from his wife. The doctors reported that she would have to spend the night and her husband stated that "I have never spent a night apart in the our 62 years of marriage" and the neuropsychologist happened to be available to speak with him. The neuropsychologists talked with the individual for a few minutes, and he decided to get a second bed set up so that the husband didn't have to experience any separation. Everyone complied with what the clinical neuropsychologist said and was an obvious solution. This example demonstrates the importance of using empathy and compassion during a neuropsychological consultation. Alternatively, in other settings, clinical neuropsychologists might have to prove or convince someone of their solution, while in the hospital or geriatric setting, patients and staff often respond quickly without questions.

There are also more individualistic approaches to using a specialty in clinical neuropsychologists, for example, working in private practice to provide a span of evaluations related to brain and behavior relationships. A private practice can provide both broad assessments for individuals and individual interventions geared toward the results of the evaluation. Also, there is a great need for research in the field which a clinical neuropsychologist can provide as they obtain detailed results

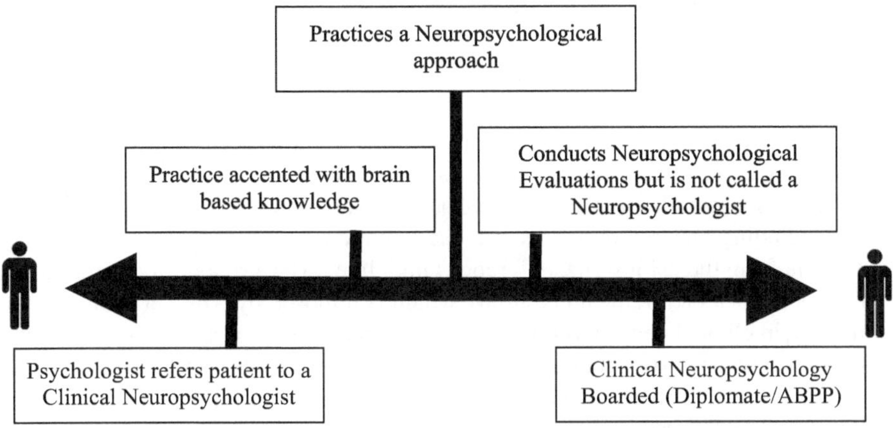

Fig. 1.3 Demonstration of the span of competency within clinical neuropsychology

from assessment evaluations of either rare disorders or more collective research focused on higher incident disorders. Both tend to be self-directed options. Just as clinicians can work in outpatient or private practice, they can also work in inpatient treatment. Clinical neuropsychologists can work across many types of inpatient treatment facilities and can both run programs and consult on specific cases. As inpatient hospitalizations are becoming shorter and shorter due to health insurance coverage restrictions having a clinical neuropsychologist available would allow for a robust use of consultation, psychotherapy, or treatment planning. Figure 1.3 demonstrates the span of competency within clinical neuropsychology.

Becoming a clinical neuropsychologist is not a simple task and includes years of dedicated schooling, practice, internship, and post-doctoral fellowships to develop competency and the expertise needed. Although most states allow licensed psychologists to call themselves neuropsychologists – without any specialized training in assessing and treating neurological and neurodevelopmental disorders – the American Board of Professional Psychology (ABPP) and its specialty board, the American Board of Clinical Neuropsychology (ABCN), set the specialty standards and demonstrate the competency of practicing neuropsychologists. The decision to become a clinical neuropsychologist can develop early in one's career and can be pursued in undergraduate studies by studying psychology and neuroscience, as well as studying other physical, social, and technological studies. From undergraduate school, the application and admissions to a doctoral program should be established with consideration to the style of the program and the amount of exposure to neuropsychology. The doctoral program should also meet the ABPP general doctoral program requirements. While in graduate school, one should look to elect courses with a foundation in neuroscience and neuropsychology. It is also important to select a mentor who can lead you in clinical and research initiatives. Pre-doctoral training should include emphasis, experience, and exposure in related neuropsychological areas (APA, 2017).

As in all psychological training, it is important to learn the basic skills in the classroom, to apply the learned material within a clinical practicum experience, to hone these skills, and then to cap off these skills in a pre-doctoral internship, followed by a 2-year post-doctoral supervised specialization (Witsken et al., 2008). This process was built upon an existing foundation of education and training guidelines, including the requirements for accreditation by the APA and the Policy Statement from the "Houston Conference Guidelines" (HCG; Sperling et al., 2017). This process is a hierarchical taxonomy which is imposed by APA for training, and education in clinical neuropsychology has set criteria within academic, clinical, and research domains across four stages of study: doctoral, internship, post-doctoral, and post-licensure (Sperling et al., 2017). The criteria set by APA assess the education and training opportunities, split into four separate levels. From highest to lowest, these levels are Major Area of Study, Emphasis, Experience, and Exposure. Across these experiences, there are several domains that should be met including assessment, intervention, consultation, supervision, research and inquiry, public interest, continuing professional development, and any additional core professional practice (Clinical Neuropsychology Specialty Petition). Together these areas with a focus on clinical neuropsychology help develop the skills needed to be a practicing clinical neuropsychologist. However, it seems the most important piece in these areas is the focus on strong supervision during the training years including practicum, internship, and post-doctoral work. It is important that any individual looking to become a clinical neuropsychologist find a supervisor who is well trained and provides strong supervision.

While the Clinical Neuropsychology Guidelines make it clear that practicum and internship should focus on general psychological information, it is helpful to highlight other areas that will be focused on during a clinical neuropsychology pre-doctoral internship. At the post-doctoral level, clinicians should begin to think about the brain-behavior relationship, neuropsychological assessment, and intervention (Clinical Neuropsychology Specialty Petition). The guidelines recommend that the clinician in training splits their time evenly between research and practice. Table 1.4 demonstrates the areas outlined in the Clinical Neuropsychology Specialty Petition.

For a doctoral program to consider itself an institution that provides neuropsychology as a Major Area of Study, it must include the following: (1) at least three separate neuropsychology courses that address the foundation of the brain-behavior relationship, (2) two separate clinical neuropsychology practicum experiences of 8 hours per week (at least 50% of time devoted to clinical contact with patients), (3) additional coursework and experience in neuropsychology, and (4) to complete and defend a dissertation project in neuropsychology (Sperling et al., 2017). For a program to provide an emphasis in neuropsychology, one to two separate courses and one clinical neuropsychology practicum experience are required, while an emphasis in neuropsychology only requires one course and one practicum experience. At the lowest level, Exposure, it is only required that either one course of study or one practicum experience is sufficient.

Table 1.4 Didactic and experiential training in clinical neuropsychology

Didactic training
1. Neurological and psychiatric diagnosis
2. Consultation to neurological and neurosurgical services
3. Direct consultation to psychiatric, pediatric, or general medical services
4. Exposure to methods and practices of neurological and neurosurgical consultation
5. Observation of neurosurgical procedures and biomedical tests
6. Participation in seminars offered to neurology and neurosurgery residents
7. Training in neuropsychological techniques, examination, interpretation of test results, report writing, as well as the integration of issues of culture, context, and diversity in interpretations
8. Training in consultation to patients and referral sources
9. Training in methods of intervention specific to clinical neuropsychology
10. Seminars, readings, etc., in neuropsychology (case conferences, journal discussion, topic-specific seminars)
11. Didactic training in neuroanatomy, neuropathology, and related neurosciences
Experimental training
1. Neuropsychological examination and evaluation of patients with actual and suspected neurological diseases and disorders
2. Neuropsychological examination and evaluation of patients with psychiatric disorders and/or pediatric or general medical patients with neurobehavioral disorders
3. Participation in clinical activities with neurologists and neurosurgeons
4. Experience at a specialty clinic setting which emphasizes multidisciplinary approaches to diagnosis and treatment
5. Direct consultation to patients involving neuropsychological assessment
6. Direct intervention with patients, specific to neuropsychological issues, and to include psychotherapy and or family therapy where indicated
7. Research in neuropsychology, i.e., collaboration on a research project or other scholarly academic activity, initiation of an independent research project or other scholarly academic activity, and presentation or publication of research data where appropriate

For internship programs, a Major Area of Study in neuropsychology requires (1) at least 50% of training time be devoted to clinical neuropsychology and (2) didactic experiences consistent with the HCG for knowledge and skill. The involvement in supervised clinical neuropsychology experience reduces to 30 to 50% at the level of Emphasis and 10 to 30% at the level of Experience. A program providing neuropsychology Exposure requires only 5 to 10% of supervised experience in clinical neuropsychology and/or didactic training. This is typically provided within clinical psychology, counseling psychology, or school psychology programs that provide a health service provider foundation for the next step of clinical neuropsychology specialty. A neuropsychology specialization also mandates post-doctoral programs with 2 years of full-time post-doctoral experience. This should focus on assessment and intervention of health service provider activities which incorporate neuropsychological theories, methods, and perspectives. The post-doctoral program must also provide clinical and research experiences as well as exposure to related medical care disciplines (e.g., psychiatry, neurology, rehabilitation). After specializing in neuropsychology and after earning a license in the field, it is also required that neuropsychologists meet annual continuing education (CE) requirements to maintain or improve competencies based on original research and clinical findings. As discussed, the finalized Taxonomy for Education and Training in Clinical Neuropsychology provides clear definitions for what constitutes a specific level of education and training, in terms of intensity and involvement, across the educational and training sequence (CNS; Sperling et al., 2017; see http://www.cospp.org/education-and-training-guidelines) (Table 1.5).

The Future of Clinical Neuropsychology

The future of neuropsychology appears to be intrinsically linked to the practice of health service psychology. Our practice is linked to understanding the brain via brain imaging studies and research that shows the impact of how neurotransmission relates to the biochemical basis of understanding our behavior. Accordingly, as we learn about the brain, we understand the chemicals that affect an individual's ability to think, function, and feel which is chemically related – therefore, we must understand psychopharmacology and the chemicals that can change and shape the client's behavior.

Brain Imaging and Neurotransmission

Research continues to inform us on how the brain works based on a variety of brain technology-reported activities as well as a number of new brain scanning techniques (Papanicolaou, 2017). There are both invasive (e.g., implanted electrodes) and non-invasive (e.g., MRI) ways to measure the brain's output. Invasive measures that require either an implant or intrusion into the brain have significant health risks such as infection and other medical complications. Some non-invasive methods typically require electrodes applied to the outer surface of one's head. These methods have some disadvantages scientifically, such as the need for an amplifier to heighten the signal of the brain waves and to remove noise from the reading, but these concerns are outweighed by an increase in safety for the participants (Ferree et al., 2001). Recent technological advances are highly supportive of non-invasive measures, as the technology can reduce noise interference and increase the ability to pick up stronger pure signals (Ferree et al., 2001). Neurofeedback is one such non-invasive neuropsychological intervention.

Health, Drugs, and Behavior

More people than ever before are prescribed medication because of the current understanding of brain behavior relationships (Lezak et al., 2012). It has become

Table 1.5 Guidelines for doctoral training in neuropsychology

Education	
May be accomplished through a PhD program in clinical neuropsychology offered by a psychology department or medical facility or through completion of a PhD program in a related specialty (e.g., clinical, school, counseling psychology) that offers sufficient specialization in clinical neuropsychology	
Required core	
Generic psychology core	
1. Statistics and methodology	4. Physiological psychology
2. Learning, cognition, and perception	5. Lifespan development
3. Social psychology and personality	6. History
Generic clinical core	
1. Psychopathology	4. Intervention techniques
2. Psychometric theory	(a) Counseling and psychotherapy
3. Interview and assessment techniques	(b) Behavior therapy/ modification
(a) Interviewing	(c) Consultation
(b) Intellectual assessment	5. Professional ethics
(c) Personality assessment	
Neurosciences: Basic human and animal neuropsychology	
1. Basic neuroscience	
2. Advanced physiological and psychopharmacology	
3. Neuropsychology of perceptual, cognitive, and executive processes	
4. Research design and research practicum in neuropsychology	
Specific clinical neuropsychology training	
1. Clinical neuropsychology and neuropathology	
2. Specialized neuropsychology assessment techniques	
3. Specialized neuropsychological intervention techniques	
4. Assessment practicum with children and/or adults	
5. Clinical neuropsychology internship of 1800 h, preferably in a university setting	
Internship	
The internship must devote at least 50% of 1-year full-time training experience to neuropsychology. In addition, at least 20% of the training must be devoted to general clinical training to ensure competent background in clinical psychology. Supervisors should be board-certified clinical neuropsychologists	

Note: Reprinted from Witsken et al. (2008)

obvious that the connection between the body-mind/brain behavior is a reality; for example, exercise and diet impact mental health outcomes related to positive neuronal growth. Unfortunately, a large population of individuals struggle with underlying brain-based mental health needs (e.g., individuals with schizophrenia). Another example of individuals with neurodiverse needs would be those who suffer from depression, another biochemical imbalance in the brain. Moreover, a widely used group of medications are stimulants for individuals with ADHD. Research has shown medications to be beneficial in all of these areas (Davis, 2011; Dunn & Retzlaff, 2005; Gautam et al., 2019). In many disorders psychotropic medication has been found to reduce behavioral problems and help the individual develop coping techniques. These examples highlight the importance of coordinating care with either a psychiatrist or a primary care physician to support the wellness of the individual in the treatment of mental disorders related to biochemical imbalances within the brain.

Psychopharmacology

The study of psychopharmacology is relevant for all health service psychologists, and some universities allow students to complete a master's in psychopharmacology. A brief overview is provided to help introduce practitioners to the study and use of medications. There are five major classes of drugs that are in use today: *antipsychotics*, *antidepressants*, *antianxiety*, *mood stabilizer*, and *stimulants*. Each drug impacts neurotransmitters including dopamine, norepinephrine, serotonin, and GABA (Dunn & Retzlaff, 2005). Drugs that are prescribed fit into a single category, although there can be benefits of a single drug across categories. It is important to note that finding a therapeutic effect from a drug may take multiple visits to either a psychiatrist or a primary care physician. Altogether, medication takes time and patients to reach the desired behavioral or cognitive change. There is a movement for some states to allow specially trained health service psychologists to prescribe psychotropic medication.

Antipsychotics
There are two types of antipsychotics: typical and atypical. Typical antipsychotics had originally been the first mental health medication in use for the treatment of schizophrenia. However, the high dosage resulted in negative side effects such as extrapyramidal motor issues (Dunn & Retzlaff, 2005). Today there are more options such as the atypical antipsychotics which work by blocking both dopamine and serotonin receptors in the brain. While overall these appear to do better with reducing side effects, weight gain is a major concern when taking this class of drugs.

Antidepressants
Antidepressants are widely used in psychology and several different types of antidepressants are available. MAO inhibitors inhibit the enzyme monoamine oxidase decreasing the depression symptoms. While MAO decreases depression symptoms, it can have dangerous side effects related to specific food, which would require a dietary change. Next are the selective serotonin reuptake inhibitors (SSRI) which prevent the reuptake of serotonin and increase neurotransmission decreasing depression. Recently drug companies invented second-generation reuptake inhibitors

which impact both dopamine and norepinephrine. It should be noted with all antidepressants that during the first few weeks of use, they may increase an individual's chance of suicide. Adults and children alike using these medications should be closely monitored for the first month of using antidepressants.

Antianxiety

Historically, barbiturates were prescribed to aid in sleeping and managing anxiety. Barbiturates have a long-standing place in history yet they are highly addictive and are often not used in clinical practice. Today instead benzodiazepines are prescribed to aid in the treatment of those with anxiety disorders. This medication has high success rates with individuals as it is a GABA agonist and as it reduces neuronal firing related to anxiety (Dunn & Retzlaff, 2005). For patients using this medication, it is important to be aware of the dangers related to mixing alcohol with this type of medication since serious side effects including death may occur.

Mood Stabilizer

The primary use for mood stabilizers is to treat individuals with mood disorder such as bipolar disorder. For many years lithium was the drug of choice to treat bipolar disorder. It is a medication that has worked well, yet it has several serious side effects that must be managed in order to have healthy blood levels. Lithium also has difficult iterations with other drugs which is important to keep in mind if a patient is using this medication.

Stimulants

Stimulants are often used in the treatment of attention deficit/hyperactivity disorder and narcolepsy. This type of drug is used as a dopamine agonistic to increase dopamine in the brain and increase attention in students and adults. One major problem with this medication is that it is addictive and often can be easily abused. While many students perform exceptionally well when taking this medication, there are side effects such as weight loss and loss of appetite which can lead to other related medical problems.

Psychopharmacology Conclusions

There is an abundance of research occurring concerning the impact of drugs on behavior (e.g., Coogan et al., 2019; Gautam et al., 2019; Stirratt et al., 2015). Having safer and more tailored drugs appears to be the future of the psychopharmacology practice. Most drugs were started in the early 1930s, and researchers have continued to investigate why these drugs have been successful within the brain and how to increase the success of these drugs. Drug trials are slow and deliberate to help keep the community safe, and while new medications are being developed, the ones above can continue to be investigated for their success with one or multiple diagnosis. There is much more research to be done in the psychopharmacology world.

Prescription Privileges

There is a movement for psychologists to gain prescription privileges as part of a comprehensive healthcare delivery system. Prescription privileges which are already utilized in the armed forces are available in five states, and other states are currently considering this change. In 2016, the American Association of Retired Persons (AARP) conducted a survey looking at medication usage in older adults. The study found that 80% of individuals 65 and older use at least two medications per day (Schwarz, 2016). Currently, people use medications to manage their life; even the use of caffeine intake impacts a large population. Wide use/abuse of alcohol, food, and marijuana call for psychologists to understand the complex relationship between psychological functioning, behavior, and various subtances. In addition, pornography, social media, and sex are becoming more common addictions which psychologists can explore underlying factors and treatment approaches. One such factor appears to be that people have shown an inability to remain present during one activity; often individuals are seen multitasking between watching television and playing on their phone while engaging in a secondary activity. A second major factor is the increase for productivity, reduction in resources, and increase in overall life stressors for many individauls.

Conclusions

As each decade inches closer to the ending, the excitement toward a new decade ignites a thoughtful consideration of our knowledge of the brain and how it impacts our behavior. Future researchers and practitioners are faced with the decision to continue current intervention research or branch off into a new examination of how psychological functioning is viewed in relation to current practices. Today we have strong support for neuropsychology as it has unlocked some of the largest questions we have asked across time. It is important to understand the relationship between the brain and body, know how information is processed, and recognize that injury to different parts of the brain interferes with functioning. While still in the early infancy of treating brain injury, the field has made great strides with the assistance of advanced technology. Clearly, clinical neuropsychology is one of the major components for understanding the future of psychology. The brain is a major asset that requires stimulation, energy, and interaction with the world. However, our society has shifted in our ability to engage socially and in meaningful and healthy ways. Too often our society ignores healthy eating, exercise, and mindfulness which can lead to disease and early death. Understanding neuropsychology helps practitioners know how to appropriately treat individuals who suffer from addiction, anxiety, and psychological ailments. Neuropsychology can help us build a roadmap to being healthier and solving our daily world obstacles. While clinical neuropsychology should help us approach public health in a meaningful way, instead we are continuing to venture down a path ignoring the science of healthy living. While understanding neurotransmission and medication may be the future, it is equally important to pursue living based on healthy life choices.

Discussion Questions

1. How does the history of psychology and the advancement of clinical neuropsychology impact your role as a practicing health service provider?
2. What ethical concerns might develop from the advancement of technology and clinical neuropsychology?
3. What concerns might you have about a colleague who identifies as a clinical neuropsychologist but falls short of displaying the necessary requirements to be a clinical neuropsychologist?
4. What area of clinical neuropsychology research do you hope to apply as a health service provider?
5. When thinking about the implications of psychopharmacological interventions, why is it important to consider the patient's everyday functioning when recommending such interventions?
6. How should your understanding of the biological basis of behavior drive evidence-based interventions when practicing clinical neuropsychology?

EPPP Sample Questions

1. Practicing clinicians who help to improve societal problems should consider themselves a

   (a) Neuropsychologist
   (b) Psychologist
   (c) Health service provider
   (d) Clinical neuropsychologist

   Answer: C

2. Specialization in clinical neuropsychology should include

   (a) Coursework, practicum, internship, and a 2-year post-doctoral training
   (b) Course work, internship, and a 2-year post-doctoral training
   (c) Coursework, practicum, and 1-year internship
   (d) Practicum, internship, and a 1-year post-doctoral training

   Answer: A

3. Which wars are related to the first increased need for psychologists or health service providers?

   (a) World War I and World War II
   (b) Korean War and Civil War
   (c) Vietnam and Korean War
   (d) Cold War and World War II

   Answer: A

4. What area of study forms the foundation for clinical neuropsychology during graduate-level training?

   (a) Biological basis of behavior
   (b) Cognitive basis of behavior
   (c) Affective basis of behavior
   (d) Assessment for intervention

   Answer: A

5. In the future what is the biggest adjustment that the field of psychology will need to broaden their services for?

   (a) Drop in birth rates
   (b) Population changes
   (c) Increased life expectancy
   (d) All of the above

   Answer: D

Proactive Readings

Transcending the Past

D'Amato, R. C., & Perfect, M. (2020). History of the future of proactive school psychology: Historical review at our 75th APA anniversary to transcend the past, excel in the present, and transform the future. *School Psychology, 35*(6), 375–384. https://doi.org/10.1037/spq0000420.

D'Amato, R. C., Zafiris, C., McConnell, E., & Dean, R. S. (2011). The history of school psychology: Understanding the past to not repeat it. In M. Bray & T. Kehl (Eds.), *Oxford handbook of school psychology* (pp. 9–60). Oxford.

Halstead, W. C. (1947). *Brain and intelligence: A quantitative study of the frontal lobes*. Chicago University Press.

Excelling in the Present

D'Amato, R. C., Fletcher-Janzen, E., & Reynolds, C. R. (Eds.). (2005). *Handbook of school neuropsychology*. New York, NY:Wiley.

Goldstein, L. H., & McNeil, J. E. (2013). *Clinical neuropsychology: A practical guide to assessment and management for clinicians*. Hoboken, NJ: Wiley.

Perfect, M., & D'Amato, R. C. (2020). Introduction to special issue on the history of the future of proactive school psychology: Transcending the past, excel in the present, and transform the future. *School Psychology, 35*(6), 363–366. https://doi.org/10.1037/spq0000419.

Transforming the Future

Hans, J. (2011). *Clinical neuroanatomy: Brain circuitry and its disorders*. Springer.

Kent, P. L. (2020) Evolution of clinical neuropsychology: Four challenges, *Applied Neuropsychology: Adult*, 27(2), 121–133, DOI: 10.1080/23279095.2018.1493483

Hilsabeck, R. C., & Rivera-Mindt, M. (2020). Editorial from the TCN department of culture and gender in neuropsychology: Updates, future directions, and next steps, *The Clinical Neuropsychologist, 34*(5), 863–872, DOI: 10.1080/13854046.2020.1772886

Power, E., & D'Amato, R. C. (2018). Should our future include the integration of evidence-based neuropsychological services into school settings? In D. Flanagan & E. McDonough (Eds.), *Contemporary intellectual assessment: Theories, tests, and issues* (4th ed., pp. 1017–1045).

References

Albert, M. S., & Moss, M. B. (1988). *Geriatric neuropsychology*. Guilford Press.

American Medical Association. (2014). *ICD-10-cm documentation: A how-to guide for coders, physicians and healthcare facilities*. American Medical Association.

American Psychological Association. (2017). *Standards of accreditation for health service psychology*. American Psychological Association.

Benton, A. L. (2000). *Exploring the history of neuropsychology: Selected papers*. Oxford Press.

Broca, P. (1960/1865). Remarks on the seat of the faculty of articulate language, followed by an observation of aphasia. In G. von Bonin (Trans.), *Some papers on the cerebral cortex* (pp. 49–72). Charles C. Thomas.

Coogan, A. N., Schenk, M., Palm, D., Uzoni, A., Grube, J., Tsang, A. H., … Oster, H. (2019). Impact of adult Attention Deficit Hyperactivity Disorder and medication status on sleep/wake behavior and molecular circadian rhythms. *Neuropsychopharmacology, 44*(7), 1198–1206. https://doi.org/10.1038/s41386-019-0327-6

D'Amato, R. C., & Dean, R. S. (1988). School psychology practice in a department of neurology. *School Psychology Review, 18*, 416–420. https://doi.org/10.1080/02796015.1988.12085356

D'Amato, R. C., Dean, R. S., & Holloway, A. F. (1987). A decade of employment trends in neuropsychology. *Professional Psychology: Research and Practice, 18*, 653–655. https://psycnet.apa.org/doi/10.1037/0735-7028.18.6.653

D'Amato, R. C., & Hartlage, L. C. (Eds.). (2008). *Essentials of neuropsychological assessment: Rehabilitation planning for intervention* (2nd ed.). Springer.

D'Amato, R. C., & Rothlisberg, B. A. (Eds.). (1992/1997). *Psychological perspectives on intervention: A case study approach to prescriptions for change*. Republished by Waveland Press.

Darmstadt, G. L., Bhutta, Z. A., Cousens, S. N., Adam, T., Walker, N., & Bernis, L. D. (2005). Evidence-based, cost-effective interventions: How many newborn babies can we save? *Lancet, 365*(9463), 977–988. https://doi.org/10.1016/S0140-6736(05)71088-6

Davis, A. C., & D'Amato, R. C. (2005). Evaluating and using contemporary neuropsychological batteries: The NEPSY and the Dean Woodcock neuropsychological assessment system. In R. C. D'Amato, E. Fletcher Janzen, & C. Reynolds (Eds.), *Handbook of school neuropsychology* (pp. 264–286). Wiley.

Davis, A. S. (Eds.). (2011). *Handbook of pediatric neuropsychology*. New York, NY: Springer.
Davis, A. S., Johnson, J. A., & D'Amato, R. C. (2005). Evaluating and using long standing neuropsychological batteries: The Halstead-Reitan and the Luria-Nebraska neuropsychological batteries. In R. C. D'Amato, E. Fletcher-Janzen, & C. Reynolds (Eds.), *Handbook of school neuropsychology* (pp. 236–263). Wiley.
Davis, J. M., & D'Amato, R. C. (Eds.). (2014). *Neuropsychology of Asians and Asian-Americans: Practical and theoretical considerations* (Part of the issues of diversity in clinical neuropsychology series). Springer.
Dean, R. S., & Noggle, C. A. (2013a). *Neuropsychology of cancer and oncology*. Springer.
Dean, R. S., & Noggle, C. A. (2013b). *The neuropsychology of pathology*. Springer.
Dean, R. S., & Reynolds, C. R. (1997). Cognitive processing and self-report of lateral preference. *Neuropsychology Review, 7*(3), 127–142.
Dunn, T., & Retzlaff. (2005). Understanding psychopharmacology with learners. In R. C. D'Amato, E. Fletcher-Janzen, & C. R. Reynolds (Eds.), *Handbook of school neuropsychology* (pp. 804-826). Wiley.
Ferree, T. C., Luu, P. L., Russell, G. S., & Tucker, D. M. (2001). Scalp electrode impedance, infection risk, and EEG data quality. *Clinical Neurophysiology, 112*(3), 536–544. https://doi.org/10.1016/s1388-2457(00)00533-2
Gautam, S., Jain, A., Gautam, M., Gautam, A., & Jagawat, T. (2019). Clinical practice guidelines for Bipolar Affective Disorder (BPAD) in children and adolescents. *Indian Journal of Psychiatry, 61*(Suppl 2), 294. https://doi.org/10.4103/psychiatry.IndianJPsychiatry_570_18
Kennedy, C. H., & Moore, J. L. (2010). *Military neuropsychology*. Springer.
Larner, A., & Leach, J. P. (2002). Phineas Gage and the beginnings of neuropsychology. *Advances in Clinical Neuroscience and Rehabilitation, 2*(3), 26. https://doi.org/10.1007/978-0-387-79948-3_615
Lee, P. G. (2010). *Neuropsychology of epilepsy and epilepsy surgery*. Oxford Press.
Lezak, M. D., Howieson, D. B., Bigler, E. D., & Tranel, D. (2012). *Neuropsychological assessment* (5th ed.). Oxford.
MacNeil Horton, A., & Wedding, D. (2008). *The neuropsychology handbook*. Springer.
Meier, M. J. (1974). Some challenges for clinical neuropsychology. In R. Reitan & L. Davison (Eds.), *Clinical neuropsychology: Current status and applications* (pp. 289–323). VH Winston & Sons.
Panksepp, J., & Biven, L. (2012). *The archaeology of mind: Neuroevolutionary origins of human emotions*. Norton & Company.
Papanicolaou, A. C. (2017). *The Oxford handbook of functional brain imaging in neuropsychology and cognitive neurosciences*. Oxford University Press.
Parks, R. W., Levine, D. S., & Long, D. L. (1998). *Fundamentals of neural network modeling: Neuropsychology and cognitive neuroscience*. MIT Press.
Power, E., & D'Amato, R. C. (2018). Should our future include the integration of evidence-based neuropsychological services into school settings? In D. Flanagan & E. McDonough (Eds.), *Contemporary intellectual assessment* (4th ed., pp. 1017–1045). Guilford.
Reitan, R. M., & Wolfson, D. (1985). *The Halstead-Reitan neuropsychological test battery: Theory and clinical interpretation*. Neuropsychology Press.
Reswick, J. B., & Rogers, J. E. (1976). Experience at rancho Los amigos hospital with devices and techniques to prevent pressure sores. In R. Kenedi & M. Cowden (Eds.), *Bed sore biomechanics* (pp. 301–310). Palgrave/SpringerLink.
Root, K. A., D'Amato, R. C., & Reynolds, C. R. (2005). Providing neurodevelopmental, collaborative, consultative, and crisis intervention school neuropsychology services. In R. C. D'Amato, E. Fletcher-Janzen, & C. R. Reynold (Eds.), *Handbook of school neuropsychology* (pp. 15–40). Wiley.
Rothlisberg, B. A., D'Amato, R. C., & Palencia, B. N. (2003). Assessment of children for intervention planning following traumatic brain injury. In C. R. Reynolds & R. W. Kamphaus (Eds.),

Handbook of psychological and educational assessment of children: Personality, behavior and context (2nd ed.). Guilford.
Rowley, G., & Fielding, K. (1991). Reliability and accuracy of the Glasgow coma scale with experienced and inexperienced users. *The Lancet, 337*(8740), 535–538.
Schultz, D. P., & Schultz, S. E. (2015). *A history of modern psychology*. Cengage Learning.
Schwarz, C. (2016, April). AARP survey highlights prescription drug use among older adults. *Medicare Rights Center.* https://blog.medicarerights.org/aarp-survey-highlights-prescription-drug-use-among-older-adults/
Semrud-Clikeman, M., Wilkinson, A., & Wellington, T. (2005). Evaluating and using qualitative approaches to neuropsychological assessment. In R. C. D'Amato, E. Fletcher-Janzen, & C. R. Reynolds (Eds.), *Handbook of school neuropsychology* (pp. 287–302). Wiley.
Smith, A. D., & Moulin, C. J. A. (2012). *Neuropsychology*. SAGE.
Stirratt, M. J., Dunbar-Jacob, J., Crane, H. M., Simoni, J. M., Czajkowski, S., Hilliard, M. E., ... Ogedegbe, G. (2015). Self-report measures of medication adherence behavior: Recommendations on optimal use. *Translational Behavioral Medicine, 5*(4), 470–482. https://doi.org/10.1007/s13142-015-0315-2
American Academy of Pediatrics. (2006). The Apgar score. *Pediatrics, 6*(4),220-223. https://doi.org/10.1016/j.adnc.2006.04.008.
Thornicroft, G., & Tansella, M. (2004). Components of a modern mental health service: A pragmatic balance of community and hospital care: Overview of systematic evidence. *The British Journal of Psychiatry, 185*(4), 283–290. https://doi.org/10.1192/bjp.185.4.283
D'Amato, R. C., Power, E. M., & Tincup, M. J. (2021). Appendix A: Sample neuropsychological questionnaire. In R. C. D'Amato, A. S. Davis, E. M. Power, & E. C. Eusebio (Eds.), *Understanding our biological basis of behavior: Developing evidence-based interventions for clinical, counseling and school psychologists.* Springer Nature.
Webb, F. M. (2011). *The handbook of sport neuropsychology*. Springer.
Witsken, D., D'Amato, R. C., & Hartlage, L. C. (2008). Understanding the past, present, and future of clinical neuropsychology. In L. Hartlage & R. C. D'Amato (Eds.), *Essentials of neuropsychological assessment: Rehabilitation planning for intervention* (2nd ed., pp. 1–30). Springer.
Zaroff, C., & D'Amato, R. C. (Eds.). (2015). *The neuropsychology of men: From neurodevelopment to evidence-based interventions* (Part of the issues of diversity in clinical neuropsychology series). Springer.
D'Amato, R. C., Creapeau-Hobson, F., Huang, L.V., & Geil, M. (2005). Ecological neuropsychology: An alternative to the deficit model for conceptualizing and serving students with learning disabilities. *Neuropsychology Review, 15*(2), 97–103. https://doi.org/10.1007/s11065-005-7092-5

Chapter 2
Understanding the Development of the Central Nervous System and Its Relationship to Clinical Practice

Margaret Semrud-Clikeman

Learning Objectives

1. To understand the basic neuroanatomy of the brain.
2. To understand the development of the brain and how it affects later functioning.
3. To understand the relation of early experience and culture to the development of the brain.
4. To relate basic knowledge of the central nervous system to clinical practice.

Overview

The goal of this chapter is to review the basic development of the central nervous system and to relate this development to clinical practice. The chapter will begin with a basic neuroanatomy of the brain starting with a discussion of the structure and function of the four lobes. In addition, this structure and function will be discussed as it relates to stages within a neurotypical child's development. Multicultural and ethnic differences will be discussed as they relate to neuroanatomy. Finally, a foundation for later chapters on errors in neurodevelopment will be provided to assist the clinical, school, and counseling psychologist in understanding why this neurodevelopment is crucial for the child's adjustment.

M. Semrud-Clikeman (✉)
Department of Pediatric Clinical Behavioral Neuroscience, University of Minnesota Medical School, Minneapolis, MN, USA

R. C. D'Amato et al. (eds.), *Understanding the Biological Basis of Behavior*,
https://doi.org/10.1007/978-3-030-59162-5_2

Basic Brain Anatomy

To understand the development of the central nervous system (CNS), it is first important to have a basic knowledge of brain anatomy. The brain is composed of two hemispheres that include four lobes (frontal, temporal, occipital, and parietal), the cerebellum, and the brain stem. In addition, it also includes the basal ganglia, limbic system, and ventricles. The neurons that make up the brain include the nuclei (the gray matter on the outside of the brain) and the axons (the white matter internal to the brain). The brain is surrounded and cushioned by the meninges and cerebrospinal fluid (CSF). There are three meninges: pia mater (the most interior and contains small blood vessels), arachnoid (a spiderlike web between the pia and dura mater), and the dura mater (a tough exterior meninge which attaches to the bones covering the cranium and has the blood vessels that nourish the brain). The cerebrospinal fluid serves to protect against injury by providing a cushion as well as diffusing materials into and away from the brain and lies within the ventricles as well as within the subdural space between the dura mater and arachnoid meninges. Infections can attack the meninges and are referred to as meningitis. These infections have serious consequences for the developing brain particularly with the first year of life and can result in death or intellectual disability, hydrocephalus, seizures, deafness, and hyperactivity (Swaiman & Ashwal, 2017). Hydrocephalus is generally remediated through a shunt being placed in the ventricles and draining to the stomach. Hydrocephaly can range from mild to severe with the age of the child at the time of the shunt being placed as well as other medical conditions being present affecting the level of difficulty (Fletcher et al., 2000).

Ventricles The four ventricles are cavities that are filled with CSF. The largest ventricles are the lateral ventricles that are in the forebrain of the cortex. The third ventricle is connected to the lateral ventricles and in the deep portion of the brain in the diencephalon. In turn the fourth ventricle is connected to the brain stem and drains into the spinal cord.

Brain Stem The brain stem includes five areas: fourth ventricle, medulla oblongata, pons, midbrain, and diencephalon (see Fig. 2.1). The medulla oblongata is directly connected to the spinal cord. Sensory and motor nuclei from the cranial nerves are located here. As you may recall, the right side of the body is controlled by the left hemisphere and the left side of the body by the right. The medulla is where these pathways cross. This is true for auditory, visual, kinesthetic, and motor systems.

The reticular activating system (RAS) runs through the medulla and plays an important role in arousal as well as in maintaining consciousness and attention. It receives input from most sensory systems as well as connects to all levels of the CNS. The raphe system that secretes serotonin (an important neurotransmitter) runs through the medulla as well as the pons and midbrain sections. This region also contains the locus ceruleus which produces 70 percent of norepinephrine in the

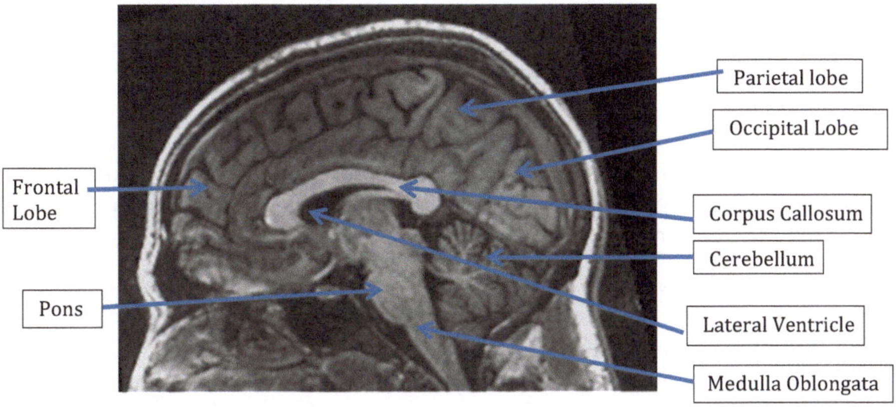

Fig. 2.1 Sagittal view of the brain showing the major structures

brain and modulates other neurotransmitters (Carlson & Birkett, 2017). Norepinephrine plays an important role in vigilance, while serotonin plays a role in mood, attachment, and aggression to name a few (Pliszka, 2016). The RAS projects to the limbic system and is affected by these neurotransmitters.

The pons is between the medulla and the midbrain and lies above the cerebellum and serves as a bridge between the hemispheres. Major sensory and motor pathways course through this area from the spinal cord to the cortex. The pons works in concert with the cerebellum and receives input from the motor cortex modulating movements (Brodal, 2016). Input from the limbic system also occurs at the level of the pons and appears to influence emotional and motivational factors on motor activity (Brodal, 2016).

The midbrain serves as a major relay for sensory-motor fibers. The midbrain includes the superior colliculi that are important for vision orientation and the inferior colliculi that are involved in the integration of auditory and kinesthetic input. Several cranial nerves also traverse through the midbrain particularly those for eye movement and sensory movement of the face.

The diencephalon is the most superior region of the brain stem and contains the major relax center for all sensory systems except smell. It includes the thalamus, hypothalamus, pituitary gland, internal capsule, the third ventricle, and the optic nerve (Semrud-Clikeman & Ellison, 2009). The thalamus is a crucial structure receiving input from several sensory sources including the visual, auditory, pain, pressure, touch, and temperature. The hypothalamus, which lies anterior and below the thalamus, is important for the autonomic nervous system which controls eating, sexual function/dysfunction, drinking, sleeping, temperature, rage, and violence as well as motivational aspects of behavior. The pituitary gland also is in this region and responds to hypothalamic directions in secreting hormones (cortisol, etc.) that regulate bodily functions. The hypothalamus and pituitary gland along with the adrenal gland above the kidney make up the hypothalamic-pituitary-adrenal (HPA) axis. This system is influenced by serotonin and activates during times of stress making it difficult for the child to respond to changing situations (Pliszka, 2016; Puig et al., 2013). It can also change brain structure in young children due to stress experienced during important developmental times—this effect will be discussed later in the chapter.

Finally, the internal capsule is like a highway where fibers connect the cortex to lower brain regions. In addition, major fibers connect the frontal lobes to the thalamus and then to the pons. The optic nerve also converges in the diencephalon and forms the optic chiasm.

Cerebellum The cerebellum (also referred to as the hindbrain) connects to the midbrain, pons, and medulla. It receives sensory information about where the body is in space and the position of the limbs. It also receives input from the semicircular canals in the ear concerning orientation and balance. It works without conscious awareness for smooth and complex motor activity. Injury to the cerebellum can cause problems with movement (dystaxia) and speech (dysarthria), nystagmus (blurred vision and dizziness), and hypotonia (low muscle tone; Swaiman & Ashwal, 2017).

The Cortex

The cortex is the highest functional division of the brain and makes up about 80 percent of the human brain. It is comprised of two hemispheres that have anatomical as well as functional differences. The right and left hemispheres differ in terms of the efficiency in processing certain tasks with the left hemisphere being more efficient in language and sequential thinking and the right in wholistic processing. The right hemisphere is more adept at processing novel information, while the left hemisphere works more efficiently with pre-existing learning (Semrud-Clikeman & Ellison, 2009). Gender differences are present with women showing less lateralization then men and men showing stronger visual-spatial reasoning skills (Semrud-Clikeman & Fine, 2009).

There are large bundles of myelinated fibers that connect the various regions of the cortex. The two hemispheres are connected through the corpus callosum (large white matter fibers) as well as smaller pathways connecting the temporal lobes (anterior commissure) and parietal region (posterior commissure). There are also long pathways that connect the frontal lobes to the occipital lobes via the parietal lobes (superior longitudinal fasciculus) and the frontal lobes to the temporal lobes (inferior longitudinal fasciculus).

Frontal Lobes The frontal lobes are the most sophisticated part of the brain and are important for motor as well as reasoning, planning, and monitoring of behavior. They mature the slowest of all of the lobes and continue developing into the mid-twenties. There are many connections between the frontal lobes and all parts of the brain and particularly with the limbic system that is involved in emotion and motivation. Damage to this regions can cause problems with executive function, behavioral/emotional control, and impaired judgment (Lezak et al., 2004). Connections from the prefrontal region of the brain allow for the individual to compare past and present experiences as well as to learn from experience. Consequently damage to this region (often seen in traumatic brain injury and concussions) results in impaired judgment, poor insight, and often impulsive behavior (Gazzaniga et at., 2013).

Parietal Lobes The parietal lobes play an important role in the perception of tactile and sensory information. They are important in recognizing the source, quality, and severity of pain, discrimination of light pressure and vibration, proprioception, and kinesthetic sense. The parietal lobes also integrate complex sensory information and allow for analysis of the information such as visual-motor integration.

Occipital Lobes The occipital lobes are in the posterior portion of the brain and are important for visual information and interpretation. The functions are important for complex visual perception. In addition, the current perception is paired with past learning for interpretation of meaning as well as recognition and appreciation of what is being seen. Damage to this region can result in problems with recognizing objects, faces, and drawings (Gazzaniga et al., 2013).

Limbic System The limbic system is a collection of structures deep in the cortex and includes the hippocampus, amygdala, septum, and cingulate gyrus (Carlson & Birkett, 2017). It is an important system that assists in formulating an emotional response to fearsome or threatening situations, monitoring sexual response, remembering recent and past events, and responding to need states (Pliszka, 2016). The cingulate gyrus has been associated with error checking and self-monitoring (Semrud-Clikeman et al., 2006), while feelings of anxiety, rage, and fear are associated with the amygdala (Semrud-Clikeman & Ellison, 2009). The hippocampus is crucial for learning and memory with the emotional tone of memories provided by interaction with the amygdala.

Basal Ganglia The basal ganglia are a collection of gray matter structures within the cerebral hemispheres and include the caudate, putamen, and globus pallidus. This structure connects to the cortex and the thalamus as well as to the brain stem. Serotonin pathways from the raphe nuclei in the brain stem connect to the basal ganglia and inhibit motor and emotional reactions (Gazzaniga et al., 2013). The basal ganglia (particularly the caudate) have been implicated in attention deficit hyperactivity disorder (Castellanos & Proal, 2012; Semrud-Clikeman et al., 2006).

The Developing Brain

The previous section provides a brief overview of the structural areas of the brain and is important for understanding the infant brain that changes with experience and development. The fetal brain grows at an astonishing rate prior to birth with estimates of 250,000 brain cells forming each minute through mitosis (Nyardi et al., 2013). The fastest brain growth is between 25 and 40 weeks of gestation (Gazzaniga et al., 2013). The human brain also grows in predictable stages beginning with the neural tube at 25 days of gestation through birth. The following sections will discuss the various stages of development throughout gestation and into early childhood.

Neural Tube Formation The neural tube forms approximately 2 weeks within conception and is completed around 1 month of gestation. It is the foundation for the brain and spinal cord. The neural plate is formed and looks like the shape of a keyhole with the broad end at the anterior portion of the plate. Neurulation is a complex process where the cells in the neural plate give rise to the neural tube and later the CNS. There are three primary layers in the early embryo—ectoderm (proximal layer), mesoderm (middle layer), and endoderm (distal layer). The endoderm serves as the genesis for the gut and digestive organs, while the mesoderm is the foundation for the circulatory system. We are most concerned with the ectodermal cells that become the CNS. The ectodermal cells that lie ventrally to the neural plate form the neural crest. The neural crest becomes the peripheral nervous system, while the neural tube (the most central part of the neural plate) becomes the CNS (Gilbert, 2000) (Fig. 2.2). Illustration done by Richard Magnusson.

By day 23 the neural tube is formed with the anterior portion becoming the brain and the posterior portion the spinal cord. For a video as to this process, please access http://www.lsic.ucla.edu/classes/lifesci/central/ps107/lectures/ns-slide_2.html. The neural tube folds over with the most anterior portion becoming the forebrain, the hypothalamus and thalamus and interbrain, then the midbrain, and finally the spinal cord (Squire et al., 2008).

When the neural tube fails to close in the anterior section, the child's brain will not be encased in the skull and an encephalocele will form. An encephalocele is a sac-like projection of the brain and meninges through the skull frequently at the back of the head. These children generally do not survive. If the neural tube does not close at the caudal portion of the tube, spina bifida is present. There are levels of spina bifida that are determined by how much of the spinal cord is affected. The most common and mildest form shows very few clinical signs and generally looks like a dimple, or hairy patch on the back above the buttocks. It is not generally discovered without an X-ray. The more severe form is the meningocele where fluid leaks out of the spine and the skin bulges out. Generally there are no other clinical symptoms. The most rare and severe form is the myelomeningocele and is the common understanding of spina bifida. In this case the spinal nerves are out of the spinal canal with resulting damage ranging from lack of feeling to paralysis. The skin is open in this case, and the sac-like projection is unprotected from infection, etc.

Spina bifida is a common severe birth defect with a prevalence of 1 per 1000 in the USA. Rates are higher in Hispanics and whites of European descent and lower in Ashkenazi Jews, Asians, and African Americans. Mothers with diabetes or seizure disorders have a higher rate of spina bifida in children. The prognosis for children with spina bifida is much better in recent years with improved surgical techniques and early diagnosis leading to corrective surgery during pregnancy.

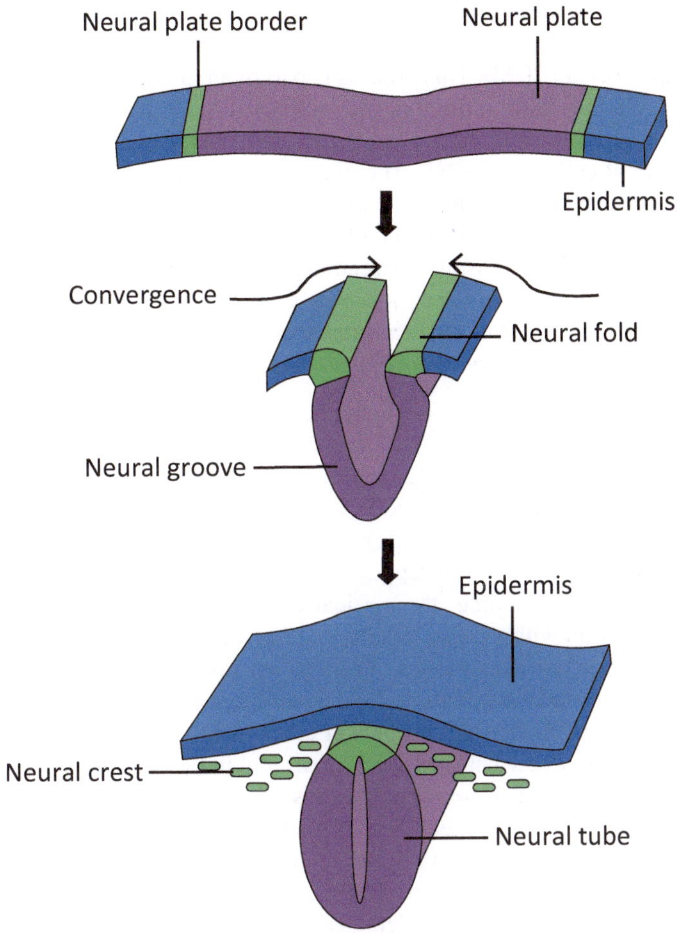

Fig. 2.2 An illustration of the neural plate during embryogenesis

Moreover, studies found that as many as 70 percent of cases could be prevented by increasing intake of folic acid prior to and during pregnancy (Wasserman & Holmbeck, 2016).

Children with spina bifida frequently have average to above average measures of intelligence with stronger language than visual perceptual skills. Difficulties are present in visual-motor integration, attention, and executive functioning (particularly comprehension, planning and organization, and decision-making (Hampton et al., 2013). A sizable minority of children with spina bifida also shows with learning disabilities (Ris et al., 2007).

Cell Migration Cell migration occurs throughout gestation and is regulated by physical as well as chemical processes (Carlson & Birkett, 2017). It begins at about 4 weeks when the neural tube closes. Stem cells proliferate inside the neural tube and are the foundation for all of the structures of the brain. The migration process is rapid, and the cortical layers of the brain are visible by the fifth month of fetal development (Squire et al., 2008). This process is part of an intricate neuron-glial interaction. Glial cells are brain cells that are supportive cells in the CNS and are not involved in impulses. They generally provide support for neurons and are the most common type of cells in the CNS. The neurons are guided along the glial fibers by a chemical process to their proper location (Kolb & Whishaw, 2003). During this process the cortex thickens and sulci (ridges) and gyri (valleys) begin to appear. The longitudinal fissure (long fissure between the hemispheres) is evident at 10 weeks, the lateral sulcus (fissure between the frontal and temporal lobe) at 14 weeks, and a sulcus between the parietal and occipital lobes at 14 weeks. The central sulcus (between the frontal and parietal lobes) appears at 20 weeks of gestation.

During the prenatal and early postnatal periods, the neurons differentiate and got to genetically predetermine regions of the brain. When this system does not work as planned, neurons will go the wrong location or make inappropriate synaptic connections. Schizophrenia has been linked to cells incorrectly placed particularly in the frontal lobes (Buchsbaum et al., 2006). Learning disabilities have also been linked to misplaced cells or to cells that replicated too much (Galaburda & Kemper, 1979).

During this period of time, the cortical mantle is also being established. The cortex has six layers with the first developing neurons on the inside and later developing neurons passing over the first layer to migrate to layers 2 through 6. This process is called cortical lamination. Each layer has a distinctive group of cells that are defined by their inputs and outputs (Purves et al., 2001). It is estimated that approximately 2/3 of new neurons reach their goal in the brain while the others die or disappear. This process is important because more neurons are produced than are necessary with necessary cell death important for this process of neuronal proliferation and migration (Gazzaniga et al., 2013). It has been hypothesized that there is a limited amount of what is termed "trophic substance" which keeps the neurons alive. Thus, when this substance is depleted, the fetal neurons which are left will die (Brodal, 2016).

When migration is disrupted by environmental or toxic events, the child can suffer from serious neuropsychological deficits. Maternal stress, alcohol and other substance abuse, and poverty can cause significant disruption to the developing brain and result in lifelong disabilities (Johnson et al., 2016; Porter & Dyer, 2017). These disabilities can be cognitive, behavioral, and/or emotional in nature.

Formation of Synapses and Axon Development Neurons continue to develop throughout gestation. Axons (or the long portion of the neuron that connects with other neurons and conducts impulses away from the cell nucleus) follow what are termed "pioneer axons" which set the pattern of growth and direction. These pioneer axons have a high concentration of chemicals that propel the axons to the correct destination and are thought to have chemoaffinity between these axon ends and the neurons (Brodal, 2016). These axons grow rapidly while migrating and form pathways that connect the two hemispheres. As we discussed earlier, there are three commissures that connect the hemispheres. The anterior commissure appears around 3 months of gestation, while the corpus callosum develops much more slowly and in fact some believe is not fully formed until early adolescence (Witelson, 1990).

Dendrites are those neuronal structures that conduct neural impulses toward the cell body of the neuron. They often have many branches that connect to other neurons for neuronal transmission. The more dendrites, the more intercommunication there is possible. Dendrites also have spines, which are protrusions that receive input from an axon. Again, the more spines are present, the more signals, which are possible between neurons. Dendrites and spines grow much more slowly than axons and are visible at around the seventh month of gestation. While axons grow prior to finding their home, dendrites do not develop until the cells are at the destination. Dendrites also continue to develop postnatally and can be affected by environmental stimulation.

While the development of synapses is poorly understood, they are generally seen around the fifth month of gestation (Carlson & Birkett, 2017). Synaptogenesis, or the development of synapses, occurs during gestation. Babies are born with over 100 billion neurons with each neuron having many branches. This makes a possible quadrillion connections through synapses. Initially only 17 percent of neurons are linked in a baby's brain (Carlson & Birkett, 2017). These connections increase dramatically in the first few years of life, and by the age of 2, the frontal lobes have 50 percent more synapses than are present in adults (Gazzaniga et al., 2013). Synapses are eliminated as the child grows and the brain becomes more efficient in function and shows more refinement of ability. In this case less is more as the synapses that remain provide more precise neuronal connections. Unused synapses basically die away if they don't wire up to axons. This process of pruning is termed apoptosis and basically reduces gray matter in the brain throughout childhood as the brain becomes more efficient (Giedd et al., 1994; Gogtay et al., 2004). It is also during this period that the migration of cells and apoptosis can be disrupted by environmental, genetic, and viral infections. These synaptic networks become elaborate in the postnatal period as dendritic arborization (increase in dendritic spines that look basically like limbs of a tree) increases. During the third trimester of gestation, the brain enters a growth spurt that continues until 2 years of age.

Myelination At the same time, as apoptosis and synaptogenesis are occurring, the axons are becoming coated with a fatty substance called myelin that makes up the white matter. This process proceeds from deep in the brain to the outside and from posterior to anterior. Initially most neurons are not myelinated and have dendritic spines. Myelination continues throughout childhood and into adolescence and the early twenties (Gogtay et al., 2004). It occurs in the primary sensory and motor cortices first (prior to birth), and then the secondary areas of the basic senses (auditory discrimination, motor planning, visual discrimination, sensory discrimination) complete myelination by the age of 4 months postnatally. The association areas of the frontal and parietal lobes do not complete myelination until much later and for some individuals not until the twenties (Fredrik et al., 2007). Subcortical structures such as the amygdala (emotional processing) and the hippocampus (memory) increase in volume until around the age of 30 and then begin to gradually decline (Nyraradi et al., 2013). These changes also occur in the caudate and in cortical thickness (Fair et al., 2013).

There are sensitive periods during this development when the brain changes drastically. During these periods the brain is fairly "plastic" and responds to environmental changes and experiences in a more exaggerated manner. The length of these periods varies depending on the child. The experiences the child is engaged in can change the function and complexity of these circuits for better or for worse (Holtmaat & Svoboda, 2009).

Gender Effects The study of gender effects in the fetus is in its infancy. A literature search of these key terms found no articles. The studies that do exist are for infants and toddlers as well as adults. Males have been found to be at higher risk for learning disabilities, ADHD, and autism (Schore, 2017). Male brains develop more slowly than female brains putting them at higher risk for difficulties in childhood and adulthood (Schneider et al., 2011). It has been suggested that one of the reasons that males are more often diagnosed with schizophrenia is that the brain deficits begin in the fetal period when the brain becomes sexually differentiated through hormones (Holden, 2005). In addition it has been accepted in neuroscience research that males are prone to psychiatric difficulties that appear earlier in development while female difficulties most frequently appear later in life (Llorente et al., 2009). Schore (2017) suggests that gender differences in brain development are related to differences in sex hormones, social experiences, and the rate of brain maturation particularly in the right hemisphere. He goes on to suggest that the *"stress-regulating circuits of the male brain mature more slowly than those of the female in the prenatal, perinatal, and postnatal critical periods, and that this is reflected in normal gender differences in right-brain attachment functions"* (p. 19). He goes on to hypothesize that due to this slower maturation process, males are more vulnerable to stress, brain injury, and environmental effects than females particularly since the right hemisphere is important for social and emotional development.

Using animal studies there is emerging evidence that the male fetus may also be at higher risk for neurodevelopmental problems when exposed to substances during pregnancy. It has been found that male rats showed a decrease in the dopaminergic system that resulted in increased dysregulation while females, showing the same decrease, showed less dysregulation (Dow-Edwards & Torres-Reveron, 2012). Additional studies have found that males exposed to cocaine in utero show problems with attention, emotional control, impulsivity, and general dysregulation while females do not show these same difficulties (Kestler et al., 2012). These authors suggest that because male brains develop more slowly, their brains are at higher risk for damage from cocaine than are females.

Culture Effects Cognitive development occurring after birth occurs within a culture or ethnic group (Gauvain & Perez, 2015). Neurodevelopment prior to birth is less likely to be affected by culture with the exception of nutrition and prenatal practices. The influence of culture can transform the brain as the child is exposed to environmental stimuli. Culture-based learning affects not only skills and abilities but also how emotion is expressed and perceived (Kennepol, 1999). It has been hypothesized that cultural influences on brain organization (after birth) relate to the making of appropriate neuronal connections based on experience in the culture, activating specific neural networks that are developed through cultural experiences, and learning how to adapt appropriate to the culture to novel environments (Luria, 1980). Luria goes on further to state that the "social contact and objective activity by the child" are related to the development of the association areas that develop with experience (p. 31).

Changes in brain structure have been found based on cultural experience in studies of stroke patients from China (Yu-Huan, Ying-Guan, & Gui-Quing, 1990). Aphasia was more common in these patients following a right-sided lesion for patients from a majority ethnic group, the Han (crossed aphasia). The Han language is basically nonphonetic and picture based. Crossed aphasia was rarely seen in the Western European population. Wernicke's aphasia is rarely seen in the Han population. Yu-Huan et al. (1990) suggest that for this population language is lateralized in the right or both hemispheres rather than most predominately in the left hemisphere. What is not known is whether this difference is passed on genetically and there is altered brain development in utero.

Additional findings are present in Japan particularly in languages which are logographic. In this case Japanese use a phonetic language for reading and a logographic language for everyday written Japanese. In aphasics with left-sided lesions, they can read fluently using the phonetic language but not the logographic language possibly implicating a right-hemisphere language system (Elman et al., 1981).

These areas begin to highlight some possible adjustments that are made from cultural contexts. Further studies have also found commonalities among cultures in neurodevelopment and organization (Gauvain & Perez, 2015). For the most part, human brain structure has not changed in the past 50,000 to 10,000 years (Harris, 1983). Reading and writing skills are recent developments in our evolution, and thus these areas may be more susceptible to culture and environmental changes. It has been hypothesized by Kennepol (1999) that the basic neural structures are preprogrammed to develop in a flexible manner following interaction with the environment (Semrud-Clikeman & Bledsoe, 2014). One of the difficulties in this area is the dearth of empirical studies to verify these conclusions which are based on behavioral data. There is ethnographic and social experimental evidence that culture may be transmitted genetically as well as through experience (Perez-Arce, 1999).

Many children whose parents have immigrated to another country are now bilingual. One study evaluated the brain differences in Spanish-English bilinguals (Felton et al., 2017). Findings were that thicker right than left cortices were present for bilinguals with monolinguals showing the reverse pattern. For bilinguals the mid-anterior and central portions of the corpus callosum had a greater volume compared to the one-language speakers. Thus, changes in structures were likely present with experience. It is not clear whether these differences are later genetically inherited or whether they are based solely on environmental input at early ages. Further study in this area is certainly needed particularly in the USA as ethnic minorities continue to grow and prosper and our understanding of the neurological basis of language is crucial.

Development of Higher-Order Cognitive Abilities

Challenges to Brain Development

Brain development can be affected by malnutrition, disease, injury, and inadequate stimulation as well as experiencing neglect and abuse during this very sensitive developmental period (Porter & Dyer, 2017). Disruption can result in problems with infant regulation both physical and emotional (Kouros et al., 2014). Enrichment activities (toys, social stimulation, novel experiences) have been found to improve changes in brain structure, function, and gene expression (Hirase & Shinohara, 2014). It has been hypothesized that poverty can shape the brain at many levels including at the molecular, neural, and cognitive levels (Lipina et al., 2011). Thus, brain development is transactional in nature where the genetic and environmental influences interact to produce the individual (Shonkoff & Garner, 2012). Socioeconomic status (SES) has been found to have a larger influence on brain development than genetics for individuals at the low end but not for those in high-SES environments (Chiang et al., 2011; Turkheimer et al., 2003). This vulnerability can be moderated by genetic influences explaining why children from the same family show different responses to the same environment with some more resilient than others (Ellis et al., 2011).

To complicate matters further, epigenetic research has found that the environment itself plays a role in how the genetic code is expressed (Johnson et al., 2016). Maternal care can affect the development of the brain in that there is more efficient regulation for negative feedback from the hypothalamic-pituitary-adrenal (HPA) axis that allows for a better regulated stress response and cognitive performance (Essex et al., 2013). Better maternal care resulted in better emotional regulation and cognition. Of even greater concern is the emerging finding that this modification can be transmitted across generations as well as in gene expression in the brain (Essex et al., 2013; Sheridan & McLaughlin, 2014).

Stress can also negatively impact the fetal and infant brain. Children growing up in low-SES environments are more likely to be exposed to family conflict, many people in the same household and many changes in who lives in the home, neighborhood disruption, and anger all making for the experience of "toxic stress" (Evans et al., 2011; Lupien et al., 2009). This stress is thought to program the HPA axis leading to excessive secretion of glucocorticoids (Lupien et al., 2009). This chronic stress on a child's brain development can lead to hyper or hypo activity of the HPA axis leading to changes in the prefrontal cortex (important for insight and impulse control), the amygdala, and the hippocampus (Lupien et al., 2009). This excessive glucocorticoid exposure can affect plasticity and hence neurogenesis in the hippocampus and synapsis. This is particularly devastating to the child's development as it affects the child's ability to cope, to develop coping mechanisms, and to undermine cognitive development (McEwen & Gianaros, 2010).

Children raised in poverty are more likely to be disciplined more harshly and inconsistently as well as experiencing less nurturing and positive reinforcement

(Conger et al., 2010). Studies of children in institutions or who have documented maltreatment have found smaller gray and white matter volume in childhood and less hippocampal volume in adulthood (Belsky & deHaan, 2011).

Susceptible Cognitive Areas of Development The areas that are most susceptible to changes based on poverty and stress include basic skills of language, literacy, and executive functioning. Language is based in the left temporal lobe and has been found to be strongly associated with childhood SES (Noble et al., 2007). Research has found that higher-SES children have more neural specialization for reading, and when a reading disability is present in these children, compensatory systems are more readily available for remediation (Raizada et al., 2008). For lower-SES children, lack of experience and exposure to literacy seems to result in neural differences particularly in the language centers of the brain (D'Angiulli et al., 2012).

Learning and memory can also be associated with SES. The hippocampus is the main structure that supports learning and memory and has many glucocorticoid receptors. If you recall, glucocorticoids are part of the HPA axis and respond to stress. Too much glucocorticoids can interfere with hippocampal development. Neuroimaging has found that higher-SES children have larger hippocampi with low-SES children showing smaller hippocampi even when they reach their fifth decade of life (Jednorog et al., 2012; Staff et al., 2012). An intriguing recent finding has been that family income and learning may be mediated by hippocampal differences and are inversely related (Hair et al., 2015). In addition, educational experiences being related to hippocampal volume decrease with individuals with less education showing greater hippocampal volume loss than those with higher educational attainment (Noble et al., 2012). Thus, nurturance, educational experience, and enrichment have effects on the hippocampus, which is a crucial structure for new learning to take place.

The amygdala is responsible for emotional processing. Functional neuroimaging studies have found that children from lower-SES backgrounds as well as those from nonoptimal environments have less regulated functioning in the amygdala (Kim et al., 2013). In addition, problems with attachment, maternal depression, and difficulty with bonding have been found to be related to a larger amygdala in childhood and adolescence. A larger amygdala is associated with more emotional dysregulation and poorer emotional control (Gilliam et al., 2015).

In addition to the hippocampus and amygdala, the prefrontal cortex is an important structure for executive function, insight into behavior, impulse control, and higher-order planning and reasoning. Aspects that have been found to be related to smaller prefrontal cortex development include deprivation, stress, negative parenting, and less use of language to explain concepts and ideas (Hair et al., 2015). One interesting study using a longitudinal design found a relationship between low SES in childhood and later problems with aggression and conduct to smaller prefrontal volume (Holz et al., 2015). Studies have also found that when high levels of cortisol are present (the HPA axis), children are in deprived and higher stress environments (Blair et al., 2011). Thus the prefrontal cortex is exquisitively sensitive to stress, the HPA axis, and deprivation as well as poor parenting.

Summary Thus, poverty and family stress can alter the brain's trajectory and place the child at high risk for emotional and behavioral problems. Particular structures that are vulnerable are in the limbic system, the language system, and the prefrontal cortex. These structures basically allow the child to adapt to his/her environment and the changing requirements of that environment. When these structures are compromised, the resulting adaptation of the child and eventually the adult is less than optimal. From the research the key factor is poverty and stress rather than ethnicity or culture that shapes the child's brain and resulting mental health. What is most alarming is that this brain change appears to alter the genetics of the child and can be passed down to ensuing generations almost guaranteeing continuing poverty and poor functioning. Interventions to improve living conditions and stress are indicated for these children in order to circumvent the inevitability of these difficulties for future generations. It is not clear whether these difficulties can be reversed, but public policy and interventions by schools and psychologists would seem to be a first step toward making life more palatable for these children and their families. Clinical, counseling, and school psychologists need to be aware of these effects on a child's development and brain in assisting parents to understand the resulting trauma that can result from excessive stress and environmental challenge.

The Importance of Understanding Neurodevelopment for the Clinician

While it is not expected that general clinicians in psychology (school, counseling, and clinical) have extensive training in neurodevelopment, it is not uncommon for these professionals to see children who have various disorders for therapy and/or assessment. Moreover, chronic diseases such as diabetes and genetic disorders often are accompanied by neuropsychological deficits that can translate into difficulties with adaptation and emotional functioning. More and more children with significant medical diseases are now surviving and frequently experience emotional difficulty from the stress of their disease and treatment as well as family stress. Children who recover from cancer, leukemia, organ transplants, and brain injuries frequently experience difficulty with memory and attention as well as impulse control. These issues often translate into problem socially as well as emotionally and frequently require psychotherapy.

Genetic disorders also pose risks to neurodevelopment for children. There is evidence for a predisposition for depression and anxiety for children with families with a history of these disorders. This is true also for schizophrenia and bipolar disorder. Further children with genetic disorders such as Hurler's disease, adrenoleukodystrophy, Williams syndrome, and others are surviving, and treatments have been developed. While these treatments are lifesaving, they also take a toll on the brain and can result in difficulty with attention, memory, vision, hearing, and mobility. These aspects often can affect the child's adaptation, and psychotherapy is frequently recommended for the child and his/her family.

Biological and Environmental Factors

Several other factors can also impact the child's functioning and result in referral to specialists. The effect of stress on the fetus was discussed earlier. Nutritional deficiencies, particularly in the last trimester of the pregnancy, can affect brain size and weight resulting in fewer brain cells. Maternal hypotension can be as dangerous for the fetus as hypertension. Both of these disorders can cause difficulty with migration of cells and proliferation of synapses and circulation problems in the fetal brain resulting in stroke-like areas to be present.

The use of alcohol during pregnancy has been widely publicized as having serious consequences for the fetal brain. It has been estimated that over 40,000 children are born with fetal alcohol effects of some degree each year (Streisguth et al., 2004; Luu et al., 2017). Fetal alcohol syndrome effects can vary from mild to very severe depending on how much the mother drank and when (Boys et al., 2016). The psychologist will see these children in psychotherapy, and it is important to recognize that impulse control and emotional control are part and parcel of these disorders and usual behavioral interventions are often insufficient for treatment. It is also important for the clinician to be aware that alcohol often results in frontal lobe symptoms where learning from mistakes and insights into behavior are negatively impacted.

Birth complications can also result in difficulties in the child. Prematurity can affect the child in many ways. While many premature infants may progress well, there are some that experience significant problems with attention and executive functioning around the age of 9 or 10. Birth complications have been strongly implicated in schizophrenia and psychosis including low and high birth weight, breech presentation, vacuum extraction, placenta infarcts, and others (Liu et al., 2019). The clinician is well advised to obtain a comprehensive pregnancy and delivery history to fully appreciate these risk factors.

This is a very brief description of these disorders from a neurodevelopmental perspective. Chapter 4 will discuss these areas in much more detail. It is important to recognize that the frontal lobe is most susceptible to problems in neurodevelopment. These difficulties may not show up until 9 or 10 when independence and emotional control are expected. The clinician working with these children will profit from understanding the development of these structures and how it impacts later development particularly in the emotional and social domains.

Conclusions

Neurodevelopment is becoming a more and more important aspect for clinicians as children with various disorders are now surviving and thriving following treatment. It is also important in helping parents to understand why their child is not learning at the expected pace or why their child is experiencing significant problems with emotional control, impulsivity, attention, and hyperactivity. Depression and anxiety have been linked for some children to neurodevelopmental and genetic causes. Fetal alcohol syndrome, genetic disorders, prematurity, environmental toxins, and other impacts on the fetus and baby have also been found to impact neurodevelopment with these children frequently requiring psychotherapy and/or assessment to progress as far as they can.

As described above there are critical periods in fetal neurodevelopment with the first 2 weeks crucial for the formation of the neural tube and then later the synaptogenesis and selective cell death that occurs to form synapses and to trim back neurons that have not found their place. Birth complications can cause significant problems for the child's neurodevelopment as can stress and domestic violence. Stress, poverty, violence, and substance abuse appear to be far more predictive of later neurodevelopmental difficulty than the effects of culture or ethnicity. Research has indicated that the ethnicity of the child is not as important as poverty, stress, and domestic violence in predicting later neurodevelopmental disorders. These findings are critically important as some mistakenly lay learning and adjustment difficulties on children of poverty as a result of ethnicity and culture rather than to environmental factors that can be corrected. Support of children, and their families, who are in adverse situations can improve their future. It is sobering to recall that continued stress over long periods of time can result in genetic transformation of the telomeres of the chromosomes that is then transmitted to the next generation. It would appear that one of the more ready solutions for these difficulties is political and requires the will to change how we work with children and families who are in poverty and who live in dangerous situations. I can recall one of my clients saying to me (he was 9): *"how do you expect me to practice my reading at night when I can hear shots and fighting outside my window?"* From the mouths of babes!

Discussion Questions

1. Describe the lobes of the brain, their function, and their development.
2. Describe the process during the first 2 weeks of gestation. Describe the difficulties that can arise from defects in development during this time.
3. What are apoptosis and synaptogenesis? Describe these processes and how important they are for neurodevelopment.
4. Describe the gender differences in brain development. Are there any? If not why not?
5. What effects does poverty and violence have on the developing brain? Why do you think these aspects affect the developing fetus to that extent? How would you work with these children and their families?
6. The frontal lobe takes the longest to develop. How do you think this increased length of development is necessary for this structure? How do these findings map onto the work of Erickson, Freud, and Piaget?
7. How would you work with a child who has survived treatment for a life-threatening disease? What types of educational information would be most helpful for him/her and his/her family?

8. What role do you believe culture has in supporting the neurodevelopment of the child? What gender differences may also affect neurodevelopment?
9. The limbic system is an important aspect of neurodevelopment. How would you work with a child who is very dysregulated and who has difficulty learning from his/her mistakes? What areas of the brain would be most affected to result in these difficulties?
10. Why is this information important for the clinician to master even when not in neuropsychological practice?

EPPP Sample Questions

1. What is the main function of the meninges?
   (a) To provide cushioning for the brain
   (b) To provide air between the brain and skull
   (c) To take away waste and unneeded substances
   (d) To facilitate consciousness and attention
2. The brain stem involves several functions including:
   (a) Thinking, eating, and sleeping
   (b) Body movement, thinking, and eating
   (c) Respiration, swallowing, blood pressure
   (d) Breathing, thinking, moving
3. Injury to the cerebellum can mostly result in:
   (a) Movement disturbances
   (b) Emotional disturbance
   (c) Out-of-body feelings
   (d) Learning problems
4. The neural tube is the foundation for:
   (a) The brain and spinal cord
   (b) The brain stem and hippocampus
   (c) The basal ganglia and hippocampus
   (d) The brain stem and basal ganglia
5. The basal ganglia are made up of:
   (a) Globus pallidus, neural tube, putamen
   (b) Caudate, brain stem, hippocampus
   (c) Putamen, globus pallidus, brain stem
   (d) Caudate, putamen, globus pallidus

Answers: A, C, A, A, D

Proactive Readings

Transcending the past

Galaburda, A. M., & Kemper, T. L. (1979). Cytoarchitectonic abnormalities in developmental dyslexia: A case study. *Annals of Neurology, 6*, 94–100.

Lupien, S. J., McEwen, B. S., Gunnar, M. R., & Heim, C. (2009). Effects of stress throughout the lifespan on the brain, behavior, and cognition. *Nature Review of Neuroscience, 10*, 434–445.

Excelling in the Present

Kim, P., Evans, G. W., & Angstadt, M. (2013). Effects of childhood poverty and chronic stress on emotion regulatory brain function in adulthood. *Proceedings of the National Academy of Science USA, 110*, 18442–18447.

Puig, J., Englund, M. M., Simpson, J. A., & Collins, W. A. (2013). Predicting adult physical illness from infant attachment: A prospective longitudinal study. *Health Psychology, 32*, 409–417.

Transforming the Future

Porter, C. L., & Dyer, W. J. (2017). Does marital conflict predict infants' physiological regulation? A short-term prospective study. *Journal of Family Psychology, 31*, 475–484.

Sheridan, M. A., & McLaughlin, K. A. (2014). Dimensions of early experience and neural development: Deprivation and threat. *Trends in Cognitive Science, 18*, 580–585.

References

Belsky, J., & deHaan, M. (2011). Annual research review: Parenting and children's brain development: The end of the beginning. *Journal of Child Psychology & Psychiatry, 52*, 409–428. https://doi.org/10.1111/j.1469-7610.2010.02281.x

Blair, C., Raver, C., Granger, D., Mills-Koonce, R., & Hibel, L. (2011). Allostasis and allostatic load in the context of poverty in early childhood. *Development and Psychopathology, 23*(3), 845–857. https://doi.org/10.1017/s0954579411000344

Boys, C. J., Bjorke, J., Dole, K. N., Dalnes, C., Terwey, S., & Chang, P.N. (2016). Improving educational outcomes in fetal alcohol syndrome disorder through interagency collaboration. *Journal of Pediatric Neuropsychology, 2*, 50–57. https://doi.org/10.1007/s40817-016-0011-2

Brodal, P. (2016). *The central nervous system* (Vol. 5). Oxford.

Buchsbaum, M. S., Friedman, J., Buchsbaum, B. R., Chu, K.-W., Hazlett, E. A., Newmark, R., … Gorman, J. (2006). Diffusion tensor imaging in schizophrenia. *Biological Psychiatry, 60*(11) 1181–1187. https://doi.org/10.1016/j.biopsych.2005.11.028

Carlson, N. A., & Birkett, M. A. (2017). In C. Palendorf (Ed.), *Physiology of behavior* (Vol. 12). Pearson Education.

Castellanos, F. X., & Proal, E. (2012). Large-scale brain systems in ADHD: Beyond the prefrontal-striatal model. *Trends in Cognitive Science, 16*(1), 17–26. https://doi.org/10.1016/j.tics.2011.11.007

Chiang, M.-C., McMahon, K. L., & de Zubicaray, G. I. (2011). Genetics of white matter development: A DTI study of 705 twins and their siblings aged 12 to 29. *NeuroImage, 54*(3), 2308–2317. https://doi.org/10.1016/j.neuroimage.2010.10.015

Conger, R. D., Conger, K. J., & Martin, M. J. (2010). Socioeconomic status, family processes, and individual development. *Journal of Marriage and Family, 72*(3), 685–704. https://doi.org/10.1111/j.1741-3737.2010.00725.x

D'Angiulli, A., Van Roon, P. M., & Weinberg, J. (2012). Frontal EEG/ERP correlates of attentional processes, cortisol, and motivational states in adolescents from lower and higher socioeconomic status. *Frontiers in Human Neuroscience, 6*, 306. https://dx.doi.org/10.3389%2Ffnhum.2012.00306

Dow-Edwards, D., & Torres-Reveron, A. (2012). Sex differences in the effects of cocaine exposure on dopaminergic systems during brain development. In M. Lewis & L. Kestler (Eds.), *Gender differences in prenatal substance exposure* (pp. 55–76). American Psychological Association.

Ellis, B. J., Boyce, W. T., Belsky, J., Bakermans-Kranenburg, M. J., & van Ijzendoorn, M. (2011). Differential susceptibility to the environment: An evolutionary-neurodevelopmental theory. *Development and Psychopathology, 23*(1), 7–28. https://doi.org/10.1017/s0954579410000611

Elman, J. L., Takahashi, K., & Tohsaku, Y. H. (1981). Lateral asymmetries for the identification of concrete and abstract Kanji. *Brain and Language, 19*(3), 290–300. https://doi.org/10.1016/0028-3932(81)90070-1

Essex, M. J., Boyce, W. T., & Hertzman, C. (2013). Epigenetic vestiges of early developmental adversity: Childhood stress exposure and DNA methylation in adolescence. *Child Development, 84*(1), 58–75. https://doi.org/10.1111/j.1467-8624.2011.01641.x

Evans, G. W., Brooks-Gunn, J., & Klebanov, P. K. (2011). Stressing out the poor: Chronic physiological stress and the income-achievement gap. *Community Investments, 23*, 22–27.

Fair, D. A., Nigg, J. T., Iyer, S., Bathula, D., Mills, K. L., Dosenbach, N., et al. (2013). Distinct neural signatures detected for ADHD subtypes after controlling for micromovements in resting state functional connectivity MRI data. *Frontiers in Systems Neuroscience, 6*, 80. https://doi.org/10.3389/fnsys.2012.00080

Felton, A., Vazquez, D., Ramos-Nunez, A. I., Greene, M. R., Macbeth, A., Hernandez, A. E., & Chiarello, C. (2017). Bilingualism influences structural indices of interhemispheric organization. *Journal of Neurolinguistics, 42*, 1–11. https://doi.org/10.1016/j.jneuroling.2016.10.004

Fletcher, J. M., Dennis, M., & Northrup, H. (2000). Hydrocephalus. In K. O. Yeates, D. M. Ris, & H. G. Taylor (Eds.), *Pediatric neuropsychology* (pp. 25–46). Guilford.

Fredrik, E., Macoveanu, J., Olesen, P., Tegner, J., & Klingberg, T. (2007). Stronger synaptic connectivity as a mechanism behind development of working memory-related brain activity during childhood. *Journal of Cognitive Neuroscience, 19*(5), 750–760. https://doi.org/10.1162/jocn.2007.19.5.750

Galaburda, A. M., & Kemper, T. L. (1979). Cytoarchitectonic abnormalities in developmental dyslexia: A case study. *Annals of Neurology, 6*, 94–100. https://doi.org/10.1002/ana.410060203

Gauvain, M., & Perez, S. (2015). Cognitive development and culture. In L. S. Liben, U. Muller, & R. M. Lerner (Eds.), *Handbook of child psychology and developmental science: Cognitive processes* (Vol. 2, 7th ed., pp. 854–896). Wiley.

Gazzaniga, M. S., Ivry, R. B., & Mangun, G. R. (2013). *Cognitive neuroscience: The biology of the mind* (4th ed.). W.W. Norton & Company.

Giedd, J. N., Castellanos, F. X., Casey, B. J., Kozuch, P., King, A. C., Hamburger, S. D., & Rapoport, J. L. (1994). Quantitative morphology of the corpus callosum in Attention Deficit Hyperactivity Disorder. *American Journal of Psychiatry, 151*(5), 665–669. https://doi.org/10.1176/ajp.151.5.665

Gilbert, S. F. (2000). *Developmental biology* (Vol. 6). Sinauer Associates.

Gilliam, M., Forbes, E. E., Gianaros, P. J., Erickson, K. I., Brennan, L. M., & Shaw, D. S. (2015). Maternal depression in childhood and aggression in young adulthood: Evidence for mediation by offspring amygdala–hippocampal volume ratio. *Journal of Child Psychology & Psychiatry, 56*(10), 1083–1091. https://doi.org/10.1111/jcpp.12364

Gogtay, N., Giedd, J. N., Lusk, L., Hayashi, K. M., Greenstein, D., Vaituzis, A. C., … Thompson, P. M. (2004). Dynamic mapping of human cortical development during childhood through early adulthood. *PNAS, 101*(21), 8174–8179. https://doi.org/10.1073/pnas.0402680101

Hair, N. L., Hanson, J. L., Wolfe, B. L., & Pollak, S. D. (2015). Association of child poverty, brain development, and academic achievement. *JAMA Pediatrics, 169*(9), 822–829. https://doi.org/10.1001/jamapediatrics.2015.1475

Hampton, L. E., Fletcher, J. M., Cirino, P., Blaser, S., Kramer, L. A., & Dennis, M. (2013). Neuropsychological profiles of children with aqueductal stenosis and spina bifida myelomeningocele. *Journal of the International Neuropsychological Society, 19*(2), 127–136. https://dx.doi.org/10.1017%2FS1355617712001117

Harris, J. L. (1983). *Cultural anthropology*. Harper & Row.

Hirase, H., & Shinohara, Y. (2014). Transformation of cortical and hippocampal neural circuit by environmental enrichment. *Neuroscience, 280*(7), 282–298. https://doi.org/10.1016/j.neuroscience.2014.09.031

Holden, C. (2005). Sex and the suffering brain. *Science, 308*(5278), 1574–1577. https://doi.org/10.1126/science.308.5728.1574

Holtmaat, A., & Svoboda, K. (2009). Experience-dependent structural synaptic plasticity in the mammalian brain. *Nature Review of Neuroscience, 30*, 14964–14971.

Holz, N. E., Boecker, R., & Hohm, E. (2015). The long-term impact of early life poverty on orbitofrontal cortex volume in adulthood: Results from a prospective study of over 25 years. *Neuropsychopharmacology, 40*(4), 996–1004. https://doi.org/10.1038/npp.2014.277

Jednorog, K., Altarelli, I., & Monzalvo, K. (2012). The influence of socioeconomic status on children's brain structure. *PLoS One, 7*(10), https://doi.org/10.1371/annotation/47661de2-2c53-4396-9f88-06b5ad233566

Johnson, S. B., Riis, J. L., & Noble, K. G. (2016). Poverty and the developing brain. *Pediatrics, 137*(4), e20153075. https://doi.org/10.1542/peds.2015-3075

Kennepol, S. (1999). Toward a cultural neuropsychology: An alternative view and a preliminary model. *Brain and Cognition, 41*(3), 365–380. https://doi.org/10.1006/brcg.1999.1138

Kestler, L., Bennett, D. S., Carmody, D. P., & Lewis, M. (2012). Gender-dependent effects of prenatal cocaine exposure. In M. Lewis & L. Kestler (Eds.), *Gender differences in prenatal substance exposure* (pp. 11–29). American Psychological Association.

Kim, P., Evans, G. W., & Angstadt, M. (2013). Effects of childhood poverty and chronic stress on emotion regulatory brain function in adulthood. *Proceedings of the National Academy of Science USA, 110*(46), 18442–18447. https://doi.org/10.1073/pnas.1308240110

Kolb, B., & Whishaw, I. Q. (2003). *Fundamentals of human neuropsychology* (5th ed.). Worth Publishers.

Kouros, C. D., Papp, L. M., Goeke-Morey, M. C., & Cummings, E. M. (2014). Spillover between marital quality and parent-child relationship quality: Parental depressive symptoms as moderators. *Journal of Family Psychology, 28*(3), 315–325. https://doi.org/10.1037/a0036804

Lezak, M. D., Howieson, D. B., & Loring, D. W. (2004). *Neuropsychological assessment* (4th ed.). Oxford University Press.

Liu, Y., Mendonca, M., Johnson, S., & O'Reilly, H. (2019). Testing the neurodevelopmental trauma and developmental risk factor models of psychosis using a naturalistic experiment. *Psychological Medicine*. https://doi.org/10.1017/S0033291719003349

Lipina, S. J., Simonds, J., & Segretin, M. S. (2011). Recognizing the child in child poverty. *Vulnerable Child Youth Studies, 6*(1), 8–17. https://doi.org/10.1080/17450128.2010.521598

Llorente, R., Lopez Gallardo, M., Berzal, A. L., Prada, C., Garcia-Segura, L. M., & Viveros, M.-P. (2009). Early maternal deprivation in rats induces gender-dependent effects on developing hippocampal and cerebellar cells. *International Journal of Developmental Neuroscience, 27*(3), 233–241. https://doi.org/10.1016/j.ijdevneu.2009.01.002

Lupien, S. J., McEwen, B. S., Gunnar, M. R., & Heim, C. (2009). Effects of stress throughout the lifespan on the brain, behavior, and cognition. *Nature Review of Neuroscience, 10*(6), 434–445. https://doi.org/10.1038/nrn2639

Luria, A. B. (1980). *Higher cortical functions in man* (2nd ed.). Basic Books.

Luu, T. M., Mian, M. O. R., & Nyut, A. M. (2017). Long-term impact of premature birth. *Clinics in Perinatology, 44*(2), 305–315. https://doi.org/10.1016/j.clp.2017.01.003

McEwen, B. S., & Gianaros, P. J. (2010). Central role of the brain in stress and adaptation: Links to socioeconomic status, health, and disease. *Annals of the New York Academy of Sciences, 1186*, 190–222. https://doi.org/10.1111/j.1749-6632.2009.05331.x

Noble, K. G., Grieve, S. M., & Korgaonkar, M. S. (2012). Hippocampal volume varies with educational attainment across the life span. *Frontiers in Human Neuroscience 9*(6), 307. https://doi.org/10.3389/fnhum.2012.00307

Noble, K. G., McCandliss, B., & Farah, M. J. (2007). Socioeconomic gradients predict individual differences in neurocognitive abilities. *Developmental Science, 10*, 464–480. https://doi.org/10.1111/j.1467-7687.2007.00600.x

Nyardi, A., Li, J., Hickling, S., Foster, J., & Oddy, W. H. (2013). The role of nutrition in children's neurocognitive development from pregnancy through childhood. *Frontiers in Human Neuroscience, 7*, 97–110. https://doi.org/10.3389/fnhum.2013.00097

Perez-Arce, P. (1999). The influence of culture on cognition. *Archives of Clinical Neuropsychology, 14*(7), 581–592. https://doi.org/10.1093/arclin/14.7.581

Pliszka, S. (2016). *Neuroscience for the mental health clinician* (Vol. 2). Guilford.

Porter, C. L., & Dyer, W. J. (2017). Does marital conflict predict infants' physiological regulation? A short-term prospective study. *Journal of Family Psychology, 31*(4), 475–484. https://psycnet.apa.org/doi/10.1037/fam0000295

Puig, J., Englund, M. M., Simpson, J. A., & Collins, W. A. (2013). Predicting adult physical illness from infant attachment: A prospective longitudinal study. *Health Psychology, 32*(4), 409–417. https://psycnet.apa.org/doi/10.1037/a0028889

Purves, D., Augustine, G. J., Fitzpatrick, D., Katz, L. C., LaMantia, A.-S., McNamara, J. O., & Williams, S. M. (2001). *Neuroscience* (2nd ed.). Sinauer Associates.

Raizada, R. D. S., Richards, T. L., Meltzoff, A. N., & Kuhl, P. K. (2008). Socioeconomic status predicts hemispheric specialization of the left inferior frontal gyrus in young children. *NeuroImage, 40*(3), 1392–1401. https://doi.org/10.1016/j.neuroimage.2008.01.021

Ris, D. M., Ammerman, R. T., Waller, N., Walz, N. C., Oppenheimer, S., Brown, T. M., et al. (2007). Taxonicity of nonverbal learning disabilities. *Journal of the International Neuropsychological Society, 13*(1), 50–58. https://doi.org/10.1017/s1355617707070087

Schneider, S., Peters, J., Bromberg, U., Brassen, S., Menz, M. M., Miedl, S. F., et al. (2011). Boys do it the right way: Sex-dependent amygdala lateralization during face processing in adolescents. *NeuroImage, 56*(3), 1847–1853. https://doi.org/10.1016/j.neuroimage.2011.02.019

Schore, A. N. (2017). All our sons: The developmental neurobiology and neuroendocrinology of boys at risk. *Infant Mental Health Journal, 38*(1), 15–52. https://doi.org/10.1002/imhj.21616

Semrud-Clikeman, M., & Bledsoe, J. (2014). Understanding the neuroscience of clients with Asian heritage. In M. Davis & R. D'Amato (Eds.), *Neuropsychology of Asians and Asian Americans: Practical and theoretical considerations* (pp. 117–134). Springer.

Semrud-Clikeman, M., & Ellison, P. A. T. (2009). *Child neuropsychology: Assessment and intervention*. Springer.

Semrud-Clikeman, M., & Fine, J. G. (2009). Neuroimaging in women. In E. Fletcher-Janzen & C. R. Reynolds (Eds.), *The neuropsychology of women* (pp. 31–67). Kluwer.

Semrud-Clikeman, M., Pliszka, S. R., Lancaster, J., & Liotti, M. (2006). Volumetric MRI differences in treatment-naïve vs chronically treated children with ADHD. *Neurology, 67*(6), 1023–1027. https://doi.org/10.1212/01.wnl.0000237385.84037.3c

Sheridan, M. A., & McLaughlin, K. A. (2014). Dimensions of early experience and neural development: Deprivation and threat. *Trends in Cognitive Science, 18*(11), 580–585. https://doi.org/10.1016/j.tics.2014.09.001

Shonkoff, J. P., & Garner, A. S. (2012). The lifelong effects of early childhood adversity and toxic stress. *Pediatrics, 129*(1), 1–59. https://doi.org/10.1542/peds.2011-2663

Squire, L. R., Berg, D., Bloom, F. E., duLac, S., Gosh, A., & Spitzer, N. C. (2008). *Fundamental neuroscience* (Vol. 3). Elsevier.

Staff, R. T., Murray, A. D., Ahearn, T. S., Mustafa, N., Fox, H. C., & Whalley, L. J. (2012). Childhood socioeconomic status and adult brain size: Childhood socioeconomic status influences adult hippocampal size. *Annals of Neurology, 71*, 653–660. https://doi.org/10.1002/ana.22631

Streissguth, A. P., Bookstein, F. L., Barr, H., Sampson, P. D., O'Malley, K., & Young, J. K. (2004). Risk factors for adverse life outcomes in fetal alcohol syndrome and fetal alcohol effects. *Journal of Developmental and Behavioral Pediatrics, 4*, 228–238.

Swaiman, K. F., & Ashwal, S. (2017). *Pediatric neurology*. Mosby.

Turkheimer, E., Haley, A., Waldron, M., D'Onofrio, B., & Gottesman, I. I. (2003). Socioeconomic status modifies heritability of IQ in young children. *Psychological Science, 14*, 623–628. https://doi.org/10.1046%2Fj.0956-7976.2003.psci_1475.x

Wasserman, R. M., & Holmbeck, G. N. (2016). Profiles of neuropsychological functioning in children and adolescents with spina bifida: Associations with biopsychosocial predictors and functional outcomes. *Journal of the International Neuropsychological Society, 22*(8), 804–816. https://doi.org/10.1017/s1355617716000680

Witelson, S. F. (1990). Structural correlates of cognitive function in the human brain. In A. B. Scheibel & A. F. Wechsler (Eds.), *Neurobiology of higher cognitive function* (pp. 167–184). Guilford Press.

Yu-Huan, H., Ying-Guan, Q., & Gui-Quing, Z. (1990). Crossed aphasia in Chinese: A clinical survey. *Brain and Language, 39*, 347–356. https://doi.org/10.1016/0093-934x(90)90144-6

Chapter 3
Why Should We Care About Functional Neuroanatomy?

Eleazar Cruz Eusebio and Anna Pignatiello

Learning Objectives

1. To understand why functional neuroanatomy developed.
2. To understand how functional neuroanatomy developed.
3. To understand the practical and clinical uses of functional neuroanatomy in addressing and prioritizing an individual's problem set, needs, and subsequent interventions.
4. To explain how to use a multicultural approach to functional neuroanatomy to help guide treatment from assessment to intervention.
5. To understand the implications and future directions of functional neuroanatomy.

Overview

The purpose of this chapter is to provide the history and background of functional neuroanatomy and its critical role in working with the biological basis of behavior of individuals in clinical, counseling, and school settings. This chapter will address the importance of examining the client or student from a multicultural perspective. It will identify the areas of growth and implications of clinical practice within the psychological fields. Finally, it will address the future of functional neuroanatomy

E. C. Eusebio (✉)
School Psychology, Prince George's County Public Schools, Upper Marlboro, MD, USA

A. Pignatiello
Department of School Psychology, The Chicago School of Professional Psychology, Chicago, IL, USA

R. C. D'Amato et al. (eds.), *Understanding the Biological Basis of Behavior*,
https://doi.org/10.1007/978-3-030-59162-5_3

after decades of expansion and research in practice, in an attempt to give the reader a better understanding of where we are with functional neuroanatomy and the biological basis of behavior.

Functional Neuroanatomy and the Biological Basis of Behavior

School, clinical, and counseling psychologists are essentially experts in helping others with emotional regulation and changing behaviors that may be intrusive to their life at school, in the workplace, at home, or in the community. As a psychologist or counselor, people come to us to understand why they or a loved one are engaging in inappropriate behaviors, or why they are not performing up to standards in school or the work place, and what can be done to help them. It is important to understand the underlying biological bases of an individual's behavior in order to create a more personalized and accurate treatment plan or educational plan. As stated in Chap. 2, various parts of the brain are associated with emotion. In this chapter, there will be more focus on the circuitry of the brain and its connection to behavior. One way to think of the circuitry of the brain is to compare it to wires that connect different parts of machinery. While the individual parts of the brain are generally used for specific functions, the neurological circuitry is what connects those different parts. Complications in these circuits can cause clinical implications which school, clinical, and counseling psychologists commonly encounter when working with their clients. Through understanding networking and connections of the various areas of the brain, mental health professionals can better support their clients through evidence-based interventions and psychoeducation. See Tables 3.1 and 3.2 for more specific information about brain lobes, structures, and their functions.

When a student or client is brought to the attention of the practitioner, it is often because they are engaging in some sort of negative behavior. For example, a teacher may come to a school psychologist describing a student who is impulsive and never stays in her seat, or a student who never pays attention and is constantly daydreaming. One may jump to thinking that the child has attention-deficit/hyperactivity disorder (ADHD) and an exhausted parent or teacher may want to move quickly toward medication. Practitioners who understand the biological basis of behavior will know to dig deeper. While prescribing medication may not be within the realm of some psychologists, having this understanding will strengthen the skill of case conceptualization and aid those involved on the decision as to whether medication is necessary, and if this is a child with ADHD or not. Given the brief description of the child, a psychologist may begin to think of frontal lobe circuitry and possible implications in the anterior cingulate, orbitofrontal, dorsolateral, and ventrolateral cortexes. All of these areas are involved with various functions, such as self-regulation of behavior, decision making, planning, monitoring, focusing and sustaining attention, motivation, self-awareness, and self-restraint (Torregrossa, Quinn, & Taylor, 2008). A

Table 3.1 Brain lobes and hemisphere functions, notes, and structures

Brain lobes and hemispheres			
Brain structure	Function	Notes	Damage
Frontal lobe	Responsible for emotional regulation, reasoning, risk taking, expressive language, muscle movement, planning, judgment, decision-making, and attention	Located at the front section of the brain; ultimate control and information processing center; interprets and acts on information processes by sensory areas; often seen as the most understood brain lobe	Executive processing problems, attention concerns, sexual issues/habits, apathy, overall socialization, ability to attend, and frontotemporal dementia
Temporal lobe	Serves as primary auditory cortex; important for hearing, recognizing sounds and language, and memories; it is the auditory center of the brain	Located in the bottom section of the brain; above the ear; the hippocampus is housed in the temporal lobe; long-term memory and conscious memory can be found here	Disturbance of sensation and perception, inability to attend to sights and sounds, and memory loss; speech perception problems, language issues, and emotional problems
Parietal lobe	Tactile/sensory *(senses)* and body processing center; it is responsible for understanding pressure, touch, temperature, and pain; includes academic abilities with sound symbols in reading, math and spatial reasoning	Located in the top and rear of cerebral cortex in the middle section of the brain; behind the frontal lobe; its role is in self-awareness and attention has recently been highlighted in research	Impaired attention, academic dysfunction, tactile and sensory processing issues; socialization issues relating to self-awareness may be affected, and difficulty writing and problems connecting words in speech
Occipital lobe	Is responsible for processing, understanding, and remembering visual perceptions; allows for the interpretation of depth, distance, location, and identity of objects	Located in the rearmost lobe of the cerebral hemisphere, this is the brain's smallest lobe but remains a unique and indispensable part of the brain's sensory system	Problems with sight, visual hallucinations, and illusions. Lesions on the occipital lobe can result in a "hole" in your vision known as a scotoma. Extensive damage can result in total blindness
Left hemisphere	Processes verbal information and language sequentially; interprets actions logically and analytically that are detail-oriented to math/science; hemisphere typically used during traditional learning activities (e.g., verbal lectures)	Typically associated with logic, processing science/math, and written information; controls right side of body (contralateral) including right field vision and motor skills	Problems with language (aphasia), judgment, and motor planning. Trouble reading and writing and changes in speech. Deficits in planning, organization, and memory

(continued)

Table 3.1 (continued)

Brain lobes and hemispheres			
Brain structure	Function	Notes	Damage
Right hemisphere	Processes visual/nonverbal information simultaneously, holistically, and globally; includes nonverbal functions, such as depth perception, tactile/sensory perception, creativity, art, emotional thought, nonverbal memory, and face recall	Typically associated with art awareness, creativity, music awareness, intuitiveness; includes novel and nonverbal abilities, impulsivity, center for imagination, and adventure. Controls left side of body (contralateral) including left field vision and motor skills	Problems with emotional recognition, such as recognizing faces and emotions; semantic processing; and other cognitive processing skills such as attention, memory, and executive functioning has been related to ADHD

Table 3.2 Brain structures, functions, and location/damage notes

Brain structure	Function	Notes
Angular gyrus	Combines sensory inputs; allows visual patterns to be covered to suitable auditory structures; word reading	Part of the language system in the left temporal lobe; damage causes inability to read and speak; problems writing
Amygdala	Processes emotions (aggression) rage, fear; relates to risk and loss abilities.	Almond-shaped mass; deep in the temporal lobes; relates to survival abilities
Auditory cortex	Responsible for hearing and processing sounds	Part of the temporal lobe, on the posterior superior temporal gyrus; Brodmann's areas 41 and 42
Broca's area	Produces speech through control of the motor cortex, in left frontal lobe; allows for ability to sing and comprehend speech	Damage disrupts speaking; located in the inferior frontal gyrus
Cerebral cortex	Allows for learning, thinking, and enabling adaptability; information processing center	Damage disrupts a person's ability to think, manage emotions, and behave appropriately
Corpus callosum	White mass axon fibers which connect both hemispheres for processing and communication of efficient brain functioning	Arched mass of white matter found deep in the longitudinal fissure; damage leads to disconnection of the hemispheres and processing problems
Hippocampus	Involves memory and learning; including visual, spatial (right hemispheric), and verbal (left hemisphere)	Medial region of the temporal lobe; damage impacts specific types of memory
Hypothalamus	Regulates thirst, hunger, body temperature, sexual behavior (hormone release); controls/regulates maintenance reflexes (eating); homeostasis linked to emotion	Located next to the third ventricle; helps govern endocrine system, monitors glands; controls hunger; linked to emotion and rewards

(continued)

Table 3.2 (continued)

Brain structure	Function	Notes
Medulla	Responsible for controlling autonomic functions such as breathing, heart rate, and blood pressure	Major relay point for information going to and from the brain and spinal cord; located directly above the spinal cord in the lower part of the brainstem
Midbrain	Serves as relay station for auditory and visual information including eye movement; smallest region of the brain	Controls eye movement and body movement; degeneration of this area is associated with Parkinson's disease
Motor cortex	Allows for processing of body movements; controls body parts; sends messages out to body, controls body movement	Premotor, primary, and supplemental motor areas responsible for movement from initiation to execution
Pituitary gland	Regulates hormone release related to growth, blood pressure, and reproduction; small bean-shaped gland	Located at the base of the brain; controlled by hypothalamus
Pons	Responsible for autonomic functions such as breathing and sleep cycles; integration of motor impulses, and postural and kinesthetic information	Portion of the brain stem, located above the medulla oblongata and below the midbrain; damage relates to nerve palsies, vertigo, facial paralysis, and gaze palsy
Prefrontal cortex	Plays a critical role in executive functioning, including working memory, planning complex behavior, decision-making, and moderating social behavior	Behind forehead and controls motor cortex; damage results in short-term memory, impulse control, and long-term planning
Reticular formation	Helps control behavioral arousal and consciousness	Network of interconnected nuclei located throughout the brainstem; damage can cause coma or death
Sensory cortex	Responsible for receiving and interpreting sensory information from the body	Behind and parallel to motor cortex. Modulates speech and clarity; includes touch, proprioception, and temperature
Spinal cord	Connects the brain to the body; long thin tubular structure made up of nervous tissue	Pathway to neural fibers; damage can lead to paralysis and/or death
Thalamus	Acts as a switchboard between sensory neurons and higher brain regions to relay sensory information	Deals with sight, hearing, touch, taste. Transmits replies from higher brain to cerebellum and medulla
Limbic system	Regulates autonomous and endocrine function, and consolidates memories. Set of brain structures that deal with emotion and memory; links emotion (fear and anger), basic motives (food and sex)	Located on both sides of the thalamus beneath the medial temporal lobe. Supports emotion, behavior, long-term memory, and olfactory functioning. Damage can cause hormonal imbalance and emotional dysfunction
Wernicke's area	Assists in the processing of speech. Responsible for auditory coding and understanding	Damage disrupts language comprehension

Adapted from D'Amato et al. (2005), Das et al. (1994), Hale and Fiorello (2004), Hynd and Willis (1988), Goodwin (1989), and Lezak et al. (2012)

disconnection or miscommunication between these areas with the rest of the brain may look like inattention or hyperactivity (Torregrossa et al., 2008). However, these areas are also involved with functions, such as judgment of another's feelings, self-regulation of behavior, emotional processing, anticipation, use of feedback, response inhibition, and emotional regulation. If the child looks like she is never paying attention, maybe she is hypervigilant. If she has poor concentration, it may not be due to ADHD, but instead she may have experienced a traumatic event which has negatively impacted her ability to sustain attention. Understanding the biological and physical differences of these complications is significant for identifying and implementing appropriate supports.

With the current increase in awareness of how toxic stress and adverse events during childhood can impact brain development, we look at the communication between the limbic system and the prefrontal cortex; however, several areas of the brain are activated when responding to stressful situations. Two major parts of the limbic system are the amygdala and hippocampus. Together these areas create and store memories and produce emotional responses. Research in neuroimaging has shown that the amygdala and hippocampus are altered in children who experience toxic stress and adverse events (De Bellis & Zisk, 2014; Souza-Queiroz et al., 2016). This type of alteration leads to a disruption in communication between the limbic system and the prefrontal cortex, which can then lead to the fight, flight, or freeze reaction instead of processing through appropriate decision making and problem solving (De Bellis & Zisk, 2014). Thus, experiencing neglect or chronic stressors during childhood increases the risk of significant problems with cognitive, affective, behavioral, physiological, relational, and self-attributional functioning (Kinniburgh et al., 2005; Perry & Hambrick, 2008). Psychoeducation can help individuals to understand their emotional and behavioral responses and work toward healthy emotional regulation. It can also aid parents and educators to promote and create predictable, consistent, and nurturing environments that lead to healthy brain development.

During childhood and adolescence, healthy environments that are stimulating and allow for opportunities of creativity and critical thinking can lead to positive neural growth (Cozolino, 2013; De Bellis & Zisk, 2014). Cozolino (2013) explains how social experiences affect brain function and development and argues as to why this is closely related to how humans learn throughout their lifetime. With his book, *The Social Neuroscience of Education*, Cozolino (2013) explains the brain-body connection and highlights the benefits of centering education on building secure and healthy attachments and how it impacts learning. Many of the behavioral aspects in his book, which are focused on teachers and the field of education, can be generalized and applied to other fields. For example, teacher burnout is explained as a hit to self-esteem and emotional well-being which leads to lowered job satisfaction and poor performance. In other words, when humans feel a decreased sense of self-worth, an emotional response to environmental factors, their behavior reflects that (i.e., career change or poor job performance). As Albert Bandura (1997) once stated, "The work we do determines whether a substantial part of our lives is repetitively boring, burdensome, and distressing, or lastingly challenging and self-fulfilling" (p. 422).

Functional neuroanatomy has provided researchers and clinicians with a greater understanding of how the brain is connected to behavior. With this understanding, health service psychologists can evaluate more comprehensively and create and implement additional sound and sustainable interventions and supports for those with whom they work. This information is invaluable when considering how to psychologically approach situations, no matter the complexity. Functional neuroanatomy has provided psychological practitioners with the knowledge base to provide support at individual, family, small group, and system-wide levels, while, at the same time, it has increased awareness and reliability in differential diagnosis.

History of Functional Neuroanatomy

The American Psychological Association (APA) promotes psychology programs to include history of psychology in the curriculum. It is important to study the history of functional neuroanatomy in order understand where we have been, how we have gotten to where we are currently, and where we are going in the future of the field of psychology. Having a deeper understanding of how the field has developed also allows for a more in-depth understanding and sound practice of one's theoretical orientation. The American Psychological Association (APA) also requires graduate programs to include history in the curriculum of the program (APA, 2006). The study of neuroanatomy dates back to pre-World War II with psychologists, such as Broca and Wernicke, who studied localization of brain functions (Hebben, Milberg, & Kaufman, 2010). After the war, major contributions were made to the field of clinical neuropsychology due to the large number of soldiers experiencing symptoms of post-traumatic stress disorder (PTSD), then viewed as "shell shock" or "soldier's heart," and traumatic brain injuries (Substance Abuse and Mental Health Services Administration, 2014). Researchers and clinicians thus began working toward a deeper understanding of the brain and its connection to emotional, behavioral, and physical responses.

Some of the most notable clinicians and researchers include, but are not limited to, Ward Halstead, Ralph Reitan, Alexander Luria, and Edith Kaplan. Halstead and Reitan created the assessment *Halstead-Reitan Neuropsychological Test Battery* (HRNTB), which has been updated several times and is still used in adult clinical neuropsychology today (Horton & Reynolds, 2015). The original core subtests of the HRNTB were created by Halstead and then updated by Reitan, who was his mentee. The development of both the original battery and the updated subtests were significant milestones in the field of neuropsychology. Reitan's contributions to the HRNTB allowed for assessment and treatment of individuals who suffered from brain damage and established that performances were related to the brain rather than related to behavior. Because of his research and practice, the role of clinical neuropsychologists in the healthcare system was recognized and welcomed for the first time. Horton and Reynolds (2015) argue, "every clinical neuropsychologist working today owes a debt to Reitan's contributions."

Alexander Luria (1902–1977) is another neuropsychologist who is well known for his significant contributions to contemporary neuropsychology through his findings on the function and organization of the brain (Hazin & Tarcísio da Rocha Falcão, 2014). Luria has contributed to the field in various ways, including the theory of extracortical organization of higher mental functions (Kotik-Friedgut, 2006). This theory laid the foundation for consideration of cross-cultural differences of brain development and structure. Thus, it is now well accepted today that social, cultural, and historical factors all play a vital role in neural development and must be considered throughout the evaluation process. Luria established that an evaluation should include both qualitative and quantitative measures.

Additionally, psychologist Edith Kaplan has contributed to the field of neuropsychology in many domains, most notable through her focus on apraxia, aphasia, and developmental issues (Oscar-Berman & Fein, 2013). Kaplan also developed a predoctoral and postdoctoral clinical neuropsychological internship-training program during her time as the director of Clinical Neuropsychological Services at the Boston VA Medical Center (1976–1987). Along with Luria, Kaplan added to the assessment domain by emphasizing the importance of qualitative data collection and analysis alongside of quantitative data. Kaplan and colleagues developed the Boston Process Approach (later called the Boston Hypothesis Testing Approach) which laid emphasis on the importance of *how* an individual arrives at an answer and initiated the concept of "testing the limits" (Miller, 2013).

Nearly all domains of the psychology field have changed and developed over the last several decades, including evaluation procedures and assessment tools. Much of the development in these areas is due to the research that has been dedicated to functional neuroanatomy. Because of the work of the previously mentioned individuals, and so many more, functional neuroanatomy has played a significant role in the progress of the fields of adult clinical neuropsychology, pediatric neuropsychology, and school neuropsychology. Miller (2013) addresses the work of Rourke (1982) who researched the history of clinical neuropsychology and described three stages in which the field went through: (1) the single test approach, (2) the test battery/lesion specification stage, and (3) the functional profile stage. The single test approach is described as a stage wherein researchers were utilizing a single measure to determine if a patient had brain damage (Miller, 2013). Psychologists were concerned, at the time, with overall brain functioning versus assessment of diverse domains of functioning. The test battery/lesion specification stage was a time in history when clinicians moved away from the single test approach and began to utilize several test batteries to measure a number of cognitive processes in order to discover neuropsychological dysfunction in patients (Miller, 2013). Much of the credit for the progress made during this stage is given to the previously mentioned psychologists, Ward Halstead, Ralph Reitan, Alexander Luria, and Edith Kaplan. Finally, the functional profile stage is noted as the time when neuroimaging techniques began to tie into assessment procedures for cognitive functioning. The developments made during this stage lead to a more comprehensive approach to neuropsychological assessment.

The study of functional neuroanatomy has evolved over time from a very narrow view of functioning and assessment, to a greater understanding of the brain-body connection and how it relates to emotion and behavior. Today, rather than approaching an evaluation to determine whether there is a presence of brain dysfunction or not, comprehensive assessments are often conducted to look more so at patterns of strengths and weaknesses.

Functional Neuroanatomy and Multicultural Issues

As our world becomes increasingly more diverse, practitioners, researchers, and scholars must all address the broadening of our growing multicultural society and continue to be informed of all of the diverse populations and cultures that make up the world's population. In the United States alone, our population is expected to grow more slowly in future decades than it did in the previous century. However, the total population of over 330 million at the time of publication of this textbook is projected to reach the 400 million threshold in 2051 and 417 million in 2060. In addition, around the time the 2020 Census was conducted, more than half of the nation's children were part of a minority race or ethnic group. This proportion is expected to continue to grow so that by 2060, just 36 percent of all children (people under age 18) will be single-race non-Hispanic White, compared with 52 percent today the U.S. population as a whole is expected to follow a similar trend, becoming majority-minority in 2044. The minority population is projected to rise to 56 percent of the total in 2060, compared with 38 percent in 2014 (United States Census Bureau, 2015). When examining functional neuroanatomy in practice, clinicians must understand the importance of the various multicultural factors and variables of the client in front of them. As the populations become more majority-minority in the next few decades, the biological basis of behavior as seen from the multicultural perspective will also diversify. Human beings are not a homogenous species and the diverse cultures that make up society are factors that can affect the utility of functional neuroanatomy from assessment to intervention.

Pediatric clinical neuropsychology is a subspecialty within the field of clinical neuropsychology that is concerned with the study and understanding of brain-behavior relationships in children and adolescents with known or suspected brain neurodevelopmental disorder, disease, injury, learning disability, or other acquired or congenital disorder affecting brain function and development. As a subspecialty, it has more access to the use of functional neuroanatomy in as many pediatric clinical neuropsychologists work in hospitals, clinics, or specialized practices that have access to equipment, such as a functional MRI (fMRI) and brain scanning technology. However, school and counseling psychologists can also vastly benefit from the use of functional neuroanatomy, but currently do not have the access to the same technology.

What remains a constant is that all of these subspecialties within the field of psychology work with the regular population of individuals from every socioeconomic, ethnic, sociocultural of all genders, beliefs, and walks of life. Therefore, psychologists must take a strong stance on looking at the diverse multicultural components that make up an individual and impact their presentation from a functional neuroanatomy sense. For example, the brain of an individual who experienced early childhood trauma in the form of abuse or neglect may look and present vastly different in an fMRI versus the brain of a regular functioning individual. Therefore, sociocultural components and factors must be taken into effect when examining and assessing individuals with the assistance of functional neuroanatomy.

So, what does a brain scan discover in an individual who reportedly experiences any kind of trauma? First, it is essential to provide a general overview of what a brain scan is in practice. For the purposes of clinical practice, brain scans that identify functional neuroanatomy come from brain scan technology that covers a diverse group of methods for imaging the brain. In psychiatric clinical practice, brain scans are mostly used to rule out visible brain lesions that may be causing psychiatric symptoms. In the schools and counseling psychology, brain scan technology can be used on a consult basis with the professionals who conduct the studies. In research, psychologists use brain scan technology to learn about the pathologies of the brain in mental illness. A common method is magnetic resonance imaging (MRI) which allows clinicians to look at the changes in the volume and structure of different areas of the brain, and integrity of the pathways connecting them.

Then there is functional MRI (fMRI) which examines blood flow in different areas and regions of the brain as a measure of their dynamic function, mostly in response to a task or event, such as thinking about a traumatic event or viewing of a short video that produces stress and raises cortical levels in the brain. Practitioners use brain circuitry to look at how people can be proactive by teaching clients to learn fear and safety, for example. Researchers who want to use functional neuroanatomy through a multicultural lens may also want to add variables in the research that address socioeconomic status, cultural norms, and any array of methodology that addresses the diversity of the subjects. At the current stage of the technology and research, psychiatrists, psychologists, and neuroscientists only use these methods for researching the brain changes in mental illness, and not for making diagnoses. In order to make broader conclusions about the data, practitioners and researchers must combine data from people with a mental illness to determine how, on average, different areas of their brain may differ in volume or function from others. This is further confounded when adding varying degrees of what makes up a groups' multicultural profile and the makeup and constellation of that group can be very complex. To summarize, brain imaging has been a very useful tool in understanding the aberrations in structure and function of a brain with PTSD, but it does not diagnose the condition.

Why Functional Neuroanatomy Is Critical to Professional Psychological Practice

Functional Neuroanatomy is not only critical to the professional practice of psychology, but it has become essential for professionals to utilize it to optimize their assessment, treatment, progress monitoring, and interventions for the client or patient. The 1990s was declared the "Decade of the Brain" in the United States and is now nearly three decades old (Goldstein, 1994). Although there have been great strides taken since then to explore and understand the brain better, there is still a lot of work to be done. Perhaps, the biggest push is in the area of brain scan technology. Although this chapter does not discuss the various technologies that exist, it will address why technology plays a role in why functional neuroanatomy is critical to professional psychological practice. See Chap. 5, (Noggle & Davis, 2021) for comprehensive coverage on neuroimaging.

Using technology to determine the functional neuroanatomy and clinical treatment planning for individuals go hand-in-hand. The data collected from brain scans is only as good as the technology that creates the images needed to examine the brain. However, it is important to note that technology, such as the MRI can only detect changes in blood flow without using a radioactive tracer. When a particular site in the brain is more active, blood flows to that area (Schooler et al., 2018). This blood brings oxygen to the brain cells that are working harder and, subsequently, thought to be working more efficiently. By tracking variations in blood flow, functional MRI can detect activity in the brain as it happens (Filippi, 2015).

So how is this critical to professional psychological practice? The bottom line is that if a client is seen for a severe condition of depression, anxiety, or even psychosis, brain technology can now utilize real-time data in the form of images to detect whether different parts of the brain are being utilized or maybe even neglected as the absence of active blood flow also predicts potential hypotheses for the practitioner.

Scientists have started to discover which areas of the brain are involved in different mental health conditions, such as depression, anxiety, and post-traumatic stress disorder (PTSD; Akiki et al., 2017); more clear data has been collected as to which areas of the brain are involved. For example, PTSD appears to be heavily involved with activity in the amygdala, which is, subsequently, involved in processing fear as well as lowered activity in parts of the frontal lobes (Zotev et al., 2018). This is essential to psychological practice because, with this data and analysis, we can now proceed to better confirmation of diagnoses and, subsequently, better and more accurate treatment plans.

Some technologies, like Positron Emission Tomography (PET) imaging and functional MRI (fMRI), measure the activity of the brain either at rest or while a person performs specific tasks (Filippi, 2015). Other technologies, such as the already discussed MRI, measure the brain's structure and the corresponding size and shape of its various components. All of these technologies play a massive role in how strong a hypothesis can be made leading to better outcomes due to stronger decisions on diagnoses and treatment.

Given the scientific and technological advantages we have to guide treatment based on functional neuroanatomy, we must remember that there is variation in brain activity among people with the same diagnosis. Ultimately, brain scans can be useful and supplemental to better outcomes through confirmation of diagnosis and treatment based on empirical data. However, caution should be taken in considering this a perfect science at this time.

Functional Neuroanatomy and Its Relationship to the Future

Research has indicated very specific reviews and critiques of cross-linguistic brain imaging studies of conditions, such as developmental dyslexia (Lallier et al., 2017). Inquiries arise as to the predictions that should be tested in future brain imaging studies of typical and atypical reading in order to refine the current neurobiological understanding of developmental dyslexia. This is only one example of where functional neuroanatomy can go in the future in terms of identifying, understanding, and treating complex mental health and disabling conditions. Watson, Kirkcaldie, and Paxinos (2010) posed that the future of functional neuroanatomy needs to be considered with caution so that the future generation of scientists that we are training are more optimistic and open-minded by realizing the limitation of the scientific tools in the past, present, and future. They emphasized that they become more motivated to look forward for proper application of the future technologies in discovering the etiologies and treatments of the Central Nervous System (CNS) disorders. Ultimately, we need to increase the amount of research in the areas of functional neuroanatomy to obtain larger sample sizes of individuals with specific mental illnesses and their symptomatology. Watson et al. posed that we must not rely on the scientific tools alone, but, in addition, on stronger clinical judgment based on the best diagnostic and treatment measures we can obtain.

A number of functional neuroanatomy studies have been conducted on Tourette syndrome (Stern et al., 2000), anxiety (Etkin, 2009), and bipolar disorder (Strakowski et al., 2005; Cerullo et al., 2009). The future of functional neuroanatomical studies look to include other psychiatric disorders and a host of research on emotional regulation, working memory, and specific learning disabilities.

Conclusions

As mentioned, the study and practice of functional neuroanatomy is not perfect and we have many more opportunities to improve the accessibility of what researchers and practitioners are looking to find. Most notably, functional neuroanatomy could use a tremendous boost in funding for researchers to build lasting outcomes that are specific to the field. Also, the number of individuals who have a diagnosed mental illness and who are willing to be a part of research must be willing to participate in larger participant pools for research fidelity and validity.

With all the improvements and changes in technology, it remains to be seen, but the future of functional neuroanatomy will likely follow suit with much exciting research and trials conducted with larger numbers of participants. As long as there are practitioners and researchers interested and looking to advance the research in cooperation and collaboration of better outcomes for more diverse and multicultural populations, there will be a better and more substantial set of research agendas willing to advance the field of functional neuroanatomy.

Discussion Questions

1. Why is it important to understand the history of neuroanatomy? When might knowledge of historical events and developments in the field come into play?
2. What are the practical and clinical uses of functional neuroanatomy in addressing and prioritizing an individual's problem set, needs, and subsequent interventions?
3. Thinking of Luria's theory of extra-cortical organization of higher mental functions, how might one's culture impact the development of cognitive functioning? Why is it important to consider cultural, social, and historical accounts when assessing children and adults?
4. How have Halstead/Reitan and Luria historically influenced the area of understanding functional neuroanatomy?
5. What are the implications and future directions of functional neuroanatomy?
6. How does using a multicultural approach to functional neuroanatomy help guide treatment from assessment to intervention?

EPPP Sample Questions

1. One of the major parts of the brain that stores memories is the:
   (a) Anterior cingulate
   (b) Hippocampus
   (c) Parietal lobe
   (d) Cerebellum

2. Two main functions of the prefrontal cortex are:
   (a) Language and movement
   (b) Vision and memory
   (c) Planning and decision making
   (d) Speech and balance
3. The Boston Process Approach was developed by:
   (a) Luria
   (b) Kaplan
   (c) Halstead
   (d) Reitan
4. The principle of extracortical organization of higher mental functions paved the way for:
   (a) Examining "shell shock" after World War II
   (b) Consideration of cross-cultural differences of brain structure and function
   (c) The creation of the *Halstead-Reitan Neuropsychological Test Battery* (HRNTB)
   (d) The concept of "testing the limits"
5. Early childhood toxic stress may cause an adolescent to have a "fight, flight, or freeze" response to an adverse stimuli. When looking at an fMRI of this adolescent in comparison to a same aged youth who did not experience early childhood toxic stress, you may notice:
   (a) More activity in the occipital lobe of the child who experienced toxic stress
   (b) Less activity around the amygdala of the child who experienced toxic stress
   (c) Less activity in the frontal lobe of the child who experienced toxic stress
   (d) Less blood flow near the hippocampus of the child who experienced toxic stress

   Answers: B, C, B, B, C

Proactive Readings

Transcending the Past

Etkin, A. (2009). Functional neuroanatomy of anxiety: A neural circuit perspective. In *Behavioral neurobiology of anxiety and its treatment* (pp. 251–277). Springer.

Goldstein, M. (1994). Decade of the brain. An agenda for the nineties. *Western Journal of Medicine*, *161*(3), 239.

Excelling in the Present

Hebben, N., Milberg, W., & Kaufman, A. (2010). *Essentials of neuropsychological assessment* (2nd Ed.) Wiley.

Hazin, I., & Tarcísio da Rocha Falcão, J. (2014). Luria's neuropsychology in the 21st century: Contributions, advancements, and challenges. *Psychology & Neuroscience, 7*(4), 433–434. https://doi.org/10.3922/j.psns.2014.4.01

Watson, C., Kirkcaldie, M., & Paxinos, G. (2010). *The brain: An introduction to functional neuroanatomy*. Academic Press.

Transforming the Future

De Bellis, M. D., & Zisk, A. (2014). The biological effects of childhood trauma. *Child and Adolescent Psychiatric Clinics, 23*(2), 185–222.

Souza-Queiroz, J., Boisgontier, J., Etain, B., Poupon, C., Duclap, D., D'Albis, M.,. .. Houenou, J. (2016). Childhood trauma and the limbic network: A multimodal MRI study in patients with bipolar disorder and controls. *Journal of Affective Disorders, 200*, 159–164. doi:https://doi.org/10.1016/j.jad.2016.04.038

References

Akiki, T. J., Averill, C. L., & Abdallah, C. G. (2017). A network-based neurobiological model of PTSD: Evidence from structural and functional neuroimaging studies. *Current Psychiatry Reports, 19*(11), 1–10. https://doi.org/10.1007/s11920-017-0840-4

Bandura, A. (1997). *Self-efficacy: The exercise of control*. Freeman.

Cerullo, M. A., Adler, C. M., Delbello, M. P., & Strakowski, S. M. (2009). The functional neuroanatomy of bipolar disorder. *International Review of Psychiatry, 21*(4), 314–322. https://doi.org/10.1111/j.1399-5618.2012.01022.x

Cozolino, L. (2013) *The social neuroscience of education: Optimizing attachment and learning in the classroom*. W.W. Norton & Co. Inc.

D'Amato, R. C., Fletcher-Janzen, E., & Reynolds, C. R. (Eds.). (2005). *Handbook of school neuropsychology*. Wiley.

Das, J. P., Naglieri, J. A., & Kirby, J. R. (1994). *Assessment of cognitive processes: The PASS theory of intelligence*. Allyn & Bacon.

De Bellis, M. D., & Zisk, A. (2014). The biological effects of childhood trauma. *Child and Adolescent Psychiatric Clinics, 23*(2), 185–222. https://doi.org 10.1016/j.chc.2014.01.002

Etkin, A. (2009). Functional neuroanatomy of anxiety: A neural circuit perspective. In *Behavioral neurobiology of anxiety and its treatment* (pp. 251–277). Springer. https://doi.org/10.1007/7854_2009_5

Filippi, M. (2015). *Oxford Textbook of Neuroimaging*. Oxford University Press. https://doi.org/10.1093/med/9780199664092.001.0001

Goldstein, M. (1994). Decade of the brain. An agenda for the nineties. *Western Journal of Medicine, 161*(3), 239.

Goodwin, D. M. (1989). *A dictionary of neuropsychology.* Springer-Verlag Publishing. https://doi.org/10.1007/978-1-4613-8944-6

Hale, J. B. & Fiorello, C. A. (2004). *School neuropsychology: A practitioner's handbook.* Guilford.

Hazin, I., & Tarcísio da Rocha Falcão, J. (2014). Luria's neuropsychology in the 21st century: Contributions, advancements, and challenges. *Psychology & Neuroscience, 7*(4), 433–434. https://doi.org/10.3922/j.psns.2014.4.01

Hebben, N., Milberg, W., & Kaufman, A. (2010). *Essentials of neuropsychological assessment* (Essentials of psychological assessment series) (2nd ed.). Wiley.

Horton, A., & Reynolds, C. (2015). Ralph M. Reitan: Evidenced based before evidence based was cool. *Archives of Clinical Neuropsychology : The Official Journal of the National Academy of Neuropsychologists, 30*(8), 740–747. https://doi.org/10.1093/arclin/acv070

Hynd, G. W., & Willis, W. G. (1988). *Pediatric neuropsychology.* Grune & Stratton/W B Saunders Co.

Kinniburgh, K. J., Blaustein, M., Spinazzola, J., & van der Kolk, B. A. (2005). Attachment, self-regulation, and competency: A comprehensive intervention framework for children with complex trauma. *Psychiatric Annals, 5*(35), 424–430. https://doi.org/10.3928/00485713-20050501-08

Kovelman, I., Baker, S. A., & Petitto, L. A. (2008). Bilingual and monolingual brains compared: A functional magnetic resonance imaging investigation of syntactic processing and a possible "neural signature" of bilingualism. *Journal of Cognitive Neuroscience, 20*(1), 153–169. https://doi.org/10.1162/jocn.2008.20011

Kotik-Friedgut, B. (2006). Development of the Lurian approach: A cultural neurolinguistic perspective. *Neuropsychology Review, 16*, 43–52. https://doi.org/10.1007/s11065-006-9003-9

Lallier, M., Molinaro, N., Lizarazu, M., Bourguignon, M., & Carreiras, M. (2017). Amodal atypical neural oscillatory activity in dyslexia: A cross-linguistic perspective. *Clinical Psychological Science, 5*(2), 379–401. https://doi.org/10.1177/2167702616670119

Lezak, M. D., Howieson, D. B., Bigler, E. D., & Tranel, D. (2012). *Neuropsychological assessment* (5th ed.). Oxford University Press.

Miller, D. (2013). *Essentials of school neuropsychological assessment* (Essentials of psychological assessment series) (2nd ed.). Wiley.

Noggle, C. A. & Davis, A. S. (2021). Advances in Neuroimaging. In R. C. D'Amato, A. S. Davis, E. M. Power, & E. C. Eusebio (Eds.), *Understanding the Biological Basis of Behavior: Developing Evidence-Based Interventions for Clinical, Counseling and School Psychologists.* Springer Nature. https://doi.org/10.1007/978-3-030-59162-5

Oscar-Berman, M., & Fein, D. (2013). Edith Kaplan: Educational background and her impact on neuropsychology. In L. Ashendorf, R. Swenson, & D. J. Libon, *The Boston Process Approach to Neuropsychological Assessment: A Practitioner's Guide.* Oxford University Press.

Perry, B. D. & Hambrick, E. P. (2008). The neurosequential model of therapeutics. *Reclaiming Children and Youth, 17*(3), 38–43.

Rourke, B. P. (1982). Central processing deficits in children: Toward a developmental neuropsychological model. *Journal of Clinical Neuropsychology, 4*, 1–18. https://doi.org/10.1080/01688638208401112

Schooler, G. R., Davis, J. T., Daldrup-Link, H. E., & Frush, D. P. (2018). Current utilization and procedural practices in pediatric whole-body MRI. *Pediatric Radiology, 48*(8), 1101–1107. https://doi.org/10.1007/s00247-018-4145-5

Souza-Queiroz, J., Boisgontier, J., Etain, B., Poupon, C., Duclap, D., D'Albis, M., . . . Houenou, J. (2016). Childhood trauma and the limbic network: A multimodal MRI study in patients with bipolar disorder and controls. *Journal of Affective Disorders, 200*, 159–164. doi:https://doi.org/10.1016/j.jad.2016.04.038.

Strakowski, S. M., Delbello, M. P., & Adler, C. M. (2005). The functional neuroanatomy of bipolar disorder: A review of neuroimaging findings. *Molecular Psychiatry, 10*(1), 105.

Stern E., Silbersweig D. A., Chee K. Y., Holmes A., Robertson M. M., Trimble M, Frith C. D., Frackowiak R. S., Dolan R. J. (2000) A functional neuroanatomy of tics in Tourette syndrome. *Archive of General Psychiatry, 57*(8), 741–748. https://doi.org/10.1001/archpsyc.57.8.741

Substance Abuse and Mental Health Services Administration. (2014). *Trauma-informed care in behavioral health services* (Treatment Improvement Protocol (TIP) Series 57. HHS Publication No. (SMA) 13-4801). Substance Abuse and Mental Health Services Administration. https://www.ncbi.nlm.nih.gov/books/NBK207202/.

Torregrossa, M. M., Quinn, J. J., & Taylor, J. R. (2008). Impulsivity, compulsivity, and habit: The role of orbitofrontal cortex revisited. *Biological Psychiatry, 63*(3), 253–255. https://doi.org/10.1016/j.biopsych.2007.11.014

United States Census Bureau. (2015). *New census bureau report analyzes U.S. population projections*. https://www.census.gov/newsroom/press-releases/2015/cb15-tps16.html.

Watson, C., Kirkcaldie, M., & Paxinos, G. (2010). *The brain: An introduction to functional neuroanatomy* (1st ed.). Academic Press.

Zotev, V., Phillips, R., Misaki, M., Wong, C. K., Wurfel, B. E., Krueger, F., ... & Bodurka, J. (2018). Real-time fMRI neurofeedback training of the amygdala activity with simultaneous EEG in veterans with combat-related PTSD. *NeuroImage: Clinical, 19*, 106–121. https://doi.org/10.1016/j.nicl.2018.04.010

Chapter 4
Understanding Typical and Atypical Neurodevelopment in Children and Adults

Cynthia A. Riccio, Linda Huilin Sun, and Alyssa Gonzalez

Learning Objectives

- Understand neurodevelopmental trajectories from conception through adulthood.
- Understand effects of alterations to typical neurodevelopment and critical time periods.
- Understand the relation of neurodevelopment to the manifestation of skill development and behavior.
- Understand how experiences and culture can impact neurodevelopment, function, and behavior.
- Understand how knowledge of typical and atypical development can inform professional practice for clinical, counseling, and school psychologists.

Overview

Basic to the understanding of brain-behavior associations is the understanding that brain development precedes and is necessary for behaviors to occur. This is most evident when neurodevelopment is considered from a longitudinal perspective beginning at conception. In effect, research indicates extraordinary changes to brain structure and function throughout development that parallels the capacity and typical development of behaviors be they motor, cognitive, academic, or social emotional. It has been argued that understanding the developmental trajectory for typical development provides the basis for understanding and potentially intervening when what is observed is atypical (Morgan et al., 2018). This chapter highlights what is

C. A. Riccio (✉) · L. H. Sun · A. Gonzalez
Department of Educational Psychology, Texas A&M University, College Station, TX, USA
e-mail: criccio@tamu.edu; lindahuilinsun@tamu.edu; alygon@tamu.edu

R. C. D'Amato et al. (eds.), *Understanding the Biological Basis of Behavior*,
https://doi.org/10.1007/978-3-030-59162-5_4

known about typical and atypical development across the life span, with consideration of neural development as a foundation that interacts with environmental stressors, trauma or disease, or intervention.

Typical Neurodevelopment in Children and Adults

The brain is best described as a diverse neural network or an "integrated complex system" (Grayson & Fair, 2017, p. 16). Research has shown early maturation of primary brain regions (i.e., those developed first) associated with sensory and motor functions, followed by gradual development of brain regions associated with higher-order functions such as self-regulation and social cognition well into adulthood (Khundrakpam et al., 2013; Raznahan et al., 2011). Functional systems or distributed networks underlie complex behaviors (e.g., Anderson et al., 2013; Goldman-Rakic, 1987, 1988; Mesulam, 1990); this conceptualization is not new and adds to the understanding of the interactions between neural networks or systems and resulting behavior. The recent emphasis on connectivity, as well as the integration of distributed neural activity or hubs, and functional systems (Khundrakpam et al., 2013; Mill et al., 2017) is consistent with this conceptualization. Connectivity refers to the anatomical links formed by synapses throughout the brain or the functional interactions between brain regions measured by neuroimaging techniques (Müller et al., 2011). It is influenced by genetic code, intrauterine environment (i.e., the health of the mother), and later by environmental and genetic influences that arise at differing points in time (Insel, 2014). Neural development continues, is malleable, and can be altered to some extent by exposure or experience across the life span. In effect, behavior both depends on, and to some extent determines, the integrity of the neural system. Briefly, the course of the typical neurodevelopmental trajectory is summarized here, followed by consideration of atypical trajectories. Neurocognitive correlates, as well as factors that influence neurodevelopmental trajectories, are also discussed.

Prenatal to Early Childhood

From the time of conception, there are significant neural changes occurring that set the foundation for functional systems as neurons multiply, move to locations, and take on functions set by genetic code. The earlier chapter by Semrud-Clikeman in this volume provides an in-depth description of the processes involved. Generally, by the end of the second trimester, the focus is less on neuronal increases but on the establishment of connections between neurons through the development of axons and dendrites (Collin & van den Heuvel, 2013; Stiles & Jernigan, 2010). Cell growth continues at a rapid rate until early childhood and then slows down (Tanaka et al., 2012). The neural system becomes more efficient as myelination continues and connections are strengthened through activity and exposure (Stiles & Jernigan, 2010). At the same time, there is cell proliferation, cell loss, pruning, and synaptic plasticity. Infancy and early childhood experiences are critical for development of motor skills (Marrus et al., 2017), language (D'Angiulli et al., 2012), higher-order thinking, and social cognition (Eggebrecht et al., 2017); hence, the importance of early intervention programming (Hirase & Shinohara, 2014), including nutritional programs (Prado & Dewey, 2015), during this time period fosters neurodevelopment.

Childhood

Myelination, brain growth, and the establishment of connections continue well into childhood. Gray matter increases and then decreases with gray matter peaking at different ages for different brain regions (i.e., growth is nonlinear; Giedd et al., 1996, 1999; Giedd & Rapoport, 2010; Mills et al., 2016; Sowell et al., 2002). Overall, females gain whole brain volume faster than males, but males eventually attain greater volume (Giedd et al., 1996, 1999; Sowell et al., 2002). Notably the peak ages for temporal and frontal lobe growth, critical to cognition and self-regulation, occur in preadolescence (Tanaka et al., 2012), but not in parallel. Growth in the frontal and temporal lobes is also important for the continued development of language and communication skills. Greater white matter growth (i.e., connectivity) has been found in the frontal lobes as compared to the temporal lobes (Tanaka et al., 2012). The onset of puberty marks the end of the critical period for language and spatial skills development (Gur et al., 2012; Johnson & Newport, 1989).

Adolescence to Young Adult

Although historically it was posited that the brain, and particularly the neocortex, was fully developed by adolescence, it is now believed that the adolescent brain undergoes changes that allow for a transition from basic processing to complex processing (Selemon, 2013). The transition to adolescence yields both decreases in gray matter and increases in white matter. Cortical thinning (i.e., selective pruning) typically is associated with volume reductions during adolescence (Tamnes et al., 2017). Although counterintuitive, the prefrontal cortex in particular has been shown to have large volume decreases (Gogtay et al., 2004; Sowell et al., 2003). The observed decreases in gray matter and gyrification are posited to reflect needed modifications to the cortex for cognitive development (Klein et al., 2014). At the same time, connectivity continues to develop, allowing for increased cognitive control and decision-making (Dwyer et al., 2014). In addition to significant changes in the frontal and prefrontal regions, there are changes to amygdala volumes implicated in the stress response and hippocampal growth needed for learning and memory, as well as stress reactivity in youth 12–14 years of age (Goddings et al., 2014). Whitaker et al. (2016) highlighted the importance of myelination of hubs in association cortex areas in adolescence. A hub is a set of brain regions in which neurons communicate with each other, and the association cortex refers to the cerebral surfaces of the brain which enable cognition. At age 14, the association cortex is less myelinated than primary cortices, but it has a faster rate of myelination from age 14–24 (Whitaker et al., 2016). The connections made in young adulthood take on more individual, as opposed to universal, characteristics, most likely influenced by individual experiences (Kaufmann et al., 2017).

These changes in brain structure allow for shifts in strategy use and academic gains in both reading (Eden, 2016) and mathematics (Peters & De Smedt, 2018). As math becomes more complex, for example, bilateral regions of the prefrontal cortex, the anterior cingulate, and other regions associated with executive functioning, particularly working memory, are activated; these same patterns are not evident in children or in adults (Peters & De Smedt, 2018). At the same time, the interactions between continued brain maturation, hormonal stress reactivity, and sensitivity to corticosterone during, or at least coinciding with, puberty result in increased plasticity and vulnerability (Aoki et al., 2017; Herting & Sowell, 2017; Juraska & Willing, 2017; Romeo, 2017). Just as adolescents experience more pronounced negative alterations to the limbic and cortical structures and functions from stress-related problems or substance use, they have potential to be more responsive to intervention as well (Holder & Blaustein, 2014). In fact, puberty sets the stage for the improved functioning in areas of concept formation, task-switching, and inhibition, either as a function of hormonal changes, neural reorganization, or both (Juraska & Willing, 2017). These changes signal a critical period for developmental plasticity, with the potential for positive or negative results (Anderson et al., 2008; Aoki et al., 2017; Pechtel et al., 2014).

Historically, the focus has been on negative outcomes; however, the underlying brain mechanisms and factors leading to resilience in conjunction with adolescence have been studied as well. Resilience encompasses those processes by which individuals rise above or develop ways that allow themselves to have positive quality of life in the face of adversity (Parsons et al., 2016; Wallander & Koot, 2016). Burt et al. (2016), as well as others (e.g., Cicchetti & Rogosch, 2007; Curtis & Cicchetti, 2003), examined the structural brain correlates of resilience in adolescence. Results indicated that neurobiological effects (e.g., genetics, stress hormone changes, EEG asymmetry), as well as environmental risk, affect, brain function, and resilience (Cicchetti & Rogosch, 2007). The study of structural correlates has focused on the prefrontal cortex (Burt et al., 2016; Curtis & Cicchetti, 2003) with indications of differences in gray matter volume in the right prefrontal areas, as well as the right middle frontal gyrus between groups identified as evidencing high or low resilience (Burt et al., 2016). Further, these differences were not due to differences in cognitive ability or personality factors. This supports the role of the prefrontal cortex in emotional, behavioral, and stress regulation, as well as executive function and control (Aron et al., 2014; Burt et al., 2016; Whelan et al., 2012).

Adulthood and Aging

The changes that occur in adolescence and into young adulthood result in reorganization of neural networks; brain development in adulthood shifts toward consolidating roles and functions imperative to success in adulthood. During this phase of life, there is continued synaptogenesis and pruning, with completion of neurodevelopment (Arnett, 2005). Association cortices and frontolimbic systems undergo significant and important changes that allow for improved functioning in the executive, social, attention, and reward processes (Taber-Thomas & Perez-Edgar, 2015). From multi-echo functional magnetic resonance imaging (fMRI), it is evident that blood oxygen level-dependent (BOLD) signals significantly decrease from adolescence to middle age and then stabilize (Kundu et al., 2018). These changes are most evident in prefrontal cortices, the parietal cortex, and the cerebellum, consistent with neurodevelopmental integration of brain function (i.e., networks or hubs) through middle age. As such, differences in neurodevelopment during early adulthood to middle age may contribute to deviations in functioning in aging individuals, and outcomes from earlier deviations will manifest during this period of development (Taber-Thomas & Perez-Edgar, 2015).

There is little additional brain growth in adulthood with the majority of research on younger adults and then with older adults (Petrican, Taylor, & Grady, 2017). What is known is that there is general, slow cell degeneration that is not balanced by cell proliferation, with cortical development usually completed around age 25 (Insel, 2014). As an individual ages, gray matter reduces in volume, and the cortex begins to thin, especially in the frontal lobes (Raz et al., 1997). Further, over time, there is degrading of connectivity as synaptic pruning continues and connections not used can be lost (Petrican et al., 2017). As such, connectivity established by early adulthood is degraded during later middle age and older adulthood in most individuals; processing speed is one of the processes most sensitive to this change (Van Gorp et al., 1990).

Although much of the research focuses on dementia, these changes are not specific to dementia but also have been identified in early stages of mild cognitive impairment (Ruan et al., 2016; Farias et al., 2013). The changes may be subtle; however, a faster rate of change (i.e., altered developmental rate) is associated with more rapid conversion to dementia (Daly et al., 2000) with more pronounced associations between decreased volume and neurocognitive function as the individual transitions to dementia (Farias et al., 2013). In older adults, total brain volume, hippocampal volume, and dorsolateral prefrontal volume are associated with neurocognitive status (Farias et al., 2013).

Neurodevelopmental Manifestation in Neuropsychological Function

As may be evident from the above, behavioral function parallels neural development across the life span and allows for understanding of emerging skills and behaviors (Insel, 2014). With regard to performance on specific neuropsychological tasks, it is difficult to isolate demands as neuropsychological tasks tend to be cognitively complex (i.e., tap into multiple neurocognitive demands) and do not readily map onto specific brain regions (Newman et al., 2007). Various cross-sectional studies have linked neuropsychological function to typical neurodevelopment. For example, Newman et al. examined performance on various tasks with modulated gray matter probability maps among healthy adults. Results indicated significant associations between specific structures of the frontal lobe and performance on trail-making tasks and verbal fluency tasks, supporting the importance of frontal circuitry in executive function. Additionally, longitudinal studies on preterm infants have added to the understanding of brain-behavior relationships (Thompson et al., 2013). For example, the altered shape and volume of the hippocampus from infancy to childhood are associated with verbal memory function (Thompson et al., 2013). Similarly, changes in the structure of the arcuate fasciculus in infancy correlate with later language development (Mullen et al., 2011; Salvan et al., 2017).

In adolescence, as noted already, performance on neuropsychological tasks improves, particularly those relying on the prefrontal cortex (i.e., cognitive control, inhibition, cognitive flexibility, decision-making; Durston & Casey, 2006, Dwyer et al., 2014; Taylor et al., 2013). Because of the importance of the frontal lobes in executive function and cognition, much research has been done on the brain-behavior correlates of the frontal lobe and neuropsychological function. Notably, different aspects of executive function, as with other neurocognitive domains, develop at differing rates rather than simultaneously or in a linear fashion (see Romine & Reynolds, 2005). When neural development occurs in the expected trajectory, function follows; however, sometimes this is not the case.

Abnormal Neurodevelopment and Function

Neurodevelopmental Models and Atypical Development

For most disorders, or when there is a deviation from what is considered normal development or behavior, there is a presumption that the difference or deviation in behavior or function is the result of some variability in the development or function of the neural system (Insel, 2014). This is consistent with the conceptualization of neurodevelopmental disorders reflecting atypical development of the central nervous system that becomes evident in childhood and may persist into adulthood (Bishop & Rutter, 2008). This is a necessary presumption if we are to assume that medication will "correct" the dysfunction by altering the neurochemical environment of the brain or that any intervention will have long-term effects on brain function. Moreover, variations in brain structure have been identified for individuals with neurodevelopmental disorders (e.g., Fletcher & Grigorenko, 2017; Park et al., 2018).

Neurodevelopmental models (e.g., Armstrong, 2006; Ball et al., 2015; Insel, 2014; Johnson et al., 2016; Werchan & Amso, 2017) posit multiple factors associated with risk and resiliency for individuals whose development does not follow the expected trajectory. These include the etiological factors (e.g., genetics, premature/term birth, disease and disease processes, injury or insult), child and family factors, and environmental stressors, all of which contribute to educational and mental health outcome (Armstrong, 2006; Ball et al., 2015; Guilfoyle et al., 2017). An ecological approach is suggested to understanding interactions among these factors in neurodevelopment (Gottwald et al., 2016; Werchan & Amso, 2017).

Etiological factors, genetic influences, child and family factors, and other environmental factors may facilitate or impede neurodevelopment at different points in the trajectory (see Fig. 4.1). Current research on neurodevelopmental disorders provides evidence of genetic contributions to cortical patterns associated with connectivity (Parikshank et al., 2015), as well as inhibitions (Márin, 2012), with neurodevelopmental disorders, early neural development for the fetus is significantly impacted not only by genetics but also by any complication in the pregnancy and maternal health (e.g., Gerner & Baron, 2015). Most studied in preterm infants,

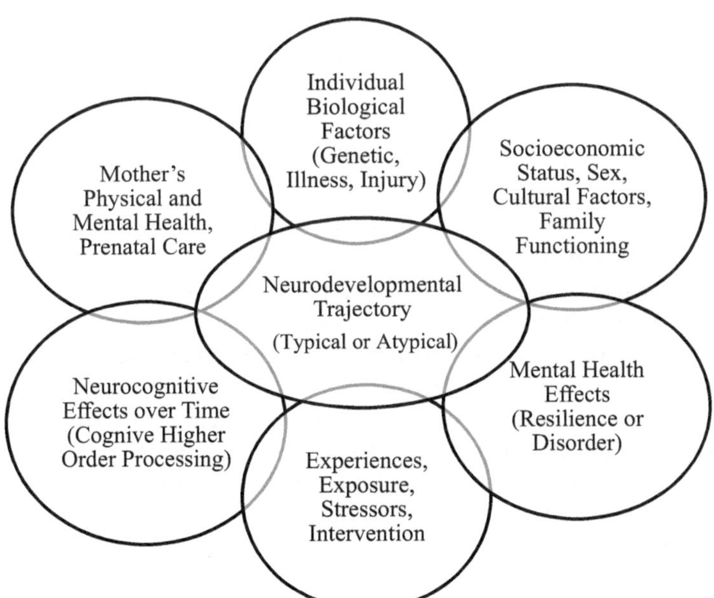

Fig. 4.1 Factors affecting and affected by the neurodevelopmental trajectory from conception across the life span

even subtle brain anomalies are predictive of altered neurodevelopmental function as early as 2 years of age (Counsell et al., 2008). This is exemplified by rises in certain disorders in conjunction with high rates of occurrence of disease, as with the rise in rates of autism spectrum disorder (ASD) in children whose mothers had atopic diseases and inflammation (e.g., Theoharides et al., 2016).

In effect, neurodevelopmental trajectories are influenced by a combination of psychosocial and environmental factors, particularly in the early years but continuing across the life span, making it difficult to predict outcome (Batelle et al., 2018; Insel, 2014). Trauma at the level of the central nervous system may result from not only physical injury but also prolonged stress. Studies have identified bidirectional interactions between disease or disorder and psychological stress (e.g., Chiang et al., 2009; Tang et al., 2014). Neurodevelopment associated with language and executive functioning is considered especially vulnerable to environmental factors (Conant et al., 2017; Demir & Küntay, 2014; Noble et al., 2007). In much the same way as risk factors account for outcome variance, child and family protective factors also can account for variance (e.g., Monaghan et al., 2015; Hilliard et al., 2012).

The models for neurodevelopmental disorders like ADHD, learning disabilities, or ASD hypothesize some change or alteration in neurodevelopment (e.g., in cell migration, proliferation, pruning, or connectivity) that occurred prenatally and resulted in the observed atypical neurodevelopment (e.g., Finn et al., 2014; Schweren et al., 2016). Differences in brain structure (i.e., cortical thickness, surface area) have been found, for example, between those with ADHD, ASD, schizophrenia, and healthy individuals (Park et al., 2018). These structural differences, in turn, give rise to network wide effects with both convergence and divergence across groups (Park et al., 2018), thus affecting connectivity. It has been suggested that brain connectivity serves as a consistent marker of atypical development (Lewis et al., 2014; Lewis et al., 2017). For example, many factors associated with preterm births are associated with neurodevelopmental disorders, and many children born preterm manifest neurodevelopmental disorders (Johnson & Marlow, 2014). Indications of these differences in trajectory may be present at birth or emerge over time in response to environmental demands, when age-expected behaviors fail to develop. For disorders later in life (e.g., Alzheimer, Parkinson's), it is believed that the symptoms experienced are later manifestations of the underlying brain processes, possibly genetically coded. With current methodologies, neural changes can be detected prior to symptom presentation for many degenerative disorders such as Alzheimer's disease (Ferreira & Busatto, 2011; Insel, 2014).

There are different ways in which alternative trajectories to neurodevelopment and associated behavior may manifest. Changes in neurodevelopment may present as delays, such that the outcome of neurodevelopment is the same or fairly similar but delayed or an altered trajectory with differing outcomes (Insel, 2014; Shaw et al., 2010). When neurodevelopment is delayed, the shape of the curve is the same, but key benchmarks are achieved and peak neuroanatomical variations occur at later ages (Shaw et al., 2010). The rate of change may vary, yet the same transition points are reached nonetheless. Alternatively, with more pronounced deviation in development, there is clear deviation from the typical trajectory that does not ever reach the same transition points. Shaw and colleagues pointed out that some aspects of neurodevelopment may be typical or delayed, while others may be altered in terms of rate and shape. It is important to keep in mind that the neurodevelopmental trajectory is dynamic and effects of genetic predisposition, ecological factors, and any pre-occurring conditions are synergistic. As with earlier neurodevelopmental trajectories, differing profiles for older adults and progression to dementia have been proposed with a continued focus on connectivity within systems and between networks; however, additional research is warranted. Notably, symptoms may not be apparent until later ages or after disease onset or injury. Examples of how differing patterns may present is provided in Table 4.1 and discussed in depth for ADHD, ASD, schizophrenia, and chronic illness/TBI.

Table 4.1 Examples of alterations to the typical neurodevelopmental trajectory

	Attention deficit hyperactivity disorder	Autism spectrum disorders	Schizophrenia spectrum disorders	Chronic illness and traumatic brain injury
Alteration	Generally delayed from early childhood with typical developmental benchmarks met at later points in time	Atypical development in some areas, but highly variable in presentation; some developmental benchmarks delayed, others not met	Initially typical development with subtle differences; trajectory shifts with onset of disorder	Presumed typical neurodevelopment up to onset of disease process or injury; how trajectory altered is then a function of disease/injury factors and treatment effects
Brain behavior correlates	Cortical maturation and volume, particularly in ventromedial prefrontal region, delayed but reach typical levels in adulthood	Rapid cell proliferation and increased cortical thickness followed by thinning; decreased connectivity	Marked cortical thinning; altered reorganization of neural networks in adolescence; loss of gray matter following first psychotic episode	Imaging and activation reflect the focal or diffuse effects on the central nervous system
Variation	Not all individuals with ADHD remit in adulthood; those with continued symptoms tend to have thinner cortex; variation may be function of gene-environment interaction	Differences across the spectrum reflect individual differences in rate and trajectory; also impacted by co-occurring disorders	Extent of deviation in reorganization of networks in early sensitive developmental stages, as well as continued effects of psychotic episodes and environment/treatment contribute to variation in trajectory and outcome	Effects on trajectory may be focal or diffuse depending on the disease/injury and any treatment effects/rehabilitation or ongoing disease processes

Attention Deficit Hyperactivity Disorder (ADHD) ADHD is one of the most common neurodevelopmental disorders with an extensive research base. Research continues to examine genetic contributions and neurobiological markers for this highly heterogeneous group. Heritability estimates of 75–80% (Faraone et al., 2005) account for much of the variance. The remaining variance, based on research, is derived from other factors and influences on neurodevelopment (see Fig. 4.1). In particular, maternal physical and mental health, low birthweight, maternal substance use, physical abuse, neglect, stressful life events, exposure to neurotoxins, and so on have emerged as contributing to symptom presentation (e.g., Braun et al., 2006; Humphreys et al., 2019; Nikolas & Burt, 2010). Despite these differences, there is evidence of an expected trajectory for individuals with ADHD.

ADHD is most often conceptualized as presenting with a delayed trajectory (Shaw et al., 2010). This is evident from cross-sectional and longitudinal studies of brain development (e.g., Krain & Castellanos, 2006; Valera et al., 2007) with indications that those with ADHD lag behind in cortical maturation by about 3 years, particularly in the prefrontal region (Shaw et al., 2010). At the same time, there is evidence that the primary motor cortex develops slightly earlier (Shaw et al., 2010). Notably, children with ADHD also lag behind on neurocognitive measures of inhibition; however, there is improvement with age and increased volumes in the anterior cingulate, striatum, and medial temporal lobe (McAlonan et al., 2009). Thus, behavioral indicators of ADHD are believed to reflect "maturational delay" of the prefrontal cortex, which subserves inhibition, working memory, and temporal processing (Barkley, 2015; Toplak et al., 2006).

The conceptualization of ADHD as delayed maturation is consistent with symptom improvement with age in most individuals (e.g., Barkley, 2015; Faraone et al., 2006). While about half of the individuals with ADHD continue to have some residual symptoms, only about 15–20% retain the diagnosis in early adulthood at age 25 (Faraone et al., 2006). Shaw et al. (2010) examined cortical development in individuals with ADHD in remission. Results indicated normalization of cortical thickness, including in the lateral prefrontal cortex over time. Other studies have yielded similar results in brain activity such that activation patterns for children with ADHD tend to be more similar to younger healthy peers (e.g., Fernández et al. 2009; Shaw et al., 2010). In contrast, there was no normalization, particularly in the medial prefrontal wall as well as in ventromedial volume (Albaugh et al., 2019), in those individuals with continued behavioral symptoms (Shaw et al., 2010). This is consistent to findings with regard to executive function of continued deficits in those with continued ADHD symptomology (Halperin et al., 2008; Makris et al., 2007). Thus, when ADHD symptoms persist, there are likely persistent alterations in the trajectory of cortical maturation specific to the prefrontal cortex.

Autism Spectrum Disorders (ASD) In the past decade, there has been increased attention to ASD and consideration of the associated deficits in social cognition and restricted repetitive behaviors (American Psychiatric Association, 2013). ASD is associated with a broad range of prenatal and perinatal conditions yielding heterogeneous atypical trajectories. There is, for example, evidence of an altered rate of neurodevelopment in ASD (Shaw et al., 2006; Wolff et al., 2012; Zielinski et al., 2014). For individuals with ASD, the rate of accelerated cell growth in childhood occurs earlier and more rapidly, with some indications of dysregulation in the process (Courchesne et al., 2003; Mosconi et al., 2009; Redcay & Courchesne, 2005). This rapid growth plateaus and is followed by increased cortical thinning in adolescence to reach typical ranges (Redcay & Courchesne, 2005). Research indicates the rapid cell growth of both white and gray matter occurs prior to age two (e.g., Courchesne et al., 2003), with some indications that this overgrowth occurs at the level of the amygdala as well, and is associated with deficits in joint attention (Mosconi et al., 2009), while decreased amygdala volume is associated with anxiety in conjunction with ASD (Herrington et al., 2017). Shen et al. (2017) demonstrated the relations between cerebrospinal fluid volume in 6-month-old infants and later ASD symptom severity. From the components of ASD, symptoms related to social cognition are associated structurally with the length of the posterior superior temporal sulcus (Hotier et al., 2017).

Consistent with current emphasis on connectivity, another area implicated in ASD is the resting state interhemispheric connectivity in the auditory cortex (Dinstein et al., 2011). Differences in the establishment of connections for children with ASD can be seen as early as six months of age (Wolff et al., 2012). Further, there is evidence of decreased long range connectivity, giving rise to decreased efficiency (Zielinski et al., 2014) as well as disruption in hubs and regions associated with social interaction (e.g., Bernhardt et al., 2014). Kana et al. (2017) found significantly weaker connectivity in areas of the brain associated with social processing, particularly the anterior cingulate cortex. Differences also have emerged between children with ASD as compared to typically developing children for the corpus callosum suggesting white matter pathology, which was associated with decreased social responsiveness (Aoki et al., 2017). Similarly, the neural networks that involve non-motor cerebellar function also are implicated such that early cerebellar dysfunction could influence the neurodevelopment of other brain regions (e.g., Wang et al., 2014). These changes in the trajectory not only reduce efficiency of cognitive processes but also result in disruption in those hubs and regions associated with social interaction (e.g., Bernhardt et al., 2014; Kana et al., 2017). It should be noted that not all research replicated these findings (e.g., Zwaigenbaum et al., 2014), likely reflecting the heterogeneity of individuals with ASD and the high rate of comorbidity with intellectual disability or language impairment (i.e., child factors).

Schizophrenia Spectrum As with other disorders, schizophrenia is highly heritable yet presumably affected by other factors. As with ADHD and ASD, a multitude of environmental factors further contribute to the gene-environment interaction to influence symptom severity (Meyer-Lindenberg & Tost, 2014). Although schizophrenia most often manifests in late adolescence or early adulthood, some signs of atypical neurodevelopment have been noted much earlier (Meyer-Linderberg & Tost, 2014). Some studies trace the alterations associated with schizophrenia risk in neurodevelopment to the second trimester of gestation (e.g., Piper et al., 2012);

however, it is not until the cortical restructuring of adolescence (i.e., myelination, synaptic pruning) that these effects are likely to become evident (Huttenlocher, 1990). Deviations from the typical rate of neurodevelopmental are evident in schizophrenia with excessive decreases in cortical gray matter prior to the presentation of psychosis (Brent et al., 2013; Reichenberg & Harvey, 2007), as well as at onset of psychosis (Pantelis et al., 2005). There is also evidence of more pronounced thinning at a higher rate than expected particularly in frontotemporal and frontoparietal regions with some normalization possible (Thompson et al., 2001; Vidal et al., 2006).

Alterations in cortical peaks and thinning also have emerged in studies of childhood-onset schizophrenia (Gogtay et al., 2008; Rapoport & Gogtay, 2008). With childhood-onset schizophrenia, findings indicate a typical trajectory up until preadolescence or adolescence (e.g., Thompson et al., 2001; Vidal et al., 2006). In adolescence, differences emerge, with cortical thinning of gray matter in the parietofrontal region more pronounced and at a faster rate and not continuing into adulthood (Greenstein et al., 2006; Vidal, et al., 2006). The resulting effect of the rapid thinning in the frontotemporal regions is similar to the cortical deficit pattern in adult-onset schizophrenia (e.g., Shaw et al., 2010). Excessive loss of gray matter is evident in some cases prior to the onset of psychosis, with the greater loss of gray matter followed by more rapid thinning after the first psychotic episode, indicative of the altered rate of degeneration as with older adults. In addition, the volumetric increase in white matter in adolescents with childhood-onset schizophrenia represents a clear deviation from typical development (Gogtay et al., 2008). In particular, volumetric gains in white matter, the pathways for connectivity, have been found to be absent in the right hemisphere and minimal in the left hemisphere (Gogtay et al., 2008).

Local connectivity with disrupted connections has been found to be associated with psychosis as well (Wang et al., 2018). As with ASD, connectivity is compromised, and abnormal development of hub regions, particularly in adolescence, coincides with vulnerability for schizophrenia onset (Whitaker et al., 2016). Meyer-Lindenberg and Tost (2012) found that individuals with schizophrenia did not evidence the hierarchical hubs of typical adults; adults with schizophrenia had few prefrontal hubs. Similarly, differences in functional connections have been found such that dysconnectivity may interfere with attention and executive functions in adults with schizophrenia (Bassett et al., 2008). These findings are consistent with theories of network insufficiency in schizophrenia (Callicott et al., 2003; Callicott et al., 2003).

Alternatively, there may be progressive changes to the central nervous system further altering the trajectory with psychotic episodes over time (Pantelis et al., 2005). The changes may be a manifestation of neurodevelopmental disorganization at some earlier point that affects connectivity and synaptic pruning (Meyer-Lindenberg & Tost, 2014). Thus, the atypical trajectories associated with schizophrenia may arise initially from genetic or prenatal factors; however, other factors at vulnerable points of neurodevelopment contribute to outcome.

Altered by Chronic Illness or Trauma Consideration is also needed when the trajectory is altered as a result of chronic illness or injury. The presumption often is that neurodevelopment proceeded in the typical fashion until the onset of the disease process or Traumatic Brain Injury (TBI). Thus, typical development is disrupted by a disease or injury, and subsequent neurodevelopmental changes arise from the changes in neural function and connectivity. With chronic illnesses, these changes may be the result of observable structural changes due to (a) neurosurgery for a tumor or intractable epilepsy (Riccio et al., 2015); (b) a vascular injury associated with a stroke in sickle cell (Daly et al., 2008); (c) decreased oxygen available to the brain in conjunction with cardiac abnormalities, respiratory conditions, or anemia (Congdon et al., 2012); (d) acute alterations in glucose levels as may occur with diabetes (Savage et al., 2010); (e) treatment effects as with chemotherapy and radiation (Kaiser et al., 2014); or (f) in association with traumatic brain injury shearing of white matter (Kinnunen et al., 2010). With chronic illness or TBI, while some effects may be transient, there may be both immediate effects and subsequent late effects on neurodevelopmental trajectory and function (Armstrong, 2006).

For those with chronic illness, family context, including socioeconomic status, parent mental health, and family functioning, impacts not only disease factors and access to care but also the child's mental health (e.g., Anclair et al., 2017; Whittemore et al., 2012). Further, the relation between illness-related fears and concerns with services and supports available for the child and other family members is synergistic (e.g., Lagor et al., 2013). While some children with chronic illness are resilient (Hilliard et al., 2012), it is not infrequent for these children to present with behavioral concerns and psychological adjustment issues (Pinquart & Shen, 2011). Continued disease effects (i.e., remission or recurrence) and treatment effects play a role in the trajectory for those with chronic illness. Similarly, TBI, depending on severity, may interrupt the typical neurodevelopmental trajectory or exacerbate an already atypical trajectory with effects on cognitive, affective, and behavioral function (Prins et al., 2013). Physical changes to the central nervous system may be subtle or evident in axonal injuries with disruption to neural networks (Wolf & Koch, 2016). Over time and in conjunction with other factors, the interruption and deviation from the typical neurodevelopmental trajectory may have a cascade effect, with further deviations long term.

Neurodevelopment and Multicultural Issues

The need to consider cultural and linguistic differences in the field of neuropsychology and neurodevelopment has garnered additional attention in the past 20 years, with competencies in understanding the influences of diversity and culture considered necessary components for a mental health professional (Hessen et al., 2018). This need is fueled by the rapid growth of individuals in the United States with diverse backgrounds and the urgency for the field of neuropsychology to respond quicker to this shift in needs. Between 2000 and 2010, the Hispanic population experienced a significant increase, amassing a 43 percent gain in numbers and contributing to over half of all growth in the total US population (U.S. Census Bureau, 2011). Similarly, the Asian population experienced an increase in numbers by 43 percent. Although the populations of each group comprised only 16 percent and 5 percent of the entire US population by 2010 (U.S. Census Bureau, 2011), the need for helping professionals has become dire. Many states lack the required number of mental health professionals required to satisfy the needs of individuals who lack diverse backgrounds; however, this gap increases when individuals with diverse backgrounds are considered.

When working with individuals with diverse backgrounds, it is vital to consider language and culture. Individuals who have migrated to a host country might speak the host country's language, but they might not perform as well as native-born individuals on neuropsychological assessments due to their language background. Peviani et al. (2016) examined the performance of Italian-born and foreign-born individuals with epilepsy on a full neuropsychological battery. The results indicated that the difference in ethnicity/culture impacted the performance of the individuals and the number of years an individual had spent in Italy did not impact these scores. Additionally, the language background of the individual did impact the neuropsychological performance of participants, with foreign-born Italian speakers exhibiting significant large task-related variability and low performance on language-related tasks (Peviani et al., 2016).

Within the past 15 years, cultural neuroscience has emerged as a subfield (Azar, 2010) to consider the role of culture in neurodevelopment and function. Freeman et al. (2009), for example, used fMRI with American and Japanese adults as they viewed silhouettes of people in dominant and submissive postures. They hypothesized differences in neural activity as a result of the conflicting values placed on being dominant or submissive in these two cultures. Results indicated the dominant postures resulted in activation of the limbic system for the American participants. In contrast, the same activation pattern occurred for the Japanese in response to the submissive posture. Further, extent of activation correlated with self-reported values on dominance and submissiveness (Freeman et al., 2009).

Research has shown that culture and language play a role in performance on neuropsychological assessments, so as the population of the United States becomes more heterogeneous, it is important to take these differences into account when creating or using neuropsychological assessments (Brickman et al., 2006). These differences must be integrated not only into the assessment creation process but also in the norming process as well, and this process should be under the purview of an individual who is culturally competent or an expert in a particular culture (Brickman et al., 2006). This would include consideration of differential impact, as well as ensuring that the proportion in the norming sample is consistent with the census.

Not only can language result in changes among groups of individuals, but also culture can impact the thought process of individuals which can influence their decision-making. Bakos et al. (2010) examined the performance of Brazilians and Americans on the Iowa Gambling Task (Bechara, 2007), which is a psychological task that attempts to simulate real-life decision-making. Both ethnic groups consisted of a group of younger adults and a group of older adults. The researchers found differences in performance between the Brazilians and Americans; however, there were no differences when considering age group and country impacts on learning during the task (Bakos et al., 2010). This suggests there are cultural differences for this task and supports the need to ensure validation of instruments for different cultures not only on this task but also on other psychological tasks.

It was first hypothesized that initial language acquisition could only occur during a specific and critical period: from early infancy to puberty (Lenneberg, 1967). Johnson and Newport (1989) investigated whether or not this held true for second-language acquisition. The researchers hypothesized that if there was also a critical period in which second-language acquisition was feasible, children would acquire a second language quicker than adults, and they also would achieve higher proficiency. After examining native Chinese and Korean speakers who had moved to the United States between the ages of 3 and 39, a linear relationship was found between test performance on English grammar and age of arrival in the United States up to the age of puberty, suggesting a critical period of second-language acquisition. Beyond puberty, performance on the grammar tasks was found to be low, variable, and unrelated to the individual's age of arrival in the United States (Johnson & Newport, 1989). Although the end of the critical period of second-language acquisition has been variable, ranging from 12 to 18 (Muñoz & Singleton, 2011), there undoubtedly exists a critical period not only for first-language acquisition but also for second-language acquisition, suggesting that with age comes increased difficulty in acquiring language (Johnson & Newport, 1989; Muñoz & Singleton, 2011).

Different patterns of behavior across cultures are the result of the differing values cultures place on certain practices and behaviors, such that the reinforcement of these behaviors leads to their expression among individuals of a particular culture. These expectations of culture can then influence the neurodevelopment of an individual, impacting and interacting with experiences, mental health, prenatal care, and biological factors. Taken together, these factors determine typical or atypical neurodevelopment, and presentation between cultures may present differently. For example, Western cultures exhibit more individualized ideals and dominance, whereas Eastern cultures typically exhibit a focus on submission and collectivism (Oyserman & Lee, 2008) with differences manifesting in neuropsychological performance as well as brain activity (e.g., Chiao, 2009; Freeman et al., 2009).

Many individuals hold the belief that individuals who speak the same language, but come from different cultures, would perform similarly on various tasks; however, this is not always the case. Buré-Reyes and colleagues tested (2013) Spanish speakers from four different countries on various neuropsychological tests. Results further supported findings of within-group differences and the need to not only account for differences across groups with regard to language but also in regard to subgroups of individuals from differing cultures (Buré-Reyes et al., 2013).

Similarly, research has shown differences in social and executive functioning across three Eastern cultures (Lewis et al., 2009). In the Lewis et al. study, Korean children tended to exhibit the most executive control when compared to not only Western counterparts but also Chinese and Japanese counterparts. The Korean participants neared ceilings on most of the executive functioning tasks; however, they did not perform as well on false-belief tasks, with only about a one-third pass rate and nearly no correlation between executive function and social understanding. For the Japanese children, the correlation between executive function and false beliefs was nearly zero. In the Chinese sample, a weak and borderline significant correlation was found between executive functioning and false beliefs. These results indicate differences between ethnic groups of similar backgrounds, suggesting that culture underpins executive and social processes (Lewis et al., 2009).

Differences in executive functioning also can be found among individuals with differing linguistic backgrounds, with bilingual individuals exhibiting a faster rate of development compared to monolingual individuals (Bialystok & Viswanathan, 2009). Despite this fact, bilingual individuals exhibit deficits in lexical access (Pelham & Abrams, 2014). Pelham and Abrams (2014) examined whether acquiring a second language after childhood resulted in cognitive gains for these individuals. Results indicated that both early and late bilinguals evidenced equivalent cognitive effects on both the lexical access task and executive functioning. This suggests that cognitive effects of bilingualism are not solely associated with acquisition in youth, but rather proficient use of two languages (Pelham & Abrams, 2014).

Differences exist not only between individuals with different ethnicities but also among individuals with similar ethnicities and language. Flores et al. (2017) investigated cognition between Hispanic and non-Hispanic White individuals using the NIH Toolbox Cognition Battery (Gershon et al., 2013). Their findings indicated that Spanish-speaking Hispanics performed worse on tests of fluid cognition compared to English-speaking Hispanics and suggest the importance of language over ethnic affiliation (Flores et al., 2017). Research has focused on whether neuropsychological assessments consider cultural differences and how they might impact diagnostic accuracy (Daugherty et al., 2017; Veliu & Leathem, 2017). Results indicated that misdiagnoses and false positives often occur when common neuropsychological assessments are administered to groups of individuals with diverse backgrounds (Norman et al., 2011). Thus, it is important to tailor neuropsychological assessments to the cultures of individuals completing them.

Understanding the differences between cultural groups is vital for helping professionals to meet the needs of the ever-changing US population. A lack of knowledge and understanding can be dangerous, as it can impact diagnosis and thus treatment for individuals with diverse backgrounds. It is the utmost responsibility of a professional to provide the best treatment possible without inflicting harm unto a client, and failing to consider cultural differences can prove irresponsible. Additionally, there exists a need to not only incorporate more culturally competent professionals in the field but also culturally adapted assessments as well. This will enhance the quality of information received during assessment from individuals with diverse backgrounds and the treatment of these individuals as well. The current burgeoning research in the area of cultural neuroscience only can improve what is known about the interaction of culture and function (Azar, 2010; Chiao, 2009). Further, there is increased attention to and consideration of the impact of cultural and linguistic differences in the practice of neuropsychology (Olson & Jacobson, 2015).

Why Understanding Neurodevelopment in Children and Adults Is Critical to Professional Psychological Practice

The knowledge of neurodevelopment informs psychological practice in assessment, therapy, academic intervention, as well as prevention (Fletcher & Grigorenko, 2017). In addition to understanding the developmental trajectories of psychological and cognitive processes, researchers have begun to look at the neural substrates underlying both typical and atypical trajectories (Rapoport & Gogtay, 2008). Professional psychologists may refer to the trends of typical development to assess for the developmental appropriateness of behaviors (Merzenich et al., 2014). With various neuroimaging techniques, neuropsychology provides additional information to existing knowledge of developmental milestones and stage theories by visualizing the continuous changes in the brain over time as well as regions most implicated in performing different activities (Klingberg et al., 2005; Shaywitz et al., 2004). Professional psychologists play a critical role in communicating this information to their clients to set realistic yet challenging expectations in intervention and encourage a growth-oriented mindset.

Advances in neuropsychology have enabled psychologists to understand broad abilities as being comprised of distinct cognitive processes (Antonenko et al., 2014). Studies have looked at the brain metabolism of individuals while they are performing tasks with different theorized cognitive demands. The neural activities associated with different behaviors have been identified and in support of some classical conceptualizations of cognition and psychopathology (Goldapple et al., 2004; Huey et al., 2015; McFarland, 2017). While considering the whole brain, distinct skills have been mapped onto different brain regions and networks. For example, in the process of reading, the left dorsolateral prefrontal cortex is most implicated in auditory or phonological processes (Kovelman et al., 2011), while the left occipito-temporal cortex is implicated in the visual recognition of written words and symbols (Vogel et al., 2014). Comprehension is associated with the anterior temporal lobe (Ferstl, Neumann, Bogler, & Von Carmon, 2008) and right frontal regions (Bailey et al., 2016). In assessment and intervention, professional psychologists can use this knowledge to analyze individuals' processing strengths and difficulties (Fletcher & Grigorenko, 2017). This provides a deeper and more fine-tuned understanding of individual characteristics. Psychologists may target specific processing difficulties or provide accommodations to compensate for them, especially with the help of plasticity-based interventions.

The central message from the neurodevelopmental perspective is the brain's plasticity or ability to change as individuals interact with the environment regardless of age or developmental stage (Citri & Malenka, 2008; Kani et al., 2017; Saggar et al., 2012). In the adaptive sense, neuroplasticity enables learning and rehabilitation. Many evidence-based intervention methods have been found to modify the brain structurally and functionally. For example, changes in brain activity region were observed in children with reading difficulties after they received evidence-based intervention for 105 hours, which increased their reading skills (Shaywitz et al., 2004). Their brain activation pattern was compared to that of typically developing children before and after intervention and was found to have normalized following intervention. Activity increased in the left hemisphere and decreased in the right hemisphere. Taken together, their brain activation pattern normalized toward that of typically developing children. Similar findings emerged in adults with dyslexia (Eden et al., 2004). Initial research suggests differing mechanisms and brain plasticity in response to treatments for core components of ASD (Ventola et al., 2013). Similarly, individuals with ASD who participated in intervention showed improvement in facial affect recognition, as well as normalized activation pattern, with increased activity in brain regions associated with social cognition (Bolte et al., 2016). Cognitive rehabilitation correlates with normalizing connectivity involving the cingulate cortex in those with multiple sclerosis (Parisi et al., 2014).

The same effects have been found with mental health interventions. For example, individuals who participated in mindful meditation training showed a reduction of depression symptoms as well as changed functional connectivity between brain regions; reduced connectivity was found between areas associated with depression (Yang et al., 2016). Cognitive behavioral therapy also has been found to lead to behavioral and neurological changes in individuals with anxiety disorders and depression (Freyer et al., 2011; Höflich et al., 2012; Ritchey et al., 2011). Although deficits are not fully remediated clinically, the brain processes in clinical population are found to normalize over the course of intervention to resemble that of healthy individuals. In older adults, memory strategy training, as well as physical exercise, has been found to reduce loss of structural and functional connectivity often seen in individuals not provided with intervention (Brehmer et al., 2014). The changes enabled by neural plasticity may elucidate the mechanism through which interventions promote symptom reduction or functional improvement, and the validity of the intervention may be supported by the observed neurological changes (Slagter et al., 2011).

Potential new directions in translating neurodevelopmental science to practice involve designing plasticity-based interventions and adding neuroimaging technology to diagnostic procedures (Eldar & Bar-Haim, 2010; Porto et al., 2009; Teipel et al., 2018). Plasticity-based interventions are often computer-automated programs that target specific cognitive skills and provide opportunities for repeated practice. Individuals may complete these treatment activities individually on their electronic devices (Merzenich et al., 2014). As such, intervention can be a low-cost, systematic, and accessible option compared to most psychologist-direction intervention. These interventions provide opportunities for individuals to repeatedly activate specific brain networks, thereby remediating specific skill deficits. Remediation of specific skills may generalize and help alleviate clinical symptoms.

Attention training is an example of efficacious plasticity-based approach that reduces internalizing symptoms (Fergus & Bardeen, 2016). Individuals complete computerized tasks that require them to pay attention to external stimuli, reducing their excessive self-focus and interference by emotional stimuli. At the same time, normalization in brain activity related to attentional control has been observed following intervention (Eldar & Bar-Haim, 2010). In neurorehabilitation for individuals with schizophrenia, while some symptoms may be targeted by medication, social and cognitive deficits may persist. Cognitive training targeting working memory and cognitive flexibility has been shown to increase brain activation in networks associated with these skills (Wykes, et al., 2002). Neurorehabilitation can be more complex than merely having clients repeatedly perform a task they are not proficient at (Merzenich et al., 2014). By analyzing a complex ability into multiple components or processes, improving a domain-general component or lower-level process may help individuals improve their broad ability on the whole. For example, children with specific language impairment improved on language measures following intervention on selective auditory attention, which is not a linguistic skill but an attention construct (Stevens et al., 2008).

On the diagnostic side, studies have looked at neural activity patterns as a predictor or biomarker of various psychological disorders (Fonseka et al., 2018; O'Halloran et al., 2017; Teipel et al., 2018). This has the potential to contribute to the incremental validity in assessment relying on rating scales and standardized testing. In some cases, individuals who do not differ on traditional rating scales and standardized tests have been found to differ at the level of brain activity during neuroimaging tasks. At the group level, differences can be found between those who are genetically predisposed to psychological disorders and those who are not. Risk for psychopathology could be visualized in neuroimaging studies. For example, differences exist between individuals exposed to early adversity and individuals who were not (Bryck & Fisher, 2012). Differences also have been found between clinically depressed individuals in remission and healthy individuals who have never been clinically depressed (Höflich et al., 2012). These techniques may evolve to predict responsiveness to treatment and explore characteristics of non-responders (Fonseka et al., 2018; Ritchey et al., 2011). On the other hand, individuals with different clinical diagnoses may show similar brain activation patterns while performing tasks that are affected by their symptoms; this points to the need to reconsider the nature of their disorders and refine diagnostic criteria (Black et al., 2015).

From the constellation of factors that influence the neurodevelopmental trajectory, within professional practice, there is the need to consider environmental factors, as well as sex differences (Lenroot et al., 2007) and variance accounted for by intellectual ability (Shaw et al., 2006). For those with medical involvement, the integrated health perspective with a collaborative treatment approach across home-school-medical-community is recommended to ensure consideration of disease factors and processes (e.g., Asarnow et al., 2015; Godoy et al., 2017; Kolko & Perrin, 2014). Further, given the potential impact on and of others around the individual affected, efforts need to address not only the individual but also educate and address the concerns of caregivers, siblings, and peers (Guilfoyle et al., 2017).

Future Directions in Understanding Neurodevelopment in Children and Adults

There are many unknowns in the future, and understanding of neurodevelopment will require continued research to address changes in culture and environment that impact individuals at critical points in development. Although potential risks have been known, only in the past decade has significant research been conducted on neurodevelopmental risks in conjunction with pesticides, pollution, additives, and other neurotoxins (see Riccio & Sullivan, 2016). As indicated, experience and exposure to different stimuli can be key to changes and reorganization and critical periods of time. The effect of stimulation through electronic means as an intervention has demonstrated some positive effects, yet the long-term effects of children interacting via tablet and games on neurocognitive processes are as yet unknown. Certainly, the identification of a gaming as a disorder (World Health Organization, 2020) suggests interaction with electronics is not always positive. Even if not at the level of a disorder, there are indications of gray matter volume differences in association with internet gaming, particularly in association with a childhood history of ADHD (Lee et al., 2018).

There is great potential for further technological advances to foster better understanding of the brain-behavior-environment relations in both prevention and intervention for atypical neurodevelopmental trajectories (Bednarz & Kana, 2018). Some sensitive or critical periods for plasticity and change have been identified already. Increases in functional technology continue to add to understanding the complexities of neural networks as widely distributed functional systems (Anderson et al., 2013; Batelle et al., 2018; Grayson & Fair, 2017; Mill et al., 2017). There is, however, a need for additional longitudinal studies of children and adults to better understand the typical trajectory and how to best intervene when it is apparent that trajectory has been altered (Morgan et al., 2018). As yet, there remains minimal research on differences in connectivity across the life span (Petrican et al., 2017). Better understanding of intra- and inter-network connectivity may lead to insights regarding age-related changes in cognitive performance (Park & Reuter-Lorenz, 2009). Further consideration of connectivity profiles may improve understanding of mechanisms that underlie behavioral performance (Petrican et al., 2017). Additionally, with increased understanding of normative and atypical developmental trajectories, as well as factors that foster positive changes in the trajectory, better prevention and intervention approaches to positively impact outcome may be possible (Grayson & Fair, 2017). Continued research only can inform both science and practice; however, considerations need to be given to all the potential confounds and considerations (Bednarz & Kana, 2018).

Conclusions

As discussed in this chapter, the neurodevelopmental trajectory begins at conception and continues across the life span. When there are variations or deviations from the neurotypical trajectory, the greatest effects are evidenced at the times of greatest plasticity. From a neurodevelopmental perspective, these stages add to vulnerability as well as the potential for effective reorganization or rehabilitation. Many factors contribute to outcome with significant interaction effects; it is not sufficient to focus on the child or genes but also to consider other influences. A developmental perspective of function and behavior across the life span is imperative. The need for ongoing monitoring of neurocognitive functioning, as well as social-emotional development and quality of life, has been commonly suggested for children with chronic illnesses (Compas et al., 2017; Schraegle & Titus, 2017); similar ongoing monitoring of those with neurodevelopmental disorders may be informative. Understanding the bidirectional interaction of brain-behavior relations and the typical neurodevelopmental trajectory can inform early identification and early intervention, taking advantage of neuroplasticity to affect outcome (Insel, 2014).

Discussion Questions

1. What are some things parents can do with their newborns to promote optimal neuropsychological functioning in years to come?
2. At what point should parents begin to grow concerned about their child's behavior and development?
3. How do you think the shift from believing the brain is fully developed in the early 20s to learning the brain is not fully developed until the late 20s impacts societal expectations of adolescence and adulthood?
4. What is one way adults can combat the effects of neurological degradation during the aging process?
5. How can a disease or injury impair neuropsychological development or functioning?
6. What educational outcomes can be impacted by deviations in typical neuropsychological functioning? How do you think they will be affected?
7. In your opinion, to what degree is understanding cultural differences relevant in neuropsychology? What can you do to enhance your knowledge of different cultures?

EPPP Sample Questions

1. What does "neural connectivity" encompass?

   (a) The anatomical and functional interaction of neurons within and across brain regions that allows for complex behavior
   (b) The connection between neurons that form a center or system
   (c) The determination of the integrity of the neural system
   (d) The connections that are made and lost in childhood

2. Which of these patterns of change in neural development is necessary to transition from basic processing to complex processing in adolescence?
   (a) Decreases in gray matter, increases in white matter, and selective cortical pruning
   (b) Susceptibility to changes as a result of experience, intervention, disease or trauma
   (c) Increased cell growth, arborization, and myelination throughout the brain
   (d) Consolidation of neural networks in the association cortex
3. Neurodevelopmental models generally adopt a framework that emphasizes:
   (a) Typical versus atypical development
   (b) Etiological factors, child and family factors, and other ecological factors that facilitate or impede neurodevelopment at different points in the trajectory
   (c) The primary contribution of genetic makeup in shaping the trajectory of neurodevelopment
   (d) Identification of functional systems most vulnerable to alterations in trajectory
4. For individuals with chronic illness, the neurodevelopmental trajectory most often is characterized by:
   (a) Initially typical development with some subtle differences that gradually alter the trajectory to a more significant extent, leading to symptom presentation.
   (b) Generally delayed neurodevelopment from early childhood in some areas, but not all; however, typical benchmarks are eventually met.
   (c) Presumed typical neurodevelopment up to the onset of the disease process with alterations in trajectory thereafter a function of the disease process and treatment effects.
   (d) Atypical development in some areas early on, with highly variable presentation such that some trajectories may be intact while others are not.
5. The concepts of plasticity and vulnerability apply to neural development in that:
   (a) Plasticity is what explains the effects of exposure and intervention on altering brain function.
   (b) When the neural system is most in flux or stressed (e.g., puberty), there is the potential for greater change in connectivity as a result of exposure or intervention; however, effects can be both positive and negative.
   (c) Plasticity is greatest for different functional systems at different times from conception across the life span.
   (d) Plasticity is greatest in childhood with neural function locked in by adolescence.

Answers: A, A, A, C, B

Proactive Readings

Transcending the Past

Goldman-Rakic, P. S. (1987). Development of cortical circuitry and cognitive function. *Child Development, 58,* 601–622.

Mesulam, M. M. (1990). Large-scale neurocognitive networks and distributed processing for attention, language, and memory. *Annals of Neurology, 28*(5), 597–613.

Excelling in the Present

Anderson, M. L., Kennison, J., & Pessoa, L. (2013). Describing functional diversity of brain regions and networks. *NeuroImage, 73*, 50–58.

Insel, T. R. (2014). Mental disorders in childhood: Shifting the focus from behavioral symptoms to neurodevelopmental trajectories. *Journal of the American Medical Association, 311,* 1727–1728.

Transforming the Future

Antonenko, P. D., van Gog, T., & Paas, F. (2014). Implications of neuroimaging for educational research. In *Handbook of research on educational communications and technology* (pp. 51–63). Springer.

Bednarz, H. M., & Kana, R. K. (2018). Advances, challenges, and promises in pediatric neuroimaging of neurodevelopmental disorders. *Neuroscience Biobehavioral Review, 90,* 50–69. https://doi.org/10.1016/j.neubiorev.2018.03.025

References

Albaugh, M. D., Ivanova, M., Chaarani, B., Orr, C., Allgaier, N., Althoff, R. R., … Potter, A. S. (2019). Ventromedial prefrontal volume in adolescence predicts hyperactive/inattentive symptoms in adulthood. *Cerebral Cortex, 29*, 1866–1874. https://doi.org/10.1093/cercor/bhy066

American Psychiatric Association. (2013). Diagnostic and statistical manual of mental disorders (5th ed.). https://doi.org/10.1176/appi.books.9780890425596

Anclair, M., Hjärthag, F., & Hiltunen, A. (2017). Cognitive behavioural therapy and mindfulness for health-related quality of life: Comparing treatment for parents of children with chronic conditions – A pilot feasibility study. *Clinical Practice & Epidemiology in Mental Health, 13*, 1–9. https://doi.org/10.2174/1745017901713010001

Anderson, M. L., Kennison, J., & Pessoa, L. (2013). Describing functional diversity of brain regions and networks. *NeuroImage, 73*, 50–58. https://doi.org/10.1016/j.neuroimage.2013.01.071

Anderson, S. L., Tomada, A., Vincow, E. S., Valente, E., Plocari, A., & Teicher, M. H. (2008). Preliminary evidence for sensitive periods in the effect of childhood sexual abuse on regional brain development. *Journal of Neuropsychiatry, 20*, 292–301. https://doi.org/10.1176/jnp.2008.20.3.292

Antonenko, P. D., van Gog, T., & Paas, F. (2014). Implications of neuroimaging for educational research. In *Handbook of research on educational communications and technology* (pp. 51–63). Springer.

Aoki, C., Romeo, R. D., & Smith, S. S. (2017). Adolescence as a critical period for developmental plasticity. *Brain Research, 1654*, 85–86. https://doi.org/10.1016/j.brainres.2016.11.026

Aoki, Y., Yoncheva, Y. N., Chen, B., Nath, T., Sharp, D., Lazar, M., … DiMartino, A. (2017). Association of white matter structure with autism spectrum disorder and Attention-Deficit/Hyperactivity Disorder. *Journal of the American Medical Association Psychiatry, 74*, 1120–1128. https://doi.org/10.1001/jamapsychiatry.2017.2573

Armstrong, F. D. (2006). Neurodevelopment and chronic illness: Mechanisms of disease and treatment. *Mental Retardation and Developmental Disabilities Research Reviews, 12*, 168–173. https://doi.org/10.1002/mrdd.20114

Arnett, J. J. (2005). The developmental context of substance use in emerging adulthood. *Journal of Drug Issues, 35*, 235–254. https://doi.org/10.1177%2F002204260503500202

Aron, A. R., Robbins, T. W., & Poldrack, R. A. (2014). Inhibition and the right inferior frontal cortex: One decade on. *Trends in Cognitive Science, 18*, 177–185. https://doi.org/10.1016/j.tics.2013.12.003

Asarnow, J. R., Rozenman, M., Wiblin, J., & Zeltzer, L. (2015). Integrated medical behavioral care compared with usual primary for child and adolescent behavioral health: A meta-analysis. *JAMA Pediatrics, 169*, 929–937. https://doi.org/10.1001/jamapediatrics.2015.1141

Azar, B. (2010). Your brain on culture. *Monitor on Psychology, 41*, 44–45.

Bailey, S., Hoeft, F., Aboud, K., & Cutting, L. (2016). Anomalous gray matter patterns in specific reading comprehension deficit are independent of dyslexia. *Annals of Dyslexia, 66*, 256–274. https://doi.org/10.1007/s11881-015-0114-y

Bakos, D. S., Denburg, N., Fonseca, R. P., & Parente, M. A. D. M. P. (2010). A cultural study on decision making: Performance differences on the Iowa gambling task between selected groups of Brazilians and Americans. *Psychology & Neuroscience, 3*, 101–107. http://dx.doi.org/10.3922/j.psns.2010.1.013

Ball, G., Pazderova, L., Chew, A., Tusor, N., Merchant, N., Arichi, T., … Counsell, S. J. (2015). Thalamocortical connectivity predicts cognition in children born preterm. *Cerebral Cortex, 25*, 4310–4318. https://doi.org/10.1093/cercor/bhu331

Barkley, R. (2015). *Attention-Deficit Hyperactivity Disorder: A handbook for diagnosis and treatment*. Guilford.

Bassett, D. S., Bullmore, E., Verchinski, B. A., Mattay, V. S., Weinberger, D. R., & Mery-Lindenberg, A. (2008). Hierarchical organization of human cortical networks in health and schizophrenia. *Journal of Neuroscience, 28*, 9239–9248. https://doi.org/10.1523/JNEUROSCI.1929-08.2008

Batelle, D., Edwards, A. D., & O'Muircheartaigh, J. (2018). Annual research review: Not just a small adult brain: Understanding later neurodevelopment through imaging the neonatal brain. *Journal of Child Psychology and Psychiatry, 59*, 350–371. https://doi.org/10.1111/jcpp.12838

Bechara, A. (2007). *Iowa gambling task: Professional manual*. Psychological Assessment Resources.

Bednarz, H. M., & Kana, R. K. (2018). Advances, challenges, and promises in pediatric neuroimaging of neurodevelopmental disorders. *Neuroscience Biobehavioral Review, 90*, 50–69. https://doi.org/10.1016/j.neubiorev.2018.03.025

Bernhardt, B., Valk, S., Silani, G., Bird, G., Frith, U., & Singer, T. (2014). Selective disruption of sociocognitive structural brain networks in autism and alexithymia. *Cerebral Cortex, 24*, 3258–3267. https://doi.org/10.1093/cercor/bht182

Bialystok, E., & Viswanathan, M. (2009). Components of executive control with advantages for bilingual children in two cultures. *Cognition, 112*, 494–500. https://doi.org/10.1016/j.cognition.2009.06.014

Bishop, D., & Rutter, M. (2008). Neurodevelopmental disorders: Conceptual issues. In M. Rutter (Ed.), *Child and adolescent psychiatry* (pp. 32–41). Wiley-Blackwell.

Black, J. M., Myers, C. A., & Hoeft, F. (2015). The utility of neuroimaging studies for informing educational practice and policy in reading disorders. *New Directions for Child and Adolescent Development, 2015*(147), 49–56. https://doi.org/10.1002/cad.20086

Bölte, S., Bartl-Pokorny, K. D., Jonsson, U., Berggren, S., Zhang, D., Kostrzewa, E., Falck-Ytter, T., Einspieler, C., Pokorny, F. B., Jones, E. J., Roeyers, H., Charman, T., & Marschik, P. B. (2016). How can clinicians detect and treat Autism early? Methodological trends of technology use in research. *Acta Paediatrics, 105*(2):137–144. https://doi.org/10.1111/apa.13243

Braun, J. M., Kahn, R. S., Froehlich, T., Auinger, P., & Lanphear, B. P. (2006). Exposures to environmental toxicants and Attention Deficit Hyperactivity Disorder in U. S. children. *Environmental Health Perspectives, 114*, 1904–1909. https://doi.org/10.1289/ehp.9478

Brehmer, Y., Kalpouzos, G., Wenger, E., & Lövdén, M. (2014). Plasticity of brain and cognition in older adults. *Psychological Research, 78*, 790–802. https://doi.org/10.1007/s00426-014-0587-z

Brent, B. K., Thermenos, H. W., Keshavan, M. S., & Seidman, L. J. (2013). Gray matter alterations in Schizophrenia high-risk youth and early-onset Schizophrenia: A review of structural MRI findings. *Child and Adolescent Psychiatric Clinics of North America, 22*, 689–714. https://doi.org/10.1016/j.chc.2013.06.003

Brickman, A. M., Cabo, R., & Manly, J. J. (2006). Ethical issues in cross-cultural neuropsychology. *Applied Neuropsychology, 13*, 91–100. https://doi.org/10.1207/s15324826an1302_4

Bryck, R. L., & Fisher, P. A. (2012). Training the brain: Practical applications of neural plasticity from the intersection of cognitive neuroscience, developmental psychology, and prevention science. *The American Psychologist, 67*(2), 87–100. https://doi.org/10.1037/a0024657

Buré-Reyes, A., Hidalgo-Ruzzante, N., Vilar-López, R., Gontier, J., Sánchez, L., Pérez-García, M., & Puente, A. E. (2013). Neuropsychological test performance of Spanish speakers: Is performance different across different Spanish-speaking subgroups? *Journal of Clinical and Experimental Neuropsychology, 35*(4), 404–412. https://doi.org/10.1080/13803395.2013.778232

Burt, K. A., Whelan, R., Conrod, P. L., Banaschewski, T., Barker, G. J., Bokde, A. L. W., … the IMAGEN Consortium. (2016). Structural brain correlates of adolescent resilience. *Journal of Child Psychology and Psychiatry, 57*, 1287–1296. https://doi.org/10.1111/jcpp.12552

Callicott, J. H., Egan, M. F., Mattay, V. S., Bertolino, A., Bone, A. D., Verchinski, B., & Weinberger, D. R. (2003). Abnormal fMRI response of the dorsolateral prefrontal cortex in cognitively intact siblings of patients with schizophrenia. *American Journal of Psychiatry, 160*, 709–719. https://doi.org/10.1176/appi.ajp.160.4.709

Callicott, J. H., Mattay, V. S., Verschinski, B. A., Marenco, S., Egan, M. F., & Weinberger, D. R. (2003). Complexity of prefrontal cortical dysfunction in Schizophrenia: More than up and down. *American Journal of Psychiatry, 160*, 2209–2215. https://doi.org/10.1176/appi.ajp.160.12.2209

Chiang, L.-C., Ma, W.-F., Huang, J.-L., Tseng, L.-F., & Hsueh, K.C. (2009). Effect of relaxation-breathing training on anxiety and asthma signs/symptoms of children with moderate-to-severe Asthma: A randomized controlled trial. *International Journal of Nursing Studies, 46*, 1061–1070. https://doi.org/10.1016/j.ijnurstu.2009.01.013

Chiao, J. Y. (2009). Cultural neuroscience: A once and future discipline. *Progress in Brain Research, 20*, 287–304. https://doi.org/10.1016/s0079-6123(09)17821-4

Cicchetti, D., & Rogosch, F. A. (2007). Personality, adrenal steroid hormones, and resilience in maltreated children: A multi-level perspective. *Development and Psychopathology, 19*, 787–809. https://doi.org/10.1017/s0954579407000399

Citri, A., & Malenka, R. (2008). Synaptic plasticity: Multiple forms, functions, and mechanisms. *Neuropsychopharmacology, 33*, 18–41.

Collin, G., & van den Heuvel, M. (2013). The ontogeny of the human connectome: Development and dynamic changes of brain connectivity across the life span. *The Neuroscientist, 19*, 616–626. https://doi.org/10.1177/1073858413503712

Compas, B. E., Jaser, S. S., Reeslund, K., Patel, N., & Yarboi, J. (2017). Neurocognitive effects in children with chronic health conditions. *American Psychologist, 72*, 326–338. https://psycnet.apa.org/doi/10.1037/amp0000042

Conant, L. L., Liebenthal, E., Desai, A., & Binder, J. R. (2017). The relationship between maternal education and the neural substrates of phoneme perception in children: Interactions between socioeconomic status and proficiency level. *Brain and Language, 171*, 14–22. https://doi.org/10.1016/j.bandl.2017.03.010

Congdon, E. L., Westerlund, A., Algarin, C. R., Peirano, P. D., Gregas, M., Lozoff, B., & Nelson, C. A. (2012). Iron deficiency in infancy is associated with altered neural correlates of recognition memory at 10 years. *The Journal of Pediatrics, 160*(6), 1027–1033. https://doi.org/10.1016/j.jpeds.2011.12.011

Counsell, S. J., Edwards, A. D., Chew, A. T., Anjari, M., Dyet, L. E., Srinivasan, L., … Cowan, F. M. (2008). Specific relations between neurodevelopmental abilities and matter microstructure in children born preterm. *Brain, 131*, 3201–3208. https://doi.org/10.1093/brain/awn268

Courchesne, E., Carper, R., & Akshoomoff, N. (2003). Evidence of brain overgrowth in the first year of life in the Autism. *Journal of the American Medical Association, 290*, 337–344. https://doi.org/10.1001/jama.290.3.337

Curtis, W. J., & Cicchetti, D. (2003). Moving research on resilience into the 21st century: Theoretical and methodological considerations in examining the biological contributors to resilience. *Development and Psychopathology, 15*, 773–810. https://doi.org/10.1017/s0954579403000373

D'Angiulli, A., Van Roon, P. M., & Weinberg, J. (2012). Frontal EEG/ERP correlates of attentional processes, cortisol, and motivational states in adolescents from lower and higher socioeconomic status. *Frontiers in Human Neuroscience, 6*, 306. https://dx.doi.org/10.3389%2Ffnhum.2012.00306

Daly, B., Kral, M., & Brown, R. (2008). Cognitive and academic problems associated with childhood cancers and sickle cell disease. *School Psychology Quarterly, 23*, 230–242. https://psycnet.apa.org/doi/10.1037/1045-3830.23.2.230

Daly, E., Zaitchik, D., Copeland, M., Schmahmann, J., Gunther, J., & Albert, M. (2000). Predicting conversion to Alzheimer's disease using standardized clinical information. *Archives of Neurology, 57*, 675–680. https://doi.org/10.1001/archneur.57.5.675

Daugherty, J. C., Puente, A. E., Fasfous, A. F., Hidalgo-Ruzzante, N., & Pérez-Garcia, M. (2017). Diagnostic mistakes of culturally diverse individuals when using North American neuropsychological tests. *Applied Neuropsychology: Adult, 24*, 16–22. https://doi.org/10.1080/23279095.2015.1036992

Demir, Ö. E., & Küntay, A. C. (2014). Cognitive and neural mechanisms underlying socioeconomic gradients in language development: New answers to old questions. *Child Development Perspectives, 8*, 113–118. https://doi.org/10.1111/cdep.12069

Dinstein, I., Pierce, K., Eyler, L., Solso, S., Malach, R., Behrmann, M., & Courchesne, E. (2011). Disrupted neural synchronization in toddlers with Autism. *Neuron, 70*, 1218–1225. https://doi.org/10.1016/j.neuron.2011.04.018

Durston, S., & Casey, B. J. (2006). What have we learned about cognitive development from neuroimaging? *Neuropsychologia, 44*, 2149–2157. https://doi.org/10.1016/j.neuropsychologia.2005.10.010

Dwyer, D. B., Harrison, B. J., Yücel, M., Whittle, S., Zalesky, A., Pantelis, C., … Fornito, A. (2014). Large-scale brain network dynamics supporting adolescent cognitive control. *Journal of Neuroscience, 34*(42), 14096–14107. https://doi.org/10.1523/JNEUROSCI.1634-14.2014

Eden, G. F. (2016). Early identification and treatment of dyslexia a brain-based perspective. *Perspectives on Language and Literacy, 42*(1), 7.

Eden, G. F., Jones, K. M., Cappell, K., Gareau, L., Wood, F. B., Zeffiro, T. A., … Flowers, D. L. (2004). Neural changes following remediation in adult developmental dyslexia. *Neuron, 44*(3), 411–422. https://doi.org/10.1016/j.neuron.2004.10.019

Eggebrecht, A. T., Elison, J. T., Feczko, E., Todorov, A., Wolff, J. J., Kandala, S., … IBIS Network. (2017). Joint attention and brain functional connectivity in infants and toddlers. *Cerebral Cortex, 27*, 1709–1720. https://doi.org/10.1093/cercor/bhw403

Eldar, S., & Bar-Haim, Y. (2010). Neural plasticity in response to attention training in anxiety. *Psychological Medicine, 40*(04), 667. https://doi.org/10.1017/s0033291709990766

Faraone, S. V., Biederman, J., & Mick, E. (2006). The age dependent decline of Attention Deficit Hyperactivity Disorder: A meta-analysis of follow-up studies. *Psychological Medicine, 36*, 159–165. https://doi.org/10.1017/s003329170500471x

Faraone, S. V., Perlis, R. H., Doyle, A. E., Smoller, J. W., Goralnick, J. J., Holmgren, M. A., & Sklar, P. (2005). Molecular genetics of Attention-Deficit/Hyperactivity Disorder. *Biological Psychiatry, 57*, 1313–1323. https://doi.org/10.1016/j.biopsych.2004.11.024

Farias, S. T., Park, L. Q., Harvey, D. J., Simon, C., Reed, B. R., Carmichael, O., & Mungas, D. (2013). Everyday cognition in older adults: Associations with neuropsychological performance and structural brain imaging. *Journal of the International Neuropsychological Society, 19*, 430–441. https://doi.org/10.1017/s1355617712001609

Fergus, T. A., & Bardeen, J. R. (2016). The attention training technique: A review of a neurobehavioral therapy for emotional disorders. *Cognitive and Behavioral Practice, 23*(4), 502–516. https://doi.org/10.1016/j.cbpra.2015.11.001

Fernández, A., Quintero, J., Hornero, R., Zuluga, P., Navas, M., Gómez, C., … Ortiz, T. (2009). Complex analysis of spontaneous brain activity in attention-deficit/hyperactivity disorder: Diagnostic implications. *Biological Psychiatry, 65*, 561–577. https://doi.org/10.1016/j.biopsych.2008.10.046

Ferreira, L. K., & Busatto, G. F. (2011). Neuroimaging in Alzheimer's disease: Current role in clinical practice and potential future applications. *Clinics, 66*, 19–24. https://dx.doi.org/10.1590%2FS1807-59322011001300003

Ferstl, E. C., Neumann, J., Bogler, C., & von Cramon, D. Y. (2008). The extended language network: A meta-analysis of neuroimaging studies on text comprehension. *Human Brain Mapping, 29*, 581–593. https://doi.org/10.1002/hbm.20422

Finn, E. S., Shen, X., Holahan, J. M., Scheinost, D., Lacadie, C., Papdemetris, X., … Constable, R. T. (2014). Disruption of functional networks in dyslexia: A whole-brain, data-driven analysis of connectivity. *Biological Psychiatry, 76*, 397–404. https://doi.org/10.1016/j.biopsych.2013.08.031

Fletcher, J. M., & Grigorenko, E. L. (2017). Neuropsychology of learning disabilities: The past and the future. *Journal of the International Neuropsychological Society, 23*(9–10), 930–940. https://dx.doi.org/10.1017%2FS1355617717001084

Flores, I., Casaletto, K. B., Marquine, M. J., Umlauf, A., Moore, D. J., Mungas, D., … Heaton, R. K. (2017). Performance of Hispanics and non-Hispanic whites on the NIH toolbox cognition battery: The roles of ethnicity and language backgrounds. *The Clinical Neuropsychologist, 31*(4), 783–797. https://doi.org/10.1080/13854046.2016.1276216

Fonseka, T. M., Macqueen, G. M., & Kennedy, S. H. (2018). Neuroimaging biomarkers as predictors of treatment outcome in major depressive disorder. *Journal of Affective Disorders, 233*, 21–35. https://doi.org/10.1016/j.jad.2017.10.049

Freeman, J. B., Rule, N. O., Adams, R. B., Jr., & Ambady, N. (2009). Culture shapes a mesolimbic response to signals of dominance and subordination that associates with behavior. *NeuroImage, 47*(1), 353–359. https://doi.org/10.1016/j.neuroimage.2009.04.038

Freyer, T., Klöppel, S., Tüscher, O., Kordon, A., Zurowski, B., Kuelz, A., … Voderholzer, U. (2011). Frontostriatal activation in patients with Obsessive-Compulsive Disorder before and after Cognitive Behavioral Therapy. *Psychological Medicine, 41*(01), 207–216. https://doi.org/10.1017/s0033291710000309

Gerner, G., & Baron, I. S. (2015). Pregnancy complications and neuropsychological outcomes: A review. *Child Neuropsychology, 21*, 269–284. https://doi.org/10.1080/09297049.2014.910301

Gershon, R. C., Wagster, M. V., Hendrie, H. C., Fox, N. A., Cook, K. F., & Nowinski, C. J. (2013). NIH toolbox for assessment of neurological and behavioral function. *Neurology, 80*(11 Suppl 3), S2–S6. https://doi.org/10.1212/wnl.0b013e3182872e5f

Giedd, J. N., Blumenthal, J., Jeffries, N. O., Castellanos, F., Liu, H., Zijdengox, A., … Rapoport, J. (1999). Brain development during childhood and adolescence: A longitudinal MRI study. *Nature Neuroscience, 2*, 861–863. https://doi.org/10.1038/13158

Giedd, J. N., & Rapoport, J. L. (2010). Structural MRI of pediatric brain development: What have we learned and where are we going. *Neuron, 67*, 728–734. https://doi.org/10.1016/j.neuron.2010.08.040

Giedd, J. N., Vaituzis, A. C., Hamburger, S. D., Lange, N., Rajapakse, J. C., Kaysen, D., … Rapoport, J. L. (1996). Quantitative MRI of the temporal lobe, amygdala, and hippocampus in normal human development: Ages 4–18 years. *Journal of Comparative Neurology, 366*, 223–230. https://doi.org/10.1002/(sici)1096-9861(19960304)366:2%3C223::aid-cne3%3E3.0.co;2-7

Goddings, A.-L., Mills, K. L., Clasen, L. S., Giedd, J. N., Viner, R. M., & Blakemore, S.-J. (2014). The influence of puberty on subcortical brain development. *NeuroImage, 88*, 242–251. https://doi.org/10.1016/j.neuroimage.2013.09.073

Godoy, L., Long, M., Marschall, D., Hodgkinson, S., Bokor, B., Rhodes, H., … Beers, L. (2017). Behavioral health integration in health care settings: Lessons learned from a pediatric hospital primary care system. *Journal of Clinical Psychology in Medical Settings, 24*, 245–258. https://doi.org/10.1007/s10880-017-9509-8

Gogtay, N., Giedd, J. N., Lusk, L., Hayashi, K. M., Greenstein, D., Vaituzis, A. C., … Thompson, P. M. (2004). Dynamic mapping of human cortical development during childhood through early adulthood. *Proceedings of the National Academy of Science, 101*, 8174–8179. https://doi.org/10.1073/pnas.0402680101

Gogtay, N., Lu, A., Leow, A. D., Klunder, A. D., Lee, A. D., Chavez, A., … Thompson, P. M. (2008). Three-dimensional brain growth abnormalities in childhood-onset Schizophrenia visualized by using tensor-based morphometry. *Proceedings of the National Academy of Science, 105*, 15979–15984. https://doi.org/10.1073/pnas.0806485105

Goldapple, K., Segal, Z., Garson, C., Lau, M., Bieling, P., Kennedy, S., & Mayberg, H. (2004). Modulation of cortical-limbic pathways in major depression. *Archives of General Psychiatry, 61*(1), 34. https://doi.org/10.1001/archpsyc.61.1.34

Goldman-Rakic, P. S. (1987). Development of cortical circuitry and cognitive function. *Child Development, 58*, 601–622. https://doi.org/10.2307/1130201

Goldman-Rakic, P. S. (1988). Topography of cognition: Parallel distributed networks in primate association cortex. *Annual Review of Neuroscience, 11*, 137–158. https://psycnet.apa.org/doi/10.1146/annurev.ne.11.030188.001033

Gottwald, J. M., Achermann, S., Marciszko, C., Lindskog, M., & Gredebäck, G. (2016). An embodied account of early executive-functioning development. *Psychological Science, 27*, 1600–1610. https://psycnet.apa.org/doi/10.1177/0956797616667447

Grayson, D. S., & Fair, D. A. (2017). Development of large-scale functional networks from birth to adulthood: A guide to the neuroimaging literature. *NeuroImage, 160*, 15–31. https://doi.org/10.1016/j.neuroimage.2017.01.079

Greenstein, D., Lerch, J., Shaw, P., Clasen, L., Giedd, J., Gochman, P., … Gogtay, N. (2006). Childhood onset Schizophrenia: Cortical brain anomalies as young adults. *Journal of Child Psychology and Psychiatry, 47*, 1003–1012. https://doi.org/10.1111/j.1469-7610.2006.01658.x

Guilfoyle, S. M., Wagner, J. L., Modi, A. C., Junger, K. F., Barrett, L. E., Riisen, A. C., … Weyand, C. (2017). Pediatric epilepsy and behavioral health: The state of the literature and directions for evidence-based interprofessional care, training, and research. *Clinical Practice in Pediatric Psychology, 5*, 79–90. https://psycnet.apa.org/doi/10.1037/cpp0000169

Gur, R. C., Richard, J., Calkins, M. E., Chiavacci, R., Hansen, J. A., Bilker, W. B., … Gur, R. E. (2012). Age group and sex differences in performance on a computerized neurocognitive battery in children age 8−21. *Neuropsychology, 26*(2), 251. https://dx.doi.org/10.1037%2Fa0026712

Halperin, J. M., Trampush, J. W., Miller, C. J., Marks, D. J., & Newcorn, J. H. (2008). Neuropsychological outcome in adolescents/young adults with childhood ADHD: Profiles of persisters, remitters and controls. *Journal of Child Psychology and Psychiatry, 49*(9), 958–966. https://doi.org/10.1111/j.1469-7610.2008.01926.x

Herrington, J. D., Maddox, B. B., Kerns, C. M., Rump, K., Worley, J. A., Bush, J. C., … Miller, J. S. (2017). Amygdala volume differences in Autism Spectrum Disorder are related to anxiety. *Journal of Autism and Developmental Disorders, 47*, 3682–3691. https://doi.org/10.1007/s10803-017-3206-1

Herting, M. M., & Sowell, E. R. (2017). Puberty and structural brain development in humans. *Frontiers in Neuroendocrinology, 44*, 122–137. https://doi.org/10.1016/j.yfrne.2016.12.003

Hessen, E., Hokkannen, L., Ponsford, J., van Zandvoort, M., Watts, A., Evans, J., & Haaland, K. Y. (2018). Core competencies in clinical neuropsychology training across the world. *The Clinical Neuropsychologist, 32*, 642–656. https://doi.org/10.1080/13854046.2017.1413210

Hilliard, M. E., Harris, M. A., & Weissberg-Benchell, J. (2012). Diabetes resilience: A model of risk and protection in Type 1 Diabetes. *Current Diabetes Reports, 12*, 739–748. https://doi.org/10.1007/s11892-012-0314-3

Hirase H., & Shinohara Y. (2014). Transformation of cortical and hippocampal neural circuit by environmental enrichment. *Neuroscience, 280*, 282–298. https://doi.org/10.1016/j.neuroscience.2014.09.031

Höflich, A., Baldinger, P., Savli, M., Lanzenberger, R., & Kasper, S. (2012). Imaging treatment effects in depression. *Reviews in the Neurosciences, 23*, 227–252. https://doi.org/10.1515/revneuro-2012-0038

Holder, M. K., & Blaustein, J. D. (2014). Puberty and adolescence as a time of vulnerability to stressors that alter neurobehavioral processes. *Frontiers in Neuroendocrinology, 35*, 89–110. https://dx.doi.org/10.1016%2Fj.yfrne.2013.10.004

Hotier, S., Leroy, F., Boisgontier, J., Laidi, C., Mangin, J.-F., Delorme, R., … Houenou, J. (2017). Social cognition in Autism is associated with the neurodevelopment of the posterior superior temporal sulcus. *Acta Psychiatrica Scandinavica, 136*, 517–525. https://doi.org/10.1111/acps.12814

Huey, E. D., Lee, S., Lieberman, J. A., Devanand, D. P., Brickman, A. M., Raymont, V., … Grafman, J. (2015). Brain regions associated with internalizing and externalizing psychiatric symptoms in patients with penetrating traumatic brain injury. *The Journal of Neuropsychiatry and Clinical Neurosciences, 28*, 104–111. https://doi.org/10.1176/appi.neuropsych.15060150

Humphreys, K. L., Watts, E. L., Dennis, E. L., King, L. S., Thompson, P. M., & Gotlib, I. H. (2019). Stressful life events, ADHD symptoms, and brain structure in early adolescence. *Journal of Abnormal Child Psychology, 47*, 421–432. https://doi.org/10.1007/s10802-018-0443-5

Huttenlocher, P. R. (1990). Morphometric study of human cerebral cortex development. *Neuropsychologia, 28*, 517–527. https://doi.org/10.1016/0028-3932(90)90031-i

Insel, T. R. (2014). Mental disorders in childhood: Shifting the focus from behavioral symptoms to neurodevelopmental trajectories. *Journal of the American Medical Association, 311*, 1727–1728. https://doi.org/10.1001/jama.2014.1193

Johnson, J. S., & Newport, E. L. (1989). Critical period effects in second language learning: The influence of maturational state on the acquisition of English as a second language. *Cognitive Psychology, 21*(1), 60–99. https://doi.org/10.1016/0010-0285(89)90003-0

Johnson, S., & Marlow, N. (2014). Growing up after extremely preterm birth: Lifespan mental health outcomes. *Seminars in Fetal and Neonatal Medicine, 19*(2), 97–110. https://doi.org/10.1016/j.siny.2013.11.004

Johnson, S. B., Riis, J. L., & Noble, K. G. (2016). State of the art review: Poverty and the developing brain. *Pediatrics, 137*(4), https://doi.org/10.1542/peds.2015-3075.

Juraska, J. M., & Willing, J. (2017). Pubertal onset as a critical transition for neural development and cognition. *Brain Research, 1654*, 87–94. https://doi.org/10.1016/j.brainres.2016.04.012

Kaiser, J., Bledowski, C., & Dietrich, J. (2014). Neural correlates of chemotherapy-related cognitive impairment. *Cortex, 54*, 33–50. https://doi.org/10.1016/j.cortex.2014.01.010

Kana, R. K., Sartin, E. B., Stevens, C., Jr., Deshpande, H. D., Klein, C., Klinger, M. R., & Klinger, L. G. (2017). Neural networks underlying language and social cognition during self-other processing in Autism Spectrum Disorders. *Neuropsychologia, 102*, 116–123. https://doi.org/10.1016/j.neuropsychologia.2017.06.008

Kani, A. S., Shinn, A. K., Lewandowski, K. E., & Öngür, D. (2017). Converging effects of diverse treatment modalities on frontal cortex in schizophrenia: A review of longitudinal functional magnetic resonance imaging studies. *Journal of Psychiatric Research, 84*, 256–276. https://doi.org/10.1016/j.jpsychires.2016.10.012

Kaufmann, T., Alnaes, D., Doan, N., Brandt, C., Andreassen, O., & Westyle, L. (2017). Delayed stabilization and individualization in connectome development related to psychiatric disorders. *Nature Neuroscience, 20*, 513–515. https://doi.org/10.1038/nn.4511

Khundrakpam, B. S., Reid, A., Brauer, J., Carbonell, F., Lewis, J., Ameis, S., … Evans, A. C. (2013). Developmental changes in organization of structural brain networks. *Cerebral Cortex, 23*, 2072–2085. https://doi.org/10.1093/cercor/bhs187

Kinnunen, K. M., Greenwood, R., Powell, J. H., Leech, R., Hawkins, P. C., Bonnelle, V., … Sharp, D. J. (2010). White matter damage and cognitive impairment after traumatic brain injury. *Brain, 134*, 449–463. https://doi.org/10.1016/j.bbadis.2017.05.020

Klein, D., Rotarska-Jagiela, A., Genc, E., Sritharan, S., Mohr, H., Roux, F., … Uhlhaas, P. J. (2014). Adolescent brain maturation and cortical folding: Evidence for reductions in gyrification. PLoS One (15)9, https://doi.org/10.1371/journal.pone.0084914

Klingberg, T., Fernell, E., Olesen, P. J., Johnson, M., Gustafsson, P., Dahlstrom, K., … Westerberg, H. (2005). Computerized training of working memory in children with ADHD: A randomized, controlled trial. *Journal of the American Academy of Child & Adolescent Psychiatry, 44*, 177–186. https://doi.org/10.1097/00004583-200502000-00010

Kolko, D. J., & Perrin, E. (2014). The integration of behavioral health interventions in children's health care: Services, science and suggestions. *Journal of Clinical Child and Adolescent Psychiatry, 43*, 216–228. https://doi.org/10.1080/15374416.2013.862804

Kovelman, I., Norton, E. S., Christodoulou, J. A., Gaab, N., Lieberman, D. A., Triantafyllou, C., … Gabrieli, J. D. (2011). Brain basis of phonological awareness for spoken language in children and its disruption in dyslexia. *Cerebral Cortex, 22*(4), 754–764. https://doi.org/10.1093/cercor/bhr094

Krain, A. L., & Castellanos, F. X. (2006). Brain development and ADHD. *Clinical Psychology Review, 26*, 433–444. https://doi.org/10.1016/j.cpr.2006.01.005

Kundu, P., Benson, B. E., Rosen, D., Frangou, S., Leibenluft, E., Luh, W.-M., … Ernst, M. (2018). The integration of functional brain activity from adolescence to adulthood. *Journal of Neuroscience, 4*, 3559–3570. https://doi.org/10.1523/jneurosci.1864-17.2018

Lagor, A. F., Williams, D. J., Lerner, J. B., & McClure, K. S. (2013). Lessons learned from a mindfulness-based intervention with chronically ill youth. *Clinical Practice in Pediatric Psychology, 1*, 146–158. https://psycnet.apa.org/doi/10.1037/cpp0000015

Lee, D., Namkoong, K., Lee, J., & Jung, Y. C. (2018). Preliminary evidence of altered gray matter volume in subjects with internet gaming disorder: Associations with history of childhood Attention-Deficit Hyperactivity Disorder symptoms. *Brain Imaging and Behavior,* online first: https://doi.org/10.1007/s11682-018-9872-6.

Lenneberg, E. H. (1967). *Biological foundations of language*. Wiley.

Lenroot, R. K., Gogtay, N., Greenstein, D. K., Wells, E. M., Wallasce, G. I., Clasen, L. S., … Giedd, J. N. (2007). Sexual dimorphism of brain developmental trajectories during childhood and adolescence. *NeuroImage, 7*, 1065–1073. https://doi.org/10.1016/j.neuroimage.2007.03.053

Lewis, C., Koyasu, M., Oh, S., Ogawa, A., Short, B., & Huang, Z. (2009). Culture, executive function, and social understanding. *New Directions for Child and Adolescent Development, 123*, 69–85. https://doi.org/10.1002/cd.236

Lewis, J. D., Evans, A. C., Pruett, J. R., Botteron, K., Zwaigenbaum, L., Estes, A., … Piven, J. (2014). Network inefficiencies in autism spectrum disorder at 24 months. *Translational Psychiatry, 4*, e388. https://doi.org/10.1038/tp.2014.24

Lewis, J. D., Evans, A. C., Pruett, J. R., Jr., Boteron, K. N., McKinstry, R. C., Zwaigenbaum, L., … Piven, J. (2017). The emergence of network inefficiencies with Autism Spectrum Disorder. *Biological Psychology, 82*, 176–183. https://dx.doi.org/10.1016%2Fj.biopsych.2017.03.006

Makris, N., Biederman, J., Valera, E. M., Bush, G., Kaiser, J., Kennedy, D. N., … Seidman, L. J. (2007). Cortical thinning of the attention and executive function networks in adults with Attention-Deficit Hyperactivity Disorder. *Cerebral Cortex, 17*, 1364–1375. https://doi.org/10.1093/cercor/bhl047

Márin, O. (2012). Interneuron dysfunction in psychiatric disorders. *Nature Reviews Neuroscience, 13*, 107–120. https://doi.org/10.1038/nrn3155

Marrus, N., Eggebrecht, A. T., Todorov, A., Elison, J. T., Wolff, J. J., Cole, L., … Emerson, R. W. (2017). Walking, gross motor development, and brain functional connectivity in infants and toddlers. *Cerebral Cortex, 28*(2), 750–763. https://doi.org/10.1093/cercor/bhx313

McAlonan, G. M., Cheung, V., Chua, S. E., Oosterlaan, J., Hung, S.-F., Tang, C.-P., … Leung, P. W. L. (2009). Age-related grey matter volume correlates of response inhibition and shifting in attention-deficit hyperactivity disorder. *British Journal of Psychiatry, 194*, 123–129. https://doi.org/10.1192/bjp.bp.108.051359

McFarland, D. J. (2017). How neuroscience can inform the study of individual differences in cognitive abilities. *Reviews in the Neurosciences, 28*, 343–362. https://doi.org/10.1515/revneuro-2016-0073

Merzenich, M. M., Van Vleet, T. M., & Nahum, M. (2014). Brain plasticity-based therapeutics. *Frontiers in Human Neuroscience, 8*, 385. https://dx.doi.org/10.3389%2Ffnhum.2014.00385

Mesulam, M. M. (1990). Large-scale neurocognitive networks and distributed processing for attention, language, and memory. *Annals of Neurology: Official Journal of the American Neurological Association and the Child Neurology Society, 28*(5), 597–613. https://doi.org/10.1002/ana.410280502

Meyer-Lindenberg, A., & Tost, H. (2014). Neuroimaging and plasticity in schizophrenia. *Restorative Neurology and Neuroscience, 32*, 119–127. https://doi.org/10.3233/RNN-139014

Mill, R. D., Ito, T., & Cole, M. W. (2017). From connectome to cognition: The search for mechanism in human functional brain networks. *NeuroImage, 160*, 124–139. https://doi.org/10.1016/j.neuroimage.2017.01.060

Mills, K., Goddings, A. L., Herting, M., Meuwese, R., Blakemore, S. J., Crone, E., … Tamnes, C. K. (2016). Structural brain development between childhood and adulthood: Convergence across four longitudinal samples. *NeuroImage, 141*, 273–281. https://doi.org/10.1016/j.neuroimage.2016.07.044

Monaghan, M., Clary, L., Stern, A., Hilliard, M. E., Streisand, R. (2015) Protective factors in young children with Type 1 Diabetes. *Journal of Pediatric Psychology, 40*(9), 878–887. https://doi.org/10.1093/jpepsy/jsv041

Morgan, S. E., White, S. R., Bullmore, E. T., & Vértes, P. E. (2018). A network neuroscience approach to typical and atypical brain development. *Biological Psychiatry, 3*, 754–766. https://doi.org/10.1016/j.bpsc.2018.03.003

Mosconi, M. W., Cody-Hazlett, H., Poe, M. D., Gerig, G., Gimpel-Smith, R., & Piven, J. (2009). Longitudinal study of amygdala volume and joint attention in 2- to 4-year-old children with Autism. *Archives of General Psychiatry, 66*, 509–516. https://doi.org/10.1001/archgenpsychiatry.2009.19

Mullen, K. M., Vohr, B. R., Katz, K. H., Schenider, K. C., Lacadie, C., Hampson, M., … Ment, L. R. (2011). Preterm birth results in alterations in neural connectivity at age 16 years. *NeuroImage, 54*, 2563–2570. https://doi.org/10.1016/j.neuroimage.2010.11.019

Müller, R. A., Shih, P., Keehn, B., Deyoe, J., Leyden, K., & Shukla, D. (2011). Underconnected, but how? A survey of functional connectivity MRI studies in Autism Spectrum Disorders. *Cerebral Cortex, 21*, 2233–2243. https://doi.org/10.1093/cercor/bhq296

Muñoz, C., & Singleton, D. (2011). A critical review of age-related research on L2 ultimate attainment. *Language Teaching, 44*, 1–35. https://doi.org/10.1017/S0261444810000327

Newman, L. M., Trivedi, M. A., Bendlin, B. B., Ries, M. L., & Johnson, S. C. (2007). The relationship between gray matter morphometry and neuropsychological performance in a large sample of cognitively healthy adults. *Brain Imaging and Behavior, 1*, 3–10. https://doi.org/10.1007/s11682-007-9000-5

Nikolas, M. A., & Burt, S. A. (2010). Genetic and environmental influences on ADHD symptom dimensions of inattention and hyperactivity: A meta-analysis. *Journal of Abnormal Psychology, 119*, 1–17. https://doi.org/10.1037/a0018010

Noble, K. G., McCandliss, B. D., & Farah, M. J. (2007). Socioeconomic gradients predict individual differences in neurocognitive abilities. *Developmental Science, 10*, 464–480. https://doi.org/10.1111/j.1467-7687.2007.00600.x

Norman, M. A., Moore, D. J., Taylor, M., Franklin, D., Jr., Cysique, L., Ake, C., … Hnrc Group. (2011). Demographically corrected norms for African Americans and Caucasians on the Hopkins verbal learning test–revised, brief visuospatial memory test–revised, stroop color and word test, and Wisconsin card sorting test 64-card version. *Journal of Clinical and Experimental Neuropsychology, 33*(7), 793–804. https://doi.org/10.1080/13803395.2011.559157

O'Halloran, L., Nymberg, C., Jollans, L., Garavan, H., & Whelan, R. (2017). The potential of neuroimaging for identifying predictors of adolescent alcohol use initiation and misuse. *Addiction, 112*, 719–726. https://doi.org/10.1111/add.13629

Olson, K., & Jacobson, K. (2015). Cross-cultural considerations in pediatric neuropsychology: A review and call to attention. *Applied Neuropsychology-Child, 4*, 166–177. https://doi.org/10.1080/21622965.2013.830258

Oyserman, D., & Lee, S. S. (2008). Does culture influence what and how we think? Effects of priming individualism and collectivism. *Psychological Bulletin, 134*(2), 311–342. https://doi.org/10.1037/0033-2909.134.2.311

Pantelis, C., Yücel, M., Wood, S. J., Velakoulis, D., Sun, D., Berger, G., Stuart, G. W., Yung, A., Phillips, L., McGorry, P. D. (2005). Structural brain imaging evidence for multiple pathological processes at different stages of brain development in schizophrenia. *Schizophrenia Bulletin, 31*(3):672–696. https://doi.org/10.1093/schbul/sbi034

Parikshank, N. N., Gandal, M. J., & Geschwind, D. H. (2015). Systems biology and gene networks in neurodevelopmental and neurodegenerative disorders. *Nature Reviews Genetics, 16*, 441–458. https://doi.org/10.1038/nrg3934

Parisi, L., Rocca, M. A., Valsasina, P., Panicari, L., Mattioli, F., & Filippi, M. (2014). Cognitive rehabilitation correlates with the functional connectivity of the anterior cingulate cortex in patients with multiple sclerosis. *Brain Imaging and Behavior, 8*, 387–393. https://doi.org/10.1007/s11682-012-9160-9

Park, D. C., & Reuter-Lorenz, P. (2009). The adaptive brain: Aging and neurocognitive scaffolding. *Annual Review of Psychology, 60*, 173–196. https://doi.org/10.1146/annurev.psych.59.103006.093656

Park, M. T. M., Raznahan, A., Shaw, P., Gogtay, N., Lerch, J. P., & Chakravarty, M. M. (2018). Neuroanatomical phenotypes in mental illness: Identifying convergent and divergent cortical phenotypes across Autism, ADHD, and Schizophrenia. *Journal of Psychiatry and Neuroscience, 43*, 201–212. https://doi.org/10.1503/jpn.170094

Parsons, S., Kruijt, A.-W., & Fox, E. (2016). A cognitive model of psychological resilience. *Journal of Experimental Psychopathology, 7*, 296–310. https://doi.org/10.5127%2Fjep.053415

Pechtel, P., Lyons-Ruth, K., Anderson, C. M., & Teicher, M. H. (2014). Sensitive periods of amygdala development: The role of maltreatment in preadolescence. *NeuroImage, 97*, 236–244. https://doi.org/10.1016/j.neuroimage.2014.04.025

Pelham, S. D., & Abrams, L. (2014). Cognitive advantages and disadvantages in early and late bilinguals. *Journal of Experimental Psychology: Learning, Memory, and Cognition, 40*(2), 313. https://doi.org/10.1037/a0035224

Peters, L., & De Smedt, B. (2018). Arithmetic in the developing brain: A review of brain imaging studies. *Developmental Cognitive Neuroscience, 30*, 265–279. https://doi.org/10.1016/jdcn.2017.05.002

Petrican, R., Taylor, M. J., & Grady, C. L. (2017). Trajectories of brain system maturation from childhood to older adulthood: Implications for lifespan cognitive functioning. *NeuroImage, 163*, 125–149. https://doi.org/10.1016/j.neuroimage.2017.09.025

Peviani, V., Scarpa, P., Toraldo, A., & Bottini, G. (2016). Accounting for ethnic-cultural and linguistic diversity in neuropsychological assessment of patients with drug-resistant epilepsy: A retrospective study. *Epilepsy & Behavior, 64*, 94–101. https://doi.org/10.1016/j.yebeh.2016.09.011
Pinquart, M., & Shen, Y. H. (2011). Behavior problems in children and adolescents with chronic physical illness: A meta-analysis. *Journal of Pediatric Psychology, 36*, 1003–1016. https://doi.org/10.1093/jpepsy/jsr042
Piper, M., Beneyto, M., Burne, T. H., Eyles, D. W., Lewis, D. A., & McGrath, J. J. (2012). The neurodevelopmental hypothesis of Schizophrenia: Convergent clues from epidemiology and neuropathology. *Psychiatric Clinics of North America, 35*, 571–584. https://doi.org/10.1016/j.psc.2012.06.002
Porto, P., Oliveira, L., Mari, J., Volchan, E., Figueira, I., & Ventura, P. (2009). Does cognitive behavioral therapy change the brain. A systematic review of neuroimaging in anxiety disorders. *The Journal of Neuropsychiatry and Clinical Neuroscience, 21*, 114–125. https://doi.org/10.1176/appi.neuropsych.21.2.114
Prins, M. L., Alexander, D., Giza, C. C., & Hovda, D. A. (2013). Repeated mild traumatic brain injury: Mechanisms of cerebral vulnerability. *Journal of Neurotrauma, 30*(1), 30–38. https://doi.org/10.1089/neu.2012.2399
Prado, E. L., & Dewey, K. G. (2015). Nutrition and brain development in early life. *Nutrition Review, 72*, 267–284. https://doi.org/10.1111/nure.12102
Rapoport, J. L., & Gogtay, N. (2008). Brain neuroplasticity in healthy, hyperactive, and psychotic children: Insights from neuroimaging. *Neuropsychopharmacology, 33*, 181–197. https://doi.org/10.1038/sj.npp.1301553
Raz, N., Gunning, F. M., Head, D., Dupuis, J. H., McQuain, J., Briggs, S. D., Loken, W. J., Thornton, A. E., Acker, J. D. (1997). Selective aging of the human cerebral cortex observed in vivo: Differential vulnerability of the prefrontal gray matter. *Cerebral Cortex, 7*(3), 268–282. https://doi.org/10.1093/cercor/7.3.268
Raznahan, A., Lerch, J., Lee, N., Greenstein, D., Wallace, G., Stockman, M., … Giedd, J. N. (2011). Patterns of coordinated anatomical change in human cortical development: A longitudinal neuroimaging study of maturational coupling. *Neuron, 72*, 873–884. https://doi.org/10.1016/j.neuron.2011.09.028
Redcay, E., & Courchesne, E. (2005). When is the brain enlarged in Autism? A meta-analysis of all brain size reports. *Biological Psychiatry, 58*, 1–9. https://doi.org/10.1016/j.biopsych.2005.03.026
Reichenberg, A., & Harvey, P. D. (2007). Neuropsychological impairments in Schizophrenia: Integration of performance-based and brain imaging findings. *Psychological Bulletin, 133*, 833–858. https://doi.org/10.1037/0033-2909.133.5.833
Riccio, C., Pliego, J., Cohen, M., & Park, Y. (2015). Executive function performance for children with epilepsy localized to the frontal or temporal lobes. *Applied Neuropsychology: Child, 4*, 277–284. https://doi.org/10.1080/21622965.2014.923774
Riccio, C. A., & Sullivan, J. R. (2016). *Pediatric neurotoxicology: Academic and psychosocial outcomes*. Springer.
Ritchey, M., Dolcos, F., Eddington, K. M., Strauman, T. J., & Cabeza, R. (2011). Neural correlates of emotional processing in depression: Changes with cognitive behavioral therapy and predictors of treatment response. *Journal of Psychiatric Research, 45*, 577–587. https://doi.org/10.1016/j.jpsychires.2010.09.007
Romeo, R. D. (2017). The impact of stress on the structure of the adolescent brain: Implications for adolescent mental health. *Brain Research, 1654*, 185–191. https://doi.org/10.1016/j.brainres.2016.03.021
Romine, C., & Reynolds, C. R. (2005). A model of the development of frontal lobe functioning: Findings from a meta-analysis. *Applied Neuropsychology, 12*, 190–201. https://doi.org/10.1207/s15324826an1204_2
Ruan, Q., D'Onofrio, G., Sancarlo, D., Bao, Z., Greco, A., & Yu, Z. (2016). Potential neuroimaging biomarkers of pathologic brain changes in mild cognitive impairment and Alzheimer's

disease: A systematic review. *BMC Geriatrics, 16*(1), 104. https://dx.doi.org/10.1186%2Fs12877-016-0281-7

Saggar, M., King, B. G., Zanesco, A. P., Maclean, K. A., Aichele, S. R., Jacobs, T. L., … Saron, C. D. (2012). Intensive training induces longitudinal changes in meditation state-related EEG oscillatory activity. *Frontiers in Human Neuroscience, 6*(256). https://doi.org/10.3389/fnhum.2012.00256

Salvan, P., Tournier, J. D., Batalle, D., Falconer, S., Chew, A., Kennea, N., … Counsell, S. J. (2017). Language ability in preterm children is associated with arcuate fasciculi microstructure at term. *Human Brain Mapping, 38*, 3836–3847. https://doi.org/10.1002/hbm.23632

Savage, E., Farrell, D., McManus, V., & Grey, M. (2010). The science of intervention for type 1 diabetes in childhood: Systematic review. *Journal of Advanced Nursing, 66*, 2604–2619. https://doi.org/10.1111/j.1365-2648.2010.05423.x

Schraegle, W. A., & Titus, J. B. (2017). The influence of endophenotypic, disease-specific, and environmental variables on the expression of anxiety in pediatric epilepsy. *Epilepsy & Behavior, 75*, 90–96. https://doi.org/10.1016/j.yebeh.2017.07.008

Schweren, L. J. S., Hartman, C. A., Zwiers, M. P., Heslenfeld, D. J., Franke, B., Oosterlaan, J., … Hoekstra, P. J. (2016). Stimulant history predicts frontal-striatal structural connectivity in adolescents with Attention-Deficit/Hyperactivity Disorder. *European Psychopharmacology, 26*, 674–683. https://doi.org/10.1016/j.euroneuro.2016.02.007

Selemon, L. D. (2013). A role for synaptic plasticity in the adolescent development of executive function. *Translational Psychiatry, 3*, e238. https://doi.org/10.1038/tp.2013.7

Semrud-Clikeman, M. (this volume). Understanding the development of the central nervous system and its relationship to clinical practice. In R. D'Amato, A. S. Davis, E. M. Power, & E. C. Eusebio (Eds.), *Understanding the biological basis of behavior*. Springer.

Shaw, P., Gogtay, N., & Rapoport, J. (2010). Childhood psychiatric disorders as anomalies in neurodevelopmental trajectories. *Human Brain Mapping, 31*, 917–925. https://doi.org/10.1002/hbm.21028

Shaw, P., Greenstein, D., Lerch, J., Clasen, L. S., Lenroot, R., Gogtay, N., … Giedd, J. N. (2006). Intellectual ability and cortical development in children and adolescents. *Nature, 440*, 676–679. https://doi.org/10.1038/nature04513

Shaywitz, B. A., Shaywitz, S. E., Blachman, B. A., Pugh, K. R., Fulbright, R. K., Skudlarski, P., … Gore, J. C. (2004). Development of left occipitotemporal systems for skilled reading in children after a phonologically- based intervention. *Biological Psychiatry, 55*(9), 926–933. https://doi.org/10.1016/j.biopsych.2003.12.019

Shen, M. D., Kim, S. H. L., McKinstry, R. C., Gu, H., Hazlett, H. C., Nordahl, C. W., … Piven, J. (2017). Increased extra-axial cerebrospinal fluid in high risk infants who later develop Autism. *Biological Psychiatry, 82*, 186–193. https://dx.doi.org/10.1016%2Fj.biopsych.2017.02.1095

Slagter, H. A., Davidson, R. J., & Lutz, A. (2011). Mental training as a tool in the Neuroscientific study of brain and cognitive plasticity. *Frontiers in Human Neuroscience, 5*. https://doi.org/10.3389/fnhum.2011.00017

Sowell, E. F., Peterson, B. S., Thoompson, P. M., Welcome, S. E., Henkenius, A. L., & Toga, A. W. (2003). Mapping cortical change across the human life span. *Nature Neuroscience, 6*, 309–315. https://doi.org/10.1038/nn1008

Sowell, E. R., Trauner, D. A., Gamst, A., & Jernigan, T. L. (2002). Development of cortical and subcortical brain structures in childhood and adolescence: A structural MRI study. *Developmental Medicine and Child Neurology, 44*, 4–16. https://doi.org/10.1017/s0012162201001591

Stevens, C., Fanning, J., Coch, D., Sanders, L., & Neville, H. (2008). Neural mechanisms of selective auditory attention are enhanced by computerized training: Electrophysiological evidence from language-impaired and typically developing children. *Brain Research, 1205*, 55–69. https://doi.org/10.1016/j.brainres.2007.10.108

Stiles, J., & Jernigan, T. (2010). The basics of brain development. *Neuropsychological Review, 20*, 327–348. https://dx.doi.org/10.1007%2Fs11065-010-9148-4

Taber-Thomas, B., & Perez-Edgar, K. (2015). Emerging adulthood brain development. In *The Oxford handbook of emerging adulthood* (pp. 126–141). Oxford University Press.

Tamnes, C. H., Goddings, A. L., Meuwese, R., Blakemore, S. J., Dalh, R., … Mills, K. L. (2017). Development of the cerebral cortex across adolescence: A multisample study of inter-related longitudinal changes in cortical volume, surface area, and thickness. *Journal of Neuroscience, 37*, 3402–3412. https://doi.org/10.1523/jneurosci.3302-16.2017

Tanaka, C., Matsui, M., Uematsu, A., Noguchi, K., & Miyawaki, T. (2012). Developmental trajectories of the fronto-temporal lobes from infancy to early adulthood in health individuals. *Developmental Neuroscience, 34*, 477–487. https://doi.org/10.1159/000345152

Tang, V., Michaelis, R., & Kwan, P. (2014). Psychobehavioral therapy for epilepsy. *Epilepsy & Behavior, 32*, 147–155. https://doi.org/10.1016/j.yebeh.2013.12.004

Taylor, S. J., Barker, L. A., Heavey, L., & McHale, S. (2013). The typical developmental trajectory of social and executive functions in late adolescence and early adulthood. *Developmental Psychology, 49*, 1253–1265. https://doi.org/10.1037/a0029871

Teipel, S., Kilimann, I., Thyrian, J. R., Kloppel, S., & Hoffmann, W. (2018). Potential role of neuroimaging markers for early diagnosis of dementia in primary care. *Current Alzheimer Research, 15*(1), 18–27.https://doi.org/10.2174/1567205014666170908093846

Theoharides, T. C., Tsilioni, I., Patel, A. B., & Doyle, R. (2016). Atopic diseases and inflammation of the brain in the pathogenesis of Autism Spectrum Disorders. *Translational Psychiatry, 6*(6), https://doi.org/10.1038/tp.2016.77

Thompson, D. K., Adamson, C., Roberts, G., Faggian, N., Wood, S. J., Warfield, S. K., … Inder, T. E. (2013). Hippocampal shape variations at term equivalent age in very preterm infants compared with term controls: Perinatal predictors and functional significance at age 7. *NeuroImage, 70*, 278–287. https://doi.org/10.1016/j.neuroimage.2012.12.053

Thompson, P. M., Vidal, C., Giedd, J. N., Gochman, P., Blumenthal, J., Nicolson, R., … Rapoport, J. L. (2001). Mapping adolescent brain change reveals dynamic wave of accelerated gray matter loss in very early-onset Schizophrenia. *Proceedings of the National Academy of Sciences, 98*(20), 11650–11655. Mapping adolescent brain change reveals dynamic wave of accelerated gray matter loss in very early-onset schizophrenia.

Toplak, M. E., Dockstader, C., & Tannock, R. (2006). Temporal information processing in ADHD: Findings to date and new methods. *Journal of Neuroscience Methods, 151*(1), 15–29. https://doi.org/10.1016/j.jneumeth.2005.09.018

Tost, H., & Meyer-Lindenberg, A. (2012). Puzzling over schizophrenia: Schizophrenia, social environment and the brain. *Nature medicine, 18*(2), 211–213. https://doi.org/10.1038/nm.2671

U.S. Census Bureau. (2011, March). *Overview of race and Hispanic origin: 2010*. http://www.census.gov/prod/cen2010/briefs/c2010br-02.pdf

Valera, E. M., Faraone, S. V., Murray, K. E., & Seidman, L. J. (2007). Meta-analysis of structural imaging findings in Attention-Deficit/Hyperactivity Disorder. *Biological Psychiatry, 61*, 1361–1369. https://doi.org/10.1016/j.biopsych.2006.06.011

Van Gorp, W. G., Satz, P., & Mitrushina, M. (1990). Neuropsychological processes associated with normal aging. *Developmental Neuropsychology, 6*(4), 279–290. https://doi.org/10.1080/87565649009540467

Veliu, B., & Leathem, J. (2017). Neuropsychological assessment of refugees: Methodological and cross-cultural barriers. *Applied Neuropsychology: Adult, 24*(6), 481–492. https://doi.org/10.1080/23279095.2016.1201483

Ventola, P. E., Oosting, D., Anderson, L. C., & Pelphrey, K. A. (2013). Brain mechanisms of plasticity in response to treatments for core deficits in Autism. *Progress in Brain Research, 207*, 255–272. https://doi.org/10.1016/b978-0-444-63327-9.00007-2

Vidal, C. N., Rapoport, J. L., Hayashi, K. M., Geaga, J. A., Sui, Y., McLemore, L. E., … Thompson, P. M. (2006). Dynamically spreading frontal and cingulate deficits mapped in adolescents with Schizophrenia. *Archives of General Psychiatry, 63*, 25–34. https://doi.org/10.1001/archpsyc.63.1.25

Vogel, A. C., Petersen, S. E., & Schlaggar, B. L. (2014). The VWFA: It's not just for words anymore. *Frontiers in Human Neuroscience, 8*, 1–10. https://doi.org/10.3389/fnhum.2014.00088

Wallander, J. L., & Koot, H. M. (2016). Quality of life in children: A critical examination of concepts, approaches, issues, and education. *Clinical Psychology Review, 45*, 131–143. https://doi.org/10.1016/j.cpr.2015.11.007

Wang, C., Lee, J., Ho, N. F., Lim, J. K. W., Poh, J. S., Rekhi, G., … Zhou, J. (2018). Large-scale network topology reveals heterogeneity in individuals with at risk mental state for psychosis: Findings from the longitudinal youth-at-risk study. *Cerebral Cortex, 28*, 1–10. https://doi.org/10.1093/cercor/bhx278

Wang, S. S.-H., Kloth, A. D., & Badura, A. (2014). The cerebellum, sensitive periods, and Autism. *Neuron, 83*, 581–532. https://dx.doi.org/10.1016%2Fj.neuron.2014.07.016

Werchan, D. M., & Amso, D. (2017). A novel ecological account of prefrontal cortex functional development. *Psychological Review, 124*, 720–739. https://doi.org/10.1037/rev0000078

Whelan, R., Conrod, P., Poline, J.-B., Banaschewski, T., Barker, G. J., Belgrave, M. A., … the IMAGEN Consortium. (2012). Adolescent impulsivity phenotypes characterized by distinct brain networks. *Nature Neuroscience, 15*, 920–935. https://doi.org/10.1038/nn.3092

Whitaker, K., Vértes, P., Romero-Garcia, R., Vása, F., Moutoussis, M., Prabhu, G., … Bullmore, E. T. (2016). Adolescence is associated with genomically patterned consolidation of the hubs of the human brain connectome. *Proceedings of the National Academy of Science, 113*, 9105–9110. https://doi.org/10.1073/pnas.1601745113

Whittemore, R., Jaser, S., Chao, A., Jang, M., & Grey, M. (2012). Psychological experience of parents of children with type 1 diabetes. *The Diabetes Educator, 18*, 562–579. https://doi.org/10.1177/0145721712445216

Wolf, J. A., & Koch, P. F. (2016). Disruption of network synchrony and cognitive dysfunction after traumatic brain injury. *Frontiers in Systems Neuroscience, 10*, 43. https://doi.org/10.3389/fnsys.2016.00043

Wolff, J. J., Gu, H., Gerig, G., Elison, J. T., Styner, M., Gouttard, S., … Piven, J. (2012). Differences in white matter fiber tract development present from 6 to 24 months in infants with Autism. *American Journal of Psychiatry, 169*(6), 589–600. https://doi.org/10.1176/appi.ajp.2011.11091447

World Health Organization (2020). International statistical classification of diseases and related health problems (11th ed.). https://icd.who.int/

Wykes, T. I. L., Brammer, M., Mellers, J., Bray, P., Reeder, C., Williams, C., & Corner, J. (2002). Effects on the brain of a psychological treatment: Cognitive remediation therapy: Functional magnetic resonance imaging in Schizophrenia. *The British Journal of Psychiatry, 181*(2), 144–152. https://doi.org/10.1017/s0007125000161872

Yang, C., Barrós-Loscertales, A., Pinazo, D., Ventura-Campos, N., Borchardt, V., Bustamante, J., … Walter, M. (2016). State and training effects of mindfulness meditation on brain networks reflect neuronal mechanisms of its antidepressant effect. *Neural Plasticity, 2016*, 1–14. https://doi.org/10.1155/2016/9504642

Zielinski, B. A., Prigge, M. B., Nielsen, J. A., Froehlich, A. L., Abildskov, T. J., Anderson, J. S., … Alexander, A. L. (2014). Longitudinal changes in in cortical thickness in Autism and typical development. *Brain, 1376*, 1799–1812. https://doi.org/10.1093/brain/awu083

Zwaigenbaum, L., Young, G. S., Stone, W. L., Dobkinbs, K., Ozonoff, S., Brian, J., … Messigner, D. (2014). Early head growth in infants at risk for Autism: A baby siblings research consortium study. *Journal of the American Academy of Child and Adolescent Psychiatry, 53*, 1053–1062. https://doi.org/10.1016/j.jaac.2014.07.007

Chapter 5
Advances in Neuroimaging

Chad A. Noggle and Andrew S. Davis

Learning Objectives

- To understand the difference between structural and functional imaging techniques.
- To understand how different imaging techniques work.
- To comprehend the differences between CT and MRI in terms of when one is preferred over the other.
- To understand how aspects of the brain change in appearance across MRI sequences.
- To comprehend that each imaging technique provides in terms of research and clinical application.

Overview

Over the course of the past two to three decades, there has been tremendous growth within the cognitive neurosciences. While differences may be noted between the various subfields, the primary foundation of each remains the study of the neurophysiological basis of cognition and behavior. A primary reason for the rapid expansion of these fields has been the equally rapid advancement of neuroimaging techniques. This has ranged from improvements in existing technologies to the

C. A. Noggle (✉)
Division of Clinical Psychology, Neuroscience Institute-Department of Psychiatry, Southern Illinois University-School of Medicine, Springfield, IL, USA

Outpatient Behavioral Health, Blessing Health System, Quincy, IL, USA
e-mail: cnoggle@siumed.edu

A. S. Davis
Department of Educational Psychology, Ball State University, Muncie, IN, USA

R. C. D'Amato et al. (eds.), *Understanding the Biological Basis of Behavior*,
https://doi.org/10.1007/978-3-030-59162-5_5

emergence of new ones allowing enhanced investigation of brain structure and functionality related to cognition and behavior. Included with this we have seen growth in the clinical utilization of neuroimaging and methods of analysis. Additionally, using neuroimaging data has become part of the standard of care for neuropsychologists, and thus it is essential that they understand both the underlying physiological basis of the various techniques and how to interpret and incorporate results and diagnostic impressions. To not get lost in the minutia of the historical background of neuroimaging, Table 5.1 outlines the key developments.

History of Neuroimaging and Neurodiagnostic Procedures

Modern-day advancements in neuroimaging have provided an increased ability to connect neuroanatomical structure and function with clinical presentations, refining our understanding of the roles neural regions and circuitry play in specific neurocognitive and behavioral tasks, which in turn has led to improvements in clinical practice (Noggle et al., 2008). Consequently, as advances in neuroimaging capabilities continue, their incorporation into clinical practice via differential diagnosis, data interpretation, and treatment planning will increase (Noggle et al., 2011). Truly, it is these advances that have been at the vanguard of the exponential growth in our understanding of the biological basis of behavior. The following chapter will outline various structural and functional imaging techniques and their role in this endeavor.

Neuroimaging and Neurodiagnostic Procedures and the Biological Basis of Behavior

Structural neuroimaging involves those technologies and methods by which we visualize the architectural integrity of various systems and structures of the brain. These technologies permit the robust visualization, evaluation, and diagnosis of gross intracranial disease, abnormalities, and injuries. This may include the identification of tumors, cerebrovascular concerns, and degenerative processes, among other etiologies. Computed tomography (CT), magnetic resonance imaging (MRI), magnetic resonance spectroscopy (MRS), diffusion tensor imaging (DTI), and magnetic resonance angiography (MRA) constitute the primary methods of structural neuroimaging. Images generated by these techniques are rendered in either two- or three-dimensional orientations. This is possible due to these technologies operating on a digital pixel/voxel system to display images. Pixels are similar to those units by which televisions and cameras operate; thus images can be rendered in two-dimensional form. Furthermore, these pixels range in value along a color continuum from black to bright white, which correspond with tissue density. When displayed in two-dimensional form, images are portrayed in such a way that the anterior

Table 5.1 Historical developments in neuroimaging

1895	Wilhelm Roentgen, a physicist, developed and demonstrated the first radiograph
1902	The electrocardiograph machine was first developed
1918	Walter Dandy, a neurosurgeon, first performed ventriculography and pneumoencephalography (PEG)
1924	Berger developed the electroencephalograph to detect electrical activity from the surface of a human skull
1927	Moniz, a neurologist, accomplished the first cerebral arteriogram
1936	EEG developed to establish patterns to diagnose epilepsy
1950	Erwin Hahn first detected spin echoes and free induction decay, the building block of MRI
1952	Herman Carr produced a one-dimensional NMR spectrum based on Hahn's techniques
1959	Jay Singer first studied blood flow by NMR
1961	Oldendorf developed the basis for computerized tomography (CT)
1968	Cohen first measured magnetoencephalography (MEG)
1971	Paul Lauterbur first outlined the theory and mechanics of MRI; he published the theory in March of 1973
1972–1974	Damadian, an internist, published works on MRI tumor detection. He then applies for and receives a patent on the technology
1973	Hounsfield and Cormack applied Oldendorf's technique to diagnostics with CT
1973	Lauterbur, a physicist, published the first spatially differentiated MR images
1973	Ter-Pogossian, Hoffman, and Phelps developed the first human PET scanner
1977	First MRI body scan of a human completed
1980	Bottomley increased magnetic field strength, creating the first 1.5 T MRI/MRS scanner which was the first high-field device
1982	Bottomley performed the first localized MRI scan of the human heart and brain
1986	Dumoulin and Hart developed MR angiography
1988	Villringer successfully applied contrast in conjunction with MRI serving as the basis for perfusion MRI
1990	Ogawa discovered principles underlying fMRI; oxygen-depleted blood with dHb attracted to a magnetic field
1991–1992	Diffusion tensor imaging and tractography developed and first brain images published
1992	Hajnal, Young, and Bydder described the use of FLAIR sequencing to evaluate white matter
1992	Arterial spin labeling developed by Detre and Koretsky
1997	Susceptibility-weighted imaging developed by Reichenbach and Haacke
1999	Combined use of MEG and fMRI first reported – basis of multimodal approach

region of the brain (i.e., frontal) will be at the top portion of the scan, the left hemisphere will present on the right, and the right hemisphere will present on the left.

Whereas pixels are associated with two-dimensional images, voxels are units by which three-dimensional images are rendered, as they correspond with a particular degree of volume. Volumetric measurements can be obtained of the entire brain or specific structures which has advanced the ability to ascertain structural neurological abnormalities in psychiatric disorders such as autism spectrum disorder. Aside from this difference (i.e., two-dimensional vs. three-dimensional), interpretation is slightly altered as hemispheres present on the screen as they do in the skull. As such, the left hemisphere is portrayed on the left and the right hemisphere on the right side of the screen. Images are rendered with this orientation (i.e., looking down through the top of the skull through the brain referred to as the horizontal plane). A coronal plane would be as if a person was standing in front of you and you were looking at the brain through the back of their head. Notice that within this description, the left hemisphere would still present on the left of the screen. The final plane is the sagittal, which corresponds to looking through the side of a person's head at their brain while that person is standing beside you.

Computed Tomography (CT)

Computed tomography (CT) scanning provides visualization of the brain based on the differential absorption of x-rays. CT was the first modern-day neuroimaging technique developed. Despite CT being surpassed by MRI in the imagery produced pertaining to neuroanatomy and pathology, CT remains the most widely available, cheapest, and convenient imaging tool, and it tends to be utilized as the first tool in emergent/acute trauma situations (Koenigsberg et al., 2007). During examination, patients lie on a table which moves in and out of a cylindrical apparatus which internally projects x-rays through the patient's head to receptors on the opposite side of the cylinder from which they are cast. These receptors measure the trace x-ray received. The denser the tissue through which the x-ray is passing, the greater the degree of x-ray absorption. These measurements can then be used to construct images of the patient's brain. With CT, bone and hard tissue absorb a high amount of x-rays, air and water absorb very little, and soft tissue is somewhere in between. As a result, CT scans reveal the gross features of the brain but do not resolve its structure well. In general, CT can discriminate variance in density as small as 2 mm in diameter (Zillmer & Spiers, 2001). These variations are depicted by the contrast between shades which range from black (hypodense) to bright white (hyperdense). There are some concerns about late effects of CT scans in regard to the amount of radiation uptake experienced by the patient, such as various forms of cancer. Specific concerns have been noted when considering the use of CT in the pediatric population, and limited use of radiographic techniques such as CT and MRI in children and adolescents is recommended (Durham et al., 2006; Thierry-Chef et al., 2006).

CT Interpretation

When interpreting CT, investigation of expected symmetry of the brain as well as areas of hyperdensity and hypodensity that may speak to structural integrity is a common first step as it highlights any neuroanatomical abnormalities. While subtle asymmetries are common [many times favoring the left over the right (e.g., frontal, temporal, and occipital horns)], gross asymmetry should be seen as a probable sign of underlying pathology. A normal unenhanced head CT scan will show midline position of the third and fourth ventricles and the septum pellucidum/fornix positioned between the lateral ventricles (Koenigsberg et al., 2007).

Asymmetries can occur from a number of underlying abnormalities (e.g., prenatal complication, tumor, degeneration, etc.) that would require further investigation, including possible alternative imaging. In regard to density, lighter appearance corresponds with increased density (i.e., hyperdensity), whereas darker coloring corresponds with decreased density (i.e., hypodensity); there should be clear discrimination between the density of the white matter (centrum semiovale, corona radiata, internal capsule, and brachium pontis) and gray matter (Koenigsberg et al., 2007). In CT, gray and white matter attenuation tends to be much more similar when compared to MRI which can result in problems distinguishing between these areas (Kaplan & Saddock, 1998). Therefore, CT is often insensitive to subtle disease states, especially subcortical white matter processes. While all findings are interpreted, factors such as age should be considered. For example, no focal white matter low densities should be seen in young patients (Koenigsberg et al., 2007), whereas in patients over 60 years of age, this may be more common secondary to the effects of small vessel ischemic changes.

Further interpretation of points of hyper- and hypodensity can also be indicative of pathology. Acute hemorrhage and tumors will appear hyperdense (i.e., white on CT scans), while necrosis from an old infarct, ischemic infarction, and even edema will present as hypodense (i.e., dark on CT scans). Such determinations must be made in comparison to the surrounding tissue. As noted by Kurth and Bigler (2008), one of the first steps to interpretation and identification of abnormality is knowing what a "normal" brain should look like, as this knowledge provides a template against which one can compare images. As part of its summary, Table 5.2 provides expected appearances of cerebral structures on CT as well as MRI.

Utility of CT

CT is the study of choice for suspected infarction, especially if there are concerns of acute hemorrhage. The speed at which results are rendered and detectable on the scan allows for more immediate intervention if needed which is critical with infarction and hemorrhage. On CT, acute hemorrhage is detected as high attenuation owing to clot retraction with separation of the high-density erythrocytes from lower-density plasma (Koenigsberg et al., 2007). In comparison, edema is identified as low attenuation due to the increased amount of water present. Edema can be further differentiated by where it occurs. Cytotoxic edema is associated with hypodensity in the gray matter, usually associated with infarction or diffuse anoxia, whereas vasogenic edema is associated with low attenuation in white matter tracts (Koenigsberg et al., 2007). However, CT of small ischemic strokes of an acute nature may not be conclusive due to similar densities on imaging. In this instance

Table 5.2 Appearance based on sequence used

Tissue/structure	CT	T1	PD	T2	DWI	FLAIR
Gray matter[a]	Lt. gray	Mod. gray	Lt. gray	Intermediate	Brighter	Lt. gray
White matter[a]	Darker gray	Bright	Dark gray	Mod. dark	Darker	Dark
Gray abnormal white matter	Varies	Dark	Lt. gray	Brighter	Bright	Bright
CSF or water[b]	Black	Very dark	Inter. gray	Bright	Dark	Dark
Fat	Dark	Bright	Intermediate-bright	Intermediate	Not sensitive	Very bright
Air	Black	Signal void	Signal void	Signal void	Signal void	Signal void
Bone or calcification	Bright	Signal void	Signal void	Signal void	Signal void	Signal void
Edema[b]	Darker	Dark	Bright	Bright	Bright	Bright
Demyelination, scarring, or gliosis	Gray	Dark	Bright	Bright	Bright	Bright
Ca^{2+} bound to protein	Bright	Bright	Dark	Dark	Not sensitive	Variable
Proteinaceous fluid	Black	Bright	Variable	Variable	Dark	Dark

Note: This table is based on information from Kurth and Bigler (2008) and Blumenfeld (2002)
[a]Patterns do not hold true per se until after the second decade of life [Kurth & Bigler, 2008 (see Barkovich & Maroldo, 1993)]
[b]In comparison to parenchyma

the anatomical effect of the event may only be observed 3 to 4 days later, as the stroke evolves. This involves an initial hyperdense state of the lesion which soon resolves appearing isodense. Finally, as necrosis occurs in relationship to the penumbra, the lesion takes on a hypodense appearance. In comparison, contrast MRI may be more sensitive to this form of acute stroke (Snyder & Nussbaum, 1999).

CT may also be used to identify structural abnormalities and mass effect and even complement MRI in the evaluation of neoplasms, but in many instances, unless it is contraindicated, MRI becomes the technique of choice. This is due to the refined imagery that may be obtained on MRI in comparison to CT and the various sequences and planes of view that further differentiate abnormalities. In regard to neoplasms, certain tumors may absorb the same amount of radiation as surrounding brain tissue and may thus not be visible. An infusion of intravenous iodine may help to distinguish some tumors and areas of inflammation, causing such entities to appear whiter than the normal surrounding brain tissue. In essence, the iodine remains excluded from the blood-brain barrier except in breakdown, such as inflammation or tumor. However, while CT with contrast is available and can be used for refined imagery, MRI is preferred unless contraindicated (Koenigsberg et al., 2007). Table 5.3 provides a comparison of CT and MRI.

Table 5.3 Clinical preference of CT versus MRI

Clinical presentation	Preferred method of imaging
Possible acute stroke (ischemic; hemorrhagic)	CT
Chronic stroke (ischemic; hemorrhagic)	MRI
Acute head trauma	CT
Chronic head trauma	MRI
Skull fracture	CT (x-ray may be used)
Neoplasm	MRI
Demyelinating disease	MRI
Necrosis	Either
Seizures and epilepsy	Idiopathic (neither); symptomatic (MRI)
	Cryptogenic (neither)
Atrophy and neurodegeneration	MRI
Infectious processes of the CNS	MRI
Neurodevelopmental disorders	MRI
Calcified lesions	CT
Brainstem lesions	MRI
Claustrophobic or obese patients (>250 lb)	CT
Pacemaker, or metallic fragments in body	CT
Lower cost	CT
Speed	CT[a]

This table is based on information obtained from Blumenfeld (2002) and Kurth and Bigler (2008)
[a]Some MRI scans/techniques are as quick as CT

Magnetic Resonance Imaging (MRI)

Magnetic resonance imaging (MRI) is another structural imaging technique. MRI is superior to CT in a multitude of ways. While both CT and MRI offer an anatomical view of the brain, the clarity of their imagery and thus utility differ significantly. Even the technological underpinnings by which they work differ. MRI works as the human body, including the brain, is comprised mostly of water and thus contains a high concentration of hydrogen nuclei. These nuclei are comprised of both protons and neutrons. Protons, which constitute the nuclei of hydrogen atoms, are normally arranged in a random fashion. Yet, when they encounter a strong static magnetic field, such as the one produced by modern MRI scanners, the hydrogen nuclei within that field line up in a parallel formation termed equilibrium. Upon achieving equilibrium, radio waves are emitted from the MRI scanner to disturb this alignment. This causes the hydrogen nuclei to start to fall out of alignment only to have the magnetic field reapplied to reestablish equilibrium. This is done in rapid fashion causing a spinning action to the nuclei. As the hydrogen nuclei fall back into alignment, they produce a detectable radio signal. The intensity of the signal is thus dependent upon the intensity of the detected radio signal which, itself, is dependent on the concentration of hydrogen in the tissue. For example, in a standard T2 MRI scan, the bone appears black compared to how bright the brain appears given its richness in hydrogen.

Once data is recorded and analyzed, a three-dimensional visualization of hydrogen responsiveness demonstrates the density of regions and structures throughout the brain. As an end result, images obtained via MRI can be analyzed much like those of CT in that asymmetries, hyperdensities, and hypodensities can be seen. MRI's ability in spatial detection of data in three-dimensional space provides images of neuroanatomical structures superior to that rendered by CT, thereby providing for more accurate and finite diagnosis of underlying pathology (Pykett, 1982). In addition, various MRI sequences and weightings are available that allow for differential sensitivity to structural and pathological entities. Common MRI sequences are summarized in Table 5.4.

While MRI has been in use since the 1980s, recent advances in the technology have been observed secondary to development of magnet and field gradient designs at higher field strengths of 3 teslas (T) and, more recently, 7 T (DeLano & Fisher, 2006; Machann et al., 2008; Nakada, 2007; Schmitz et al., 2005). Teslas refer to the magnetic field, and the corresponding number refers to the strength of said field. When MRI was first developed, imaging suffered from the inherently low signal intensity in which only 5 hydrogen protons of every 1 million within a voxel contributes to the magnetic resonance signal at 1.5 T in comparison to 10 at 3 T (Moseley et al., 2009). The number of hydrogen protons activated out of every million in a voxel is referred to as the signal-to-noise ratio (SNR). Beyond increasing the SNR, higher tesla exposure (i.e., higher magnetic field strength) produces a linear increase in the chemical shift, which has made MR spectroscopy more of a routine clinical use (Henning et al., 2008; Mikulis & Roberts, 2007). MR spectroscopy is discussed in greater detail below. In addition, longer proton relaxation times, T1s, are observed at higher fields, again typically a linear response. Because of the longer T1s, inflow methods such as MR angiography and postcontrast agent T1-shortening effects are better visualized at higher fields (DeLano & Fisher, 2006). The longer T1 values have also been important in the development of arterial spin labeling or non-contrast-enhanced perfusion MRI for clinical use in such diseases as stroke when used at high field (Golay & Petersen, 2006; Jahng et al., 2007).

Interpreting MRI Scans

Interpretation in MRI largely resembles the approach taken in CT. However, two key points must be noted. First, MRI has multiple sequencing capabilities that may portray structural areas differently. As such, one must be mindful of what "normal" is as it pertains to that form of sequencing. For example, while CSF and areas with increased fluid content present as dark on T1, on T2 they will present as bright. The second key point is that when evaluating a lesion of the brain that is seen on MRI, the specific location of the lesion must be identified (Koenigsberg et al., 2007) because MRI obtains and renders images on multiple planes. Thus, failure to recognize in what plane a lesion is detected can lead to inaccurate interpretation. Oftentimes, a regimented progression through the anatomy may prove useful in

Table 5.4 Various MRI sequences and weightings

T1 sequencing	T1 sequencing is generally the default scan sequence and provides exceptional anatomical details including atrophy and degeneration (McDonald, Saykin, & Ahles, 2008). In this sequence, fluid is dark given its hypodensity, whereas hyperdensity is brighter
T2 sequencing	T2 sequencing is often likened to a negative of a picture. Whereas in the T1 sequence, fluid and other hypodense areas are dark; within the T2 sequence they are bright. As such, the ventricular spaces on a T2 sequence will be bright white. The basis for the reversal is that the T2 sequence is intended to differentiate fluid [e.g., cytotoxic or vasogenic edema, hydrocephalus ex vacuo, encephalomalacia (Kurth & Bigler, 2008)]. In general, it is more sensitive to differences between damaged tissue and intact tissue and so is useful for detecting lesions (Kolb & Whishaw, 2003). White matter hyperintensities are most commonly identified through this sequencing and are commonly linked with cognitive deficits (de Groot et al., 2000, 2001). This is due to the reliance of the system on subcortical integrity. As such, when the white matter is impacted, neuronal processes slow and become less efficient diffusely
Proton density sequencing	Proton density sequencing in a way is a mixture of T1 and T2 sequences, as it represents a middle ground between the two in regard to proton relaxation times (Blumenfeld, 2002). It has been most commonly used in the differentiation of gray and white matter because of its shared T1 and T2 properties; however, fluid-attenuated inversion recovery magnetic resonance (FLAIR) is now commonly relied upon to make this discrimination (Kurth & Bigler, 2008)
Gradient echo (GRE) Sequencing	GRE can resemble T1, proton density, or T2 sequences depending on scanner parameters; thus, clarification of these parameters is noted prior to interpretation/review. This sequence is sensitive to the detection and identification of blood products making it a top choice in situations requiring detection of subtle hemorrhage [e.g., suspected diffuse axonal injury or primary brainstem traumatic injury (Kurth & Bigler, 2008)]
FLAIR	FLAIR has in many ways proven superior to proton density sequencing in the differentiation of gray and white matter. Much of this is due to its sensitivity to the detection of water content, particularly in the context of restricted motion of water molecules, such as gliosis, demyelination, a lesion situated near CSF, acute subarachnoid hemorrhage, and tissue with increased protein content such as a chronic hematoma (Kurth & Bigler, 2008). It has also proven effective in the identification of visible pathology such as microvascular and inflammatory lesions (McDonald et al., 2008)

(continued)

Table 5.4 (continued)

Diffusion-weighted imaging	Diffusion-weighted imaging (DWI) is sensitive to and provides visualization of brain structures based on restriction in the motion of water protons (Mori, 2002). Diffusion is an essential physical property of a living system, which facilitates the transport of molecules through membranes (Pagani et al., 2008). The brain constitutes an environment in which water molecules are not free to diffuse equally in all directions as a result of the presence of cell membranes (Elster & Burdette, 2001). These barriers provide pathways in which protons are able to move quickly through the tissue, allowing the intracellular medium to remain. As such, water diffusivity depends on the characteristic of the medium where the molecules move (Pagani et al., 2008). DWI as a technology measures the microscopic random translational motion of these water molecules (Le Bihan et al., 1992). Where these protons maintain a higher speed of movement, those areas will be dark on DWI. However, where proton movement is slowed, these areas will appear bright and are indicative of various forms of pathology (Kurth & Bigler, 2008) such as demyelination and other white matter disease and neoplasms (Elster & Burdette, 2001). Of particular interest is evidence that DWI can identify both diffuse and isolated/focal ischemic infarcts (Gledhill et al., 2000; Le Bihan et al., 1992) and cytotoxic edema (Kurth & Bigler, 2008), among others. This is because alterations of the microdynamics of cellular transport between subcompartments may change diffusivity, which can be detected in comparison to surrounding tissue of anticipated similar diffusivity (Pagani et al., 2008). As a result, research has shown DWI to be significantly more useful in revealing diffuse microstructural injuries, as found on autopsy, in comparison to standard MRI (Medana & Esiri, 2003)
Perfusion-weighted imaging	Cerebral perfusion constitutes the volume of blood flowing through a definite volume of tissue during a specified time frame (Pagani et al., 2008). Given this, perfusion-weighted imaging provides visualization of the brain through the calculation of blood flow. It is commonly used following infarction and in differentiating radiation necrosis with recurrent tumor (Kurth & Bigler, 2008). This is made possible by the sensitivity of MRI to not only the detection of blood flow in large vessels (Wetzel & Bongartz, 1999) but also perfusion as it takes place in small vessels (Cha, 2003)
MRI contrast enhancement	Contrast is used in conjunction with MRI to identify focal areas of blood-brain barrier compromise. As noted by Kurth and Bigler (2008), contrast can assist in the visualization and evaluation of regions of injury following CVA, contusion, shearing injury, sepsis, infection, or differential identification of neoplasms

Imaging Techniques: General Description
Computed tomography (CT) is a structural-based, diagnostic imaging test used to create detailed images of organs, bones, soft tissue, and blood vessels, including the brain. It is an x-ray-based technology which produces cross-sectional images based on the absorption of said x-rays.
Magnetic resonance imaging (MRI) is a structural-based, diagnostic imaging test that produces highly detailed pictures of the body and brain. MRI uses a powerful magnetic field to manipulate hydrogen nuclei to produce a measurable signal of density.
Magnetic resonance spectroscopy (MRS) is a noninvasive, functional imaging technique used for measuring biochemical changes in the brain, especially the presence of tumors. MR spectroscopy compares the chemical composition of normal brain tissue with abnormal tumor tissue.

(continued)

Table 5.4 (continued)

Diffusion tensor imaging (DTI) is a structural-based, diagnostic imaging test focused on evaluation of the integrity of white matter. DTI is an extension of diffusion-weighted imaging.
Magnetic resonance angiography (MRA) is a structural-based, diagnostic imaging test that permits evaluation of the integrity of blood vessels in order to identify abnormalities or diagnose atherosclerotic disease. The technology uses the combination of powerful magnetic fields and radio waves to produce images.
Electroencephalogram (EEG) is a noninvasive functional imaging technique that measures electrical activity of the brain primarily useful in the evaluation of seizures and sleep disorders, though it can be used in a number of other presentations.
Magnetoencephalography (MEG) is a noninvasive, functional imaging technique that measures and localizes brain activity through the detection of electromagnetic effects within the brain.
Functional MRI (fMRI) is a noninvasive, functional imaging technique that measures brain activity by detecting changes in blood oxygenation and flow that occur in response to neural activity, thereby permitting visualization of what parts of the brain are involved in a particular mental process.
Positron emission tomography (PET) is an invasive, functional imaging technique that demonstrates brain activity by visualizing the uptake of radioactive tracers injected into the bloodstream. These tracers attach to targeted compounds which are processed at higher levels in active brain areas, thereby showing which areas are active.

Imaging technique	Primary disease/condition use
Computed tomography (CT)	Acute stroke
	Acute head injury
	Subacute/chronic stroke when MRI cannot be used
	Subacute/chronic head injury when MRI cannot be used
	Other instances where MRI cannot be used
Magnetic resonance imaging (MRI)	Subacute/chronic stroke
	Subacute/chronic head injury
	Aneurysms
	Brain tumors
	MS
	Hydrocephalus
	Epilepsy
	Dementia/degenerative processes
Magnetic resonance spectroscopy (MRS)	Brain tumors – biochemical changes
	Metabolic issues
Diffusion tensor imaging (DTI)	White matter disease (e.g., multiple sclerosis)
	Epilepsy
	Traumatic brain injury
	Brain tumors
	Arteriovenous malformations
Magnetic resonance angiography (MRA)	Vascular abnormalities/blocked arteries
Electroencephalogram (EEG)	Seizures/epilepsy
	Sleep disorders

(continued)

Table 5.4 (continued)

Imaging technique	Primary disease/condition use
Magnetoencephalography (MEG)	Seizures/epilepsy
	Pre-surgical mapping
Functional MRI (fMRI)	Epilepsy
	Dementias
	Movement disorders
Positron emission tomography (PET)	Cancer/tumors
	Dementias
	Movement disorders
	Pre-epilepsy surgery

promoting a thorough review of the structures and systems while assisting in maintaining an orientation to locality. Following a systematic approach to evaluating each structure (e.g., brainstem, midbrain, cortical gray regions, white matter, lobes, meninges, vasculature, bone, etc.) reduces the possibility of missing important secondary or tertiary findings in instances where primary etiology is quite noticeable (Kurth & Bigler, 2008).

In those instances where lesions or pathology are identified, multiplanar review can help identify the full extent (e.g., volume) of the affliction. Furthermore, utilization of differential sequencing can prove invaluable in the determination of potential lesion pathology. For example, Koenigsberg et al. (2007) noted that when evaluating a cystic lesion, one must determine if the lesion follows CSF signal characteristics on all pulse sequences. If the lesion does not, it is considered atypical and would warrant further evaluation (e.g., doing an MRI with contrast or a PET scan). In comparison, if a space-occupying lesion does follow CSF signal characteristics, it may likely represent an arachnoid cyst, among other things, which could be further differentiated by utilizing diffusion-weighted imaging. This is just one example of how combinations of findings from different sequencing types can help to better differentiate pathology. In fact, MRI signal patterns are discernible for a wide variety of manifestations. Cerebral edema, neoplasm, abscess, infarcts, and demyelinating processes all demonstrate a nonspecific pattern of decreased signal on T1-weighted images and increased signal on proton density and T2-weighted images, such that a differential diagnosis with a high degree of accuracy can be determined by linking this information with anatomical location, morphology, and a degree of contrast medium enhancement (Koenigsberg et al., 2007). Of course, interpretation must also take into account clinical presentation and disease history which highlights the interplay between neuropsychological assessment and neuroimaging.

Utility of MRI

As a result of its capabilities in rendering high contrast between tissues and multiplanar imaging, MRI is generally the study of choice to evaluate lesions in the brain and spine within the clinical setting. In fact, over the past decade, the role of MRI in the diagnosis and follow-up of a large number of pediatric neurological diseases has continued to grow (Vloet et al., 2008). However, the use of MRI in children poses technical and interpretive challenges due to age-dependent, neuroanatomical differences associated with varying degrees of brain maturation (Patrick et al., 2007). Just as neuropsychological interpretation of data must be considered from a developmental perspective, so too does the interpretation of MRI within the pediatric population. Furthermore, despite its increased resolution, MRI may miss calcification and fractures, which is better viewed on CT (Cummings & Mega, 2003). Additionally, CT is better than MRI for evaluating meningeal tumors, acute intracranial hemorrhage, and acute parenchymal infarction (Snyder & Nussbaum, 1999). While CT and MRI may both be useful in the identification of infarcts in the cortical and subcortical zones of the brain following stroke, CT can only identify an infarct grossly, whereas MRI is better suited for the identification of extensive atherosclerosis in the capillaries that appears as patches of increased signal in the white matter (Kaplan & Saddock, 1998). MRI has also been critical in implementation of medications that assist with recovery of cognitive function – especially with evaluation of ischemic penumbra following stroke and the addition of neuroprotective agents that minimize brain damage until oxygenation is restored (Heilman & Valenstein, 2003). Specific neurologic conditions also tend to maintain a characteristic appearance on MRI, especially in the deep subcortical zones, whereas consistency in the image can be lost in CT at times. However, the nature of the technology can make it difficult to obtain adequate images, as movement negatively impacts visual depictions. In those instances in which MRI results are deemed essential, sedation may be employed (Sury et al., 1999).

Magnetic Resonance Spectroscopy (MRS)

In addition to traditional MRI, new structural neuroimaging techniques have emerged in recent years. Whereas traditional MRI permits the visualization of brain anatomy, magnetic resonance spectroscopy (MRS) provides a noninvasive way of investigating brain chemistry. Although MRS can be performed using a number of different nuclei, 1H spectroscopy is by far the most refined, permitting the measurement of important brain metabolites such as N-acetylaspartate (NAA), creatine (Cr), and choline (Cho) as well as molecules with weaker signals such as glutamate (Glu), glutamine (Gln), myo-inositol (mI), and lactate (Lac) (Govindaraju, Young, & Maudsley, 2000). The utility of MRS data, however, is largely dependent on the post-scan quantification method used as there is prominent overlap in peaks along with limited SNR in vivo (Gillard et al., 2005).

Resonance (peaks) areas are related to the metabolite concentrations, and variations are associated with different etiologies. For example, decrease of NAA, an amino acid present mostly in neurons and regarded as a marker of neuronal structural and functional health and integrity, is observed in various cerebral pathologies such as ischemia, brain tumors, gliosis, dementia, trauma, and multiple sclerosis. Longitudinal MRS studies in stroke have found acute decreases in NAA and a continuing fall during the first week after the onset (Saunders, 2000). Improvements of NAA levels have also been associated with neurological improvements such as reversed ischemia and recovery from brain injury, making it an established clinical outcome marker (Eliassen et al., 2008). MRS has even shown a capacity for demonstrating effectiveness of rehabilitation and intervention (Mountz, 2003).

While NAA speaks to the integrity and health of neurons, analysis of total creatine resonance permits evaluation of the energetic status of cells and is often used as a standard or reference for relative quantification of other metabolites due to its relative consistency with location in the brain, age, and physiological conditions. However, Cr levels do change in certain pathologies such as tumors and stroke although this must only be considered in relation to history. Total choline resonance in MRS is a marker of cell membrane integrity and viability. It has been shown to be elevated in dementia, multiple sclerosis, healthy aging, and tumors (Rudkin & Arnold, 1999).

Diffusion Tensor Imaging (DTI)

Diffusion-weighted imaging/diffusion tensor imaging (DWI/DTI) is a technological advancement which allows researchers and clinicians to assess human white matter pathways in vivo. In discussing the two, it is important to note they are related. DWI largely refers to the obtained imagery data or the contrast of the acquired images. DWI has become an essential neuroimaging tool in the detection of acute hyperintense lesions of the brain. With a high diagnostic sensitivity and specificity (90% and above) to ischemic and infarction events following onset of stroke, DWI has significantly affected acute and long-term patient management strategies (Saur et al., 2003; Schaefer et al., 2002).

DWI works by measuring the diffusion of water molecules and random motion present due to thermal energy (Crosson et al., 2010). Within tissue, diffusion is restricted by cell membranes as well as tissue boundaries, resulting in diffusion anisotropy, which is diffusion along a preferred direction. For example, in white matter fiber bundles, the myelin sheath surrounding axons prevents diffusion across the axon, restricting water diffusion only along the longitudinal axis of the axon. Therefore, the directionality of diffusion provides information about local fiber orientation (Crosson et al., 2010).

DTI is the mathematical modeling process that arises from those images by calculating the spatial orientation of fibers and the strength of diffusion along each of the three axes. A scalar describing the proportion of the diffusion along a particular direction (relative to all other directions) is called fractional anisotropy, or FA. *Mean diffusivity* (MD) then measures the average speed with which the molecules traveled during a given time interval. Together, FA and MD maps can be used in clinical settings to acquire information about the structural organization of tissues not present in conventional MRI (Crosson et al., 2010). In this way, DTI may be used to not only evaluate the volume of white matter but also trace fiber tracts within the brain, a technique known as tractography (Crosson et al., 2010). Specifically, because water diffusion in white matter and peripheral nerves is anisotropic, DTI is now becoming an accepted measurement of structural integrity and functional connectivity of the underlying white matter tracts and pathways in the brain (Mori & Zhang, 2006; Mukherjee & McKinstry, 2006). In some instances, DTI has been found to be superior to high-resolution MRI, being of such sensitivity that it can even demonstrate neuroanatomical connections between brain regions involved within a particular network (Pierpaoli et al., 1996). For example, DTI has identified abnormalities in hippocampal formation tissue in patients with temporal lobe epilepsy that, in some cases, did not have any structural abnormality on high-resolution MRI (Lee et al., 2000). Furthermore, it has been used to evaluate the subcortical impact of presentations including neurodevelopmental disorders and tumors (Mori, 2002).

This advancement is permitting the revisiting of our understanding of functional networks and has demonstrated that the use of DTI tractography is a valuable tool to define the anatomical networks required to perform good analysis of effective connectivity. Using DTI tractography, Jbabdi et al. (2005) propose a model for the structure of the brain which considers anatomical connections between various cerebral regions as being geodesic with respect to a metric given by the inverse of the diffusion tensor. Using this geodesic method, they are able to construct a path connecting every pair of brain regions. However, the brain is obviously not fully connected, and, consequently, they needed to determine whether a given geodesic really represents a white matter fiber tract or not. This is why they also propose the use of probablistic fiber tracking, which combines a term that represents the data fit and another term that represents the data confidence.

Magnetic Resonance Angiography (MRA)

Magnetic resonance angiography (MRA) is used to study and provide imaging of blood flow in various vessels and is a powerful tool in the clinical conceptualization of vascular diseases. This is accomplished in two different ways: the time-of-flight technique and the phase-contrast (PC) technique. The time-of-flight technique (TOF) utilizes the inflow-outflow of the moving spins (similar to the spin that occurs in standard MRI when protons are exposed to the magnetic pulse) within the targeted area to provide volumetric imagery of the blood flow, whereas the PC technique utilizes the flow-induced phase variations of the MRA signal caused by the motion of the blood (Koenigsberg et al., 2007). The resulting images for both techniques display points of blood flow as bright in contrast to the surrounding tissue. TOF is the most commonly used variation and can be either two-dimensional or three-dimensional.

Clinically, MRA has been most commonly used in the evaluation of lesions of the carotid artery bifurcation and the circle of Willis, as well as arteriovenous brain malformations (Al-Shahi et al., 2003; Byrne, 2005). While investigation of lesions of the carotid artery bifurcation is most commonly used in adults to investigate atherosclerosis, evaluation of the circle of Willis or for unruptured aneurysms or malformations may be done in both adults and children. Within this investigational role, MRA has demonstrated an approximate 90% sensitivity to detecting congenital aneurysms 5 mm or larger (Huston et al., 1994; Ronkainen et al., 1995). In pediatric patients with aneurysms or arteriovenous malformations (AVM), seizures, headaches, cerebral hemorrhage, neurological deficits, and intellectual deterioration are commonly present (Duran et al., 2002); thus, MRA can be essential in diagnostic determinations and treatment planning in this population.

Functional Imaging Techniques

The emergence of functional imaging techniques has shown even greater promise in the clarification of pathophysiology, symptom genesis, and mechanisms of recovery (McAllister, 2005). Functional neuroimaging is the class of techniques that provide volumetric, spatially localized measures of neural activity from across the brain and time (Bede et al., 2018; Koenigsberg et al., 2007). Price and Friston (2003) note that functional neuroimaging has two primary advantages over structural neuroimaging: (1) functional neuroimaging technologies measure neurophysiological change that precedes behavioral output in which the prior is not dependent on the latter; and (2) the whole brain is depicted regardless of regional activity allowing for more reliable and specific determination of functional origin. More recently, there has been a growing interest in how activity in one brain region relates to activity in other regions, that is, functional connectivity (Williams & Henson, 2018).

Functional neuroimaging can be divided into two primary divisions: electromagnetic techniques and hemodynamic techniques. Electromagnetic techniques primarily involve electroencephalography (EEG) and magnetoencephalography (MEG), whereas hemodynamic techniques largely focus on functional magnetic resonance imaging (fMRI) and positron emission tomography (PET). Each technology has its strengths and weaknesses. For example, fMRI has a greater temporal resolution than PET, but the temporal resolution of fMRI is poorer compared to EEG and MEG. PET and fMRI can image activity in deep, subcortical structures, whereas this is difficult if not impossible with EEG- and MEG-based techniques.

Electromagnetic Techniques

Neuronal communication is the basis for brain activity. Neurons communicate via electrical impulses, and electromagnetic techniques permit measurement of this electrical activity. Electroencephalography (EEG) and magnetoencephalography (MEG) represent the two primary forms of noninvasive electromagnetic functional imaging. These techniques are similar in that they both measure this aforementioned electrical activity, albeit in different ways. More specifically, EEG and MEG measure the ionic currents caused by the information exchange of neurons as active neurons generate small, fluctuating electrical currents. During EEG, synchronized electrical activity of thousands of active neurons is detected by means of electrodes that are attached to the scalp. The electric currents inside the head also produce small magnetic field oscillations that are the sources of the MEG signal. Both EEG and MEG signals are mainly produced by postsynaptic ionic currents of synchronically active pyramidal cortical neurons. However, due to the differences in these technologies and the properties of the neural sources of the respective signals that are measured, EEG and MEG are differentially sensitive and clinically useful. EEG is most sensitive to activity generated on top of the cortical sulci, while MEG is more sensitive to activity in the sulci. In this way, both techniques can provide complementary information about neural activity (Babiloni, Pizzella, Gratta, Ferretti, & Romani, 2009). However, both EEG and MEG are limited in their ability to capture activity in deep brain structures.

Electroencephalography (EEG)

Electroencephalography (EEG) measures electrical activity from neuronal populations via electrodes on the scalp, specifically postsynaptic potentials of tens of thousands of neurons firing simultaneously (Williams & Henson, 2018). This is based on the principle that varying states of arousal correspond with brain wave changes in polarity, shape, and frequency such that irregularities may speak to underlying pathology (Knight, 1997). Due to physics of the measurement, EEG activity predominantly reflects postsynaptic potentials of pyramidal neurons near the cortical surface, although subcortical contributions are also present, and secondary currents and volume conduction complicate the pattern (Williams & Henson, 2018). The EEG is capable of detecting changes in electrical activity in the brain on a millisecond level. This is a strength with EEG in that it can measure neuronal activity with significant temporal detail. Where the technology struggles is that it has poor spatial resolution due to blurring that occurs when electrical fields are propagated through regions of different conductivities (e.g., CSF, skull, and scalp) to EEG electrodes, making it difficult to infer location of active brain regions (Williams & Henson, 2018) although in some situations, electrocorticography allows for direct placement of the electrodes on the brain. EEG signals usually reflect two types of brain activities, spontaneous and event-related activities. Spontaneous EEG reflects neuronal responses that occur unprovoked. In other words, when reports reference spontaneous EEG records, they are discussing neuronal activity in the absence of any identifiable stimulus, with or without behavioral manifestations. Within the clinical setting, spontaneous EEG has long been used to evaluate seizure disorders and diffuse presentations such as encephalopathies and even neurodegenerative processes. Consequently, evidence has emerged that speaks to the relationship between spontaneous EEG and cognitive functioning (Romei et al., 2008).

In contrast to spontaneous EEG, event-related potentials (ERPs) are associated with specific stimuli or thoughts. Measurements of ERPs are more difficult as they correspond with lower amplitude changes, ranging from less than a microvolt to several microvolts, compared to tens of microvolts for spontaneous EEG (Xue et al., 2010). Two techniques are utilized to detect ERPs, *time-locked averaging* techniques and *spectral analysis* techniques. Time-locked averaging techniques are usually used to detect *evoked activities*, which are time-locked to the presentation of stimuli (Xue et al., 2010). Time-locked averaging techniques reduce interference from random background noise while preserving the event-related signals in the EEG. In addition to time-locked responses, there may also be signals in the EEG called induced activity that are related to stimulus processing without a well-defined temporal relation to the event (Xue et al., 2010). To detect induced activity, spectral analysis must be used, in which EEG recordings are decomposed into a number of frequency (sinusoidal) components, such as delta (0–3 Hz), theta (4–7 Hz), alpha (8–12 Hz), beta (12–30 Hz), gamma (30–50 Hz), and high gamma (80–150 Hz).

EEG is most typically utilized to evaluate the presence of seizures, especially those of temporal and frontal origin as well as those occurring secondary to space-occupying lesions (Mesulam, 2000). While techniques such as PET and SPECT have shown utility in the evaluation of seizures, EEG remains the gold standard method of assessment, largely due to its clinical sensitivity. When evaluating patients with epileptiform-based seizures, 70% of the time EEG will be abnormal; however, sensitivity increases to 95% after three EEGs are performed (Mesulam, 2000). From a practice-based standpoint, when EEGs do not show epileptiform activity, prolonged monitoring with 24-hour closed-circuit television (CCTV) electroencephalographic monitoring may be necessary. This is particularly useful for individuals who purely have non-epileptiform seizure activity. In fact, the clinical utility of video EEG in both adults and children was established in reports nearly 30 years ago (e.g., Holmes et al., 1982), not only in differentiating epileptic and non-epileptic seizure activity but also in the demonstration of the electrical underpinnings of a variety of pediatric phenomena (Duthowny et al., 1988).

A normal EEG reading consists of four frequencies: delta waves (below 4 Hz), theta waves (4–8 Hz), alpha waves (8–13 Hz), and beta waves (over 13 Hz) (Mesulam, 2000). At any point in time, based on level of arousal and focus, there is an inner mixing of multiple waves, with one or two waves being predominately seen. Wave activity corresponds with the nature of the arousal level. For example, Kaplan and Saddock (1998) report that normal activity consists of alpha waves in the posterior brain regions with the eyes closed and a mixture of theta, alpha, and beta activity in the anterior regions. Once the eyes are opened, the posterior alpha waves become random. If during wakefulness delta waves are recorded, then this is generally associated with structural lesions. In comparison, if they are seen during sleep, then their presence is viewed as normal. When dealing with epileptogenic seizure focus, abnormal discharges (spikes or spike-wave complexes) that are rhythmical in nature will commonly be seen (Kaplan & Saddock, 1998). It is worth noting that aside from epileptiform activity, electrical slowing represents the other primary abnormality seen on EEG.

The primary clinical utility of EEG is to assist in the diagnosis of seizure activity and/or disorders, sleep disorders, and level of coma or presence of brain impairment.

Whereas PET can demonstrate changes in activation based on cognitive tasks and region utilized, similar changes or at least alterations to the same degree cannot be seen on EEG (Knight, 1997). However, EEG readings are limited to activity immediately below the scalp, which may distorted by bone tissue. Distortions may also occur with movement. As a result, EEG provides excellent temporal resolution but poor spatial resolution (Heilman & Valenstein, 2003). Quantitative EEG is an overlapping referential term that has been applied to a group of interrelated technologies that revolve around a mathematical approach to EEG known as spectral analysis (Wallace et al., 2001). Within the context of these technologies, the EEG signal is digitally processed, with the contributing measurements from each electrode being quantified and thus depicting a map of differential wavelengths across the cortical landscape. The resulting analyses provide two separate variable measurements. The first, similar to standard EEG, depicts the relative strength of the brain waves from an amplitude and spectral power standpoint as they present across the various scalp locations (Thornton & Carmody, 2008). The second type of variable addresses the relationship between electrode pairs, which allows for the assessment of the coordination of brain activity across separate brain regions (Thornton & Carmody, 2008). An additional approach to clinical investigation is applying probability statistics to the topographical mapping technique (Nuwer, 1997). Known as discriminant functions, these mathematical outcomes can predict the severity of a clinical condition (Leon-Carrion et al., 2008). This approach utilizes a topographic map as its basis, and the map can be compared to a normative database, allowing for inferences to be made based on deviation from the normal distribution (Ricker & Arenth, 2008).

Clinically, QEEG has demonstrated sensitivity to the identification of electrical alterations in TBI (Thatcher et al., 1989) that some have associated with neurophysiological alterations such as diffuse axonal injury (DAI) and neurochemical and/or metabolic alterations, particularly in the acute phase of mild or moderate head injury and even in the context of a post-concussive syndrome (Nuwer, 1997). Furthermore, QEEG has been found capable of discriminating injury severity based on the predominance and arrangement of slow-band (usually increased) and fast-band (usually decreased) amplitudes as well as changes in EEG coherence (Kotchoubey et al., 2005). QEEG has been correlated with specific diagnostic categories, both in healthy controls and clinical populations (Thatcher et al., 2001; Thatcher et al., 2005). In addition to QEEG's use in the diagnosis of pathological alterations, it has also been utilized in the guidance and assessment of EEG biofeedback training (Hammond et al., 2004).

Magnetoencephalography (MEG)

Magnetoencephalography (MEG) is an imaging technique that uses sensitive devices called superconducting quantum interference devices (SQUIDs) to measure the magnetic fields produced by electrical activity in the brain. More specifically, MEG measures magnetic induction produced by the postsynaptic electrical activity in neuronal populations measured by EEG. Due to the different properties of magnetic and electrical fields, the activity recorded by MEG is less affected by secondary currents and more sensitive to superficial sources (Williams & Henson, 2018). MEG sensors cannot however detect the radial component of those currents (Williams & Henson, 2018). As with EEG, MEG records brain activity with fine temporal resolution. In comparison to EEG, MEG is less affected by blurring due to different tissue types. In this way, MEG demonstrates superior spatial resolution compared to EEG. There are many uses for MEG, including assisting surgeons in localizing a pathology, assisting researchers in determining the function of various parts of the brain, neurofeedback, and others (Vidaurre et al., 2016; Williams & Henson, 2018).

Hemodynamic Techniques

Hemodynamic techniques assess brain functioning through the analysis of changes in metabolic demand and cerebral blood flow. In general, increase in neuronal activity within a particular brain region elicits an increase in metabolic demand for glucose and oxygen. This increased metabolic demand stimulates increased cerebral blood flow to the activated region. It is these hemodynamic shifts that are assessed by various functional imaging techniques primarily including functional magnetic resonance imaging (fMRI) and positron emission tomography (PET). In general, these techniques present with excellent spatial resolution while exhibiting poor temporal resolution.

Functional Magnetic Resonance Imaging (fMRI)

Functional magnetic resonance imaging (fMRI) is a hemodynamic technique for measuring brain activity that works by detecting the changes in blood oxygenation and flow that occur in response to neural activity. This is based on the principle that when a brain area is more active, it consumes more oxygen, and to meet this increased demand, blood flow increases to the active area. In this way, fMRI can be used to produce activation maps showing which parts of the brain are involved in a particular mental process. In a way, the technology is a bridge between the unipolar focus of MRI and PET. Whereas MRI looks at magnetically structured/organized hydrogen protons to determine density, and PET investigates underlying cerebral metabolism (glucose in the case of PET in lieu of oxygen), fMRI incorporates both of these techniques. However, in comparison to PET, fMRI focuses on wider metabolic factors in the context of a three-dimensional and spatially related origin (Noggle et al., 2008). As such, while there remain some issues in respect to validity, reliability, and standardization, fMRI is expected to continue to evolve into a potentially essential clinical assessment tool for pediatric patients in regard to neurosurgical planning, understanding and managing neurological disease, developing new therapies, and monitoring rehabilitation outcomes (Brown, 2007).

Functional MRI has become the dominant functional imaging method in cognitive neuroscience due to its low invasiveness, lack of radiation exposure, and wide availability. The three most common fMRI techniques are blood-oxygen-level dependent (BOLD fMRI), contrast fMRI, and perfusion fMRI. BOLD fMRI remains the most widely used. BOLD fMRI detects the difference in magnetic susceptibility between oxygenated hemoglobin and deoxygenated hemoglobin. In this way, BOLD contrast is derived primarily from the paramagnetic properties of deoxygenated hemoglobin (deoxyhemoglobin). Hemoglobin is diamagnetic when oxygenated but paramagnetic when deoxygenated. The magnetic property of blood therefore depends on its oxygenation level. In the end, the BOLD signal is the result of a complex interplay between changes in regional cerebral oxygen extraction, blood flow, and blood volume (Crosson et al., 2010). Although BOLD fMRI is an indirect measure of neuronal activities, there is strong empirical evidence that the BOLD signals are highly correlated with neuronal activities (Logothetis, Pauls, Augath, Trinath, & Oeltermann, 2001). Because the BOLD signals are usually stronger and require less time to acquire than perfusion signals, BOLD fMRI is more popular than perfusion fMRI. In comparison to BOLD fMRI, contrast fMRI requires injection of contrast agents, such as iron oxide coated with sugar or starch. The signals associated with contrast agents are thus proportional to the cerebral blood volume (CBV). This method can provide relatively strong signals, but is less favorable than BOLD fMRI as it is more invasive.

Finally, perfusion fMRI, sometimes referred to as arterial spin labeling (ASL), provides a measure of cerebral blood flow, using an endogenous tracer, blood water, to noninvasively measure tissue perfusion to evaluate the tissue viability or functionality (Golay et al., 2004; Liu & Brown, 2007). In ASL, two sets of images are alternately acquired, a set of labeling images and a set of control images. In the labeling experiment, arterial blood spins on the proximal side of the imaging slab are inverted. After a short delay of a second or so, to allow arterial blood that is tagged in this fashion to perfuse throughout the brain, images are acquired from the imaging slab. In the control imaging experiment, no arterial blood is inverted, and after the same short delay, images are acquired from the imaging slab. After pairwise subtraction of control from labeling images, MRI signals from static brain tissue can be cancelled, leaving signal only from the labeled inflowing blood water perfusing brain tissue. The difference image from pair-wise subtraction of control images from labeling images is referred to as a perfusion-weighted image, which depicts cerebral blood flow (Crosson et al., 2010).

From an empirical standpoint, fMRI is advancing knowledge pertaining to the neural substrates of cognitive processes from the mechanisms underlying memory (e.g., Owen, 1998) and language (e.g., Bechtel & Stufflebeam, 2001) as well as those pertaining to psychosocial functionality (e.g., Ward, 2006). Furthermore, it has provided for the growth of our understanding of the neurophysiological underpinnings of various neurological presentations ranging from ADHD (Schulz et al., 2005; Silk et al., 2005; Konrad et al., 2006), antisocial behavior (Fu & McGuire,

1999), dyslexia (Temple et al., 2003), additional forms of psychopathology (e.g., depression and anxiety; Mayberg et al., 2005), to schizophrenia (Yu et al., 2015), among others.

Positron Emission Tomography (PET) and Single-Photon Emission Computed Tomography (SPECT)

Positron emission tomography (PET) and single-photon emission computed tomography (SPECT) have comparable sensitivity in the detection of neurological pathology, though they are built on slightly different scientific principles. Both can detect pathology including but not limited to movement disorders in both children and adults (Ilgin, 1998), seizure foci (Rowe et al., 1989), and DAI (Abdel-Dayem et al., 1987) among others. While both can be used in the evaluation of neoplasms of the brain, SPECT is more limited in comparison to PET as the radionuclide utilized in the latter increases its ability to differentiate tumors. For example, when using 18F-fluoro-2-dexoy-D-glucose (FDG), PET has demonstrated sensitivity to assessing the metabolic activity of a variety of tumors (Ell, 2006; Shields, 2006), which has proven effective in differentiating not only type but also grade of the neoplasm, which helps guide intervention (Wong et al., 2002). In comparison, there is some evidence available that suggests SPECT's utility in differentiating lymphoma from toxoplasmosis (Ruiz et al., 1994).

PET uses trace amounts of short-lived radioactive material to map functional processes in the brain. When the material undergoes radioactive decay, a positron (a positively charged electron) is emitted. When this positron collides with an electron, the two particles annihilate each other, and produce two photons traveling in opposite directions. This repelling creates a small traceable amount of energy that can subsequently be measured. Once data is computed and analyzed, images can be rendered in axial, coronal, or sagittal planes that demonstrate chemical utilization (e.g., glucose uptake) during specific tasks, which suggests activation and subsequently the extent to which that region is involved in that function (Hoffman, 2001). Regional cerebral blood flow serves as a primary dependent measure. In the end, PET demonstrates a spatial resolution of around 4 mm throughout the brain, which is quite good. The weakness however is that PET also demonstrates very poor temporal resolution, with delays of more than 30 seconds.

PET has demonstrated its utility clinically and scientifically in healthy brains as well as those with neuropathological disease. This utility is directly related to the importance of glucose (which PET measures) to the brain, as well as its sensitivity to injury. For example, disruption in glucose metabolism can be viewed up to 6 months after injury (Snyder & Nussbaum, 1999). However, when reviewing uptake levels, a developmental perspective must be applied. As noted by Kaplan and Saddock (1998), PET studies on brain development have identified that glucose content is at its nadir in the sensorimotor cortex, thalamus, brainstem, and cerebellar vermis at 5 weeks or younger. At 3 months, the majority of regions of the cortex, with the exception of the frontal and association cortices, which increase at 8 months old, show increased glucose metabolism. Adult levels of glucose metabolism are achieved at 1 year old and increase above adult levels until age 9. Then, glucose metabolism begins to decrease until the late teens.

Clinically, PET has been most prominently used in tumor workup using F-deoxyglucose in combination with cyclotron-produced nucleotides to identify increased glucose metabolism in the involved cortical region (Hoffman, 2001). Alterations in metabolism can be utilized for differentiation. In general, high-grade neoplasms demonstrate increased metabolism, whereas low-grade neoplasms demonstrate relatively decreased activity (Koenigsberg et al., 2007). There has been high correlation between metabolic activity determined by PET and histological grade of the neoplasm (DiChiro, 1986). Furthermore, PET has demonstrated capability in distinguishing tumor recurrence from radiation necrosis in which focal areas of decreased metabolic activity help diagnose areas of radiation necrosis, whereas tumor recurrence shows increased metabolic activity (Koenigsberg et al., 2007). Unfortunately, because PET imaging requires cyclotron-produced nucleotides and is expensive, its use has been limited to major research entities to expand the understanding of regional involvement in particular functions; however, clinically there remains utility as suggested above.

Single-photon emission computed tomography (SPECT) requires a radioactive tracing compound that helps to localize neuronal activity as well as binding sites of neurotransmitters by evaluating difference in cerebral blood flow within the brain (Heilman & Valenstein, 2003). In action, SPECT detects single photons that are emitted which speak to underlying metabolic processes, and, in turn, neurocognitive actions. In comparison to PET, SPECT imaging tends to be far more accessible owing to advances in computer technology and the stability of the radionucleotides used in this form of imaging in comparison to cyclotron-produced nucleotides. The radionucleotides used in SPECT release gamma radiation in a 360 degree direction that is picked up by external detectors that create multiplanar reformations via computation that is believed to be proportional to blood flow (Kuhl et al., 1982).

Clinically, SPECT has demonstrated utility in the evaluation of both seizures and TBI. Just as PET has demonstrated sensitivity to the identification of diminished glucose metabolism and outcome following trauma (Snyder & Nussbaum, 1999), correlations have been found between post-traumatic lesions and decreased regional cerebral blood flow identified with SPECT (Abdel-Dayem et al., 1987). Research has looked at the potential of SPECT to characterize prognosis of focal lesions following head trauma as well as cases of more widespread diffuse axonal injury (Koenigsberg et al., 2007). In regard to seizures, both SPECT and PET have demonstrated associated perfusion or metabolic activity defect with the same region of focal EEG abnormality in up to approximately 80% of patients (Rowe et al., 1989). SPECT, in particular, has been proven useful in demonstrating metabolic changes both within and outside the confines of the ictal phase with some delineation evident between types of seizure presentation (Nehlig et al., 2004). Furthermore, both PET and SPECT studies are typically superimposed on pre-study CT or MRI for better anatomical and functional information, which creates outcomes similar to what is rendered in fMRI.

Conclusions

Advances in structural and functional imaging in recent decades have propelled the cognitive neurosciences ahead by leaps and bounds. Utilization of these technologies within the research setting has expanded our understanding of the biological basis of behavior, with each technology making its own contribution. Within the clinical setting, the contributions of both structural and functional imaging cannot be overstated. The concept of neuroimaging can be intimidating and overwhelming for new clinicians. It is essential, however, that neuropsychologists have a full understanding of both the methodology and clinical implications of neuroimaging. While it is generally not necessary for a clinical neuropsychologist to be able to read a scan, it is necessary they be able to extrapolate relevant information from the report of the scan. Understanding the methodology of how the neuroradiologist arrived at their results and impressions will allow the neuropsychologist to extrapolate relevant information to help them address the referral question, provide differential diagnosis, determine prognosis, and facilitate design of interventions. Additionally, understanding the concept of neuroimaging is critical as neuropsychologists continue their learning as, discussed earlier, much of current literature about the biological basis of behavior is now relying upon neuroimaging. For example, research is underway looking at the relationship between susceptibility-weighted imaging (SWI) and brain injury-related concerns. In essence, these technologies continue to advance; we will likely see an even greater role of them both in research and clinic practice.

Discussion Questions

1. What are the strengths, limitations, and clinical use of EEG and MEG? How are they similar? How are they different?
2. What are the strengths and limitations of CT and MRI? In what instances is CT preferred? In what instances would MRI be preferred?
3. What are the strengths and weaknesses of fMRI and PET?
4. What useful information is provided by diffusion-weighted images and diffusion tensor imaging?
5. In what way is MRS unique compared to other imaging techniques? How does MRS work?
6. How could you use neuroimaging to facilitate differential diagnosis? How about for suggesting prognosis and designing interventions? Provide some specific examples.

EPPP Sample Questions

A 62-year-old, right-handed, Caucasian male presents with sudden onset left facial droop and slurring of speech. The BEST imaging technique when he first presents to the emergency room is what?

A. EEG
B. CT
C. MRI
D. PET

What neuroimaging technique is LEAST likely to be used in the evaluation of a neoplasm of the brain?

A. MRI
B. PET
C. EEG
D. fMRI

What neuroimaging technique is BEST at evaluating the integrity of white matter tracts in the brain?

A. CT
B. EEG
C. DTI
D. MRI

Non-epileptiform seizures are best identified by:

A. Failure on PVTs and/or SVTs
B. Standard, time-limited EEG
C. MRI
D. 24–72-hour closed-circuit television (CCTV) electroencephalographic monitoring

The integrity of the circle of Willis is best evaluated using which technique?

A. MRA
B. MRI
C. fMRI
D. PET

Answers: B, D, D, D, A

Proactive Readings

Transcending the Past

- Bigler, E. D. (1996). *Neuroimaging I: Basic Science*. Springer.
- Bigler, E. D. (1996). *Neuroimaging II: Clinical.* Springer.

Excelling in the Present

- Cabeza, R., Kingstone, A., & Gazzaniga, M. S. (2006). *Handbook of Functional Neuroimaging of Cognition, 2nd Edition.* MIT Press.
- Lebby, P. C. (2013). Brain Imaging: A Guide for Clinicians (2013). Oxford.

Transforming the Future

- Chappell, M. & Jenkinson, M. (2018). *Introduction to Neuroimaging Analysis.* Oxford.
- Sanelli, P., Schaefer, P. W., & Loevner, L. A. (2015). *Neuroimaging: The Essentials.* Wolters Kluwer Health.

References

Abdel-Dayem, H. M., Sadek, S. A., & Kouris, K. (1987). Changes in cerebral perfusion after acute head injury: Comparison of CT with Tc-99m HM-PAO SPECT. *Radiology, 165*, 221–226. https://doi.org/10.1148/radiology.165.1.3498184

Al-Shahi, R., Bhattacharya, J. J., Currie, D. G., Papanastassiou, V., Ritchie, V., Roberts, R. C., … Warlaw, C. P. (2003). Prospective, population-based detection of intracranial vascular malformations in adults: The Scottish Intracranial Vascular Malformation Study (SIVMS). *Stroke, 34*, 1163–1169. https://doi.org/10.1161/01.str.0000069018.90456.c9

Babiloni, C., Pizzella, V., Gratta, C. D., Ferretti, A., & Romani, G. L. (2009). Fundamentals of electroencephalography, magnetoencephalography, and functional magnetic resonance imaging. *International Review in Neurobiology, 86*, 67–80. https://doi.org/10.1016/s0074-7742(09)86005-4

Barkovich, A. J. & Maroldo, T. V. (1993). Magnetic resonance imaging of normal and abnormal brain development. *Topics in Magnetic Resonance Imaging, 5*(2), 96–122.

Bechtel, W., & Stufflebeam, R. S. (2001). Epistemic issues in procuring evidence about the brain: The importance of research instruments and techniques. In W. Bechtel, P. Mandik, J. Mundale, & R. S. Stufflebeam (Eds.). Philosophy and the neurosciences: A reader. Blackwell Publishers Limited.

Bede, P., Querin, G., & Pradat, P.-F. (2018). The changing landscape of motor neuron disease imaging: The transition from descriptive studies to precision clinical tools. *Current Opinions in Neurology, 31*, 431–438. https://doi.org/10.1097/WCO.0000000000000569

Blumenfeld, H. (2002). *Neuroanatomy through clinical cases*. Sinauer Associates, Inc.

Brown, G. G. (2007). Functional magnetic resonance imaging in clinical practice: Look before you leap. *Neuropsychology Review, 17*, 103–106. https://doi.org/10.1007/s11065-007-9027-9

Byrne, J. V. (2005). Cerebrovascular malformations. *European Radiology, 15*, 448–452. https://doi.org/10.1007/s00330-004-2634-4

Cha, S. (2003). Perfusion MR imaging: Basic principles, and clinical applications. *Magnetic Resonance Imaging Clinics of North America, 11*(3), 403–413. https://doi.org/10.1016/s1064-9689(03)00066-7

Crosson, B., Ford, A., McGregor, K. M., Meinzer, M., Cheshkov, S., Li, X., … Briggs, R. W. (2010). Functional imaging and related techniques: An introduction for rehabilitation researchers. *Journal of Rehabilitation Research & Development, 47*(2), 1–33. https://doi.org/10.1682/jrrd.2010.02.0017

Cummings, J. L. & Mega, M. S. (2003). *Neuropsychiatry and Behavioral Neuroscience*. Oxford University Press.

de Groot, J. C., de Leeuw, F. E., Oudkerk, M., Hofman, A., Jolles, J., & Breteler, M. M. (2001). Cerebral white matter lesions and subjective cognitive dysfunction: The Rotterdam Scan Study. Neurology, 56(11), 1539–1545. https://doi.org/10.1212/wnl.56.11.1539

de Groot, J. C., de Leeuw, F. E., Oudkerk, M., van Gijn, J., Hofman, A., Jolles, J., & Breteler, M. M. (2000). Cerebral white matter lesions and cognitive function: The Rotterdam Scan Study. Annals of neurology, 47(2), 145–151. https://doi.org/10.1002/1531-8249(200002)47:2<145::aid-ana3>3.3.co;2-g

DeLano, M. C., & Fisher, C. (2006). 3T MR imaging of the brain. *Magnetic Resonance Imaging Clinics of North America, 14*(1), 77–88. https://doi.org/10.1016/j.mric.2006.01.004

DiChiro, G. (1987). Positron emission tomography using F-18-fluorodeoxyglucose in brain tumors: A powerful diagnostic and prognostic tool. *Investigational Radiology, 22*, 360–371. https://doi.org/10.1097/00004424-198705000-00002

Duran, M., Schoenberg, S. O., Yuh, W. T., Knopp, M. V., van Kaick, G., & Essig, M. (2002). Cerebral arteriovenous malformations: Morphologic evaluation by ultrashort 3D gadolinium-enhanced MR angiography. *European Radiology, 12*, 2957–2964. https://doi.org/10.1007/s00330-002-1418-y

Durham, S. R., Liu, K. C., & Selden, N. R. (2006). Utility of serial computed tomography imaging in pediatric patients with head trauma. *Journal of Neurosurgery, 105*(suppl 5), 365–369. https://doi.org/10.3171/ped.2006.105.5.365

Duchowny, M. S., Resnick, T. J., Deray, M. J., & Alvarez, L. A. (1988). Video EEG diagnosis of repetitive behavior in early childhood and its relationship to seizures. Pediatric Neurology, 4(3), 162-164. https://doi.org/10.1016/0887-8994(88)90004-5

Eliassen, J. C., Boespflug, E. L., Lamy, M., Allendorfer, J., Chu, W. J., & Szaflarski, J. P. (2008). Brain-mapping techniques for evaluating poststroke recovery and rehabilitation: A review. *Top Stroke Rehabilitation, 15*, 427–450. https://doi.org/10.1310/tsr1505-427

Ell, P. J. (2006). The contribution of PET/CT to improved patient management. *British Journal of Radiology, 79*, 32–36. https://doi.org/10.1259/bjr/18454286

Elster, A. D., & Burdette, J. H. (2001). *Questions and answers in magnetic resonance imaging* (2nd ed.). Mosby.

Gillard, J. H., Waldman, A., & Barker, P. (2005). In J. H. Gillard, A. D. Waldman, & P. B. Barker (Eds.), *Clinical MR neuroimaging: Diffusion, perfusion, and spectroscopy*. Cambridge University Press.

Gledhill, K., Moore, K. R., Jacobs, J. M., & Orrison, W. W., Jr. (2000). Cerebrovascular disease. In W. W. Orrison Jr. (Ed.), *Neuroimaging* (Vol. 1). W.B. Saunders.

Golay, X., Hendrikse, J., & Lim, T. C. (2004). Perfusion imaging using arterial spin labeling. *Topics in Magnetic Resonance Imaging, 15*(1), 10–27. https://doi.org/10.1097/00002142-200402000-00003

Golay, X., & Petersen, E. T. (2006). Arterial spin labeling: Benefits and pitfalls of high magnetic field. *Neuroimaging Clinics of North America, 16*(2), 259–268. https://doi.org/10.1016/j.nic.2006.02.003

Govindaraju, V., Young, K., & Maudsley, A. A. (2000). Proton NMR chemical shifts and coupling constants for brain metabolites. *NMR Biomedicine, 13*, 129–153. https://doi.org/10.1002/1099-1492(200005)13:3<129::AID-NBM619>3.0.CO;2-V

Hammond, C., Walker, J., Hoffman, D., Lubar, J., Trudeau, D., Gurnee, R., & Horvat, J. (2004). Standards for the use of quantitative electroencephalography (QEEG) in neurofeedback: A position paper of the International Society for Neuronal Regulation. *Journal of Neurotherapy, 8*(1), 5–29. https://doi.org/10.1300/J184v08n01_02

Heilman, K. M., & Valenstein, E. (2003). *Clinical neuropsychology* (4th ed.). Oxford University Press.

Henning, A., Schär, M., Kollias, S. S., et al. (2008). Quantitative magnetic resonance spectroscopy in the entire human cervical spinal cord and beyond at 3 T. *Magnetic Resonance Medicine, 59*(6), 1250–1258. https://doi.org/10.1002/mrm.21578

Hoffman, J. M. (2001). New advances in brain tumor imaging. *Current Opinions in Oncology, 13*, 148–153. https://doi.org/10.1097/00001622-200105000-00003

Holmes, G. L., McKeever, M., & Russman, B. S. (1982). Prolonged EEG and videotape monitoring in children. *American Journal of Diseases of Children, 136*(7), 608–611.

Huston, J., Nichols, D. A., Luetmer, P. H., Goodwin, J. T., Meyer, F. B., Wiekers, D. O., & Weaver, A. L. (1994). Blinded prospective evaluation of sensitivity of MR angiography to know intracranial aneurysms: Importance of aneurysm size. *American Journal of Neuroradiology, 15*(9), 1607–1614.

Ilgin, N. (1998). Functional imaging of neurotransmitter systems in movement disorders. *Quarterly Journal of Nuclear Medicine, 42*, 179–192.

Jahng, G. H., Weiner, M. W., & Schuff, N. (2007). Improved arterial spin labeling method: Applications for measurements of cerebral blood flow in human brain at high magnetic field MRI. *Medical Physics, 34*(11), 4519–4525. https://doi.org/10.1118/1.2795675

Jbabdi, A., Mandonnet, E., Duffau, H., Capelle, L., Swanson, K. R., Pelegrini-Issac, M., … Benali, H. (2005). Simulation of anisotropic growth of low-grade gliomas using diffusion tensor imaging. *Magnetic Resonance in Medicine, 54*, 616–624. https://doi.org/10.1002/mrm.20625

Kaplan, H. I., & Saddock, B. J. (1998). *Synopsis of psychiatry: Behavioral sciences/clinical psychiatry* (8th ed.). Williams & Wilkins.

Knight, R. T. (1997). Electrophysiologic methods in behavioral neurology and neuropsychology. In T. E. Feinberg & M. J. Farrah (Eds.), *Behavioral neurology and neuropsychology*. McGraw-Hill.

Koenigsberg, R. A., Bianco, B. A., Faro, S. H., Stickles, S., Hershey, B. L., Siegal, T. L., … Tsia, F. Y. (2007). Neuroimaging. In C. G. Goetz (Ed.), *Textbook of clinical neurology*. Saunders Elsevier.

Kolb, B., & Whishaw, I. Q. (2003). *Fundamentals of human neuropsychology* (3rd ed.). Worth Publishers.

Konrad, K., Neufang, S., Hanisch, C., Fink, G. R., & Herpetz-Dahlmann, B. (2006). Dysfunctional attentional networks in children with ADHD: Evidence from an event-related fMRI study. *Biological Psychiatry, 59*, 643–651. https://doi.org/10.1016/j.biopsych.2005.08.013

Kotchoubey, B., Lang, S., Mezger, G., Schmalohr, D., Schneck, M., Semmler, A., … Birbaumer, N. (2005). Information processing in severe disorders of consciousness: Vegetative state and minimally conscious state. *Clinical Neurophysiology, 116*(10), 2441–2453. https://doi.org/10.1016/j.clinph.2005.03.028

Kuhl, D. E., Barrio, J. R., Huang, S.-C., Selin, C., Achemus, R. F., & Leas, J. L. (1982). Quantifying local cerebral blood flow by N-isopropyl-p-123 I-iodoamphetamine (IMP) tomography. *Journal of Nuclear Medicine, 23*, 196–203.

Kurth, S., & Bigler, E. (2008). Structural neuroimaging in clinical neuropsychology. In J. E. Morgan & J. H. Ricker (Eds.), *Textbook of clinical neuropsychology*. Taylor & Francis.

Le Bihan, D., Turner, R., Douek, P., & Patronas, N. (1992). Diffusion MR imaging: Clinical applications. *American Journal of Roentgenology, 159*, 591–599.

Lee, J. S., Lee, D. S., & Kim, S. K. (2000). Localization of epileptogenic zones in F-18-FDG brain PET of patients with temporal lobe epilepsy using artificial neural networks. *IEEE Transactions on Medical Imaging, 19*, 347–355. https://doi.org/10.1109/42.848185

Leon-Carrion, J., Martin-Rodriguez, J., Damas-Lopez, J., Martin, J., & Dominguez-Morales, M. (2008). A QEEG index of level of functional dependence for people sustaining acquired brain injury: The Seville Independence Index (SINDI). *Brain Injury, 22*(1), 61–74. https://doi.org/10.1080/02699050701824143

Liu, T. T., & Brown, G. G. (2007). Measurement of cerebral perfusion with arterial spin labeling: Part 1. Methods. *Journal of the International Neuropsychological Society, 13*(3), 517-525. https://doi.org/10.1017/S1355617707070646

Logothetis, N. K., Pauls, J., Augath, M., Trinath, T., & Oeltermann, A. (2001). Neurophysiological investigation of the basis of the fMRI signal. *Nature, 412*, 150–157. https://doi.org/10.1038/35084005

Machann, J., Schlemmer, H. P., & Schick, F. (2008). Technical challenges and opportunities of whole-body magnetic resonance imaging at 3T. *Physical Medicine, 24*(2), 63–70. https://doi.org/10.1016/j.ejmp.2008.01.011

McAllister, T. W. (2005). Mild brain injury and the post-concussion syndrome. In J. Silver, T. W. McAllister, & S. C. Yudofsky (Eds.), *Textbook of traumatic brain injury*. American Psychiatric Publishing.

McDonald, B. C., Saykin, A. J., & Ahles, T. A. (2008). Brain imaging investigation of chemotherapy-induced neurocognitive changes. In C. A. Meyers & J. R. Perry (Eds.), *Cognition and cancer*. Cambridge University Press.

Medana, I. M., & Esiri, M. M. (2003). Axonal damage: A key predictor of outcome in human CNS diseases. *Brain, 126*, 515–530. https://doi.org/10.1093/brain/awg061

Mayberg, H. S., Lozano, A. M., Voon, V., McNeely, H. E., Seminowicz, D., Hamani, C., Schwalb, J. M., & Kennedy, S. R. (2005). Deep brain stimulation for treatment-resistant depression. *Neuron, 45*, 651–660. https://doi.org/10.1016/j.neuron.2005.02.014

Mesulam, M. M. (2000). *Principles of behavioral and cognitive neurology*. Oxford University Press.

Mikulis, D. J., & Roberts, T. P. (2007). Neuro MR: Protocols. *Journal of Magnetic Resonance Imaging, 26*(4), 838–847. https://doi.org/10.1002/jmri.21041

Mori, S. (2002). Principles, methods, and applications of diffusion tensor imaging. In A. W. Toga & J. C. Mazziotta (Eds.), *Brain mapping: The methods*. Academic.

Mori, S., & Zhang, J. (2006). Principles of diffusion tensor imaging and its applications to basic neuroscience research. *Neuron, 51*(5), 527–539. https://doi.org/10.1016/j.neuron.2006.08.012

Moseley, M. E., Liu, C., Rodriguez, S., & Brosnan, T. (2009). Advances in magnetic resonance neuroimaging. *Neurology Clinical, 27*(1), 1–24. https://doi.org/10.1016/j.ncl.2008.09.006

Mountz, J. M. (2003). Nuclear medicine in the rehabilitative treatment evaluation in stroke recovery. Role of diaschisis resolution and cerebral reorganization. *Eura Medicophysica, 43*, 221–239.

Mukherjee, P., & McKinstry, R. C. (2006). Diffusion tensor imaging and tractography of human brain development. *Neuroimaging Clinics of North America, 16*(1), 19–43. https://doi.org/10.1016/j.nic.2005.11.004

Nakada, T. (2007). Clinical application of high and ultra high-field MRI. *Brain Development, 29*(6), 325–335. https://doi.org/10.1016/j.braindev.2006.10.005

Nehlig, A., Valenti, M. P., Thiriaux, A., Hirsh, E., Marescaux, C., & Namer, I. J. (2004). Ictal and interictal perfusion variations measured by SISCOM analysis in typical childhood absence seizures. *Epileptic Disorders, 6*, 247–253.

Noggle, C. A., Davis, A. S., & Barisa, M. (2008). Neuropsychology and neuroimaging: Integrating and understanding structure and function in clinical practice. In L. Hartlage & R. C. D'Amato (Eds.), *Essentials of neuropsychological assessment: Treatment planning for rehabilitation* (2nd ed.). Springer.

Noggle, C. A., Horwitz, J., & Davis, A. S. (2011). Neuroimaging and pediatric neuropsychology: Implications for clinical practice. In A. Davis (Ed.), *Handbook of pediatric neuropsychology* (pp. 1065–1076). Springer.

Nuwer, M. (1997). Assessment of digital EEG, quantitative EEG, and EEG brain mapping. *Neurology, 49*, 277–292.

Owen, A. M. (1998). Memory: Dissociating multiple memory processes. *Current Biology, 8*, Rb50–R852. https://doi.org/10.1016/s0960-9822(07)00529-5

Pagani, E., Bizzi, A., Di Salle, F., De Stefano, N., & Filippi, M. (2008). Basic concepts of advanced MRI techniques. *Neurological Science, 29*, S290–S295. https://doi.org/10.1007/s10072-008-1001-7

Patrick, P. D., Mabry, J. L., Gurka, M. J., Buck, M. L., Boatwright, E., & Blackman, J. A. (2007). MRI patterns in prolonged low response states following traumatic brain injury in children and adolescents. *Brain Injury, 21*(1), 63–68. https://doi.org/10.1080/02699050601111401

Pierpaoli, C., Jezzard, P., Basser, P. J., Barnett, A., & Di Chiro, G. (1996). Diffusion tensor MR imaging of the human brain. *Radiology, 201*, 637–648. https://doi.org/10.1148/radiology.201.3.8939209

Price, C. J., & Friston, K. J. (2003). Functional neuroimaging studies of neuropsychological patients. In T. E. Feinberg & M. J. Farah (Eds.), *Behavioral neurology and neuropsychology* (2nd ed.). McGraw-Hill.

Pykett, I. L. (1982). NMR imaging in medications. *Scientific American, 246*(5), 78–88. https://doi.org/10.1038/scientificamerican0582-78

Ricker, J. H., & Arenth, P. M. (2008). Functional neuroimaging in clinical neuropsychology. In J. E. Morgan & J. M. Ricker (Eds.), *Textbook of clinical neuropsychology*. Taylor & Francis.

Romei, V., Brodbeck, V., Michel, C., Amedi, A., Pascual-Leone, A., & Thut, G. (2008). Spontaneous fluctuations in posterior alpha-band EEG activity reflect variability in excitability of human visual areas. *Cerebral Cortex, 18*(9), 2010–2018. https://doi.org/10.1093/cercor/bhm229

Ronkainen, A., Puranen, M. I., & Hernesniemi, J. A. (1995). Intracranial aneurysms: MR angiographic screening in 400 symptomatic individuals with increased familial risk. *Radiology, 193*, 35–40. https://doi.org/10.1148/radiology.195.1.7892491

Rowe, C. C., Berkovic, S. F., Sia, S. T. B., Austin, M., McKay, W. J., Kalnins, R. M., & Bladin, P. F. (1989). Localization of epileptic foci with postictal single photon emission computed topography. *American Neurology, 26*, 660–668. https://doi.org/10.1002/ana.410260512

Rudkin, T. M., & Arnold, D. L. (1999). Proton magnetic resonance spectroscopy for the diagnosis and management of cerebral disorders. *Archives of Neurology, 56*, 919–926. https://doi.org/10.1001/archneur.56.8.919

Ruiz, A., Ganz, W. I., Donovan, P. J., Camp, A., Landry, H., Mallin, W., & Sfakianakis, G. N. (1994). Use of thallium-201 brain SPECT to differentiate cerebral lymphoma from Toxoplasma encephalitis in AIDS patients. *American Journal of Neuroradiology, 15*, 1885–1894.

Saunders, D. E. (2000). MR spectroscopy in stroke. *British Medical Bulletin, 56*, 334–345. https://doi.org/10.1258/0007142001903256

Saur, D., Kucinski, T., Grzyska, U., et al. (2003). Sensitivity and interrater agreement of CT and diffusion weighted MR imaging in hyperacute stroke. *AJNR American Journal of Neuroradiology, 24*(5), 878–885.

Schaefer, P. W., Hunter, G. J., He, J., et al. (2002). Predicting cerebral ischemic infarct volume with diffusion and perfusion MR imaging. *AJNR American Journal of Neuroradiology, 23*(10), 1785–1794.

Schmitz, B. L., Aschoff, A. J., Hoffmann, M. H., et al. (2005). Advantages and pitfalls in 3 T MR brain imaging: A pictorial review. *AJNR American Journal of Neuroradiology, 26*(9), 2229–2237.

Schulz, K. P., Newcorn, J. H., Fan, J., Tang, C., & Halperin, J. M. (2005). Brain activation gradients in ventrolateral prefrontal cortex related to persistence of ADHD in adolescent boys. *Journal of the American Academy of Child & Adolescent Psychiatry, 44*, 47–54. https://doi.org/10.1097/01.chi.0000145551.26813.f9

Shields, A. F. (2006). Positron emission tomography measurement of tumor metabolism and growth: Its expanding role in oncology. *Molecular Imaging and Biology, 8*, 141–150. https://doi.org/10.1007/s11307-006-0039-2

Silk, T., Vance, A., Rinehart, N., Egan, G. O., Boyle, M., & Cunnington, R. (2005). Fronto- parietal activation in ADHD, combined type: fMRI study. *British Journal of Psychology, 187*, 282–283. https://doi.org/10.1192/bjp.187.3.282

Snyder, P. J., & Nussbaum, P. D. (Eds.). (1999). *Clinical neuropsychology: A pocket handbook for assessment*. American Psychological Association.

Sury, M. R., Hatch, D. J., Deeley, T., Dicks-Mireaux, C., & Chong, W. K. (1999). Development of a nurse-led sedation service for paediatric magnetic resonance imaging. *Lancet, 353*, 1667–1771. https://doi.org/10.1016/s0140-6736(98)08383-4

Temple, E., Deutsch, G. K., Poldrack, R. A., Miller, S., Tallal, P., Merzenich, M. M., & Gabrieli, J. D. E. (2003). Neural deficits in children with dyslexia ameliorated by behavioral remediation: Evidence from functional MRI. *Proceedings of the National Academy of Sciences, 100*, 2860–2865. https://doi.org/10.1073/pnas.0030098100

Thatcher, R. W., North, D., & Biver, C. (2005). EEG and intelligence: Relations between EEG coherence, EEG phase delay and power. *Clinical Neurophysiology, 116*(9), 2129–2141. https://doi.org/10.1016/j.clinph.2005.04.026

Thatcher, R. W., North, D. M., Curtin, R. T., Walker, R. A., Biver, C. J., Gomez, J. F., & Salazar, A. M. (2001). An EEG severity index of traumatic brain injury. *The Journal of Neuropsychiatry and Clinical Neurosciences, 13*, 77–87. https://doi.org/10.1176/jnp.13.1.77

Thatcher, R. W., Walker, R. A., Gerson, L., & Geisler, F. (1989). EEG discriminate analysis of mild head trauma. *EEG and Clinical Neurophysiology, 73*, 93–106. https://doi.org/10.1016/0013-4694(89)90188-0

Thierry-Chef, I., Simon, S. L., & Miller, D. L. (2006). Radiation dose and cancer risk among pediatric patients undergoing interventional neuroradiology procedures. *Pediatric Radiology, 36*(suppl 14), 159–162. https://doi.org/10.1007/s00247-006-0206-2

Thornton, K. E., & Carmody, D. P. (2008). Efficacy of traumatic brain injury rehabilitation: Interventions of QEEG-guided biofeedback, computers, strategies, and medications. *Applied Psychophysiological Biofeedback, 33*, 101–124. https://doi.org/10.1007/s10484-008-9056-z

Vidaurre, D., Quinn, A. J., Baker, A. P., et al. (2016). Spectrally resolved fast transient brain states in electrophysiological data. *NeuroImage, 126*, 81–95. https://doi.org/10.1016/j.neuroimage.2015.11.047

Vloet, T. D., Konrad, K., Herpertz, S., & Herpertz-Dahlman, B. (2008). Structural and functional MRI findings in children and adolescents with antisocial behavior. *Behavioral Sciences and Law, 26*, 99–111. https://doi.org/10.1002/bsl.794

Wallace, B. E., Wagner, A. K., Wagner, E. P., & McDeavitt, J. T. (2001). A history and review of quantitative electroencephalography in traumatic brain injury. *Journal of Head Trauma Rehabilitation, 16*(2), 165–190. https://doi.org/10.1097/00001199-200104000-00006

Ward, J. (2006). *The Student's Guide to Cognitive Neuroscience*. Psychology Press.

Wetzel, S., & Bongartz, G. (1999). MR angiography: Supra-aortic vessles. *European Radiology, 9*(7), 1277–1284. https://doi.org/10.1007/s003300050834

Williams, N., & Henson, R. N. (2018). Recent advances in functional neuroimaging analysis for cognitive neuroscience. *Brain and Neuroscience Advances, 2*, 1–4. https://doi.org/10.1177/2398212817752727

Wong, T. Z., van der Westhuizen, G. J., & Coleman, R. E. (2002). Positron emission tomography imaging of brain tumors. *Neuroimaging Clinics of North America, 12*, 615–626. https://doi.org/10.1016/s1052-5149(02)00033-3

Xue, G., Chen, C., Lu, Z.-L., & Dong, Q. (2010). Brain imaging techniques and their applications in decision-making research. *Xin Li Xue Bao, 42*(1), 120–137. https://doi.org/10.3724/SP.J.1041.2010.00120

Yu, Q., Erhardt, E. B., Sui, J., Du, Y., He, H., Hjelm, D., et al. (2015). Assessing dynamic brain graphs of time-varying connectivity in fMRI data: Application to healthy controls and patients with schizophrenia. *Neuroimaging, 107*, 345–355. https://doi.org/10.1016/j.neuroimage.2014.12.020

Zillmer, E., & Spiers, M. (2001). *Principles of neuropsychology*. Wadsworth.

Part II
Using Research to Guide Neuropsychologically-Based Practice

Chapter 6
Designing Single Subject Research-Based Interventions for Clinical Neuropsychology Practice

Fan Wu

Learning Objectives

- To comprehend the history of single subject-based designs.
- To understand major single subject-based design types and how they should be utilized.
- To learn how to apply multicultural issues in designing single subject-based interventions.
- To comprehend why designing single subject-based interventions is critical to professional psychological practice.
- To understand future directions of single subject-based interventions in clinical neuropsychology practice.

Designing Single Subject Research-Based Interventions for Clinical Neuropsychology Practice

The purpose of this chapter is to introduce human service psychologists to **single subject-based interventions** used in clinical neuropsychology practice. This chapter first highlights the historical and theoretical foundations of single subject-based designs, followed by presenting a clinical neuropsychology case. The case will be presented to demonstrate various single subject-based design types. Multicultural issues in designing single subject-based interventions and why it is

F. Wu (✉)
Office of the Provost, University of Houston, Houston, TX, USA
e-mail: fwu7@uh.edu

R. C. D'Amato et al. (eds.), *Understanding the Biological Basis of Behavior*,
https://doi.org/10.1007/978-3-030-59162-5_6

critical to design single subject-based interventions for professional psychological practice will be discussed. At the end, future directions and questions for discussion will be provided.

Clinical neuropsychology is a specialty in professional psychology (American Psychological Association; APA, 2010). According to the National Academy of Neuropsychology (2001), clinical neuropsychology is the applied science of brain-behavior relationships. A clinical neuropsychologist uses his or her knowledge in psychology, neurology, cognitive science, human behavior, and physiology to assess, diagnose, and treat diverse clients with neurological, medical, neurodevelopmental, psychiatric, cognitive, and learning disorders (D'Amato et al., 2005; Witsken et al., 2008). A clinical neuropsychologist also evaluates clients' strengths and weaknesses in neurocognition, behaviors, and emotions and their relationship to normal and abnormal central nervous system functioning (National Academy of Neuropsychology, 2001). A variety of research methodologies including single subject-based designs may be used in clinical neuropsychology research and interventions.

Single subject-based designs have been used in many areas of research, such as psychology, psychiatry, education, and social work. The designs have been referred to as "*single-case designs*" or "*intrasubject-replication designs*" (Kazdin, 2020). These designs are unique because you can conduct experiments with the single subject as well as evaluate the intervention effects with large groups (Kazdin, 2020). Single subject-based design is usually not the primary methodology used or taught in psychology. Common views of single subject-based designs include (1) they are not true experiments; (2) they cannot show causal relations between variables; and (3) they cannot generalize conclusions that extend beyond the small sample. The reality is that single subject designs can be used as important methodological tools to evaluate research questions with individuals or groups. Single subject research may not be used as a replacement for other methodologies, though it makes unique and overlapping contributions just like other methodologies. Therefore, it is important for researchers and clinicians to appreciate the strengths and unique features of single subject-based designs, despite their limitations.

History of Designing Single Subject-Based Interventions

Although single subject-based designs are underused currently by psychologists and clinicians, they have made key advances in psychology since the earliest days. They are efficient, flexible, and powerful tools. This section will first briefly introduce the history of single subject-based designs in experimental and clinical psychology contexts, followed by an overview of experimental analysis of behavior and applied behavior analysis.

Experimental Psychology

Tracing the history of psychological research not far into the past, one would find out that many traditional research studies investigated individuals though single subject-based design is usually viewed as a non-traditional psychological research method (Kazdin, 2020). In the late 1880s and early 1900s, most researchers in experimental psychology only use one or a few subjects to draw inferences. A few prominent psychologists have used single subject-based design in different areas.

- Wundt (1832–1920) studied sensation and perception and believed that reactions and perceptions can be reported based on deep investigation of one or several subjects' changes on stimulus conditions presented.
- Ebbinghaus (1850–1909) used himself as a subject and studied learning and memory of nonsense syllables in changing conditions. His findings provided fundamental knowledge about human memory.
- Pavlov (1849–1936) is a physiologist whose experiments were mostly based on studying one or a few subjects at a time and made major contribution in psychology of learning. Classical conditioning is one of his classic examples, which is an experiment of a dog starting to salivate in response to the stimulus after a few repetitions with the presence of the stimulus and then the food.
- Thorndike (1874–1949) conducted experiments with a few animals at a time. One example is the investigation of cats escaping from puzzle boxes through "trial and error" learning. The experimental designs that were used by these researchers are a few examples of single subject-based designs.

With the development of statistical methods and appreciation of large group comparison, the accepted research designs changed from single subjects to large sample sizes (Kazdin, 2020).

Clinical Psychology

The investigation of single subjects played an important role in clinical psychology because some definitions of clinical psychology emphasize the study of the individual explicitly (e.g., Watson, 1951). The personality psychologist Allport (1961) recommended the intensive investigation of the individual as a supplement to group comparisons because these two methods provide separate and unique information. Freud (1856–1939) used psychoanalysis as a personality theory and a treatment tool developed from single subjects. He studied individual cases extensively and conceptualized developmental stages, psychological processes, and symptom development (Kazdin, 2020). German psychiatrist Kraepelin (1855–1926) collected thousands of case studies from psychiatric patients who were hospitalized and identified various disorders based on these cases. His elaborations of various types of psychological disorders contributed to the development of a contemporary psychiatric diagnostic model (Zilboorg & Henry, 1941).

In summary, experimental and clinical psychology evolved from single subject designs. Scientific investigations of perception, learning, memory, and psychological disorders are a few examples. Therefore, single subject designs have provided valuable and unique contributions to the advancement of many disciplines (Kazdin, 2020).

The Experimental Analysis of Behavior

The development of single subject research can be tracked to Skinner (1904–1990). Skinner's research focused on animal behaviors, consequences of those behaviors, and the subsequent performances that were influenced by the consequences. He also developed a set of concepts that described behavior processes, such as reinforcement, punishment, discrimination, and response differentiation (e.g., Skinner, 1938, 1953). These behavior processes formed operant conditioning, and Skinner's research was considered as the experimental analysis of behavior (Kazdin, 2020). Investigations in the experimental analysis of behavior usually use a single subject, such as a rat, a pigeon, or any other animals. Sidman (1960) referred these designs as "intrasubject-replication designs," which evaluates the effect of a variable that is repeated over time. Researchers usually compare performances before, during, and after an independent variable is presented. In the 1950s and 1960s, the connection between single subject-based designs and operant conditioning research became obvious. It is important to be aware of this connection in order to understand the history and development of single subject-based designs.

Applied Behavior of Analysis

As laboratory applications of **operant conditioning** developed, the use of operant conditioning was extended to human behaviors (see Kazdin, 2020). The extension started mainly with (1) adults with psychiatric disorders; (2) adults functioning normally in the community; (3) children diagnosed with intellectual or developmental disabilities; and (4) children diagnosed with autism (e.g., Ferster, 1961). Research findings suggested using operant conditioning for therapies and interventions. Starting from the late 1960s, applied behavior analysis emerged from the extension of experimental analysis of behavior and operant conditioning to children, adolescent, and adults in various applied areas (Cooper et al., 2007; Kazdin, 2001). In applied behavior analysis, interventions used to change behavior rely on operant conditioning, whereas single subject-based designs were used to evaluate these interventions. Single subject-based designs have been used for various interventions and used to evaluate interventions in diverse settings.

Single Subject Design Types and Utilization Recommendations

Interventions and evaluations are important new topics for single subject-based designs. Accountability in providing services and in evaluating interventions in applied settings is another critical issue (Kazdin, 2020). This section will first give an overview of evidence-based interventions and increased evaluation and accountability, followed by an introduction of a case and demonstrations of various single subject-based design types.

Evidence-Based Interventions

Evidence-based interventions (EBIs) refer to interventions that are based on strong empirical evidence. The specific definitions of EBI vary in different countries, professions, organization, and disciplines. Therefore, the interventions selected can vary widely. Table 6.1 includes EBI criteria that are used frequently, which was adapted from Kazdin (2020).

The APA Division 16 Task Force on Evidence-Based Interventions in School Psychology provides procedures and coding manuals with comprehensive criteria for evaluating EBIs in school settings (Kratochwill & Stoiber, 2002). However, there are still challenges in promoting and implementing EBIs in professional practice (Kratochwill & Shernoff, 2003). The adoption of EBIs in professional practice may be constrained by (1) limited time and resources; (2) some clinicians may prefer following clinical judgment rather than implementing EBIs; and (3) lack of training among psychologists (Power & D'Amato, 2018). Although it is challenging to implement EBIs in clinical neuropsychology practice, the MTSS approach is recommended by some psychologists (e.g., Traughber & D'Amato, 2005).

Increased Evaluation and Accountability in Single Subject Designs

Evidence-based intervention (EBI) is a part of the movement of increased evaluation and accountability in intervention work (Kazdin, 2020). Cost control and funding agencies promote this movement, and third-party payers are interested in EBIs and treatment costs as well. There is an increased interest in obtaining data about what has been provided and what effects have been showing. Given the subjective

Table 6.1 Criteria used to establish an evidence-based intervention (EBI)

• Random assignment of subjects to treatment and control/comparison conditions (e.g., no treatment, routine care, treatment as usual for the setting)
• Well-specified sample with inclusion and exclusion criteria
• Well-specified intervention procedures in treatment manuals
• Multiple outcome measures (if there are raters, they are not aware of the different conditions)
• Statistically significant differences between treatment and control/comparison conditions
• Two or more randomized controlled studies attest to the treatment effects
• The studies include replication of the findings beyond the original investigators

nature of the clinicians' impressions of their own treatment progress, user-friendly and well-validated measures have been developed to be used in clinical work. For example, the Outcome Questionnaire 45 (OQ-45; Lambert et al., 1996) is an adult self-report scale used to evaluate treatment progress. It has been applied to over 10,000 clients and has shown empirical evidence (e.g., Lambert et al., 2001). It is important to use **evaluations** in clinical work to make sure that the outcomes of the interventions have been achieved. If the **outcomes** of the interventions have not been achieved, when and how to alter the intervention process becomes essential. Single subject-based designs provide many options to facilitate the evaluation of interventions in clinical settings.

A Case Illustrating Single Subject Design Types

A case from Power et al. (2016) will be used to demonstrate various single subject-based designs. A 15-year-old Hispanic male met the IDEA 2004 eligibility criteria for intellectual disability and Autism to receive special education services. Power and colleagues found that the intervention entitled *Social Stories* significantly increased the participant's frequency of eye contact and the knowledge of eye contact, but not social emotional reciprocity.

ABAB Designs and Illustration

ABAB designs are the most basic single subject-based designs. ABAB designs examine an intervention's effects by alternating the baseline condition (A phase) when there is no intervention, with the intervention condition (B phase; Kazdin, 2020). The A and B phases are repeated one more time to form four phases). If performance improves in B phase after the intervention is provided, reverts to A phase when intervention is removed, and reinstates in the second B phase when intervention is provided, we can say that the effects of the intervention are clear. Figure 6.1 shows hypothetical data for an ABAB design with the 15-year-old boy's case as a background. The numbers show frequency of eye contact per hour with or without the intervention of Social Stories. There are four phases involved.

In Fig. 6.1, it is clear that the frequency of eye contact increased during the first intervention phase. However, it is not clear that the intervention Social Stories causes this change. Other factors cannot be fully ruled out with only these two phases. Therefore, we need to repeat the baseline and intervention phases one more time. In the third phase, the intervention is withdrawn and the baseline condition is restored. In the last phase, the intervention is applied and the frequency of eye contact is reinstated. The third and the last phases are used to test whether the frequency of eye contact is as predicted as from the second phase. From Fig. 6.1, we can tell that our prediction is mostly correct. The frequency of eye contact drops back to the

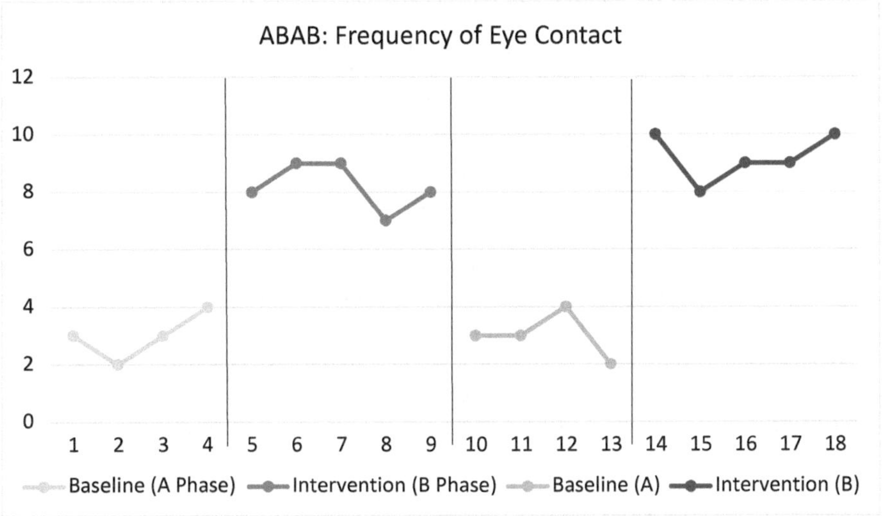

Fig. 6.1 ABAB design: Frequency of eye contact

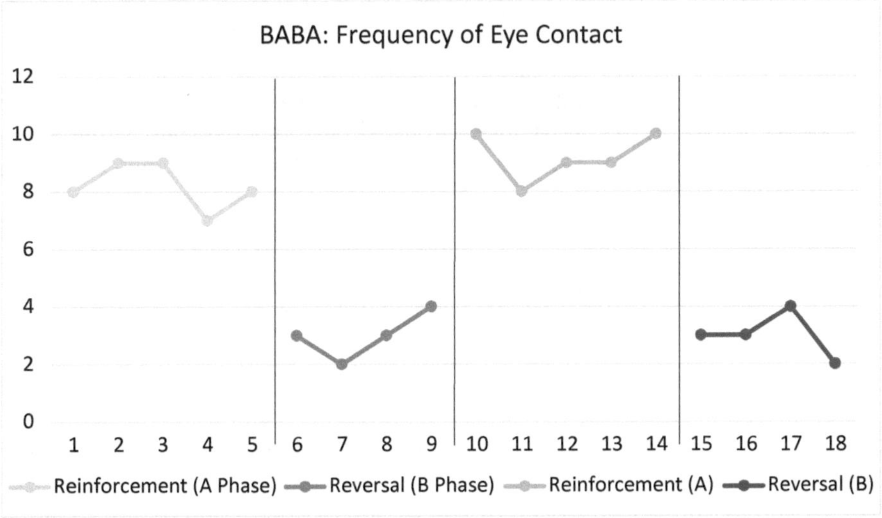

Fig. 6.2 BABA design: Frequency of eye contact

baseline level when the intervention is withdrawn and reinstates when the intervention is applied.

The ABAB design may also be changed to a BABA design (see Fig. 6.2). Using the same case and hypothetical data, Social Stories can be used as reinforcement at the beginning, and by removing this reinforcement, the results reverse. There are also four phases involved.

In Fig. 6.2, it is clear that the frequency of eye contact decreases during the first reversal phase. However, it is not clear that the withdrawal of intervention Social Stories causes this reverse. Other factors cannot be fully ruled out with only these two phases. Therefore, we need to repeat the reinforcement and reversal phases one more time. In the third phase, the reinforcement is provided and the reinforcement condition is restored. In the last phase, the reinforcement is removed and the frequency of eye contact drops back to reversal condition. The third and the last phases are used to test whether the frequency of eye contact is as predicted as from the second phase. From Fig. 6.2, we can tell that our prediction is mostly correct. The frequency of eye contact drops back to the reversal level when the reinforcement is withdrawn and reinstates when the reinforcement is provided.

In general, a four-phase design (ABAB or BABA) is considered better than a two-phase design due to validity. ABAB designs may vary in the number of interventions they include and sometimes researchers include more than one intervention (B and C phases) in the same intervention design (Kazdin, 2020). One strength of single subject-based designs in clinical practice is the possibility to see one intervention's effect and then to change or add another intervention to improve the outcome. Examples include ABCBCA or ABCABC designs.

Figure 6.3 shows hypothetical data for an ABCBCA design with the same 15-year-old boy's case as a background. The numbers show frequency of eye contact per hour with or without the intervention of Social Stories (B phase) and Dolphin-Assisted Therapy (C phase). There are six phases involved.

In Fig. 6.3, it is clear that the frequency of eye contact increased during the first intervention phase (B phase). However, it is not clear that the intervention Social Stories causes this change. Other factors cannot be fully ruled out with only these

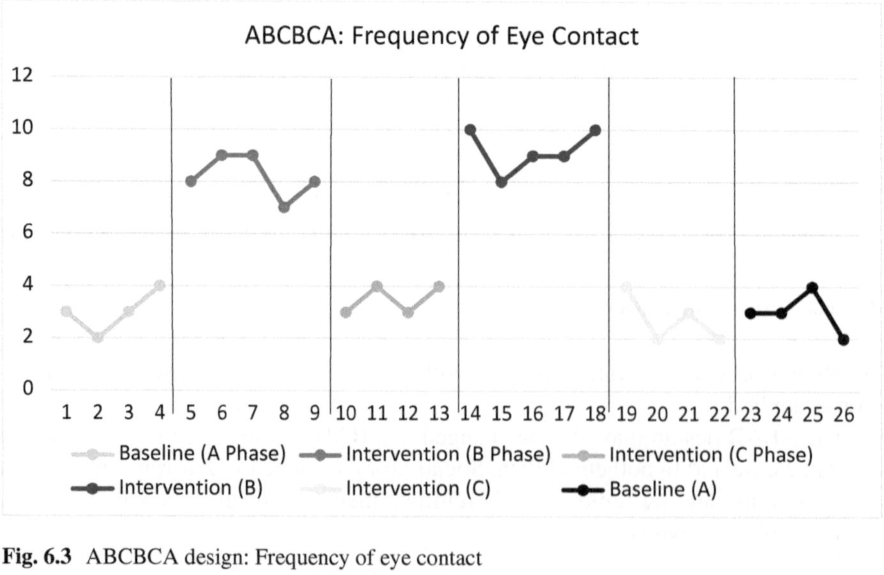

Fig. 6.3 ABCBCA design: Frequency of eye contact

two phases. In the third phase, the intervention Social Stories is withdrawn, and the intervention Dolphin-Assisted Therapy is provided. The frequency of eye contact drops back to baseline status (C phase). In order to explain this change better, Social Stories is provided again in the fourth phase, and the frequency of eye contact is reinstated. Dolphin-Assisted Therapy is provided again in the fifth phase, and the frequency of eye contact drops back to baseline status. The fourth and fifth phases are used to test whether the frequency of eye contact is as predicted as from the second and third phases. In the last phase, no intervention is provided, and the frequency of eye contact drops back to baseline status. From Figure 6.3, we can tell that the frequency of eye contact drops back to the baseline level when the intervention Social Stories is withdrawn and when Dolphin-Assisted Therapy is provided. It means that Dolphin-Assisted Therapy is not effective for the 15-year-old boy. The frequency of eye contact increases when the intervention Social Stories is applied, which means Social Stories is effective.

Understanding Multiple-Baseline Designs with a Case Illustration

Multiple-baseline designs are very different from ABAB designs. Researchers introduce the intervention to different baselines at various points in time (Kazdin, 2020). The characteristics of multiple-baseline designs include (1) the intervention is effective if each baseline changes when the intervention is applied; (2) the intervention will not be withdrawn once it is implemented to change a behavior; and (3) no ethnical or practical concerns like ABAB designs). Multiple-baseline designs can be across behaviors, individuals, situations, settings, or time. Figure 6.4 shows hypothetical data for a multiple-baseline design across individuals. The numbers show frequency of eye contact per hour with or without the intervention Social Stories. Individual A is the same 15-year-old boy. Individual B is a 13-year-old boy and individual C is a 14-year-old girl.

For multiple-baseline design across individuals, the **multiple baselines** refer to the number of individuals whose behaviors are observed (Kazdin, 2020). The procedures include (1) at the beginning of the design, each person's baseline performance of the same behavior is observed; (2) after the behavior becomes stable, the intervention is applied to one of the individuals, while others remain in the baseline conditions; (3) when behaviors become stable for everyone, another person receives the intervention; and (4) it continues until everyone receives the intervention. The intervention effect is demonstrated when each individual's performance is changed at the time when the intervention is provided and not before.

In Fig. 6.4, it is clear that the frequency of eye contact increases after the intervention is applied across individuals A, B, and C. Therefore, we can tell that the intervention Social Stories is effective for individuals A, B, and C. Multiple-baseline designs can also be across behaviors, situations, settings, or time. The procedures are similar to multiple-baseline designs across individuals.

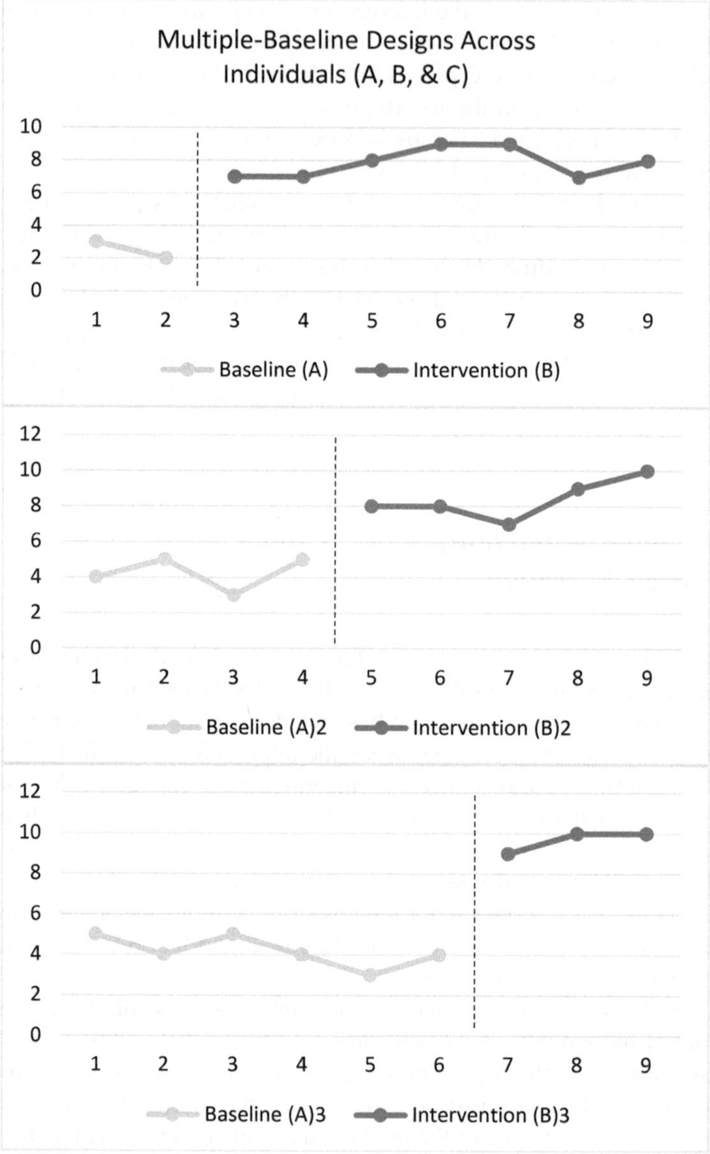

Fig. 6.4 Multiple-baseline design: Frequency of eye contact

Changing-Criterion Designs with a Case Illustration

For changing-criterion designs, the intervention effect is demonstrated by showing gradual behavior changes over the course of the intervention phase (Kazdin, 2020). Changing-criterion designs are unique because they do not require withdrawing or withholding the intervention and the behavior improves in steps to match a performance criterion that is specified as part of the intervention. After the baseline phase, the intervention phase that includes several subphases starts. If performance meets the criterion, a new subphase starts with a new criterion, and this continues in the following subphases in which the criterion is changed repeatedly. Figure 6.5 shows hypothetical data for a changing-criterion design using the 15-year-old boy's case. The numbers show frequency of eye contact per hour with or without the intervention of Social Stories. Within the intervention phase, there are several subphases (vertical dashed lines). In each subphase, a criterion for performance is specified (horizontal dashed line). As performance meets the criterion, a new criterion is made, and criterion is changed repeatedly over the course of the design.

In Fig. 6.5, it is clear that the frequency of eye contact increases during the first intervention phase (B1). However, it is not clear that the intervention Social Stories causes this change. Other factors cannot be fully ruled out with only these two phases. Therefore, we need to repeat the intervention phases. In the following subphases, as performance meets the frequency of eye contact criterion, a new criterion for the frequency of eye contact is made, and the criterion is changed repeatedly over the course of the design. From Fig. 6.5, we can tell that the frequency of eye contact is increased every time when the intervention is applied and a new criterion is made. In most cases, at least two subphases during intervention are required, and three or more subphases are recommended. A subphase can be brief (2 to 5 days or sessions) if performance meets new criterion and shows low variability (Kazdin, 2020). If not, the subphase should last longer.

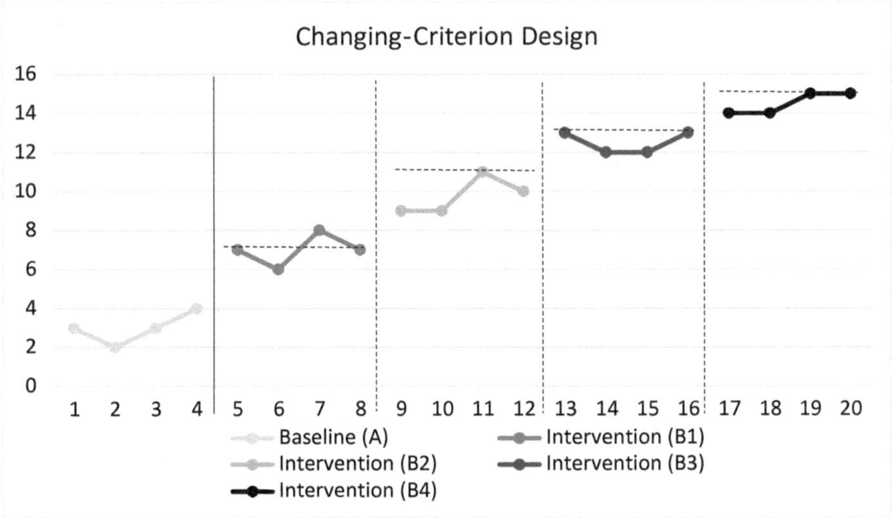

Fig. 6.5 Changing-criterion design: Frequency of eye contact

Multiple-Treatment Designs with a Case Illustration

In multiple-treatment designs, two or more interventions are implemented in the same intervention phase; however, these interventions will be administered separately so their separate effect can be evaluated (Kazdin, 2020). Figure 6.6 shows hypothetical data for a multiple-treatment design with the 15-year-old boy's case as a background. During baseline, no intervention is provided. During the intervention phase, three levels of the same intervention Social Stories are executed by the trainer 100%, 50%, and 0% of the time, respectively. In the 100% condition, the trainer follows the procedures every time as instructed by the intervention manual. In the 50% condition, the trainer follows the procedures half of the time. In the 0% condition, the procedure is not done. The numbers show frequency of eye contact per hour.

In Fig. 6.6, during baseline, no intervention is provided. The separate lines indicate different instructions. During the intervention phase, the three levels of instruction are compared. When the intervention is implemented 100% of the time, the frequency of eye contact increases the most. When the intervention is implemented 50% of the time, the frequency of eye contact is increased, but not as much as 100%. When the intervention is implemented 0% of the time, there is no real change in the frequency of eye contact. The design shows different intervention effects clearly in relation to the level of instruction.

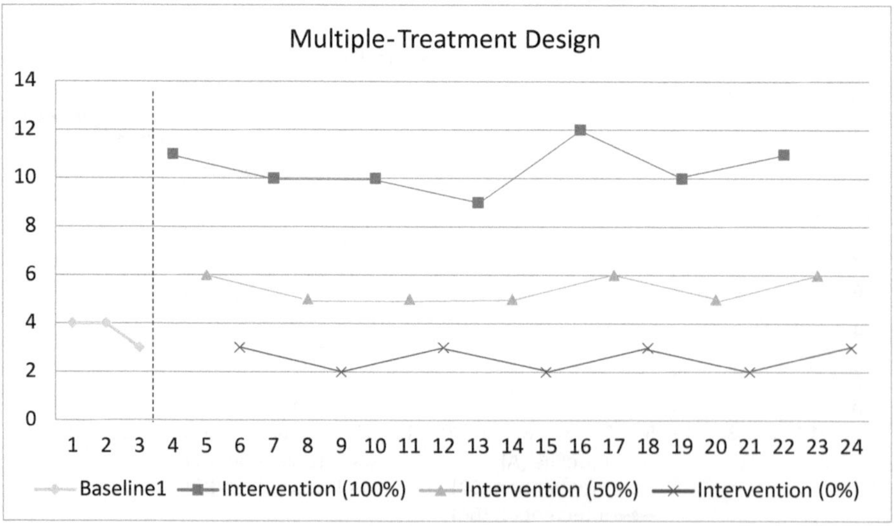

Fig. 6.6 Multiple-treatment design: Frequency of eye contact

Quasi-single-Case Experimental Designs with a Case Illustration

Quasi-experimental designs are non-randomized, pre-post-intervention designs, which can provide strong bases for drawing inferences. The key steps to evaluate a program and improve inferences are (1) collect systematic data; (2) assess behavior or program outcomes on multiple occasions; (3) consider past and future projections of performance; (4) consider the type of effect associated with treatment; and (5) use multiple and heterogeneous participants. Examples of quasi-experimental designs include (1) pre-post assessment; (2) continuous assessment helps to evaluate change; (3) continuous assessment over baseline and intervention phases helps further; (4) continuous assessment and marked changes; and (5) continuous assessment, marked changes, and multiple subjects (Kazdin, 2020).

Figure 6.7 shows hypothetical data for a continuous assessment and marked changes with the 15-year-old boy's case as a background. During baseline, no intervention is provided. During the intervention phase, the frequencies of eye contact per hour significantly increase and remain high at 2- and 18-month follow-up assessment. The stable and very clear baseline and marked changes after intervention suggest that maturation or other factors may not account for the results. The results are relatively clear within the limits of quasi-single-case experimental designs.

In Fig. 6.7, it is clear that the frequency of eye contact increases during the intervention phase. However, it is not clear that the intervention Social Stories causes this change. Therefore, 2-month and 18-month follow-ups are added. We can tell that the frequency of eye contact increases since the start of the intervention and remains stable in the 2-month and 18-month follow-up.

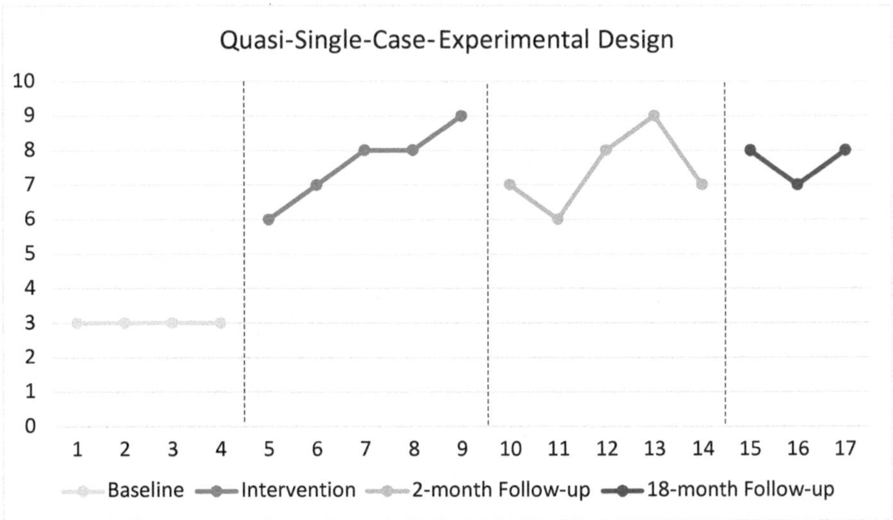

Fig. 6.7 Quasi-single-case experimental design: Frequency of eye contact

Other Design Options

In addition to the above designs, there are other design options. Combined design is an additional design option, which combines two or more design features. One of the most commonly used combined designs integrates ABAB and multiple-baseline design features. Probes and graduated withdrawal of intervention are design additions to examine transfer of training and response maintenance (Kazdin, 2020). Between-group designs are used widely in psychology, education, medicine, and other disciplines, which usually focus on quantitative research methods. Between-group designs and single subject-based designs are occasionally combined, and mixed-methods research and interventions have become more and more popular.

Why Do Multicultural Issues Need to Be Considered When Designing Single Subject-Based Interventions

Understanding Why

Demographic changes, professional ethical standards, and construct validity are three major reasons why multicultural issues are important in clinical neuropsychology practice (Rivera et al., 2010). According to Colby and Ortman (2014), the US Census Bureau projected that the United States will become more racially and ethnically diverse in the coming years, as seen in the projected increases in the percentage of the population that are minorities. The child population is even more diverse than the adult population.

According to the American Psychological Association's (APA) Guidelines on Multicultural Education, Training, Research, Practice, and Organizational Change for Psychologists (APA, 2003), "*all individuals are cultural beings who possess a cultural, racial, and ethnic heritage*" (p. 380). In APA's Ethical Principles of Psychologists and Code of Conduct (APA, 2017, p.13), Standard 9.06 (Interpreting Assessment Results) states that psychologists should "*take into account the purpose of the assessment as well as the various test factors, test-taking abilities, and other characteristics of the person being assessed, such as situational, personal, linguistic, and cultural differences, that might affect psychologists' judgments or reduce the accuracy of their interpretations*" when they interpret assessment results.

It is crucial to use proper instruments in order to design valid neuropsychological interventions. APA Ethical Standard 9.02b (APA, 2017) states that "*psychologists use assessment instruments whose validity and reliability have been established for use with members of the population tested*" (p. 13). In the past, many researchers failed to investigate the validity of clinical neuropsychological instruments in multicultural settings. Clinical neuropsychological instruments designed to measure behaviors in one culture may not be valid or effective in measuring behaviors of clients who are from other cultures. Nowadays, more and more research models have been designed to investigate the construct validity of clinical neuropsychological instruments across cultures.

Therefore, it is important for clinical neuropsychologists to focus on **multicultural issues** and provide **culturally competent** neuropsychological services to all clients. Multicultural issues needed to be considered in every aspect of clinical neuropsychological evaluation and intervention, such as gathering background information and clinical history, choosing assessments, and interpreting results (Power & D'Amato, 2018). Factors such as gender, age, ethnicity, and family have critical implications for clinical assessments (Manly et al., 2002) and single subject-based interventions.

Understanding How

In 2017, the updated version of the **Multicultural Guidelines** encouraged psychologists to consider how knowledge and understanding of identity develops from and is disseminated within professional psychological practice (APA, 2017). This new version emphasizes an ecological approach to context, identity, and intersectionality. A five-level layered ecological model is introduced, which incorporates Bronfenbrenner's (1977, 1979) ecological model that proposes five centric circles. These five levels include (1) bidirectional model of self-definition and relationships; (2) community, school, and family context; (3) institutional impact on engagement; (4) domestic and international climate; and (5) outcomes. These five levels help psychologists form an understanding of the interactions among individuals, microsystems, exosystems, and macrosystems (APA, 2017). Case studies in each level and a list of ten guidelines are provided. Table 6.2 summarizes the ten guidelines, which was quoted from the APA (2017) Multicultural Guidelines (p. 4–5).

Why Designing Single Subject-Based Interventions Is Critical to Professional Psychological Practice

Single subject-based interventions have several advantages that large sample designs may not have. A summary of the advantages includes (1) single subject-based designs can demonstrate clear causal relations between intervention and behavior change efficiently, whereas large sample designs require support in human resources, finance, and time; (2) it is more flexible to implement and evaluate interventions using single subject-based designs, which provides the opportunity to modify interventions as needed; (3) it is easier to see individual change patterns from the evaluation data using single subject-based designs, whereas large sample designs usually include pre- and post-intervention assessment without focusing on the change pattern during the whole intervention process; and (4) some statistical or methodological problems can be improved or avoided using single subject-based designs (Nock et al., 2007). Single subject-based interventions also have limitations, which should be noted when selecting design options. The limitation that is most commonly cited is a lack of generality of obtained effects. However, using multiple and heterogeneous individuals within and across studies can be implemented to demonstrate generality (Nock et al., 2007).

Table 6.2 APA (2017) Multicultural Guidelines

Guidelines
1. Psychologists seek to recognize and understand that identity and self-definition are fluid and complex and that the interaction between the two is dynamic. To this end, psychologists appreciate that intersectionality is shaped by the multiplicity of the individual's social contexts
2. Psychologists aspire to recognize and understand that as cultural beings, they hold attitudes and beliefs that can influence their perceptions of and interactions with others as well as their clinical and empirical conceptualizations. As such, psychologists strive to move beyond conceptualizations rooted in categorical assumptions, biases, and/or formulations based on limited knowledge about individuals and communities
3. Psychologists strive to recognize and understand the role of language and communication through engagement that is sensitive to the lived experience of the individual, couple, family, group, community, and/or organizations with whom they interact. Psychologists also seek to understand how they bring their own language and communication to these interactions
4. Psychologists endeavor to be aware of the role of the social and physical environment in the lives of clients, students, research participants, and/or consultees
5. Psychologists aspire to recognize and understand historical and contemporary experiences with power, privilege, and oppression. As such, they seek to address institutional barriers and related inequities, disproportionalities, and disparities of law enforcement, administration of criminal justice, educational, mental health, and other systems as they seek to promote justice, human rights, and access to quality and equitable mental and behavioral health services
6. Psychologists seek to promote culturally adaptive interventions and advocacy within and across systems, including prevention, early intervention, and recovery
7. Psychologists endeavor to examine the profession's assumptions and practices within an international context, whether domestically or internationally based, and consider how this globalization has an impact on the psychologist's self-definition, purpose, role, and function
8. Psychologists seek awareness and understanding of how developmental stages and life transitions intersect with the larger biosociocultural context, how identity evolves as a function of such intersections, and how these different socialization and maturation experiences influence worldview and identity
9. Psychologists strive to conduct culturally appropriate and informed research, teaching, supervision, consultation, assessment, interpretation, diagnosis, dissemination, and evaluation of efficacy as they address the first four levels of the Layered Ecological Model of the Multicultural Guidelines
10. Psychologists actively strive to take a strength-based approach when working with individuals, families, groups, communities, and organizations that seeks to build resilience and decrease trauma within the sociocultural context

Recommendations for the Future

The characteristics of single subject-based interventions include (1) focus on one or a few subjects; (2) focus on overt behavior; (3) use of visual inspection; and (4) can be used for psychological or behavioral interventions (Kazdin, 2020). These characteristics make single subject-based interventions great options for clinical neuropsychology practice. Not to mention single subject-based designs focus on individuals, have special strengths in evaluation, provide ongoing feedback while the intervention is applied, and provide extended interventions for tests of generality.

In the future, it is believed that single subject-based designs can be better applied in two broad contexts: the different levels of analyses and the different methodologies including between-group and qualitative research (D'Amato & Perfect, 2020; Kazdin, 2020). Depending on the research questions, researchers need to choose appropriate levels of analysis, such as individual level (e.g., single subject-based designs), group level (e.g., between-group designs), or groups of studies (e.g., meta-analysis). Different levels of analyses could lead to different methodologies. When it is appropriate, researchers are encouraged to combine different levels of analyses and different methodologies with single subject-based designs in order to help in answering the research questions.

Conclusions

This chapter introduced single subject-based interventions for clinical neuropsychology practice. We first highlighted the historical and theoretical foundations of single subject-based designs. A clinical neuropsychology case was presented to demonstrate various single subject-based design types. Multicultural issues in designing single subject-based interventions and why it is critical to design single subject-based interventions for professional psychological practice were discussed. At the end, future directions and questions for discussion were provided.

Discussion Questions

- What are the strengths of single subject-based designs?
- What are the limitations of single subject-based designs?
- Why is it important to use evidence-based interventions in clinical neuropsychology practice?
- What are the major single subject-based design types?
- Why multicultural issues are important in designing single subject-based interventions for clinical neuropsychology practice?

EPPP Sample Questions

1. Which of the following is NOT a prominent psychologist who has used single subject-based designs in experimental psychology?

   A. Freud
   B. Pavlov
   C. Ebbinghaus
   D. Wundt

2. Which of the following is NOT a criterion used to establish an evidence-based intervention?
   A. Random assignment of subjects to treatment and control/comparison conditions
   B. Statistical significant differences between treatment and control/comparison conditions
   C. Secondary progressive
   D. One or more randomized controlled studies attest to the treatment effects
3. Which of the following is a common type of single subject-based design?
   A. Multiple-treatment design
   B. Changing-criterion design
   C. Multiple-baseline design
   D. All of the above
4. Which of the following is included in Bronfenbrenner's ecological model?
   A. Microsystems
   B. Exosystems
   C. Macrosystems
   D. All of the above
5. What are some of the constraints of adopting evidence-based interventions in professional practice?
   A. Limited time and resources.
   B. Some clinicians may prefer following clinical judgment rather than implementing evidence-based interventions.
   C. Lack of training among psychologists.
   D. All of the above.

   Answers: A, D, D, D, D

Proactive Readings

Transcending the Past

American Psychological Association (2010). *Clinical neuropsychology*. https://www.apa.org/ed/graduate/specialize/neuro

Perfect, M., & D'Amato, R. C. (2020). Introduction to special issue on the history of the future of proactive school psychology: Transcending the past, excel in the present, and transform the future. *School Psychology, 35*(6), 363-366. https://doi.org/10.1037/spq0000419

Excelling in the Present

American Psychological Association (2017). *Multicultural guidelines: An ecological approach to context, Identity, and Intersectionality*. http://www.apa.org/about/policy/multicultural-guidelines.pdf

Kazdin, A. E. (2020). *Single-case research designs: Methods for clinical and applied settings* (3rd ed.). Oxford University Press.

Transforming the Future

D'Amato, R. C., & Perfect, M. (2020). History of the future of proactive school psychology: Historical review at our 75th APA anniversary to transcend the past, excel in the present, and transform the future. *School Psychology*, 35(6), 375–384. https://doi.org/10.1037/spq0000420

Power, E., & D'Amato, R. C. (2018). Should our future include the integration of evidence-based neuropsychological services into school settings? In D. P. Flanagan & E. M. McDonough (Eds.), *Contemporary intellectual Assessment: Theories, tests, and issues* (4th ed.; pp. 1017–1045). New iYork, NY: Guilford.

References

D'Amato, R. C., & Perfect, M. (2020). History of the future of proactive school psychology: Historical review at our 75th APA anniversary to transcend the past, excel in the present, and transform the future. *School Psychology, 35*(6), 375–384. https://doi.org/10.1037/spq0000420

Allport, G. W. (1961). *Pattern and growth in personality*. Holt, Reinhart & Winston.

American Psychological Association. (2003). Guidelines on multicultural education, training, research, practice, and organizational change for psychologists. *American Psychologist, 58*, 377–402.

American Psychological Association. (2010). *Clinical neuropsychology*. https://www.apa.org/ed/graduate/specialize/neuro

American Psychological Association. (2017). *Multicultural guidelines: An ecological approach to context, identity, and intersectionality*. http://www.apa.org/about/policy/multicultural-guidelines.pdf

Bronfenbrenner, U. (1977). Toward an experimental ecology of human development. *American Psychologist, 32*(7), 513–531. https://doi.org/10.1037/0003-066X.32.7.513

Bronfenbrenner, U. (1979). *The ecology of human development: Experiments by nature and design*. Harvard University Press.

Colby, S. L., & Ortman, J. M. (2014). Projections of the size and composition of the U.S. population: 2014 to 2060. In *Current Population Reports* (pp. 25–1143). U.S. Census Bureau.

Cooper, J. O., Heron, T. E., & Heward, W. L. (2007). *Applied behavior analysis* (2nd ed.). Pearson.

D'Amato, R. C., Fletcher-Janzen, E., & Reynolds, C. R. (Eds.). (2005). *Handbook of school neuropsychology*. Wiley.

Ferster, C. B. (1961). Positive reinforcement and behavioral deficits of young children. *Child Development, 32*, 437–456. https://psycnet.apa.org/doi/10.1111/j.1467-8624.1961.tb05042.x

Kazdin, A. E. (2020). *Single-case research designs: Methods for clinical and applied settings* (3rd ed.). Oxford.

Kazdin, A. E. (2001). *Behavior modification in applied settings* (6th ed.). Wadsworth/Thomson Learning.

Kratochwill, T. R., & Stoiber, K. C. (2002). Evidence-based interventions in school psychology: Conceptual foundations of the Procedural and Coding Manual of Division 16 and the Society for the Study of School Psychology Task Force. *School Psychology Quarterly, 17*(4), 341–389. https://psycnet.apa.org/doi/10.1521/scpq.17.4.341.20872

Kratochwill, T. R., & Shernoff, E. S. (2003). Evidence-based practice: Promoting evidence-based interventions in school psychology. *School Psychology Quarterly, 18*(4), 389–408. https://psycnet.apa.org/doi/10.1521/scpq.18.4.389.27000

Lambert, M. J., Hansen, N. B., & Finch, A. E. (2001). Patient-focused research: Using patient outcome data to enhance treatment effects. *Journal of Consulting and Clinical Psychology, 69*(2), 159–172.

Lambert, M. J., Hansen, N. B., Umpress, V., Lunnen, K., Okiishi, J., Burlingame, G. M., … Reisinger, C. (1996). *Administration and scoring manual for the outcome questionnaire (OQ 45.2)*. American Professional Credentialing Services.

Manly, J. J., Jacobs, D. M., Touradji, P., Small, S. A., & Stern, Y. (2002). Reading level attenuates differences in neuropsychological test performance between African American and white elders. *Journal of the International Neuropsychological Society, 8*(3), 341–348. https://doi.org/10.1017/s1355617702813157

National Academy of Neuropsychology. (2001). *NAN definition of a clinical neuropsychologist*. https://www.nanonline.org/docs/PAIC/PDFs/NANPositionDefNeuro.pdf

Nock, M. K., Michel, B. D., & Photos, V. (2007). Single-case research designs. In D. McKay (Ed.), *Handbook of research methods in abnormal and clinical psychology* (pp. 337–350). Sage.

Power, E. M., & D'Amato, R. C. (2018). Should our future include the integration of evidence-based neuropsychological services into school settings? In D. P. Flanagan & E. M. McDonough (Eds.), *Contemporary intellectual assessment: Theories, tests, and issues* (p. 1017–1045). The Guilford Press.

Power, E. M., Hill, A. K., D'Amato, R. C., & Losoff, R. (2016, August). *Social stories ™ as a neuropsychological intervention for an adolescent with autism Spectrum disorder*. Poster session presented at the American Psychological Association convention, Denver, CO.

Rivera Mindt, M., Byrd, D., Saez, P., & Manly, J. (2010). Increasing culturally competent neuropsychological services for ethnic minority populations: A call to action. *The Clinical Neuropsychologist, 24*(3), 429–453. https://doi.org/10.1080/13854040903058960

Sidman, M. (1960). *Tactics of scientific research*. Basic Books.

Skinner, B. F. (1938). *The behavior of organisms: An experimental analysis*. Appleton-Century-Crofts.

Skinner, B. F. (1953). *Science and human behavior*. Free Press.

Traughber, M. C., & D'Amato, R. C. (2005). Integrating evidence-based neuropsychological services into school settings: Issues and challenges for the future. In R. C. D'Amato, E. Fletcher-Janzen, & C. R. Reynolds (Eds.), *Handbook of school neuropsychology* (pp. 827–857). Wiley.

Watson, R. I. (1951). *The clinical method in psychology*. Harper.

Witsken, D., D'Amato, R., & Hartlage, L. (2008). Understanding the past, present, and future of clinical neuropsychology. In R. C. D'Amato & L. C. Hartlage (Eds.), *Essentials of neuropsychological assessment: Rehabilitation planning for intervention* (pp. 103–118). Springer.

Zilboorg, G., & Henry, G. W. (1941). *A history of medical psychology*. Norton.

Chapter 7
Qualitative Research-Based Interventions for Clinical Neuropsychology Practice

Mary (Rina) M. Chittooran and Gertina J. van Schalkwyk

Learning Objectives

- To provide a rationale for qualitative research-based interventions in clinical neuropsychology.
- To identify applications of qualitative research designs to clinical neuropsychology.
- To describe the relationship between qualitative assessments and clinical neuropsychology interventions.
- To describe qualitative research-based interventions in clinical neuropsychology.
- To discuss multicultural considerations for assessment and intervention in clinical neuropsychology.
- To discuss implications for present and future professional practice.

Introduction

Clinical neuropsychology "*is an applied science concerned with the behavioral expression of brain dysfunction*" (Lezak, 1995, p. 7); that is, the primary focus of this discipline is the biological basis of behavior (Lezak et al., 2012), sometimes referred to as brain-behavior relationships. Interventions in clinical

M. M. Chittooran (✉)
School of Education, Saint Louis University, St. Louis, MO, USA
e-mail: mary.chittooran@slu.edu

G. J. van Schalkwyk
Department of Psychology, University of Macau, (Retired Head of Department), Macao, Macao Special Administrative Region (SAR), People's Republic of China

R. C. D'Amato et al. (eds.), *Understanding the Biological Basis of Behavior*,
https://doi.org/10.1007/978-3-030-59162-5_7

neuropsychology may be based on data that are quantitative, qualitative, or a combination of the two; however, the purpose of this chapter is to address the application of **qualitative methodologies** to interventions designed to address neuropsychological deficits that are identified through qualitative assessments (Rhodes et al., 2008; Witsken et al., 2008).

Qualitative research relates to the application of exploratory, interactive, and discovery-oriented methodology to observing behavior in natural settings where it emerges or evolves in the social world rather than being fixed according to predetermined categories or typologies (Willig, 2008; Yehl, 2009). Multiple qualitative methods have emerged over the past 30–40 years allowing researchers and practitioners to better understand neuropsychological phenomena and gain new perspectives by exploring meanings about the behavior and experiences of clients in interaction with others in their social world. Relying on complex reasoning that moves dialectically between deductive, inductive, and abductive methods, qualitative research provides rich descriptions of complex phenomena (e.g., sensitive topics, culturally defined experiences), tracks unique or unexpected events, illuminates experiences and interpretations by actors/participants, and uncovers patterns that are not immediately apparent with the confirmatory, controlled designs that are typical of quantitative research (Popay, 2006). Petticrew and Roberts (2006) propose the utility of qualitative methodologies for studying the lived experiences of individuals diagnosed with a neuropsychological disorder (e.g., Walsh et al., 2016) and for systematic reviews of the literature focusing on the effectiveness of evidence-based interventions and programs (e.g., das Nair et al., 2014) as they relate to quality-of-life issues, healthcare disparities, and multicultural competencies (e.g., Baquedano & Fabar, 2017; Braun & Clarke, 2014; Johnson, 2016; Lloyd et al., 2006).

The application of qualitative methodologies to clinical neuropsychology is still relatively new; however, this is not entirely surprising, given that the field itself is young (Witsken et al., 2008) and that, for many years, **quantitative approaches** were the default for assessment and intervention in psychology. However, despite lingering concerns about bias, validity, and lack of generalizability, qualitative methodologies, which were once marginalized (Karasz & Singelis, 2009), are being increasingly utilized (Kidd, 2002) in clinical neuropsychology. Such methodologies have also been endorsed by the American Psychological Association (2006) in its call for evidence-based practices (EBP) in psychology, "the use of systematically collected data, clinical expertise, and patient preferences by decision-makers (including clinicians, administrators and policy makers) when making decisions and considering service options" (Hunsley, 2015; Roberts & Yeager, 2004). In a similar vein, there has been a demand for more evidence-based interventions (EBI) in applied psychology, specifically in school psychology (Traughber & D'Amato, 2005) and in other fields related to psychology and education, such as reading and clinical child and adolescent psychology (e.g., Kratochwill & Shernoff, 2003). In other words, over the past few decades, there has been a growing recognition that applied psychology must be informed by both **qualitative and quantitative evidence** supported by clinical judgments of service providers as well as client perspectives; this thought is echoed by Sandelowski and Barroso (2007) who stated that "qualitative research is… viewed as essential to achieving the goal of evidence-based practice: namely to use the best evidence available as a foundation for practice without methodological prejudice" and that research findings are critical for "*developing valid and culturally sensitive instruments and effective participant-centred interventions*" (pp. 4–5).

Underlying the majority of qualitative methods is the assumption that all behavior – also potentially dysfunctional behavior or behavior emerging from neuropsychological deficits—is co-constructed and reciprocal, evolving from the interactions between individuals and their network of relationships (Chan, 2004; Gergen, 2001; Lock & Strong, 2010). Individuals interact with the environment based on the meanings it has for them. These meanings result from interactions with others, specifically significant others, social discourses, and culture-specific artifacts, and are often stored in memories that may not be easily accessible but still affect behavior. Conceptualizing an intervention for clinical neuropsychology practice therefore needs to take cognizance of these underlying meanings emerging from clients' ecological systems in order to address how they live with the dysfunction in their everyday lives.

Rationale for Qualitative Research Methods in Clinical Neuropsychology

Qualitative methods have significant utility in clinical neuropsychology in that they can present researchers and practitioners with a host of new insights regarding how individuals experience, and function optimally within the constraints of, their diagnosed disorder (e.g., Johnson, 2016; Walsh et al., 2016). They can allow clients with diagnosed neuropsychological disorders to express and interpret their actions, interactions, and co-actions leading to transformations typically expected as outcomes of clinical interventions (Bertrando & Arcelloni, 2006; Lloyd et al., 2006). Furthermore, combined with quantitative methods in a mixed-method approach (Creswell & Plano-Clark, 2011), the practitioner could integrate experimental and experiential evidence to comprehensively study brain-behavior relationships in a client. For instance, a practitioner working with a client experiencing cognitive impairment following a traumatic brain injury could collect numerical data (e.g., frequency of seizures, dosing schedules) as well as idiographic data (e.g., obtained through storytelling and clinical interviews) to analyze the case and conceptualize appropriate interventions. In fact, there is some research that shows limited success of interventions based only on quantitative data; for example, Burns et al. (2016) found almost no effects for interventions based on cognitive, numeric data alone and only moderate effects for those in reading and mathematics, suggesting that it was time to look at other more effective paradigms for research and intervention.

Qualitative methodology is a natural fit for applications to clinical neuropsychology in that qualitative researchers and practitioners typically attempt to understand a phenomenon from the perspective of the individual, interpret the meanings they bring to their behavior and experiences, examine a phenomenon holistically, and do so in naturalistic settings, rather than in laboratory or artificial settings (Tracy, 2010), using experimental methods and randomized controlled sampling. While quantitative approaches provide us with normative data that tell us how clients function in comparison to their peers, qualitative assessments can give us information about how they complete tasks and how their life histories and cultural backgrounds influence test performance (Semrud-Clikeman et al., 2005). Further, according to Semrud-Clikeman et al. (2005), qualitative approaches enhance rapport between clients and clinicians, thereby leading to improved understanding of clients' presenting problems and richer, thicker data regarding their strengths and deficits. Interventions that are based on these methods therefore allow us to engage in treatment planning that is based on research evidence, is tailored to clients, is based on their complex, unique needs (Hunsley, 2015), and ideally is a result of **interdisciplinary collaboration** (Cleary & Scott, 2011). Such collaboration across disciplines may be associated with varying conceptualizations of the problem and consequently varying approaches to intervention. Different research questions call for alternative methodologies, and different methodologies can provide a greater variety of evidence for practice.

Qualitative Research Methods and the Biological Basis of Behavior

The design and implementation of all qualitative, research-based interventions in clinical neuropsychology must consider the biological basis of behavior or the brain-behavior relationships that are the hallmark of this discipline (Witsken et al., 2008). That is, it is assumed by neuropsychologists that post-injury behaviors are at least partially the result of the location, timing, and severity of the injury. However, where quantitative, objective methods allow us to localize injury and directly examine brain functioning (e.g., with neuroimaging techniques), qualitative methods allow us only to examine clients' direct or indirect *experiences* of living with a neuropsychological deficit. At best, therefore, we can only make educated inferences about the impact of brain injury on a client, even if we attempt to strengthen those inferences by having multiple data collection points or multiple informants. Finally, a focus on brain-behavior relationships means that clinical neuropsychologists using qualitative methods must attend to improvements in **observable behaviors** such as reading out loud or completing math calculations and connect them back to corresponding improvements in brain function, if any (Davis, 2006).

Advances in medical technology and improvements in the psychometric properties of neuropsychological measures have shifted the focus away from the brain injury to the behavioral changes stemming from that injury. Unlike neuroimaging techniques which can help identify and localize structural brain injury or defects, clinical neuropsychology allows us to use a variety of measures to determine the *impact* that such injuries might have on the daily living activities of individuals so that interventions can be designed to ameliorate the impact of those injuries.

Qualitative Research Designs in Clinical Neuropsychology

This section explicates how a number of commonly used qualitative research designs can allow us to generate data that can subsequently serve as a foundation for evidence-based interventions (Creswell, 2007; McCaslin & Scott, 2003; Willig, 2008). For example, using *ethnography*, the researcher focuses on collective/communal behavior in a naturalistic context (e.g., Lasanen et al., 2017; Rashid, 2016), reporting on the "way of life" and how people interact with one another and more specifically with an individual who has a neuropsychological impairment. The central question for the neuropsychology researcher or practitioner could be: "*What are the lived experiences of a client living with traumatic brain injury within a particular cultural context*?" Conducting fieldwork in a naturalistic setting in a different culture allows researchers to adopt direct observation, participant observation, and unstructured interviewing as methods to gain an understanding of clients' experiences in a particular **cultural setting**.

Phenomenology as a method aims to describe, understand, and relay the deep meaning and essence of a phenomenon (e.g., a diagnosed neuropsychological deficit) as experienced by an individual (e.g., Johnson, 2016). In this study, the central question for the researcher or practitioner could be: "*What are the lived experiences of clients regarding a quality or phenomenon* (e.g., a diagnostic procedure for neuropsychological assessment)?" For example, Baquedano and Fabar (2017) employed what they called neurophenomenology to adapt measures in cognitive science experiments using interview data and first-person accounts alongside behavioral outcomes to elaborate the final design. The **phenomenological method** relies on in-depth interviewing that could also form part of a case study design or narrative inquiry.

Narrative inquiry has become a widely accepted qualitative approach to studying personal and human dimensions of experiences that occur over time. In this approach, storytelling is accepted as the central means by which people make sense of their lives and translate knowing into telling (Diez-Itza et al., 2016; Kulkofsky & Klemfuss, 2008; Whiffin et al., 2017). Narrative approaches take into account the relationship between individual experiences and the cultural context, prevalent discourses in society, and stored discursive cues with a focus on how elements in individuals' stories are sequenced. They also account for how memories of the past shape perceptions of the present and vice versa and how both past and present memories shape perceptions of the future (Clandinin & Connelly, 2000). In this case, the central question for the researcher or practitioner in clinical neuropsychology could be: "*How does the person diagnosed with traumatic brain injury remember the* *specific events that preceded or followed that injury and what kind of story does he or she construct related to that injury*?"

Case study methodology, another popular qualitative approach, allows the researcher to select a case that allows for in-depth exploration of an event, process, or behavior. A case serves as a unit of analysis and forms a "bounded system" that allows the researcher to define its boundaries; to decide, in advance, what will and will not be examined (Miles et al., 2014); and in so doing to predetermine the "limits" of a case. Typically, interviewing is used to collect first-person accounts from a client (Yin, 2009) although the researcher may choose to use a variety of data-gathering approaches such as observations and document analysis. In clinical neuropsychology practice, the central question for a case study design could be: "What actually occurred and was experienced by a client diagnosed with traumatic brain injury in a particular time and space (i.e., in a bounded system)?" Following the replication logic for multiple case studies and an iterative and interpretive stance for pattern matching, one could also expand the study developing a cross-case synthesis (Weber, 2008).

Using Qualitative Assessments as a Basis for Interventions in Clinical Neuropsychology

We now turn to various types of qualitative assessments that may be used to **generate data** about a client that can serve as the basis for interventions in clinical neuropsychology. Such assessments can often serve as a rich source of information about a client's functioning, especially if they supplement quantitative data (Semrud-Clikeman et al., 2005). We use the example of Sam, a 10-year-old boy who is experiencing disinhibition, problems with impulse control, severe headaches, and impaired academic functioning after falling headfirst off the climbing equipment at his elementary school and hitting his head on the concrete surround. We end with an explication of the **Collage Life Story Elicitation Technique** (CLET; van Schalkwyk, 2010, 2013), a unique qualitative, arts-based approach that has potential applications for research, assessment, and interventions in clinical neuropsychology

Behavioral Observations. Informal observations of behavioral and other changes may be one of the first ways in which we become aware that an individual has experienced a neurological insult. Subsequent planned observations, both structured and semi-structured, direct and indirect, may then be used to gather additional qualitative data about that individual's functioning in a variety of academic skills (e.g., math calculation), social-behavioral areas (e.g., social skills), settings (e.g., at home), times of the day (e.g., first thing in the morning), and during social interactions (e.g., conversations with parents). Data generated from these observations can be used to inform the development of qualitative interventions, perhaps in a pre-post format so that change can be documented. For instance, Sam could be systematically observed by his classroom teacher to identify behavior patterns, frequency of verbal outbursts, and degree and kind of class participation. Interventions could include continuing observations of Sam's behavior to determine academic and behavioral changes that suggest whether or not the intervention is effective.

Clinical Interviews. These are verbal, ideally face-to-face conversations between two or more individuals for the purpose of gathering information about the functioning of a client from the perspective of the client or others who live and work with the client; in fact, clinical interviews are often referred to as conversations with a purpose. Semrud-Clikeman, Wilkinson, and Wellington (2005) state that clinical interviews are a critical part of qualitative assessments in neuropsychology, in that they provide data on "developmental, medical, and educational histories as well as the family structure and background" (p. 288), timelines, and previous interventions. Zuluaga et al., (2013) promote the use of the clinical interview in gathering data that can be used as part of the assessment process, in developing diagnoses, and in setting up interventions in clinical neuropsychology. The data that can result from the judicious use of a clinical interview reflect the kind of narrative, non-numeric information that is the hallmark of clinical neuropsychology. The clinical neuropsychologist who works with Sam can use clinical interviews with him and his caregivers to gather baseline information, tailor an intervention to areas of strengths and weaknesses, document his progress under treatment, and record outcomes.

Questionnaires. A questionnaire is used to gather qualitative information from an individual, typically in the form of written responses to several complex questions, and may be used when setting up a clinical interview might be problematic (e.g., difficulty scheduling a mutually convenient time). Questionnaires may be completed by the individual, a family member, or a professional who works with him or her. While questionnaires can be completed at the convenience of the respondent, they may prove to be a cumbersome, time-consuming way to gather information. They do not allow for probing and clarifying questions that would be possible with a face-to-face interview and may be too difficult for respondents who have trouble writing. In the case of Sam, his parents might complete a detailed questionnaire about premorbid behaviors so that the clinical neuropsychologist can use the findings to compile an in-depth profile of his academic and behavioral functioning and then design a treatment plan.

Checklists. These are qualitative measures that can be used during observations or structured interactions with a child to document the presence or absence of certain behaviors (e.g., out-of-seat behaviors). The advantage of checklists is that they are easy to use; one simply checks off a behavior on a list of predetermined behaviors when it is observed. The disadvantage of a checklist is that there is no easy way to quantify exactly how many times the behavior occurred or how to record a novel behavior that is particular to a child that is not on the checklist (e.g., facial twitching). The clinical neuropsychologist working with Sam could ask his teachers to use a checklist to identify behaviors of concern and could then compare findings across teachers. In the classroom, teachers who implement positive reinforcement for target behaviors could use the checklist periodically to determine quickly if change has occurred. Checklists used in this way to identify behaviors that have occurred are often followed by behavior rating scales that can provide more quantitative detail about those behaviors.

Rating Scales. While rating scales are designed to allow us to gather quantitative information, typically along a Likert scale, related to a respondent's perceptions of some phenomenon (e.g., one's own self-esteem), some do include a comment section or several open-ended questions that yield useful qualitative information about an individual. It must be cautioned, however, that while such qualitative information can serve to amplify quantitative information about a client, data analysis can be time-consuming. In the case of Sam, a norm-referenced assessment of his behaviors on a rating scale completed by his parent, teacher, and Sam himself can allow us to gather information about Sam relative to his age or grade peers; however, the qualitative portion of the rating scale can allow the clinical neuropsychologist to gather a more holistic picture of his functioning that can then inform the design and implementation of interventions.

Document analysis may be used in qualitative assessment to triangulate information gathered through other means such as observations or interviews. For example, clinical neuropsychologists can examine student classwork, behavioral logs, and cumulative academic records. A homeroom teacher, who is perfectly positioned to gather continuous information about a child's functioning in the classroom, may conduct a series of qualitative assessments of a child's behaviors and submit those records to the clinician for document analysis. Sam could be encouraged to keep a simple journal, depending on his writing capabilities, to allow for expression of events, emotions, and responses to intervention that would allow him to track his own progress as well as share with his clinician.

Self-monitoring can be an effective way to gather qualitative data and can be used in a variety of ways to monitor the progress of an intervention. For example, if Sam's doctor sends him home with a new headache medication, he can record his dosing schedule and reactions to the drug and may then be asked to periodically share the log with the clinical neuropsychologist who may determine that a change in medication is needed. Self-monitoring can be modified according to age and developmental level; for example, adolescents often do well with self-monitoring because they are able to take responsibility for their behaviors. Children may be shown a chart of faces, each with a different emotion (angry, sad, happy), and are asked to mark the face that best represents how they feel about a particular event or experience. Faces can also be arranged in sequence from least happy (with an angry expression) to most happy (with a beaming, open-mouthed smile) so that children can record the intensity of their emotions when words are not adequate. The information thus generated can be used throughout a behavioral intervention and may also be transmitted to the clinician for evidence of treatment acceptability and success.

Using the Collage Life Story Elicitation Technique (CLET)

The CLET is an innovative qualitative technique aimed at eliciting **autobiographical memories** and **life stories** by prompting narrative processes through collage making and providing a space for participants' voices to be heard (van Schalkwyk,

2013). Participating in the CLET gives voice to clients' subjective meaning making as they tell their stories through visual representations of a topic under investigation using both nonverbal (visual) and verbal modes of communication. The CLET comprises a semi-structured interview process unfolding in five sequential steps each building upon the other and aiming to elicit rich narratives about a particular behavior or topic such as motivation for action/behavior. For example, conceptualizing an intervention for a client living with a traumatic brain injury, the five steps of the CLET would focus on exploring the client's experiences, perceptions, and behavior emanating from living with the consequences of the injury.

In the CLET interview, the first step entails the construction of a collage about the behavior to be explored. For collage making, the client (i.e., the storyteller) cuts images from cultural resources such as locally relevant magazines to generate visual narratives and bring to awareness the intrapsychic information that is often difficult to access merely through verbal means (van Schalkwyk, 2013; Waller, 2006). After completing a collage (Step 1), the participant engages in generating verbal stories for each of the images on the collage (Step 2). Three prompts guide the storytelling phase, namely (i) "Tell the story of this image," (ii) "What does this image mean to you?" and (iii) "How does the image relate to the behavior we are exploring?" The length of the story for each image is not important, but the content will be analyzed thematically to examine, for example, the client's capacity for problem-solving or cognitive integration of experiences. In Step 3, the clinical neuropsychologist asks the participant (i) to position himself/herself in the collage and (ii) to reflect upon the silent voice(s). Observing and interpreting the client's self-positioning on the collage and in relation to the focus topic could represent the underlying perceptions of self in the world and agency, or it could represent the client's defenses as a way of protection against troubling/distressing memories. Prompting for missing images—that is, something the person wished to add to her/his collage but could not find—further explores the client's problem-solving strategies. Step 4 involves asking the client to reflect upon two (or more) images on the collage with apparently opposing meanings and telling about the contradictions evident in the nonverbal story. Juxtaposing also explores underlying conflicts that clients may potentially have but are not yet aware of either in their behavior or interpretation of the behavior of others. The final step in the CLET (Step 5) concludes the inquiry and engages the client in reflection and debriefing. In this step, the clinician can also prompt the participant to add stories should he/she wish to do so (van Schalkwyk, 2017).

As is common in visual research methods, data analysis requires an iterative and interpretive stance for pattern matching, explanation building, and cross-case synthesis (Braun & Clarke, 2014; van Schalkwyk, 2017; Weber, 2008). Systematically analyzing and interpreting the three units of analysis (i.e., the collage, the verbal storytelling, and field notes), first independently and then collectively, gives the clinical neuropsychologist access to **different layers of meanings** that could be affecting the client's functioning in the present and in different settings (van Schalkwyk, 2017). For example, one could read the collage for information about significant individuals and groups, objects in the world, settings and events, self-positioning, hidden plots, and metaphors. The reading of the collage helps to generate assumptions and/or questions (hypotheses) to explore further in the verbal storytelling (i.e., the textual data evolving from transcribing the micro-narratives performed in Steps 2–5 of the CLET) or using other assessment tools.

In a clinical neuropsychology setting, the practitioner could use the CLET for intake screening to explore experiences and particular behavior or actions of a client living with a neuropsychological deficit; in the case of Sam, the CLET might be a useful adjunct to other forms of data collection. The CLET could also be used at any other point during the process and in collaborating with the client to interpret the underlying meanings or as outcome evaluation to explore transformations following an intervention specific to the behavior or functioning. Conducting the CLET in a single sitting, however, could be difficult depending on the nature and extent of the neuropsychological deficit and/or trauma. Therefore, the clinician could conduct two to three interviews following the five steps outlined above. It is important to complete all five steps as each step brings to the fore a different aspect of the client's experiences and perceptions of living with the dysfunctional behavior in question.

The CLET is not a diagnostic tool, and there is no actual testing of hypotheses or psychometric properties. Rather, the focus is on generating thick descriptions of the performances and representations so as to build a credible case by continuously focusing on explicating the memories about the topic/behavior under investigation and to recognize the patterns linking the behavior to the contexts in which it is or should be performed. Thus, as with other qualitative approaches in neuropsychological clinical practice, the CLET should be used in conjunction with more nomothetic measures, particularly to explore evidence for the assumptions and questions generated during the CLET analysis (van Schalkwyk, 2017). For example, in a case where the client is diagnosed with cognitive impairment due to lesions in the prefrontal cortex or early onset dementia as a result of HIV/AIDS, the CLET could only provide access to the client's perceptions and experiences of her/his condition and not the nature or degree of deficit. For the latter, a mixed-method approach should be followed to gain a better understanding of the particularities of an impairment or disorder and to plan an intervention. As mentioned previously, the CLET is not a diagnostic, but a screening tool that encourages narrative/discursive performances otherwise difficult to elicit where interpretations are aimed at generating provisional assumptions about possible areas of concern, challenges, or problems.

Qualitative Research-Based Interventions in Clinical Neuropsychology

Clinical neuropsychologists have conducted numerous intervention studies and have offered guidelines for the design of effective qualitative interventions. Perhaps the most important of these acknowledges that quantitative data alone cannot provide complete explanations for, or effectively manage, a client's functioning post-injury; neither, of course, do qualitative data by themselves. If interventions are to be truly effective, they must be based on a comprehensive assessment of an individual's functioning that includes *both* **quantitative** and **qualitative** measures of the following: medical information, results of norm- and criterion-referenced neuropsychological assessments in a variety of areas, family history, client and family perceptions based on clinical interviews, personality variables, and cognitive processes such as attention, memory, and academic achievement (e.g., Goldstein & Naglieri, 2008; Harvey, 2012; Saleh et al., Niarhos, 2018). Researchers like Goldstein and Naglieri (2008) have stated that effective interventions must be "*multidisciplinary, multimodal, and maintained over a long period" (and that) "the most effective short-term interventions .... reflect the combined use of medical, behavioral, and environmental techniques*" (p. 869).

Prigitano et al., (1995) offered a series of recommendations for developing interventions, many of which are still relevant today. For example, they discussed the importance of setting up rigorous scientific investigations; assessing reliability and validity of measures; asking research questions that would provide answers to clinical, daily practice; applying findings from medical studies of the brain to setting up neuropsychological interventions (e.g., a relationship exists between decreased blood flow in the frontal areas of the brain and disinhibited behaviors in individuals with TBI); studying brain-behavior relationships across the lifespan; and, assessing premorbid behaviors as well as non-neurological factors that might have an impact on post-injury functioning,

Interventions in clinical neuropsychology must be based on a **theoretical framework** that can guide the way interventions are conceptualized and implemented. For example, Bell and Halligan (2004) state that rehabilitation in the neurosciences requires a metatheory of rehabilitation to integrate social, neural, and psychological explanations for how to target interventions and assess their effects. Goldstein and Naglieri (2008) have promoted the use of the PASS (planning, attention, simultaneous, successive) theory to design and implement effective interventions for children with ADHD and found that subjects were more reflective and less impulsive and showed improvement in math and reading when their PASS profiles were considered in setting up interventions. Gay's (2013) theoretical discussion of **culturally responsive pedagogy** could drive the development of teaching interventions grounded in the cultural background of a student who has suffered a traumatic brain injury.

Authors such as Semrud-Clikeman and Teeter Ellison (2009) have advocated for a broad-based set of interventions that are designed to remediate weaknesses that are identified through neuropsychological assessment. Other authors have called for interventions to build on a client's existing strengths and compensate for areas of deficit, in other words, to "work around" a task, function, or process. Children and adults with a brain injury are taught to modify their environments, change the way they access those environments, or learn to adapt to a new way of life. In fact, neuropsychological rehabilitation does not have to be an either-or proposition; it can include both compensation and remediation, so that the individual may compensate for deficits by learning new ways of doing things while he or she simultaneously works on remediating areas of deficit, that is, restoring lost function to the maximum level possible (Murphy & Vaidya, 2004).

In addition to clinical outcomes, clinical neuropsychologists using qualitative methods must be mindful of **process issues**. For example, traditional research in the social sciences has silenced many groups marginalized and oppressed in society by making them passive objects of study (individuals *to* whom research is done), rather than active participants with agency (those *with* whom research is done) as Tisdall et al., (2009) have stated. Qualitative methods require that we examine closely not only how we represent participants in our work, but how we prioritize whose purpose is being served with the research, how we manage power and control in our relationships, and the dynamics of ethics and politics in our work. The reflexive researcher/practitioner, therefore, engages the participant as co-researcher interpreting the actions, experiences, and meanings that evolve seamlessly within the social world where the behavior originates.

Mixed-Method Interventions Researchers who understand that quantitative or qualitative data alone cannot provide all the answers have successfully conducted, and found evidence for, mixed-method interventions designed to ameliorate a variety of problems, including those in the area of executive functions. For instance, Dekker et al. (2011) described a neuropsychological intervention with 46 eighth grade boys who had executive function problems. Half of the participants were assigned to a neuropsychological intervention group and the other half to a homework support group. Components of the intervention included psychoeducation and goal management training, while measures included objective neuropsychological tests as well as qualitative information from multiple informants such as students, parents, and teachers. Preliminary results showed that children receiving the intervention made greater improvements in executive functions; further, children showed greater satisfaction in the neuropsychological intervention group. Other studies have also reported success with mixed-method interventions for executive functions; for example, Kuruyer et al. (2017) studied eight elementary-age students experiencing reading difficulties in a pre-post, single-subject design using a reading enrichment intervention. The researchers used neuroimaging (fMRIs) to study brain activation during reading tasks as well as neuropsychological measures of attention and memory (e.g., Stroop Test, Digit Span Cancellation Test) to assess cognitive processes and neural structures and found that the students showed improvement in attention and memory that translated to improvements in reading skills. Faramarzi and Sadri (2014) designed mixed-method interventions for 30 second grade girls with dyscalculia that included objective measures of pre- and post-intervention performance as well as qualitative approaches, such as reinforcement, storytelling, and specific instructional practices like teaching students to plan and pay attention, and found significant difference between groups.

While many mixed-method interventions are reported to improve academic skills as well as cognitive function, some researchers, e.g., Butler et al. (2008) studying children who had survived cancer, found that along with medication and other therapies, children who received team-based, cognitive rehabilitation interventions that were psychologically based showed improvements in academic functioning but not in neurocognitive functioning. Similarly, Burns et al. (2016), in a meta-analysis of 37 studies that utilized neuropsychological interventions, determined that there was evidence for improvements in reading fluency and phonological/phonemic awareness but not for cognitive functioning. Despite this somewhat inconsistent evidence for the impact of mixed-method interventions, Butler and his colleagues (2008) have stated, "it is essential that we take a holistic approach to brain injury rehabilitation that attends to basic physiology, patient characteristics, the nature of the neurocognitive involvement, family-related functioning, the overall psychosocial environment, and with children/adolescents in particular, schooling and academic variables" (p. 257).

Several authors have discussed the importance of language in gathering data and setting up interventions in clinical neuropsychological settings. A shift toward recognition of the discursive and interpretive aspects of clinical interventions over the past 30+ years has given qualitative research a firm basis on which to design evidence-based interventions for neuropsychological practice. This turn in clinical practice and research acknowledges the importance of language as social action (Burr, 2003). Thus, language is perhaps the most familiar vehicle for data collection in the qualitative paradigm finding expression in narrative approaches to intervention (White, 2005) and storytelling as a way in which people make sense of their lives in the here and now. Narrative approaches in clinical practice, however, rely heavily on clients' ability to verbalize their subjective meanings in collaboration with the clinician. The challenge is finding ways to elicit trustworthy and detailed narratives that could serve as a resource for understanding clients' needs, plan interventions, and evaluate the effectiveness of outcomes following an intervention. Depending on the nature of the neuropsychological disorder, individuals often struggle to produce a coherent story (Bohn & Bernsten, 2008), have difficulty verbalizing or making sense of their past experiences, may be reticent to express meanings related to a specific traumatic experience, or lack the language proficiency to engage in transformative (therapeutic) dialogue.

Although language is the central component for much of qualitative data collection, we should not focus only on the *lingua franca* of the client and clinician. Rather, in all qualitative approaches, there are also nonverbal languages evident in various art forms and artifacts which people use to co-construct subjective and intersubjective meanings of their experiences. These nonverbal representations provide alternative explanations, descriptions, and perceptions (Gergen, 2001; Lock & Strong, 2010) that are often not evident when merely talking or verbalizing and that may provide confirmatory evidence of clients' verbal perceptions of their experiences. Because of their projective content, visual and arts-based research methods (Gerstenblatt, 2013; Mitchell, 2008) could help the practitioner gain access to personalized accounts of the participant's experiences, including those that have been suppressed due to their challenging content (van Schalkwyk, 2010), but may still have an impact on present behavior and relationships. Such methods in qualitative assessment therefore create space for clients' voices to emerge through the use of videos, photographs, drawings, cultural artifacts, visual graphics, and collage making (Gerstenblatt, 2013; Hiles & Chemak, 2008; Mitchell, 2008). These methods could assist clients diagnosed with neuropsychological deficits to make sense of their lived experiences as well as enable them to distance themselves from sensitive topics or challenging and suppressed experiences and become more willing to work with and through difficult memories during a neuropsychological intervention (Keat, Streickland, & Marinak, 2009; Knowles & Cole, 2008; Weber, 2008). Immersion in **multimodal performances** (i.e., both verbal and nonverbal storytelling) of the individual with neuropsychological challenges could thus help the researcher and clinician see linkages among strands of meanings and synthesize disparate observations for a holistic conceptualization of evidence-based interventions.

Clinical neuropsychologists have offered some additional cautions when it comes to developing interventions. For example, researchers like Davis (2006) studied neuropsychological interventions for psychopathology which are often comorbid with neurological impairment. Additionally, Lange (2018) discussed the comorbidity of ADHD and developmental coordination disorder. Each argued for the importance of assessing and intervening with comorbid conditions because both were likely to cause disruption in functional activities of daily living. It is also likely that the impact of comorbid conditions is multiplicative, rather than additive.

Qualitative and mixed-method interventions with adults have found successes that are similar to those obtained with children. For example, Porter et al. (2017) used graph theory and cognitive instruction to assess impact in adult patients with TBI and found changes in brain function, including improved connectivity and new neural pathways. Other interventions that are growing in popularity include direct instruction in planning and specific academic skills and the incorporation of response to intervention strategies (Feifer, 2008). Interventions involving cognitive strategy training and biofeedback have been increasingly popular, particularly with practitioners, for example, studies have shown that children with ADHD who had a comprehensive assessment, including tests of intelligence, attention, and social-behavioral functioning, as well as clinical interviews and observations followed by direct cognitive instruction tended to do better on subsequent classroom tasks than children who did not (Goldstein & Naglieri, 2008). Clinical neuropsychologists are also asking that closer attention be paid to interventions that focus on long-term academic and behavioral changes in a client's response to brain injury, as well as the immediate, intermediate, and long-term psychosocial consequences of the injury (Goldstein & Naglieri, 2008; Louis & Isaac, 2016; Prigitano et al., 1995). In addition, Goldstein and Naglieri (2008) found that psychosocial interventions for ADHD were often better accepted by clients than were medications. Since treatment acceptability is related to treatment integrity and both are associated with superior outcomes for the recipients of treatments, it is important to use interventions that are likely to have high acceptability for clients. Other directives about interventions relate to a continuing emphasis on evidence-based practices, greater home-school collaboration (Davis, 2006), and both short-term and long-term evaluations of the effectiveness of interventions.

There are a number of other interventions that due to space limitations cannot be discussed in this chapter but which are described elsewhere (e.g., Dekker et al.,

2011; Eslinger, 2002; Hunter & Donders, 2007). These include interventions such as cognitive rehabilitation, pharmacological treatments for certain conditions including autism and ADHD, neurofeedback, neuroimaging techniques such as the use of fMRIs, computer games in rehabilitation, and developmentally appropriate interventions for adolescents that involve self-monitoring, peer interaction, and/or the use of social media.

Multicultural Considerations and Qualitative Research Methods

In a world that is becoming increasingly diverse, clinical neuropsychologists and others in the social sciences are being called by professional organizations like the American Board of Clinical Neuropsychology and the American Psychological Association to be **culturally sensitive** and **culturally competent** (Chittooran, 2011) and work with the heterogeneity of their clients to serve them most effectively. Unlike quantitative researchers who attempt to understand the world as it is, qualitative researchers attempt to understand it from the perspective of those who live and function in that world. This suggests that clinical neuropsychologists who use qualitative interventions to work with individuals from culturally diverse backgrounds must be particularly careful to treat them with dignity and respect, set aside their biases, and not judge them for behaviors that may differ from their own. In addition to an open and accepting attitude toward culturally diverse populations, there are certain specific behaviors that are important as well (Banks & Banks, 2014; Gollnick & Chinn, 2017); for example, language and communication styles can vary widely across cultures. Issues in this area could include the degree of formality and acceptable forms of address (e.g., using titles, avoiding first names), knowing which individuals to whom communication should be addressed (e.g., the oldest male in any group, never the female), understanding issues such as loss of face (e.g., not speaking to and through children in order to communicate with adults who do not speak the language), and nonverbal communication (e.g., maintaining a respectful physical distance from families).

Other issues that may pose conflicts have to do with the nature of relationships between professionals and families (e.g., families deferring to the clinical neuropsychologist's decisions instead of being true collaborative partners in their child's education, lack of willingness to challenge professional decisions, even if they disagree with them). Clinical neuropsychologists working with school professionals, such as teachers and counselors, must also remember that treatment **integrity** and treatment **acceptability** may be related to cultural differences. For example, teachers in a particular community may not follow an agreed-upon intervention because it conflicts with long-held cultural values. Incentivizing interventions may not be seen as appropriate in classrooms where achievement is the norm or where children are simply expected to follow adult directives, without professionals having to resort to extrinsic motivators to ensure compliance. Gender status is important; for example, boys tend to experience more delays than girls do in a variety of areas

(Dekker et al., 2011), or perhaps boys in certain cultural groups are expected to be strong and not have to seek assistance, resulting in families not being amenable to professional intervention. Ethical issues and religious or spiritual considerations cannot be ignored (e.g., values conflicts, acceptance of poor outcomes because "it's God's will"). Other cultural variables (e.g., social class, educational level, generational status, disability) will also have an impact on the success of interventions. A more extensive discussion of cultural issues in designing and implementing interventions is beyond the scope of this chapter; however, **cultural sensitivity** should underlie everything we do with clients and their families, regardless of our cultural differences.

Implications for Professional Practice

The move toward qualitative and mixed-methods in clinical neuropsychology has implications for professional practice. These changes have resulted in recognition that **quantitative methods alone** cannot yield adequate information about strengths and weaknesses of clients and must be supplemented by qualitative methods (e.g., Dykens, 2015). This in turn has resulted in increased collaboration across disciplines such as education and the neurosciences (e.g., Dubinsky, 2010; Feifer, 2008; Koch et al., 2013; Tommerdahl, 2010). Similarly, there appears to be a greater degree of collaboration between professionals and stakeholders (e.g., O'Brien et al., 2016); that is, individuals with a stake in the outcomes, such as the client, his or her family, and teachers, are invited to provide feedback and input at each step along the way, thereby enhancing treatment integrity and treatment acceptability.

Interventions designed to treat neurological injury have become increasingly complex. For example, the ability to study brain structure and function, along with the increasing sophistication of neuropsychological measures, has allowed practitioners to design and assess the impact of interventions in a variety of settings in a way that was previously not possible. Advances in medical technology and the neurosciences have allowed us to use neuropsychological approaches to examine changes in the brains of individuals in response to interventions (Witsken et al., 2008), thereby providing confirmatory evidence of the reciprocal relationship between the brain and behavior.

In response to changes in neuropsychological research and practice, training programs in school psychology, clinical psychology, neuropsychology, and related fields have begun to include more courses in intermediate and advanced qualitative research as well as data-based, **multidimensional interventions**. Training programs are offering field placements and internships that provide students with a range of experiences that will better prepare them for the world of work. Institutions of higher learning are staffing their programs with qualified, competent faculty and are developing curricula, majors, and certificates designed to graduate well-prepared professionals. Professional bodies including the American Psychological

Association have promoted specialty groups such as its Society for Clinical Neuropsychology (Division 40), and a number of peer-reviewed journals (e.g., the American Academy of Clinical Neuropsychology's *The Clinical Neuropsychologist*) have been established to serve the needs of researchers and practitioners in this growing field.

Implications for the Future

Clinical neuropsychology in years to come is likely to look different than it does today. Continued advances in medicine and its application to human behavior, combined with the use of qualitative methodologies, will result in even better ways to assess, diagnose, and intervene with children and adults with neurological deficits; this, in turn, will result in improved outcomes for these populations. The influx of qualitative research methodologies is likely to increase as well. Researchers (e.g., Alderfer & Sood, 2016; Chittooran et al., in press; Dubois et al., 2012; Madill & Gough, 2008) have promoted the acceptance of such methodologies in specialties as wide-ranging as education, school psychology, pediatric psychology, and clinical practice, as well as the integration of mixed methods that incorporate a variety of research paradigms so that we are better able to resolve the multiplicity of our clients' presenting problems. The kind of **ecological neuropsychology** that D'Amato and Wang (2015) call for, rather than a medically driven neuropsychology, will take hold as neuropsychologists consider clients within the context of their daily lives, so that they do not separate individuals from their presenting problems nor do they try to treat these problems independently of their home, school, or work environments.

Evidence-based approaches will become more common as time goes on and as calls for professional accountability increase. As evidence-based approaches gain a firmer foothold and as research evidence accumulates, so inevitably will interventions based on **collaborations** across research paradigms and disciplines (e.g., Koch et al., 2013). Similarly, as teachers become more familiar with the applicability of neuropsychology to classroom instruction and as collaborations between teachers and school psychologists increase, we are likely to see a greater number of classroom interventions, for example, in reading and math, that are based on **neuropsychological data** (Burns et al., 2016). Researchers (e.g., Cleary & Scott, 2011; Witsken et al., 2008) suggest that advances in clinical neuropsychology will inevitably contribute to improved school psychological services, in that we not only have greater access to client data than we had previously but also data that vary in complexity and depth. Cleary and Scott (2011) have advocated for the use of neuropsychological information to enhance school psychology practice in several ways: interprofessional collaboration to develop and plan interventions based on neuropsychological assessments that integrate knowledge from various disciplines, the use of remedial and/or compensatory interventions that integrate neurodevelopmental principles as well as scientifically validated interventions, transparency and clarity of communication of neurodevelopmental principles and assessment results to all stakeholders, and the conduct of research regarding the efficacy of consultation and interventions in neuropsychological settings. Meta-analyses of quantitative studies (e.g., Burns et al., 2016) and meta-syntheses of qualitative studies (e.g., Sandelowski & Barroso, 2003; Walsh et al., 2016) are likely to increase as research productivity and output increase.

There are several areas of behavior in which research data and subsequently effective interventions are lacking; for example, there is very little research on the families of children with neurodevelopmental disorders (e.g., Dykens, 2015). As our definition of families expands, we can expect to see a growing emphasis on the needs of the child within the family and the ways in which family dynamics play a role in the success or failure of an intervention. International attention to the needs of immigrants, refugees, and English language learners will inevitably translate to improved efforts on their behalf as well as superior outcomes in all areas of functioning. Hiring, staffing, and professional development efforts will also continue to keep pace with changes in this burgeoning field.

Case Study

We present here a brief case study of 16-year-old Lia to illustrate the concepts presented in this chapter. We hope that an examination of the complexities of this case along with the guiding questions we have provided will allow readers to think about how qualitative methods can be used in conjunction with quantitative methods, not only to gather evidence-based data on a child but also to design an intervention that is likely to yield positive outcomes and ultimately enhance the functioning of the child.

Lia is a first-generation, 16-year-old Asian female in the 11th grade at West Oakfield High School in a small town in the United States. Over the summer, she was in a car accident when another car hit the passenger side of the car where she was sitting (without a seatbelt) and sent her flying through the windshield and sustaining serious injuries, which have since been treated. In addition to medical tests and treatment, Lia was administered a flexible battery assessment that included various subtests from the Halstead-Reitan Neuropsychological Battery designed to assess attention, memory, and planning, the Wechsler Intelligence Scale for Children-Fifth Edition, the Wechsler Individual Achievement Test (Third Edition), the Behavior Assessment Checklist completed by both her parents and homeroom teacher, behavioral observations in formal and informal settings, and clinical interviews with Lia, her family, and her teachers. She was diagnosed with a traumatic brain injury (TBI) with injury mainly to the cerebral cortex. She is currently functioning in the superior range of intellectual ability but demonstrated significant weaknesses on WISC-V subtests that required her to plan, remember, and use judgment. Her skills in reading comprehension and math reasoning have been affected, but her skills in reading recognition and math calculation have not. Receptive language shows some deficits, but oral and written expression show significant deficits.

Lia is also in physical therapy for injuries to her back and meets weekly with a school psychologist to help her adjust to her injury. Lia is described as being moody, difficult to live with, and impatient with herself. Her relationship with her parents, two younger brothers, and friends has deteriorated. This is the year that Lia was to apply to a premed program, but she has told her family that she wants to take a year off to "*decide what I'm going to do with myself, IF anything.*" Lia used to play forward on the school soccer team but has had to stay out for the season and is not happy about that at all. Lia's parents are doing everything they can for her but are worried about their daughter and her future. The happy, sunny girl they all knew has disappeared, only to be replaced by a moody, young woman who seems to be miserable most of the time.

- What is the presenting problem(s)? Which problem(s) is a priority? Which is causing the most disruption to Lia's daily functioning? To others?
- Is additional assessment necessary? If so, what kinds of assessment? In what areas? By whom?
- What are the clinician's overall goals for Lia? Specific objectives? Goals and objectives can relate to one or more areas of functioning (e.g., academic, behavioral, social-emotional, motor). Is there a timeline?
- Are there particular elements of the situation that demand specific kinds of data collection (quantitative, qualitative, or mixed methods)? Can they be used by themselves or concomitantly with other approaches?
- Are there particular qualitative methodologies that the clinician might use (e.g., observations or clinical interviews) that might be particularly suited to the proposed intervention? To Lia's age and developmental status?
- Is the proposed intervention multidimensional? Multimethod? Multidisciplinary?
- Has the clinician considered issues of treatment acceptability? Treatment integrity? What are some facilitating factors? Barriers to success?
- Are there limits to the clinician's professional competence? If there are, with which professionals does he or she need to collaborate? On what parts?
- Is the clinician paying attention to the context in which interventions will be implemented? What factors in Lia's home and school environment need to be considered? Are there cultural factors that are being overlooked?
- Is the clinician incorporating the perspectives of all those who have relevant information to share about the phenomenon under study (i.e., Lia, her family, school personnel)?
- Has the clinician developed a detailed intervention plan that includes a rationale, details of each component of the intervention, persons responsible, and a timeline?
- Does the clinician have a plan for evaluation of the effectiveness of the intervention? What about modification of the intervention, given the results of this evaluation?
- Is there a plan for dissemination of the results of the intervention? Who should receive the information? In what form?

Conclusions

This chapter has addressed how clinical neuropsychologists can use **qualitative data** to design and implement interventions that will contribute to **effective outcomes** for children and their families. While quantitative approaches have stayed at the forefront of clinical neuropsychology for many years, both researchers and practitioners are realizing that these numeric, post-positivistic approaches are no longer fully adequate to make sense of phenomena under investigation and that we need to expand our repertoire to include *qualitative and mixed-method approaches* to assess and plan for clients. The field of clinical neuropsychology has grown dramatically. Just a little over 20 years ago, Prigatano et al., (1995) stated how important it was to have interventions that could be **replicated** and that were based on **hypotheses** for behavior. Today, however, we are developing interventions that are grounded in our daily lives, do not have to be replicated in exactly the same way, and do not have to be based on explanatory, testable hypotheses for behavior. The question to be asked, instead, is: *Are the interventions we use based on data, do they provide insight into the functioning of individuals, do they help us use those insights to add to our clinical judgments about clients, and are they, at the very least, founded on evidence-based information about what might be going on with the children and adults who are in our charge*? While a continued paradigmatic shift is inevitable and progress may be slow, we must be vigilant so that we can continue to develop **effective evidence-based interventions** for clinical neuropsychology practice and so enhance outcomes for children and families.

Discussion Questions

1. What are the benefits of conducting qualitative research as it relates to neuropsychology?
2. What types of qualitative research designs serve as the foundation for evidence-based interventions?
3. Describe the type of qualitative assessments that can be beneficial during a neuropsychological evaluation.
4. Discuss the process of using the Collage Life Story Elicitation Technique (CLET).
5. What are some multicultural factors to consider during a qualitative assessment, such as the CLET?

EPPP Sample Questions

1. Qualitative methods in neuropsychology rely on complex reasoning moving dialectically between ______ and used in conjunction with quantitative methods in a(n)_____:
   (a) deductive, inductive and abductive methods; mixed-method design
   (b) abductive methods; experimental design
   (c) confirmatory, controlled designs; qualitative design
   (d) evidence-based approaches; mixed-method design
2. Which of the following would provide comprehensive data about brain-behavior relationships in a client?
   (a) Frequency of seizures
   (b) Idiographic data
   (c) Experimental and experiential evidence
   (d) Observations of behavior in naturalistic settings
3. Which of the following would provide information about the way in which a person with a traumatic brain injury constructs reality preceding or following that injury?
   (a) Rating scales
   (b) Narrative inquiry
   (c) Case study methodology
   (d) Behavioral observations
4. Interventions utilizing mixed methods allow the clinical neuropsychologist to study:
   (a) A variety of problems, including those in executive functioning
   (b) Cognitive processes involved in reading
   (c) Neural structures relevant to attention and memory
   (d) Primarily goal management training
5. Qualitative, research-based interventions in clinical neuropsychology in multicultural settings should:
   (a) Use artifacts that are culturally relevant to the client
   (b) Treat clients with dignity despite their cultural differences
   (c) Provide advice to families that they can follow at home
   (d) All of the above

   Answers: A, C, B, A, D

Proactive Readings

Transcending the Past

Burr, V. (2003). *Social Constructionism* (2nd ed.). Routledge.
D'Amato, R. C. & Perfect, M. (2020). History of the future of proactive school psychology: Historical review at our 75th APA anniversary to transcend the past, excel in the present, and transform the future. *School Psychology 35*(6), 375–384. DOI:10.1037/spq0000420.
Eslinger, P. J. Ed. (2002). *Neuropsychological interventions: Clinical research and practice*. Guilford.

Excelling in the Present

Clandinin, D. J., & Connelly, F. M. (2000). *Narrative Inquiry*. Jossey-Bass.
Nastasi, B. K., Chittooran, M. (R.) M., Arora, P., & Song, S. (2020). Infusing global and intercultural perspectives to transform school psychology and school psychologists. *School Psychology, 35*(6), 440–450. DOI: 10.1037/spq0000403
Willig, C. (2008). *Introducing qualitative research in psychology* (2nd ed.). Open University Press.

Transforming the Future

Popay, J. (Ed.). (2006). *Moving beyond effectiveness in evidence synthesis: Methodological issues in the synthesis of diverse sources of evidence.* National Institute for Health and Clinical Excellence. http://www.nice.org.uk/page.aspx?o=530093
Yin, R. K. (2013). *Case Study Research: Design and Methods* (5th ed.). Sage Inc.

References

Alderfer, M. A., & Sood, E. (2016). Using qualitative research methods to improve clinical care in pediatric psychology. *Clinical Practice in Pediatric Psychology, 4*(4), 358–361. https://doi.org/10.1037/cpp0000164
Baquedano, C., & Fabar, C. (2017). Modeling subjects' experience while modelling the experimental design: A mild-neurophenomenology-inspired approach in the piloting phase. *Constructivist Foundations, 12*(2), 166–180.
Bell, V., & Halligan, P. (2004). Neuropsychological interventions: Clinical research and practice. *Brain, 127*(1), 237–238. https://doi.org/10.1093/brain/awh026

Banks, J. A., & Banks, C. A. M. (2014). Multicultural education: Issues and perspectives (7th ed.). Wiley.
Bertrando, P., & Arcelloni, T. (2006). Hypotheses are dialogues: Sharing hypotheses with clients. *Journal of Family Therapy, 28*, 370–387. https://doi.org/10.1111/j.1467-6427.2006.00358.x
Bohn, A., & Berntsen, D. (2008). Life story development in childhood: The development of life story abilities and the acquisition of cultural life scripts from late middle childhood to adolescence. *Developmental Psychology, 44*, 1135–1147. http://dx.doi.org/10.1037/0012-1649.44.4.1135
Braun, V., & Clarke, V. (2014). What can "thematic analysis" offer health and wellbeing researchers? *International Journal of Qualitative Studies in Health and Wellbeing, 9*, 1–2. https://doi.org/10.3402/qhw.v9.26152
Burns, M. K., Peterson-Brown, S., Haegele, K., Rodriguez, M., Schmitt, B., Coper, M., … VanDerHeyden, A. M. (2016). Meta-analysis of academic interventions derived from neuropsychological data. *School Psychology Quarterly, 31*(1), 28–42. doi: 10.1037/spq0000117
Burr, V. (2003). *Social constructionism* (2nd ed.). Routledge.
Butler, R. W., Sahler, O. J. Z., Akins, M. A., Alderfer, M. A., Katz, E. R., Phipps, S., & Noll, R. B. (2008). Interventions to improve neuropsychological functioning in childhood cancer survivors. *Developmental Disabilities Research Reviews, 14*, 251–258. doi: 10.1002/ddrr.33
Chan, E. (2004). Narratives of experience: How culture matters to children's development. *Contemporary Issues in Early Childhood, 5*(2), 145–159. https://doi.org/10.2304/ciec.2004.5.2.3
Chittooran, M. M. (2011, April). *Culturally competent research with children: Implications for the public good.* Paper presented at the Annual Meeting of the American Educational Research Association, New Orleans, LA.
Chittooran, M. M., D'Amato, R. C., & Wang, A. (in press). Research and publication in global settings: An editorial perspective. In C. Hatzichristou & B. Nastasi (Eds.), *Handbook of school psychology in a global context*. Springer.
Clandinin, D. J., & Connelly, F. M. (2000). *Narrative inquiry*. Jossey-Bass.
Cleary, M. J. & Scott, A. (2011). Developments in school neuropsychology: Implications for school psychological practice. *Journal of School Health, 81*(1), 1–7. DOI: 10.1111/j.1746-1561.2010.00550.x
Creswell, J. W. (2007). *Qualitative inquiry and research design: Choosing among five approaches* (2nd ed.). Sage.
Creswell, J. W., & Plano-Clark, V. L. (2011). *Designing and conducting mixed methods research*. Sage.
D'Amato, R. C., & Wang, Y. Y. (2015). Using a brain-based approach to collaborative teaching and learning with Asians. *[In G. J. van Schalkwyk and R. C. D'Amato's Special Issue, Facilitative collaborative knowledge co-construction.] New Directions for Teaching and Learning, 2*(143), 41–60. doi: 10.1002/tl.20132.doi:
Das Nair, R., Martin, K.-J., & Sinclair, E. J. (2014). A meta-synthesis of qualitative research on perceptions of people with long-term neurological conditions about group-based memory rehabilitation. *Neuropsychological Rehabilitation, 25*(4), 479–502. https://doi.org/10.1080/09602011.2014.971820
Davis, A. S. (2006). The neuropsychological basis of childhood psychopathology. *Psychology in the Schools, 43*(4), 503–512. https://doi.org/10.1002/pits.20164
Dekker, S. J., Krabbendam, L., Gemmink, M. M., De Groot, R. H. M., & Jolles, J. (2011, June). *Implementation of a neuropsychological intervention in secondary school: Targeting executive problems in young adolescent boys*. Poster presented at the 3rd biennial conference of the International Mind, Brain, and Education Society, San Diego, CA.
Diez-Itza, E., Martínez, V., & Antón, A. (2016). Narrative competence in Spanish-speaking adults with Williams syndrome. *Psicothema, 28*(3), 291–297. https://doi.org/10.7334/psicothema2015.190
Dubinsky, J. (2010). Neuroscience education for prekindergarten-12 teachers. *The Journal of Neuroscience, 30*, 8057–8060.

DuBois, J. M., Beskow, L., Campbell, J., Dugosh, K., Festinger, D., Hartz, S., … Lidz, C. (2012). Restoring balance: A consensus statement on the protection of vulnerable research participants. *American Journal of Public Health, 102*(12), 2220–2225. https://doi.org/10.2105/AJPH.2012.300757

Dykens, E. M. (2015). Family adjustment and interventions in neurodevelopmental disorders. *Current Opinion in Psychiatry, 28*(2), 121–126. https://doi.org/10.1097/YCO.0000000000000129

Eslinger, P. J. (Ed.). (2002). *Neuropsychological interventions: Clinical research and practice*. Guilford.

Faramarzi, S., & Sadri, S. (2014). The effect of basic neuropsychological interventions on performance of students with dyscalculia. *Neuropsychiatria i Neuropsychologia, 9*(2), 48–54.

Feifer, S. G. (2008). Integrating Response to Intervention (RTI) with neuropsychology: A scientific approach to reading. *Psychology in the Schools, 45*(9), 812–825.

Gay, G. (2013). Teaching to and through cultural diversity. *Curriculum Inquiry, 43*(1), 48–70. http://dx.doi.org/10.1111/curi.12002

Gergen, K. J. (2001). Psychological science in a postmodern context. *American Psychologist, 56*(10), 803–812. https://doi.org/10.1037//0003-066X.56.10.803

Gerstenblatt, P. (2013). Collage portraits as a method of analysis in qualitative research. *International Journal of Qualitative Methods, 2013*, 294–309. doi: 10.1177/160940691301200114

Goldstein, S., & Naglieri, J. (2008). The school neuropsychology of ADHD: Theory, assessment, and intervention. *Psychology in the Schools, 45*(9), 859–884. https://doi.org/10.1002/pits.20331

Harvey, P. D. (2012). Clinical applications of neuropsychological assessment. *Dialogues in Clinical Neuroscience, 14*(1), 91–99. doi: 10.31887/DCNS.2012.14.1/pharvey

Hiles, D., & Cermák, I. (2008). Narrative psychology. In C. Willig & W. Stainton-Rogers (Eds.), *The Sage handbook of qualitative research psychology* (pp. 147−164). Sage.

Hunsley, J. (2015). *The role of assessment in providing evidence-based treatments* (Power Point Slides). Lincoln, NE: Clinical Assessment Webinar Series, Buros Center for Testing.

Hunter, S. J., & Donders, J. (Eds.). (2007). *Pediatric neuropsychological intervention*. Cambridge University Press.

Johnson, H. F. (2016). Exploring the lived experience of people with dementia through interpretative phenomenological analysis. *The Qualitative Report, 21*(4), 695–711.

Karasz, A., & Singelis, T. M. (2009). Qualitative and mixed method research in cross-cultural psychology. *Journal of Cross-Cultural Psychology, 40*(6), 909–916. doi: 10.1177/0022022109349172

Keat, J. B., Strickland, M. J., & Marinak, B. A. (2009). Child voice: How immigrant children enlightened their teachers with a camera. *Early Childhood Education Journal, 37*, 13–21. https://doi.org/10.1007/s10643-009-0324-1

Kidd, S. A. (2002). The role of qualitative research in psychology journals. *Psychological Methods, 7*(1), 126–138. doi: 10.1037//1082-989X.7.1.126

Knowles, J. G., & Cole, A. L. (2008). *Handbook of the arts in qualitative research: Perspectives, methodologies, examples, and issues*. Sage.

Koch, K. R., Timmerman, L., Peiffer, A. M., & Laurienti, P. J. (2013). Convergence of two independent roads leads to collaboration between education and neuroscience. *Psychology in the Schools, 50*(6), 577–588. doi: 10.1002/pits.21692

Kratochwill, T. R., & Shernoff, E. S. (2003). Evidence-based practice: Promoting evidence-based interventions in school psychology. *School Psychology Quarterly, 18*(4), 389–408. https://doi.org/10.1521/scpq.18.4.389.27000

Kulkofsky, S., & Klemfuss, J. Z. (2008). What the stories children tell can tell about their memory: Narrative skills in young children's suggestibility. *Developmental Psychology, 44*(5), 1442–1456. https://doi.org/10.1037/a0012849

Kuruyer, H. G., Akyol, H., Karli Oguz, K., & Has, A. C. (2017). The effect of an enrichment reading program on the cognitive processes and neural structures of children having reading difficulties. *International Electronic Journal of Elementary Education, 9*(4), 809–828.

Lange, S. M. (2018). ADHD and comorbid Developmental Coordination Disorder: Implications and recommendations for school psychologists. *Contemporary School Psychology, 22*(1), 30–39.

Lasanen, M., Määttä, K., & Uusiautti, S. (2017). 'I am not alone' – An ethnographic research on the peer support among northern-Finnish children with hearing loss. *Journal of Early Child Development and Care*. https://doi.org/10.1080/03004430.2017.1371704

Lezak, M. D. (1995). *Neuropsychological assessment* (3rd ed.). Oxford University Press.

Lezak, M. D., Howieson, D. B., Bigler, E. D., & Tranel, D. (2012). *Neuropsychological assessment* (5th ed.). Oxford University Press.

Lloyd, V., Gatherer, A., & Kalsy, S. (2006). Conducting qualitative interview research with people with expressive language difficulties. *Qualitative Health Research, 16*(10), 1386–1404. https://doi.org/10.1177/1049732306293846

Lock, A., & Strong, T. (2010). *Social constructionism: Sources and stirrings in theory and practice*. Cambridge University Press.

Louis, P. T., & Isaac, A. E. (2016). Implementing psychosocial intervention to improve the neuropsychological functioning of students with learning disabilities. *Pertanika Journal of Social Sciences and Humanities, 24*(1), 9–114.

Madill, A., & Gough, B. (2008). Qualitative research and its place in psychological science. *Psychological Methods, 13*(3), 254–271. doi: 10.1037/a0013220

McCaslin, M. L., & Scott, K. W. (2003). The five-question method for framing a qualitative research study. *The Qualitative Report, 8*(3), 447–461. http://www.nova.edu/ssss/QR/QR8-3/mccaslin.pdf

Miles, M. B., Huberman, A. M., & Saldana, J. (2014). *Qualitative data analysis: A methods sourcebook* (3rd ed.). Sage.

Mitchell, C. (2008). Getting the picture and changing the picture: Visual methodologies and educational research in South Africa. *South African Journal of Education, 28*, 365–383.

Murphy, K., & Vaidya, A. (2004). Recommendations for best practice in cognitive rehabilitation therapy: Acquired brain injury. *Society for Cognitive Rehabilitation*, 2–58.

O'Brien, N., Heaven, B., Teal, G., Evans, E. H., Cleland, C., Moffatt, S., … Moynihan, P. (2016). Integrating evidence from systematic reviews, qualitative research, and expert knowledge using co-design techniques to develop a web-based intervention for people in the retirement transition. *Journal of Medical Internet Research, 18*(8), e210. https://doi.org/10.2196/jmir.5790

Petticrew, M., & Roberts, H. (2006). *Systematic reviews in the social sciences: A practical guide*. Blackwell Publishing.

Popay, J. (Ed.). (2006). *Moving beyond effectiveness in evidence synthesis: Methodological issues in the synthesis of diverse sources of evidence*. National Institute for Health and Clinical Excellence. http://www.nice.org.uk/page.aspx?o=530093

Porter, S., Torres, I. J., Panenka, W., Rajwani, Z., Fawcett, D., Hyder, A., & Virji-Babul, N. (2017). Changes in brain-behavior relationships following a 3-month pilot cognitive intervention program for adults with traumatic brain injury. *Heliyon, 3*(8). https://doi.org/10.1016/j.heliyon.2017.e00373

Prigitano, G. P., Parsons, O. A., & Bortz, J. J. (1995). Methodological considerations in neuropsychological research: 17 years later. *Psychological Assessment, 7*(3), 396–403. https://doi.org/10.1037/1040-3590.7.3.396

Rashid, M. (2016). *After a child's traumatic brain injury: An ethnographic study of being a parent*. Unpublished doctoral thesis, University of Alberta.

Rhodes, R. L., D'Amato, R. C., & Rothlisberg, B. A. (2008). Utilizing a neuropsychological paradigm for understanding educational and psychological tests. In C. R. Reynolds & E. Fletcher-Janzen (Eds.), *Handbook of Clinical Child Neuropsychology* (3rd ed.; pp. 321–348). Plenum.

Roberts, A. R., & Yeager, K. (Eds.). (2004). *Evidence-based practice manual: Research and outcome measures in health*. Oxford University Press.

Saleh, A., Fuchs, S., Warren, D. T., & Niarhos, F. (2018). Evaluating the consistency of scales used in adult attention deficit hyperactivity disorder assessment of college-aged adults. *Journal of American College Health, 66*(2), 98–105. https://doi.org/10.1080/07448481.2017.1377206

Sandelowski, M., & Barroso, J. (2003). Toward a metasynthesis of qualitative findings on motherhood in HIV-positive women. *Research in Nursing & Health, 26*(2), 153–170. doi: 10.1002/nur.10072

Sandelowski, M., & Barroso, J. (2007) *Handbook for Synthesizing Qualitative Research*. Springer.

Semrud-Clikeman, M., & Teeter Ellison, P. A. (2009). *Assessment and interventions for neurodevelopmental disorders* (2nd ed.). Springer.

Semrud-Clikeman, M., Wilkinson, A., & Wellington, T. M. (2005). Evaluating and using qualitative approaches to neuropsychological assessment. In R. C. D'Amato, E. Fletcher-Janzen, & C. R. Reynolds (Eds.), *Handbook of school neuropsychology* (pp. 287–302). Wiley.

Tisdall, E. K. M., Davis, H. M., & Gallagher, M. (2009). *Researching with children and young people: Research design, methods and analysis*. Sage.

Tommerdahl, J. (2010). A model for bridging the gap between neuroscience and education. *Oxford Review of Education, 36*, 97–109. http://dx.doi.org/10.1080/03054980903518936

Tracy, S. J. (2010). Qualitative quality: Eight "Big-Tent" criteria for excellent qualitative research. *Qualitative Inquiry, 16*(10), 837–851. https://doi.org/10.1177/1077800410383121

Traughber, M. C., & D'Amato, R. C. (2005). Integrating evidence-based neuropsychological services into school settings: Issues and challenges for the future. In R. C. D'Amato, E. Fletcher-Janzen, & C. R. Reynolds (Eds.), *Handbook of school neuropsychology* (pp. 827–857). Wiley.

van Schalkwyk, G. J. (2010). Collage Life Story Elicitation Technique: A representational technique for scaffolding autobiographical memories. *The Qualitative Report, 15*(3), 675–695. http://www.nova.edu/ssss/QR/QR15-3/vanschalkwyk.pdf

van Schalkwyk, G. J. (2013). Assessing individual or family dynamics through the Collage Life-story Elicitation Technique (CLET). In B. Gerrard & M. Soriano (Eds.), *School-based family counseling: Transforming family-school relationships* (pp. 419–439). Institute for School-Based Family Counseling.

van Schalkwyk, G. J. (2017). *The Collage Life-story Elicitation Technique (CLET): A workbook for researchers and practitioners*. Unpublished manuscript available from the author at gjvsumac@gmail.com

Waller, D. (2006) Art therapy for children: How it leads to change. *Clinical Child Psychology and Psychiatry, 11*(2), 271–282. http://dx.doi.org/10.1177/1359104506061419

Walsh, J., Corcoran, J., Crooks, P., Cooke, N., & Cummings, C. (2016). The lived experience of bipolar disorder: A systematic review and meta-synthesis. *Journal of Psychiatry and Mental health, 1*(2), 2–7. https://doi.org/10.16966/2474-7769.102

Weber, S. (2008). Using images in research. In J. G. Knowles & A. L. Cole (Eds.), *Handbook of the arts in qualitative research: Perspectives, methodologies, examples and issues* (pp. 41–54). Sage.

Whiffin, C. J., Ellis-Hill, C., Bailey, C., Jarrett, N., & Hutchinson, P. J. (2017). We are not the same people we used to be: An exploration of family biographical narratives and identity change following traumatic brain injury. *Journal of Neuropsychological Rehabilitation*. https://doi.org/10.1080/09602011.2017.1387577

White, M. (2005). Children, trauma and subordinate storyline development. *The International Journal of Narrative Therapy and Community Work, 2005*(3&4), 10–21.

Willig, C. (2008). *Introducing qualitative research in psychology* (2nd ed.). Open University Press.

Witsken, D., Stoeckel, A., & D'Amato, R. C. (2008). Leading educational change using a neuropsychological response-to-intervention approach: Linking the past, present, and future. *Psychology in the Schools, 45*(9), 781–798. doi: 10.1002/pits.20326

Yehl, A. (2009). Personal, thorough, and accessible: A review of Carla Willig's Introducing Qualitative Research in Psychology. *The Weekly Qualitative Report, 2*(16), 95–98. http://www.nova.edu/ssss/QR/WQR/willig.pdf

Yin, R. K. (2009). Case study research: Design and methods. Sage Inc.: California Neuropsychological Data. *School Psychology Quarterly, 31*(1), 28–42.

Zuluaga, P., Lopero, I., & Tobon, O. (2013). Clinical interview's functionality in evaluation, diagnosis and neuropsychological evaluation. *Revista Colombiana des ciencias sociales, 4*(2). https://doi.org/10.21501/issn.2216-1201

Chapter 8
Designing Quantitative Evidence-Based Interventions for Clinical Neuropsychology Practice

Andrew S. Davis, Cathrine M. Short, Amanda R. Slonaker, and Jacob Yuichung Chan

Learning Objectives

- To understand the difference between qualitative and quantitative interventions.
- To understand the Boston Process and Lurian approach to quantitative interventions.
- To understand how a quantitative approach such as applied behavior analysis can be used.
- To understand the use of cognitive rehabilitation.
- To understand how quantitative interventions are used to address academic concerns.
- To understand the importance of and how to assess acculturation.

Introduction to Quantitative Evidence-Based Interventions

Although the process of neuropsychological assessment may differ slightly for each clinician, there are several commonalities. These generally include a careful consideration of assessment scores and/or observable behaviors in the context of the patient's background information, including medical, educational, vocational, legal, psychiatric, and psychosocial history, as well as the production of a written report to document their findings. Another prototypical consideration is the generation of

A. S. Davis (✉) · C. M. Short · A. R. Slonaker
Department of Educational Psychology, Ball State University, Muncie, IN, USA
e-mail: davis@bsu.edu

J. Y. Chan
Department of Counseling Psychology, Social Psychology, and Counseling,
Ball State University, Muncie, IN, USA

R. C. D'Amato et al. (eds.), *Understanding the Biological Basis of Behavior*,
https://doi.org/10.1007/978-3-030-59162-5_8

evidence-based interventions and accommodations to help the patient and their family cope with identified deficits. Although many different types or recommendations may be provided, neuropsychologists are generally comfortable with quantitative interventions. Quantitative interventions are those that rely upon empirical data; for neuropsychologists this is typically generated through the use of valid and reliable neuropsychological tests that produce norm-referenced scores. This familiarity with quantitative interventions in the field of neuropsychology is, in part, due to the fact that most neuropsychologists come to the field with a thorough grounding in the field of tests and measurements, which is essential for understanding the psychometrics of the tests that they use. Entire texts are dedicated to the use of evidence-based interventions to treat neurological and psychiatric disorders. Indeed, these texts are essential to the practice of many applied psychologists, including counseling psychologists and school psychologists. The purpose of this chapter is not to provide the reader with a list of detailed interventions, but to rather discuss the process through which quantitative neuropsychological data can be used to generate recommendations for practitioners, the patient, and their families. Two theoretical approaches, the Boson Process Approach, and Lurian theory will be discussed as an approach to using quantitative interventions.

Boston Process Approach

Just like other psychologists, neuropsychologists use a variety of theoretical approaches and orientations in their practice. One of these, the Boston Process Approach, has gained popularity over the years, and in the past decades more standardized tests are starting to incorporate this approach. The Boston process approach was founded by Edith Kaplan in the 1960s (Libon et al., 2013) and is likely one of the most widely used ways of approaching and interpreting neuropsychological assessments. Indeed, a key principle in neuropsychological assessment is that it is important to understand why a deficit is present in addition to discovering that a deficit exists. Often, by the time a patient reaches a neuropsychologist they are likely to have seen other professionals such as teachers, nurses, physicians, school psychologists, or therapists. For example, if a child is having trouble reading, the teacher and/or the parent/guardian may realize it and attempt to intervene in the school. Usually, a referral will only be made to a neuropsychologist if those interventions are unsuccessful. As such, in this type of situation, the role of the neuropsychologist is not to determine that the child is having trouble reading but to determine what is causing the problem. The use of quantitative measures to uncover neurological processing deficits that may be contributing to a functional problem is at the heart of many neuropsychological assessments, and the Boston Process Approach provides a roadmap to accomplish this goal. Once a quantitative deficit, normative or intraindividual, has been uncovered, neuropsychologists can then start to consider how best to accommodate or intervene for that deficit.

The Boston Process Approach has largely become embedded throughout modern neuropsychology practice including forming the structural basis for some neuropsychological tests. For example, the *Delis-Kaplan Executive Function Systems* (D-KEFS; Delis et al., 2001a) uses the process approach to assess the individual functions of cognitive tasks that are deemed higher-level (Homack et al., 2005). Kaplan (1988) demonstrated that the use of single-score methods do not allow neuropsychologists to tap independent fundamental cognitive skills of executive functions. The D-KEFS allows for aspects of executive functions to be assessed independently for performance and impairments (Delis et al., 2001b). It also allows for more in-depth interpretation of functioning by providing error analyses that are converted into either scaled scores or cumulative percentages (Homack et al., 2005). The D-KEFS is an excellent example of a modern test that uses the Boston Process Approach, and this can be illustrated via their Trail Making Test (TMT). The TMT has five conditions, although only one of them is truly designed to measure executive functioning (Condition 4). The other four conditions are useful in interpreting performance on Condition 4. For example, poor performance on the fifth condition, Motor Speed, could inform the neuropsychologist that poor performance on Condition 4 was actually due to a motor speed deficit as opposed to a cognitive set-shifting deficit. This process allows clinicians to determine which executive functions are impaired versus spared to aid in differential diagnoses by examining profiles seen in different disorders and conditions (Homack et al., 2005).

Lurian Model

Alexander Romanovich Luria is one of the most important neuropsychologists of the twentieth century. Indeed, from a historical perspective his ideas have become so ingrained into modern practice it is difficult to imagine a time when assessment practice did not incorporate his philosophy. Luria (1973) described how mental functioning is hierarchical, involves many areas of the brain, and can be distinguished into three functional units that work together to produce the type of behavior that neuropsychologists now largely attempt to measure via a quantitative approach. The first unit Luria (1973) described involved the regulation of tone, walking, and mental capacities. It can be seen as the unit that regulates a person's alertness. Luria (1973) noted that the neuroanatomical areas that are captured under the first functional unit are the reticular formation, brainstem, limbic system, caudate nucleus, hippocampus, thalamus, hypothalamus, and the prefrontal cortex. The second functional unit involves receiving information, analyzing it, and storing it away for future retrieval and are controlled by the more posterior regions of the cortex, such as the temporal lobe, occipital lobe, and parietal lobe (Luria, 1973). The third functional unit involves the "programming, regulation, and verification" of information (Luria, 1973, p. 79). These functions comprised in unit three are regulated by areas anterior to the precentral gyrus, including the primary motor strip, premotor area, and frontal lobes (Luria, 1973).

Several neuropsychological tests have been adapted from Luria's theories, including the *NEPSY-II* (Korkman et al., 2007) and the *Kaufman Assessment Battery for Children, Second Edition* (KABC-II; Kaufman & Kaufman, 2004). Luria's theories are uniquely suited for neuropsychologists who want to use quantitative interventions. For example, an elderly adult who has been struggling with independent living secondary to cerebrovascular concerns may yet be able to reside independently with interventions in the home. Designing these types of interventions without knowing the etiology of the patient's difficulty with his activities of daily living is likely to be less efficacious than if the neuropsychologist can help the patient, and perhaps the patient's family, through interventions or accommodations targeting the exact problem. In this case, the problem could be that the patient does not exhibit sufficient arousal, vigilance, or directed attention (Unit 1) when completing financial activities, they may be struggling with the sequential nature of medication management (Unit 2), or integrating new complex medical information into their decision making process regarding informed consent (Unit 3). All of these difficulties are likely to interfere with the patient being able to manage their own finances, adhere to their medication regiment, and/or be able to provide informed consent for medical procedures yet are likely to require different interventions depending upon which unit(s) is contributing to the functional impairment.

Quantitative Evidence-Based Interventions for Neurodevelopmental Disorders

Neurodevelopmental disorders are a category of disorders in which the central nervous system is disrupted in some way that results in a developmental behavioral and/or neurocognitive delay for the individual relative to their peers. Although typically associated with children, neurodevelopmental disorders can be life-long and pervasive. This disruption in neurodevelopment can lead to impairment in a variety of domains, including motor, sensory, language, memory, overall cognitive abilities, and spatial skills, etc. These disruptions can also lead to and/or exacerbate psychiatric and physiological concerns in the individual. As such, neurodevelopmental disorders represent an ideal intersection of neurological, psychiatric, academic, and psychosocial dysfunction that is best addressed via a neuropsychological approach to intervention.

Individuals with Autism Spectrum Disorder

One neurodevelopmental disorder that has been extensively discussed in the literature due to its increasing prevalence is autism spectrum disorder (ASD). A well-studied quantitative approach to managing behaviors manifested in ASD is applied behavior analysis (ABA). ABA has been defined in the literature in many different ways. Furman and Lepper (2018) stated that ABA is "the scientific study of behavior change, using the principles of behavior, to evoke or elicit a targeted behavioral change" (p. 104). Cooper et al. (2007) noted that ABA "is the science in which tactics derived from the principles of behavior are applied systematically to improve socially significant behavior and experimentation is used to identify the variables responsible for behavior change" (p. 20). ABA can also be considered the most empirically researched and validated interventions for those with ASD (Tiura et al., 2017).

To use ABA as an evidence-based intervention, one generally completes a functional behavior assessment to hypothesize what is leading to behaviors occurring as well as possible reinforcements and/or punishments that could alter the target behavior. Once a system has been chosen on how to alter the behavior, there must be a plan set up for how to evaluate and analyze the behavior change to see if the intervention is effective (Cooper et al., 2007). In general, the earlier the intervention is put into place, the better chance of positive outcomes (Axelrod et al., 2012; Tiura et al., 2017). Early intensive behavioral interventions (EIBI) that use ABA principles focuses on operant learning, improving deficits in language, imitation skills, pre-academic skills, social skills, and self-help and other adaptive abilities (Peters-Scheffer et al., 2011). A meta-analysis by Peters-Scheffer et al. (2011) noted that children with ASD who completed EIBI outperformed those who received other treatments, such as eclectic treatment, parent-directed ABA, and treatments as usual (public early intervention, nursery provision, or school-based interventions) in the areas of adaptive skills, expressive language, receptive language, nonverbal IQ, and IQ scores.

Tiura et al. (2017) provided ABA therapy to 35 participants with ASD and measured their developmental functioning (cognitive, communication, social-emotional, adaptive, and physical) using the *Developmental Profile, Third Edition* (DP-3; Alpern, 2007). They assessed growth predictor variables including cognitive functioning, age at entry, diagnosis severity, treatment hours, primary language, gender, and parent's level of education. Tiura et al. found cognitive functioning assessed at the entry of ABA therapy was the most predictive variable of children's growth rates in all five developmental domains. More specifically, they noted that the higher the cognitive functioning at the entry of ABA therapy, the faster the growth rates in all domains assessed. Other variables that predicted developmental domain growth included diagnosis severity predicted physical development growth, speaking English as the primary language predicted social-emotional and physical development growth, and male gender predicted faster adaptive and physical development growth (Tiura et al., 2017). These results indicate that developmental growth depends not only on access and completion of ABA therapy but also diagnosis severity, the language primarily spoken by the child, and the gender of the child.

Individuals with Traumatic Brain Injuries

Traumatic brain injury (TBI) is broadly defined for individuals with damage to brain tissue resulting from external forces such as accidents, falls, violence, sport activities, or penetration of the skull by a foreign object (NIH Consensus with

Traumatic Brain Injury, 1999). According to the Centers for Disease Control and Prevention (CDC), about 2.87 million TBI-related emergency department (ED) visits, hospitalizations, and deaths were recorded in the United States in 2014. Additionally, an average of 155 people die in the United States each day from injuries associated with having had a TBI within that same year (CDC, 2019). Psychologists and neuropsychologists are often part of a rehabilitation team and are tasked to provide assessment and intervention (Ricker, 2010). The following section discusses evidence-based interventions for TBI.

Behavior Management

Patients with TBI often exhibit behavioral disturbances such as agitation, aggression, and various types of impaired social functioning (Ricker, 2010); given the dependence of socially appropriate behavior on inhibition, planning, and other executive functions it stands to reason this is a significant concern for many patients with TBI. Behavior management may be broadly based on operant learning theory's key components of reinforcement, punishment, or a combination of both (Wood & Alderman, 2011). Behavior management intervention strategies include, but are not limited to, redirection and verbal praise for prosocial behavior, time-out procedure, and checklist with token rewards and have been tested and applied to adults, adolescents, and children with TBI (Carnevale et al., 2006; Slifer & Amari, 2009).

Cognitive Rehabilitation

According to the Brain Injury Special Interest Group of the American Congress of Rehabilitation Medicine, cognitive rehabilitation is defined

> as a systematic, functionally oriented service of therapeutic activities that is based on assessment and understanding of the patient's brain-behavioral deficits. Specific interventions may have various approaches, including (1) reinforcing, strengthening, or reestablishing previously learned patterns of behavior; (2) establishing new patterns of cognitive activity through compensatory cognitive mechanisms for impaired neurologic systems; (3) establishing new patterns of activity through external compensatory mechanisms such as personal orthoses or environmental structuring and support; and (4) enabling persons to adapt to their cognitive disability, even though it may not be possible to directly modify or compensate for cognitive impairments, in order to improve their overall level of functioning and quality of life" (Cicerone et al., 2000, pp 1596-1597).

Hart (2010) described that cognitive rehabilitation has two approaches – restorative and compensatory. Restorative approaches aim at restoring damaged functioning to the pre-injury stage and involve retraining using repetitive activities (e.g. forced-use technique) while compensatory approaches seek to avoid damaged functions and focus on intact functions or creative strategies. Attention, language, memory, and executive function are some of the targeted areas where cognitive rehabilitation has found success in both children and adults with TBI (Cicerone et al., 2011; Cimolin et al., 2012). This highlights the importance of considering quantitative data in considering both premorbid functioning as well as measuring these cognitive domains.

Psychotherapy

The comorbidity of mental health issues such as depression, anxiety, posttraumatic stress disorder (PTSD), and suicide among patients with TBI has been long established (Brenner et al., 2011; Hart et al., 2011; Moore et al., 2006). Psychotherapy, especially cognitive behavioral therapy (CBT), has been the focus of treatment for mental health issues related to TBI. Vanderploeg et al. (2019) recently conducted a review of the literature and reported that CBTs have been superior to cognitive rehabilitation in treating postconcussive symptoms (e.g., dizziness, light and noise sensitivity, poor attention, forgetfulness, depression) among patients with a history of TBI. In addition, specific forms of CBT or cognitive therapy (CT) have been shown to be effective in working with people with TBI. For example, Bédard et al. (2012) incorporated mindfulness-based components into cognitive therapy and found that the treatment was efficacious in reducing depression in their sample with TBI. Cognitive Processing Therapy (CPT), a cognitive therapy, has been widely studied and endorsed by the Veteran Administration for the treatment of PTSD (Hamblen et al., 2019). Chard et al. (2011) and Walter et al. (2014) have provided quantitative evidence, including RCTs, supporting the effectiveness of CPT on treating people with PTSD and TBI.

Individuals Presenting with Strokes

According to the Centers for Disease Control, stroke (cerebrovascular accident) is the fifth leading cause of death in the U.S. and is a major cause of serious disability for adults (CDC, 2019). Stroke is defined as "an acute neurological dysfunction of vascular origin with sudden or at least rapid occurrence of symptoms and signs corresponding to the involvement of focal areas of the brain" (World Health Organization, 1989, p. 1412). The two main categories of stroke are cerebral infarction or ischemic stroke and hemorrhage (Caplan, 2010). Psychologists are often tasked with assessment and intervention in both acute and postacute rehabilitations (Caplan, 2010).

Cognitive Rehabilitation

Similar to patients with TBI, cognitive rehabilitation has been shown to be beneficial for patients with stroke. Lincoln et al. (2012) stated that psychologists tend to provide rehabilitation for attention, memory, executive functioning, and perceptual impairments. Again, the two main approaches are restorative and compensatory (or restitution and compensation; Lincoln et al., 2012).

Constraint-Induced Movement Therapy

Backed by basic research (e.g., animal research and human subject) and subsequently clinical application, Constraint-Induced (CI) Movement Therapy has been tested and supported by quantitative evidence, including randomized clinical trials, in helping patients with stroke to improve upper extremity function (Taub et al., 1999). CI therapy operates through using intense functionally oriented task practice of the more impaired extremity while restraining the less-impaired extremity for most waking hours. For example, CI therapy involves inducing use of the more affected upper limb for a target of 90 percent of waking hours. This is done through the application of one of several methods, such as placing the hand in a mitt or the entire arm in a sling. The purpose of which is to constrain or reduce the use of the less-impaired limb for a few weeks in order to strengthen the use of the more impaired limb (Wolf et al., 2006).

Psychotherapy

Poststroke depression has been reported for decades in the US and abroad (Caplan, 2010; Jørgensen et al., 2016; Limampai et al., 2017) and studies of correlates of poststroke depression have been published (Taylor-Rowan et al., 2019). Similarly, poststroke anxiety has been well recorded (Caplan, 2010; Cumming et al., 2016). Despite the established record of poststroke depression and anxiety and the ample evidence available in justifying the use of psychotherapy, findings of its effectiveness in helping patients with poststroke mental health issues have been inconsistent (Kootker et al., 2017; Lincoln & Flannaghan, 2003). This is incompatible with the belief of general health care professionals that psychotherapy and its specific or related components (e.g., problem-solving techniques; motivational interviewing) are effective in treating poststroke mental health issues (Hildebrand, 2015). While typical treatments on poststroke depression have focused on pharmacologic options, the efficacy and safety of pharmacotherapy in poststroke depression remains controversial. Thus, it is important to review the evidence that does exist for the efficacy and effectiveness of psychotherapeutic interventions. For instance, there is emerging evidence that psychotherapy is effective for poststroke depression. Wang et al. (2018) conducted a meta-analysis (23 RCTs) and showed that cognitive behavioral treatment (CBT) had significantly decreased depressive symptoms and increased patient's remission and response rates among poststroke patients. In addition, CBT was shown to improve patients' poststroke anxiety, neurological functional deficits, and activities of daily living. However, the generalizability of these findings to a U.S. sample is unclear as none of the studies included in the meta-analysis were conducted in the U.S. The majority of the studies were conducted in China (with two conducted in Europe). Wang et al. concluded that RCTs with higher quality are needed to draw more affirmative conclusions.

Quantitative Evidence-Based Interventions for Academic and Vocational Functioning

Research is clear that use of quantitative evidence-based interventions for academic and vocational functioning enhances outcomes. However, areas of deficit can impact performance. As such, interventions and strategies to improve performance are imperative to ensure success in school and into adulthood.

Learning and Memory Functioning

Learning and memory play an important role in daily functioning, particularly in the school or academic setting. A meta-analysis by Schaffer and Geva (2016) conducted on memory strategies and interventions indicated that multiple strategies serve to improve memory. Such strategies include silent rehearsal, mnemonics, semantic clustering, and retrieval practice. While academic and vocational deficits may occur due to difficulties with learning and memory, it is important to consider that such strategies can be used in conjunction with interventions specifically aimed to address specific learning disorders, particularly with regard to reading, mathematics, and written expression. As such, the following interventions for dyslexia, dyscalculia, and dysgraphia are provided to illustrate how quantitative interventions could assist with the learning and retention of information for students within the academic setting as well as for adolescents and adults in vocational settings.

Dyslexia

Dyslexia is a neurodevelopmental disorder which affects basic reading and spelling skill development, including phonological awareness (D'Mello & Gabrieli, 2018; Mather & Wendline, 2012). The American Psychiatric Association (2013) identifies dyslexia to be characterized by difficulties with word recognition accuracy and fluency, decoding words, and spelling words (APA, 2013). Early intervention is of utmost importance given neurological sensitive periods; however, interventions can be effective from childhood through adulthood (Mather & Wendline, 2012). Indeed, multiple neuroimaging studies demonstrate neuroplasticity, or the brain's ability to change based on experience, for children and adults with dyslexia (Gaab et al., 2007; Krafnick et al., 2011; Shaywitz et al., 2004). Decades of research on reading has demonstrated the effectiveness of quantitative interventions, and neuropsychologists can facilitate this process by helping to identify the genesis of the deficit.

Learning to read and spell in the English language is contingent on the learning of the alphabetic principle: graphemes, or letters, are represented by phonemes, or units of sound. As such, individuals with dyslexia may benefit from phonological-based approaches (Duff & Clarke, 2011) depending upon the underlying neurological processing difficulty. Direct instruction in phonological awareness has been shown to remediate deficits in reading accuracy and decoding (D'Mello & Gabrieli, 2018). A meta-analysis conducted by the National Institute of Child Health and Human Development (2000) concluded that systematic phonics instruction yielded improvement in both reading and spelling skills. This was particularly evident for children in early grades (i.e., kindergarten and 1st grade), demonstrating the importance of early intervention. Specific phonics instruction methods include teaching letter–sound relationships and the use of letters and sounds to read and spell. Using a systematic approach, students are taught the alphabetic system and its application to reading and spelling (NICHD, 2000).

Fluency difficulties can persist for children as they get older, particularly as the academic environment necessitates reading more complex material (Gabrieli, 2009). Difficulty with fluency can also limit vocational success, particularly when employers assume the individual is able to read instructions and/or novel information at a rate commensurate with their peers and may misattribute a fluency difficulty to noncompliance or laziness. However, there is research that demonstrates improved reading fluency with intervention. The aforementioned meta-analysis by NICHD (2000) indicated repeated readings (i.e., a student repeatedly reads a passage and receives corrective feedback when needed) to be a fluency intervention with a significant effect for students with reading fluency difficulties. Of note, though, is that the effects of fluency intervention were within the greater context of broad reading instruction.

Dyscalculia

Dyscalculia is a neurodevelopmental disorder characterized by difficulty learning math facts, processing information using numbers, as well as accurate and fluent mathematical calculations (APA, 2013; Faramarzi & Sadri, 2014). A review of literature by Faramarzi and Sadri (2014) indicates that students with dyscalculia have difficulties with multiple aspects of neuropsychological functioning, including attention, executive functions, memory, language, and visual-spatial processing;

these abilities are essential for numerical accuracy (e.g., attending to information, visual reproduction of numbers and information), spatial processing, as well as mathematical reasoning (Wilkey et al., 2018). As such, when interventions for these areas are implemented, there has been improvement in math skills (Faramarzi & Sadri, 2014). This highlights the importance of considering quantitative-based neuropsychological assessment data when examining patients with these known or suspected conditions as it could be important to ascertain which function is impaired (and to what extent) prior to selecting the appropriate intervention.

A review of literature by Monei and Pedro (2017) indicated that researchers have demonstrated that individualized training for students with mathematical difficulties improved skills, including interventions focused on numerical knowledge, fluently and automatically retrieving and using math facts, as well as mental and written calculation. Strategies used also involved specific practice, feedback, and instruction on reading directions such that students learned to identify key points within the math problems (e.g., through circling or underlining key points) as well as the use of diagrams (Monei & Pedro, 2017). Improvement in learning math facts has been shown with the Cover-Copy-Compare method (Joseph et al., 2011; Skinner et al., 1997). In this method, the student is provided a sheet of math facts for practice, the math facts are studied, each fact is covered for a brief moment, the student copies the fact from memory, and then the fact copied from memory is compared to the original math fact with the correct answer (Joseph et al., 2011). Incremental rehearsal also has been shown to develop a student's fluency and automaticity in learning basic math facts (Burns, 2005). Improvement in accurate mathematical calculations has been demonstrated through the use of strategic number counting instruction. Using this method, the student is presented with cards with basic math facts but no answer. The student is then required to use a number line to figure out the problem if needed. The cards are reviewed as the student demonstrates the ability to remember the answer to the math fact (Fuchs et al., 2009).

While there are multiple types of interventions to remediate math difficulties, it is important to keep in mind that multiple factors may influence math performance and thus intervention for these types of conditions is often best paired with quantitative assessment data. For example, if a student has trouble remembering multiple steps to a problem, strategies for developing working memory may be helpful, such as breaking instruction into "chunks." Strategies to manage anxiety also can help students should math be a source of anxiety (Gillum, 2014).

Dysgraphia

Dysgraphia is a term often used to describe difficulties with handwriting, spelling, and written expression (Prunty & Barnett, 2017). Ideas are communicated through writing which is essential for students as well as many vocations. Handwriting skills are typically acquired during the first three years of school for production of a written product. As students age, writing becomes more complex and the process requires retrieving symbols and spelling of words from memory to write ideas (Rosenblum, 2018).

Interventions for dysgraphia should focus on the specific area of deficit which, similar to the other academic areas reviewed in this chapter, can often be determined via quantitative assessment. Identified deficits could include formation of letters in handwriting, spelling of words, or expressing ideas in written form. The Cover-Copy-Compare method, as outlined previously for learning math facts, can be used in the learning of spelling. Using this method, students review a sheet with words, cover the words, write the words from memory, and then compare their written words to the original correct words (Joseph et al., 2011). Integrated writing instruction is a classroom approach to writing instruction designed to improve students' writing through multiple methods including the following: Status-checking, mini-lessons, student writing, peer and teacher conferences, and group sharing. The teacher checks in with students about their goals and status of a writing project, and a mini-lesson is conducted pertaining to the writing process to explicitly teach a skill or strategy. Students then have time allotted to work on their writing project. During the time students are writing, the teacher briefly meets with individual students regarding their project, or at the end of the writing block, students participate in a peer editing process. At the conclusion of the writing session, students have the opportunity to share their work with the class (MacArthur et al., 1993).

Quantitative Evidence-Based Interventions for Neuropsychological Domains

Comprehensive neuropsychological assessments typically assess a wide number of neurological, psychiatric, psychosocial, educational, legal, and vocational areas. Some of these are considered neuropsychological domains such as attention, memory, language, executive functioning, processing speed, sensory-motor functioning, and visual-spatial analysis. There are multiple tests that can quantitatively assess these areas. This section briefly reviews some of these domains and illustrate how quantitative interventions can be applied.

Attention

Attention deficits can result in decreased academic performance in school and vocational functions; indeed, as discussed previously in the Luria section, a patient who cannot attend to relevant stimuli will generally not have an opportunity to fully employ their processing and problem-solving skills. There are multiple interventions and strategies that have been shown to help students better attend to instruction thus reducing the risk of poor academic performance, and many of these quantitative interventions can be applied to vocational functioning as well.

Whole class strategies and interventions are abundant. Research has shown the importance of obtaining students' attention prior to providing instruction (Ford et al., 2001). The use of proximity, where the teacher is near students, increases attention and supervisors could employ this vocational instruction as well. Providing the opportunity for students to make a choice in the lesson or activity can increase engagement in academics as well as attention span (Powell & Nelson, 1997). A reduction in assignment length can improve attention. For example, an assignment can be broken into shorter assignments rather than one long assignment (DuPaul & Ervin, 1996).

Multiple interventions have demonstrated effectiveness on improving attention at the individual level as well. Results of a meta-analysis indicate that self-monitoring in addition to reinforcement interventions improve attention to tasks, accuracy with academic tasks, as well as decrease disruptive behaviors (Reid et al., 2005). The daily report card is another intervention used for improving attention. This entails a list of the student's behaviors to target for intervention with a goal with detailed criteria for meeting that goal. Immediate feedback is provided by the teacher to the student based on the targeted behaviors on the daily report card. A reward is sometimes provided if the student meets one or more of the goals (Pyle & Fabiano, 2017). In addition, mindfulness-based interventions have increased in popularity in recent years with many studies showing a reduction in inattention for both children and adults (Poissant et al., 2019).

Executive Functions

Executive functions refer to the abilities needed to self-regulate and direct one's own behavior, which include planning, organization, self-control, working memory, and goal direction (Hofmann et al., 2012; Miciak et al., 2019). Significant correlations have been found between executive functions and academic achievement (Duckworth & Seligman, 2005; Jacob & Parkinson, 2015), social competence (Morgan & Lilienfeld, 2000), emotional regulation (Carlson & Wang, 2007), and vocational functioning (Yeates et al., 2016). This highlights the importance of taking into account quantitative neuropsychological assessment data when considering academic and vocational interventions.

Executive functions play an important role for students starting at a young age into adulthood. Rothlisberger et al. (2011) established that early intervention programs focused on executive functions, such as working memory, cognitive flexibility, and interference control, demonstrated student gains in all areas measured. Intervention tasks used as a part of the intervention program included adapted versions of dimensional card sorting, listening recall, Simon Says, matching figures, mazes, and attention training. In addition, research indicates that physical exercise can improve executive functions (Pritchard Orr et al., 2018; Vonk et al., 2019). Improvement in executive functions and emotional regulation also has been shown through mindfulness-based interventions (Poissant et al., 2019).

Processing Speed

Processing speed plays a key role in learning and execution of academic and vocational tasks at a timely rate. It involves perceiving information, processing information, and/or forming or executing a response (Braaten & Willoughby, 2014). In school, students with adequate processing speed are able to fluently read and understand material as well as perform basic and complex mathematical operations to solve problems (Benner et al., 2012). In contrast, deficits in processing speed can result in decreased academic performance as well as in the understanding of language across settings (Leonard et al., 2007).

Language-based interventions are showing promise to develop processing speed skills as well as language skills in children. One such intervention is Language for Thinking (Engelmann & Osborn, 2002), which can be used across grade levels to address receptive and expressive language skills. This programmatic approach teaches students concepts, vocabulary, and sentence structure, which they encounter throughout their school day in textbooks and assignments. Results have shown not only improvement in language and processing speed skills but also a reduction in behavior difficulties and anxiety (Benner et al., 2012). Cognitive training, specifically with regard to visual speed processing training, has demonstrated positive effects on improved processing speed performance in adults. In a study by Wolinsky et al. (2013), a visual speed of processing training computerized program implemented over 10 hours of time was shown to maintain or improve multiple cognitive functions, including processing speed.

Visual-Spatial Functioning

Visual-spatial functioning is often assessed via copying and drawing tasks as well as through nonmotoric activities which require the mental manipulation of visual stimuli. Visual-spatial skills are involved in writing and copying tasks (Carlson et al., 2013). Further, visual-spatial and spatial relation skills are helpful for individuals to orient to the environment and objects in space (e.g., judge distance, distinguish shapes and objects; Nadkarni, Sumi, & Ashok, 2012). In a study by Carlson et al. (2013), students with higher visual spatial integration skills demonstrated stronger performance in both mathematics and written expression. Nadkarni et al. (2012) used a transfer-of-training approach, which focused on remediating skills through repeated practice of visual-spatial skills including matching shapes, constructing designs with blocks, copying pictures, and copying geometric shapes. Results demonstrated that students improved not only their visual-spatial skills but also their academic abilities. Training for visual spatial skills via puzzle problem-solving methods using visual and verbal prompts during instruction was found to improve visual spatial functioning as well (Chabani & Hommel, 2014).

Multicultural Considerations in Quantitative Evidence-Based Interventions

One of the greatest difficulties in using evidence-based interventions is the group upon which they were developed may not capture the individual variation in a particular patient for whom the neuropsychologist would like to use the intervention. Even if the patient has the same disorder as the group upon which the evidence-based intervention was established, the patient is likely to have at least somewhat different demographics; this is a substantial concern given the relationship that has been found between patient demographics and the measurement of cognitive processing (Boone et al., 2007; Flores et al., 2017; Krch et al., 2015). When neuropsychologists want to apply quantitative evidence-based interventions they are encouraged to consider factors such as socioeconomic status, parental level of education, parental occupation, race, ethnicity, and culture that could impact the efficacy of the intervention; in essence, the patient's background may be different than that of the group(s) for which an intervention has been shown to be effective. One way to quantify cultural differences is by using a measure of acculturation. According to Alegria (2009), acculturation is a multidimensional process where one adopts the cultural norms, values, and even lifestyle of the majority culture. Wang et al. (2019) noted that acculturation is a process of change in either the dominant or nondominant group that results in cultures interacting and crossing. Understanding acculturation in the context of interventions is critical, especially for children, because it has been noted that level of acculturation is positively correlated with academic achievement (Salamonson et al., 2008). In adults, differences between parental and adolescent acculturation was found to be negatively associated with family functioning, and negative family functioning was in turn associated with poor mental health outcomes (Lawton et al., 2018). To assess acculturation, there are various measures that can be used based upon the culture with which the patient identifies. These include the East Asian Acculturation Measure (EAAM; Barry, 2001), Acculturation Rating Scale for Mexican Americans, Second Edition (ARSMA-II; Cuellar et al., 1995), and Bicultural Involvement Questionnaire – Short Version (BIQ-S; Szapocznik et al., 1980). In addition to assessing acculturation to help interpret quantitative assessment scores to implement effective interventions, assessing acculturation stress can be informative as well. Acculturation stress can be defined as the conflict one faces between their native culture and the majority culture (Berry, 1992). This conflict can occur for various reasons, such as differing expectations in relation to social situations and behaviors, discrimination, and different languages, values, and norms (d'Abreu et al., 2019). When this type of conflict arises, it can disrupt a person's daily functioning in many areas. These areas can include family dynamics, school, and peer relationships (d'Abreu et al., 2019). Assessing which of these areas is affected can contribute to the proper interventions being set in place.

Conclusions

The process of neuropsychological assessment is complex and is most effective when a wide range of data is collected. This data is generally used to ascertain an etiology, establish a diagnosis (or diagnoses), make prognoses, and then generate recommendations. This last step provides the neuropsychologist the opportunity to link assessment results to interventions. Although many neuropsychologists do not directly carry out the interventions themselves, the recommendation of quantitative interventions helps ensure that they have been well-validated through empirical study. Indeed, the effectiveness of quantitative interventions can generally be measured, which is why they fit in well with the general ethos underlying the psychometric approach of many neuropsychologists. This approach can be effectively employed with both the Boston Process and Lurian approach which reflects some of the widely used tests in our field. Quantitative interventions easily lend themselves to the treatment of behavioral concerns for individuals with autism spectrum disorder as well as other neurodevelopmental disorders. They are also widely used in the field of cognitive rehabilitation for the treatment of acquired injuries such as stroke and traumatic brain injury. School psychologists and pediatric neuropsychologists have a wide array of evidence-based interventions from which to choose when working with children with dyslexia, dyscalculia, and/or dysgraphia. Finally, one of the most important considerations for working with patients with known or suspected neurological or psychiatric problems is their cultural background. A patient's cultural experiences have a significant influence on their performance on standardized neuropsychological measures and thus should be considered when interpreting test performance. Using a quantitative approach such as measuring acculturation or cultural stress allows for more exact understanding of this process.

Discussion Questions

1. Discuss the strengths and weaknesses of using the Boston Process Approach during a clinical neuropsychological evaluation.
2. Compare and contrast the Boston Process Approach and the Lurian Model as they pertain to a clinical neuropsychological evaluation.
3. What are some salient features of Applied Behavior Analysis (ABA)?
4. Discuss the various evidence-based interventions needed for individuals with Traumatic Brain Injuries (TBIs).
5. Why is it important to consider one's acculturation process during a clinical neuropsychological evaluation?
6. Discuss the importance of understanding and utilizing quantitative, evidence-based interventions in clinical neuropsychology.

EPPP Sample Questions

1. Which of the following would best encapsulate the Boston Process approach?
   (a) A neuropsychologist administers a measure of intelligence to predict academic performance
   (b) A neuropsychologist interprets a score designed to measure a higher-order function by first considering the scores on lower-order measures
   (c) Understanding the correlation between neuropsychological test data and estimates of premorbid functioning
   (d) Using embedded measures to understand a patient's level of effort and/or determine if malingering is present
2. Which of the following would not describe one of Luria's three functional units?
   (a) Simultaneous processing
   (b) Successive processing
   (c) Attention processing
   (d) Visual processing
3. "The scientific study of behavior change, using the principles of behavior, to evoke or elicit a targeted behavioral change" (Furman & Lepper, 2018) is describing:
   (a) Skinner's verbal behavior principal
   (b) Classical condition
   (c) Applied behavior analysis
   (d) Cognitive-behavior therapy
4. A multidimensional process where one adopts the cultural norms, values, and even lifestyle of the majority culture is best describing:
   (a) Assimilation
   (b) Cultural stress
   (c) Acculturation
   (d) All of the above
5. In cognitive rehabilitation the process of avoiding damaged functions and focusing on intact functions or creative strategies is best termed:
   (a) Restorative
   (b) Compensatory
   (c) Therapeutic
   (d) Ameliorative

Answers: B, D, C, C, B

Proactive Readings

Transcending the Past:

Kaplan, E. (1988). A process approach to neuropsychological assessment. In T. Boll & B. K. Bryant (Eds.), *Clinical neuropsychology and brain function: Research, measurement, and practice* (pp. 125–167). American Psychological Association.
Luria, A. R. (1973). The three principal functional units. *The working brain: An introduction to neuropsychology* (pp. 43–101). Penguin Books.
Naglieri, J. A., & Gottling, S. H. (1997). Mathematics instruction and PASS cognitive processes: An intervention study. *Journal of Learning Disabilities, 30*(5), 513–520. https://doi.org/10.1177/002221949703000507

Excelling in the Present:

Lezak, M. D., Howieson, D. B., Bigler, E. D., & Tranel, D. (2012). *Neuropsychological assessment* (5th ed.). Oxford.
Axelrod, S., McElrath, K. K., & Wine, B. (2012). Applied behavior analysis: Autism and beyond. *Behavioral Interventions, 27*, 1–15. https://doi.org/10.1002/bin.1335
Boone, K. B., Victor, T. L., Wen, J., Razani, J., & Pontón, M. (2007). The association between neuropsychological scores and ethnicity, language, and acculturation variables in a large patient population. *Archives of Clinical Neuropsychology, 22*, 355–365. https://doi.org/10.1016/j.acn.2007.01.010

Transforming the Future:

Kaufman, A. S. (2008). Neuropsychology and specific learning disabilities: Lessons from the past as a guide to present controversies and future clinical practice. In E. Fletcher-Janzen and C. R. Reynolds (Eds.), *Neuropsychological perspectives on learning disabilities in the era of RTI: Recommendations for diagnosis and intervention*. (pp. 1–13). John Wiley & Sons Inc.
Tan, Y. W., Burgess, G. H., & Green, R. J. (2020). The effects of acculturation on neuropsychological test performance: A systematic literature review. *The Clinical Neuropsychologist, 1-31*. https://doi.org/10.1080/13854046.2020.1714740

References

Alegria, M. (2009). The challenge of acculturation measures: What are we missing? A commentary on Thomas & Hoffman-Goetz. *Social Science and Medicine, 69*(7), 996–998. https://doi.org/10.1016/j.socscimed.2009.07.006

Alpern, G. D. (2007). *Developmental profile, third edition (DP-3)*. Stoelting.

American Psychiatric Association (APA). (2013). *Diagnostic and statistical manual of mental disorders* (5th ed.). Author.

Axelrod, S., McElrath, K. K., & Wine, B. (2012). Applied behavior analysis: Autism and beyond. *Behavioral Interventions, 27*, 1–15. https://doi.org/10.1002/bin.1335

Barry, D. T. (2001). Development of a new scale for measuring acculturation: The east Asian acculturation measure (EAAM). *Journal of Immigrant Health, 3*(4), 195–196. https://doi.org/10.1023/A:1012227611547

Bédard, M., Felteau, M., Marshall, S., Dubois, S., Gibbons, C., Klein, R., & Weaver, B. (2012). Mindfulness-based cognitive therapy: Benefits in reducing depression following a traumatic brain injury. *Advances in Mind-Body Medicine, 26*, 14–20.

Benner, G. J., Ralston, N. C., & Feuerborn, L. (2012). The effect of the language for thinking program on cognitive processing and social adjustment of students with emotional and behavioral disorders. *Preventing School Failure, 56*(1), 47–54. https://doi.org/10.1080/1045988X.2011.555794

Berry, J. W. (1992). Acculturation and adaptation in a new society. *International Migration, 30*(1), 69–85.

Boone, K. B., Victor, T. L., Wen, J., Razani, J., & Pontón, M. (2007). The association between neuropsychological scores and ethnicity, language, and acculturation variables in a large patient population. *Archives of Clinical Neuropsychology, 22*, 355–365. https://doi.org/10.1016/j.acn.2007.01.010

Braaten, E., & Willoughby, B. (2014). *Bright kids who can't keep up: Help your child overcome slow processing speed and succeed in a fast-paced world*. Guilford Press.

Brenner, L. A., Ignacio, R. V., & Blow, F. C. (2011). Suicide and traumatic brain injury among individuals seeking veterans health administration services. *The Journal of Head Trauma Rehabilitation, 26*, 257–264. https://doi.org/10.1097/HTR.0b013e31821fdb6e

Burns, M. K. (2005). Using incremental rehearsal to increase fluency of single-digit multiplication facts with children identified as learning disabled in mathematics computation. *Education and Treatment of Children, 28*, 237–249.

Caplan, B. (2010). Rehabilitation psychology and neuropsychology with stroke survivors. In R. G. Frank, M. Rosenthal, & B. Caplan (Eds.), *Handbook of rehabilitation psychology* (pp. 63–94). American Psychological Association. https://doi.org/10.1037/15972-004

Carlson, A. G., Rowe, E., & Curby, T. W. (2013). Disentangling fine motor skills' relations to academic achievement: The relative contributions of visual-spatial integration and visual-motor coordination. *The Journal of Genetic Psychology, 174*(5), 514–533. https://doi.org/10.1080/00221325.2012.717122

Carlson, S. M., & Wang, T. S. (2007). Inhibitory control and emotion regulation in preschool children. *Cognitive Development, 22*(4), 489–510. doi:10.1016/j.cogdev.2007.08.002

Carnevale, G. J., Anselmi, V., Johnston, M. V., Busichio, K., & Walsh, V. (2006). A natural setting behavior management program for persons with acquired brain injury: A randomized controlled trial. *Achieve of Physical Medicine and Rehabilitation, 87*, 1289–1297. https://doi.org/10.1016/j.apmr.2006.06.010

CDC. (2019, June). *Traumatic brain injury & concussion*. https://www.cdc.gov/traumaticbraininjury/index.html

Chabani, E., & Hommel, B. (2014). Effectiveness of visual and verbal prompts in training visuospatial processing skills in school age children. *Instructional Science, 42*, 995–1012. DOI 10.1007/s11251-014-9316-7

Chard, K. M., Schumm, J., McIlvain, S., Bailey, G., & Parkinson, R. (2011). Exploring the efficacy of a CPT-cognitive only (CPT-C) focused residential treatment program for veterans with PTSD and traumatic brain injury. *Journal of Traumatic Stress, 24*, 347–351. https://doi.org/10.1002/jts.20644

Cicerone, K. D., Dahlberg, C., Kalmar, K., Langenbahn, D. M., Malec, J. F., Bergquist, T. F., … Morse, P. A. (2000). Evidence-based cognitive rehabilitation: Recommendations for clinical practice. *Achieve of Physical Medicine and Rehabilitation, 81*, 1596–1615. https://doi.org/10.1053/apmr.2000.19240

Cicerone, K. D., Langenbahn, D. M., Braden, C., Malec, J. F., Kalmar, K., Fraas, M., . . . Ashman, T. (2011). Evidenced-based cognitive rehabilitation: Updated review of the literature from 2003 through 2008. *Archives of Physical Medicine and Rehabilitation, 92*, 519–530. https://doi.org/10.1016/j.apmr.2010.11.015

Cimolin, V., Beretta, E., Piccinini, L., Turconi, A. C., Locatelli, F., Galli, M., & Strazzer, S. (2012). Constraint-induced movement therapy for children with hemiplegia after traumatic brain injury: A quantitative study. *The Journal of Head Trauma Rehabilitation, 27*, 177–187. DOI: 10.1097/HTR.0b013e3182172276

Cooper, J. O., Heron, T. E., & Heward, W. L. (2007). *Applied behavior analysis*. Pearson.

Cuellar, I., Arnold, B., & Maldonado, R. (1995). Acculturation rating scale for Mexican Americans-II: A revision of the original ARSMA scale. *Hispanic Journal of Behavioral Sciences, 17*, 275–305. https://doi.org/10.1177/07399863950173001

Cumming, T. B., Blomstrand, C., Skoog, I., & Linden, T. (2016). The high prevalence of anxiety disorders after stroke. *American Journal of Geriatric Psychiatry, 24*, 154–160. https://doi.org/10.1016/j.jagp.2015.06.003

d'Abreu, A., Castro-Olivo, S., & Ura, S. K. (2019). Understanding the role of accultrative stress on refugee youth mental health: A systematic review and ecological approach to assessment and intervention. *School Psychology International, 40*(2), 107–127. https://doi.org/10.1177/0143034318822688

D'Mello, A. M., & Gabrieli, J. D. E. (2018). Cognitive neuroscience of dyslexia. *Language, Speech, and Hearing Services in Schools, 49*, 798–809. https://doi.org/10.1044/2018_LSHSS-DYSLC-18-0020

Delis, D. C., Kaplan, E., & Kramer, J. H. (2001a). *Delis Kaplan executive function system*. The Psychological Corporation.

Delis, D. C., Kaplan, E., & Kramer, J. H. (2001b). *D-KEFS examiners manual*. The Psychological Association.

Duckworth, A. L., & Seligman, M. E. (2005). Self-discipline outdoes IQ in predicting academic performance of adolescents. *Psychological Science, 16*(12), 939–944. https://doi.org/10.1111/j.1467-9280.2005.01641.x

Duff, F. J., & Clarke, P. J. (2011). Practitioner review: Reading disorders: What are the effective interventions and how should they be implemented and evaluated? *The Journal of Child Psychology and Psychiatry, 52*(1), 3–12. https://doi.org/10.1111/j.1469-7610.2010.02310.x

DuPaul, G. J., & Ervin, R. A. (1996). Functional assessment of behaviors related to attention-deficit/hyperactivity disorder: Linking assessment to intervention design. *Behavior Therapy, 27*, 601–622. https://doi.org/10.1016/S0005-7894(96)80046-3

Engelmann, S., & Osborn, J. (2002). *Language for thinking: Teacher's guide*. SRA/McGraw-Hill.

Faramarzi, S., & Sadri, S. (2014). The effect of basic neuropsychological interventions on performance of students with dyscalculia. *Neuropsychologia, 9*(2), 48–54.

Flores, I., Casaletto, K. B., Marquine, M. J., Umlauf, A., Moore, D. J., Mungas, D., … Heaton, R. K. (2017). Performance of Hispanics and non-Hispanic whites on the NIH toolbox cognition battery: The roles of ethnicity and language backgrounds. *The Clinical Neuropsychologist, 31*(4), 783–797. https://doi.org/10.1080/13854046.2016.1276216

Ford, A. D., Olmi, D. J., Edwards, R. P., & Tingstrom, D. H. (2001). The sequential introduction of compliance training components with elementary-aged children in general education classroom settings. *School Psychology Quarterly, 16*, 142–157. https://doi.org/10.1521/scpq.16.2.142.18702

Fuchs, L. S., Powell, S. R., Seethaler, P. M., Cirino, P. T., Fletcher, J. M., Fuchs, D., & Hamlett, C. L. (2009). The effects of strategic counting instruction, with and without deliberate practice, on number combination skill among students with mathematics difficulties. *Learning and Individual Differences, 20*(2), 89–100. https://doi.org/10.1016/j.lindif.2009.09.003

Furman, T. M., & Lepper, T. L. (2018). Applied behavior analysis: Definitional difficulty. *The Psychological Record, 68*, 103–105. https://doi.org/10.1007/s40732-018-0282-3

Gaab, N., Gabrieli, J. D. E., Deutsch, G. K., Tallal, P., & Temple, E. (2007). Neural correlates of rapid auditory processing are discurpted in children wtih developmental dyslexia and ameliorated with training: An fMRI study. *Restorative Neurology and Neuroscience, 25*(3–4), 295–310. https://doi.org/10.1007/s40732-018-0282-3

Gabrieli, J. D. E. (2009). Dyslexia: A new synergy between education and cognitive neuroscience. *Science, 325*(5938), 280–283. https://doi.org/10.1126/science.1171999

Gillum, J. (2014). Assessment with children who experience difficulty in mathematics. *Support for Learning, 29*(3), 275–291. https://doi.org/10.1111/1467-9604.12061

Hamblen, J. L., Norman, S. B., Sonis, J. H., Phelps, A. J., Bisson, J. I., Nunes, V. D., … Schnurr, P. P. (2019). A guide to guidelines for the treatment of posttraumatic stress disorder in adults: An update. *Psychotherapy, 56*(3), 359–373. https://doi.org/10.1037/pst0000231

Hart, T. (2010). Cognitive rehabilitation. In R. G. Frank, M. Rosenthal, & B. Caplan (Eds.), *Handbook of rehabilitation psychology* (pp. 285–300). American Psychological Association. https://doi.org/10.1037/15972-017

Hart, T., Brenner, L., Clark, A. N., Bogner, J. A., Novack, T. A., Chervoneva, I., … CarlosArango-Lasprilla, J. C. (2011). Major and minor depression after traumatic brain injury. *Achieve of Physical Medicine and Rehabilitation, 92*, 1211–1219. https://doi.org/10.1016/j.apmr.2011.03.005

Hildebrand, M. W. (2015). Effectiveness of interventions for adults with psychological or emotional impairment after stroke: An evidence-based review. *American Journal of Occupational Therapy, 69*(1), 6901180050p1-6901180050p9. https://doi.org/10.5014/ajot.2015.012054

Hofmann, W., Schmeichel, B. J., & Baddeley, A. D. (2012). Executive functions and self-regulation. *Trends in Cognitive Sciences, 16*, 174–180. https://doi.org/10.1016/j.tics.2012.01.006

Homack, S., Lee, D., & Riccio, C. A. (2005). Test review: Delis-Kaplan executive function system. *Journal of Clinical and Experimental Psychology, 27*, 599–609. https://doi.org/10.1080/13803390490918444

Jacob, R., & Parkinson, J. (2015). The potential for school-based interventions that target executive function to improve academic achievement: A review. *Review of Educational Research, 85*(4), 512–552. https://doi.org/10.3102/0034654314561338

Jørgensen, T. S. H., Wium-Andersen, I. K., Wium-Andersen, M. K., Jørgensen, M. B., Prescott, E., … Osler, M. (2016). Incidence of depression after stroke, and associated risk factors and mortality outcomes, in a large cohort of Danish patients. *JAMA Psychiatry, 73*(10), 1032–1040. https://doi.org/10.1001/jamapsychiatry.2016.1932

Joseph, L. M., Konrad, M., Cates, G., Vajcner, T., Eveleigh, E., & Fishley, K. M. (2011). A meta-analytic review of the cover-copy-compare and variations of this self-management procedure. *Psychology in the Schools, 49*(2), 122–136. https://doi.org/10.1002/pits.20622

Kaplan, E. (1988). A process approach to neuropsychological assessment. In T. Boll & B. K. Bryant (Eds.), *Clinical neuropsychology and brain function: Research, measurement, and practice* (pp. 125–167). American Psychological Association.

Kaufman, A. S., & Kaufman, N. L. (2004). *Kaufman assessment battery for children, second edition manual.* AGS Publishing.

Kootker, J. A., Rasquin, S. M. C., Lem, F. C., van Heugten, C. M., Fasotti, L., & Geurts, A. C. H. (2017). Augmented cognitive behavioral therapy for poststroke depressive symptoms: A randomized controlled trial. *Archives of Physical Medicine and Rehabilitation, 98*, 687–694. https://doi.org/10.1016/j.apmr.2016.10.013

Korkman, M., Kirk, U., & Kemp, S. (2007). *NEPSY-II: Clinical and interpretive manual.* Pearson.

Krafnick, A. J., Flowers, D. L., Napoliello, E. M., & Eden, G. F. (2011). Gray matter volume changes following reading intervention in dyslexic children. *NeuroImage, 57*(3), 733–741. https://doi.org/10.1016/j.neuroimage.2010.10.062

Krch, D., Lequerica, A., Arango-Lasprilla, J. C., Rogers, H. L., DeLuca, J., & Chiaravalloti, N. D. (2015). The multidimensional influence of acculturation on digit symbol-coding and Wisconsin card sorting test in Hispanics. *The Clinical Neuropsychologist, 29*(5), 624–638. https://doi.org/10.1080/13854046.2015.1063696

Lawton, K. E., Gerdes, A. C., & Kapke, T. (2018). The role of acculturation differences and acculturation conflict in Latino family mental health. *Journal of Latina/o Psychology, 6*(2), 94–114. https://psycnet.apa.org/record/2017-09410-001

Leonard, L. B., Weismer, S. E., Miller, C. A., Francis, D. J., Tomblin, J. B., & Kail, R. V. (2007). Speed of processing, working memory, and language impairment in children. *Journal of Speech, Language, and Hearing Research, 50*, 408–428. https://doi.org/10.1044/1092-4388(2007/029)

Libon, D. J., Swenson, R., Ashendorf, L., Bauer, R. M., & Bowers, D. (2013). Edith Kaplan and the Boston process approach. *The Clinical Neuropsychologist, 27*(8), 1223–1233. https://doi.org/10.1080/13854046.2013.833295

Limampai, P., Wongsrithep, W., & Kuptniratsaikul, V. (2017). Depression after stroke at 12-month follow-up: A multicenter study. *International Journal of Neuroscience, 124*, 887–892. https://doi.org/10.1080/00207454.2016.1277344

Lincoln, N. B., & Flannaghan, T. (2003). Cognitive behavioral psychotherapy for depression following stroke. A randomized controlled trial. *Stroke, 34*, 111–115. https://doi.org/10.1161/01.STR.0000044167.44670.55

Lincoln, N. B., Kneebone, I. I., Macniven, J. A. B., & Morris, R. C. (2012). *Psychological management of stroke*. Wiley.

Luria, A. R. (1973). The three principal functional units. In *The working brain: An introduction to neuropsychology* (pp. 43–101). Penguin Books.

MacArthur, C., Graham, S., & Schwarz, S. (1993). Integrating strategy instruction and word processing into a process approach to writing instruction. *School Psychology Review, 22*, 671–681. https://doi.org/10.1080/02796015.1993.12085681

Mather, N., & Wendline, B. J. (2012). *Essentials of dyslexia assessment and intervention*. Wiley.

Miciak, J., Cirino, P. T., Ahmed, Y., Reid, E., & Vaughn, S. (2019). Executive functions and response to intervention: Identification of students struggling with reading comprehension. *Learning Disability Quarterly, 42*(1), 17–31. https://doi.org/10.1177/0731948717749935

Monei, T., & Pedro, A. (2017). A systematic review of interventions for children presenting with dyslexia in primary schools. *Educational Psychology in Practice, 33*(3), 277–293. https://doi.org/10.1080/02667363.2017.1289076

Moore, E. L., Terryberry-Spohr, L., & Hope, D. A. (2006). Mild traumatic brain injury and anxiety sequelae: A review of the literature. *Brain Injury, 20*, 117–132. https://doi.org/10.1080/02699050500443558

Morgan, A. B., & Lilienfeld, S. O. (2000). A meta-analytic review of the relation between antisocial behavior and neuropsychological measures of executive function. *Clinical Psychology Review, 20*(1), 113–136. https://doi.org/10.1016/S0272-7358(98)00096-8

Nadkarni, S., Sumi, S., & Ashok, D. (2012). Enhancing eye-hand coordination with therapy intervention to improve visual-spatial abilities using 'the re-training approach' in children with down syndrome: Three case studies. *Disability, CBR & Inclusive Development, 23*(2), 107–120. https://doi.org/10.5463/DCID.v23i2.87

National Institute of Child Health and Human Development, NIH, DHHS (NICHD). (2000). *Report of the National Reading Panel: Teaching children to read: Reports of the subgroups (00–4754)*. U.S. Government Printing Office. https://www.nichd.nih.gov/sites/default/files/publications/pubs/nrp/Documents/report.pdf

NIH Consensus with Traumatic Brain Injury. (1999). Consensus conference. Rehabilitation of persons with traumatic brain injury. NIH consensus development panel on rehabilitation of persons with traumatic brain injury. *JAMA, 282*, 974–983.

Peters-Scheffer, N., Didden, R., Korzilius, H., & Sturmey, P. (2011). A meta-analytic study on the effectiveness of comprehensive ABA-based early intervention programs for children with Autism spectrum disorders. *Research in Autism Spectrum Disorders, 5*, 60–69. https://doi.org/10.1016/j.rasd.2010.03.011

Poissant, H., Mendrek, A., Talbot, N., Khoury, B., & Nolan, J. (2019). Behavioral and cognitive impacts of mindfulness-based interventions on adults with attention-deficit hyperactivity disorder: A systematic review. *Behavioural Neurology, 2019*, 1–16. https://doi.org/10.1155/2019/5682050

Powell, S., & Nelson, B. (1997). Effects of choosing academic assignments on a student with attention deficit hyperactivity disorder. *Journal of Applied Behavior Analysis, 30*, 181–183. https://doi.org/10.1901/jaba.1997.30-181

Pritchard Orr, A. B., Keiver, K., Bertram, C. P., & Clarren, S. (2018). FAST club: The impact of a physical activity intervention on executive function in children with fetal alcohol spectrum disorder. *Adapted Physical Activity Quarterly, 35*, 403–423. https://doi.org/10.1123/apaq.2017-0137

Prunty, M., & Barnett, A. L. (2017). Understanding handwriting difficulties: A comparison of children with and without motor impairment. *Cognitive Neuropsychology, 34*(3–4), 205–218. https://doi.org/10.1080/02643294.2017.1376630

Pyle, K., & Fabiano, G. A. (2017). Daily report card intervention and attention deficit hyperactivity disorder: A meta-analysis of single-case studies. *Exceptional Children, 83*(4), 378–395. https://doi.org/10.1177/0014402917706370

Reid, R., Trout, A. L., & Schartz, M. (2005). Self-regulation interventions for children with Attention-Deficit/Hyperactivity Disorder. *Exceptional Children, 71*(4), 361–377.

Ricker, J. H. (2010). Traumatic brain injury in adults. In R. G. Frank, M. Rosenthal, & B. Caplan (Eds.), *Handbook of rehabilitation psychology* (pp. 43–62). American Psychological Association.

Rosenblum, S. (2018). Inter-relationships between objective handwriting features and executive control among children with developmental dysgraphia. *PLoS One, 13*(4), e0196098. https://doi.org/10.1371/journal.pone.0196098

Rothlisberger, M., Neuenschwander, R., Cimeli, P., Michel, E., & Roebers, C. M. (2011). Improving executive functions in 5- and 6-year-olds: Evaluation of a small group intervention in prekindergarten and kindergarten children. *Infant and Child Development, 21*, 411–429. https://doi.org/10.1002/icd.752

Salamonson, Y., Everett, B., Koch, J., Andrew, S., & Davidson, P. M. (2008). English-language acculturation predicts academic performance in nursing students who speak English as a second language. *Research in Nursing and Health, 31*(1), 86–94. https://doi.org/10.1002/nur.20224

Schaffer, Y., & Geva, R. (2016). Memory outcomes following cognitive interventions in children with neurological deficits: A review with a focus on under-studied populations. *Neuropsychological Rehabilitation, 26*(2), 286–317. https://doi.org/10.1080/09602011.2015.1016537

Shaywitz, B. A., Shaywitz, S. E., Blachman, B. A., Pugh, K. R., Fulbright, R. K., Skudlarski, P., … Gore, J. C. (2004). Development of left occipitotemporal systems for skilled reading in children after phonlogically-based intervention. *Biological Psychiatry, 55*(9), 926–933. https://doi.org/10.1016/j.biopsych.2003.12.019

Skinner, C. H., McLaughlin, T. F., & Logan, P. (1997). Cover, copy, and compare: A self-managed academic intervention effective across skills, students, and settings. *Journal of Behavioral Education, 7*, 295–306. https://doi.org/10.1023/A:1022823522040

Slifer, K. J., & Amari, A. (2009). Behavior management for children and adolescents with acquired brain injury. *Developmental Disabilities Research Reviews, 15*, 144–151. https://doi.org/10.1002/ddrr.60

Szapocznik, J., Kurtines, W. M., & Fernandez, T. (1980). Bicultural involvement and adjustment in Hispanic-American youths. *International Journal of Intercultural Relations, 4*, 353–365. https://doi.org/10.1016/0147-1767(80)90010-3

Taub, E., Uswatte, G., & Pidikiti, R. (1999). Constraint-induced movement therapy: A new family of techniques with broad application to physical rehabilitation–a clinical review. *Journal of Rehabilitation Research and Development, 36*(3), 237–251.

Taylor-Rowan, M., Momoh, O., Ayerbe, L., Evans J. J., Stott, D. J., & Quinn, T. J. (2019).Prevalence of pre-stroke depression and its association with post-stroke depression: a systematic review and meta-analysis. *Psychological Medicine, 49*, 685–696. doi:10.1017/S0033291718002003

Tiura, M., Kim, J., Detmers, D., & Baldi, H. (2017). Predictors of longitudinal ABA treatment outcomes for children with Autism: A growth curve analysis. *Research in Developmental Disabilities, 70*, 185–197. https://doi.org/10.1016/j.ridd.2017.09.008

Vanderploeg, R. D., Belanger, H. G., Curtiss, G., Bowles, A. O., & Cooper, D. B. (2019). Reconceptualizing rehabilitation of individuals with chronic symptoms following mild traumatic brain injury. *Rehabilitation Psychology, 64*, 1–12. https://doi.org/10.1037/rep0000255

Vonk, M., Wikkerink, S., Regan, K., & Middleton, L. E. (2019). Similar changes in executive function after moderate resistance training and loadless movement. *PLoS One, 14*(2), e0212122. https://doi.org/10.1371/journal.pone.0212122

Walter, K. H., Dickstein, B. D., Barnes, S. M., & Chard, K. M. (2014). Comparing effectiveness of CPT to CPT-C among U.S. veterans in an interdisciplinary residential PTSD/TBI treatment program. *Journal of Traumatic Stress, 27*, 438–445. https://doi.org/10.1002/jts.21934

Wang, L., Bordon, J. J., Wang, K. T., & Yeung, J. G. (2019). Acculturation, enculturation, perceived discrimination, and well-being: A comparison between U.S. raised and non-U.S. raised Asian students. *Asian American Journal of Psychology, 10*(1), 22–32. https://doi.org/10.1037/aap0000117

Wang, S., Wang, Y., Zhang, Q., Wu, S., Ng, C. H., Ungvari, G. S., … Xiang, Y. (2018). Cognitive behavioral therapy for post-stroke depression: A meta-analysis. *Journal of Affective Disorders, 235*, 589–596. https://doi.org/10.1016/j.jad.2018.04.011

Wilkey, E. D., Pollack, C., & Price, G. R. (2018). Dyscalculia and typical math achievement are associated with individual differences in number-specific executive function. *Child Development, 91*, 596. https://doi.org/10.1111/cdev.13194

Wolf, S. L., Winstein, C. J., Miller, J. P., Taub, E., Uswatte, G., Morris, D., … Nichols-Larsen, D. (2006). Effect of constraint-induced movement therapy on upper extremity function 3 to 9 months after stroke -the EXCITE randomized clinical trial. *JAMA, 296*(17), 2095–2104. https://doi.org/10.1001/jama.296.17.2095

Wolinsky, F. D., Vander Weg, M. W., Howren, M. B., Jones, M. P., & Dotson, M. M. (2013). A randomized controlled trial of cognitive training using a visual speed of processing intervention in middle aged and older adults. *PLoS One, 8*(5), e61624. https://doi.org/10.1371/journal.pone.0061624

World Health Organization. (1989). Stroke – 1989: Recommendations on stroke prevention, diagnostics and therapy. Report of the who task force on stroke and other cerebrovascular disorders. *Stroke, 20*, 1407–1431. DOI: 10.1161/01.str.20.10.1407

Wood, R. L., & Alderman, N. (2011). Applications of operant learning theory to the management of challenging behavior after traumatic brain injury. *Journal of Head Trauma Rehabilitation, 26*, 202–211. doi: 10.1097/HTR.0b013e318217b46d

Yeates, G., Rowberry, M., Dunne, S., Goshawk, M., Mahadevan, M., Tyerman, R., … Tyerman, A. (2016). Social cognition and executive functioning predictors of supervisors' appraisal of interpersonal behavior in the workplace following acquired brain injury. *NeuroRehabilitation, 38*, 299–310. https://doi.org/10.3233/NRE-161321

Part III
Linking Assessment to Intervention in Clinical, Counseling, and School Psychology

Chapter 9
Using a Standardized Neuropsychological Model to Guide a Qualitative and Quantitative Assessment for Evidence-Based Interventions

Elizabeth M. Power and Rik Carl D'Amato

Learning Objectives

- To be able to defend the empirical and rational arguments for using clinical neuropsychology as your paradigm for approaching evaluations and neuropsychological services.
- To understand the importance of knowing your personal psychological paradigm from which you practice.
- To be able to explain how to use an Eastern or qualitative approach to neuropsychological assessment with a focus on the uniqueness of planning, conceptualization, and formulation for individual clients.
- To be able to explain how to use a Western or quantitative approach to neuropsychological assessment with a focus on the uniqueness of planning, conceptualization, and formulation for individual clients.
- To understand the difference between a fixed-battery and flexible-battery in a neuropsychological evaluation and explain when different batteries should be considered.
- To be able to tell which areas should be evaluated for assessment and evidence-based intervention when providing comprehensive clinical neuropsychological services.
- To differentiate the assessments used at the primary, secondary, and tertiary levels that lead to evidence-based interventions in a comprehensive neuropsychological evaluation.

E. M. Power (✉)
Department of Educational/School Psychology, The College of Saint Rose, Albany, NY, USA
e-mail: powere@strose.edu

R. C. D'Amato
Department of School Psychology, The Chicago School of Professional Psychology & Presence Learning, Chicago, IL and New York, NY, USA

R. C. D'Amato et al. (eds.), *Understanding the Biological Basis of Behavior*,
https://doi.org/10.1007/978-3-030-59162-5_9

The Professional Practice of Clinical Neuropsychology

Clinical neuropsychology is the study of brain-behavior relations. It stems from the early ideas that all behavior could be categorized into one of two major paradigms – those developing from *nature* (i.e., the biogenetic or organic approach) or *nurture* (i.e., the environmental approach). With a focus on understanding our behavior and its relationship to overall brain integrity, clinical neuropsychology has developed into one of the most sophisticated areas of psychology, with strong links to medicine, psychopharmacology, school psychology, counseling, consulting, and rehabilitation (D'Amato et al., 2005; Davis, 2011). Some have argued persuasively that *all psychologists* must be comprehensively trained in this seminal area if we are to effectively practice any type of psychology (D'Amato & Rothlisberg, 1997; Power & D'Amato, 2018).

Leaders in psychological training, such as the American Psychological Association (APA) require the biological basis of behavior to be both included by accredited doctoral programs and as part of the health service provider definition for psychological practice (APA, 2017). This is understandable given the interplay and overlap between psychology, medicine, and the brain. Almost 100 years ago, one of our most seminal leaders argued that psychometric testing should be viewed as a *significant psychological dimension* important in understanding the practice of clinical neurology (Wechsler, 1928). For better or for worse, all psychologists utilize some type of ***model*** which is related to how they conceptualize, diagnose, and treat individuals, groups, systems, etc. While some may claim to be eclectic or more recently ecological, the data they collect, the way they interpret this information, and the type of evidence-based interventions they select all relate to **the approach** they explicate (Nicholson et al., 2011). Thus, while all psychologists are trained in various psychotherapeutic approaches, such as cognitive-behavioral, client-centered/humanistic, and psychoanalytic, the way an individual practices psychology reveals the belief system they utilize (D'Amato & Rothlisberg, 1997). The purpose of this chapter is to review various paradigms used within clinical neuropsychology and offer an integrative ecological model that allows one to effectively understand and practice clinical neuropsychology applied to meet a variety of societal needs (D'Amato et al., 2011). This could include providing neuropsychological services at the primary, secondary, or tertiary levels with patients from any and all age groups. Without at least a beginning understanding of the integrity of the central nervous system and its functioning, psychologists are not able to provide suitable psychological services to meet the needs of the general public (Hynd & Semrud-Clikeman, 1990). The knowledge of this book allows all health service providers a comprehensive understanding of the biological basis of behavior. This opens doors to services in a variety of unique and additional settings (D'Amato et al. 2005).

Neurology and Psychiatry

Neurology concerns the assessment and rehabilitation of abnormalities of the nervous system. This emphasis includes both the central and peripheral nervous systems, as well as their communication with muscles. Moreover, emotional and psychological functions are often impacted by neurological disorders (e.g., multiple sclerosis). Some have defined neurological difficulties as clearly related to nerve function problems (Hartlage & D'Amato, 2008). In fact, higher-order psychological functions are likely to be the initial symptom of central nervous system impairment (D'Amato & Dean, 1988). Recent technological advances (e.g., CT scans) have paved the way for advances and integration of disciplines that have helped clinical neuropsychology become prominent as part of rehabilitation services in many subareas of medicine.

> *Historically, psychiatry and neurology were the same field, and only recently have two separate specialties emerged. For many patients, however, the distinction is arbitrary. Diseases of the brain can produce severe psychological disturbances, and the causes are only beginning to be understood* (Kolb & Whishaw, 2003, p. 748).

A related specialty is that of the psychiatrist. Given the complexity of societal functioning and problems in human development, psychiatry has ballooned into being a critical specialty which is in great demand. Moreover, this has forced many psychiatrists to have a singular focus on psychopharmacology. However, the specialty was originally delineated to focus on community mental health within the general population and a small number of psychiatrists do regulary provide psychoptherapetic services. Related to this notion is the fact that many psychological advances, such as the development of consultation have psychiatric roots (Caplan et al., 1995). Because of the shortage of psychiatrists, some have advocated that psychologists seek further education and training to be able to prescribe medication to clients (McGrath et al., 2004). For a comprehensive overview of neurological and psychiatric disorders, see Hartlage and D'Amato (2008).

Neurologists work to describe, understand, and treat neurological abnormalities (D'Amato & Dean, 1988). Although neurological examinations involve a variety of evaluative techniques, they routinely include a broad physical examination (including an extensive history), basic laboratory tests (e.g., urine analysis), and an in-depth neurological exam. The neurological exam is a universal standardized procedure that may be divided into a series of assessments concerning (a) cranial nerves, (b) reflexes, (c) motor functions, (d) sensory functions, (e) cerebellar functions, (f) cerebrovascular functions, and (g) the patient's mental status and language (D'Amato & Dean, 1988). Based on this comprehensive examination, more specific and/or advanced tests may be ordered. These procedures may involve assessment of brain functioning, brain structure, or psychological processes. The neuropsychologist's chief role in the medical/neurologic setting involves the use of psychometric assessments to offer an objective baseline of the patient's impaired functioning and remaining adaptive behaviors (Hartlage & D'Amato, 2008a, b).

More than 100 years of seminal research has made clear that we should conceptualize psychiatric (organic) and neurological (environmental) as two ends of a single continuum (Lezak et al., 2012; Schultz & Schultz, 2016). This makes clear the need to conceptualize disorders on an interactive, continuum given our current level of understanding of neuropsychiatric disorders (Hartlage & D'Amato, 2008a). It seems important to hypothesize this as a spectrum such as the autism spectrum disorder conceptualization with two distinct, yet related ends. In fact, the very notion of a disconnected dichotomy with psychiatric at one end, unconnected to neurologic at the other end, seems static and is not in line with the multidimensional brain-related notions of influential researchers (Reitan, 1985; Luria, 1966; Dean, 1986a, 1986b; Kolb & Whishaw, 2003; Kaufman, 2001). If conceptualized as an interactive continuum, and not as an all-or-none occurrence, this allows neuropsychologists to answer more than yes/no questions regarding brain damage (Hartlage & D'Amato, 2008a, b). This makes conceptual sense because an organic disorder when left untreated often leads to environmental or functional changes. For example, a clinical neuropsychologist may prescribe a child who presents with depression with an antidepressant medication (i.e., organic end). While symptoms of depression may subside, the practitioner must also consider the other end of the spectrum (i.e., behavioral and environmental), which impacts his or her depression, such as imparied social skills. If a child is depressed, they may stop contact with their friends. This often causes friends to cut off contact with them. If they have improved neurotransmission with this medication, they may feel like establishing relationships. Now, although they may no longer feel depressed, they created an environment of depression which interferes with their ability to interact with friends. If viewed along a continuum, a clinical neuropsychologist must comprehensively address organic and environmental/behavioral issues. This data allows the neuropsychologist to analyze, integrate, and interpret the patient's abilities related to known behavioral patterns associated with specific neurologic or psychiatric disorders (D'Amato & Dean, 1988; Hartlage & D'Amato, 2008a, b).

Instruments Used in Neuropsychological Practice

Neurologists and other trained health service psychologists utilize a variety of techniques to assess a patient's behavioral and cognitive functioning. It is important for a clinical neuropsychologist to be aware of many of the traditional scales used in most medical facilities to evaluate brain functioning.

Specialized Techniques

Using these techniques may be a part of a clinical neuropsychologist's role related to neuropsychological rehabilitation. Most neuropsychologists will assess and/or review a patient's mental status, lateral preference, and scores from the APGAR, Glasgow Coma Scale, and the Ranchos Los Amigos Levels of Cognitive Functioning Scale.

Mental Status Exam

During a neurological examination, a patient's mental status is measured through a structured assessment of their behavioral and cognitive functioning. During this examination, the following functions are assessed: level of consciousness, attention, motor functioning, speech, mood, affect, thoughts/perception, attitude, insight, reaction level to the examiner, and higher cognitive abilities (Martin, 1990). The mental status exam is equivalent to a physical exam; it occurs as a series of observations. The observations may occur at different times throughout an appointment, in that they may be ordered differently for each client. In the end, the findings help to describe a client's appearance, cognition, and emotion. The mental status exam assists clinicians in determining psychiatric diagnoses. For example, a person with dementia might present with difficulty speaking, which will be evident when the client is expected to answer questions. Upon recording responses to questions and observations, the clinician should take such responses into consideration when offering a final diagnosis/decision.

APGAR

The APGAR test was developed in 1952 and has become a standard tool used immediately following the delivery of a baby. The APGAR provides scores for a baby's breathing effort, heart rate, muscle tone, reflexes, and skin color at 1 and 5 min post-delivery (Apgar, 1966). As a result of the use of medication and anesthesia during delivery, the APGAR was established to provide a quick and accurate assessment of an infant's status post-birth. In addition to identifying signs of distress, the APGAR works well to identify metabolic imbalance (Apgar, 1966). For each of the systems assessed using this test, the infant is assigned a number (0–2). For example, if a baby is not breathing at birth, they are assigned a *0* to indicate that they are not breathing. If a baby engages in active motion, they are assigned a *2* to indicate such behavior (Finster & Wood, 2005). It should be noted that the APGAR score was invented to assess the baby's condition at birth, and should not be used as a predictor of long-term outcomes (Montgomery, 2000). However, low APGAR scores could indicate significant problems, such as the presence of a disability (Nelson & Ellenberg, 1981), and should be considered when making clinical formulations. This score lacks psychometric sophistication and displays reliability concerns so judicious use is recommended (Dean & Gray, 1991).

Glasgow Coma Scale

The *Glasgow Coma Scale* (GCS) was first presented in 1974 to aid in determining one's level of consciousness (Sternbach, 2000). This tool provides a practical method for assessing impairment of consciousness, especially at patient presentation or following a traumatic brain injury (TBI). It is used by trained staff at the site of an injury, as well as in hospitals to measure eye opening, verbal response, and motor response (Teasdale et al., 2014). Patients are measured on a quantitative scale between numbers 1 and 6, depending on the function being assessed. If a patient is not testable, they are given a rating of *NT* to indicate that they are *not testable.* For example, eye opening is measured at ratings of *not testable, none (1), to pressure (2), to sound (3), and spontaneous (4;* Teasdale et al., 2014). The total GCS score is a sum of the eye opening, verbal, and motor response subscores. The GCS is used to determine cognitive functioning in adults; however, there is a modified version of the GCS for children (Hynd & Willis, 1988). While it is critical to understand this scale, many patients admitted to a hospital with a TBI will have the absence of a coma and yet suffer long-term coma-like brain injuries (Kolb & Whishaw, 2003). There is a significant relationship between a patient's short- or long-term coma and their need for comprehensive rehabilitation (Lezak et al., 2012). Clinical neuropsychologists who focus on traumatic brain injuries and other medical issues use information from patient histories as a key to understanding client rehabilitation. See Table 9.1 for Glasgow Coma Scale levels.

Ranchos Los Amigos

The Ranchos Los Amigos Levels of Cognitive Functioning Scale, also known as the Ranchos scale, is a tool used to rate recovery in patients with brain injuries. The scale assists in describing cognitive and behavioral patterns found in brain-injured patients (Lin & Wroten, 2017). This Ranchos Scale is often used in a more comprehensive fashion, both initially following an injury as well as throughout the recovery

Table 9.1 Glasgow Coma Scale

Behavior	Response	Score
Eye opening response	Open spontaneously	4
	Open to verbal command	3
	Open to pain	2
	No response	1
Verbal response	Oriented to time, place, and person	5
	Confused	4
	Inappropriate words	3
	Incomprehensible sounds	2
	No response	1
Motor response	Obeys commands	6
	Localizing to pain	5
	Withdrawal from pain	4
	Abnormal flexion to pain	3
	Abnormal extension to pain	2
	No response	1

period (Lin & Dulebohn, 2017). The Ranchos Scale provides an easy way to describe a person's level of activity. When assessing an individual's responses, their reactions are described to occur at various cognitive functioning levels. See Table 9.2 for the various levels of the Ranchos Los Amigos Scale.

Lateral Preference

Understanding lateral preference has historically been a conundrum for clinical neuropsychologists because early on they thought that there would be a clear relationship between a patient's handedness and significant cerebral dysfunctions (Dean & Reynolds, 1997; Rothlisberg & Dean, 1985). Thus, a number of questionnaires or rating scales were developed to evaluate laterality functions, such as handedness, footedness, and eyedness. The most popular assessment for lateral preference is the *Lateral Preference Schedule* (Dean, 1978). This tool is an easy and quick self-report measure that takes approximately 15 min to complete (Davis, 2008). Within that assessment, the following factors provide understanding for individuals with mixed laterality being most significant. Numerous early studies by Dean and colleagues attempted to understand the relationship of all lateral senses to the brain (e.g., handedness, footedness, visually-guided; e.g., see Dean & Reynolds, 1997)). For example, researchers have evaluated verbal performance discrepancies, cued auditory asymmetries, and functional lateralization of the brain (Dean, 1979, 1982, 1984). Dean, Schwartz, and Smith (1981) found

Table 9.2 Levels of cognitive functioning for the Ranchos Scale

Level	Cognitive functioning response
Level 1	**No reaction**: Person is unconscious and does not respond to sight, sound, touch, or movement
Level 2	**Generalized reaction**: Person begins to respond slowly to sensory stimuli (may include chewing, sweating, moaning)
Level 3	**Localized reaction**: Person wakes on and off, makes more movements that are different each time
Level 4	**Confusion/Agitation**: Person is very active but not yet able to comprehend the situation; behavior may be bizarre or uncooperative
Level 5	**Confusion/Inappropriate**: Person may be able to attend for a few minutes; person becomes less agitated; responds to simple commands more consistently
Level 6	**Confusion/Appropriate**: Person is more motivated but still depends on others; person begins to recognize and be more aware of others
Level 7	**Automatic/Appropriate**: Person seems to act appropriately in hospital or home; person can follow a schedule with some assistance
Level 8	**Purposeful/Appropriate**: Person is cognizant of problems with cognition and memory; person may start to compensate for problems; person can learn things at a slower rate

significant differences between groups of individuals with learning difficulties in factors related to: (1) general handedness, (2) visually-guided activites (3) fine motor, (4) eye preference, (5) ear preference, (6) activities of strength, and (7) fine motor. When one considers that we are *contralaterally wired*, that is, where the right side of the body relates to the left hemisphere and the left side of the body relates to the right hemisphere, it makes conceptual sense to think that functions on one side of the body would relate to continuity of cognitive processing. Many studies show that children with neurodiversity display unique patterns of lateral preference (Dean et al., 1981; Rothlisberg & Dean, 1985).

How to Differentiate Neuropsychology from Neurology

People generally confuse, and thus cannot differentiate between the fields of neurology and clinical neuropsychology (Lezak et al., 2012). This is made even more complex by the fact that some neurologists are termed *"behavioral"* neurologists. Although there is a great deal of overlap relating to lower and higher cognitive functions, there are significant differences in the way data are interpreted and used by these specialists. The neurological history and related physical examination, which is typically the first step in a comprehensive medical/physical health evaluation, tends to be the platform which the medical specialist uses to begin to hypothesize potential concerns and test-related areas to see if concerns are similar to a constellation of issues related to a specific medical disorder (Kolb & Whishaw, 2003). All medical practitioners, including pediatricians, family practice physicians, neurologists, and psychiatrists use this examination as their first step in understanding a patient's abilities. This procedure is used to evaluate and track the basic functions of human growth, development, and aging. The emphasis of the medical practitioner will change given the nature of their specialized examination. Undoubtedly, a neurologist will focus on neurological disorders whereas a psychiatrist will focus on psychiatric disorders. However, this is where specialists utilize the knowledge of one another. If a neurologist suspects a psychological disturbance they may ask for consultation from a psychiatrist or clinical neuropsychologist. As previously stated, they may ask a question as simple as if the patient's presenting disorder appears to be primarily organic or functional in origin. Given the complexity of human functioning, and the overlap between these areas, this is not as easy a question as one might think (Hartlage & D'Amato, 2008a, b; Rothlisberg et al., 2003). But in general, neurologists focus on the larger issues relating to the initial diagnosis and later treatment of disorders of the nervous system, focusing on the multifaceted diagnosis of various neurological diseases discussed below (D'Amato, Fletcher-Janzen, & Reynolds, 2005). The complexity of this neurodiagnostic process is extremely challenging and requires considerable training, expertise, and experience (Dean, 1986; Lezak et al., 2012).

The Neurological Examination

The neurological exam often is broken down into two parts, the patient's *history* and the general *physical* examination (Kolb & Whishaw, 2003). While the history may overlap extensively with a clinical neuropsychologist, the physical examination is quite different. While some basic abilities such as walking, talking, writing, and cognitive processing may be observed by both specialists, the neurologist assesses many more complex medical/physical abilities such as (1) sounds of the heart and blood vessels, (2) pupillary reflexes, (3) gag reflexes, (4) smell, (5) taste, (6) corneal reflexes, (7) muscle stretch reflexes, (8) sensitivity to touch, and (9) blood pressure. Typically, most if not all cranial nerves are evaluated. They then go on to evaluate higher cognitive functions such as mental manipulation, reading, writing, mathematics, and problem-solving, and current issues. Motor systems in various parts of the body are further examined as well as a sensory examination that reviews areas such as touch, pain, temperature, and vibration.

The Challenge of Diagnosis before Rehabilitation

Entire books are written about this critical examination which covers significant findings related to vascular disorders, traumatic brain injuries (TBI), epilepsy, tumors, headaches, infections, disorders of motor neurons and the spinal cord, and disorders of sleep (See Chap. 1, Van Damme & D'Amato, 2021). Most of these disorders are relatively common, life-changing, and relate to significant changes in neuropsychological functioning (Hartlage & D'Amato, 2008a). The clinical neuropsychological examination while covering some of the same areas of neurology, views functioning from a different lens. They consider individuals in light of the ability they have or need to develop to return to life and be successful *with others*, *in work*, and *in life* (Rothlisberg et al., 2003). While a neurologist may diagnose a patient as having a TBI, the clinical neuropsychology will work with a team planning a rehabilitation program that will help them relearn skills and abilities, and return to life and work (if such a move is possible). However, while it is important to remember that advanced medicine based on cutting-edge technology is amazing, "*the most sensitive measure of cerebral integrity is behavior and behavior analysis consistently finds dysfunction that is not seen in MRI, especially in cases of closed head injury and epilepsy*" (Kolb & Whishaw, 2003; p. 762). Thus, the practice of clinical neuropsychology has continued to grow at an enormous rate and has developed into a critical health service provider postdoctoral specialty. See Chap. 1 for a discussion of growth and needed specialization areas.

A neuropsychological evaluation includes the consideration of many domains, in addition to the deliberation of neuroanatomy and corresponding functions. The comprehensive evaluation focuses on the skills that can be found within the different lobes of the brain. For instance, the frontal lobe of the brain often concerns executive processes, such as task initiation, organization, and long-term planning.

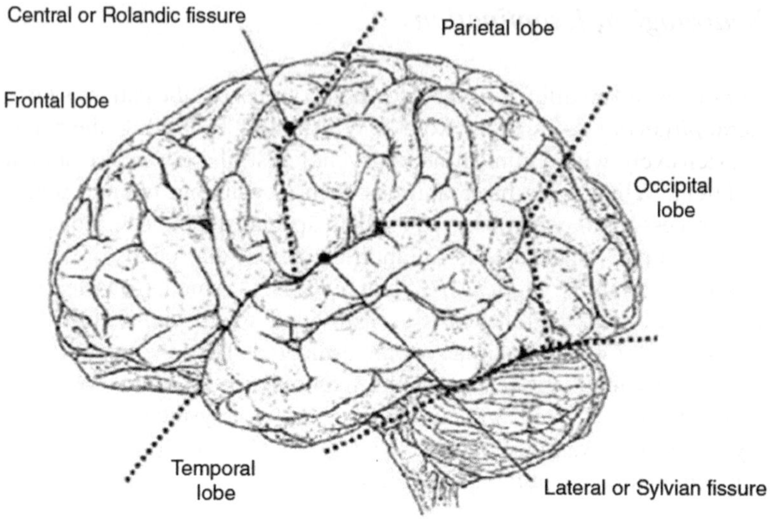

Fig. 9.1 Lobes of the Brain. (*Source*: Reprinted with permission from Power & D'Amato, 2018)

The other lobes of the brain are the occipital, temporal, and parietal lobes. Figure 9.1 shows the lobes of the brain, in addition to the central and lateral fissures. See Chap. 3 for discussion of functional neuroanatomy. Recent research has shown that many disorders that were originally thought to be related to behavior really have a neuropsychological foundation (Lezak et al., 2012). Table 9.3 illustrates various disorders that have neuropsychological underpinnings.

History of Neuropsychological Assessment for Evidence-Based Intervention

Qualitative and Quantitative Approaches to Practice

Two distinct approaches – *qualitative* and *quantitative* – have been utilized in helping us understand the biological basis of each individual's functioning. Many credit Halstead (1947) as developing the approach to using comprehensive and standardized measures for all individuals with neuropsychological impairment. He advocated a comprehensive, wide-range battery which he developed with his student Reitan (Reitan & Wolfson, 1985) and then at one point, these measures were the most widely used neuropsychological batteries in the world. There are several factors that need to be evaluated and each person who undergoes this evaluation is administered the batteries in the same fashion (Johnson & D'Amato, 2011).

Table 9.3 Disorders found to have neuropsychological underpinnings

Alcoholism	Language disorders
Alzheimer disease	Learning disorders: Reading, mathematics, written expression
Asthma	Malnutrition
Aphasia	Migraines/headaches
Attention deficit disorder (ADD) and attention deficit/hyperactivity disorder (ADHD)	Motor skill disorders
Behavioral/personality disorders	Multiple sclerosis
Cancer	Muscular dystrophy
Dementia not otherwise specified	Parkinson disease
Diabetes	Perceptual disorders
Eating disorders	Pervasive developmental disorders
Epilepsy	Pick disease
Fetal alcohol syndrome	Prematurity
Genetic and chromosomal disorders: Phenylketonuria (PKU), Down syndrome	Seizure disorders
Hearing/auditory disorders	Traumatic brain injuries (as a result of motor vehicle accidents, pedestrian-vehicle accidents, contact/ noncontact spores, accidental injuries, abuse, assault)
HIV/AIDS	Vascular disorders
Huntington disease	Vision problems
Hypertension	Zika virus
Infants' exposure to prenatal toxins	

Coronavirus-19 (COVID)

The Need for Innovation in Clinical Neuropsychology

Understanding the brain is a quandary because every brain is unique and standardized instruments including neuropsychological testing, as well as use of an MRI, do not easily differentiate the unique or impaired brain components. Therefore, we need to use informal and qualitative assessments to help us determine a client's strengths and weaknesses (D'Amato et al., 2011). For example, Rhodes, D'Amato, and Rothlisberg (2008) have advocated using the Thematic Apperception Test (TAT) in unique ways such as having clients write stories or having clients tell stories, and then interpreting data from a neuropsychological perspective. The uniqueness of the brain requires this type of approach. Similarly, Teglasi (2015) has called for the use of storytelling which collects information which may not be offered in any other format. To be an effective health service psychologist, one must approach neuropsychological needs armed with innovative assessment for intervention skills (D'Amato et al., 2005). Another example is van Schalkwyk's collage technique for understanding the core of a client's neuropsychological profile. See Chap. 7 for more in-depth coverage of related techniques.

How Qualitative Data Should Link to the Biological Basis of Behavior

To understand an individual's neuropsychological strengths and weaknesses, a practitioner must use an ecological approach. An ecological framework is based on evidence that no single factor can explain or predict behaviors (Perfect & D'Amato, 2020; Spooner & Pachana, 2006). Neuropsychologists spend a great deal of time using informal and formal methods that inform clinical decisions. In addition to standardized test batteries, the collection of qualitative information, such as one's developmental history, provide critical details to assist in impression formulation and/or diagnosis. Historically, organic and environmental variables are considered essential within an evaluation (D'Amato et al., 2011; D'Amato, 1990). The *nature* versus *nurture* debate is one of the oldest issues in the field of psychology (Hartlage & D'Amato, 2008b). While many are divided on the issue of which contributes more to our development, it is often assumed that both neurobiology and environment influence our thoughts and behavior (Collins et al., 2000). Figure 9.2 illustrates the systems, contexts, settings, sources, and methods from which we should draw information regarding a client. As displayed, social, developmental, and medical historical data provide rich information regarding a client's systems, contexts, and settings. D'Amato and colleagues have developed a questionnaire that helps one know what questions to ask in an interview; the questionnaire is availabe in both pediatric and adult formats (for children see Tincup et al, 2005; for adults see

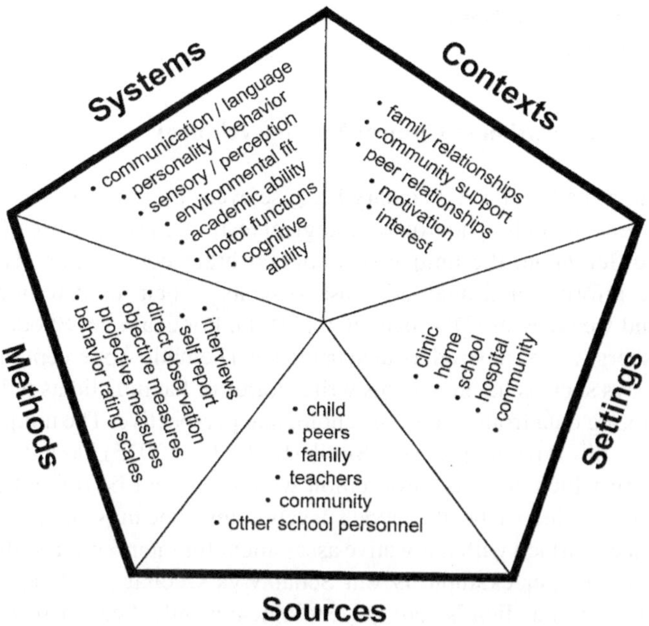

Fig. 9.2 Organic and environmental areas to consider during an evaluation

Appendix A, D'Amato et al., 2021) during a comprehensive neuropsychological evaluation. This questionnaire covers all relevant areas in detail and is completed using a multi-step process which includes some one-to-one interviewing and some completion of the form in advance by the patient. This questionnaire includes sentence completion tasks, self-ratings of behavior, and short response questions. The authors recommend that readers practice using the form prior to conducting a formal evaluation. Neuropsychologists also use informal approaches to determine a client's current functioning and status, such as a neurological examination, mental status examination, and other direct behavioral observations of a client.

Behavioral Observations

During any psychological evaluation, it is necessary to observe and document behavior that occurs during testing. Observations of individuals during the evaluation process can provide valuable insight into qualitative information, such as how one approaches a problem. Each person approaches test items differently, and such behaviors can offer information regarding self-esteem, frustration, communication skills, academic approaches, and more. During an evaluation, it is common for health service psychologists to keep track of motor skills, activity level, and language. It is also beneficial to document consistency in performance, mood, frustration tolerance, cognitive flexibility, motivation, degree of cooperativeness, anxiety, and the need for redirection (Aylward & Carson, 2005). Entire book chapters have been offered that deal with *how* and *what* to observe with individuals during the evaluation process (see e.g., Sattler & D'Amato, 2002a, 2002b). Observations are perhaps the most important aspect of the psychological evaluation process and behaviors displayed during this greatly influence the outcome of the evaluation. For example, if an individual has difficulty sitting still for too long, they may be likely to rush through test items resulting in lower performance. Many view the "*relationship*" as essential to success and the client-psychologist interactions are vital to understanding the dynamics and uniqueness of each client (D'Amato & Rothlisberg, 1997/1992; Gaddes & Edgell, 1994; Luria, 1970, 1980). Another related example is *The Boston Process Approach*, developed by Kaplan (1988) which emphasizes the importance of watching clients approach problems during assessment. This process-oriented approach allows for neuropsychologists to consider qualitative aspects rather than solely considering a client's quantitative numerical test scores. Qualitative aspects of behavior should always be considered when results are interpreted and impressions are formulated. Related to behavioral observations of a client, it is necessary to consider a client's motivation during an evaluation. This can be one of the most critical areas when conceptualizing a client. Figure 9.3 demonstrates which components of motivation should be considered. Ornstein and Sobel (1987) have claimed that what a person can learn is also affected and organized by emotions and motivation – so to understand the voice of a client, an understanding of aspects such as the client's motivation, attention, relevance, satisfaction, and confidence will be

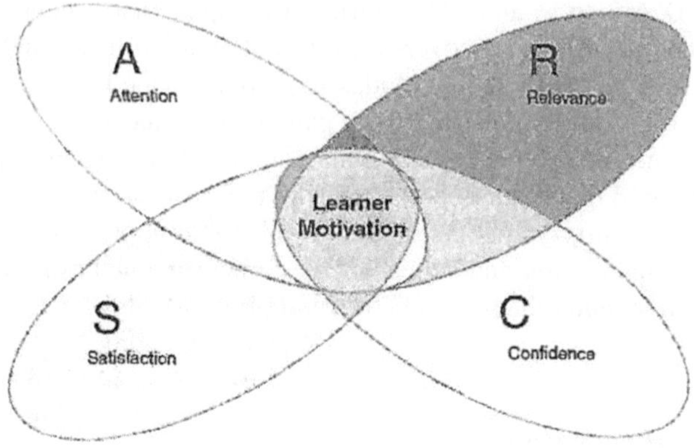

Fig. 9.3 Visual display of the components of a client's motivation

needed to determine future learning. Figure 9.3 shows how learner motivation must be understood within the context of attention (A), relevance (R), satisfaction (S), and confidence (C).

Visual display of the components of a learner's motivation. From D'Amato and Wang (2015). Copyright © John Wiley & Sons, Inc. Reprinted with permission

Review of History/Clinical Interview

To understand a client comprehensively involves the collection of an individual's detailed history. This history provides a professional with information, such as medical/ health history, developmental milestones, and social functioning (see D'Amato et al., 2005, Appendix A, p. 859, for an example). The history is also essential for gathering information about an individual's culture. Cultural factors, such as age, gender, education, income, and other related factors, should always be taken into consideration during a neuropsychological evaluation. Such implications assist the clinician in determining outcomes. There are different ways of collecting this information. Historically, a neuropsychological understanding of a client seemed to represent a continuum with organic (factors within the child) at one end and environmental factors (outside the child) at the other. What makes neuropsychology unique is that we consider environmental outcomes, biogenetic factors, and outcome behaviors and how these influence/are influenced by one's perceptions, memory, affect, and problem-solving (see Fig. 9.4).

A detailed social, developmental, and medical history is one of the most critical elements of a neuropsychological evaluation (Davis, 2011). This information is typically collected during a clinical interview with a client, family, and/or child (D'Amato et al., 2005). This interview is typically conducted prior to the administration of formal assessments and assists in the development of a practitioner-client

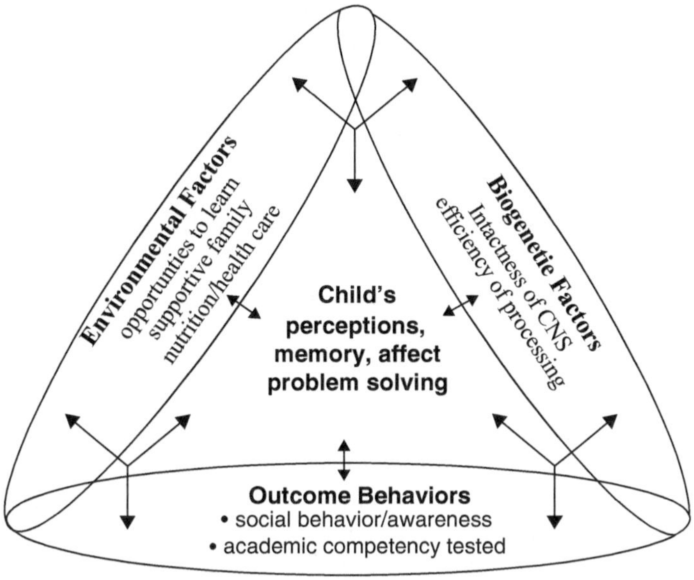

Fig. 9.4 Impact of environmental, biogenetic, and outcome factors

relationship. As previously discussed, many medical specialists and psychological practitioners view the clinical interview and process as the most important activity with a client (Lezak et al., 2012). Clinical interviews may be unstructured, structured, or semistructured (Jones, 2011). During unstructured interviews, questions are not standardized and can be asked in any order. Practitioners usually determine the questions to ask and allow the clients to answer in any format they choose. Structured interviews consist of a standardized list of questions that are asked in a sequence (First, 2014). Semistructured interviews are a mix of both structured and unstructured formats, in that questions are pre-determined, but are asked in a less-uniformed manner. Detailed history collection can take a significant amount of time, which is often why neuropsychologists will ask clients/guardians to complete forms prior to the initial interview. Questions during the interview process or on forms will vary depending on the age of the client. For example, if a neuropsychologist is conducting a pediatric evaluation, they might ask questions that relate more to marital status of parents and/or custody/supervision. Questions on forms, and during the interview process, will often pertain to one's medical (e.g., history of medical/psychiatric disorders), developmental (e.g., ages at which developmental milestones were reached), and social (e.g., current relationship and social status) history. If the client is school-age, additional information about academic and/or school functioning will also be considered. A comprehensive clinical interview is typically the first step in determining initial diagnosis and treatment. While current functioning and environment are often essential in determining impressions, a detailed family and medical history can assist in differential diagnosis. Questions asked during a clinical interview, in addition to administration of assessments, can assist in determining if any such disorders might be the cause of weaknesses in neuropsychological functioning (Hartlage & D'Amato, 2008a, b; Davis, 2011; Lezak et al., 2012). It also allows the clinical to determine the informal and formal assessments that will be administered during the evaluation.

Neuropsychological Models of Assessment for Intervention

Luria and His Functional Integrative Systems

Deciding how to comprehend behavior and relate it to brain functioning is a difficult undertaking at best (Reynolds & French, 2005). Few researchers agree how this should be done and numerous models are available historically (e.g., Orton, Halstead) to help us understand brain functioning (D'Amato et al., 2005; Davis, 2011; Reynolds, 1981a, 1981b). One of the most prominent models offered in the literature is by Luria (1966, 1970, 1973, 1980) and this is the model the authors advocate learning for a comprehensive understanding of how the brain processes information. Luria reported that he was influenced by others such as Vygotsky and Piaget although he had a clear focus on the frontal lobes and informal, data-based procedures (Reynolds & French, 2005). Luria proposed a functional system view of the brain dividing it into three major components he termed *blocks of the brain.* **Block I**, often called the arousal and attention unit, is concerned with energy level, and tone, and is composed of the brainstem, including the reticular formation, the midbrain, pons, and medulla, and relates to basic life functions. **Block II** is composed of the parietal, occipital, and temporal lobes, called the association areas of the cortex, and relates to information processing. **Block III** is composed of the remaining area including the sensorimotor strip and the frontal lobes, and corresponds with executive functioning, including the formation of intentions and programming behavior (Luria, 1970, 1980). The most critical component of this theory is the fact that each block of the brain is *not* seen as functioning independently (Reynolds, 1981a, 1981b). Moreover, there is a dynamic interaction between the areas, and a weakness in one area of the brain may interact and affect the functioning of other brain areas (Christian, 1975). A popular quote from Luria (1964) explains:

When one or another link has been lost, the whole functional system will be disturbed in a particular way, and systems of disturbance of one or another higher (mental) function will have a completely different structure, depending on the location of the damage (Luria, 1964, p. 6).

Luria's work influenced the development of many cognitive and neuropsychological tests including those of the *Kaufman-Assessment Battery for Children*, *The Cognitive Assessment System*, and the *NEPSY* (Flanagan & McDonough, 2018; Kaufman & Kaufman, 1983; Naglieri & Das, 1996).

Hemispheric Processing or Cerebral Specialization

Since the beginning of time individuals have sought to understand the brain and its relationship to behavior (Lezak et al., 2012; Schultz & Schultz, 2016). Initially, scientists believed the essence of our abilities were controlled by our heart. While this makes intuitive sense, they quickly discovered that the brain was the moderator of our functioning. Early on, researchers noted that the brain had two sides or hemispheres. Chapter 1 covers in-depth these many initial historical neuropsychological theories. Beginning in the late 1950s and moving into the 1960s, a number of prominent researchers sought to understand the differences between the *Right hemisphere* of the brain and the *Left hemispheric* of the brain (Carmon & Bechtoldt, 1969; Reitan, 1955; Sperry, 1974; Stark, 1961; Wada, 1949). In fact, many popular brain-based books have been written relating our hemispheric processing styles to learning, relationship success, and job accomplishments (Sattler & D'Amato, 2002a, 2002b). For example, see Dweck (2015; *Mindset: The new psychology of success*). Clearly, understanding the brain and how it works is critical to successful learning and living (Sousa, 2005, 2006). Some authors have even advocated that women tend to be more verbal and men tend to be more nonverbal while others have seen men as being less emotional and women as being more expressive (Zaroff & D'Amato, 2015).

It seems that most individuals have preferential processing modes or styles which may be assessed at simple and complex levels. Perhaps the simplest level is to assess if individuals prefer to be *verbal* or *nonverbal* processers. Some have advocated that traditional Western society tends to be more verbal and abstract whereas Eastern society tends to be more nonverbal, visual, and tactical (Reynolds, 1981a, 1981b; van Schalkwyk & D'Amato, 2015a, 2015b). Processing modes have been applied to learning with reading instruction seen as relating to a simultaneous/wholistic or whole word approaches to learning in contract to those who learn best sequentially and phonetically (Reynolds & French, 2005). Kaufman and his colleagues (e.g., Kaufman & Horn, 1996; Kaufman & Kaufman, 2014; Power & D'Amato, 2018) have developed cognitive, educational, and executive functioning measures that relate to processing style while Naglieri and colleagues (2014), and others have made similar attempts (Flanagan & McDonough, 2018; Reynolds, 1981a, 1981b). Both research groups have found promising results related to both assessment of individuals and intervention using specialized research-based techniques (Power & D'Amato, 2018; Work & Hee-Sook, 2005). While we have made great strides in these areas we still have much to learn. It would seem necessary to establish if different patient brain processing style may relate to the ability of individuals to profit from various therapies based on neuropsychological profiles. For example, will patients with certain learning styles profit from using a computer-based-phonetic reading approach, would individuals with certain personality profiles profit most from dialectic behavioral therapy, or would patients with an autism spectrum disability do best in a small group opposed to a traditional classroom approach? (Gisi & D'Amato, 2000; Rothlisberg et al., 2003; Sattler & D'Amato, 2002a, 2002b; Work & Hee-Sook, 2005; Table 9.4).

Table 9.4 Right hemisphere and left hemisphere processing modes, functions, and memory/learning[a]

Function	References
Right hemisphere	
Processing modes	
Simultaneous	Sperry (1974)
Holistic	Sperry (1969); Dimond and Beaumont (1974)
Visual/nonverbal	Sperry (1974); Savage and Thomas (1993)
Imagery	Seamon and Gazzaniga (1973)
Spatial reasoning	Sperry (1974); Polzner et al. (1990)
Nonverbal functions	
Depth perception	Carmon and Bechtoldt (1969)
Melodic perception	Shankweller (1966)
Tactile perception (integration)	Boll (1974b)
Haptic perception	Witelson (1974)
Nonverbal sound recognition	Milner (1962)
Motor integration	Kimura (1967)
Visual constructive performance	Parsons et al. (1969)
Pattern recognition	Eccles (1973)
Memory/learning	
Nonverbal memory	Stark (1961)
Face recognition	Milner (1967)
	Hecaen and Angelergues (1962)
Left hemisphere	
Processing modes	
Sequential	Sperry et al. (1969)
Temporal	Mills (1977); Efron (1963)
Analytic	Morgan et al. (1971); Eccles (1973)
Verbal functions	
Speech	Wada (1949); Reitan (1955); Posner et al. (1988)
General language/verbal abilities	Gazzaniga (1970); Smith (1974)
Calculation/arithmetic	Reitan (1955); Eccles (1973); Gerstmann (1957)
Abstract verbal thought	Gazzaniga and Sperry (1962)
Writing (composition)	Sperry (1974); Hecaen and Marcie (1974)
Complex motor functions	Dimond and Beaumont (1974)
Body orientation	Gerstmann (1957)
Vigilance	Dimond and Beaumont (1974)
Memory/learning	
Verbal paired associates	Dimond and Beaumont (1974)
Short-term verbal recall	Kimura (1961)
Abstract and concrete words	McFarland et al. (1978); Seamon and Gazzaniga (1973)
Verbal mediation/rehearsal	Dean (1983); Seamon and Gazzaniga (1973)
Learning complex motor functions	Dimond and Beaumont (1974)

[a]Adapted from Power and D'Amato (2018). Please see the original source of the table for a listing of all references cited above

Understanding Multicultural Issues in a Neuropsychological Context

In recent years, there has been a push for more social justice in the world, including the acceptance of diverse views of relationships and changing societal mores. An understanding of these changes must lead to the consideration of important environmental and familial factors – if not considered, subjective perspectives can lead to misdiagnosis and erroneous understanding of clients. Recently the definition of a *typical family* has changed. For example, health service providers should no longer assume that every client has a mother and a father. Historically, while some may refer to a *mother* as the individual who solely produced the child, others may consider this person a primary caretaker, nurturer, and provider. Parents might be composed of two mothers or two fathers, which is an essential detail to consider as part of a comprehensive neuropsychological evaluation. Details of egg or sperm donorship are crucial to share with a health service provider as that can mean the difference in a diagnosis. Genetic features of disorders may go overlooked if not sought out thoroughly. Additionally, health psychology service providers need to more carefully consider the aspect of gender when writing reports and working in therapeutic environments. For instance, many individuals who identify as transgender prefer to be referred to by pronouns that do not correspond with their biological sex organs. Other individuals who are transgender prefer more ambiguous pronouns, such as *ze* or *they.*

Many neuropsychologists don't consider multicultural components and end up making recommendations for certain populations that are inappropriate and ineffective. Within certain Asian cultures, family is considered to be one of the highest priorities (van Schalkwy & D'Amato, 2015a, b). If an elderly man who is Asian requires memory interventions and significant care, it is very important to consider the setting in which the care is offered. For example, a neuropsychologist might recommend that this client receive clinical care outside of the home instead of considering that the care takes place under the family's guidance and within the home. It is necessary to consider multicultural factors when making recommendations for neuropsychological interventions (Davis & D'Amato, 2014). The future must focus on evidence-based interventions with a *multicultural* lens.

Understanding and Comparing Quantitative and Qualitative Interventions

Health service psychologists that can provide comprehensive neuropsychological practices often utilize more than a single approach. In fact, the authors of this chapter advocate that all skilled neuropsychological practitioners must understand and be able to utilize both quantitative and qualitative models of assessment (D'Amato et al., 2005). The qualitative Lurian/Eastern approach is considered an informal, skill-driven, and client-centered model, whereas the Actuarial/Western approach advocates a statistical, standardized, and test-score based model (Power & D'Amato, 2018).

Which Approach is Best?

Both approaches are quite inimitable and erudite practitioners will be able to select tasks or tests from each approach and integrate them to understand, diagnose, and offer evidence-based services to clients (Traughber & D'Amato, 2005). Table 9.3 compares and contrasts both approaches with detailed words describing each unique paradigm. As is true with most of psychology, it is best to consider these paradigms as *ends of a continuum* with both ends being distinctly different but with integration of both methods possible; the authors of this chapter advocate selection of techniques from both ends of the continue and offer such an approach as a *best practice* in neuropsychological assessment for evidence-based practice (Kratochwill & Stoiber, 2002; Sattler & D'Amato, 2002a, 2002b). Thus, one should work to understand and utilize data from patients, selected from *both ends* of the model to offer wide-ranging assessments. In total, practitioners should use an integrated or mixed battery *collecting data* that is most relevant to understanding behavior and working for evidence-based change. For instance, following Luria's model, one may begin with observations and use flexible and informal tasks to understand patient functioning (Luria, 1966, 1970, 1973). Then this basic understanding of the patient could be used to select objective, psychometric tests that offer fixed data which can be used to diagnose, monitor, and program plan for rehabilitation. This model demonstrates how services from both ends of the continuum may be integrated to offer sophisticated neuropsychological services (e.g., biofeedback, counseling, adaptive skill evaluations) that can track psychological progress. The most important part of such an integrated examination is the appropriate diagnosis of the patient (Power & D'Amato, 2018), and the selection of suitable rehabilitation techniques (Rothlisberg et al., 2003; Sattler & D'Amato, 2002a, 2002b), which may be documented behaviorally (Burns, 2008). Psychological and/or behavioral change must be the focus of any evidence-based neuropsychological interventions (D'Amato & Rothlisberg, 1997/1992) (Table 9.5).

Depth of Neuropsychological Examinations

The most unique feature of the clinical neuropsychological perspective in both assessment and intervention is its comprehensive and in-depth nature. It integrates both internal (i.e., what the client is feeling) and external (i.e., how the client is behaving) aspects of behavior. It also integrates the medical aspects of functioning in tandem with a psychological and historical understanding of behavior. Accordingly, neuropsychological evaluations are one of the most time-consuming

Table 9.5 Lurian/Eastern versus Actuarial/Western approach

Lurian/Eastern approach:	North American/Western approach:
Theory-driven	Not overall a priority theory; data-driven
Attempts to support or confirm a theory	Attempts to disconfirm specific hypotheses
Synthetical	Analytical
Observation-oriented	Evaluation-oriented
Single-case-oriented	Group comparison-oriented
Describe behaviors	Evaluates behaviors
Subjective	Objective
Looks for patterns of functioning	Looks for differential diagnosis
Qualitative in nature	Quantitative in nature
Flexible	Fixed
Process-oriented	Product-oriented
Focuses on individualized activities	Focuses on multiple tests/procedure
Links behavioral data to functioning	Links psychometric data to diagnoses
Considers the functional system	Considers discrete brain-related areas
Clinical-theoretical	Actuarial-standardized

and most expensive in the field of psychology. Many insurance agencies track and dictate how long neuropsychologists may spend with clients given the complexity of neuropsychological functioning. For instance, for an individual referred for an evaluation of dementia, the insurance company approved only 1 hour of historical interview, 2 hours of testing, and 1 hour for a report/summary. In reality, neuropsychologists require up to 12–15 hours to complete a wide-band comprehensive evaluation, which includes historical intake, testing, data interpretation, report/summary, and client feedback. Given the extensive administration time of some of the batteries, neuropsychologists have trained psychometrists to ensure efficiency. Most psychometrists have a college-level or Master's degree in psychology. Often neuropsychologists will use extensively trained psychometrists to assist in assessment administration, which may be video recorded.

Each health service neuropsychologist must dissect human behavior into areas that can be evaluated and integrated to understand the complexity of each unique individual. We advocate that human behavior be understood within nine major domains. For heuristic purposes, we advocate that each of these nine major sections be viewed as pieces of a puzzle and when put together, an individual's functioning can be understood. Table 9.6 demonstrates the areas that should be assessed during a neuropsychological evaluation, which include **(1) Perceptual/sensory, (2) Motor functions, (3) Intelligence/cognitive abilities, (4) Executive functioning/attention, (5) Memory, (6) Communication/language, (7) Academic achievement, (8) Personality/behavior/family, and (9) Classroom/work environment.** Perceptual/ sensory systems refer to visual, auditory, and kinesthetic behaviors, such as touch discrimination or sense of smell. Motor functions include strength, speed, coordination, and lateral preference (i.e., right versus left). Intelligence/cognitive abilities encompass verbal and nonverbal capabilities, such as language skills, concept

Table 9.6 What areas should be assessed from a neuropsychological perspective?

1. Perceptual/sensory	**6. Communication/language skills**
Visual	Phonological processing (awareness and phonics)
Auditory	Listening comprehension
Tactile/kinesthetic	Expressive vocabulary
Integrated	Receptive vocabulary
	Speech/articulation
	Pragmatics
2. Motor functions	**7. Academic achievement**
Strength	Preacademic skills
Speed	Academic skills
Coordination	Rapid automatic naming
Lateral preference	Reading decoding
3. Intelligence/cognitive abilities	Reading fluency
Verbal functions	Reading comprehension
Language skills	Arithmetic computation
Concepts/problem-solving	Arithmetic concepts and applications
Numerical abilities	Social studies
Integrative functioning	Language arts
Nonverbal functions	Science
Receptive perception	Written language
Expressive perception	**8. Personality/behavior/family**
Abstract reasoning	Adaptive behavior
Spatial manipulation	Daily living
Construction	Development
Visual	Play/leisure
Integrative functions	Environmental/social
	Parental/family
	School/work environment
	Peers
	Community
	Patient history
	Coping/tolerance
	Family interpersonal style
	Happiness/resiliency
	Internalizing/externalizing symptoms
	Psychopathology
	Social skills
	Projective/expressive
4. Executive functioning/attention	**9. Classroom/work environment**
Sustained attention	Learning environment fit
Inhibition	Peer reactions
Shifting set	Community reactions

(continued)

Table 9.6 (continued)

Planning	Teacher/staff reactions
Flexibility	Classroom dispositions
Initiation	Direct behavioral observations
Organization	
5. Memory	
Short-term memory	
Long-term memory	
Working memory	
Retrieval fluency	

problem-solving, and reasoning. Executive functioning/attention refers to abilities such as sustained attention, inhibition, organization, and cognitive flexibility. Memory encompasses short-term, long-term, and working memory, in addition to retrieval fluency. Communication/language skills refers to all aspects of language, including phonological processing, listening comprehension, expressive language, receptive language, speech/articulation, and pragmatic language. Academic achievement refers to all academic skills, including those related to reading, mathematics, written language, and other relevant subjects in schools. The personality/behavior/family domain refers to adaptive behavior, environment, social skills, patient history, and internalizing/externalizing behaviors. Classroom/work environment refers to learning environments, reactions from various systems, classroom dispositions, and direct behavioral observations. Within the field of neuropsychology, there is much disagreement about exactly which areas should be evaluated. Each author calls for specific areas that they find critical to functioning. Authors may argue about how they would define memory (short-term vs. long-term) or how they would identify executive functioning (shifting set vs. planning). However, in general, most functional neuropsychological areas overlap in some type of systematic fashion.

Understanding a Qualitative Model to Guide Assessment for Interventions

As previously detailed, the qualitative approach should direct how a patient is approached, what questions are asked, which data are collected, how data are organized, and how such data are understood – these ideas were first introduced in Table 9.3. The conceptualization of the patient, differential diagnosis, and rehabilitation development and/or interventions will also be driven by the approach selected (Hynd & Semrud-Clikeman, 1990). This section of the chapter offers and explains specific questions which may be used to collect information from this approach. In addition, some tests have been built from this approach and although controversial, some of these instruments will be discussed (D'Amato et al., 2005; Davis, 2011; Power & D'Amato, 2018).

The best known advocate of this approach for assessment and rehabilitation was Luria (1970, 1973, 1980). It is clear from his accounts with patients that Luria gleaned a great deal of information from his informal clinical interactions with his patients. This led him to a selection of assessment tasks and tests that explained patient strengths, difficulties, cerebral impairment, and an approach to rehabilitation. He clearly linked all of his assessment procedures to his intervention/rehabilitation activities. Much like working with behavioral approaches (e.g., applied behavioral analysis), the data collected in this approach is used for direct interventions (Nicholson et al., 2011; D'Amato & Rothlisberg, 1997/1992). Luria argued for the collection of information based on 12 areas and they are briefly discussed:

1. The preliminary conversation (attention and care to detail linked to purposeful investigation)
2. The determination of cerebral dominance (processing modes and functions of hemispheres)
3. Investigation of motor functions (including the hands and speech)
4. Investigation of acoustic-motor organization (including perception, reproduction, regulation of pitch relationships, and rhythmic structures)
5. Investigation of the higher cutaneous and kinesthetic functions (including cutaneous sensation, muscle, and joint sensation)
6. Investigation of higher visual functions (including visual perception of objects, spatial orientation, and intellectual operations)
7. Investigation of impressive speech (including phonemic hearing, word comprehension, and understanding grammatical structures)
8. Investigation of expressive speech (including speech sounds, repetitive speech, and narrative speech)
9. Investigation of writing and reading (including phonetic analysis and writing and reading)
10. Investigation of arithmetical skills (including number structures and arithmetical operations)
11. Investigation of mnestic (memory) processing (including the learning process, retention, retrieval, and logical memorization)
12. Investigation of intellectual processes (including understanding of thematic pictures and texts, concept formation, and discursive intellectual activity)

(Christensen & Luria, 1975; Hynd & Semrud-Clikeman, 1990). For a more comprehensive review, please see Luria, 1966, 1973, 1980 or Christensen, 1975.

The qualitative approach focuses on the distinctiveness of the individual under evaluation and seeks to match the procedures used with the individual's unique profile. Glozman (1999) has argued that "Luria's neuropsychological assessment is recognized today by the world's scientific community to be the most comprehensive and flexible method of neuropsychological evaluation available, which is also based on an understanding of the factors underlying complex psychological activities" (p. 23). Sample tasks that could be used in a neuropsychologically based model have also been offered by others including Gaddes and Edgell (1994). Gaddes and Edgell offer tasks to evaluate auditory processes and aphasic signs in oral speech

(17 questions; p. 411), visual processes (13 questions; pp. 411–412), tactile processes (6 questions; p. 412), and motor-expressive processes (6 questions; pp. 412–413). For example, to evaluate auditory processes/abilities, the 6 questions Gaddes and Edgell use are reprinted below:

1. Can he recite all the letters of the alphabet?
2. Can he associate all the phonetic sounds of all the letters?
3. Can he name common objects without hesitation?
4. Can he describe the use of common objects?
5. How many nouns can the child produce in one minute?
6. Can he construct a meaningful sentence if given three words?

Reprinted from Gaddes and Edgell (p. 411).

Similarly, Luria (1970) provided a list of evaluation activities that Gaddes and Edgell (1994) advocated have used to assess the neuropsychological processes that underlie arithmetic. These steps included asking the student (1) to count aloud (to check memory of number in the correct sequence), (2) to recognize quantities, (3) to read and write single digits, (4) to read and write multidigit numbers (to show an understanding of the decimal system), (5) to recognize relative values, (6) to show competence in the basic arithmetic skills, and (7) to attempt more complex calculations (Luria, 1970, as cited in Gaddes & Edgell, 1994, p. 419).

These approaches can be used to understand a client and offer psychological interventions based on neuropsychological principals principles at primary, secondary, and tertiary levels. It should be obvious that this type of data collection may provide a wealth of information that can be used to understand the complete neuropsychological functioning of a client for rehabilitation or intervention. It is important to use the client's strengths to support his or her needs. Clearly, client individualization and uniqueness is the focus of evaluation for intervention in this distinctive approach.

Understanding a Quantitative Model to Guide Assessment for Interventions

In contrast to a qualitative model, the North American/Western Approach focuses on hypothesis-testing and data collection. This standardized model is evaluation-oriented, uses group norms, is fixed, product-oriented, and links psychometric data to use for diagnosis and intervention. This approach fits well with the current Western psychological paradigm which is statistical, data-based, and research-oriented (Flanagan & McDonough, 2018; Schultz & Schultz, 2016). These assessments offer many data collection tools, including structured interviews, questionnaires, and norm-referenced tests. Clinical neuropsychologists are taught the importance of using quantitative assessments because with these measures it is easier to generalize results to a broader audience (D'Amato et al., 2005).

Additionally, quantitative assessments offer more evidence or clear proof of neuropsychological impairment. Table 9.7 provides examples of quantitative assessments that fall under each of the neuropsychological domains.

Within a comprehensive evaluation, clinical neuropsychologists will typically choose between a *fixed-* and/or *flexible*-battery approach. A fixed-battery approach refers to a systematic administration of a consistent and standardized battery to all individuals, regardless of the referral question. A practitioner using a flexible-battery approach determines assessments based on individual referral problems and uses different batteries each time (Sattler & D'Amato, 2002a, 2002b). Often, many clinical neuropsychologists will choose to use an **integrative model**, allowing them to incorporate unique elements from each approach. By selecting an integrative model, a clinical neuropsychologist can emphasize the person being assessed, as

Table 9.7 Quantitative assessments for neuropsychological evaluation

Neuropsychological domains	Example of quantitative assessment
Perceptual/sensory	*Dean-Woodcock Sensory Motor Battery*
	Bender Visual-Motor Gestalt Test, Second Edition
	Wide Range Assessment of Visual Motor Abilities
Motor functions	*Bruininks-Oseretsky Test of Motor Proficiency, Second Edition*
	Bayley Scale of Infant and Toddler Development, Third Edition
	Grooved Pegboard
Intelligence/cognitive abilities	*Wechsler Adult Intelligence Scale, Fourth Edition*
	Kaufman Assessment Battery for Children, Second Edition
	Cognitive Assessment System, Second Edition
Executive functioning/ attention	*Delis-Kaplan Executive Function System*
	The NEPSY, Second Edition
	Tests of Variables of Attention
Memory/learning	*Children's Memory Scale*
	Wide Range Assessment of Memory & Learning, Second Edition
	Test of Memory and Learning, Second Edition
Communication/language skills	*Peabody Picture Vocabulary Test, Fourth Edition*
	Expressive One-Word Picture Vocabulary Test, Fourth Edition
	Comprehensive Assessment of Spoken Language, Second Edition
Academic achievement	*Wechsler Individual Achievement Test, Third Edition*
	Woodcock-Johnson Fourth Edition, Tests of Achievement
	Kaufman Test of Educational Achievement, Third Edition
Personality/behavior/family	*Behavior Assessment System for Children, Third Edition (parent, teacher, & child versions)*
	Autism Spectrum Rating Scale (parent and teacher ratings)
	Minnesota Multiphasic Personality Inventory – 2 (MMPI-2)
Classroom/work environment	*Time on-task observations*
	Structured teacher interview
	Dynamic Indicators of Basic Early Literacy Skills

well as their fit with their environment. The authors advocate for using an integrative model as it allows for the efficiency of selecting instruments that will be most likely to facilitate treatment planning (Power & D'Amato, 2018).

Qualitative and quantitative approaches represent both the different views of neuropsychological services and demonstrate how data can be used in a unique fashion to achieve similar or identical progress (Power & D'Amato, 2018). Health service psychologists typically select assessment approaches from one end of the quantitative/qualitative continuum and do not understand that best interventions stem from an *integration* of both ends of services. For example, one can assess the perceptual/sensory system from Eastern and Western approaches using diverse assessments. Using an Eastern approach, a clinical neuropsychologist can gain understanding about a client's sensory system by asking questions about sensory responses to stimuli, such as clothing. From a Western perspective, a clinical neuropsychologist can administer the *Sensory Processing Measure* (Miller-Kuhaneck et al., 2007) to determine an individual's sensory processing when compared to a normative sample. Using an **integrative model** ensures a comprehensive approach that will lead to more accurate clinical formulations.

Why Health Service Providers Need to Select an Assessment Model for Intervention

Within the fields of clinical and counseling psychology clinical psychology, most practitioners treat one client at a time based on a specific referral problem. This model stems from a medical/deficit model, in that assessments and interventions are completed at the time of the initial presentation of the problem (D'Amato et al., 2005a). From this view, psychology is a deficit model and a problem must occur before a solution is offered. Some researchers have advocated that the medical/deficit model should be changed to reflect a more ecological approach to individual and systemic change focusing on **positive mental health** (See Perfect & D'Amato, 2020). Nonetheless, many comprehensive health service psychologists, such as school and community-based psychologists, use a multitiered approach to assess and provide services to clients who have a need for services at increasing levels of intensity.

Primary, Secondary, and Tertiary Prevention for Intervention

The authors of this chapter not only advocate for using an **integrative model** for assessment, but a model that also allows prevention and intervention for individuals at-risk and clinically significant for neuropsychological weaknesses (Nicholson et al., 2011). Using a multitiered approach to assessment and intervention allows for psychologists to provide academic, behavioral, and social/emotional screening with valid assessment measures and ongoing monitoring if improvement has not been made (Semrud-Clikeman, 2005). This inclusive health service psychology model focuses on three levels of service which all help service provider psychologists study in social and community psychology. See Fig. 9.5 for a visual representation of tiers of psychological service delivery.

By using an integrative, comprehensive, and multitiered approach, clinical neuropsychologists can ensure that services are provided for preventative and intervention at all levels. *Primary prevention* refers to a psychological activity that is offered to all individuals. Stated another way, it may be viewed as preventing a problem with **healthy** individuals (Walker & Shinn, 2002). An example of this would be the screening of all children in the first few years of life for developmental delays. Another example is the education of breast cancer for communities through flyers, television commercials, the use of national spokespeople, and the wearing of ribbons during breast cancer awareness month. The goal is to reach 100% of the population through these preventative means. *Secondary prevention* focuses on a targeted group based on unique characteristics relating to an activity or identified issue (Løberg, 1989). For instance, blood pressure screening for those who have relatives with high blood pressure risk factors. Another example of secondary prevention is using adult mentors who meet with at-risk youth twice a week in an after-school program for an academic year (Walker & Shinn, 2002). *Tertiary intervention* refers to targeted intervention, or reducing the severity of a problem once it has occurred. An example would be offering an evidence-based psychological intervention (Hardy et al., 2017) for those who have a disability or disorder, such as those who manifest with depression. Most clinical, counseling, and school psychologists operate primarily at the tertiary level, which restricts the type of outreach psychologists can have. It is important to provide primary, secondary, and tertiary evidence-based services if a health service psychologist hopes to impact societal change (D'Amato

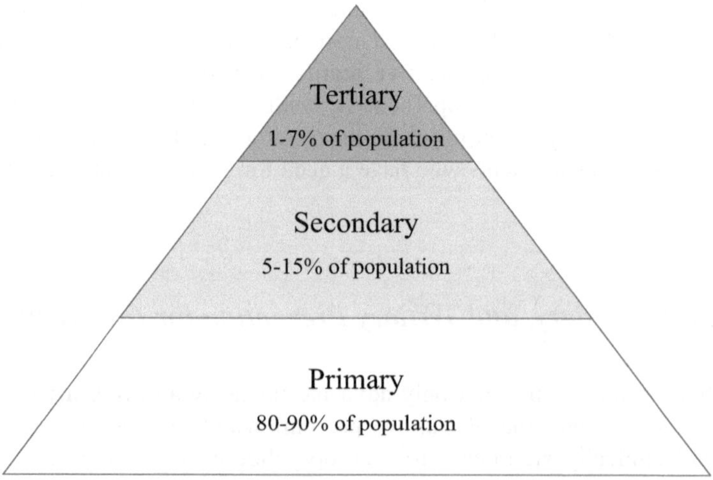

Fig. 9.5 Tiers of psychological service delivery

et al., 2011). For example, a clinical psychologist may conduct a neuropsychological evaluation of a client and offer treatment, including medication management, through an inpatient psychiatric facility (Walker & Shinn, 2002). A counseling psychologist may diagnose an individual with depression and offer dialectal behavior therapy (DBT) as a treatment. A school psychologist might find a student eligible under the educational criteria of an emotional disability and offer comprehensive educational services, including behavioral therapy through an individualized education plan.

As stated previously, psychologists who work in schools typically operate using a multitiered approach referred to as multitiered system of supports (MTSS), formerly referred to as response to intervention (Power & D'Amato, 2018). The **MTSS model** allows school psychologists to assess and monitor all students at primary, secondary, and tertiary levels. The primary tier offers screening for all students in academic, behavioral, and social/emotional functioning. If students are performing well, depending on how the institution defines their standards, they continue to receive the traditional, research-based curriculum. Typically, about 80% of students in a school system will fall at the primary level (Walker & Shinn, 2002). Some students, usually between 10% and 15%, will require a little extra assistance in meeting their goals. Within this secondary tier, these students are delivered interventions and support in small group settings, such as reading groups. Students receiving support at the tertiary level are those who present with significant challenges and who have not responded to interventions at the primary or secondary levels. Students, usually about 5% of the school population, at the tertiary level typically require individualized assistance from counselors or therapists (Walker & Shinn, 2002). Within the secondary and tertiary tiers, all students are progress monitored to determine their response to evidence-based interventions. Power and D'Amato (2018) advocate for using a neuropsychologically driven approach to MTSS, referred to as the *Neuropsychologically-Based Multi-Tiered System of Supports (NB-MTSS) model*. The NB-MTSS model assists practitioners in analyzing ***why*** skill weaknesses exist and evaluates the specific brain-based abilities that are needed for these unique skills. This approach also focuses on processing both strengths and weaknesses. This model consists of assessment of specific neuropsychological processes, as well as considering the standardized information from a school curriculum.

Integrating Clinical Neuropsychological Batteries into Interventions

The purpose of this chapter has been to explain how neuropsychological assessment should relate to appropriate evidence-driven interventions. As an example, Table 9.8 lists specific neuropsychological assessment procedures across the quantitative and qualitative areas which cover primary, secondary, and tertiary components of comprehensive health service psychology providers. A neuropsychological evaluation assists health service providers in understanding how the brain impacts behavior (Davis, 2011). Throughout a neuropsychological evaluation, multiple components of brain-based behavior are assessed, including: memory/learning, language, attention/executive functioning, visual-motor functioning, perceptual/sensory, intelligence/cognitive abilities, academic achievement, personality/behavior, and classroom/work environment. When completing such an evaluation, a health service provider must consider the referral problem and determine which assessments will be administered. For example, Table 9.8 demonstrates areas that might be assessed if someone was referred for deficits in reading. Not only is this academic area assessed, but other related abilities, such as executive function, memory/learning, and language are evaluated since these processes impact reading skills. This model is appropriate to use at all levels, from pediatric to geriatric cases. For example, individuals who have sustained brain damage from strokes may require neuropsychological assessment and intervention for deficits in language, reading, motor, and attention/executive functioning. Related to the area of reading, individuals with strokes may struggle with vocabulary, reading fluency, and reading comprehension activities. Assessments described in section "Neuropsychological models of assessment for intervention" will assists health service psychologists in determining appropriate evaluation procedures that can then be linked to evidence-based interventions. Assessment is a wide-ranging multistage process which starts with understanding the areas that need to be evaluated and then developing a system to utilize measures related to the areas under consideration. As an example, if a health service psychologist does not have a working understanding of the five components of reading (Witsken et al., 2008), they will not know the appropriate areas in which to evaluate. If an individual with a stroke has difficulty recalling words to use in conversation, an appropriately trained clinician will know to assess the area of vocabulary. It is essential that health service psychologists have extensive knowledge of test batteries, including specific skill-focused assessments (e.g., *Gray Oral Reading Test, Fifth Edition*) and broad measures (e.g., *Woodcock Johnson, Fourth Edition, Tests of Achievement*) to select time-efficient measures or batteries. Assessment in neuropsychology allows health service psychologists to better understand their client's needs through diagnosis, treatment, and intervention.

Evidence-Based Neuropsychological Interventions

A comprehensive neuropsychological evaluation will provide a rich amount of data to assist practitioners in determining recommendations for treatment. This chapter focuses on how client data can be organized both quantitatively and qualitatively to offer a standardized neuropsychological approach to assessment, covering case conceptualization, and treatment planning. Recommendations for interventions should always be linked to the significant weaknesses revealed within the evaluation. Recommendations should be clear, solution-focused, tailored to specific clients, and proven effective based on research (Power & D'Amato, 2018). Evidence-Based

Table 9.8 Neuropsychological evaluation procedures related to evidence-based reading intervention

Areas that should be evaluated, With relevant references	Evaluation tools
	Reading
Phonemic Awareness (eg., sound comparison, segmentation, blending): D'Amato, Fletcher-Janzen, and Reynolds (2005); Fletcher, Lyon, Fuchs, & Barnes (2007); Joseph (2005); Shaywitz (2003)	**DIBELS Initial Sound Fluency, Phoneme Fluency*** • **aimsweb: Test of Early Literacy*** • **IGDI: Alliteration, Rhyming*** • **Rigby Read*** • CTOPP-2: Elision, Blending Words** • KTEA-3: Nonsense Word Decoding** • WIAT-III: Pseudoword Decoding ** • WJ IV COG: Sound Blending*** • HRNB: Speech Sounds Perception Test*** • NEPSY- II: Phonological Processing***
Phonological awareness/ Phonics (letter names/ sounds and word recognition): Fletcher et al. (2007); Shaywitz (2003); Sousa (2005)	**DIBELS: Letter Naming Fluency, Nonsense Word Fluency*** • WJ IV ACH: Letter-Word Identification** • WIAT-III: Word Reading, Psuedoword Decoding** • WRAT4: Reading/ Word Calling** • GORT-5** • WJ IV COG: Word Attack*** • TOWER-2*** • DAS-II: Phonological Processing*** • NEPSY-II: Phonological Processing***
Vocabulary: D'Amato, Fletcher-Janzen And Reynolds (2005); Joseph (2005); Shaywitz (2003); Sousa (2005)	**DIBELS: Word Use Fluency, Word Naming*** • **IGDI: Picture Naming*** • **Rugby Read*** • KTEA-3: Reading Vocabulary** • WJ IV ACH: Oral Reading, Sentence Reading Fluency** • CREVT-3*** • CELF-5*** • DAS-II: Word Definition*** • KABC-II: Expressive Vocabulary, Verbal Knowledge*** • PPVT-4*** • NEPSY-II: Word Generation*** • WISC-V: Vocabulary, Word Reasoning***
Reading fluency: Fletcher et al. (2007); Shaywitz (2003); Sousa (2005)	**Classroom words correct per minute*** • **Informal assessment of words read correct/per minute*** • **aimsweb: Reading CBM*** • **DIBELS: Oral Reading Fluency*** • **WJ IV ACH: Reading Fluency*** • **WIAT-II: Oral Reading Fluency*** • GORT-5** • TOWRE-2** • Test of Reading Fluency**

(continued)

Table 9.8 (continued)

Reading Comprehension: Fletcher et al. (2007); Shaywitz (2003); Sousa (2005)	**DIBELS: Retell Fluency, Daze*** **• AIMSweb: Reading Maze passage*** **• WJ IV ACH: Passage Comprehension, Reading Recall*** **• Rigby Read*** • TORC-4** • OWLS-2: Reading Comprehension** • WIAT-III: Reading Comprehension** • KTEA-3: Silent Reading Fluency, Reading Comprehension** • GORT-5**
Phonological access (rapid Automatic naming): Hale and Fiorello (2004)	**Timed naming activities: Naming numbers, letters, animals, foods*** **• IGDI: Picture Naming*** • CTOPP-2: Rapid Letter Naming, Rapid Number Naming** • KTEA-3: Associational Fluency, Object Naming Facility, Letter Naming Facility** • WJ IV OL: Rapid Picture Naming** • DAS-II: Speeded Naming*** • NEPSY-II: Speeding Naming***
Oral Language/ listening comprehension: Semrud-Clickeman (2005); Shaywitz (2003); Sousa (2005)	**DIBELS: Retell Fluency*** • WIAT-II: Oral Expression** • KTEA-3: Oral Expression** • CELF-5*** • EOWPVT-4*** • OWLS-2: Oral Expression** • WJ IV ACH: understanding directions** • WJ IV OL: understanding directions** • PPVT-4*** • NEPSY-II: Comprehension of Instructions, Word Generation*** • WIAT-III: Listening Comprehension** • KTEA-3: Listening Comprehension** • OWLS-2: Listening Comprehension** • DAS-II: Verbal Comprehension*** • KABC-II: Expressive Vocabulary, Verbal Knowledge, Riddle***
	Additional neuropsychological areas to evaluate for reading
Short-/long -term and working memory: Fletcher et al. (2007); Hale And Fiorello (2004); Shaywitz (2003)	**Ability to follow two- and three-part directions*** • WJ IV ACH: Reading Recall/ Reading Recall-Delayed** • NEPSY-II Sentence Repetition, Narrative Memory*** • HRNB: Speech Sounds perception Test*** • DAS-II: Recall of Digits, Recall of Objects*** • WISC-V: Naming speed literacy, Naming Speed Quantity*** • KABC-II: Number Recall, Hand Movements, Atlantis/Atlantis-Delayed, Rebus/Rebus-Delayed, Word Order***

(continued)

Table 9.8 (continued)

Receptive/expressive language: Shaywitz (2003); Semrud-Clikeman (2005); Sousa (2005)	**Observations of conversation: turn taking, tangential conversation,time to process information*** • PPVT-4*** • EOWPVT-4, ROWPVT-4*** • CELF-5*** • **Comprehensive Assessment of Spoken Language*** • WJ IV ACH: understanding directions, Reading Recall** • NEPSY-II: Body Part Naming and Identification*** • HRNB: Aphasia Screening Test***
Areas that should be evaluated, With relevant references	Evaluation tools
Attention/executive functions: Fletcher et al. (2007); Hale And Fiorello (2004); Semrud-Clickeman (2005)	**Informal classroom observations (e.g., time on task)*** • **Performance on N-backs*** • WJ IV ACH: Understanding directions** • WJ IV COG: Numbers reversed, Planning*** • WISC-V: Working Memory subtests*** • NEPSY-II: Animal Sorting Inhibition, Auditory Attention, Response Set*** • HRNB: Category Test*** • Tower of London*** • D-KEFS*** • Task of Executive Control*** • Conners CPT 3*** • Trail Making Test/Stroop Test*** • TEA-Ch*** • CAS2: Planning Subsets*** • KABC-II: Rover, World Order, Pattern Reasoning, Story Completion***
Visual-motor functioning: D'Amato, Fletcher-Janzen, and Reynolds (2005); Fletcher et al. (2007); Hale and Fiorello (2004)	**Classroom observations: tracing; copying from board or from paper on desk*** • Bender Gestalt-II*** • Beery VMI-6*** • Rey-Osterrieth Complex Figure Test*** • WISC-V: Visual Spatial Subsets*** • KABC-II: Triangles, Block Counting, Gestalt Closure*** • DTVP-2*** • MVPT-3*** • BOT-2*** • NEPSY-II: Arrows, Design Copying*** • HRNB: Finger Tapping Test*** • HRNB: Trails A***
	Math
Math computation: D'Amato. Fletcher-Janzen, and Rynolds (2005); Fletcher et Al. (2007)	**Classroom problems correct per minute*** • **aimsweb: Math Computation*** • **Review of assignments/homework*** • KeyMath3: Basic Concepts, Operations** • KTEA-3: Math Computation, Math Fluency** • WJ IV ACH: Calculations**

(continued)

Table 9.8 (continued)

	• WIAT-III: numerical Operations** • WRAT4: Arithmetic** • WISC-V: Arithmetic**
Math problem solving: D'Amato, Fletcher-Janzen, and Reynolds (2005); Fletcher et al. (2007)	**Classroom exercises correct per minute*** **• aimsweb: Math Concepts and Applications*** **• Review of assignments/homework*** • WJ IV ACH: Applied Problems** • WIAT-III: Math Reasoning** • KTEA-3: Math Concepts and Applications** • KeyMath3: Applications** • WISC-V: Arithmetic***
	Additional neuropsychological areas to evaluate for math
Attention/executive functions	See this category for reading
Short-/long-term and working memory	See this category for reading
	Writing
Handwriting: D'Amato, Fletcher-Janzen, and Reynolds (2005); Fletcher et al. (2007)	**Classroom work samples*** **• aimsweb: Written Expression CBM*** • WJ IV ACH: Writing Fluency, Writing Samples** • KTEA-3: Written Expression, Writing Fluency** • WIAT-III: Alphabet Writing Fluency, Sentence Composition, Essay Composition** • TOWL-4** • OWLS-2** • NEPSY-II: Design Copying***
Spelling: Fletcher et al. (2007)	**Classroom words correct per timing*** **• aimsweb: Spelling CBM*** • KTEA-3: Spelling** • WJ IV ACH: Spelling** • WIAT-III: Spelling** • WRAT-IV: Spelling**
Written composition: Fletcher et al. (2007)	**Classroom timed work sample*** **• aimsweb: Written Expression CBM*** • WIAT-III: Essay Composition** • KTEA-3: Written Expression** • TOWL-4** • OWLS-II** • NEPSY-II: Design Copying***

Interventions (EBIs) refer to treatments that have been shown to be effective after an analysis of statistical outcomes (Kratochwill & Stoiber, 2002). Outcome data must demonstrate that the effects are clearly linked to the activities and not to unrelated, external events. Many students-in-training, as well as practitioners, focus on collecting EBIs as part of their professional growth and development (Kazdin, 2011; Løberg, 1989). EBIs can be found by searching through scholarly peer-reviewed journal articles to determine treatment effectiveness. Many books and book chapters are also available that focus on EBIs related to various paradigms, such as neuropsychology (D'Amato & Rothlisberg, 1997/1992; Davis & D'Amato, 2014; Power & D'Amato, 2018; Zaroff & D'Amato, 2015).

Furthermore, various databases, such as those created by the Institute of Education Science (IES), the Evidence-Based Practices (EPB) Resource Center provide a wide range of intervention resources that have been reviewed using thorough systematic guidelines. For example, the IES created a database called ***What Works Clearinghouse*** (WWC) which provides critical features of EBIs that aide in determining effectiveness (Traughber & D'Amato, 2005). According to WWC, the results of an intervention study can fall into three categories: (1) meets WWC standards without reservations, (2) meets WWC standards with reservations, or (3) does not meet WWC standards (US Department of Education, n.d.). For the study to meet WWC standards, the study must make clear that it had the following characteristics: groups randomly assigned, low sample attrition, and low/no confounding factors or concerns with outcomes. By selecting EBIs, clinical neuropsychologists can be expected to produce desirable, measurable outcomes in psychological practice areas (Traughber & D'Amato, 2005). The **future** of health service psychology will relate to understanding, offering, and documenting the growth of clients based on EBIs.

Developing and Monitoring Client Goals

To ascertain if an intervention is effective for a client, a clinical neuropsychologist should also determine how to monitor if a treatment has been successful (US Department of Education, n.d.). Similar to initial comprehensive evaluations, assessment data should relate directly to **progress monitoring** techniques, which should then drive the choice of an intervention for a client. Progress monitoring techniques assist in quantifying the rate of improvement or response to the intervention. For example, if a client is undergoing treatment for depression, not only should the clinical neuropsychologist keep detailed notes of a person's affect and presentation, but they should also consider using a quantitative method, such as a self-rating scale during every therapeutic session (Sattler & D'Amato, 2002a, 2002b). The use of treatment goals should also be utilized by clinical neuropsychologists to aide in determining intervention effectiveness (Cooper & Law, 2018). Goals refer to general statements of what the clinical neuropsychologist and client want to accomplish within sessions (Burns, 2008). Goals can be broken down into achievable objectives, which refer to specific strategies or steps that need to happen to attain the defined goals.

Numerous acronyms may be used to aid in analyzing, documenting, monitoring, and planning in this area. Many practitioners use **SOAP** (Subjective, Objective, Analysis, Plan) notes for summarizing, documenting, reviewing, and planning treatment. **S = Subjective Statements** are notes about the individual with examples such as *Ethan appeared distracted but worked diligently to remain focused*; **O = Objective Data** focus on test scores, and percentages of goals/objectives achieved. *Ethan was able to appropriately express his anger 2 of the 4 times discussed (50%)*; **A = Analysis of Session** includes documentation of how the client responded to treatment; *Ethan struggled with* discussing his anger but did complete two emotional processing STOP worksheets. **P = Plan for the Future** reminds the therapist what needs to be addressed in upcoming sessions. *Ethan needs additional practice in dealing with anger in group situations.* Heuristicially, the SOAP approach can be remarkable for documentation, analysis, and planning of critical therapeutic activities. Often, Another example of a popular acronymn that clinical neuropsychologists use is **SMART** goal setting to verify clear objectives. The acronym SMART stands for: Specific, Measurable, Attainable, Relevant, and Timely (O'Neill & Conzemius, 2006). Goals that are written in this format allow for objective evidence to be demonstrated when monitoring the progress of interventions. Examples of SMART goals for various settings can be found in Table 9.9. It is impossible to monitor progress if clear goals are not established and data are not collected to support progress in a comprehensive health service psychology capacity. Without goals, practitioners and clients do not understand what is being accomplished. It is crucial that goals are related directly to assessment for intervention with data that should stand on an evidence-based intervention foundation.

Table 9.9 Examples of SMART goals by setting

Setting	Goal example
Schools	By May 2020, when given four paragraphs of expository material at the third-grade level, Jacob will read the text aloud at 112 words correct per minute with 95% accuracy in 3 out of 5 opportunities
Therapy	By April 2021, Jose will make 10 requests for items using visual support (e.g., worksheets, menu choices) in a therapy session
	By June 2021, without visual support or adult guidance, Steven will verbally identify five coping strategies in a therapy session that he can use instead of hitting another peer to get attention
Home	Janet will lose 5 pounds by June 1 by eliminating sugar from her diet
	Janet will lose 5 pounds by June 1 by walking 10,000 steps each day

Conclusions

Neuroscience research has made clear that a comprehensive understanding of client behavior cannot be developed without considering how the **brain processes** information. Although they may not realize it, each health service psychologist subscribes to following a practice model; these are unique and individualized models that drive how clients are undersood and services are offered. Through a comprehensive **neuropsychological paradigm**, health service psychologists can use qualitative and quantitative assessments to determine a client's strengths and weaknesses *for* intervention. Through such a model, practitioners can yield richer assessment results with clients, that assists in driving brain-based interventions and progress monitoring tools to document clinical goals. This richness should stem from an integration of Eastern and Western models to assist in identifying appropriate EBIs. The goal of health service psychology, particularly with those who practice from a neuropsychological perspective, should be to help *improve the well-being* of all individuals in society.

Discussion Questions

1. Why is it critical to understand the biological basis of behavior when approaching assessment?
2. Although many psychologists report using an eclectic approach to service, why is it essential to choose a specific model of practice as a health service provider?
3. What are the benefits and limitations of using Eastern/qualitative assessment paradigm for intervention?
4. What are the benefits and limitations of using Western/quantitative assessment paradigm for intervention?
5. What are the differences between primary, secondary, and tertiary prevention/intervention? How would you conceptualize a case demonstrating knowledge of primary, secondary, and tertiary assessment and intervention?
6. What are the advantages of using a flexible-battery over a fixed-battery in a neuropsychological evaluation?
7. Why is it important to consider the relationship between assessment and intervention during a neuropsychological evaluation?

EPPP Sample Questions

1. The right hemisphere of the brain primarily controls all the following functions except for:
   (a) Body orientation
   (b) Pattern recognition
   (c) Depth perception
   (d) Nonverbal memory
2. A client with a traumatic brain injury who received a Level 4 rating on the Rancho Los Amigos Scale of Cognitive Functioning:.
   (a) Is nonresponsive to visual or auditory stimuli and seems to be in a state of deep sleep.
   (b) Is confused and incoherent, may exhibit bizarre behavior, and is unable to care for him/herself.
   (c) Is alert and oriented and can remember and integrate remote and recent events but may have some impairment in judgment, planning, and abstract reasoning.
   (d) Is functioning at an intellectual level that is superior for their age, education, and demographic background.
3. Programs designed to prevent the development of a physiological or psychological disorder are mainly described as:
   (a) Primary intervention
   (b) Tertiary prevention
   (c) Secondary prevention
   (d) Crisis prevention
4. Achieving a score indicating no coma and appropriate brain functioning on the Glasgow Coma Scale suggests that:
   (a) The individual definitively has no long-term effects of a TBI
   (b) The individual definitively has long-term effects of a TBI
   (c) The individual has minor effects of a TBI
   (d) The individual may have effects of a TBI
5. According to the Neuropsychologically-Based Multi-Tiered System of Supports (NB-MTSS) model, the following assessment can be used to assess phonemic awareness:
   (a) WISC-V comprehension
   (b) DAS-II word definitions
   (c) DIBELS initial sound fluency
   (d) NEPSY-2 word generation

Answers: A, B, B, D, C

Proactive Readings

Transcending the Past

- Gaddes, W. H., & Edgell, D. (1994). *Learning disabilities and brain function: A neuropsychological approach* (3rd ed.). Springer-Verlag.
- Halstead, W. C. (1947). *Brain and intelligence: A qualitative study of the frontal lobes*. University of Chicago Press.
- Luria, A. R. (1966). *The working brain: An introduction to neuropsychology*. Basic Books.

Excelling in the Present

- D'Amato, R. C., Fletcher-Janzen, E., & Reynolds, C. R. (Eds.). (2005b). *Handbook of school neuropsychology*. Wiley.
- Davis, A. S. (2011). (Ed.). *Handbook of Pediatric Neuropsychology*. Springer.
- Lezak, M. D., Howieson, D. B., Bigler, E. D., & Tranel, D. (2012). *Neuropsychological Assessment*. Oxford University Press.

Transforming the Future

- Casaletto, K. B., & Heaton, R. K. (2017). Neuropsychological assessment: Past and future. *Journal of the International Neuropsychological Society*, 23(9–10), 778–790. https://www.ncbi.nlm.nih.gov/pmc/articles/PMC6296381/
- Power, E., & D'Amato, R. C. (2018). Should our future include the integration of evidence-based neuropsychological services into school settings? In D. P. Flanagan & E. M. McDonough (Eds.), Contemporary intellectual Assessment: Theories, tests, and issues (4th ed.; pp. 1017–1045). Guilford.
- Perfect, M., & D'Amato, R. C. (2020). Introduction to special issue on the history of the future of proactive school psychology: Transcending the past, excel in the present, and transform the future. *School Psychology*, *35*(6), 363–366.

References

Apgar, V. (1966). The newborn (APGAR) scoring system. *Pediatric Clinics of North America, 13*(3), 645–650. https://doi.org/10.1016/S0031-3955(16)31874-0

Aylward, G. P., & Carson, A. D. (2005, April). Use of the test observation checklist with the Stanford-Binet intelligence scales for early childhood, 5th Ed (early SB5). Symposium conducted at the meeting of the National Association of School Psychologists, Atlanta, Georgia.

Brugha, T. S., Bebbington, P. E., & Jenkins, R. (1999). A difference that matters: Comparisons of structured and semi-structured psychiatric diagnostic interviews in the general population. https://doi.org/10.1017/S0033291799008880

Burns, D. D. (2008). *Feeling good: The new mood therapy*. Harper.

Caplan, G., Caplan, R. B., & Erchul, W. P. (1995). A contemporary view of mental health consultation: Comments on 'Types of Mental Health Consultation' by Gerald Caplan (1963). *Journal of Educational and Psychological Consultation, 6*(1), 23–30. https://doi.org/10.1207/s1532768xjepc0601_2

Carmon, A., & Bechtoldt, H. P. (1969). Dominance of the right cerebral hemisphere for stereopsis. *Neuropsychologia, 7*(1), 29-39. https://doi.org/10.1016/0028-3932(69)90042-6

Casaletto, K. B., & Heaton, R. K. (2017). Neuropsychological assessment: Past and future. *Journal of the International Neuropsychological Society, 23*(9–10), 778–790. https://www.ncbi.nlm.nih.gov/pmc/articles/PMC6296381/

Christensen, A. L. (1975). *Luria's neuropsychological investigation*. Spectrum.

Collins, W. A., Maccoby, E. E., Steinberg, L., Hetherington, E. M., & Bornstein, M. H. (2000). Contemporary research on parenting: The case for nature and nurture. *American Psychologist, 55*(2), 218–232. https://doi.org/10.1037/0003-066X.55.2.218

Cooper, M., & Law, D. (2018). *Working with goals in psychotherapy and counselling*. Oxford.

D'Amato, R. C., Crepeau-Hobson, F. C., Huang, L. V., & Geil, M. (2005a). Ecological neuropsychology: An alternative to the deficit model for conceptualizing and serving students with learning disabilities. *Neuropsychology Review, 15*(2), 97–103. https://doi.org/10.1007/s11065-005-7092-5

D'Amato, R. C., Fletcher-Janzen, E., & Reynolds, C. R. (Eds.). (2005b). *Handbook of school neuropsychology*. Wiley.

D'Amato, R. C., & Hartlage, L. C. (Eds.). (2008a). *Essentials of neuropsychological assessment: Rehabilitation planning for intervention* (2nd ed.). Springer.

D'Amato, R. C. E., & Rothlisberg, B. A. E. (Eds.) (1997/1992). *Psychological perspectives on intervention: A case study approach to prescriptions for change.* Waveland Press.

D'Amato, R. C., Zafiris, C., McConnell, E., & Dean, R. S. (2011). The history of school psychology: Understanding the past to not repeat it. In M. A. Bray & T. J. Kehle (Eds.), *The Oxford handbook of school psychology* (pp. 9–46). Oxford University Press.

D'Amato, R. C. (1990). A neuropsychological approach to school psychology. *School Psychology Quarterly, 5*(2), 141–160. https://psycnet.apa.org/doi/10.1037/h0090608

D'Amato, R. C., & Dean, R. S. (1988). School psychology practice in a department of neurology. *School Psychology Review, 17*(3), 416–420. https://doi.org/10.1080/02796015.1988.12085356

D'Amato, R. C., & Wang, Y. Y. (2015). Using a brainbased approach to collaborative teaching and learning with Asians. *New Directions in Teaching and Learning, 143*, 41–60. https://doi.org/10.1002/tl.20135

Davis, A. S. (Ed.). (2011). *Handbook of pediatric neuropsychology*. Springer.

Davis, A. S. (2008). Understanding and using the Dean-Woodcock Neuropsychological Battery with children, youth, adults, and in geriatrics. In R. C. D'Amato & L. C. Hartlage (Eds.), *Essentials of neuropsychological assessment: Treatment planning for rehabilitation* (pp. 173–205). Springer.

Davis, J. M., & D'Amato, R. C. (Eds.). (2014). *Neuropsychology of Asians and Asian-Americans: Practical and theoretical considerations* (Part of the issues of diversity in clinical neuropsychology series). Springer.

Dean, R. S. (1978). Reliability and predictive validity of the Dean laterality preference schedule with preadolescents. *Perceptual and Motor Skills, 47*(3 Pt 2), 1345–1346. https://doi.org/10.2466/pms.1978.47.3f.1345

Dean, R. S. (1979, August). *Lateral preference and reading comprehension*. Paper presented at the annual meeting of the 88th American Psychological Association Convention, New York, NY.

Dean, R. S. (1982). Assessing patterns of lateral preference. *Clinical Neuropsychology, 4*(3), 124–128.

Dean, R. S. (1984). Functional lateralization of the brain. *The Journal of Special Education, 18*(3), 239–256. https://doi.org/10.1177%2F002246698401800306

Dean, R. S. (1986a). Neuropsychological aspects of psychiatric disorders. In J. E. Obrzut & G. W. Hynd (Eds.), *Perspectives in neurolinguistics, neuropsychology, and psycholinguistics: A series of monographs and treatises. Child neuropsychology* (Vol. 2, pp. 83-112). Academic Press. https://doi.org/10.1016/B978-0-12-524042-0.50010-3

Dean, R. S. (1986b). *Perspectives on the future of neuropsychological assessment.* https://digitalcommons.unl.edu/cgi/viewcontent.cgi?article=1008&context=burosfuturetesting

Dean, R. S., Schwartz, N. H., & Smith, L. S. (1981). Lateral preference patterns as a discriminator of learning difficulties. *Journal of Consulting and Clinical Psychology, 49*(2), 227–235. https://doi.org/10.1037/0022-006X.49.2.227

Dean, R. S., & Smith, L. S. (1981). Personality and lateral preference patterns in children. *Clinical Neuropsychology, 3*(4), 22–28.

Dean, R. S., & Reynolds, C. R. (1997). Cognitive processing and self-report of lateral preference. Neuropsychology Review, 7(3), 127-142.

Finster, M., & Wood, M. (2005). The Apgar score has survived the test of time. *Anesthesiology: The Journal of the American Society of Anesthesiologists, 102*(4), 855–857. https://doi.org/10.1097/00000542-200504000-00022

First, M. B. (2014). Structured clinical interview for the DSM (SCID). *The Encyclopedia of Clinical Psychology*, 1–6. https://doi.org/10.1002/9781118625392.wbecp351

Flanagan, D. P., & McDonough, E. M. (Eds.). (2018). *Contemporary intellectual assessment: Theories, tests, and issues* (4th ed.). Guilford.

Fletcher, J. M., Lyon, G. R., Fuchs, L. S., & Barnes, M. A. (2018). *Learning disabilities: From identification to intervention.* Guilford.

Gaddes, W. H. (1985). *Learning disabilities and brain function: A neuropsychological approach* (2nd ed.). Springer-Verlag.

Gaddes, W. H., & Edgell, D. (1994). *Learning disabilities and brain function: A neuropsychological approach* (3rd ed.). Springer.

Gisi, T. M., & D'Amato, R. C. (2000). What factors should be considered in rehabilitation: Are anger, social desirability, and forgiveness related in adults with traumatic brain injuries? *International Journal of Neuroscience, 105*, 121–133. https://doi.org/10.3109/00207450009003271

Glozman, J. M. (1999). Russian neuropsychology after Luria. *Neuropsychology Review, 9*(1), 33-44.

Gray, J. W., & Dean, R. S. (Eds.). (1991). *Neuropsychology of perinatal complications.* Springer.

Hale, J. B., & Fiorello, C. A. (2004). *School neuropsychology.* Guilford.

Halstead, W. C. (1947). *Brain and intelligence: A qualitative study of the frontal lobes.* University of Chicago Press.

Hardy, K. K., Olson, K., Cox, S. M., Kennedy, T., & Walsh, K. S. (2017). Systematic review: A prevention-based model of neuropsychological assessment for children with medical illness. *Journal of Pediatric Psychology, 42*(8), 815–822.https://doi.org/10.1093/jpepsy/jsx060

Hartlage, L. C., & D'Amato, R. C. (2008a). Understanding the etiology of neurological and psychiatric disorders. In A. MacNeil Horton Jr. & D. Wedding (Eds.), *The neuropsychology handbook* (3rd ed., pp. 87–108). Springer.

Hartlage, L. C., & D'Amato, R. C. (2008b). Understanding the etiology of neurological and psychiatric disorders. In A. MacNeil Horton Jr. & D. Wedding (Eds.), *The neuropsychology handbook* (3rd ed.; pp. 87–108). Springer.

Hynd, G. W., & Willis, W. G. (1988). *Pediatric neuropsychology.* Grune & Stratton.

Hynd, W. G., & Semrud-Clikeman, M. (1990). Neuropsychological assessment. In A. S. Kaufman (Ed.), *Assessing adolescent and adult intelligence* (pp. 638–696). Allen & Bacon.

Johnson, J. A., & D'Amato, R. C. (2011). Evaluating and using the Halstead-Reitan neuropsychological battery: Is it our future or our past? In A. Davis (Ed.), *Handbook of pediatric neuropsychology* (Vol. I, pp. 353–366). Springer.

Jones, K. D. (2011). The unstructured clinical interview. *Journal of Counseling & Development, 88*(2), 220–226. https://doi.org/10.1002/j.1556-6678.2010.tb00013.x
Joseph, L. M. (2005). Understanding and implementing neuropsychologically based literacy interventions. In R. C. D'Amato, E. Fletcher-Janzen, & C. R. Reynolds (Eds.), *Handbook of school neuropsychology* (p. 738–757). Wiley.
Kaplan, E. (1988). The process approach to neuropsychological assessment. *Aphasiology, 2*(3–4), 309–311. https://doi.org/10.1080/02687038808248930
Kaufman, A. S., & Horn, J. L. (1996). Age changes on tests of fluid and crystallized ability for women and men on the Kaufman Adolescent and Adult Intelligence Test (KAIT) at ages 17–94 years. *Archives of Clinical Neuropsychology, 11*(2), 97–121. https://doi.org/10.1016/0887-6177(95)00003-8
Kaufman, A. S., & Kaufman, N. L. (1983). *Administration and scoring model for the Kaufman assessment battery for children*. American Guidance Service.
Kaufman, A. S., & Kaufman, N. L. (2014). *Kaufman test of educational achievement* (3rd ed.). Pearson.
Kaufman, D. M. (2001). *Clinical neurology for psychiatrists*. Saunders.
Kazdin, A. E. (2011). *Single-case research design: Methods for clinical and applied settings* (2nd ed.). Oxford University Press.
Kolb, B., & Whishaw, I. Q. (2003). *Fundamentals of human neuropsychology* (5th ed.). Worth Publishers.
Kratochwill, T. R., & Stoiber, K. C. (2002). Evidence based interventions in school psychology: Conceptual foundations of the procedural and coding manual of division 16 and the Society for the Study of school psychology task force. *School Psychology Quarterly, 17*(4), 341–389. https://psycnet.apa.org/doi/10.1521/scpq.17.4.341.20872
Lezak, M. D., Howieson, D. B., Bigler, E. D., & Tranel, D. (2012). *Neuropsychological assessment*. Oxford University Press.
Lin, K., & Dulebohn, S. C. (2017). *Ranchos los amigos*. Treasure Island.
Løberg, T. (1989). The role of neuropsychology in secondary prevention. In T. Løberg, W. R. Miller, P. E. Nathan, & G. A. Marlatt (Eds.), *Addictive behaviors: Prevention and early intervention* (pp. 69–86). Swets & Zeitlinger Publishers.
Luria, A. R. (1964). Neuropsychology in the local diagnosis of brain damage. *Cortex*, 1(1), 3-18. https://doi.org/10.1016/S0010-9452(64)80010-1
Luria, A. R. (1966). *The working brain: An introduction to neuropsychology*. Basic Books.
Luria, A. R. (1970). The functional organization of the brain. *Scientific American, 222*, 66–78.
Luria, A. R. (1973). *The working brain*. Penguin.
Luria, A. R. (1980). *Higher cortical functions in man* (2nd ed.). Basic Books.
Martin, D. C. (1990). The mental status examination. In H. K. Walker, W. D. Hall, & J. W. Hurst (Eds.), *Clinical Methods: The History, Physical, and Laboratory Examinations (3rd ed.)*. Ch. 207. Butterworths.
McGrath, R. E., Wiggins, J. G., Sammons, M. T., Levant, R. F., Brown, A., & Stock, W. (2004). Professional issues in pharmacotherapy for psychologists. *Professional Psychology: Research and Practice, 35*(2), 158–163. https://doi.org/10.1037/0735-7028.35.2.158
Miller-Kuhaneck, H., Henry, D. A., Glennon, T. J., & Mu, K. (2007). Development of the sensory processing measure–school: Initial studies of reliability and validity. *American Journal of Occupational Therapy, 61*(2), 170–175. https://doi.org/10.5014/ajot.61.2.170
Montgomery, K. S. (2000). Apgar scores: examining the long-term significance. *The Journal of Perinatal Education, 9*(3), 5-9. https://dx.doi.org/10.1624%2F105812400X87716
Naglieri, J. A., & Das, J. P. (1996). *Das Naglieri cognitive assessment system*. Riverside.
Naglieri, J. A., Das, J. P., & Goldstein, S. (2014). *Cognitive assessment system* (2nd ed.). PRO-ED.
Nelson, K. B., & Ellenberg, J. H. (1981). Apgar scores as predictors of chronic neurologic disability. *Pediatrics, 68*(1), 36-44.

Nicholson, H., Kehle, T. J., Bray, M. A., & Heest, J. V. (2011). The effects of antecedent physical activity on the academic engagement of children with Autism spectrum disorder. *Psychology in the Schools, 48*(2), 198-213. https://doi.org/10.1177/0145445514552891

O'Neill, J., & Conzemius, A. (2006). *The power of smart goals. Using goals to improve student learning*. Solution Tree.

Perfect, M., & D'Amato, R. C. (2020). Introduction to special issue on the history of the future of proactive school psychology: Transcending the past, excel in the present, and transform the future. *School Psychology, 35*(6), 363–366.

Power, E., & D'Amato, R. C. (2018). Should our future include the integration of evidence-based neuropsychological services into school settings? In D. P. Flanagan & E. M. McDonough (Eds.), *Contemporary intellectual assessment: Theories, tests, and issues* (4th ed., pp. 1017–1045). Guilford.

Reitan, R. M. (1955). Certain differential effects of left and right cerebral lesions in human adults. *Journal of Comparative and Physiological Psychology, 48*(6), 474. https://doi.org/10.1037/h0048581

Reitan, R. M., & Wolfson, D. (1985). *The Halstead-Reitan neuropsychological test battery: Theory and clinical interpretation*. Neuropsychology Press.

Reynolds, C. R. (1981a). Neuropsychological assessment and the habilitation of learning: Considerations in the search for the aptitude x treatment interaction. *School Psychology Review, 10*(3), 343–394. https://doi.org/10.1080/02796015.1981.12084914

Reynolds, C. R. (1981b). The neuropsychological basis of intelligence. In G. Hynd & J. Obrzut (Eds.), *Neuropsychological assessment and the school-aged child*. Grune & Stratton.

Reynolds, C. R., & French, C. L. (2005). The brain as a dynamic organ of information processing and learning. In R. C. D'Amato, E. Fletcher-Janzen, & C. R. Reynolds (Eds.), *Handbook of school neuropsychology* (pp. 86–119). Wiley.

Rhodes, R. L., D'Amato, R. C., & Rothlisberg, B. A. (2008). Utilizing a neuropsychological paradigm for understanding educational and psychological tests. In C. R. Reynolds & E. Fletcher-Janzen (Eds.), *Handbook of clinical child neuropsychology* (3rd ed., pp. 321–348). Plenum.

Rothlisberg, B. A., D'Amato, R. C., & Palencia, B. N. (2003). Assessment of children for intervention planning following traumatic brain injury. In C. R. Reynolds & R. W. Kamphaus (Eds.), *Handbook of psychological and educational assessment of children: Personality, behavior and context* (2nd ed.). Guilford.

Rothlisberg, B. A., & Dean, R. S. (1985). Reading comprehension and lateral preference in normal readers. *Psychology in the Schools, 22*, 337–342.

Sattler, J. M., & D'Amato, R. C. (2002a). Brain injuries: Theory and rehabilitation programs. In J. M. Sattler (Ed.), *Assessment of children: Behavioral and clinical applications* (4th ed., pp. 401–439). Jerome M. Sattler.

Sattler, J. M., & D'Amato, R. C. (2002b). Brain·injuries: Formal batteries and informal measures. In J. M. Sattler (Ed.), *Assessment of children: Behavioral and clinical applications* (4th ed., pp. 440–469). Jerome M. Sattler.

Schultz, D. P., & Schultz, S. E. (2016). *A history of modern psychology* (11th ed.). Cengage.

Semrud-Clikeman, M., & Hynd, G. W. (1990). Right hemispheric dysfunction in nonverbal learning disabilities social, academic, and adaptive functioning in adults and children. *Psychological Bulletin, 107*(2), 196–209. https://doi.org/10.1037/0033-2909.107.2.196

Semrud-Clikeman, M. (2005). Neuropsychological aspects for evaluating learning disabilities. *Journal of Learning Disabilities, 38*(6), 563-568. https://doi.org/10.1177%2F00222194050380061301

Shaywitz, S. (2003). *Overcoming dyslexia: A new and complete science-based program for reading problems at any level.* Knopf.

Sobel, D., & Ornstein, R. (1987). Healthy pleasures. *Reading*.

Sousa, D. A. (2005). *How the brain learns to read.* Sage.

Sperry, R. W. (1974). Lateral specialization in the surgically separated hemispheres. *The neurosciences third study program*, 5-19.

Spooner, D. M., & Pachana, N. A. (2006). Ecological validity in neuropsychological assessment: A case for greater consideration in research with neurologically intact populations. *Archives of Clinical Neuropsychology, 21*(4), 327–337. https://doi.org/10.1016/j.acn.2006.04.004

Stark, R. (1961). An investigation of unilateral cerebral pathology with equated verbal and visual-spatial tasks. *The Journal of Abnormal and Social Psychology, 62*(2), 282. https://psycnet.apa.org/doi/10.1037/h0048661

Sternbach, G. L. (2000). The Glasgow coma scale. *The Journal of Emergency Medicine, 19*(1), 67–71. https://doi.org/10.1016/s0736-4679(00)00182-7

Teasdale, G., Maas, A., Lecky, F., Manley, G., Stocchetti, N., & Murray, G. (2014). The Glasgow coma scale at 40 years: Standing the test of time. *The Lancet Neurology, 13*(8), 844–854. https://doi.org/10.1016/s1474-4422(14)70120-6

Teglasi, H. (2015). *Essentials of TAT and other storytelling assessments* (2nd ed.). Wiley.

Tincup, M. J., D'Amato, R. C., Titley, J. E., & Dean, R. S. (2005). Appendix A: Sample neuropsychological questionnaire. In R. C. D'Amato, E. Fletcher-Janzen, & C. R. Reynolds (Eds.), *Handbook of school neuropsychology* (pp. 859–873). Wiley.

Traughber, M. C., & D'Amato, R. C. (2005). Integrating evidence-based neuropsychological services into school settings: Issues and challenges for the future. In R. C. D'Amato, E. Fletcher-Janzen, & C. R. Reynolds (Eds.), *Handbook of school neuropsychology* (pp. 827–857). Wiley.

U.S. Department of Education, Institute of Education Sciences, National Center for Education Evaluation and Regional Assistance, What Works Clearinghouse. https://ies.ed.gov/ncee/wwc

van Schalkwyk, G. J., & D'Amato, R. C. (Eds.). (2015a). *From the Confucian way to collaborative knowledge co-construction: New directions for teaching & learning*. Jossey-Bass/Wiley.

van Schalkwyk, G. J., & D'Amato, R. C. (Eds.). (2015b). *Facilitative collaborative knowledge co-construction: New directions for teaching & learning*. Jossey-Bass/Wiley.

Wada, J. (1949). A new method of determining the side of cerebral speech dominance: a preliminary report on the intracarotid injection of sodium amytal in man. *Igaku to Seibutsugaku*, 14, 221–222. https://doi.org/10.3171/jns.1960.17.2.0266

Walker, H. M., & Shinn, M. R. (2002). Structuring school-based interventions to achieve integrated primary, secondary, and tertiary prevention goals for safe and effective schools. In M. R. Shinn, H. M. Walker, & G. Stoner (Eds.), *Interventions for academic and behavior problems II: Preventive and remedial approaches* (pp. 1–26). NASP Publications.

Wechsler, D. (1928). Psychometric tests. In I. S. Wechsler (Ed.), *A textbook of clinical neurology* (pp. 104–116). Saunders.

Work, L. P., & Hee-Sook, C. (2005). Developing classroom and group intervention programs based on neuropsychological principles. In R. C. D'Amato, E. Fletcher-Janzen, & C. R. Reynolds (Eds.), *Handbook of school neuropsychology* (pp. 663–683). Wiley.

Zaroff, C., & D'Amato, R. C. (Eds.). (2015). *The neuropsychology of men: From neurodevelopment to evidence-based interventions* (Part of the issues of diversity in clinical neuropsychology series). Springer.

Chapter 10
Integrating Clinical Assessments to Develop Health Service Neuropsychological Interventions

Elizabeth M. Power, Rik Carl D'Amato, Jonathan Titley, Richard McNulty, Whitney Gibson, Christy Roman, Caitlin Cox Treffert, Catherine M. Van Damme, Elise M. Chalus, Jaclyn Hoffmeister, and Sydney Mitchell

Learning Objectives

- To gain a comprehensive understanding of instruments used in a neuropsychological evaluation
- To understand that neuropsychological assessment is an approach to conceptualization of clients and not a specific test
- To be able to define and explain the importance of each of the major areas of a neuropsychological evaluation
- To understand that the neuropsychological evaluation is an appraisal of the sensory systems, including seeing, hearing, feeling, touching, moving, and smelling
- To understand where assessment began and how it has changed and is moving toward the future
- To understand and be able to identify the major areas of a neuropsychological evaluation (e.g., sensory/motor)
- To be able to discuss popular instruments (e.g., NEPSY-II), why they might be selected, and which type of data they provide concerning clients
- To understand how to collect detailed information to be able to determine appropriate evidence-based interventions and plan for rehabilitation of clients

E. M. Power (✉) · S. Mitchell
Department of Educational/School Psychology, The College of Saint Rose, Albany, NY, USA
e-mail: powere@strose.edu

R. C. D'Amato · W. Gibson · C. Roman · C. Cox Treffert · C. M. Van Damme · E. M. Chalus · J. Hoffmeister
Department of School Psychology, The Chicago School of Professional Psychology, Chicago, IL, USA

J. Titley
School Psychology, California Public Schools, Rocklin, CA, USA

R. McNulty
Department of Psychology, University of Memphis, Memphis, TN, USA

R. C. D'Amato et al. (eds.), *Understanding the Biological Basis of Behavior*,
https://doi.org/10.1007/978-3-030-59162-5_10

Overview

Clinical neuropsychological assessment is the most *comprehensive assessment* available in psychology today. Nothing is understandable without some basic knowledge of the **brain**. While discussions related to **neuroanatomy** are beyond the scope of this chapter, it is important for practitioners to understand that the brain impacts every behavior and, thus, must be the paramount focus of our assessment. The chapter begins with an overview of a brief and focused history of applied neuropsychology. This chapter focused on all components of a **comprehensive neuropsychological evaluation**, with an emphasis on sensory and motor abilities. Tests used in the **cognitive** or intellectual domain are then evaluated. This is followed by a review of **academic achievement** measures. Next, comprehensive **neuropsychological batteries** are discussed. This is followed by a discussion of specialized neuropsychological tests which focus on a single area. Measures of **personality and behavior** are reviewed as used in psychology. Both *objective* and *projective* measures are discussed along with a **neuropsychological paradigm** for understanding traditional educational and psychological tests. The main focus of the chapter is to provide a significant overview of the **most important quantitative and qualitative measures of assessment.** For the purpose of this chapter, we are using quantitative measures as highly **standardized** (e.g., WISC-V) at one end of the continuum to slightly **standardized** (e.g., Kinetic Family Drawings) at the other **end** (see Fig. 1).

History of Integrated Assessments for Intervention in Clinical Neuropsychology

We can trace the knowledge and speculation of human behavior back to the fifth century when many famous philosophers, such as Plato and Aristotle (Schultz & Schultz, 2016), fought to understand aspects of human behavior, such as perception and cognition. It wasn't until individuals began linking **behavior and the brain** that they really started to focus on clinical neuropsychology (D'Amato & Perfect, 2020; Whitsken et al., 2008). Initially, practitioners observed people and their behavior and then looked at their brains once they died. Unfortunately, waiting until patients were *deceased* did not make for *effective or efficient analyses* of brain-behavior relationships. For example, Broca (1960/1865) performed an autopsy on the brain of a patient who was unable to speak intelligibly and determined that a lesion found in the patient's **frontal lobe** was linked to **expressive language** deficits. **Broca's** link between the discovered brain lesion and behavioral difficulties was the beginning of **clinical neuropsychology** as we know it today (Broca, 1960/1865; Schultz & Schultz, 2016).

Fortunately, with the development of standardized assessment within clinical neuropsychology, we are now able to determine neurological deficits based on performance on various assessments. While a number of individuals started measuring aspects of cognition in the general population, it wasn't until 1904 that Binet developed a standardized assessment to measure intelligence (D'Amato et al., 2005). This was later developed into the *Stanford-Binet*, which for a time was the **most widely used** intelligence test in the world (D'Amato et al., 2011). Intelligence tests led to the development of neuropsychological instruments, which were originally developed for **differential diagnosis** (i.e., functional or organic) or for diagnosing **brain lesions**. Pioneers, such as **Halstead** and **Luria**, contributed to monumental neuropsychological theories and assessments (Halstead, 1947). With the breakthrough of functional imaging, such as functional magnetic resonance imaging (fMRI) and computerized tomography (CT), we are now able to confirm deficits in brain functioning in less invasive formats (Noogle et al., 2008). Clinical neuropsychology has developed into **one of health service psychology's most impressive specializations** with most hospitals, programs, and researchers all needing **clinical neuropsychologists**.

Integrated Assessments for Intervention in Clinical Neuropsychology and the Biological Basis of Behavior

Comprehensive neuropsychological assessment should contain both **quantitative** and **qualitative** measures to determine functional strengths and weaknesses. As discussed in the previous chapter, quantitative (standardized) measures have been considered as more Western approaches, while qualitative (informal) measures have been considered more Eastern. For a comprehensive and ecological view of an individual's abilities, it is imperative that both quantitative and qualitative measures be integrated during a neuropsychological evaluation (Power & D'Amato, 2018). Clearly you must be able to function appropriately at **both ends of the continuum** if you are going to be effective as a professional psychologist. Outstanding clinical neuropsychologists gain equal amounts of knowledge from a measure that they consider both qualitatively and quantitatively. For example, Omar, age 9, is given the Auditory Attention and Response Set subtest on the NEPSY-2, and he performs below average according to the test manual. A careful examination actually revealed that he was *bored* during this subtest and did not display the skills that the child obviously indicated during his classroom observations and two-hour evaluation period. Clearly paying attention to only one end of the continuum can offer the practitioner false information which can lead to an inappropriate diagnosis. All practitioners need to be able to function on both ends of the continuum, as detailed in the previous chapter. Figure 10.1 is a **graphic display of the spectrum** of quantitative and qualitative measures. Entire chapters are available on how clinical neuropsychologists should utilize information they have gleaned from patients on traditional achievement, social-emotional, and intelligence tests (Rhodes et al., 2009). One of the most critical components of selecting measures for a

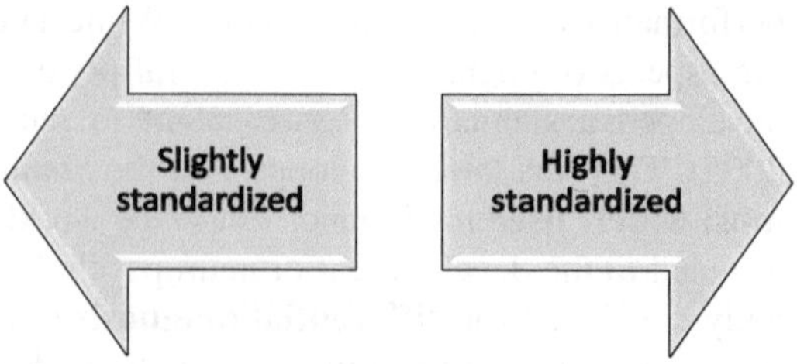

Fig. 10.1 Graphic display of the psychological assessment standardization continuum

neuropsychological evaluation is determining **which areas should be evaluated**. Some measures have been developed to be used with other related measures (e.g., WIAT-III and WISC-V); however, it is ultimately up to the practitioner to choose appropriate assessments that cover a wide range of abilities in order to determine one's neuropsychological strengths and weaknesses. A comprehensive rehabilitation **treatment plan** can only be developed when appropriate measures have been selected, scored, and interpreted (Davis, 2011; D'Amato & Hartlage, 2008; Power & D'Amato, 2018).

In this chapter, we will *introduce* comprehensive neuropsychological assessment instruments and procedures – noting an emphasis on basic neuropsychological assessment. The American Psychological Association (APA) requires that all **health service psychologists** (APA, 2017) be trained in comprehensive psychological assessment; therefore, graduate students usually complete up to five classes with many focusing on how to learn specific psychological approaches and instruments. Neuropsychological assessment represents the most comprehensive assessment available and accordingly is costly and requires post-doctoral training (see Chap. 1). However, neuropsychological assessment offers a level of understanding that far exceeds other traditional approaches (D'Amato & Rothlisberg, 1997/1992; Power & D'Amato, 2018).

Within this chapter, nine domains of the neuropsychological evaluation are explored. We review measures within the following domains: (1) **visual/spatial**, (2) **motor/perceptual/sensory**, (3) **attention/executive functions**, (4) **language/auditory**, (5) **learning/memory**, (6) **academic achievement**, (7) **neuropsychological**, (8) **cognitive**, and (9) **social/emotional/behavior**. See Fig. 10.2 for a pictorial display of evaluation domains.

There were a number of critical instruments that were not able to be discussed. It is fortunate that the area of clinical neuropsychology has hundreds and hundreds of available instruments that cover many areas that relate to the brain. However, while this chapter is extremely comprehensive it cannot possibly cover every single measure/area. Thus, it was difficult to select which instruments would be the focus of this chapter. Within this chapter, we review **28 assessments** in depth and briefly mention others while concomitantly listing critical measures in our table which space does not permit us to discuss (see Table 10.1). Given society's current focus on resiliency, trauma, and the training of non-doctoral specialists, it is essential for practitioners to be familiar with **brain-based assessments** that can be used to change the lives of infants, toddlers, children, adolescents, adults, and geriatric

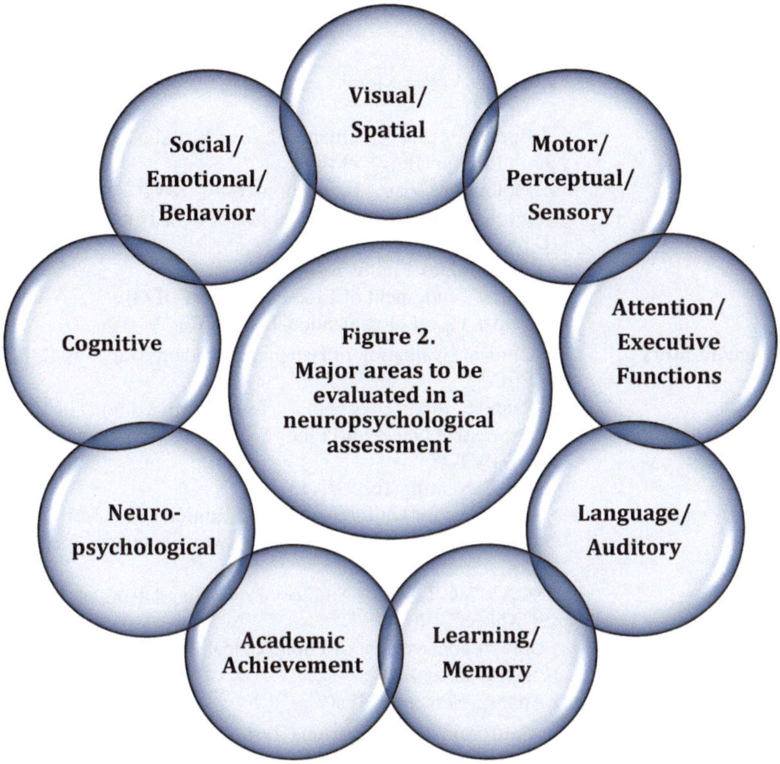

Fig. 10.2 Major areas to be evaluated in a neuropsychological assessment

populations. It is important to note that the majority of the assessments described in this chapter may be administered through a paper/pencil format. However, many assessments, such as the Minnesota Multiphasic Personality Inventory, Second Edition (MMPI-2), the Behavior Assessment Scale for Children, Third Edition (BASC-3), and the Wechsler Intelligence Scale for Children, Fifth Edition (WISC-V), can be **partially** or **entirely** administered online. For a discussion of technological applications of testing, including telepsychology, teleconsultation, and the use of technology in culturally and linguistically diverse student recruitment, see Perfect and D'Amato (2020), Fischer et al. (2019) and Germine et al. (2019).

Visual/Spatial Assessment for Intervention

Knowledge of **visual/spatial** functioning is required for a practitioner to understand a client's ability to function in the world. According to Luria (1966, 1973), there are multiple levels of visual-spatial development upon which higher-order cognitive processes are built. For example, a primary level of visual/spatial functioning is

Table 10.1 Integrated assessments for intervention in clinical neuropsychology

Domain	Assessments
Visual/spatial	✓ Bender Visual-Motor Gestalt Test, Second Edition (Bender-Gestalt II) ✓ Beery VMI Developmental Test of Visual-Motor Integration, Sixth Edition (Berry VMI-6) ✓ Motor-Free Visual Perception Test-4 (MVPT-4) • Developmental Test of Visual Perception, Third Edition (DTVP-3) • Rey Complex Figure Test (RCFT) • Benton's Judgment of Line Orientation (JLO) • Hooper Visual Organization Test (VOT)
Language/auditory	✓ Clinical Evaluation of Language Fundamentals – Fifth Edition (CELF-5) ✓ Peabody Picture Vocabulary Test, Fourth Edition (PPVT-IV) ✓ Expressive One-Word Picture Vocabulary Test, Fourth Edition (EOWPVT-4) • Boston Naming Test (BNT) • Token Test for Children – Second Edition (TTFC-2) • Comprehensive Assessment of Spoken Language, Second Edition (CASL-2) • SCAN-3:C Tests for Auditory Processing Disorders for Children (SCAN-3:C) • Comprehensive Test of Phonological Processing, Second Edition (CTOPP-2) • Aphasia Screening Test
Learning/memory	✓ California Verbal Learning Test – Second Edition (CVLT-C) ✓ Test of Memory and Learning, Second Edition (TOMAL-2) • Wide Range Assessment of Memory and Learning, Second Edition (WRAML2) • Wechsler Memory Scale – Fourth Edition (WMS-IV) • Detroit Test of Learning Aptitude – Fourth Edition (DTLA-4) • Benton Visual Retention Test, Fifth Edition • Children's Memory Scale (CMS)
Motor/perceptual/sensory	✓ Dean Woodcock Neuropsychological Assessment System ✓ Finger Tapping Test (FTT; see Halstead-Reitan) ✓ Hand Grip Strength Test (see Halstead-Reitan) • Goldman-Fristoe Woodcock Test of Auditory Discrimination • Wepman Auditory Discrimination Test • Grooved Pegboard Test • Purdue Pegboard Test • Bruininks-Oseretsky Test of Motor Proficiency, Second Edition (BOT-2) • See Halstead-Reitan Tactile Performance Test

(continued)

Table 10.1 (continued)

Domain	Assessments
Attention/executive functions	✓ Test of Everyday Attention for Children, Second Edition (TEA-Ch2) ✓ Delis-Kaplan Executive Function System (D-KEFS) • Comprehensive Trail Making Test (CTMT) • Continuous Performance Tests (CPT) • Stroop Test • Wisconsin Card Sort Test (WCST) • Tower of London
Academic achievement	✓ Kaufman Test of Educational Achievement, Third Edition (KTEA-3) ✓ Wechsler Individual Achievement Test (WIAT-III) ✓ Woodcock Johnson IV Tests of Achievement (WJ IV ACH) • Peabody Individual Achievement Test – Revised (PIAT-R) • Wide Range Achievement Test, Fourth Edition (WRAT4) • Gray Oral Reading Tests – Fifth Edition (GORT-5) • Oral and Written Language Scales, Second Edition (OWLS-II) • Process Assessment of the Learner – Second Edition (PAL-II) • Bracken Basic Concept Scale, Third Edition (BBCS-3)
Cognitive/intellectual	✓ Wechsler Intelligence Scale for Children – Fifth Edition (WISC-V) ✓ Woodcock Johnson IV Tests of Cognitive Abilities (WJ IV COG) ✓ Kaufman Assessment Battery for Children, Second Edition (KABC-2) ✓ Stanford-Binet Intelligence Scales, Fifth Edition (SB-V) • Bayley Scales of Infant and Toddler Development, Third Edition (Bayley-III) • Cognitive Assessment System – Second Edition (CAS2) • Wechsler Preschool and Primary Scale of Intelligence – Fourth Edition (WPPSI-IV) • Kaufman Adolescent and Adult Intelligence Test (KAIT) • Wechsler Adult Intelligence Scale – Fourth Edition (WAIS-IV) • Differential Ability Scales-II (DAS-II) • Battelle Developmental Inventory, Second Edition Normative Update (BDI-2 NU)
Social/emotional/ behavior	✓ Minnesota Multiphasic Personality Inventory – 2 (MMPI-2) ✓ Behavior Assessment System for Children, Third Edition (BASC-3) ✓ Thematic Apperception Test (TAT) ✓ Kinetic Family Drawing ✓ Autism Spectrum Rating Scale (ASRS) ✓ Vineland Adaptive Behavior Scales, Third Edition (Vineland-3) ✓ Sociometric techniques • Piers-Harris Children's Self-Concept Scale, Second Edition (Piers-Harris 2) • Adaptive Behavior Assessment Scale, Third Edition • Rorschach Test • Parent Stress Inventory – Second Edition • Sentence Completion Test

(continued)

Table 10.1 (continued)

Domain	Assessments
Neuropsychological function	✓ NEPSY, Second Edition (NEPSY-II) ✓ Halstead-Reitan Neuropsychological Battery • Transdisciplinary Play-Based Assessment (TPBA) • Repeatable Battery for the Assessment of Neuropsychological Status (RBANS) • Luria-Nebraska Neuropsychological Battery • Boston Process Approach • Wechsler Intelligence Scale for Children – Fourth Edition Integrated (WISC-IV Integrated)

Note: Assessments marked with a checkmark (✓) are discussed in detail, whereas those marked with a bullet (•) point are suggested for further consideration

one's ability to see images/stimuli. If a client has difficulty with the basic sense of vision, they will have difficulty reading. Other basic functions, such as manual motor performance, will also be impacted. Visual/spatial assessment is necessary to understand a client's neuropsychological processing.

Bender Visual-Motor Gestalt Test, Second Edition

Structure The Bender Visual-Motor Gestalt Test-II (Bender) is the most widely utilized visual-motor assessment in contemporary use. As an individually administered measure, it provides standard scores to children and adults in age range of 4–85 years. Overall, the **Bender** includes 16 stimulus cards, which each contain a geometric figure. During the Copy phase, an examinee is directed to copy a design while the card is displayed. Alternatively, the Recall phase requires the examinee to draw the figures from memory after they have finished copying the entire set. The Global Scoring System utilized by the Bender includes a five-point rating scale used to score examinee work on its resemblance to stimulus items. Raw scores may be converted into standard scores and percentile ranks. The Bender has been employed for a number of alternate uses. Overall, it provides information regarding visual-motor integration performance on given tasks. Alternatively, it may be used as a memory and copy test, in order to assess corresponding cognitive abilities. So too, by engaging the examinee in comparing their produced design to the stimulus design, the administrator could differentiate a potential **perceptual deficit** from one related to **motor functioning**. Namely, the ability to identify, but not correct, differences may suggest motor involvement, whereas the inability to identify differences in the figures at all might suggest deficit in the perceptual domain. Nevertheless, a few cautionary points should be noted. First, a suggestion of neurological impairment should never be made solely due to performance on the Bender. Errors on the measure may be indicative of any number of issues, including developmental delays, maturational difficulties, or perceptual/integration problems (Sattler et al., 2014). Moreover, given this assessments analysis of visual-motor performance as an integrated whole, it is best used in conjunction with other measures.

Practical Considerations The Bender allows for practitioners to assess visual-motor functioning, as well as developmental disorders. Assessment of visual-motor functioning can help identify problems, such as brain injury or other physiological disorders related to visual-motor processing.

The Beery-Buktenica Developmental Test of Visual-Motor Integration, Sixth Edition

Structure The Beery-Buktenica Developmental Test of Visual-Motor Integration, Sixth Edition (Beery VMI) is an assessment designed to determine an individual's ability to **integrate perceptual and motor abilities** (i.e., eye-hand coordination; Beery et al., 2010). It was originally designed based on the theory that sensory-motor integration is indicative of adequate development, and the assessment of such integration is **diagnostically useful** for developmental and learning disorder evaluations. The Beery VMI can be administered to children and adults 2–100 years of age. As such, it has a more extensive age range than the Bender, enabling administration to younger age ranges. While the full form includes 30 total items and spans across this age range, there is also a short form that consists of 21 items and is designed for efficient assessment of individuals 2–7 years of age. The Beery VMI may be administered either in group (i.e., for screening) or individual format (i.e., for diagnostic evaluation and eligibility determination), and administration typically takes 15 min. The test is not timed and does not require a verbal response from examinees. During administration, the examinee is asked to copy geometric figures that are presented in the test booklet and are arranged in order of increasing difficulty. A ceiling is established after the examinee fails three consecutive items. Persons under five years of age, or who have difficulty completing such tasks, may be administered the first six items of the assessment. These items require the individuals to produce their own drawing or scribble, copy the examiner's scribbles, and copy the examiner's vertical, horizontal, and circular lines. If the examinee cannot scribble, visual-perceptual items are administered, including the direction to point to a part of the body or animals pictured on a laminated card. The examiner scores each design as a 1 or a 0. In order to earn a 1 score, a constructed design must meet a set of criteria, including correct orientation, number of parts, angle size, etc. Unlike the Bender, the VMI directs examinees to create their design in a designated area, thus minimizing examinee planning. Thus, examiners could contrast performances on these measures in order to assess how the examinee approaches a task and engages in task planning (Semrud-Clikeman et al. 2005).

Practical Considerations Similar to the Bender, the VMI is utilized to assess visual-motor functioning for young children and/or impaired adults. Understanding visual-motor skills is critical when developing rehabilitation programs. While visual-motor assessments provide clarity regarding visual-motor processing, the practitioner must rule out motor abilities and their relationship to visual processing.

Structure

Motor-Free Visual Perception Test, Third Edition

The Motor-Free Visual Perception Test, Third Edition (MVPT-3; Calarusso & Hammill, 2003) is designed to measure an individual's visual perceptual ability without dependence on a motor response. It is an alternative to visual perception measures which require examinees to draw or copy stimulus items; it is considered a more **"pure" assessment of visual-perception** itself. As such, the MVPT-3 is particularly *suited* for individuals with **motor** impairments. The definition of visual perceptual ability, as understood by test authors, is based on a combination of overlapping perceptual and cognitive subskills, including spatial relationships, visual discrimination, figure-ground, visual closure, and visual memory. Specifically, spatial relationship refers to one's ability to accurately perceive objects in space with relation to oneself. Visual discrimination abilities involve differentiating object features, while figure-ground skills include differentiation of an object from its background. Likewise, visual closure refers to the gestalt ability of identifying a whole object when some of its components are missing. Lastly, visual memory is the ability to recognize an object following a brief interval of time. Because these abilities are recognized to co-occur and overlap, the MVPT-3 assessment generates one overall visual processing score, rather than separate scores for each ability. As such, it is intended solely as a **general screening** of visual perceptual abilities and does not yield subtest scores or specific strengths and weaknesses.

The MVPT-3 was designed for individuals from 4 to 94+ years of age, though reliability estimates suggest it may be inadequate for individual decision-making below age 11 (Canivez, 2005). In terms of test format, the MVPT-3 is an untimed, individually administered 65-item test. Administration is relatively straightforward, and test time averages between 20 and 30 min. As noted above, scoring yields a single score of general visual perceptual abilities and can be calculated in 10 min. Additionally, the third edition of the MVPT includes an additional "*Response Time Index*" to assist in assessing the speed of an examinee's visual perceptual skills. Stimulus items are presented through the use of a spiral-bound, test-plate easel, and each item includes four, multiple-choice options. For the majority of tasks, both stimulus and response options are presented on the same page, enabling examinees to view them at the same time. However, on memory-related tasks, the stimulus page is displayed for five seconds before being removed and replaced by a page of option items. An examinee response may include saying the option letter or pointing to the letter. The examiner records each option on the record form and calculates a raw score by subtracting the number of errors from the number of the last item attempted. Derived scores can be calculated from raw scores through the provided norm tables which include standard scores, percentile ranks, and age equivalents. Confidence intervals for standard scores can be found at the 85% and 90% level. All age groups participate in the same test format, but vary by starting point. Rather than including basal or ceiling rules, examinees complete all items associated with their respective age group. Overall, the MVPT-3 serves as an improvement over previous versions through the addition of an expanded age range in order to better assess adult populations. Additionally, the use of a nationally representative standardization sample was lacking in earlier editions and was provided for in the latest edition.

Practical Considerations The MVPT-3 allows for practitioners to assess visual processing without requiring motor responses. Making this determination is **critical** with young children as well as impaired adults and does not require the assistance of an occupational therapist. Determining if a problem is motor-driven or visual-driven will indicate the appropriate diagnosis and the need for specialized interventions.

Language/Auditory Assessment for Intervention

Similar to visual/spatial functioning, assessment of **language/auditory systems** must be demonstrated for an individual to learn in society. Assessment of language skills is one of the *strongest predictors* of future growth and development. Higher-order cognitive skills, such as reading and writing, will be impacted if one's basic auditory functioning is compromised.

Structure

Clinical Evaluation of Language Fundamentals-5

The Clinical Evaluation of Language Fundamentals, Fifth Edition (CELF-5; Semel et al., 2013) is an individually administered assessment tool designed for the diagnosis and evaluation of **language and communication disorders** in individuals 5–21 years of age. To this end, the measure is often used for the purpose of identifying and detailing the nature of language problems, determining eligibility for special education services, and informing intervention planning processes. It includes assessments of language domains such as verbal memory, reading, writing, and pragmatics, as well as verbal concepts, syntax, and morphology. Though commonly used across clinical settings, the CELF-5 includes a focus on language used within the academic context and thus may lend itself more to school-based use. The CELF-5 utilizes a tiered process of evaluation. It suggests the preliminary use of the Observational Rating Scale (ORS) in order to inform subsequent choices regarding what tests are most relevant to the referral concern. The ORS is completed by a parent, teacher, and/or student and assists in the gathering of observational information regarding an examinee's speech, language, and communication behaviors in a naturalistic environment. The CELF-5 accommodates a *flexible assessment* approach, as tests may be administered separately or collectively as a battery. Administration time for the core test battery averages between 34 and 42 min, while individual test time ranges from 5 to 15 min. Relevant tests vary according to age group (i.e., 5–8 years, or 9–21 years). Tests administered to both age groups include Word Classes, Following Directions, Formulated Sentences, Recalling Sentences, and Understanding Spoken Paragraphs. Younger age groups may also be administered the Sentence Comprehension, Linguistic Concepts, and Word Structure subtests. Older age groups may be additionally administered Word Definitions, Sentence Assembly, and Semantic Relationships subtests.

The CELF-5 yields a standardized composite score (Core Language Score), as well as five index scores, including Receptive Language, Expressive Language, Language Content, Language Structure, and Language Memory Indexes. Difference scores may also be obtained in order to consider discrepancy comparisons (e.g.,, between Receptive and Expressive Language). Additionally, suggestions for *item analysis* and *error detection* are included. After completing the assessment, an examiner can utilize extension testing by altering test items or conditions in order to identify environmental modifications or test accommodations that enhance or impair performance. For example, background noise levels or time limits may be altered. Examinees could also be afforded item repetition or visual aids in order to determine if these altered conditions significantly affect performance (Pratt, 2017). Table 10.2 lists the subtests on the CELF-5.

Practical Considerations The CELF-5 is a comprehensive measure of **language** commonly utilized by speech/language pathologists and psychologists to assess aspects of receptive, expressive, and pragmatic language. Repeated research has shown that language is one of the most important skills related to the ability to predict current and future success (Davis, 2011).

Table 10.2 Subtests on the CELF-5

Subtest	What the subtest measures
Word Classes	Understanding of relationships of words
Following Directions	Interpretation of directions; working memory
Formulated Sentences	Formulation of complex sentences
Recalling Sentences	Recall and production of sentences
Understanding Spoken Paragraphs	Sustained attention and critical thinking
Word Definitions	Definitions of words based on features
Sentence Assembly	Assembly syntactic structures
Semantic Relationships	Interpretation of sentences
Pragmatics Profile	Social and academic communication
Reading Comprehension	Reading and understanding of narratives
Structured Writing	Applied language in written format

Peabody Picture Vocabulary Test-4

Structure The Peabody Picture Vocabulary Test, Fourth Edition (PPVT-4; Dunn & Dunn, 2007) is an individually administered assessment designed to measure an examinee's **receptive vocabulary** for Standard American English. The fourth edition primarily includes updates such as an extension of easier test items and design improvements. Notably, black and white stimulus item pictures are now portrayed in color. Moreover, to support an increased accuracy of measurement and stability of scale for young children or individuals with severe impairment, the current edition has increased the number of easy test items.

Overall, the PPVT-4 is designed and normed for individuals from 2:6 to 90+ years of age and can be used for screening or diagnostic purposes. Commonly identified purposes include use with preschool students, children with expressive language disorders, cerebral palsy, and/or those with motor impairment. Moreover, due to the important role vocabulary plays in reading development, the PPVT-4 might be used as one component in a reading assessment battery. Metrics provided by the assessment include standard scores, percentile ranks, normal curve equivalents, stanines, as well as age and grade equivalent scores. The test battery limits administration of items to those that are appropriate for an examinee's ability level. As such, the PPVT-4 administration time averages between 10 and 15 min. Though an untimed test, it recommends the examiner provide a verbal prompt if no response is given in 10 s.

Of particular note, the PPVT-4 enables one to measure an individual's **receptive language improvement** over time by providing metrics and parallel forms for use in such endeavors. Specifically, a non-normative Growth Value Scale (GVS) facilitates comparisons of an individual's score change over time. Likewise, two parallel forms (A and B) are provided in order to enable one to measure an individual's receptive language improvement over time.

The process of test administration is relatively straightforward. The examiner reads a single stimulus word aloud and directs the examinee to select a picture that best corresponds to the stimulus word from an array of four picture options that are prominently displayed on each single page. Importantly, the assessment requires only a pointing response from the examinee. Overall, each individual form includes a total of 228 items, which are divided into 19 sets of 12 items a piece. The basal set is considered the lowest item set having zero to one examinee error, while a ceiling set is comprised of the highest set of items having eight or more errors. The examiner discontinues test administration after reaching the ceiling set. As such, examinees are typically administered a range of approximately 60 items that are targeted for their appropriate developmental level.

Practical Considerations Many neuropsychologists view the ability to process language and understand words as one of the **most important** considerations in clinical practice. Thus, the PPVT-4 is often viewed as an essential component of the neuropsychological evaluation process.

Expressive One-Word Picture Vocabulary Test-4 (level 2)

Structure The Expressive One-Word Picture Vocabulary Test-4 (EOWPT-4; Martin & Brownell, 2011) is an individually administered, 190-item measure used to assess the extent of an individual's **vocabulary development**. As such, it is useful as an early screening tool for vocabulary knowledge but should be used alongside complementary measures of other facets of language. The EOWPT-4 expanded the test floor and ceiling so that the fourth edition may be administered to a wider age range than previous editions, including children and adults age 2–80+ years. Results include a single total raw score, as well as standard scores, percentile ranks, and age-equivalent scores.

During this untimed test, the examinee is presented one illustration plate at a time and directed to use one word in order to name the object, action, or concept portrayed in the illustration. Test administration is untimed, affording a comfortable pace for the examinee. Basal and ceiling guidelines establish a critical range of testing, enabling testing time to be efficient – the whole test may be administered in 15–20 min. Illustrations are presented in order of increasing difficulty and correspond to vocabulary words including primarily nouns, some gerunds, verbs, and modifiers.

Practical Considerations The EOWPT-4 is commonly used to identify children with true **expressive language** disorders, such as children with Autism Spectrum Disorder. Both progress monitoring and curriculum development require knowledge of the ability to process language.

Learning/Memory Assessment for Intervention

Learning and memory are necessary functions for one to acquire and remember basic information in order to navigate the world. These processes are not only important for academic success but other occupational tasks as well. Learning and memory assessment are not always considered necessary components of comprehensive evaluations. However, if one is to understand psychopathology including categories of differential diagnoses (e.g., traumatic brain injuries) and neurodiversity, these areas must be evaluated during a comprehensive assessment.

California Verbal Learning Test-Children's Version

Structure The California Verbal Learning Test-Children's Version (CVLT-C; Delis et al., 1994) is a multifaceted neuropsychological assessment that measures the processes involved in **memory and recalling verbal information**. Quantitative (i.e., performance) and qualitative (i.e., strategies employed) components of memory and verbal information are quantified. The CVLT-C was designed to evaluate learning and memory problems in children. More specifically, it helps in determining how children approach various verbal learning/memory tasks and potential deficits that appear during assessment. Verbal memory is assessed within the parameters of a shopping task. Examinees are asked to recall items in a shopping list. Both recall and recognition of words are measured over several successive trials. The CVLT-C was designed following the success that the adult version of the California Verbal Learning Test was found to have in assessing memory and verbal information in adults. The CVLT-C can be administered to individuals ages 5 to 16 years. Additional assessment tools are available for children as young as age four. Administration of the CVLT-C requires approximately 15–20 minutes to be conducted. An additional 20 minutes is provided to accommodate for the delayed recall interval required, during which nonverbal, unrelated tasks are given to the students. The CVLT-C test includes a manual and 25 record forms. Scoring can be performed manually or via computer software. Due to the amount of data that is accumulated during the CVLT-C, use of the CVLT-C software is *recommended.* Approximately ten minutes is required to score the CVLT-C using the software. Over 20 norm-based scores are yielded from this assessment.

Practical Considerations The CVLT-C is designed to assess multiple components of verbal learning and memory. It isolates **deficient strategies** that contribute to specific learning problems and assists with designing interventions for rehabilitation purposes. It is a reasonably quick assessment to administer, albeit comprehensive.

Test of Memory and Learning, Second Edition

Structure The Test of Memory and Learning, Second Edition (TOMAL-2; Reynolds & Voress, 2008) is designed to assess the memory of individuals ranging from 5 to 59 years of age. More specifically, the TOMAL-2 assesses immediate verbal and nonverbal memory and delayed recall for **verbal memory**. Scores obtained from these individual subtests combine to create a composite memory score (Adams & Reynolds, 2009). The TOMAL-2 incorporates a multitude of additional variables as well as a varying mode of assessment presentation and response. This is to ensure that the participant is provided with visual, verbal, and motoric opportunities to be presented with the TOMAL-2 and to respond. The TOMAL-2 allows examiners to evaluate learning through the participant's quantified recall and recognition abilities of various stimuli.

The TOMAL-2 is comprised of subtests, supplementary subtests, and various summary scores. The subtests and supplementary subtests each take approximately 30 min to complete, so in totality the TOMAL-2 takes approximately one hour to administer. There are eight subtests, four verbal and four nonverbal, which yield three core indexes. The indexes are **Verbal Memory, Nonverbal Memory**, and the **Composite Memory Index** (Reynolds & Voress, 2007). There are six supplementary subtests, four verbal and two nonverbal, that may be used when a more comprehensive assessment of an individual's memory is required. Supplementary subtests in the TOMAL-2 can be substituted for a core subtest if the core subtest cannot be given or is inappropriate for a certain individual. Additionally, there is a delayed recall procedure available for two of the verbal subtests from the core battery, which yields a Verbal Delayed Recall Index. The summary scores include four core indexes and five supplementary indexes. Normative scores are provided for interpretation of the subtests and summary scores.

For the TOMAL-2, age-equivalent scores are provided for ages 5–14, and examiners must use caution in their use and interpretation. A manual is provided, along with other materials that explain how to administer the TOMAL-2 and how to calculate and interpret the results. The TOMAL-2 should be administered by an individual who has a qualification level B. Professionals can purchase the complete kit which includes a manual, 25 profile forms, 25 examiner record booklets, delayed recall cue cards, 15 vinyl chips, a Visual Selective Reminding Test Board, Picture Book A, and Picture Book B (Reynolds & Voress, 2007). The manual provides specific instructions on how to apply basal and ceiling rules, as well as appendixes for the standard scores and percentile ranks. Thorough directions for administering and interpreting the TOMAL-2 are also provided in the manual. Furthermore, standardization, reliability, and validity of the TOMAL-2 are included in the manual.

The TOMAL-2 was standardized on a sample of 1, 961 individuals from 28 states (Reynolds & Voress, 2007). Demographic characteristics of the TOMAL-2 were closest to the 2002 US Census (Reynolds & Voress, 2007). For this standardization sample, internal consistency reliability was reported, with alpha coefficients ranging from 0.67 to 0.97 for the subtests and supplementary subtests and 0.89 to 0.91 for the Verbal Delayed Recall subtests (Reynolds & Voress, 2007). Test-retest reliability coefficients ranged from 0.81 to 0.93 on the subtests, 0.68 to 0.94 on the supplementary subtests, and 0.47 to 0.88 on the Verbal Delayed Recall subtests, with the interval between testing sessions lasting for 2 weeks. Validity is also reported, with statistically significant positive correlations being shown in the manual.

Further research on the TOMAL-2 should focus on expanding the age-equivalent scores past 14 and increasing the standardization sample. This will allow for more information on memory to be collected and standardized, which will allow for knowledge about memory to be expanded on and augmented. Subtests from the TOMAL-2 can be found in Table 10.3.

Practical Considerations The TOMAL-2 is a widely used, comprehensive measure of memory and learning for individuals 5–59 years of age. The assessment of memory is often required to identify abnormalities related to neurological events and developmental disabilities. The TOMAL-2 allows a practitioner to assess **verbal versus nonverbal** memory in order to develop appropriate recommendations for rehabilitation.

Table 10.3 Subtests from TOMAL-2

TOMAL-2 subtests
Memory for Stories
Facial Memory
Word Selective Reminding
Visual Selective Reminding
Object Recall
Abstract Visual Memory
Digits Forward
Visual Sequential Memory
Paired Recall
Memory for Location
Manual Imitation
Letters Forward
Letters Backward
Memory for Stories Delayed
Word Selective Reminding Delayed

Motor/Perceptual/Sensory Assessment for Intervention

Evaluation of sensory functions is an essential element of any neuropsychological assessment, though one that is often *neglected* (Strauss et al., 2006). Alternatively, neuropsychologists often include tests of motor performance, usually focusing on the hands, during examinations. Special attention is given to comparing one side of the body to the other to determine deficits in functionality. Children experience their world through their sensory and motor skills; therefore, deficits in these areas may correlate with deficits in other areas (Rhodes et al., 2009). While many intricate parts of the brain contribute to sensory/motor functions, the parietal lobe is the primary processor of somatosensory information. The primary somatosensory cortex has different pathways – one that processes touch, pressure, and kinesthesis and another that processes pain and temperature (Hale & Fiorello, 2004). The secondary somatosensory association cortex has connections to primary areas and frontal lobes to control movements, assist with spatial perception, and guide actions in response to the environment (Davis, 2011). Sensory and motor connections allow for complex behavior to occur. Nervous system impairments revealed on **sensory-motor assessments** can significantly impact higher-order cognitive processing (Dean & Davis, 2008). Unfortunately, this remains one of the most neglected areas within neuropsychology (D'Amato et al., 2005). However, this problem can be solved by using the Dean-Woodcock Sensory-Motor Battery (DWSMB), a norm-based instrument which is a component of the Dean-Woodock Neuropsychological Battery.

Dean-Woodcock Neuropsychological Battery

Structure The Dean-Woodcock Neuropsychological Battery (DW; Dean & Woodcock, 2003) is a comprehensive set of three integrated neuropsychological measures designed to assess **sensory/motor functions, emotional, cognitive,** and **academic functioning** (D'Amato & Walker, 2007). The DW is intended for children and adults age 4–90 years. The measure consists of the DWSMB, the Dean-Woodcock Structured Neuropsychological Interview, and the Dean-Woodcock Emotional Status Examination. Furthermore, the DW may be used independently or in conjunction with the Woodcock-Johnson Tests of Cognitive Abilities and Woodcock-Johnson Tests of Achievement.

The DWSMB assesses both **sensory and motor functions** through 18 subtests. Sensory functions measured include visual acuity, visual field defects, auditory acuity, picture naming, and tactile discrimination. Scales within the sensory domain include Near-Point Visual Acuity, Visual Confrontation, Naming Pictures of Objects, Auditory Acuity, Palm Writing, Object Examination, Finger Localization, and Simultaneous Localization. Motor functions that are measured include lateral preference, gait and station, balance, visual construction, coordination, miming, fine motor function, expressive speech, and grip strength (Schneider, 2007). Scales within the motor domain include Lateral Preference Scale, Gait and Station, Romberg, Construction, Coordination, Mime Movements, Left-Right Movements, Finger Tapping, Expressive Speech, and Grip Strength. Individuals are required to engage in a series of manual tasks which are prompted by the examiner. The kit includes small materials to be used particularly during sensory function subtests. Many subtests, especially those on motor scales, do not require the use of materials. However, for scales that do require materials, such as Grip Strength and Finger Tapping, materials (e.g., dynamometer) are not included. The DWSMB is the most comprehensive portion of the DW; administration time is approximately 30–45 minutes (D'Amato & Walker, 2007). Performance on scales is rated as within normal limits and above, mildly impaired, moderately impaired, or severely impaired (Schneider, 2007). Raw scores from the DWSMB scales are transformed to W-scores and W-difference scores. According to Dean and Davis (2008), W-scores contain a greater range than cutoff scores, which increase sensitivity to elusive deficiencies. The Dean-Woodcock Structured Neuropsychological Interview consists of the practitioner asking questions to gather an individual's background information, including the client's motivation, attention, emotional capability, and information pertaining to medical disorders (D'Amato & Walker, 2007). The final portion of the assessment, the Dean-Woodcock Emotional Status Examination, is used to assess signs and symptoms of mental disorders. The DW is designed to be used by psychologists and others who have specialized training in administering neuropsychological assessments. The standardization sample for the DWSMB included 1011 participants who were screened to be free of psychiatric disorders or histories of mental health treatment (Schneider, 2007). The sample closely resembled the US

Census data, including that which related to sex, race, ethnicity, age, and handedness. A weakness of this assessment is that the 2000 US Census was used; therefore, norms need updating. Additionally, while reliability and validity are sound for the DWSMB, the data are lacking for the interview and emotional status evaluation (D'Amato & Walker, 2007) portions.

The DWSMB was developed due to the need for a *psychometrically sound*, **comprehensive neuropsychological battery** that would yield appropriate assessment of brain functioning (Dean & Davis, 2008). In fact, questions posed throughout the DW are similar to ones used during a typical neurological screening procedures, albeit with normative procedures and scores. The assessment of sensory/motor functioning, in addition to the gathering of a detailed background history, is essential in identifying potential neurological deficits. According to Davis et al. (2006), sensory/motor skills share 92% of variance with cognition, while sensory/motor skills share 90% of the variability with academic achievement. The DWSMB has been found to be successful in discerning neurologically impaired clients from typically functioning individuals (Volpe et al., 2006). Scales on the DW assist in differentiating between *signs of subcortical dysfunction* and those related to damage in the *right* hemisphere (Dean & Woodcock, 1999).

Practical Considerations Sensory/motor assessments are critical when understanding clients and are used in a variety of settings, particularly by neuropsychologists. Many test kits, such as the NEPSY-II, contain subtests related to sensory/motor functioning, but not as extensive as the DW. Additionally, the DWSMB is relatively easy to administer and subtests can be administered in any order (D'Amato & Walker, 2007). The **main advantage** of the DWSMB, and one of the greatest failings in neuropsychology in general, is that normative procedures and scoring for frequently used neurological examinations are not often followed. The DWSMB solves this quandary by offering norms in an area that is critical for understanding neurological and therefore neuropsychological functioning (Davis, 2011).

Attention/Executive Functions Assessment for Intervention

In today's society, paying attention might be one of the most important skills. The idea that one can *multitask successfully* at a high cognitive level is **erroneous**. The complexity of these areas must include an understanding of cognitive, achievement, memory/learning, and behavior. It is important to have knowledge of psychopathology for differential diagnoses (e.g., individuals with Attention-Deficit/Hyperactivity Disorder). It can be difficult to differentiate an individual with a learning disability from one with attentional difficulties.

Test of Everyday Attention for Children, Second Edition

Structure The Test of Everyday Attention for Children, Second Edition (TEA-Ch2; Manly et al., 2016) is designed to assess attentional processes in children and adolescents. It is a neuropsychological assessment that is a modification of the Test for Everyday Attention (TEA). The theoretical foundation of the TEA-Ch2 is that attention is a system of separate attentional processes and that these separate processes can be negatively impacted by different disorders (Robertson et al., 1994). The most common disorder that hinders attentional processes is attention-deficit hyperactivity disorder (ADHD). Over the past decade, research has focused on individuals with ADHD in an attempt to better understand how it affects students' attentional processes (Arnold et al., 2020).

Research has found that individuals with ADHD have structural and functional alterations in the cerebellum and the parietal lobes (Cherkasova & Hechtman, 2009). The cerebellum was once thought to mainly influence motor functioning, but over time neuroscience researchers have discovered through neuroimaging that it also influences aspects such as emotional regulation, attention shifting, working memory, and executive functions. Further research supports this new information about the cerebellum, showing that individuals with ADHD have decreased connectivity in their prefrontal cortex, superior parietal lobule, and cerebellum during a basic activation task (Geissler & Lesch, 2011). These studies show how ADHD related behavioral difficulties results from alterations in the brain, which affects attentional processes.

The TEA-Ch2 is designed to assess various **attentional processes** through **auditory and visual modalities** and uses game-like materials in order to remain current with today's world. There are two versions of this assessment dependent on a client's age (5–7 years; 8–16 years). For the children ages 5–7, there are seven subtests and administration time is approximately 35 min. The version for children ages 8–16 includes nine subtests and takes approximately 45 min to administer. The subtests on TEA-Ch2 assess *three attention factors*: selective attention, sustained attention, and attentional control/switching (Manly et al., 1999). The subtests are introduced around a story of an alien character and his dog. Long gaps are interspersed, requiring the participant to sustain attention and remember the number of "scoring" sounds. Information gathered by this subtest is critical for researchers to obtain regarding attentional processes and how it influences a student's performance. There are other components of the TEA-Ch2 that must be adhered to when it is being administered.

The TEA-Ch2 was normed on 394 children ranging from 5 to 8 years and 621 children ranging in age from 8 to 16 years; all norms were gathered from the United Kingdom. Separate norms based on sex are provided in the manual. Instructions for administering the TEA-Ch2 are available in the manual, and they must be provided verbatim. The examiner also asks if the participant understands the instructions. If the participant states that the instructions do not make sense, the examiner must paraphrase the directions. Furthermore, because this battery was normed in the United Kingdom, minor modifications of the instructions are to be made to reflect common discourse of North America (e.g., "mark" instead of "tic"). The manual delves further into the additional information about the TEA-Ch2, showing how it assesses attentional processes. According to Posner and Peterson (1990), there are at least three attentional systems in the brain, and damage to one system will not automatically lead to damage to another system. The TEA-Ch2 can help identify individuals who are experiencing attentional issues in one of the three systems. This battery provides information about **attentional processes** and sheds light on certain disorders that negatively impact an individual's attention abilities. Information such as this allows for researchers to better understand the regions of the brain that play a role in attention. It also allows for educators to provide more competent support to students who might be struggling to remain attentive in school.

Practical Considerations The TEA-Ch2 measures selective attention, sustained attention, and attentional switching using an *innovative and game-like* approach to assessment. This assessment is often used in the evaluation of children with attention problems, including attention-deficit/hyperactivity disorder (ADHD) and Autism spectrum disorder. While normed in the United Kingdom, the TEA-Ch2 is used by clinical, school, and child psychologists on an international level.

Delis-Kaplan Executive Function System

Structure The Delis-Kaplan Executive Function System (D-KEFS; Delis et al., 2001) is a neuropsychological assessment that is designed to analyze **executive functioning processes**. Executive functions are a conglomerate of higher-level processes that allow individuals to carry out certain abilities. Some of these abilities include **emotional regulation**, **cognitive flexibility, inhibitory control, planning,** and **organization**. Executive functions are housed in the **frontal lobe** of the brain, with there being some slight differences in frontal lobe development between males and females (Tanaka et al., 2012). Even though brain development occurs from four weeks of gestation, executive functions are not fully formed until the mid-twenties (Douet et al., 2014). Other research on executive functions has found that these processes also influence other areas of development.

Research on executive functions has found that individual differences in personality and cognitive ability influence an individual's health behaviors (Hall et al., 2014). This research shows how an individual's cognitive abilities might influence certain aspects of one's health such as **self-regulation**. Further research found that impairments in executive functions could contribute to late-life depression, with a correlation to the anterior thalamic radiation and uncinate fasciculus (Sexton et al., 2012). Information such as this is crucial for researchers to obtain so that executive functions can be fully understood and proper supports can be created for those who are struggling with executive *dysfunction*.

The D-KEFS (Delis et al., 2001) was designed to assess processes of executive functions and mild forms of executive dysfunction using **verbal and spatial modalities**. It can be given to individuals 8–89 years of age, with the exception being the Proverbs Tests which is designed for individuals ages 16–89 years. The D-KEFS utilizes a process-oriented approach, so that each task provides multiple scores. This approach portrays the source of any difficulties that were experienced. It allows researchers to isolate the main areas in each test that have impaired performance, allowing researchers to obtain integral information about executive function. There are nine tests that comprise the D-KEFS, and each test assesses key functions that relate to executive function.

In the Trail Making Test, the participant is asked to complete multiple conditions. The participant is asked to scan letters and numbers and mark number 3, connect numbers in ascending order, switch between connections numbers and letters, connect letters in alphabetical order, and draw a line over a dotted line in a specified period of time. The key functions assessed in the Trail Making Test are visual scanning, letter sequencing, number-letter switching, and motor speed. The executive function ability that is related to the key functions in the Trail Making Test is cognitive flexibility, or the ability to switch between thoughts fluidly. This test would be useful for researchers to use when working with an individual who has suspected frontal lobe damage. There are other vital components to the D-KEFS.

The D-KEFS takes approximately 90 min to administer. This assessment was designed to be utilized flexibly, so the tests can be administered by themselves or in combination with other D-KEFS subtests. The examiner can also decide to omit a test. Instructions for administration are given in the stimulus book; the manual is not a requirement when giving the D-KEFS. However, scoring and interpretation guidelines must be referenced in the manual.

For most of the measures, the raw scores are converted to age-scaled scores, with a mean of 10 and a standard deviation of 3. The Verbal Fluency Test has limited raw score ranges and has almost no age effects across the normative sample. For this test, raw scores are converted to percentile ranks that have been correct for the normative sample. The raw scores for the error and ratio measures also have limited ranges in normal populations; thus, they are converted to percentile ranks for each of the 16 age groups. Contrast measures are also included in the D-KEFS that provide further quantification on an individual's performance.

Contrast measures that are included in the D-KEFS quantify performance based on two factors. The first contrast measure quantifies performance on a baseline task and a higher-level task (e.g., Trail Making Contrast = Number Switching minus Motor Speed). The second contrast measure quantifies performance based on two higher-level tasks (e.g., Verbal Fluency Contrast = Letter Fluency minus Category Fluency). These scaled score differences are treated like raw scores and are then converted into scaled scores, with a mean of 10 and a standard deviation of 3. The contrast scaled scores are corrected for the entire sample. The D-KEFS also distinguishes between "*primary*" and "*optional*" measures.

The primary measures in the D-KEFS either provide an overall characterization of performance on a task or process scores for key components of the task. Optional measures provide supplemental information. If the examiner is scoring the protocol manually, mostly the primary measures can be computed. Analysis of both primary and optional measures is recommended for a more comprehensive assessment of the individual's executive function. The D-KEFS Scoring Assistant computes the standardized scores for both the primary and optional measures. Scoring and interpretation of the D-KEFS are based on a certain theoretical approach to neuropsychological assessment.

Scoring and interpretation of the D-KEFS are based on the "cognitive process" theoretical approach. This approach disfavors the reliance on a single-score method in quantifying test performance. Instead, equal importance is placed on understanding how the individual solves the tasks of the D-KEFS. Each test yields **achievement and process scores**. This allows for examiners to obtain more specific information regarding the full extent of the patient's executive functions. Although this information is crucial to expand current knowledge on executive function, additional research needs to be conducted in certain areas of the D-KEFS.

Additional research needs to be conducted on the specific ways in which the factors influence executive functions. Currently, there is a lack of strong statistical data on how the factors assessed in the D-KEFS influence executive function. Having specific information on how certain factors influence executive function would allow for many advancements to be made. This critical information would allow medical and neuroscience researchers to better understand how executive functions operate. It would also allow psychologists and educators to employ better strategies in supporting executive function development. Further research should also be conducted on the influence of neurological disorders and their influence on executive function, in order to understand the influence of these disorders and other brain deficits on executive function. Table 10.4 lists the subtests on the D-KEFS.

Table 10.4 Subtests on the D-KEFS

Subtest	What subtest measures
Trail Making Test	Visuomotor processing; psychomotor speed; attention
Verbal Fluency Test	Shifting; word generation
Design Fluency Test	Visual attention; motor speed; visuoperceptual skills
Color-Word Interference Test	Inhibition/switching; cognitive flexibility
Word Context Test	Rapid naming; reading; inhibition
Twenty Questions Test	Visual attention and perception; object recognition; categorization
Tower Test	Spatial planning; rule learning; inhibition
Proverbs Test	Verbal abstraction
Sorting Test	Concept formation; problem-solving

Practical Considerations The D-KEFS is a comprehensive neuropsychological test battery that assists in the assessment of executive functions. The scoring and interpretation are based on a cognitive process theoretical approach to neuropsychological assessment, meaning that it does not rely on a single-score method when quantifying performance (Dugbartey & Ramsden, 2003). Through this assessment, practitioners place an importance on understanding *how the examinee attempts to solve subtests*. Additionally, this assessment has been used in assessment of neurodevelopmental pathologies and adults suffering from a wide range of impairments, including brain injury.

Academic Achievement Assessment for Intervention

After development of the basic senses, academic achievement can be mastered. Today's contemporary society *requires* **academic achievement** for effective functioning, such as reading, writing, and arithmetic. Technological advancement has changed our world which also typically requires academic achievement.

Kaufman Test of Educational Achievement, Third Edition

Structure The Kaufman Test of Educational Achievement, Third Edition (KTEA-3; Kaufman & Kaufman, 2014) is an individually administered assessment of academic achievement for grades prekindergarten to 12, or ages 4:0 through 25:11 years. It is designed for the purpose of comprehensively measuring an individual's **reading, mathematics, written language, and oral language abilities**. The structure of the KTEA-3 battery includes 19 total subtests that are combined into 3 core composites and 10 supplemental composites. Additionally, an overall composite score (whose composition slightly varies by age) may be yielded from a number of subtests. Specifically, the core composites consist of Reading (Letter and Word Recognition, Reading Comprehension), Math (Math Concepts and Applications, Math Computation), and Written Language (Written Expression, Spelling). The Academic Skills Battery yields an overall composite score representative of academic functioning and is comprised of subtests that vary and increase with age (i.e., typically includes Reading, Mathematics, and Written Language composites). Among the supplemental composites are the Reading-Related Composite (Sound-Symbol, Decoding, Reading Fluency, Reading Understanding), Oral Composite (Oral Language, Oral Fluency), and four cross-domain composites (Comprehension, Expression, Orthographic Processing, and Academic Fluency). Subtests are designed to target key skill components of academic domains, facilitating analysis of an individual's strength or weakness on skill components in a given domain (i.e., phonological, decoding, word-level, comprehension abilities for reading).

Importantly, the KTEA-3 affords flexibility to practitioners in terms of subtest choice and order of administration. Examiners are not required to administer all subtests; they may choose to use a single or combination of subtests in one or more domains. As such, the practitioner may tailor the assessment to specific referral concerns. The KTEA-3 is frequently used for determining **eligibility** for special education classification, identifying academic strengths and weaknesses, or progress monitoring an academic intervention. The inclusion of examinee error analysis may be useful for facilitating instructional planning and informing the design of targeted intervention. The measure is particularly useful in addressing specific referral concerns, given its rich offering of composite score options in a wide array of academic skill domains.

The grade level is used to guide an examiner's selection of tests, as well as for locating item starting points. Because items closely resemble classroom tasks, extensive instructional feedback is not usually required. Administration format may occur through use of paper and pencil or digitally with web-based administration. In the former case, the examiner records responses in a record book; recording demands widely vary based on subtest task. On six of the subtests, the examinees write their response in a test booklet. Practitioners may hand score or utilize the web-based platform (Q-global) offered by test publishers. Several types of scores are yielded, including standard scores, percentile ranks, grade equivalents, and age equivalents. Importantly, the obtained mean KTEA-3 scores for examinees are often lower than other tests (WIAT or WJ) (Mackler, 2017). For those practitioners who wish, the KTEA-3 may be linked with Common Core State Standards in order to determine a student's performance relative to grade level expectations. Parallel forms (A and B) of the test are available to facilitate retesting and enable one to conduct pretest-posttest designed studies. However, caution should be taken when using individually administered academic achievement tests for academic progress, as many such assessments do not adequately measure short-term academic progress, especially for older grade levels. For a list of subtests on the KTEA-3, see Table 10.5.

Practical Considerations The KTEA-3 is a widely recognized and used assessment for determining one's progress in **reading, written language, mathematics,** and **oral language**. To fully understand how someone can be successful in life, the practitioner needs to know how a client can process information in a world where reading, writing, talking, hearing, and listening are all prerequisite skills to successful functioning. Tests like this are critical to allowing the clinical to understand the basic skills to life success. While similar to other standardized academic assessments, the KTEA-3 contains unique approaches to evaluation, such as use of a written language subtest which allows a client to write through a series of storytelling.

Table 10.5 Subtests from KTEA-3

Subtest
Letter and Word Recognition
Nonsense Word Decoding
Reading Comprehension
Reading Vocabulary
Word Recognition Fluency
Decoding Fluency
Silent Reading Fluency
Math Concepts and Applications
Math Computation
Math Fluency
Written Expression
Spelling
Writing Fluency
Listening Comprehension
Oral Expression
Associational Fluency
Phonological Processing
Object Naming Facility
Letting Naming Facility

Wechsler Individual Achievement Test, Third Edition

Structure The Wechsler Individual Achievement Test, Third Edition (WIAT-III) is an individually administered, **diagnostic achievement test** for individuals age 4 to 50 years. A hallmark of the WIAT-III (Wechsler, 2009) assessments includes subtests that were designed to cover and closely align with the specific learning disability areas noted by the Individuals with Disabilities Education Improvement Act of 2004 (IDEA, 2004). As such, the WIAT-III is designed to identify areas of academic strengths and weakness, assist in diagnostic and eligibility decisions related to specific learning disabilities, and inform academic intervention planning.

The structure of the WIAT-III battery includes 16 total subtests that are grouped into 4 core and 3 supplemental composites. The core composites include **Oral Language** (Listening Comprehension, Oral Expression), **Total Reading** (Word Reading, Pseudoword Decoding, Reading Comprehension, Oral Reading Fluency), **Written Expression** (Alphabet Writing Fluency, Spelling, Sentence Composition, Essay Composition), and **Mathematics** (Math Problem Solving, Numerical Operations). It also includes three supplemental composites: Basic Reading (Word Reading, Pseudoword Decoding), Reading Comprehension and Fluency (Reading Comprehension, Oral Reading Fluency), and Math Fluency (Math Fluency-Addition, Math Fluency-Subtraction, Math Fluency-Multiplication). Finally, the

Total Achievement composite is a measure of an individual's level of academic achievement relative to peers. While 13 subtests potentially contribute to this composite, actual subtest contributions vary based on the examinee's age. Importantly, the WIAT-III Total Achievement composite includes oral language subtests where other overall achievement composites do not (i.e., KTEA-3).

The WIAT-III offers a number of *unique features* relative to other academic assessment batteries. Consistent with a comprehensive assessment for a reading disability, it includes an oral reading fluency subtest with blocks of text (as opposed to single-sentence reading). Similarly, Math fluency measurements differentiate ability by procedure (addition, subtraction, multiplication). One of the most notable differences between the WIAT-III and KTEA-3 includes its assessment of written expression. While the KTEA-3 includes a detailed error analysis and single subtest score that spans writing abilities, the WIAT-III yields a more robust measurement on a finer scale of abilities. Specifically, it provides a Sentence Composition subtest that includes distinct scores on Sentence Combining and Sentence Building abilities. Moreover, it yields an overall Essay Composition score based on subscores for Word Count, Theme Development, and Text Organization and optional scores on Grammar and Mechanics. These features come at the cost of having to master the detailed and complicated task of scoring such measures in accordance with manual scoring procedures.

Examiners are encouraged to use a *customized* assessment approach and may select subtest administration based on the referral concern. Though administration time varies by subtest selection and examinee age, average administration time ranges from 1 to 17 min. Scoring may be completed by hand, with the automated Scoring Assistant CD, or via the web-based platform (Q-global). A number of derived scores are available, including standard scores, percentile ranks, grade and age equivalents, normal curve equivalents, stanines, and growth scale values. Skill analysis capabilities are provided at the item and within-item level in order to inform intervention or instructional planning. For a complete list of subtests on the WIAT-III, see Table 10.6.

Practical Considerations The WIAT-III can be used in a variety of settings to test one's reading, math, writing, and oral language. When raw scores are entered into the computer program, detailed interventions related to special education and rehabilitation are provided to the practitioner. A unique feature on the written expression subtest which may relate to some neuropsychological disorders is the fact that a verbal/written sentence prompt is provided to the client, compared to the KTEA-3 which provides the client with an unfinished story which they are asked to complete. Additionally, many practitioners appreciate using the WIAT-III in conjunction with the WISC-V because of simultaneous product development, such as co-norming.

Table 10.6 Subtests from WIAT-III

Listening Comprehension	Listens to vocabulary words and points to a picture that illustrates each word and then listens to passages and answers questions about each one
Oral Expression	Shown pictures and asked to name the concept shown in each picture and then the student says words from a given category and repeats sentences
Reading Comprehension	Reads passages aloud or silently and then answers questions about each one
Word Reading	Reads aloud a list of increasingly difficult words found within the English language
Pseudoword Decoding	Reads aloud a list of increasingly difficult nonsense words
Oral Reading Fluency	Reads passages aloud and then orally responds to comprehension questions
Sentence Composition	Combines the information from two or three sentences into one sentence, and then the student creates sentences that use specific words
Essay Composition	Writes an essay within a specified time period
Spelling	Writes single words that are dictated within the context of a sentence
Math Problem Solving	Solves untimed math problems related to basic math skills, everyday applications, geometry, and algebra
Numerical Operations	Solves untimed written math problems in basic skills, geometry, algebra, and calculus
Math Fluency-Addition	Solves written addition problems within a specified time period
Math Fluency-Subtraction	Solves written subtraction problems within a specified time period
Math Fluency-Multiplication	Solves written multiplication problems within a specified time period
Letter and Word Recognition	Identifies letters and reads grade-appropriate words
Nonsense Word Decoding	Pronounces made-up words
Reading Comprehension	Reads symbols, words, sentences, and passages appropriate to grade level and then responds to comprehension questions
Reading Vocabulary	Reads a word in the context of a picture or a sentence and then selects a word that means the same thing
Word Recognition Fluency	Reads as many words within the English language as possible within a specified time period
Decoding Fluency	Reads as many nonsense words as possible within a specified time period
Silent Reading Fluency	Silently reads questions and circles yes or no to each one within a specified time period
Math Concepts and Applications	Solves math problems that relate to real-life situations and assess skills such as number concepts, arithmetic, time and money, and measurement
Math Computation	Solves written math calculation problems

(continued)

Table 10.6 (continued)

Math Fluency	Writes answers to simple arithmetic problems that include addition, subtraction, multiplication, and division within a specified time period
Written Expression	Hears a story presented with pictures in a booklet and completes the story by writing letters, words, sentences, and an essay
Spelling	Writes single letters and spells words dictated orally
Writing Fluency	Writes simple sentences, each one describing a different picture, within a specified time period
Listening Comprehension	Listens to sentences or passages and then responds to comprehension questions
Oral Expression	Says a sentence to describe a photograph; later items require the use of specific words or phrases
Associational Fluency	Says as many words as possible that belong to a particular category within a specified time period
Phonological Processing	Responds orally to items that require manipulation of the sounds within words
Object Naming Facility	Names pictured objects as quickly as possible
Letter Naming Facility	Names upper- and lowercase letters as quickly as possible

Woodcock-Johnson IV Tests of Achievement, Fourth Edition

Structure The Woodcock-Johnson IV Tests of Achievement, Fourth Edition (WJ IV ACH; Schrank et al., 2014) is an individually administered academic assessment measure designed for individuals 2–95+ years of age. It is *part of* the comprehensive **Woodcock-Johnson IV battery suite**, which includes the Woodcock-Johnson Tests of Cognitive Abilities (WJ COG) and Tests of Oral Language (WJ OL). Like its companion assessments, the WJ IV ACH is founded on the latest developments in the Cattell-Horn-Carroll (CHC) theory of cognitive abilities, which provides a common framework for performance results and interpretation in light of *broad and narrow* abilities (e.g., Grw, Gq, Gc, Ga). It was co-normed with the WJ IV COG and WJ IV OL. As such, it remains a good option for a core battery in a *cross-battery* assessment approach. Nevertheless, the WJ IV ACH is designed to also facilitate flexible academic assessment, so subtests may be administered individually or in combination to target a specific domain or skill. In doing so, examiners may target particular subtests or clusters to selectively tailor their assessment to academic referral concerns.

The structure of the WJ IV ACH itself includes **2 batteries composed of 20 subtests**. Overall, tests are clustered across the two batteries into five main areas, including reading, mathematics, written language, academic knowledge, and cross-domain clusters. The Standard Battery is organized into four main areas: **Reading** (Letter-Word Identification, Passage Comprehension, Word Attack, Oral Reading, Sentence Reading Fluency), **Mathematics** (Applied Problems, Calculation, Math Facts Fluency), **Writing** (Spelling, Writing Samples, Sentence Writing Fluency), and **Cross-domain** clusters that include subtests from three different domain areas. The Extended Battery includes additional subtests to provide more refined coverage of the various academic skill areas, such as **Reading** (Reading Recall, Word Reading Fluency, Reading Vocabulary), **Mathematics** (Number Matrices), **Writing** (Editing, Spelling of Sounds), and **Academic Knowledge** (Science, Social Studies, Humanities).

Administration of the Standard Battery typically takes 40–50 min; the addition of the Extended Battery would require another 45 min. Individually, most subtests require approximately 5–10 minutes to administer. Three equivalent forms (A, B, C) are available for the Standard Battery in order to enable retesting without item exposure. Scores are provided exclusively through use of an online scoring and reporting program, and hand scoring is no longer possible. A number of derived scores may be yielded from raw scores, including standard scores, percentile ranks, relative performance indexes (RPIs), as well as age and grade equivalents. Broad achievement and brief achievement scores are provided to indicate an examinee's overall performance across academic areas. Additionally, the assessment potentially yields a total of *22 cluster scores* to assist in test interpretation. Various cluster scores are provided that give a broad overview of performance in academic domains (i.e., Broad Reading, Broad Math), those that tap into basic academic skills (Basic Reading Skills, Reading Fluency, Math Calculation Skills, etc.), and clusters that represent performance in an applied academic skill (Reading Comprehension, Math Problem Solving).

The WJ IV ACH may be used for the purpose of determining **achievement** and **performance** levels, measuring academic strengths and weaknesses, assisting in eligibility determinations for special education classification and services, informing recommendations for interventions, or monitoring academic progress across school years. The extremely wide breadth of academic domain coverage necessitates that each subtest be relatively brief. Nevertheless, the common CHC interpretive framework across the suite of co-normed Woodcock-Johnson batteries provides a *helpful heuristic* and makes it a good option for a core battery in a cross-battery assessment approach. For a complete list of subtests from the WJ-IV ACH, see Table 10.7.

Practical Considerations Similar to the WIAT-III, the WJ IV ACH test is co-normed with the WJ IV COG assessment. There is a theoretical model that splits neuropsychological functioning into two components. Given philosophical conceptualizations of important areas of functioning, some researchers utilize related multiple assessments in order to understand **all** necessary aspects of neuropsychological functioning. One example is using the WJ IV COG, WJ IV ACH, with the Dean-Woodcock Sensory-Motor Battery. Davis (2008) has argued for such an approach calling the integration of these batteries the Dean-Woodcock Neuropsychological Battery (Dean & Woodcock, 2003).

Table 10.7 Subtests from the WJ-IV ACH

Letter-Word Identification*	Identify and pronounce isolated letters and words
Applied Problems*	Analyze and solve practical mathematical problems
Spelling*	Write the correct spelling of words presented orally
Passage Comprehension	Read a short passage and supply the missing word
Calculation	Calculate simple to complex mathematical facts and equations
Writing Samples	Write sentences in response to a series of increasing demands
Word Attack	Apply phonics skills to pronounce phonically regular nonsense words
Oral Reading	Read sentences that gradually increase in level of difficulty
Sentence Reading Fluency	Read and comprehend sentences and then decide if the statement is true or false by marking "Yes" or "No" within a specified time period
Math Facts Fluency	Rapidly calculate single-digit addition, subtraction, and multiplication problems within a specified time period
Sentence Writing Fluency	Formulate and write simple sentences rapidly within a specified time period
Reading Recall	Read a passage silently one time and then retell the story orally
Number Matrices	Provide the missing number from a matrix
Editing	Identify errors in short written passages and correct them orally
Word Reading Fluency	Mark two words that go together in a row of four words within a specified time period
Spelling of Sounds	Spell nonsense words that conform to conventional English languages spelling rules
Reading Vocabulary	Read and provide synonyms and antonyms to various words
Science	Provide an oral response to orally presented questions that include visual stimuli
Social Studies	Provide an oral response to orally presented questions that include visual stimuli
Humanities	Provide an oral response to orally presented questions that include visual stimuli

*Subtests that are bolded comprise the General Intellectual Ability (GIA)
*Subtests that have an asterisk make up the Brief Intellectual Ability (BIA)

Cognitive/Intellectual Assessment for Intervention

Assessments of **cognitive/intellectual** functioning are a crucial component of a neuropsychological assessment. Most intellectual/cognitive assessments provide an overall **intellectual quotient** or measure of **overall ability**, which Spearman (1904) originally coined ***g***. However, there is variance in how the different aspects of intelligence are defined and measured across various assessments. Cattell (1941) introduced the theory of two-factor intelligence, including fluid intelligence (Gf) as pure general ability and crystallized intelligence (Gc) as the potential to use knowledge that was previously acquired through education, experience, and culture in adult life. This was later expanded by Schneider and McGrew (2012) to include additional more precise areas. These precise areas of intelligence often overlap with neuropsychological assessment constructs and include abilities such as visual perception, short-term memory, long-term storage and retrieval, speed of processing, auditory processing, and quantitative ability. Most researchers view intelligence as having a hierarchical structure with broad domains falling under an overall *general* factor. Under the broad domains, narrower subdomains are often conceptualized. In an effort to determine how intellectual/cognitive functioning was related to neuropsychological functioning, D'Amato et al. (1998) evaluated the overlap between cognitive and neuropsychological functioning and determined that there was *less than a 15% overlap* after conducting a canonical correlation. This means that these assessments measure unique constructs, which suggests that these measures should lead to separate plans for rehabilitation and other relevant recommendations.

Due to the varying interpretations of intelligence and how to measure the constructs, assessments approach overall ability as well as the components of what is considered ability differently, complicating the picture further. Defining intelligence has historically been a topic of conversation and debate in the field of psychology. Depending on the theoretical construct subscribed to, various assessments attempt to tap into underlying cognitive/intellectual constructs. Given that any test measuring a component of intelligence involves multiple neuropsychological processes, interpretation of cognitive assessments must be done by a skilled practitioner who knows the assessment and is able to view qualitative aspects of how the examinee approaches the task as well as integrating performance with other data collected. For example, in administering a test of fluid reasoning, the more basic psychological function of sustained attention is required to obtain an accurate assessment. Kaplan (1988) advocated for a process-oriented approach when using intelligence testing to better understand the interplay between various neuropsychological abilities and overall intelligence. Her work has not only resulted in and influenced the development of taking qualitative observations into account when interpreting measures but has also led to various *process-oriented* measures within intelligence tests to provide additional information (e.g., Wechsler Intelligence Scale for Children, Fifth Edition, Integrated, 2015). The benefit of using a **cognitive/intellectual assessment** within the context of a *broader* neuropsychological evaluation is that an individual's performance on these assessments is interpreted within the context of a broader picture of their neuropsychological profile relevant to the referral question. Best practices in assessment explain that we should never interpret an assessment within isolation of other data and information available. With this in mind, consider how the interpretation of the assessments described below would be impacted both by other data available, such as testing observations, background information, and other assessment information.

Wechsler Intelligence Scale for Children – Fifth Edition

Structure The Wechsler Intelligence Scale for Children (WISC-V; Wechsler, 2014) is designed as a measure of **intellectual ability** for children, ages 6:0–16:11. The WISC-V is the latest version of the Wechsler family of intelligence tests. The WISC-V has evolved across **multiple versions** beginning with the Wechsler-Bellevue Intelligence Scale (W-B; Wechsler, 1939). The W-B provided verbal and performance scales in addition to the overall full-scale intelligence score. Over the years, the Wechsler scales have been updated to include more specific abilities based on intelligence theories, factor analysis, and clinical studies (Wechsler, 2014). There is also currently a lower **preschool age** version, the Wechsler Preschool and Primary Scale of Intelligence, Fourth Edition (Wechsler, 2012), as well as an **adult** version, the Wechsler Adult Intelligence Scale, Fourth Edition (Wechsler, 2008). The current WISC-V includes **ten "primary"** subtests, which make up the **five primary index** areas. Seven of these subtests are used to calculate the Full Scale Intelligence Quotient (FSIQ), representing the overall "*g*" factor. The current primary indexes are made up of the Verbal Comprehension Index (VCI), Visual-Spatial Index (VSI), Working Memory Index (WMI), Fluid Reasoning Index (FRI), and Processing Speed Index (PSI). Some of the most significant changes from the WISC-V compared to the WISC-IV include the addition of eight new subtests and a number of additional supplemental index scales. There are also **six "secondary"** subtests which assist in making up additional index areas not included within the five core areas, including the Quantitative Reasoning Index (QRI), Auditory Working Memory Index (AWMI), Nonverbal Index (NVI), and Cognitive Proficiency Index (CPI). The General Ability Index is also retained as an estimate of ability without the influence of Working Memory and Processing Speed. Finally, there are "complementary indexes," which include the Naming Speed Index (NSI), Symbol Translation Index (STI), and Storage and Retrieval Index (SRI). Finally, there is an option for expansions to two of the core indexes, including the Verbal Expanded Crystalized Index (VECI) and Expanded Fluid Index (EFI). The core index areas were also changed compared to the last version to include a Visual-Spatial Index and Fluid Reasoning Index rather than only the Perceptual Reasoning Index.

The WISC-V was published in 2014 and is one of a number of recent assessments to now allow for digital administration and/or scoring. The core subtests can be completed in approximately 60 minutes on average by a skilled administrator. The normative sample includes 2,200 children aged 6:0–16:11 matched to the current US Census data for sex, race/ethnicity, parent education level, and geographic region for each age group. Compared to the fourth edition of this assessment, the factor structure has been expanded to provide separate composites for visual-spatial and fluid reasoning. See Table 10.8 for subtests from the WISC-V.

Practical Considerations Consistent with other tests, the WISC-V can be administered in sections in order to test specific abilities. The WISC-V interpretative manual uses confirmatory factor analysis to support the structure of the scale. However,

Table 10.8 Subtests from the WISC-V and corresponding cognitive domains

Subtests	Domains
Similarities	Verbal comprehension
Vocabulary	
Information	
Comprehension	
Block Design	Visual-spatial
Visual Puzzles	
Matrix Reasoning	Fluid reasoning
Figure Weights	
Picture Concepts	
Arithmetic	
Digit Span	Working memory
Picture Span	
Letter-Number Sequencing	
Coding	Processing speed
Symbol Search	
Cancellation	

based on research using exploratory factor analysis conducted by Canivez et al. (2017), the majority of the variance is explained by the overall "*g*" factor of intelligence, represented by the Full Scale IQ score. Test developers also found a lack of empirical support for the division of the Perceptual Reasoning Index from the WISC-IV into two distinct indexes in the WISC-V (i.e., Fluid Reasoning Index and Visual-Spatial Index). Therefore, it is recommended that *caution* be taken when interpreting differences between indexes, particularly when looking at the Fluid Reasoning and Visual-Spatial Indexes, as this study indicated that these indexes may not represent distinct constructs. Further research may be necessary to clarify the interpretation of these index areas, as this research was based off the standardization sample. Indeed, further research on this area may find that there is a meaningful difference in what constructs are measured for distinct populations (Canivez et al., 2017). For instance, people with certain neuropsychological profiles due to brain trauma or a specific developmental disability, such as Autism, may show distinctions in these areas.

Woodcock Johnson IV Tests of Cognitive Abilities (Level 2)

Structure The *Woodcock Johnson IV Tests of Cognitive Abilities (WJ IV COG; Schrank et al., 2014)* was collectively developed/updated by Schrank, McGrew, and Mather in 2014. This assessment is individually administered to individuals ranging from ages 2 to 90+. Preceding the *WJ IV COG* was the third edition developed in 2001. The major revisions from the previous version include renorming, more tests allowing for better flexibility, tests 1–7 used to generate a General Intellectual Ability (GIA) score, and the deletion of the diagnostic supplement replaced by additional batteries of the *WJ IV* (Mather & Wendling, 2014). There are ten subtests that compose the **Standard Battery** and eight that compose the **Extended Battery**. The purpose of the Standard and Extended Batteries are to allow flexibility in determining which tests are necessary in regard to the referral question(s). On the *WJ IV COG*, an individual's abilities are assessed through the following clusters: **Comprehension-Knowledge** (*Gc*), **Fluid Reasoning** (*Gf*), **Short-Term Working Memory** (*Gwm*), **Cognitive Processing Speed** (*Gs*), **Auditory Processing** (*Ga*), **Long-Term Retrieval** (*Glr*), and **Visual Processing** (*Gv*) (Mather & Wendling, 2014). Results of the WJ IV COG can validate **cognitive concerns** and further uncover how those **delays** specifically affect an individual's **ability to learn**. In addition, there is also a section on the assessment for examiners to reflect on the test taker's behavior. This can be helpful in deciding whether or not this test was a true representation of the individual's cognitive functioning and in measuring qualitative aspects of test taking that may influence performance. Scores for the *WJ IV COG* can be obtained through calculations by hand or computerized calculations through the Woodcock-Johnson online scoring database (Mather & Wendling, 2014). In addition to the *WJ IV COG*, there are two other assessments that make up the overall *WJ IV COG*: Tests of Oral Achievement and Tests of Achievement. These three assessments can be given independently or combined (Mather & Wendling, 2014). Combined, the three assessments can identify strengths, weaknesses, and possible academic disabilities (i.e., academic and cognitive delays) and assist in intervention. For a detailed list of subtests on the WJ IV COG, see Table 10.9.

Practical Considerations When administering the WJ IV COG, it is important to familiarize oneself with the various subtests within the assessment. One of the most valuable strengths of this assessment is the ability to pick and choose what assessments to give an individual based on the presenting concern (Mather & Wendling,

Table 10.9 Subtests on the WJ IV COG

Subtest	Description
Oral Vocabulary	Comprehension of words
Number Series	Quantitative, deductive/inductive reasoning
Verbal Attention	Short-term working memory
Letter-Pattern Matching	Speed of visual symbol discrimination
Phonological Processing	Word retrieval using phonological cues
Story Recall	Listening ability and reconstructive memory
Visualization	Visual-spatial processing
General Information	General verbal knowledge
Concept Formation	Fluid reasoning
Numbers Reversed	Working memory capacity
Number-Pattern Matching	Perceptual speed
Nonword Repetition	Phonological short-term memory
Visual-Auditory Learning	Visual-auditory associations
Picture Recognition	Visual memory

2014). Giving unnecessary tests can be a waste of time and can also add unneeded stress to the individual. This leads to another important consideration when giving the WJ IV COG: the tests that make up this assessment can be challenging and difficult to complete. Therefore, it is important to evaluate your client and know when he or she might need a break from testing. Forcing too much testing on a client leads to invalid results. A few possible break ideas may include a walk, a snack, playing a game, or tossing a ball. In addition to being able to choose which tests to give, an administrator can also choose the order in which to give the tests. This can be beneficial when working with someone who may not be entirely comfortable when first meeting with the administrator. Nonverbal tests such as ones that require the individual to point may be used first until the individual has become comfortable with the administrator (Mather & Wendling, 2014). It is also crucial to follow the administration instructions given in the manual and test booklet. However, slight accommodations may be made, when needed, due to an individual's disabilities not relevant to what is being tested. For example, if the individual lacks basic math skills and the construct being tested is related to math, then no accommodations should be made. Overall, the guidelines and instructions outlined in the manual should be strictly followed to receive accurate results.

Kaufman Assessment Battery for Children, Second Edition

Structure In 2004, Kaufman and Kaufman published the second edition of the *Kaufman Assessment Battery for Children* (*KABC-2*), an individually administered measure of cognitive and processing for children ages 3 through 18. The authors support a **"dual-theoretical"** interpretation of this assessment, including the Cattell-Horn-Carroll (CHC) interpretation or Luria's neuropsychological theory of processing. The **Lurian model** interpretation includes four index areas including **Sequential, Simultaneous, Planning,** and **Learning**. The interpretation of these index areas emphasize the **three block areas** of the brain's basic functions advocated by Luria (1970). When using the CHC model, the same subtests are used, but the scales are given different names corresponding to the different theoretical model, including Long-Term Storage and Retrieval (Glr), Short-Term Memory (Gsm), Visual Processing (Gv), and Fluid Reasoning (Gf). In addition, there is a fifth index called Crystalized Ability (Gc). Within each index area, there are two subtests that vary slightly depending on the age of the examinee. There is also an attempt with this assessment to create measures that are **less culturally biased** overall, and the examiner is provided the option of using a nonverbal scale that includes five subtests when working with children with a language deficit or learning English as a second language.

The *KABC-II* has a strong normative sample of 3025 individuals. The KABC-II has some **unique strengths** in the test development process, including that approximately 2/3 of the tryout sample were from ethnic minorities, meaning that the initial analysis of items for bias was based on a *diverse sample*. In addition to the standardization, there were multiple special group studies conducted during the normative process (i.e., students with learning disabilities in reading, writing, and math; students with ADHD; students with emotional disturbance, hearing impairments; students with intellectual disabilities, Autism, and gifted), which helps boost the *clinical validity* of the measure. The *KABC-II* was also correlated with a variety of cognitive and achievement tests, which helps demonstrate the validity of the measure in comparison to other common measures. For a detailed list of subtests on the KABC-II, see Table 10.10.

Practical Considerations The *KABC-II* is a **highly engaging** assessment for children, making it a good choice when the evaluator is concerned about how quickly a child might lose interest in assessment tasks. Many of the subtests are fun and engaging for the examinee. You will find in administering the assessment that the materials are clearly organized and labeled, making the administration process easy to learn. There are also qualitative indicators to consider when evaluating children and youth (e.g., student fails to sustain attention, is reluctant to respond, uses context clues, etc.). The manual allows for flexibility in allowing the examiner to explain tasks during teaching items in a way that the child understands. Additionally, when administering to children who have English as a second language or have limited verbal ability, the *KABC-II* includes the option of not using measures of acquired knowledge in the test battery and/or using a Nonverbal Scale. Spanish translations of some verbal directions and valid responses on verbal subtests are available in the case that it is being used with a bilingual child. This test may be appealing given the option of following a Lurian model of interpretation. This is a unique measure that is worth consideration if regularly evaluating children or youth using a **neuropsychological** approach. Occasionally, norms for tests are updated

Table 10.10 Subtests on the KABC-II

Subtests	What subtests measure
Number Recall	Sequential processing
Word Order	
Hand Movements	
Story Completion	Planning
Pattern Reasoning	
Atlantis	Learning
Atlantis-Delayed	
Rebus	
Rebus-Delayed	
Conceptual Thinking	Simultaneous processing
Face Recognition	
Rover	
Triangles	
Block Counting	
Verbal Knowledge	Knowledge
Riddles	
Expressive Vocabulary	

and all the testing materials stay the same. This is a cost-effective way to update norms based on current population trends. The Kaufman Assessment Battery for Children, Second Edition Normative Update (KABC-II NU) is an example of such an update. The authors recommend when normative updates occur that practitioners utilize such norms. It is critical that in any type of clinical practice, normative updates be used. Historically, this has been a critical problem in the field of clinical neuropsychology (D'Amato et al., 2005).

Stanford-Binet Intelligence Scales, Fifth Edition

Structure The *Stanford-Binet Intelligence Scales, Fifth Edition (SB-V)* is an individually administered assessment of **cognitive functioning** for individuals age 2 through 85+ years. The normative sample for this assessment includes 4,800 individuals matched to the 2001 US Census data with respect to age, sex, ethnicity, socioeconomic levels, and geographic region (Roid, 2003). The SB-V has a range of applications most significantly used for clinical, educational, and neuropsychological assessment. Originally, Binet and Simon created the Binet-Simon Scale to identify children's intellectual abilities with a focus on identifying mental retardation (Becker, 2003). Yet it was Terman's use of normative data and the application of a scientific approach to assessment that led to the widespread use of the Stanford-Binet Test following the initial publication in 1916 (Becker, 2003).

The first *Stanford-Binet (SB-V)* has undergone many revisions and updated editions. The current fifth edition of the SB-V, released in 2003, has developed and evolved into a valid form of measuring intellectual abilities (Roid, 2003). The *Stanford-Binet, Fifth Edition (SB-V)* assesses **cognitive functioning** across the following indexes: **Fluid Reasoning** (FR), **Knowledge** (KN), **Quantitative Reasoning** (QR), **Visual-Spatial** (VS), and **Working Memory** (WM). The *SB-V* broadly classifies performance on the overall test into ability scores of Verbal, Nonverbal, and Full Scale IQ scores. Incorporating a nonverbal quotient can provide important information for unique populations. The *SB-V* can assist in assessing individuals with **limited communication** or **low verbal** abilities (DiStefano & Dombrowski, 2016). This might include children who are still developing language skills, adults who might be losing some language skills, or students who might perform better under conditions that focus on nonverbal responses. The *SB-V* receives credit for its use of *manipulative and assessment toys* that can be used throughout the testing. The toys and pictures are often engaging and can be viewed as fun activities and games rather than standardized testing to the participant. The *SB-V* implemented a large theoretical shift from its prior editions. Prior editions supported a single use of the results; the current edition calls for a multidimensional use to best capture the individual's abilities. Specifically, the assessment allows for the assessor to report the results in three ways: the overall IQ score, the Verbal IQ and Nonverbal IQ, and/or the five indexes which collectively measure the IQ score (DiStefano & Dombrowski, 2016). This new model is helpful because it allows clinical decisions to be made about what information is useful and what is the best way to share the results in a meaningful way for the family or individual (Table 10.11).

Practical Considerations The *SB-V* is best used when assessing students who appear to have cognitive abilities that fall within the **high or low range**. Some helpful features are the increased number of manipulative that is made available in the new edition for increased participation in young children and the routing information to cut down on administration time. Given the comprehensiveness of the instrument, the assessment time varies greatly depending on the age and ability of the individual being assessed. Each subtest takes an estimated 10 min and in total can last between 45 and 75 min; however, there is also an Abbreviated Battery IQ which can produce results in 15–20 min (Roid, 2003). The assessment begins by administering two routing tests, meaning that a short task is given in the verbal and nonverbal portion to help pinpoint **the starting place** for that individual which reduces overall assessment time (Becker, 2003). These routing tests allow for a starting place to be determined on both the verbal and nonverbal portion of the *SB-V*. It is important to note that the *SB-V* is administered using age scales and point scales allowing for different starting points depending on the cognitive level of the child or adult (Roid, 2003). An important point for administrators is to remain aware of the physical layout of the subtest. Unlike other cognitive assessments, the structure is not to complete all of the tasks in Working Memory and move to the next factor. Instead the *SB-V* tests all five subtests rotationally, which can make it difficult if a ceiling or basal has not been achieved. It is important to be aware of this structure since the test can be challenging when first learning to administer the measure.

Social/Emotional/Behavioral Assessment for Intervention

Some authors have seen the area of social/emotional functioning as being paramount to understanding an individual client. Social-emotional or personality assessment is imperative to the formation of successful initial **case conceptualization** and final **intervention** or **rehabilitation** planning. Personality assessment is a required part of any comprehensive neuropsychology examination and should include both *objective and projective* measures. Integrating data from both types of these measures is challenging but necessary to fully understand the uniqueness of any individual—this integration is challenging to practitioners because of the unique

Table 10.11 Subtests from the SB-V

Verbal index	Nonverbal index
Fluid Reasoning	Fluid Reasoning
Knowledge	Knowledge
Quantitative Reasoning	Quantitative Reasoning
Visual-Spatial	Visual-Spatial
Working Memory	Working Memory

theory-driven, single-case-focused, process-oriented approach to some of the *narrative-based* measures such as the Thematic Apperception Test (TAT). Social-emotional assessment **should** meld together both the Eastern and Western approaches to evaluation (Power & D'Amato, 2018). It is important to note that **no single test**, such as the MMPI-2, should be used in isolation for neuropsychological assessment since *all* personality issues are *theme* related. It is beneficial to gather information from many **sources** in order to obtain an accurate view of each individual person. If a psychologist does not integrate information from all sources, using all types of **instruments**, significant information will be lost. The below measures can be used in conjunction with other types of formal and informal tests to produce a clear understanding of the strengths and needs of the individual being evaluated. Personality assessment covers hundreds of measures, and space and time only permit us to briefly discuss a few critical instruments. This section begins with an overview of two of the most popular personality instruments currently available, one for adults and one for children; Both are highly-standardized, objective, actuarial, and behavioral measures that frequenly have **forensic** neuropsychological applications.

Minnesota Multiphasic Personality Inventory-2

Structure The Minnesota Multiphasic Personality Inventory-2 (MMPI) is a psychological test that assesses the **personality traits** and **psychopathology** of individuals suspected of having mental health difficulties or other serious clinical issues. It is the most widely used personality psychology test in the world. The MMPI-2 (Butcher et al., 1989) is administered by a psychologist or other trained individuals on one of two forms, the MMPI-2 containing 567 true or false questions (370 items if only the standard scales are administered) or the MMPI-2-Revised Form containing 338 true or false questions. The MMPI-2 is a **self-report inventory** designed to assess a number of the **major patterns** of personality and **psychological disorders** in adolescents and adults. This test is so widely used that many individuals discuss clients in terms of scales they display in the significant to high range. For example, an individual could be referred to by the unique pattern of scores he or she displays such as having high scores on scales 4, 5, and 6. Entire books are written dealing with scale interpretation and patient profile patterns (e.g., Graham, 2011; Nichols, 2011). Books are also available that tell which types of therapeutic approaches should be used with various patient profiles. These books are user friendly as they spell out not only how to **differentially diagnose clients** but which **therapeutic approaches** have been shown to be most successful. This test is one of the most widely used measures in forensic psychology. The MMPI-2 is supported by a great deal of research, and it may be the **most researched** personality measure available today (Butcher & Williams, 2000). Another benefit of using the MMPI-2 is that it utilizes code types as the central element of interpretations. The code type is determined by the highest clinical scales in an individual's profile (McGrath et al., 1998).

There are one-point to three-point *code types* depending on how many clinical scales are to be used. Code types should only be defined if there are 5 T-score points between lowest scale in code type and next highest clinical scale in the profile. When scales in defined code types are elevated, both **symptoms** and **personality** descriptors should be included. When scales within code types are not elevated, personality descriptors, but not symptoms, are included. The *code types* will assist in writing reports, as well as accurately identify patients in the clinical and nonclinical settings (McGrath et al., 1998). The MMPI-2 should be interpreted by a clinician who meets the highest level of test user qualification (Butcher et al., 2001). The MMPI-2 form is most commonly used because it is well-known and has an extensive research base. The MMPI-2 is divided into ten clinical scales that categorize **abnormal behavior**, as well as four validity scales which assess whether the test taker's answers are true and accurate (Hathaway & McKinley, 1951). The MMPI-2 scales are presented in Table 10.12.

Table 10.12 Clinical and validity scales for the Minnesota Multiphasic Personality Inventory, Second Edition (MMPI-2)

Scale number	Scale name	Interpretation of high scores
1	**Hypochondriasis** (Hs)	Excessive bodily concern, somatic symptoms
2	**Depression** (D)	Depressed, pessimistic, irritable, demanding
3	**Hysteria** (Hy)	Physical symptoms of functional origin, self-centered, demands attention
4	**Psychopathic Deviate** (Pd)	Asocial or anti-social, rebellious, impulsive, poor judgment
5	**Masculinity-Femininity** (Mf)	Male, aesthetic interests; female, assertive, competitive, self-confident
6	**Paranoia** (Pa)	Suspicious, sensitive, resentful, rigid, may be psychotic
7	**Psychasthenia** (Pt)	Anxious, worried, obsessive, lacks self-confidence, problems in decision-making
8	**Schizophrenia** (Sc)	May have thinking disturbance, withdrawn, feels alienated and unaccepted
9	**Hypomania** (Ma)	Excessive activity, lacks direction, low frustration tolerance, friendly
0	**Social-Introversion** (Si)	Socially introverted, shy, sensitive, overcontrolled, comforting
	Validity Scale	Interpretation of Validity Scale
	Lie (L)	Identifies individuals deliberately trying to avoid answering in an honest manner
	Infrequency scale (F)	Identifies unusual or atypical ways of answering test items
	Back Infrequency scale (F^b)	Measures the same issues as F, except only on the last half of the test items
	Correction Scale (K)	Identifies psychopathology in people who otherwise would have profiles in normal range
	VRIN	Variable response inconsistency
	TRIN	True response inconsistency

Administration of the MMPI-2 takes approximately 40–90 min. However, if an individual comprehends information at a slower pace or has reading problems then administration time may take longer. Computer administration of the assessment could take less time. The MMPI-2 is intended for individuals 18 years of age and older with a sixth-grade reading level and the ability to follow standard instructions. The official language for the MMPI-2 is English; however, it is available in Spanish, Hmong, and French (Butcher et al., 2001). There are three formats that can be used, including booklet, computer, or cassette tape/CD format in individual or group settings. Individuals are required to have an eighth-grade reasoning level to appropriately answer the questions. The MMPI-2 can be broken up into sessions; however, that is not the preferred way to administer. There are a number of ways that the MMPI-2 can be scored. It can be hand scored using the administration and scoring manual. Computer scoring can be done following computerized administration or manual entry of an individual's assessment. Raw scores are converted to T-scores for clinical and validity scales (Butcher et al., 2001). Generally, scores below 65 are considered average and desirable. Scores between 55 and 64, while still within the average range, are considered to be at-risk, or mildly elevated, and may indicate some concerns with how they view themselves and their surroundings. Scores above 65 are considered clinically significant and signify moderate to high concerns.

Practical Considerations The MMPI-2 is the most widely used personality assessment in the world because it is extensively **researched**, is easily accessible, and provides **diagnostic and clinical insight** into an individual's personality traits. The comprehensive list of questions allows the assessment scores to be a valid and reliable indication of what areas of the client's life need support. Utilizing the broad validity indexes will ensure the results obtained are accurate. *For court appearances, use of this critical instrument may help achieve success.* The use of code types offers an easy way to communicate with practitioners. It allows for a fast and accurate way to talk about individual patients and their profiles. The measure is not only good for differential diagnosis but offers extensive **therapeutic treatment planning options**. The final measure that will be covered in depth requires a *different view of personality* and is **purposefully** theory driven, observation oriented, projective, flexible, process-oriented, and clinical-theoretical (Witsken et al., 2008). Due to this focus, a more **narrative** approach to personality must be used, and reliability and validity are viewed *differently* (Lanyon & Goldstein, 1997; Teglasi, 2010).

The Behavior Assessment System for Children – Third Edition

Structure The Behavior Assessment System for Children – Third Edition (BASC-3; Reynolds & Kamphaus, 2015) is a comprehensive behavior rating scale that collects information from parents, teachers, other individuals involved with the child, and the child being evaluated. The BASC-3 is designed to facilitate the **diagnosis and educational classification** of a variety of emotional and behavioral disorders in children and adolescents 2–25 years of age. Emotional and behavioral difficulties have various facets requiring assessment from many **different viewpoints**. Clinicians tend to obtain such views in a fairly ad hoc manner, using a variety of measures, observations, or other data that may prove difficult to incorporate into a total picture. This is why the **integrated assessment approach** of the BASC-3 components is desirable. Together, the BASC-3 components offer a **comprehensive system** for identifying, evaluating, monitoring, and remediating behavioral and emotional problems in children and adolescents. It can also be used to focus on an individual's strengths to reinforce positive behaviors. Each component can be used individually or in combination to formulate a plan which is best suited to the situation under study (Reynolds & Kampaus, 2015).

The BASC-3 includes a Teacher Rating Scale (TRS), which is designed to measure **adaptive and problem behaviors** in the school setting. The TRS takes approximately 10–15 minutes to complete. It can be used with teachers or other individuals who fill similar roles. There are three age-level forms: ages 2 through 5, 6 through 11, and 12 through 21. The Parent Rating Scale (PRS) is completed by the individual's parents giving insight into an individual's adaptive and problem behaviors at home and in the community. It takes approximately 10–20 minutes to complete. Both the TRS and PRS consist of statements that are to be rated using a Likert-type scale. A Self-Report for Personality (SRP) is also available, which is completed by the individual being evaluated and takes between 20 and 30 minutes to complete. It includes both true and false questions and statements that the individual rates on a Likert-type scale ranging from never to always. There are **three age-level forms**: ages 8 through 11, 12 through 21, and 18 through 25. This is one of the most popular measures in the world. The TRS, PRS, and SRP are available in English and Spanish (Reynolds & Kampaus, 2015). The BASC-3 subscales are presented in Table 1.1 and include 8 Composite scales, 28 Clinical and Adaptive scales, 9 Content scales, 5 Clinical indexes, and 5 Executive Function indexes. One of the most helpful features of this scale is that it allows the examiner to determine if the individual is **telling the truth**. In addition, clinicians are able to evaluate the *validity* of individualized responses, like **parents, teachers,** and **individuals** being assessed. See Table 10.13 for scales and indexes of BASC-3.

The BASC-3 also includes a Student Observation System (SOS), Structured Developmental History (SDH), Flex Monitor, Continuous Performance Test, Behavioral and Emotional Screening System (BESS), and Behavior Intervention Guide (Reynolds & Kampaus, 2015). The multidimensional approach to evaluating the behaviors and self-perceptions of children and adolescents is of great utility to practitioners of neuropsychology. It allows the **integration** of many perspectives that appear to be lacking in many clinical neuropsychological evaluations. It provides **deeper insight** into the behavior and emotional needs of children and adolescents to ultimately establish appropriate interventions (Rhodes et al., 2009). For example, an individual who has depression could potentially be rated clinically significant or at-risk on the following scales: anxiety, attitudes in school, depression, interpersonal relations, relation to parents, self-esteem, and/or withdrawal.

Table 10.13 Teacher Rating Scale (TRS), **Parent Rating** Scale **(PRS), and** Self-Report **(SRP) Scales and Indexes**

Scale	TRS			PRS			SRP		
Composite	P	C	A	P	C	A	C	A	Col
Adaptive Skills	•	•	•	•	•	•			
Behavior Symptoms Index	•	•	•	•	•	•			
Emotional Symptoms							•	•	•
Externalizing Problems	•	•	•	•	•	•			
Inattention/Hyperactivity							•	•	•
Internalizing Problems	•	•	•	•	•	•	•	•	•
Personal Adjustment							•	•	•
School Problems		•	•				•	•	
Scale Scores									
Activities of Daily Living				•	•	•			
Alcohol Abuse									•
Adaptability	•	•	•	•	•	•			
Aggression	•	•	•	•	•	•			
Anxiety	•	•	•	•	•	•	•	•	•
Attention Problems	•	•	•	•	•	•	•	•	•
Attitude in School							•	•	
Attitude in Teachers							•	•	
Atypicality	•	•	•	•	•	•	•	•	
Conduct Problems		•	•		•	•			
Depression	•	•	•	•	•	•	•	•	•
Functional Communication	•	•	•	•	•	•			
Hyperactivity	•	•	•	•	•	•	•	•	•
Interpersonal Relations							•	•	•
Locus of Control							•	•	•
Leadership		•	•		•	•			
Learning Problems		•	•						
Relations with Parents							•	•	•
School Maladjustment									•
Self-Esteem							•	•	•
Self-Reliance							•	•	•
Sensation Seeking								•	•
Sense of Inadequacy							•	•	•
Social Skills	•	•	•	•	•	•			
Social Stress							•	•	•
Somatization	•	•	•	•	•	•	•	•	•
Study Skills		•	•						
Withdrawal	•	•	•	•	•	•			
Content scales									
Anger Control	•	•	•	•	•	•		•	•
Bullying	•	•	•	•	•	•			

(continued)

Table 10.13 (continued)

Scale	TRS			PRS			SRP		
Composite	P	C	A	P	C	A	C	A	Col
Developing Social Disorders	•	•	•	•	•	•			
Ego Strength								•	•
Emotional Self-Control	•	•	•	•	•	•			
Executive Functioning	•	•	•	•	•	•			
Mania								•	•
Negative Emotionality	•	•	•	•	•	•			
Test Anxiety								•	•
Clinical Index									
ADHD Probability Index		•	•		•	•			
Autism Probability Index		•	•		•	•			
Clinical Probability Index	•			•					
EBD Probability Index		•	•		•	•			
Functional Impairment Index	•	•	•	•	•	•	•	•	
Executive Functioning Index									
Attention Control Index	•	•	•	•	•	•			
Behavior Control Index	•	•	•	•	•	•			
Emotional Control Index	•	•	•	•	•	•			
Overall Executive Functioning Index	•	•	•	•	•	•			
Problem Solving Index		•	•		•	•			

Note: BASC-3 forms are available for teachers, parents, children (self), adolescents, and college-age students. Coding in this table is as follows: Teacher Rating Scale (TRS); Parent Rating Scale (PRS). SRP stands for Self-Report. P stands for Preschool. C stands for Child. A stands for Adolescent. Col stands for College. The individual completing the scale is marked with a bullet

Scoring options for the BASC-3 include **electronic scoring** with **Q-global**. Manual entry consists of paper-pencil assessment format, and the raw scores or item responses are manually entered into the Q-global software. On-screen administration occurs when the test is administered to the examinee on-screen on a web-enabled computer via the Q-global software, a link to launch and administer the test at a remote location. Manual scoring is also available. Raw scores on BASC-3 rating scales and indexes are converted to *T*-scores, which are converted into five possible classification scales: *Clinically Significant, At-Risk, Average, Low Average,* and *Very Low.* An *F*-index is also included which is designed to assess the possibility that a rater has depicted a child's behavior in an extremely *negative* fashion. It consists of items representing maladaptive behaviors to which the rater responded *almost always* and adaptive behaviors to which the rater responded *never* (Whitcomb & Merrel, 2013). Gender-combined norms are preferred; however, separate-gender and Clinical norms can have advantages in some cases. The Clinical norms allow assessor to examine a child's profile for information that will aid in **differential diagnosis**. The use of Q-global will allow the generation of reports using the different norms to give insight into a variety of areas. Along with the ability to **generate**

multiple reports for one individual, **Q-global also makes scoring much easier and faster** in order to implement interventions as soon as possible (Reynolds & Kampaus, 2015).

Practical Considerations The greatest strength of the BASC-3 is the inclusion of information from the perspective of the individual, the parent, the teacher, or any other individual who is completing the measure. The analysis of behavioral information from **multiple sources and settings** is of great **utility** to practitioners in neuropsychology for differential diagnosis. The multidimensional approach gives a wide variety of information that provides a clear and accurate representation of the behavioral and emotional concerns of a child or adolescent. The BASC-3 provides a plethora of information which can be used to **guide or lead in the development** of **neuropsychological interventions** for children with behavior and emotional concerns (Rhodes et al., 2009). It can also be used as a progress monitoring tool.

Thematic Apperception Test

Structure The Thematic Apperception Test (TAT; Murray, 1943) is a **projective test** developed to facilitate the exploration of an *individual's life*, including the **ecologies** in which they live such as their dominant **drives, emotions, traits,** and **conflicts** including their life story. Projected measures are needed because they bring **unconscious emotions** to the surface providing insight concerning unknown traumas or major life events. Interestingly, Van der Kolk (2014) has used the TAT to assess individuals suffering from trauma, such as post-traumatic stress disorder (PTSD). The TAT consists of 30 cards illustrated with various scenes and people, along with 1 blank card. Specific issues are represented in the pictures involving males and females, children, adolescents, and adults. The practitioner asks the client to tell what is currently happening in the story, what has happened previously, and what will happen in the future. If these **three different views** are not discussed, the practitioner queries the individual asking specifically for details. In identifying significant needs, presses, and themes, the unconscious personality characteristics of an individual are thought to be brought to the surface. Through projective interpretation the TAT offers a better understanding of the behaviors of the individual. It also provides insight into an individual's **unconscious view of the world** (Teglasi, 2010). The **open-ended responses** from the individuals being assessed give an idea about their thoughts on authority, male/female roles, dominant personality traits, and familial relationships. This provides the **freedom** for the clients to respond realistically and openly, detailing aspects of their life that they, themselves, might not understand or be able to explain (Rhodes et al., 2009).

The TAT is the *most influential* and *widely researched* **thematic approach** which allows us to understand an individual through their narrated life story (Whitcomb & Merrell, 2013). The administration instructions for the TAT are considered unstandardized, often deviating from the original directions, which emphasize creativity and imagination. Each of the cards is numbered, and it is recommended that certain cards be given to certain age ranges. For example, for ages 8–11, the following cards are important: 1, 3BM, 7GF, 8BM, 12M, 13B, 14, and 17BM. Ultimately, the clinician needs to be selective with which cards to use to ensure they are appropriate for their specific examinee. In addition, for an examinee that has been identified as having depression, it would be appropriate to use the cards relating to depression and suicide for them to work with. After the selected battery has been given, it is appropriate to ask *clarifying questions* about the examinee's stories in order to better understand the overall themes. Some suggest querying after each card, while others say to wait until the end so as not to alter the story that the examinee is telling (Whitcomb & Merrell, 2013). Due to the **free-response style** of the TAT, the validity and reliability of the projective have been difficult to establish. This is related to the fact that each person is provided a *different test* because each individual responds to the **cards** using their own **life experiences**. The picture cards and blank card are the only procedures that allow clients to reveal their life stories in their own words. There are limited avenues to validate inferences made by individuals being assessed. Methods have been established to develop a normed approach; however, the TAT continues to be an informal assessment tool in the clinical setting. In a neuropsychological setting, it allows practitioners to get an idea of an individual's verbal behavior. One way to administer the TAT is to have the client write out their story to a single stimulus card. It will allow assessors to gather information about stimuli that elicit longer descriptions versus stimuli that evoke few words. To expand further, the use of written responses can also be used to analyze handwriting and compare the verbal descriptions with the nonverbal, written product (Rhodes et al., 2009). When administering any projective measure, it is imperative to ensure that it is an appropriate circumstance in which it may be used. When using the TAT, it is important to consider the kind of case being worked on, the type of child or individual being given the TAT, the types of problems the individual is having, the age of the individual, etc. Taking such areas into consideration will ensure that the information obtained is an accurate representation of the individual's personality. Given that the focus of this measure should be on **themes** of the client's **life**, the test is correctly named, and few measures or test authors provide the **significant insight** that this poignant measure can **uncover** as discussed by Teglasi (2010).

Practical Considerations The TAT allows clients to respond to stimuli via a free and open-ended technique. They can expose their thoughts and feelings spontaneously, with full control over how they answer, not limiting them to a specific **set of answers**. Along with a glimpse into the individual's **conscious and unconscious** personality, the assessor will also gain a better understanding of the verbal and/or written skills of those they are evaluating, which will benefit neuropsychological assessments (Lanyon & Goldstein, 1997; Rhodes et al., 2009). In sum, it is imperative to use a flexible open-ended measure that allows the individual to **project** their world and its contents onto the measure, and only tests, such as the TAT, allow such *freedom*.

Kinetic Family Drawing

Structure The use of Kinetic Family Drawings (KFD; Burns & Kaufman, 1970) in psychological assessment of children has become widespread, as it gives a plethora of **insight** into the child's perceptions. The idea behind family drawings has always been that through the process of drawing a picture representing a child's family, children provide valuable information regarding their thoughts on **family dynamics, emotional relationships,** and their *place* or *role* within the **family**. The KFD provides detailed instruction as to how the client should draw everyone in their family doing something. A list of detailed questions is available for an interview after the drawing is completed (Knoff, 2002). For analyzing drawings, seminal questions were developed by Machover (1949) and included samples such as "*what is s(he) doing*?", "*how old is s(he)*?", and "*what does s(he) worry about*?". The picture is meant to elicit the individual's attitudes toward their family, giving insight into the overall family dynamics. The practitioner should evaluate how the child is placed in relation to their family, and the interactions between family members should be closely analyzed. The KFD technique is the most widely used family drawing technique, as it has been shown to reveal **conflicts** and **difficulties** within the family, while other drawing techniques often indicate the absence of problems (Knoff, 2002; Whitcomb & Merrel, 2013). A Kinetic School Drawing (KSD; Whitcomb & Merrell, 2013), which is similar to the KFD, requires children to draw a picture of themselves, a teacher, and one or more classmates, giving insight into the child or adolescent's attitudes toward people at school, focusing on their functioning in the school environment.

The scoring of projective measures is somewhat subjective and narrative but can offer **critical components** of understanding for clients. Specific scoring systems can be utilized to offer a more objective outlook such as the Naglieri et al. (1991) Draw a Person: Screening Procedure for Emotional Disturbance (DAP:SPED) scoring system which includes a consideration of what features in a drawing are appropriate for children of various ages. For example, 5-year-old children are expected to make basic drawings of people, consisting of a head, eyes, nose, mouth, body, arms, and legs, while an older child is expected to have more details in the picture, such as a more defined neck, clothes, and arms in a particular direction. The DAP:SPED was normed on a nationwide sample of 2260 students. The sample was representative of the nation with regard to gender, race, ethnicity, geographic region, and socioeconomic status (Naglieri & Das, 1988). Although an **objective scoring system** may be used, the instructions or questions asked of the child or adolescent may vary, as well as the administrator's interpretations of the drawings, making it difficult to compare results between children who completed the KFD or KSD. *Figure drawings* are also often interpreted with regard to appropriate cognitive development, which impacts the overall interpretation of the picture (Naglieri & Das, 1988). Table 10.14 demonstrates the concept of the KFD's assessment of a child or adolescent's view of themselves and their **family relationships** through suggested interpretation of picture elements.

Table 10.14 Characteristics of Kinetic Family Drawing (KFD) photos and potential interpretations

Style of drawing	Interpretation
Edging	Seen as a clever way to stay on the edge without getting involved; likely a tendency to avoid situations
Line on top	The child's world is scary and rapid with storm clouds, darkness, and worry
Line on bottom	Serves to stabilize the child's world with a firm foundation as child's real world is unstable
Repetition	Obsessive thoughts about something or perhaps about the area around repetition
Arm extensions	Possible aids in controlling the environment
Elevated figures	Perception of dominance or power over those under him/her
Erasures	Ambivalence
On back of page	Conflict
Rotated figures	Feelings of being different
Omission of body parts	Anxiety – attempt to gain control
Omission of figures	Anxiety – attempt to gain control
Blacking out	Denying or repressing
Barriers	Objects, walls, lines between figures
Beds	Denotes depression if included with heavy shading
Fire	Combines anger and need to be loved
Lights	Children with a need for love
Electricity	Need for warmth, love, and also power
Sunshine	Warmth
"X's"	Suggests attempts at impulse control
Kites	Desire for freedom or escape; attempt to get out of or above the family
Garbage	Taking out the unwanted and dirty parts of the family
Faces turned away	Poor communication
Food	Nurturance and love
Water	Event depression
Snow	Chronic depression

Reprinted with permission from Burns and Kaufman (1972)

Practical Considerations The Kinetic Family Drawing test can provide rich **qualitative** information about a client during assessment. Themes that occur during the "story-telling" aspect regarding the figures can be telling of personal trauma or individual details about the client's life. The inclusion of qualitative and quantitative assessment provides a holistic understanding of the patient.

Autism Spectrum Rating Scale

Structure The Autism Spectrum Rating Scales (ASRS; Goldstein & Naglieri, 2013) is a behavior rating scale that collects information about the **behaviors** and **feelings** of children and adolescents from parents and teachers involved with the child or adolescent being evaluated. The ASRS is designed to **quantify observations** of children and adolescents that are associated with Autism Spectrum Disorder (ASD) or are suspected of being on the Autism spectrum between the ages of 2 and 18 years. When used in combination with other information, results from the ASRS can help determine the likelihood that a child or adolescent has *symptoms associated* with ASD; this information can then be used to determine **treatment interventions** (Goldstein & Naglieri, 2013). Treatment targets are determined based on elevated scores and include, but are not limited to, increasing the ability to maintain eye contact with adults in discussions of problem situations, reducing echolalia or the number of off-topic questions asked, developing the ability to flexibly deal with changes in routine, increasing ability to complete homework and chores successfully, and developing the ability to sit still when required.

The ASRS includes a Teacher Response Form (TRF), which gathers information from teachers about the child or adolescent's behavior in a school setting during both structured academic work and unstructured peer interactions. The most common reason for using the ASRS is to better understand a child who is having difficulty and to determine what **accommodations or modifications** are appropriate. The ASRS can also be used to see if the child is improving or for a routine check, even if there is no reason to suspect the child is struggling with a problem. The TRF takes approximately 20 minutes to complete. It can be used with teachers or other individuals who fill similar roles within the school setting. There are two age-level forms: ages 2 through 5 (70 items) and 6 through 18 (71 items). The Parent Rating Form (PRF) is completed by the child or adolescent's parents and gathers information about the child or adolescent's behavior at home or within the community. It also takes approximately 20 minutes to complete. Both the TRF and PRF consist of statements that are to be rated using a Likert-type scale. A Short-Form (15 items) is also available for both teachers and parents, which takes approximately 5 minutes to complete. The TRF, PRF, and Short-Form are available in English and Spanish (Goldstein & Naglieri, 2013).

Research has shown that the ASRS rating scales are reliable, valid, and the **first norm-referenced assessment** based on a nationally representative sample. **Information collected** from parents and teachers about the child or adolescent's behavior is extremely important, as they have the opportunity to observe the child at home, in the community, and within a school setting during both structured academic work and unstructured peer interactions. Items also assess the Diagnostic and Statistical Manual of Mental Disorders – Fifth Edition (DSM-5) symptom criteria for ASD (Goldstein & Naglieri, 2013). Responses to the various statements on the TRF, PRF, or Short-Form are combined into several subgroups of items which determine areas of need. Each group of items describes a **certain type of behavior** (see Table 10.6). The responses are then compared with what is expected for children in the *same age group* as the child or adolescent being evaluated. This information helps the assessor know if the child or adolescent is having more difficulty in a certain area than their peers. ASRS rating scales include Social/Communication, Unusual Behaviors, and Self-Regulation. Treatment rating scales include Peer Socialization, Adult, Social/Emotional, Atypical Language, Stereotypy, Behavioral Rigidity, Sensory Sensitivity, and Attention scale (Goldstein & Naglieri, 2013). See Table 10.15 for ASRS rating scales.

Scoring options for the ASRS include **electronic scoring** through the MHS online system. Manual entry consists of paper-pencil assessment format, and the raw scores or item responses are manually entered into the MHS software. On-screen administration is when the test is administered to the examinee on-screen on a web-enabled computer via the MHS software, a link to launch and administer the test at a remote location. Manual scoring is also available using the ASRS Manual. Raw scores on ASRS rating scales are converted to *T*-scores, which are converted into five possible classification scales: *Very Elevated Score*, *Elevated Score*, *Slightly Elevated Score*, *Average Score*, *and Below Average Score* (Goldstein & Naglieri,

Table 10.15 Autism Spectrum Rating Scale (ASRS) and treatment scales

ASRS RATING SCALES	Interpretation of scales
Social/ Communication	Indicates the extent to which the child or adolescent uses verbal and nonverbal communication appropriately to initiate, engage in, and maintain social contact
Unusual Behaviors	Indicates the child or adolescent's level of tolerance for changes in routine, engagement in apparently purposeless and stereotypical behaviors, and overreaction to certain sensory experiences
Self-Regulation	Indicates how well the child or adolescent controls their behavior and thoughts, maintains focus, and resists distraction
Treatment scales	**Interpretation of scales**
Peer Socialization	Indicates the child or adolescent's willingness and capacity to successfully engage in activities that develop and maintain relationships with other youth.
Adult Socialization	Indicates the child or adolescent's willingness and capacity to successfully engage in activities that develop and maintain relationships with adults
Social/Emotional Reciprocity	Indicates the child or adolescent's ability to provide an appropriate emotional response to another person in a social situation
Atypical Language	Indicates the extent to which the child or adolescent is able to utilize spoken communication in a structured and conventional way
Stereotypy	Indicates the extent to which the child or adolescent engages in apparently purposeless and repetitive behaviors
Behavioral Rigidity	Indicates the extent to which the child or adolescent tolerates changes in their environment, routines, activities, or behaviors
Sensory Sensitivity	Indicates the child or adolescent's level of tolerance for certain experiences sensed through touch, sound, vision, smell, or taste
Attention	Indicates the extent to which the child or adolescent is able to appropriately focus attention on one thing while ignoring others

2013). The use of MHS software will allow the *generation of reports* using the different norms to give **insight** into a variety of areas. Along with the ability to generate multiple reports for one individual, MHS also makes scoring much easier and faster in order to implement interventions as soon as possible.

Practical Considerations The greatest strength of the ASRS is the inclusion of information from the perspective of both the **parent and the teacher** or any other individual who is completing the measure. The analysis of behavioral and emotional information from multiple sources and settings is of great utility to practitioners in neuropsychology for differential diagnosis. The **multidimensional** approach gives a wide variety of information that provides a clear and accurate representation of the behavioral and emotional concerns of a child or adolescent within multiple settings. The ASRS provides sufficient information which can be used to guide the development of neuropsychological interventions for children with behavior and emotional concerns (Rhodes et al., 2009). It can also be used as a progress monitoring tool.

Vineland Adaptive Behavior Scales, Third Edition

Structure The Vineland Adaptive Behavior Scales, Third Edition (Vineland-3; Sparrow et al., 2016) is a leading measure of **personal** and **social skills** individuals need to **function** in their **everyday lives**. The Vineland-3 is used by practitioners to help identify individuals who have an intellectual disability or other disorders such as Autism, Asperger syndrome, developmental delays, Attention Deficit/Hyperactivity Disorder, traumatic brain injuries, hearing impairments, and dementia/Alzheimer's disease. In addition to facilitating **diagnosis**, the Vineland-3 also provides valuable information to support **educational and treatment plans** that help clients lead more fulfilling, independent lives. It focuses on what the client actually does in daily life. It is appropriate for use in the educational setting, social services, health care, medical, criminal justice, or military setting. The domain and subdomain scores and overall test score are useful for **diagnosis**, qualification for **special programs**, **progress reporting**, program and treatment **planning**, and research (Sparrow et al., 2016). The Vineland-3 is divided into 5 domains and 22 subdomains as seen in Table 10.16.

The third edition of this venerable test includes significant enhancements, providing more flexibility and relevance than ever. Everyday life has changed with advances in technology and its increased use and the evolving understanding of developmental disabilities (e.g., ASD; Fischer et al., 2019). Some Vineland-2 items have been retained, but others have been revised, and many new items have been added to Vineland-3 to make it relevant for the decisions practitioners recommend. New norms are available for all forms at all ages. There are **comprehensive** and **domain-level forms** for the **self-report, parent,** and **teacher** forms. The age range for all comprehensive forms is birth to 90+ years and for domain-level forms is 3+

Table 10.16 Vineland Adaptive Behavior Scales, Third Edition (Vineland-3) domains and subdomains

Domains	Subdomains
Communication	Receptive Expressive Written
Daily Living Skills	Personal Domestic Community
Socialization	Interpersonal Relationships Play and Leisure Coping Skills
Motor Skills (Optional)	Fine Motor Gross Motor
Maladaptive Behavior (Optional)	Internalizing Externalizing Critical Items

years. When a simpler evaluation, not requiring fine-grained results for intervention planning, is sufficient, the new domain-level versions can be administered in less time. These forms provide reliable, valid domain scores only (no subdomain scores) and are available in both Spanish and English. There are online and paper administration options for all forms/versions, as well as computerized or hand scoring for all forms/versions. Hand scoring can be tedious and complicated so it is recommended to use online scoring systems (Sparrow et al., 2016). A great deal of information is also provided which allows the easy explanation of the meaning of scores to individuals, parents, and teachers.

All Vineland-3 forms aid in diagnosing and classifying intellectual and developmental disabilities and other disorders. The scales are organized using **three domains** that correspond to the **three broad domains** of **adaptive functioning** specified by the *American Association on Intellectual and Developmental Disabilities* and by DSM-5. In addition, the Vineland-3 offers optional Motor Skills and Maladaptive Behavior domains for situations in which these areas are of concern. In any work settings, the Vineland-3 helps perform a variety of tasks including supporting **diagnosis of intellectual and developmental disabilities**, determining eligibility or qualification for special services, planning rehabilitation or intervention programs, as well as tracking and reporting educational and life progress. The Vineland-3 provides intervention guidance that will allow the practitioner to properly provide treatment (Sparrow et al., 2016).

Practical Considerations The Vineland-3 considers **life skills** to a greater degree than any measure previously discussed. The information that is provided is imperative in discovering what tasks the client is capable of performing independently. In addition to the evaluation of living skills related to intellectual capacity, the

Vineland-3 is also of use in determining the skills of children, individuals with traumatic brain injuries, and geriatric patients following neuropsychological impairment (Rhodes et al., 2009).

Sociometric Techniques

Structure Sociometric techniques include a variety of procedures used within social groups to measure such related constructs as social status, popularity, peer acceptance or rejection, and reputation. They involve gathering information directly from a **peer group concerning social dynamics**. For example, the "*Work With Rating Scale*" requires individuals to rate how much they enjoy working with people in their class on a continuum with 1 ☺ being *not at all* and 5 being *a lot* ☺. Data on various aspects of social status of the individuals within the peer group is collected directly from its members, allowing the clinician to tap directly into the ongoing social dynamics of a group (Whitcomb & Merrel, 2013). This is advantageous because there are many aspects of **social relationships** that are not easily discernable to the casual observer. Sociometric techniques are not new; they have been used in educational and clinical practice and research since the 1930s. Several important research efforts in this area occurred between the 1960s and 1980s. These studies emphasized the importance of **social functioning** and underscored the importance of clinicians who work with children having a basic knowledge of sociometric assessment methods, regardless of whether they use these techniques on a regular basis (Whitcomb & Merrel, 2013). In our current toxic society, where school violence is an everyday occurrence, sociometric techniques can be an **important diagnostic tool** when evaluating **peer relationships**. Assessing a child's social status is important because peer relationship problems during childhood may have large and lasting impacts to later adjustments in the child's life, both positive and negative. Positive peer relationships are important to a child's development and are an important avenue to consider when assessing children. Through positive peer relationships, children not only learn to interact effectively with their peers but also develop social-interactional skills that may generalize to many other situations and persons (Van der Kolk, 2014). The **peer nomination method** is usually used in which each student names one or more classmates he or she would like most to study, play, or work with. Through these nominations, four main groups can be found within the whole peer group being assessed: **popular, rejected, neglected,** and **controversial**. The popular group receives the most positive and fewest negative nominations. The rejected group receives the most negative nominations. The neglected group receives few positive or negative nominations. Finally, the controversial group has characteristics similar to popular and rejected groups (Whitcomb & Merrel, 2013). The importance of this information cannot be underestimated.

Practical Considerations Sociometric assessment has a **rich history** within developmental psychology, education, and sociology. It gathers information directly from the **peer group** being assessed and uses this information to form a **hierarchy**

that was established directly from the source. The best use of sociometric assessment is to assist in making decisions regarding additional screening, **school violence**, **psychopathology**, and assessment within a peer group setting. Sociometrics have been shown to have substantial **accuracy** in identifying at-risk children and adolescents who may be in need of additional assessment or intervention services. Individuals' understanding and rating of one another is a poignant indicator across the lifespan of leadership, accomplishment, and contentment. Some studies have shown that kindergarten teachers can predict long-term outcomes of **life success** based on rating **relationships** between and within individuals (Whitcomb & Merrel, 2013).

Comprehensive Measures of Neuropsychological Functioning

Neuropsychology is the study of brain-behavior relations. Thus, it has been difficult for individuals to develop a comprehensive battery without it being **overly broad** or **extremely complex**. The complexity of the brain makes it almost impossible for a single measure to reveal how an individual's brain *processes* information. There have been two approaches to neuropsychological assessment. One approach has been to capture all one's abilities in a single measure, such as the Halstead-Reitan Neuropsychological Test Battery, which is a measure composed of **multiple tests**. The other approach has been to select measures that evaluate the areas of concern (i.e., cognitive, achievement, and sensory/motor assessments), which has been referred to as a flexible battery approach. We begin by discussing the *NEPSY-II*, one of the newer and more focused batteries, and conclude with discussing the *Halstead-Reitan*, a comprehensive assessment which was the first neuropsychological measure which is and has been widely used.

NEPSY, Second Edition

Structure The NEPSY-II is a comprehensive neuropsychological assessment battery designed to evaluate **neuropsychological strengths and weaknesses** in children that underlie everyday functioning within and across domains (Korkman et al., 2007). This measure is theoretically based on the work of the Russian neuropsychologist, Luria (e.g., 1966, 1973), as well as more recent neuropsychological research. The NEPSY-II is unique in that many of the neuropsychological tasks have been adapted from adult measures to be more **child-friendly** and easier to administer (Titley & D'Amato, 2008). The original NEPSY was published in Finnish in 1980 for children ages 5–6 years of age. The first English version was published in 1998 for ages 3 through 12. Prior to the release of the NEPSY, a comprehensive standardized assessment specifically targeting the **neuropsychological functioning of children** did not exist in the United States. The NEPSY-II was released in 2007 and featured improvements from the original NEPSY, including an extended age range (up to 16), better **psychometrics**, an improved standardization sample, the addition of a **Social Perception** domain, and the expansion of several subtests to create improved floors and ceilings (Korkman et al., 2007). The NEPSY-II includes a standardization sample of 1,200 children approximating the demographics of the 2003 US Census (Titley & D'Amato, 2008). To further assess the clinical utility of the NEPSY-II, special group studies were conducted by independent researchers that include small convenience samples of children (260 total) with various clinical diagnoses (Korkman et al., 2007).

The NEPSY-II includes **6 domains spanning 32 subtests** which are as follows:

1. ***Attention and Executive Functioning***: This domain includes **six** subtests and is designed to measure sustained attention and higher-level cognitive skills including the ability to shift sets cognitively, flexibility in thinking, initiation, working memory, planning and organization, inhibition of incorrect automatic responses, and self-monitoring. Low performance on some subtests could be driven by other factors, including motor speed and comprehension of instructions.
2. ***Language***: This domain includes **seven** subtests designed to measure expressive and receptive language abilities, semantic knowledge, following directions, sequential processing of language, oromotor coordination, phonological awareness, segmentation, and decoding, auditory discrimination, and vocabulary knowledge and retrieval. There are also several subtests that measure processing speed as it relates to retrieval of linguistic information, but may also be impacted by slower processing overall. Factors related to short-term and working memory also come into play on several subtests.
3. ***Memory and Learning***: **Seven** subtests are included in this domain with four of the subtests including both immediate memory and delayed memory options. This is a helpful domain in differentiating between different types of memory strengths and weaknesses, as it includes both auditory rote tasks (i.e., List Memory; Sentence Repetition) and memory for a story within context (i.e., Narrative Memory) and visual memory tasks involving visual memory for designs and faces (i.e., Memory for Designs; Memory for Faces), as well as tasks that integrate auditory and visual memory systems (i.e., Memory for Names). There is also an auditory memory subtest that involves interference of other information (i.e., Work List Interference) making it a good measure of verbal working memory.
4. ***Sensorimotor:*** This domain includes **four** subtests measuring fine motor coordination, sequential motor ability, graphomotor skills, visual-spatial integration, and kinesthetic praxis (ability to perform skilled movement). Executive functioning areas may also influence performance on several subtests, including planning, self-regulation, and attention.
5. ***Social Perception***: This is a new domain, not included in the previous version of the NEPSY, which includes **two** subtests, Affect Recognition and Theory of Mind. This new area is an extremely helpful feature of this instrument. The Affect Recognition subtest is designed to measure a child's ability to identify or

recognize affect and interpret nonverbal cues and may also be impacted by visual attention and discrimination. The Theory of Mind subtest is designed to assess how well children are able to understand others' perspectives, experiences, and beliefs and also may be impacted by attention/concentration.

6. ***Visuospatial Processing***: This domain includes **six** subtests primarily designed to assess visuospatial and visuomotor skills, including visual discrimination, spatial localization, visual scanning, relationships between objects, orientation, and judging direction and distance. Several of these subtests also appear to relate to higher-order visual-spatial problem-solving and executive functioning. For example, Block Construction is similar to visual-spatial subtests of cognitive ability on other assessments. Other subtests require attention to detail and simultaneous processing.

Despite the grouping into specific domains, the NEPSY-II *does not provide* overall **domain scores**. Instead, the evaluator should interpret patterns in performance within and across domains in relation to other data. This change is one of the most difficult when attempting to understand a child's **overall neuropsychological functioning** due to the fact that the practitioner is not able to compare overall scores. As demonstrated in the description of each domain, there is considerable variability and overlap in the constructs that are measured. This provides flexibility in administration to target the specific areas addressing the referral concern but also requires careful interpretation of the patterns identified as well as considering qualitative information in determining a child's neuropsychological needs and strengths. When interpreting performance on the NEPSY-II, the evaluator should consider how more basic neuropsychological abilities, such as different areas of perception, relate to the use of higher-order reasoning abilities. Table 10.17 shows the main subtests according to neuropsychological domains on the NEPSY-2.

Practical Considerations In drawing conclusions about neuropsychological functioning, the NEPSY-II offers a variety of scores, including **Primary, Process, Contrast**, and **Behavioral Observation Scores** (Korkman et al., 2007). The Primary Scores are reported as scaled scores and are typically used as measures of overall performance on a subtest or specific ability measured within a subtest. For example, Combined Scores are a type of Primary Score used to look at performance on a task across trials involving the same measure, such as a score for time of completion or number of errors across multiple trials. Contrast Scores are used to compare two primary scores to help determine if the difference between the scores is meaningful. Process Scores are more specific in representing an aspect of a subtest that may aid in interpretation for certain children, but should be interpreted with caution, as these scores would logically tend to be less reliable due to the specific aspect of a subtest that is being measured and are more prone to indicating a low or high score due to testing error rather than a true difference. Finally, the NEPSY-II provides the option of tallying various behavioral observations, some of which may be converted into quantitative scores to compare the frequency of a behavior compared to those in the normative sample.

Table 10.17 Subtests on the NEPSY-2

Domain	Subtest
Attention and Executive Function	Animal Sorting
	Auditory Attention and Response Set
	Clocks
	Design Fluency
	Inhibition
	Statue
Language	Body Part Naming and Identification
	Comprehension of Instructions
	Oromotor Sequences
	Phonological Processing
	Repetition of Nonsense Words
	Speeded Naming
	Word Generation
Memory and Learning	List Memory and List Memory Delayed
	Memory for Designs and Memory for Designs Delayed
	Memory for Faces and Memory for Faces Delayed
	Narrative Memory
	Sentence Repetition
	Word List Interference
Sensorimotor	Fingertip Tapping
	Imitating Hand Positions
	Manual Motor Sequences
	Visuomotor Precision
Social Perception	Affect Recognition
	Theory of Mind
Visuospatial Processing	Arrows
	Block Construction
	Design Copying
	Geometric Puzzles
	Picture Puzzles
	Route Finding

As with any assessment, the NEPSY-II requires practice to become proficient with both administration and interpretation. The authors strived to create a neuropsychological assessment that could tap into the abilities of children in a way that was not overly complicated to administer, with many of the subtests being adapted from widely used adult neuropsychological and cognitive measures. When using this assessment with younger children, it is even more critical to take careful observation notes of how children approach the problems. Children may be especially creative in how they approach a task and may also be more likely than adults to misinterpret instructions or intent of a subtest. This is likely part of the reason why not all subtests on this measure have very high reliability. This **should be considered** when interpreting the assessment scores. It is always critical to interpret **the assessment within the context** of the individual and overall **evaluation data** rather than letting the test *control you*.

Another practical aspect of interpretation of the NEPSY-II is that subtests tap into **multiple domains** and the reliability of individual subtests varies. Therefore, it is critical that multiple contextual factors are considered in interpreting performance, including observations of the child during testing (e.g., attention, perseverance, strategy, etc.), standard error of measurement, and how the child's performance on this measure fits within the larger picture. The NEPSY-II interpretative manual (Korkman et al., 2007) can be a helpful resource in considering the neuropsychological functions and abilities measured by each subtest. As is true of any assessment, these measures are best used as pieces of a larger puzzle and you as the evaluator must find how the pieces fit together to form a coherent picture of the individual's neuropsychological profile. Some helpful features of the NEPSY-II are the **inclusion of recommended batteries** in the manual based on the area of the referral concern and the **flexibility for the examiner** to administer subtests either as a comprehensive neuropsychological battery or as a way to supplement information from other measures.

The Halstead-Reitan Neuropsychological Test Battery

Introduction

Halstead, one of the first clinical neuropsychologists, began a laboratory in **1935 at the University of Chicago** (see Halstead, 1947), which led to the development of the earliest full-time laboratory examining brain-behavior relationships in humans (D'Amato et al., 2005). In this laboratory, Halstead created a series of **ten tests** to identify and evaluate the wide range of deficits he observed in individuals with brain damage. A doctoral student of Halstead's, Reitan (1955, 1969, 1974) discovered that this battery was able to **differentiate** between individuals with **brain damage** and individuals **without brain damage**. This stood in stark contrast to the current zeitgeist of behaviorism, which was seen as leading the practice of psychology at the time. After some seminal research, Reitan removed three of the original ten measures due to their inability to differentiate between these individuals (Davis et al., 2005). This was the first step in the development of what was to become the most popular neuropsychological battery in the world, entitled the *Halstead-Reitan Neuropsychological Test Battery* (HRNB; Reitan, 1969). Additionally, a few new measures were added to give a more comprehensive analysis of neurological functions (Sinco, D'Amato, & Davis, 2008). Later, versions of the HRNB were created to work with children and adolescents including the *Halstead-Reitan Neuropsychological Test Battery for Older Children* (for ages 9–14) and the

Reitan-Indiana Test Battery for Children (for ages 5–8; Reitan, 1955, 1969; Reitan & Wolfson, 1985, 1992, 1993).

Halstead's **fixed battery approach** was unique because he considered the ***process*** and the ***product*** of clients. Psychologists before him had focused merely on either the product (Binet) or the process (Piaget), but it was unique to consider *both simultaneously* (Power & D'Amato, 2018). The measures he created required the client to analyze the problem's **essential components** and to define the problem itself before it could be understood. It is noteworthy that the authors did not seek to create an intelligence test, a personality measure, or an achievement test. Instead, they advocated that these neuropsychological tests be administered as part of a comprehensive battery which would include their measure as well as a standardized intelligence, personality, and achievement measure. In fact, a number of authors have studied the structure of the test and have found that intelligence, personality, and achievement factors are distinctly different than neuropsychological variables (Chittooran et al., 1993; Davis, 2011; D'Amato et al., 1988). The literature has not *clearly* indicated the relationship between **neuropsychological** and **intellectual** variables (Sattler & D'Amato, 2002a, 2002b). With this in mind, D'Amato et al. (1988) evaluated 1,181 clients and conducted a canonical correlation to evaluate the overlap of HRNB and a traditional Wechsler intelligence test. They found that some 10% of the variance was redundant indicating that a substantial amount of **innovative information** is introduced when a neuropsychological measure is added. In a demonstration that neuropsychological variables are different than traditional psychoeducational factors, Chittooran et al. (1993) argued that achievement and intelligence are *different variables* than neuropsychological abilities after studying the factor structure of almost 1000 clients using the HRNB and other achievement measures. In a related study, D'Amato et al. (1998) found that clients with learning disabilities could *be subtyped* into categories that suggested appropriate interventions for their strengths and weaknesses. These authors offered distinctive implications for suitable educational and neuropsychological programming and interventions.

This type of fixed battery approach is **enormously comprehensive**, but such extreme detail requires an *excessive amount of time* to administer, which may be difficult given the time constraints of many practicing psychologists. Therefore, such a comprehensive approach provides both a strength and a possible problem for school or pediatric practice (D'Amato, 1990).

Structure The administration and scoring of the HRNB requires training in neuropsychological test administration, test interpretation, child development, affective diagnosis, personality assessment, report writing, and psychological evaluation. As stated, Reitan and Wolfson (1986) argued that personality assessment was an important part of the neuropsychological assessment and typically included popular objective personality measures (e.g., *Minnesota Multiphasic Personality Inventory*). Those who use the HRNB should have graduate level training in the **biological bases of behavior** as well as an understanding of **medical disorders** and their related **diagnosis**. While some psychologists are trained in neuropsychological assessment, a post-doctoral specialization is required to become a clinical neuropsychologist (see Chap. 1). Remarkably, Reitan and Wolfson (1985, 1993) *advocated* that a clinical neuropsychologist must administer **at least 100** HRNB to achieve **basic proficiency** with this measure. Table 10.18 shows a complete lists of subtests available on the three versions of the Halstead-Reitan.

The subtests covered on all versions of the HRNB include the *Reitan-Indiana Aphasia Screening Test*, the *Finger Tapping Test*, the *Grip Strength Test*, the *Sensory-Perceptual Examination*, the *Tactual Performance Test*, and the *Category Test* (D'Amato, 1990).

The Category Test

This is perhaps the most unique measure from the HRNB; although it was once technologically sophisticated, projecting slides onto a television-like screen, with the advent of computers, this sophistication has passed away. The *Category Test* measures the examinee's ability to **learn general abstract principles** using sets of stimulus items. This test measures concept formation, memory, reasoning, new learning, and hypothesis testing. This test is sensitive to the detection of cerebral dysfunction and is the single test that is the *most sensitive* to the detection of *damage* occurring anywhere in the **brain**. However, the traditional version of this test is not portable. For this test, the examiner sits in front of a 10-by-8-inch colored glass screen on which a series of figures are projected. This test requires the examinee to view figures and push down on one of four levers to select an answer. If an answer is correct, the examinee will hear a bell; otherwise, the examinee will hear a buzzer.

Table 10.18 Tests of the three versions of the Halstead-Reitan Neuropsychological Test Batteries

HRNB	HRNB-C (ages 9–14)	RITB-C (ages 5–8)
Reitan-Indiana Aphasia Screening Test	*Reitan-Indiana Aphasia Screening Test*	*Reitan-Indiana Aphasia Screening Test*
Finger Tapping Test	*Finger Tapping Test*	*Finger Tapping Test*
Grip Strength Test	*Grip Strength Test*	*Grip Strength Test*
Sensory-Perceptual Examination	*Sensory-Perceptual Examination*	*Sensory-Perceptual Examination*
Tactual Performance Test	*Tactual Performance Test*	*Tactual Performance Test*
Category Test	*Category Test*	*Category Test*
Tactile Form Recognition Test	*Tactile Form Recognition Test*	*Marching Test*
Rhythm Test	*Rhythm Test*	*Color Form Test*
Speech Sounds Perception Test	*Speech Sounds Perception Test*	*Progressive Figures Test*
Trail Making Test	*Trail Making Test*	*Individual Performance Test*
		Target Test

The uniqueness of this measure relates to the fact that the individual receives **immediate figure based feedback** on the correctness of their response. A computerized version of the *Category Test* as well as a book form exists for those looking for portability. At one time, this was one of the most *popular* and *unique* measures on the HRNB (D'Amato, 1990). While this test has been *widely* copied, it seems that the unique essence of this measure continues to only be offered on this test.

The Finger Tapping Test

The *Finger Tapping Test* (also known as the *Finger Oscillation Test*) is a measure of **motor speed** (Reitan & Wolfson, 1985). This was one of Halstead's original measures. Examinees are required to press a small lever as quickly as possible for 10 s. Each hand is assessed individually, and the dominant hand is expected to perform 10% better for right-handed individuals. Higher scores on this subtest indicate a greater degree of **fine motor speed**.

The Grip Strength Test

The *Grip Strength Test* measures **upper extremity motor strength**. Examinees are instructed to squeeze a hand dynamometer as firmly as possible (Reitan & Wolfson, 1985). Like *Finger Tapping*, this test is sensitive to lateralized impairment especially in examinees with a traumatic brain injury (TBI), sensorimotor difficulties, and degenerative diseases with motor difficulties.

The Reitan-Indiana Aphasia Screening Test

The *Reitan-Indiana Aphasia Screening Test* measures **language-related** deficits. This is a modification of the *Halstead-Wepman Aphasia Screening* Test (Halstead & Wepman, 1949). Examinees must use simple math skills, produce and understand spoken language, name numbers and letters, copy basic shapes, identify body parts, and name items. This measure is a great **screener** and helps identify *pathognomonic signs* (or signs related to a specific illness). This screener is widely underutilized in psychological practice and can be used as a general screener quickly and efficiently with children, youth, and adults.

The Sensory-Perceptual Examination

The *Sensory-Perceptual Examination* examines **auditory, visual, and tactual sensory abilities**. This examination includes visual perception task, an auditory perception task, and a finger localization task. The examiner compares the sensory-perceptual function for visual, auditory, and tactual stimuli on either side of the body to assess functioning of the two cerebral hemispheres. This was an attempt to standardize the traditional behavioral neurological examination (Reitan & Wolfson, 1993). In a more recent attempt to offer *sophisticated psychometric* norms for this type of examination, Dean and Woodcock have offered the *Dean-Woodcock Sensory-Motor Battery* (Davis, 2008).

The Tactual Performance Test

The *Tactual Performance Test* (TPT) is one of the more *complex* tasks on the battery, which evaluates an examinee's **tactile discrimination**, **nonvisual-spatial awareness**, **ability to learn**, **commitment, spatial memory, psychomotor skills,** and **ability to integrate kinesthetic and tactile feedback** (Reitan & Wolfson, 1993). Historically, geometric formboard tests have been widely used in neuropsychology (Davis, 2011). First, the examinee is blindfolded and asked to use their dominant hand to place blocks in the formboard. Then, the examinee is asked to repeat the task using their nondominant hand. Finally, the examinee removes the blindfold and the formboard is taken away, and the examinee must draw the formboard from memory. This test allows the practitioner to compare the left and right hemispheres of the brain, to estimate the general efficiency of the brain, and to compare right and left times related to right and left memory (D'Amato, 1990; Davis et al., 2005; Sinco et al., 2008). **Five** scores are taken from this subtest: (1) **time** taken for performance on the dominant hand, (2) **time** taken for performance on the nondominant hand, (3) **total time** performance, (4) **memory score** for the number of correct shapes reproduced, and (5) **localization score** indicating the accuracy of location of shapes.

Review of Subtests Only on the HRNB and the HRNB-C

Four tests can be found on the HRNB and the HRNB-C and include the *Tactile Form Recognition Test*, the *Rhythm Test*, the *Speech Sounds Perception Test*, and the *Trail Making Test*.

The Tactile Form Recognition Test

The *Tactile Form Recognition Test* evaluates an examinee's ability to **discriminate shapes with their hands** (stereognosis). Errors on this test may indicate tactile or kinesthetic problems, vascular lesions, or parietal lobe dysfunction (D'Amato, 1990). During this test, the examinee's right hand is masked by a formboard that has shapes across it. The examinee is given a shape in their hand, on the side of the board they cannot see, and is asked to identify it. Difficulty on this test is rare and generally signifies *noteworthy findings*.

The Rhythm Test

The *Rhythm Test* (also known as the *Seashore Rhythm Test*) assesses the ability to **discriminate between rhythmic sounds** (D'Amato, 1990). This is a unique listening test which is different than most other instruments. It is a *nonverbal test* that measures *auditory perception, nonverbal auditory discrimination, and auditory attention*. The examinee listens to 30 pairs of rhythmic sounds and determines if the beats are the **same or different**. It was adapted from the *Seashore Test of Musical Ability* (Selz, 1981). Poor performance may indicate auditory discrimination challenges or severe attention or concentration impairment (Sinco et al., 2008). Few nonverbal listening measures are available for current use, which makes this test *impressive*.

The Speech Sounds Perception Test

The *Speech Sounds Perception Test* measures **auditory attention, concentration, and auditory-visual integration** (D'Amato, 1990). This test requires the ability to perceive speech sounds and real words and sustain attention. During this test, the examinee listens to **60 spoken nonsense words** all including the "*ee*" sound. Then, the examinee must underline on an answer sheet the matching sound. This is also a unique measure because the test offers nonsense words which must be identified and underlined on the response sheet. The number of errors makes up the score. The test does not require English language proficiency and may be helpful when working with clients who do not speak English. Research has shown that clients with left hemispheric impairment perform poorly on this test (Reitan & Wolfson, 1993; Sinco et al., 2008). This measure has proven to be extremely helpful in a school setting where *following directions* is an important activity (Power & D'Amato, 2018).

The Trail Making Test

The *Trail Making Test* measures **global** cerebral functioning and is also a measure of **processing speed, visual attention, visual perception, mental flexibility, and inhibition**. Of all the tests on the HRNB, this measure is second only to the Category Test in predicting *overall neuropsychological functioning* (Selz, 1981). This is a timed, paper and pencil test with two parts. **Part A** assesses simple cognitive processing speed, while **Part B** measures mental flexibility and complex cognitive processing. Part A requires the examinee to connect numbered circles by drawing a line in a sequential manner as fast as possible. Part B is a similar task, except that it contains both letters and numbers (D'Amato, 1990). The examinee is required to alternately connect numbers and letters (i.e., 1-A-2-B). Difficulties in standardization arise due to imprecise scoring (Sinco et al., 2008). This measure is currently available as part of other standardized cognitive tests as well as a stand-alone measure with its own norms.

Subtests Only on the RITB-C

There are multiple tests that are only included on the RITB-C. They are merely mentioned here and include the following: the *Marching Test*, the *Color Form Test*, the *Progressive Figures Test*, the *Individual Performance Test*, and the *Target Test*. For a comprehensive review, see Davis et al. (2005) and Johnson and D'Amato (2011).

Interpretation and Intervention with the HRNB

There have been a variety of approaches to **interpreting the results** of the HRNB. Reitan advocated for interpretation using **multiple levels of inference**. Reitan and Wolfson (1993) developed interpretive methods including *(1) interpreting the level of performance, (2) looking for pathognomonic signs, (3) analyzing patterns of performance, and (4) comparing right-left differences*. Interpreting the **level of performance** assists in understanding the general characteristics of a client. This method compares the level of test performance using normative standards. Indeed, one of the most popular approaches is the **pathognomonic (or sign)** approach. This approach rests on the idea that certain learning, cognitive, emotional, and/or behavioral problems relate to specific neuropsychological disorders (D'Amato et al., 2005). This approach can be used by beginning practitioners with little difficulty because the practitioner can look up specific disorders when a client presents certain unique features (Semrud-Clikeman & Teeter Ellison, 2009). However, this approach has limited reliability due to its dependence on the neurodevelopmental judgment of clinicians. The *patterns of performance* approach provides intraindividual comparisons, focusing on the strengths and weaknesses of an individual. Neuropsychological evaluations are typically the most comprehensive; therefore, a focus on both *strengths and weaknesses* is imperative (D'Amato et al., 2005). The final approach is **left-right differences** which provide intraindividual comparisons using information from a physical neurological examination. This is perhaps the most *widely used* approach to neuropsychology in general. A variety of additional data analysis can be undertaken, including the use of a neuropsychological **deficit scale, a global deficit scale,** and an **impairment index** (see Johnson & D'Amato, 2011; Reitan & Wolfson, 1992; Sinco et al., 2008).

In 1979, Reitan formalized an intervention program, the Reitan Evaluation of Hemispheric Abilities and Brain Improvement Training (REHABIT). This program provides the client with tasks that have been organized in such a way to remediate a client's specific neurological deficits based on their performance on the HRNB. Other individuals have offered a variety of interventions based on data from the HRNB. Most of these approaches advocate for the neuropsychological identification of strengths and weaknesses of individual clients (D'Amato et al., 2005; D'Amato & Hartlage, 2008; Davis, 2011; Sattler & D'Amato, 2002a, 2002b).

Practical Considerations For decades, the HRNB was the most widely used and researched neuropsychological battery in use. However, it has limited reliability and validity compared to modern batteries as well as outdated norms and instrumentation. Clearly, many of the current batteries have been *strongly influenced* by the HRNB. The HRNB provided the foundation for a comprehensive neuropsychological approach to assessment. While some may advocate using the entire battery, it would seem that the use of *specific tests* (e.g., the *Category Test, Aphasia Screening Test, Speech Sounds Perception Test, Rhythm Test*, and *TPT*) may be **warranted at this time** and certainly is recommended. The Category Test is novel in that it provides immediate feedback which allows clients to profit from mistakes or to deal ineffectively with feedback which they may perceive as cognitive criticism. The Aphasia Screening Test is comprehensive and in one measure allows you to evaluate reading, writing, arithmetic, and other necessary cognitive-processing abilities. The Speech Sounds Perception Test is an auditory assessment which evaluates a client's ability to hear, process, and identify differences in phonetic sounds. The Rhythm Test is one of the only nonverbal tests of auditory processing. Moreover, the TPT is an assessment of tactile performance using the dominant hand, nondominant hand, and both hands. Additionally, this test assesses for spatial memory. This was the first battery to argue for the importance of the brain for diagnosis and rehabilitation. Neuropsychology (and neuroscience) is on the cutting edge of psychological research today, and the HRNB helped concretize an *important shift* in our understanding of brain-behavior relations. Clearly, we have only begun to understand the **importance of our brain** as related to **functional behavior** and **mental health**. Many of these original tests have been copied and are now used in some of our current neuropsychological batteries and cognitive measures.

Multicultural Issues in Clinical Neuropsychology

This chapter provides a comprehensive examination of many popular assessment tools. The aforementioned assessments can be implemented to gain knowledge on individual's neurocognitive functioning. However, in order to gain accurate information, implementation must be conducted in a **multiculturally competent manner**. Multicultural competence in neuropsychological evaluations is no longer an asset, but a *professional requirement* (Samovar et al., 2012). Furthermore, the American Psychological Association (APA, 2017), American Academy of Clinical Neuropsychology (AACN), and the American Educational Research Association all uphold professional standards and guidelines for clinician's multicultural competence. Unfortunately, it is not atypical for an individual to *overestimate their multicultural competency,* thus resulting in limited acknowledgment and desire for further training in areas of diversity. This lack of further training can lead to multicultural issues. **Limited multicultural competence** has serious implications in neuropsychological evaluations, such as inappropriate test selection, inaccurate interpretation of assessment results such as behavioral observations and interview data, and misdiagnosis of a mental disorder (Fletcher-Janzen et al., 2000). In order to prevent these significant consequences, there are steps that clinical neuropsychologists can take to consider areas of **diversity**, such as **race, ethnicity, gender, socioeconomic status, religion, ability, and language/country of origin**. The aforementioned diversity areas all need to be considered during a neuropsychological evaluation as they will *directly impact* the assessment results and factor into the uniqueness of every individual client. Assessment results are not limited to formal tests; these also include behavioral and interview data. In a *multicultural world*, the clinical interview and behavioral observations provide vital understanding of the case. All cases require multidisciplinary input, which for children would include collecting data from their parent(s)/guardian(s), teachers, coaches, and themselves. For adult cases, depending on the reason for referral, family members and significant others may be interviewed. It is noteworthy that some hospitals *will not work with elderly clients* unless family members are present to provide additional information regarding their functioning. All **diversity** areas play a role in an individual's development in terms of their attachment and motivation for learning. Thinking metacognitively is necessary to ensure a valid, reliable, and comprehensive neuropsychological evaluation for all areas of diversity. If after self-reflection, you have personal biases that would affect the evaluation, it is extremely important that you refer out to another qualified neuropsychologist or specialist.

Race/Ethnicity

In the United States, the percentage of people identifying as only White has been steadily *decreasing* since the 1900s. It is also predicted that one in five Americans will claim a **multiracial** background by 2050 (Lee & Bean, 2004). Due to the changing racial and ethnic demographics in the United States, it is extremely important to consider differences between racial groups when conducting neuropsychological evaluations. Individuals should be treated **equitably**, not equally. This means that you would not approach parental figures of different racial and ethnic backgrounds in the same manner. Differences between cultural groups further support the need for knowledge of other **cultures**. It is criticale to conduct an in-depth social developmental history related to the client's background. Although developmental milestones are heavily acknowledged in terms of children's growth, it is crucial to understand that developmental milestones are based widely on **Eurocentric, middle-class norm**s (Kuther & Burnell, 2019). In order to obtain an accurate picture of the individual's functioning, racial and ethnic backgrounds cannot be ignored. This inclusion is also pertinent to the areas of concerns and the corresponding selection of assessments. The selection of *appropriate assessments* must be individually based, and it is essential that the client's **culture** be understood in their **context**. The assessment tool(s) should include the individual's racial and ethnic background in the sample. This may include some research on the neuropsychologist's part. It is important to use both your professional judgment and consideration of their background when selecting assessment tool(s) and when understanding historical information.

Gender and Sexuality

Society has relied heavily on the use of gender-based norms. With these norms, society has expectations for what males and females are each interested in and how they should act. However, these labels are based on a binary system of gender and are *detrimental* as many people do not fit exactly into the box that society has created. These norms have also been the main cause of gender inequality in the United States and resulted in gender stereotypes. It is important that neuropsychologists are aware of any personal biases they have regarding gender and refer out if those biases would affect their ability to complete a non-biased evaluation. When conducting a neuropsychological evaluation, it is important to consider the **culture** of the individual and gain information regarding their beliefs toward **gender**. There are typically strong social-emotional ties to cultural beliefs on gender. It is also necessary to obtain information on how the individual identifies. They may not always identify with the gender related to their biological sex or may identify non-binary, neither exclusively male nor female. When meeting with individuals, the neuropsychologist should ask them their *personal pronouns*. Each individual may identify with different pronouns, and those pronouns should be utilized when communicating with the individual and throughout the report. It is common in medical records to see biological sex noted and a statement about how the individual identifies and their use of gender pronouns. Gender identity is not something to **overlook** as it is strongly related to how one thinks about themself.

Additionally, health service psychologists have been reporting lack of preparation to adequately treat clients that identify as **lesbian, gay, bisexual, transgender, intersex, queer/questioning, asexual, and many others** (LGBTIQA+) within this community (Lyons et al., 2010). Although clients may face some common issues related to self-esteem, anxiety, and depression, it is key to understand how the gender/sexuality continuum impacts clients within this community. Recommendations for developing multicultural competencies in neuropsychological evaluations revolve around (1) gaining knowledge through consultation, professional lectures, and empirical articles; (2) not assuming clients are heterosexual; (3) advancing one's own cultural competence related to gender and sexuality; and (4) becoming fully aware of one's thoughts about individuals from the LGBTIQA+ community to increase helpful strategies and prevent unhelpful or harmful responses (Lyons et al., 2010). In this area as well of others, it is crucial that health service providers/neuropsychologists are aware of their beliefs, and if they are not able to effectively serve a client (e.g., limited training with this population), they need to **refer to a specialist**.

Language

The 2018 US Census data revealed that over **20%** of households speak another language in the home besides English. Language is typically tied heavily to one's culture. A neuropsychologist should not assume that individuals of particular backgrounds speak another language or don't speak another language. It is always important when the neuropsychologist receives a request for an evaluation that they are thorough in obtaining information about **language** despite the individual's background. When gathering information related to language, it is necessary to gather not only the information related to language proficiency but language exposed to during key developmental times. Cognitive assessments yield the *most effective results* when conducted in the language that was most exposed from infancy to early childhood.

If an individual speaks a language in which the neuropsychologist is not fluent, their first action is to attempt to find a **bilingual** neuropsychologist in the area. For a comprehensive understanding and clear recommendations for language, please see Fujii (2017). The recommendations below are adapted from this source. If a bilingual neuropsychologist is not available, there are additional considerations needed when hiring an **interpreter**. When possible, health service psychologists should select interpreters that are adequately trained to interpret during neuropsychological evaluations and be fluent and knowledgeable of the client's language/dialect. Clinicians should refer to APA and AACN's guidelines and be aware that they are responsible for the competence of the interpreter. For most effective

Table 10.19 Formats of interpretation in evaluations

Format for interpretation	Definition	When to use
Word for word	The client's responses repeated verbatim (Fujii, 2017)	This format is best to use when the client is sharing sensitive information or significant emotional details
Summary interpreting	The highlighting of key details from stories (Fujii, 2017)	This format is best when time is a concern; however, it is less accurate and requires a more experienced interpreter
Consecutive interpreting	The clinician is provided literal and cultural meanings after each statement the client says (Fujii, 2017)	It is important to note that consecutive interpreting does take time
Culture-relevant interpreting	The client's statements are translated in context to cultural relevance (Fujii, 2017)	This format is best to minimize cultural misunderstandings between the clinician and client
Cultural-expert interpreting	The interpreter serves as a cultural consultant to provide explanations to the clinician and client (Fujii, 2017)	This format is best when there are significant cultural differences between the clinician and client

communication during the interview, the interpreter should let the clinician know which interpretation they are providing and any necessary changes. There are five main formats for interpretation: (1) word for word, (2) summary interpreting, (3) consecutive interpreting, (4) culture-relevant interpreting, and (5) cultural-expert interpreting (Fujii, 2017). For a comprehensive understanding of *multicultural issues in neuropsychological evaluations*, please refer to the seminal book by Fujii (2017) which focuses on conducting culturally appropriate neuropsychological evaluations. Please see Table 10.19 for further description on formats for interpretation.

Religion

There are some religions that are common within certain ethnic groups historically (e.g., Hispanic/Latino as Christians). However, it is important to *not assume* someone's religion based on their **race or ethnicity** (e.g., assuming someone is Muslim because they are from the Middle East). Like other sections, **inclusion of religion** as part of the *social developmental history* is important. Someone's religion provides valuable information into their beliefs. Their **religion** may influence the way they dresses, jobs they seeks, beliefs of gender roles, parenting, traditions, etc. It is important to consider the individual's **religion** and their view of **mental health**. The religion of an individual is a **valuable resource** for the individual and should be acknowledged in case *conceptualization and recommendations*. Indeed, religion must be a *driving force* of the comprehensive neuropsychological evaluations given the uniqueness of our world. Some neuropsychological books focus on all components of a specific culture, including **religion** (e.g., see Davis & D'Amato, 2014).

Socioeconomic Status

Currently in the United States, at least **14%** of the population lives in poverty (United States Census Bureau, 2018). Research has demonstrated a link between lower **socioeconomic status** and lower **academic achievement** (Engle & Black, 2008; Sirin, 2005). If a child lives in poverty during early developmental periods, they are less likely to be ready for school and more likely to experience widened academic achievement gaps throughout their education even if their socioeconomic status changes (Entwisle et al., 2005). Unfortunately, when a child lives in poverty, they are faced with *increased risks* for **negative** neuropsychological factors and **decreased** opportunities for growth (Black et al., 2000; Campbell et al., 2001; Engle & Black, 2008). Examples of difficulties may include limited development of phonemic awareness and comprehension skills (Pfannenstiel et al., 2003; Snow & Burns, 2000), behavioral problems due to high family stress (Conger et al., 2000), and heightened risk of exposure to **violence** and experiences of **trauma** (Buitrago et al., 2017). Individuals of color have a higher likelihood of **living in poverty** and experiencing **income inequality** (Buitrago et al., 2017). It is important to be aware of factors related to socioeconomic status when completing a neuropsychological assessment and selecting assessment tools that have been normed on individuals with a similar socioeconomic status. Limited availability of enriching and nutritious food has long-term effect. **Malnutrition** affects brain growth and so does access to **lead paint** (D'Amato et al., 1992; Hartlage et al., 1992). It is equally important to be aware of any personal biases that could impact the way you conceptualize the case related to individuals with less or more money (e.g., assuming people who are poor have poor hygiene or assuming people who are affluent have higher self-confidence). Obviously, health service psychologists must have a **substantial focus** on understanding **multicultural issues** in neuropsychological evaluations.

Multicultural Issues Summary

This section provided a glimpse of the complexity of **culture** and **diversity factors** when understanding a client's neuropsychological evaluation. A resource that clinicians could use to determine their own developmental multicultural competency is the *Intercultural Development Inventory*® (Hammer, 2013). This 50-item questionnaire measures ones' competence and identifies what stage in which an individual's knowledge, attitude, and skills are linked. Additionally, individuals receive an *Intercultural Development Plan*® to assist with their advancement of multicultural competence, or *intercultural competence* as Hammer (2015) refers to it. If health service psychologists **do not understand** the **cultural diversity** of their clients, they typically provide neuropsychological evaluations that are problematic, have inaccurate data, and lead to **misdiagnosis** as well as general confusion.

This section is by no means an exhaustive list of all necessary components to conduct a neuropsychological evaluation in a **multiculturally competent way**. In fact, including multiculturally relevant information in an evaluation is critical. However, if the psychologist is not **multiculturally competent**, interviewing, behavioral observations, case conceptualization, assessment selection, interpretation of the results, diagnosis, and rehabilitation/intervention planning can be severely impacted. *Limited multicultural competence* has serious implications in neuropsychological evaluations. With the changing demographics in our country, ignoring **culture** and **categories of diversity,** such as **race** and **ethnicity, gender** and **gender identity, sexual orientation, religion, ability, language,** and **socioeconomic status**, in evaluations *must* **not occur**. While understanding multicultural issues is vital to be an effective health service psychologist, being able to provide accurate representation of the client's **strengths and areas of needs** reflective of their **culture** and **diversity** factors *increases the likelihood* of both client and health service psychologist success.

Conclusions

Neuropsychology is the study of brain-behavior relationships, and the purpose of this chapter was to provide a brief history of **neuropsychological assessment** and detailed information about widely used neuropsychological instruments. It is imperative that practitioners understand that neuropsychological assessment is an **approach to conceptualization** as opposed to administration of specific measures. While it is necessary to understand test administration, it is even more important to comprehend how to **conceptualize results** and make **meaningful interpretation** to understand one's neuropsychological strengths and weaknesses. In this chapter, we described the history of integrated assessment and its relation to intervention in the field of clinical neuropsychology. Next, we discussed the necessity of neuropsychological evaluation and the importance of using both **quantitative** and **qualitative** measures. The purpose of any health service psychology provider is to appropriately **differentially diagnose** in an effort to help the patient succeed in life through development of appropriate **intervention/rehabilitation**. This chapter has highlighted all of the **life domains** that must be covered for rehabilitation to be successful. The major domains of a neuropsychological evaluation were then described. The remainder of the chapter then provided an overview of **integrated assessments for intervention** in clinical neuropsychology. The majority of the assessments described in this chapter are administered through the use of a paper and pencil format. However, as we venture into the future, more assessments are becoming available **online** which will impact many aspects of the neuropsychological evaluation (D'Amato & Perfect, 2020). Additionally, our world is becoming more diverse which results in the need for health service psychologists to be **culturally competent** practitioners.

Discussion Questions

1. Why do some claim that assessment is the most important step in the health service provider continuum of services?
2. Why is it critical to consider all domains found within a neuropsychological framework?
3. Why do some laws stipulate that diagnosis cannot be determined by a single psychological measure?
4. Why is neuropsychological assessment the most comprehensive evaluation method in the health service provider field?
5. Health service providers often gravitate to diagnosis without considering cultural factors, historical events, and the influence of trauma. Why is it important to consider these faculty in relation to a differential diagnosis?
6. Why is the consideration of the biological basis of behavior with patients pivotal to the provision of ethical psychological services?

EPPP Sample Questions

1. Which of the following is not true regarding the Halstead-Reitan Neuropsychological Test Battery?
   (a) It provides information on a range of cognitive strengths and weaknesses.
   (b) It can usually be completed within 45–60 min.
   (c) It must be administered by a highly trained examiner.
   (d) The results are reflected in a combined score known as the Impairment Index.

2. An 18-year-old high school student is referred to you for personality assessment due to behavioral problems. Which of the following assessment instruments would be most appropriate to use?
   (a) WISC-V
   (b) MMPI-2
   (c) WJ-IV ACH
   (d) Halstead-Reitan

3. A 9-year-old client completed the Bender Gestalt and Beery, and their scores revealed significant deficits in their ability to process visually modified information. Their teacher reported to you that they are having trouble copying the alphabet which affects their basic handwriting abilities. Given these scores, which measure might you choose next to administer to this child in an effort to hypothesize a further diagnostic conclusion?
   (a) Kinetic Family Drawing Test
   (b) WISC-V
   (c) Aphasia Screening Test
   (d) MVPT-4

4. Which of the following domains is <u>NOT</u> one that is typically assessed during a neuropsychological evaluation?
   (a) Academic Achievement
   (b) Learning/Memory
   (c) Sensory/Motor
   (d) Vocational/Career Aptitude
5. Which is an example of a comprehensive learning and memory assessment?
   (a) WISC-V
   (b) Bender Gestalt
   (c) D-KEFS
   (d) TOMAL-2

   Answers: B, B, D, D, D

Proactive Readings

Transcending the Past

Halstead, W. C. (1947). *Brain and intelligence; A quantitative study of the frontal lobes*. University of Chicago Press.
Luria, A. R. (1966). *The working brain: An introduction to neuropsychology*. Basic Books.

Excelling in the Present

Flanagan, D. P. & McDonough, E. M. (Eds.), *Contemporary intellectual Assessment: Theories, tests, and issues* (4th ed.). Guilford.
Lezak, M. D., Howieson, D. B., Bigler, E. D., & Tranel, D. (2012). *Neuropsychological assessment*. Oxford University Press.
Perfect, M., & D'Amato, R. C. (2020). Introduction to special issue on the history of the future of proactive school psychology: Transcending the past, excel in the present, and transform the future. *School Psychology, 35*(6), 363–366. https://doi.org/10.1037/spq0000419

Transforming the Future

D'Amato, R. C., & Perfect, M. (2020). History of the future of proactive school psychology: Historical review at our 75th APA anniversary to transcend the past, excel in the present, and transform the future. *School Psychology, 35*(6), 375–384. https://doi.org/10.1037/spq0000420
Dean, R. S. (1986). Perspectives on the future of neuropsychology assessment. In B. S. Plake & J. C. Witt (Eds.), *Buros-Nebraska series on measurement and testing: Future of testing and measurement* (pp. 203–241). https://digitalcommons.unl.edu/cgi/viewcontent.cgi?article=1008&context=burosfuturetesting
Papanicolaou, A. C. (2017). *The Oxford handbook of functional brain imaging in neuropsychology and cognitive neurosciences*. Oxford University Press.

References

Adams, W., & Reynolds, R. C. (2009). *Essentials of WRAML 2 and TOMAL-2 assessment*. Wiley.

American Psychological Association. (2017). *Standards of accreditation for health service psychology*. American Psychological Association.

Becker, K. A. (2003). *History of the Stanford-Binet intelligence scales: Content and psychometrics*. Fifth Edition Assessment Service Bulletin.

Beery, K., Buktenica, N. A., & Beery, N. (2010). *Beery-Buktenica Developmental Test of Visual-Motor Integration, Sixth Edition* (Beery VMI 6).2 Pearson.

Black, M. M., Hess, C. R., & Berenson-Howard, J. (2000). Toddlers from low-income families have below normal mental, motor, and behavior scores on the revised Bayley scales. *Journal of Applied Developmental Psychology, 21*(6), 655–666. https://doi.org/10.1016/S0193-3973(00)00059-9

Broca, P. (1960). Remarks on the seat of the faculty of articulate language, followed by an observation of aphasia. In G. von Bonin (Trans.), *Some papers on the cerebral cortex* (pp. 49–72). Charles C. Thomas. (Original work published 1865).

Buitrago, K., Rynell, A., & Tuttle, S. (2017). Cycle of risk: The intersection of poverty, violence, and trauma. Retrieved from https://www.heartlandalliance.org/povertyreport/wp-content/uploads/sites/26/2017/03/FINAL_PR17_3_14.pdf

Burns, R. C., & Kaufman, S. H. (1972). *Actions, styles, and symbols in kinetic family drawings: An interpretative manual*. Brunner/Marvel Publications.

Butcher, J. N., Graham, J. R., Ben-Porath, Y. S., Tellegen, A., & Dahlstrom, W. G. (2001). *Minnesota multiphasic personality inventory–2 (MMPI-2): Manual for administration and scoring* (rev ed.). University of Minnesota Press.

Butcher, J. N., & Williams, C. L. (2000). *Essentials of MMPI-2 and MMPI-A interpretation* (2nd ed.). University of Minnesota Press.

Campbell, F. A., Pungello, E. P., Miller-Johnson, S., Burchinal, M., & Ramey, C. T. (2001). The development of cognitive and academic abilities: growth curves from an early childhood educational experiment. *Developmental Psychology, 37*(2), 231. https://psycnet.apa.org/doi/10.1037/0012-1649.37.2.231

Canivez, G. L. (2005). Review of the motor-free visual perception test, third edition. In R. A. Spies & B. S. Plake (Eds.), *The sixteenth mental measurements yearbook*. Buros Center for Testing.

Canivez, G. L., Watkins, M. W., & Dombrowski, S. C. (2017). Structural validity of the Wechsler intelligence scale for children–fifth edition: Confirmatory factor analyses with the 16 primary and secondary subtest. *Psychological Assessment: A Journal of Consulting and Clinical Psychology, 29*(4), 458–472. https://psycnet.apa.org/doi/10.1037/pas0000358

Cattell, R. B. (1941). Some theoretical issues in adult intelligence testing. *Psychological Bulletin, 38*, 592.

Cherkasova, V. M., & Hechtman, L. (2009). Neuroimaging in attention-deficit hyperactivity disorder: Beyond the frontostriatal circuitry. *Canadian Journal of Psychiatry, 54*, 651–661. https://doi.org/10.1177%2F070674370905401002

Chittooran, M. M., D'Amato, R. C., Lassiter, K. S., & Dean, R. S. (1993). Factor structure of psychoeducational and neuropsychological measures with learning disabled children. *Psychology in the Schools, 30*, 109–118. https://doi.org/10.1002/1520-6807(199304)30:2<109::AID-PITS2310300202>3.0.CO;2-Q

Colarusso, R. P. & Hammill, D.D. (2003). *Motor-Free Visual Perception Test-3 (MVPT-3)*. Academic Therapy Publications.

Conger, K. J., Rueter, M. A., & Conger, R. D. (2000). The role of economic pressure in the lives of parents and their adolescents: The Family Stress Model. In L. J. Crockett & R. K. Silbereisen (Eds.), Negotiating adolescence in times of social change (p. 201–223). Cambridge University Press.

D'Amato, R. C., & Perfect, M. (2020). History of the future of proactive school psychology: Historical review at our 75th APA anniversary to transcend the past, excel in the present, and transform the future. *School Psychology, 35*(6), 375–384. https://doi.org/10.1037/spq0000420
D'Amato, R. C., Chittooran, M. M., & Whitten, J. C. (1992). The neuropsychological consequences of malnutrition. In L. C. Hartlage, D. I. Templer, & W. G. Cannon (Eds.), *Preventable brain damage: Brain vulnerability and brain health* (pp. 193–213). Springer.
D'Amato, R. C., Dean, R. S., & Rhodes, R. L. (1998). Subtyping children's learning disabilities with neuropsychological, intellectual, and achievement measures. *International Journal of Neuroscience, 96*, 107–125. https://doi.org/10.3109/00207459808986461
D'Amato, R. C., Fletcher-Janzen, E., & Reynolds, C. R. (Eds.). (2005). *Handbook of school neuropsychology*. Wiley.
D'Amato, R. C., & Hartlage, L. C. (Eds.). (2008). *Essentials of neuropsychological assessment: Rehabilitation planning for intervention* (2nd ed.). Springer.
D'Amato, R. C., & Walker, J. M. (2007). Test review of Dean-Woodcock neuropsychological battery. In K. F. Geisinger, R. A. Spies, J. F. Carlson, & B. S. Plake (Eds.), *The seventeenth mental measurements yearbook*. Buros Institute of Mental Measurements, University of Nebraska-Lincoln. Retrieved from http://marketplace.unl.edu/buros/
D'Amato, R. C., Zafiris, C., McConnell, E., & Dean, R. S. (2011). The history of school psychology: Understanding the past to not repeat it. In M. Bray & T. Kehl (Eds.), *Oxford handbook of school psychology* (pp. 9–60). Oxford University Press.
D'Amato, R. C. (1990). A neuropsychological approach to school psychology. *School Psychology Quarterly, 5*, 141–160. https://psycnet.apa.org/doi/10.1037/h0090608
D'Amato, R. C., Gray, J. W., & Dean, R. S. (1988). A comparison between intelligence and neuropsychological functioning. *Journal of School Psychology, 26*, 283–292. https://doi.org/10.1016/0022-4405(88)90007-6
D'Amato, R. C., & Rothlisberg, B. A. (Eds.). (1997/1992). *Psychological perspectives on intervention: A case study approach to prescriptions for change*. Republished by Waveland Press: Sold to Pearson.
Davis, A. S. (2008). Understanding and using the Dean-Woodcock neuropsychological battery with children, youth, adults, and in geriatrics. In L. C. Hartlage & R. C. D'Amato (Eds.), *Essentials of neuropsychological assessment: Rehabilitation planning for intervention* (2nd ed., pp. 173–206). Springer.
Davis, A. S. (2011). *Handbook of pediatric neuropsychology*. Springer.
Davis, A. S., Finch, H. W., Dean, R. S., & Woodcock, R. W. (2006). Cortical and subcortical constructs of the Dean-Woodcock sensory motor battery: A construct validity study. *International Journal of Neuroscience, 116*(10), 1157–1171. https://doi.org/10.1080/00207450500513955
Davis, A. S., Johnson, J. A., & D'Amato, R. C. (2005). Evaluating and using long-standing school neuropsychological batteries: The Halstead-Reitan and the Luria-Nebraska neuropsychological batteries. In R. C. D'Amato, E. Fletcher-Janzen, & C. R. Reynolds (Eds.), *Handbook of school neuropsychology* (pp. 236–263). Wiley.
Davis, J. M., & D'Amato, R. C. (2014). *Neuropsychology of Asians and Asian-Americans: Practical and theoretical considerations*. Springer.
Dean, R. S., & Davis, A. S. (2008). The Dean-Woodcock neuropsychological assessment system. In A. M. Horton Jr. & D. Wedding (Eds.), *The neuropsychology handbook*. Springer.
Dean, R. S., & Woodcock, R. W. (1999). *The WJ-R and Bateria-R neuropsychological assessment: Research report number 3*. Riverside Publishing.
Dean, R. S., & Woodcock, R. W. (2003). *Dean-Woodcock neuropsychological battery*. Riverside Publishing Company.
Dean, R. S., & Woodcock, R. W. (2003). *Dean-Woodcock neuropsychological battery*. Riverside.
Delis, D. C. , Kramer, J. H. & Kaplan, E. (1994). *California Verbal Learning Test Children's Version (CVLT-C)*. Pearson.
DiStefano, C., & Dombrowski, S. C. (2006). Investigating the theoretical structure of the Stanford-Binet-fifth edition. *Journal of Psychoeducational Assessment, 24*(2), 123–136. https://doi.org/10.1177%2F0734282905285244

Douet, V., Chang, L., Cloak, C., & Ernst, T. (2014). Genetic influences on brain developmental trajectories on neuroimaging studies: From infancy to young adulthood. *Brain Imaging and Behavior, 8*, 234–250. https://doi.org/10.1007/s11682-013-9260-1
Dunn, L. M. & Dunn D. M. (2007). Peabody Picture Vocabulary Test, Fourth Edition (PPVT-4). Pearson.
Dugbartey, A. T., & Ramsden, P. (2003). Test review of Delis-Kaplan executive function system. In B. S. Plake & J. C. Impara (Eds.), *The fifteenth mental measurements yearbook*. Buros Institute of Mental Measurements. Retrieved from http://marketplace.unl.edu/buros/
Engle, P. L., & Black, M. M. (2008). The effect of poverty on child development and educational outcomes. *Annals of the New York Academy of Sciences, 1136*, 243. https://doi.org/10.1196/annals.1425.023
Entwisle, D. R., Alexander, K. L., & Olson, L. S. (2005). First grade and educational attainment by age 22: A new story. *American Journal of Sociology, 110*(5), 1458–1502. https://doi.org/10.1086/428444
Fischer, A. J., Collins, T. A., Dart, E. H., & Radley, K. C. (Eds.). (2019). *Technology applications in school psychology consultation, supervision, and training: Professional learning in school psychology series*. Routledge/Taylor & Francis Group.
Fletcher-Janzen, E., Strickland, T. L., & Reynolds, C. R. (Eds.). (2000). *Handbook of cross-cultural neuropsychology*. Springer Science & Business Media.
Fujii, D. (2017). *Conducting a culturally informed neuropsychological evaluation*. American Psychological Association. https://psycnet.apa.org/doi/10.1037/15958-000
Geissler, J., & Lesch, K.-P. (2011). A lifetime of attention-deficit/hyperactivity disorder: Diagnostic challenges, treatment and neurobiological mechanisms. *Expert Review of Neurotherapeutics, 11*(10), 1467–1484. https://doi.org/10.1586/ern.11.136
Germine, L., Reinecke, K., & Chaytor, N. S. (2019). Digital neuropsychology: Challenges and opportunities at the intersection of science and software. *The Clinical Neuropsychologist, 33*, 271–286. https://doi.org/10.1080/13854046.2018.1535662
Goldstein, S., & Naglieri, J. A. (2013). *Autism Spectrum rating scales: ASRS manual*. MHS.
Goldstein, S., & Naglieri, J. A. (2013). Autism spectrum rating scales: ASRS. MHS.
Graham, J. R. (2011). *MMPI-2: Assessing personality and psychopathology*. Oxford.
Hale, J. B., & Fiorello, C. A. (2004). *School neuropsychology*. Guilford.
Hall, A. P., Fong, T. G., & Epp, J. L. (2014). Cognitive and personality factors in the prediction of health behaviors: An examination of total, direct and indirect effects. *Journal of Behavioral Medicine, 37*, 1057–1068. https://doi.org/10.1007/s10865-013-9535-4
Halstead, W. C. (1947). *Brain and intelligence: A qualitative study of the frontal lobes*. University of Chicago Press.
Halstead, W. C., & Wepman, J. M. (1949). The Halstead-Wepman aphasia screening test. *Journal of Speech and Hearing Disorders, 14*, 9–13. https://doi.org/10.1044/jshd.1401.09
Hammer, M. R. (2013). Why should you consider using the Intercultural Development Inventory (IDI).
Hammer, M. R. (2015). The Developmental paradigm for intercultural competence research. *International Journal of Intercultural Relations, 48*(1), 12–13. https://doi.org/10.1016/j.ijintrel.2015.03.004
Hathaway, S. R., & McKinley, J. C. (1951). *Minnesota multiphasic personality inventory; manual (revised)*. Psychological Corporation.
Hartlage, L. C., Templer, D. I., & Cannon, W. G. (1992). *Preventable brain damage: Brain vulnerability and brain health*. Springer Publishing Company.
Individuals with Disabilities Education Act, 20 U.S.C. § 1400 (2004).
Johnson, J. A., & D'Amato, R. C. (2011). Evaluating and using the *Halstead-Reitan Neuropsychological Battery*: Is it our future or our past? In A. S. Davis (Ed.), *Handbook of pediatric neuropsychology* (Vol. I, pp. 353–366). Springer.
Kaplan, E. (1988). A process approach to neuropsychological assessment. In T. Boll & B. R. Bryant (Eds.), *Clinical neuropsychology and brain function: Research measurement, and practice: Master lectures*. The American Psychological Association.

Kaufman, A. S. & Kaufman, N. L. (2004). *Kaufman Assessment Battery for Children, Second Edition (KABC-2)*. Pearson.

Kaufman, A. S. & Kaufman, N. L. (2014). *Kaufman Test of Educational Achievement, Third Edition (KTEA-3)*. Pearson

Knoff, H. (2002). *The assessment of child and adolescent personality*. Guilford Press.

Korkman, M., Kirk, U., & Kemp, S. (2007). *NEPSY-II: Second edition: Clinical and interpretative manual*. Harcourt Assessment.

Kuther, T. L., & Burnell, K. (2019). A life span developmental perspective on psychosocial development in midlife. *Adultspan Journal, 18*(1), 27–39. https://doi.org/10.1002/adsp.12067

Lanyon, R. I., & Goodstein, L. D. (1997). *Personality assessment (3rd ed.)*. Wiley.

Lee, J., & Bean, F. D. (2004). America's changing color lines: Immigration, race/ethnicity, and multiracial identification. *Annual Review of Sociology, 30*, 221–242. https://doi.org/10.1146/annurev.soc.30.012703.110519

Luria, A. R. (1966). *The working brain: An introduction to neuropsychology*. Basic Books.

Luria, A. R. (1970). The functional organization of the brain. *Scientific American, 3*, 66–78. http://www.jstor.org/stable/24925755

Luria, A. R. (1973). *The working brain*. Penguin Press.

Lyons, H. Z., Bieschke, K. J., Dendy, A. K., Worthington, R. L., & Georgemiller, R. (2010). Psychologists' competence to treat lesbian, gay and bisexual clients: State of the field and strategies for improvement. *Professional Psychology: Research and Practice, 41*(5), 424–434. https://doi.org/10.1037/a0021121

Machover, K. (1949). American lectures in psychology: Vol. 25. In *Personality projection in the drawing of the human figure: A method of personality investigation*. Charles C. Thomas Publisher. https://doi.org/10.1037/11147-000

Mackler, K. (2017). Review of the Kaufman test of educational achievement, third edition. In J. F. Carlson, K. F. Geisinger, & J. L. Jonson (Eds.), *The twentieth mental measurements yearbook*. Buros Center for Testing.

Manly, T., Robertson, H. I., Anderson, V., & Nimmo-Smith, I. (1999). *Test of everyday attention for children* (TEA-Ch). Retrieved from http://eds.a.edscohost.com

Martin, N. A. & Brownell, R. (2011). *Expressive One-Word Picture Vocabulary Test-4 (EOWPT-4)*. Pearson

Mather, N., & Wendling, B. J. (2014). *Woodcock-Johnson IV tests of cognitive abilities*. Riverside.

McGrath, R. E., Powis, D., & Pogge, D. L. (1998). Code type-specific tables for interpretation of MMPI-2 Harris and Lingoes subscales: Consideration of gender and code type definition. *Journal of Clinical Psychology, 54*(5), 655–664. https://doi.org/10.1002/(SICI)1097-4679(199808)54:5%3C655::AID-JCLP11%3E3.0.CO;2-C

Murray, H. A. (1943). *Thematic apperception test*. Harvard University Press.

Naglieri, J. A., & Das, J. P. (1988). Planning-arousal-simultaneous-successive (PASS): A model for assessment. *Journal of School Psychology, 26*(1), 35–48. https://doi.org/10.1016/0022-4405(88)90030-1

Naglieri, J. A., McNeish, T., & Bardos, A. (1991). *DAP: Draw a person: Quantitative scoring system*. The Psychological Corporation.

Nichols, D. S. (2011). *Essentials of MMPI-2 assessment* (Vol. 88). Wiley.

Noogle, C. A., Davis, A. S., & Barisa, M. (2008). Neuropsychology and neuroimaging: Integrating and understanding structure and function in clinical practice. In R. C. D'Amato & L. C. Hartlage (Eds.), *Essentials of neuropsychological assessment: Treatment planning for rehabilitation* (2nd ed., pp. 79–104). Springer.

Pearson. (2019a). *Delis-Kaplan Executive Function System* (D-KEFS). Retrieved from https://www.pearsonclinical.com/psychology/products/100000618/deliskaplan-executive-function-system-d-kefs.html?origsearchtext=D-KEFS https://psycnet.apa.org/doi/10.1037/t15082-000

Pearson. (2019b). *Test of Memory and Learning* (TOMAL-2) (2nd ed.). Retrieved from https://www.pearsonclinical.ca/en/products/product-master/item-112.html

Perfect, M., & D'Amato, R. C. (2020). Introduction to special issue on the history of the future of proactive school psychology: Transcending the past, excel in the present, and transform the future. *School Psychology, 35*(6), 363–366. https://doi.org/10.1037/spq0000419

Pfannenstiel, J. C., Seitz, V., & Zigler, E. (2003). Promoting school readiness: The role of the Parents as Teachers program. *NHSA Dialog: A Research-to-Practice Journal for the early Intervention Field, 6*(1), 71–86. https://doi.org/10.1207/s19309325nhsa0601_6

Posner, M. I., & Petersen, S. E. (1990). The attention system of the human brain. *Annual Review of Neuroscience, 13*(1), 25–42. https://doi.org/10.1146/annurev.ne.13.030190.000325

Power, E., & D'Amato, R. C. (2018). Should our future include the integration of evidence-based neuropsychological services into school settings? In D. P. Flanagan & E. M. McDonough (Eds.), *Contemporary intellectual assessment: Theories, tests, and issues* (4th ed., pp. 1017–1045). Guilford.

Pratt, S. (2017). Review of the clinical evaluation of language fundamentals-fifth edition. In J. F. Carlson, K. F. Geisinger, & J. L. Jonson (Eds.), *The twentieth mental measurements year-book*. Buros Center for Testing.

Reitan, R. M. (1955). An investigation of the validity of Halstead's measure of biological intelligence. *Archives of Neurology and Psychiatry, 73*, 28–35. doi:10.1001/archneurpsyc.1955.02330070030005

Reitan, R. M. (1969). *Manual for the administration of neuropsychological test batteries for adults and children*. Author.

Reitan, R. M. (1974). Psychological effects of cerebral lesions in children of early school age. In R. M. Reitan & L. A. Davison (Eds.), *Clinical neuropsychology: Current status and applications* (pp. 53–90). Hemisphere Pub.

Reitan, R. M., & Wolfson, D. (1985). *The Halstead-Reitan neuropsychological test battery: Theory and clinical interpretation*. Neuropsychology Press.

Reitan, R. M., & Wolfson, D. (1992). Conventional intelligence measurements and neuropsychological concepts of adaptive abilities. *Journal of Clinical Psychology, 48*(4), 521–529. https://doi.org/10.1002/1097-4679(199207)48:4%3C521::AID-JCLP2270480414%3E3.0.CO;2-C

Reitan, R. M., & Wolfson, D. (1993). *The Halstead-Reitan neuropsychological test battery: Theory and clinical interpretation* (2nd ed.). Neuropsychology Press.

Reynolds, C. R., & Kampaus, R. W. (2015). *BASC 3: Behavior assessment system for children, third edition*. Pearson.

Reynolds, R. C., & Voress, K. J. (2007). Test of memory and learning, second edition. *Intelligence and General Aptitude*. Retrieved from http://eds.a.ebscohost.com

Rhodes, R. L., D'Amato, R. C., & Rothlisberg, B. A. (2009). Utilizing a neuropsychological paradigm for understanding educational and psychological tests. In C. R. Reynolds & E. Fletcher-Janzen (Eds.), *Handbook of clinical child neuropsychology* (3rd ed., pp. 321–348). Springer.

Roid, G. H. (2003). *Stanford-Binet intelligence scales*. Riverside Publishing Company.

Samovar, L. A., Porter, R. E., McDaniel, E. R. (2012). *Communication between cultures (8th ed)*. Wadsworth Publishing.

Sattler, J., Kilanowski, L. A., & Cosbey, J. (2014). Visual-motor perception and motor proficiency. In J. M. Sattler (Ed.), *Foundations of behavioral, social, and clinical assessment of children* (6th ed., pp. 395–412). Jerome M. Sattler Press.

Sattler, J. M., & D'Amato, R. C. (2002a). Brain injuries: Theory and rehabilitation programs. In J. M. Sattler (Ed.), *Assessment of children: Behavioral and clinical applications* (4th ed., pp. 401–439). J. M. Sattler Press.

Sattler, J. M., & D'Amato, R. C. (2002b). Brain injuries: Formal batteries and informal measures. In J. M. Sattler (Ed.), *Assessment of children: Behavioral and clinical applications* (4th ed., pp. 440–469). J. M. Sattler Press.

Schneider, J. M. (2007). Test review of Dean-Woodcock neuropsychological battery. In K. F. Geisinger, R. A. Spies, J. F. Carlson, & B. S. Plake (Eds.), *The seventeenth mental measurements yearbook*. Buros Institute of Mental Measurements, University of Nebraska-Lincoln. Retrieved from http://marketplace.unl.edu/buros/

Schrank, F., Mather, N., & McGrew, K., Wendling, B., & Woodcock, R. (2014). *Woodcock Johnson IV Tests of Cognitive Abilities (WJ IV COG)*. Riverside.

Schrank, F., Mather, N., & McGrew, K., Wendling, B., & Woodcock, R. (2014). *Woodcock Johnson IV Tests of Achievement (WJ IV ACH)*. Riverside.

Schultz, D. P., & Schultz, S. E. (2016). *A history of modern psychology* (11th ed.). Cengage.

Schneider, W. J., & McGrew, K. S. (2012). The Cattell-Horn-Carroll model of intelligence.

Selz, M. (1981). Halstead-Reitan neuropsychological test batteries for children. In G. W. Hynd & J. E. Obrzut (Eds.), *Neuropsychological assessment and the school-age child: Issues and procedures* (pp. 237–276). Grune & Stratton.

Semrud-Clikeman, M., & Teeter Ellison, P. A. (2009). *Child neuropsychology: Assessment and interventions for neurodevelopmental disorders* (2nd ed.). Springer.

Semrud-Clikeman, M., Wilkinson, A., & McMahon-Wellington, T. (2005). Evaluating and using qualitative approaches to neuropsychological assessment. In R. C. D'Amato, E. Fletcher-Janzen, & C. R. Reynolds (Eds.), *Handbook of school neuropsychology* (pp. 287–302). Wiley.

Snow, B., & Burns, M. (2000). Report of the National Reading Panel. Teaching children to read: an evidence-based assessment of the scientific research literature on reading and its implications for reading instruction.

Sexton, E. C., McDermott, L., Kalu, G. U., Herrmann, L. L., Bradley, M. K., Allan, L. C., … Ebmeier, P. K. (2012). Exploring the pattern and neural correlates of neuropsychological impairment in late-life depression. *Psychological Medicine, 42*, 1195–1202. https://doi.org/10.1007/S0033291711002352

Sinco, S. R., D'Amato, R. C., & Davis, A. S. (2008). Understanding and using the Halstead-Reitan neuropsychological test battery. In L. C. Hartlage & R. C. D'Amato (Eds.), *Essentials of neuropsychological assessment: Rehabilitation planning for intervention* (2nd ed., pp. 105–125). Springer.

Sparrow, S. S., Saulnier, C. A., Cicchetti, D. V., & Doll, E. A. (2016). *Vineland-3: Vineland adaptive behavior scales*. Pearson Assessments.

Spearman, C. (1904). "General intelligence:" objectively determined and measured. *American Journal of Psychology, 15*, 201–293.

Strauss, E., Sherman, E. M., & Spreen, O. (2006). *A compendium of neuropsychological tests: Administration, norms, and commentary*. American Chemical Society.

Tanaka, C., Matsui, M., Uematsu, A., Noguchi, K., & Miyawaki, T. (2012). Developmental trajectories of the fronto-temporal lobes from infancy to early adulthood in healthy individuals. *Developmental Neuroscience, 34*, 477–487. https://doi.org/10.1159/000345152

Taylor, R. (1998). Continuous norming: Improved equations for the WAIS-R. *British Journal of Clinical Psychology, 37*, 451–456. https://doi.org/10.1111/j.2044-8260.1998.tb01402.x

Teglasi, H. (2010). Essentials of psychological assessment series. In *Essentials of TAT and other storytelling techniques assessment* (2nd ed.). Wiley Inc.

Titley, J. E., & D'Amato, R. C. (2008). Understanding and using the NEPSY-II test for neuropsychological assessment for intervention. In R. C. D'Amato & L. C. Hartlage (Eds.), *Essentials of neuropsychological assessment: Rehabilitation planning for intervention* (2nd ed., pp. 149–172). Springer.

United States Census Bureau. (2018). Income and Poverty in the United States: 2018 [Data file]. Retrieved from https://www.census.gov/library/publications/2019/demo/p60-266.html

Van der Kolk, B. (2014). *The body keeps the score: Brain, mind, and body in the healing of trauma*. Penguin Books.

Volpe, A., Davis, A., & Dean, R. (2006). Predicting global and specific neurological impairment with sensory-motor functioning. *Archives of Clinical Neuropsychology, 21*(3), 203–210. https://doi.org/10.1016/j.acn.2005.12.005

Wechsler, D. (1939). *The measurement of adult intelligence*. Baltimore, MD: Williams & Wilkins. https://doi.org/10.1037/10020-000

Wechsler, D. (2003). *Wechsler intelligence scale for children* (4th ed.). Psychological Corporation.

Wechsler, D. (2008). *Wechsler adult intelligence scale* (4th ed.). NCS Pearson.

Wechsler, D. (2009). *Wechsler Individual Achievement Test, Third Edition (WIAT-III)*. Pearson.
Wechsler, D. (2012). *Wechsler preschool and primary scale of intelligence* (4th ed.). NCS Pearson.
Wechsler, D. (2014). *Wechlser Intelligence Scale for Children, Fifth Edition (WISC-V)*. Pearson.
Whitcomb, S. A., & Merrell, K. W. (2013). *Behavioral, social, and emotional assessment of children and adolescents* (4th ed.). Routledge/Taylor & Francis Group.
Witsken, D. E., D'Amato, R. C., & Hartlage, L. C. (2008). Understanding the past, present, and future of clinical neuropsychology. In *Essentials of neuropsychological assessment: Treatment planning for rehabilitation* (2nd ed., pp. 3–29). Springer.
Wiig, E. H., Semel, E., & Secord, W. A. (2013). *Clinical Evaluation of Language Fundamentals, Fifth Edition (CELF-5)*. Pearson.

Part IV
Interventions Driven by Behavioral Neuroscience

Chapter 11
Neuropsychologically Driven Evidence-Based Interventions in Clinical Psychology

Amanda Skierkiewicz and Tiffany Keller

Learning Objectives

- To understand the close relationship, similarities, and differences in the subdisciplines of clinical psychology and neuropsychology.
- To understand components of an evidence-based mindset within professional practice in clinical psychology.
- To understand the primary contributions of clinical neuropsychology to an integrative and evidence-based treatment approach to assessment and intervention.
- To understand specific issues related to multicultural competence and why it is essential to ethical practice in neuropsychology.
- To develop an understanding of how the fields of clinical psychology and neuropsychology interact in a symbiotic relationship to improve patient outcomes.

Introduction to Clinical Neuropsychological Services

In 2015, the American Psychological Association (APA) released new Standards of Accreditation (SOA) for graduate programs in psychology. Reflected heavily in these new standards are the competencies that leaders in the profession of psychology feel are critical to ethical practice of psychology with the public. For students of psychology, the successful attainment of these competencies creates the foundation for the practice of mental health in a landscape of integrated care (Smith, 2015).

A. Skierkiewicz (✉)
Neuropsychology, Landstrom Center, Schaumburg, IL, USA
e-mail: dramanda@landstromcenter.com

T. Keller
Department of School Psychology, The Chicago School of Professional Psychology, Chicago, IL, USA
e-mail: tkeller@thechicagoschool.edu

R. C. D'Amato et al. (eds.), *Understanding the Biological Basis of Behavior*,
https://doi.org/10.1007/978-3-030-59162-5_11

Health Service Psychologist is the newly adopted name for professional, licensed psychologists, trained in these competencies. Health Service Psychology is defined as "the integration of psychological science and practice in order to facilitate human development and functioning" (APA, 2017) and integrated care is the current direction in the field to better serve the public (Goodheart, 2011).

What is specifically lacking in the literature, is detail regarding how to take an integrative approach within the disciplines of clinical psychology and neuropsychology and how they can work together to provide the best outcomes for patients. The fields are often seen as separate and distinct in both applied research and in practice, although their origins and training are identical until the latter stages of training and specialization. Although both areas of practice prioritize diagnosis as the basis of all care, the primary identity in clinical psychology is that of therapist, whereas the primary identity for the neuropsychologist is evaluator or diagnostician. In this chapter, we propose aligning the distinct fields of practice and taking a more **integrative** approach to assessment, diagnosis, and treatment – one where the primary role of the clinical neuropsychologist is the diagnostician and consultant, and the clinical psychologist is treatment planner and provider. These lines, however, will not be distinct in the service of integrated care for the client. This melding is predicated on the notion that greater specificity in assessment yields far superior insight into cognitive and psychological processes, which, in turn, allows for a higher level of specificity in intervention selection to meet client needs. This chapter will explore the historical underpinnings of both clinical psychology and neuropsychology, what makes them distinct professions, how neuropsychologically-driven assessments can inform treatment planning, multicultural issues in neuropsychologically evidence-based interventions, and future directions for neuropsychological interventions as they relate to clinical psychology.

Lili is one such case example that highlights the importance of the intersectionality between clinical and neuropsychology. Lili presented as having never received psychotherapeutic or psychiatric interventions before. She is a 21-year-old college student who has a passion and talent for theatre and the arts. Academically, she has always done well, although she described quite a bit of organizational difficulties throughout her schooling. It was not until her sophomore year of college that academics became more of an issue. Lili described being "completely paralyzed by fear," feeling that she "must be perfect," "spends so much time in her head," "seems to be absorbed with anxious thoughts," and "hurts herself" – that latter behavior is not cutting or suicidality, but instead, doing things like pulling at her skin as an outlet for anxiety/to distract her mind from anxiety, and the like. As Lili's case unfolds throughout this chapter, we will highlight how her diagnostic evaluation led to targeted treatment recommendations and integrated care between neuropsychology, psychotherapy, psychiatry, and her university.

History and Foundations of Neuropsychologically Driven Evidence-Based Interventions in Clinical Psychology

Within the profession of clinical psychology, neuropsychology is a subspecialty. In practice, however, they seem to have distinct identities that can vary dramatically or closely parallel one another. Clinical psychology is an enormous umbrella under which many, sometimes disparate, yet interconnected, sub-specialties exist—in fact the APA has 54 divisions, many of which represent subdisciplines within the field. While at their foundation, neuropsychologists are indeed clinical psychologists, there are important differences in philosophy, training, and practice between the two. Although they come from the same origins and training programs, the profession and clinicians within each have taken slightly different approaches to the same goal of helping humans who are suffering with psychological maladies. What is shared, however, are the goals of thorough case conceptualization, formulation, and diagnosis-based treatment of psychological disorders. Training in clinical psychology has traditionally focused on the utilization of therapeutic frameworks to derive hypotheses, educate individuals about their syndromes, and plan and carry out interventions (Macniven, 2016).

Whereas the clinical psychologist focuses less on brain-based concerns, and historically more on personality and emotionally-based disorders, the neuropsychologist focuses more on the sequelae of brain and medical syndrome-based difficulties (Russell, 2012). The case formulation of the neuropsychologist will include added dimensions of neuropsychological data and neurological history, and there is typically less of an emphasis on the narrative history (Macniven, 2016). Of course, all psychological distress is "brain-based," including emotional and cognitive aspects, which interact and can result in a manifestation of several intermingling issues, so perhaps there is a way to better understand this when thinking about the philosophical and epistemological differences at the heart of these identities.

History of Clinical Psychology

Clinical psychology started as a discipline associated with research-based approaches to understanding the mind and behavior, using the scientific method and psychometrics to enhance understanding the individual rather than a group. Psychology split into two branches – scientific and professional – the latter specifically through the realm of clinical psychology, where the goal of the profession was to serve those suffering with mental illness and improve functioning in various settings (i.e., school, work, military; Watson, 1953). **Psychometric** approaches to understanding functioning first focused on cognitive and related sub-domains, and is the precursor to the specialty of neuropsychology. Other major fields influencing the training and practice of today's clinical psychologist include philosophy and medicine. The latter has influenced the *medical, or "disease" model* associated with many disorders, including substance abuse/dependence, ADHD, and schizophrenia. The philosophical influence is most closely associated with the *dynamic* tradition in clinical psychology that is found in many forms of personality theory, and where there is a focus on affective functioning and pathology (Watson, 1953). It is from this foundation that the basis for attachment theory, family or person-centered approaches, or the critical humanist traditions of existential and psychology of spirituality traditions arose. While all three of these major foundations were developing concurrently in the late nineteenth century, the "*clinic*" was where the psychologist practiced and put these theories and range of diagnoses and interventions to work. By the early twentieth century, clinical psychologists could be found in a multitude of settings, including hospitals, human-service agencies, and prisons. Always central among the tasks of the clinical psychologist has been **diagnostic appraisal** and **treatment** of the client (D'Amato et al., 2005; Lezak et at., 2012).

History of Clinical Neuropsychology

Neuropsychology is a specialty practice area within clinical psychology that coalesced by the 1960s, with a focus on understanding the brain-behavior relationship affecting functioning and adaptation (Lamberty & Nelson, 2012; Russell, 2012). Diagnostically, the primary goal of a neuropsychological evaluation is to identify and characterize brain-behavior relationships. This approach inherently differs from the categorical, behaviorally-defined criteria outlined in the DSM-5 (Koziol & Budding, 2012).

The roots of neuropsychology are in psychometric foundations of clinical psychology, as well as in medicine, specifically the specialties of psychiatry and neurology. The psychometric focus developed early in psychology's history by Wilhelm Wundt and Sir Francis Galton (Furr & Bacharach, 2014), which became the preferred way to create and analyze the effectiveness of measures, that categorize and differentiate levels of functioning, via systemizing observations of human behavior into units that can be measured, standardized, and compared. Psychometric data, as well as other clinically-acquired data, is used by the neuropsychologist to make inferences about the impact of brain impairment on functioning (Reynolds & Fletcher-Janzen, 2009).

Initially, the role of the neuropsychologist was to provide data pertaining to lesion location, or as to the presence or absence of brain damage (Postal & Armstrong, 2013). The advent of neuroimaging techniques shifted the focus of the field and thus the focus of the neuropsychologist. While imaging technology is able to capture great structural detail, it is not very useful in providing information about functional or degenerative processes of individual patients (Lezak et al., 2012). Thus, the field of neuropsychology turned a new corner, and psychometric results are now used to provide complex data related to an individual's adaptive functioning and what a specific impairment means for that person, and then communicate that information to the patient, their family, and any other providers (Postal & Armstrong,

2013). This goes well beyond offering a diagnosis, and includes relaying a detailed explanation of the assessment results, what those results mean in a larger, real-world context, and provision of relevant and feasible recommendations, all translated into consumable terms that the patient and family can understand.

In order to do this effectively, practitioners rely on valid and reliable instruments. The practice of psychometrics helps clinicians not only develop stronger instruments and continually evaluate their usefulness but also help discern whether a test produces scores that are psychologically meaningful and trustworthy (Furr & Bacharach, 2014). Application of quantitative methods and statistics allows clinicians to develop tests that are reliable and produce valid data. Neuropsychologists in particular, place a high value on objective and quantitative data as major contribution to the desire for specificity in the study of an individual's functioning and pathology. Not only must their instruments, which are the neuropsychologist's primary tools, be valid and reliable, but these measures must also be theoretically informed in their development. While much has been written about test descriptions and neuropsychological methodology, there is less of an emphasis placed on clinical interpretation (Russell, 2012).

Effective and accurate **measurement** of human behavior is the basis of sound neuropsychological practice. It is the foundation of science in general, and behavioral science in particular, to aid the attempt to understand or predict human behavior (D'Amato & Perfect, 2020). Development of individual targeted interventions, measurement of behavioral improvement in brain-behavior-based functioning, as well as group behavioral research, rely on sound data. While there are other forms of valuable data in the study of human behavior, such as qualitative methods, evidence-based practice and diagnosis rely heavily on quantitative data.

The development of intelligence testing and measurement of other cognitive faculties including sensory-motor functioning are the earliest manifestations of this approach and continue to be used today. Neuropsychology has developed different approaches and tools to measure brain-behavior relationships, including functional/structural approaches begun by Ward Halstead and popularized in his first battery of cognitive tests, the Halstead-Reitan (Reitan & Wolfson, 1993). Alexander Luria, in contrast, developed his theory of neural development and functioning on a process-based approach, which emphasized a qualitative approach to testing his theory with another well-known early battery of tasks, the Luria-Nebraska (Luria, 1973).

Competence in the field of neuropsychology was initially outlined by the APA Society for Clinical Neuropsychology, referred to as the Houston Conference Model, which repeatedly emphasized (1) the scientific processes, (2) psychometrics, (3) diversity/cultural factors, and (4) the relevance of changes throughout the lifespan. Notable statements include that the field of neuropsychology must be *scientist-practitioner* based, clinical neuropsychologist specializes in the application of assessment and intervention principles based on the *scientific study* of human behavior across the *lifespan* (Hannay et al., 1998).

Current State of Neuropsychology and Neuropsychological Evaluations Many older clinical psychologists and neuropsychologists were trained in an era that placed less of an emphasis on evidence-based practices and instead focused on gaining knowledge through "clinical experience." It is not difficult to see how the profession could have developed in such a way—there was less access to scientifically sound research and these methods were, at the time, less valued. Fortunately, the field has evolved in such a way that it now emphasizes scientific thinking and evidence-based practices in training. While these practices are not new, it is only recently that the field has transitioned from expertise based on *clinical experience* to an emphasis on *objective knowledge* resulting from conclusions derived from a scientist practitioner model (Bowden, 2017).

Although neuropsychological evaluations have not changed much since the 1980s, continuing to rely heavily on paper and pencil methods of assessment (albeit with ever-growing psychometric sophistication), the field has progressed significantly in its ability to accurately predict **premorbid** functioning and in determining whether or not a patient has intentionally underperformed or *malingered*. The applications of these methods have had a significant impact on practice within neuropsychology, as well as clinical and forensic psychology.

Estimating Premorbid Functioning

Assessment requires a standard by which to compare an individual's current performance, whether that is to a population average (normative) or to hypothetical averages (Franzen et al., 1997). While normative comparisons are appropriate in most evaluative contexts, in the assessment of individuals with traumatic brain injury or with known or suspected brain pathology, determining individual comparisons will be critical to assessing the level of decline (Lezak et al., 2012). It is important to consider cognitive changes ***intra*individually**, because an average or within normal limits (WNL) score can certainly represent a decline from what was a superior level of functioning for the client. In recent years, methods of estimating premorbid functioning have moved away from relying on subjective approaches and clinical judgement (Franzen et al., 1997). Methods of estimating **premorbid functioning** may include consideration of the individual's history, the use of demographic variables (i.e., age, education, occupation, sex, and ethnicity), performance on tasks thought to be more resistant to neurological insult (i.e., *hold* tests), and a combination of demographics and current functioning (Strauss et al., 2006). Word reading tests are often used as *hold* tests as they have been found to be strongly correlated with intellectual functioning, are typically resistant to acquired neurological conditions, and are able to be used across a variety of populations (Meyers et al., 2019; Price & Mechelli, 2005). Most estimates of premorbid functioning are geared toward estimating general intelligence or full-scale IQ (FSIQ). This estimate is often used to assume an individual's other areas of neuropsychological ability, though this can be problematic as some areas (e.g., executive functioning; EF) are not necessarily correlated with general intelligence and assuming a "change" in a specific area based on a more generalized impairment could be a faulty assumption (Davis et al., 2016).

Effort and Validity Testing

Effort testing involves determining whether or not an individual put forth a basic level of effort and/or complied with the demands of the test in order to do well (DeRight & Carone, 2015). The assessment of response bias has been one of the most prominent topics in clinical neuropsychology for the past 15 years (Boone, 2013). In fact, both the National Academy of Neuropsychology (NAN) and the American Academy of Clinical Neuropsychology (AACN) have published position papers regarding the use of Performance Validity Tests (PVTs) in assessments, and regard their use as important and necessary. Per a statement from a 2009 Consensus Conference hosted by AACN (Heilbronner et al., 2009), following current standards of practice should include formal measures of **response bias**. To be clear, that statement is in reference to all neuropsychological evaluations, whether clinical, forensic, school, or other. One reason behind this statement is that psychologists often falsely assume that they can detect when children and adolescents are giving subpar effort or, actively malingering, or assume that they are not sophisticated enough to *outsmart the clinician*. Some advocate that projective tests can be an important adjunct in understanding what is really going on with a client when they try to disguise their problems. For example, the Thematic Apperception Test and the Rorschach are often used in this fashion. See Chap. 10 for more details on projective measures. Research efforts have clearly established that relying on subjective behavioral observations alone is of *limited value* due to inaccuracy, and that children do indeed have the ability to be sophisticated in their deception efforts (Faust et al., 1988; Guilmette, 2013).

As an example of validity testing within an evaluation, Lili performed within normal limits on the stand-alone measures of basic effort as well as both tiers of memory tasks, resulting in a performance that is considered valid. She passed all embedded validity checks. Thus, the data would seem to support basic effort and shows no indication of active feigning. That being said, even on the basic effort tasks (and I cannot overstate how basic/easy/simple these tasks are), Lili made errors and performed more "in the grey/borderline" area of a range that, while still valid, was notable. Similar results were noted on the relatively easy memory task, including actual intrusions. In stark contrast, however, she performed better than many of the known "good effort "populations (including research controls explicitly instructed to give full effort as well as actual clinical groups whose valid performances were supported by other PVTs). Thus, I was really not at all concerned that Lili was not attempting to give her full effort or at all intending to skew the data, and instead consider that these findings suggest that some form of secondary influence was at play during the testing that the reader will want to keep in mind as they conceptualize the case (primarily anxiety-related acute emotional distress).

Lili's behavioral observations throughout testing are quite relevant to the interpretation of her results. While she was a willing participant in the evaluation and worked diligently and certainly seemingly to the best of her ability, she was easily flustered if she perceived that she did not perform well. This seemed to negatively impact her performance on subsequent subtests.

Brain-Based Understanding of Pathology and Neurodevelopment

All data gathered about a person's functioning must be considered using the developmental process as context to set expectations for typical functioning as a baseline for comparison. The **human brain** is an extremely complex organ that is not yet fully understood by researchers (Kolb & Whishaw, 2009). What makes people unique individuals (i.e., thoughts, feelings, and experiences), are stored in the brain (D'Amato et al., 2005). The field of neuropsychology attempts to understand the **intersection** between these different dimensions and potential secondary influences through a comprehensive evaluation.

Understanding the neurodevelopmental experience, for both typical and abnormal development, is of paramount importance when doing evaluations for pediatric and adolescent populations. Historically, psychological and psychiatric disorders were considered the same in both children and adults, and did not take developmental issues into account (Semrud-Clikeman & Teeter Ellison, 2009). As such, the field used adult assessments for younger populations—in essence, simply by considering them *little adults* (Noggle et al., 2013). Obviously, the brain is a highly complex organ, and our current understanding of neurobiology is really still in its infancy. However, we now know there is enough of a difference between the populations of adults and children for *pediatric neuropsychology* to be considered a subspecialty within the field.

While much about the brain is still unknown, neuroscience has advanced to the point where we can functionally and structurally understand sequential brain development (and specific variations), which can assist in determining appropriate and targeted interventions (Lezak et al., 2012; Nicholls, 2018; Riccio et al., 2010; Semrud-Clikeman & Teeter Ellison, 2009). The efficacy of many interventions are dependent on certain critical periods of development, or work best for certain dysfunctional neural systems. In the same manner that negative environmental experiences (e.g., TBI, trauma, toxin exposure) can impact the brain, *positive experiences* (e.g., enriching the environment, educational opportunities, interventions, therapeutic techniques) also have the capacity to alter brain development.

Neuropsychological principles contend that the brain is involved in all behaviors and learning processes (D'Amato et al., 2005). Mental health professionals, whether neuropsychologist or not, must carefully consider these principles in order to optimize treatment for children and adults, and produce the best outcomes, in order to enhance an individual's functioning and quality of life. Ultimately, the goal of neuropsychological evaluations is to help explain the areas of concern and provide an explanation as to *why* an individual is experiencing dysfunction and to provide salient treatment recommendations. Incorporation of neuropsychological methods (i.e., inclusion of cognitive and behavioral data into psychological and psychoeducational assessment), will provide a more holistic picture of the individual's functioning (Riccio et al., 2010). This, in turn, leads to greater specificity in intervention development improving outcomes.

Understanding People with ADHD Through a Neuropsychological Lens

The assessment and diagnosis of people with Attention-Deficit/Hyperactivity Disorder (ADHD) highlights the importance of understanding the hidden neuropsychological constructs and neurodevelopment of a disorder or syndrome. The *Diagnostic and Statistical Manual of Mental Disorders* (DSM-5; American Psychiatric Association, 2013), which is currently in its fifth edition,. attempts to standardize criteria for mental disorders in a common language. For the diagnosis of people with ADHD specifically, the DSM-5 lists 18 possible behavioral symptoms for the disorder, which allows for the condition to be subtyped (combined type, predominantly inattentive type, and predominately hyperactive-impulsive type; APA, 2013). The problem is that these behaviorally-based symptoms overlap with several other conditions. Also consider that, from a neurodevelopmental perspective, the behavioral phenotype of students with ADHD can change as a child ages or the environmental demands increase or decrease. Thus, the behavioral method of diagnosing people with ADHD is unstable and capricious (Koziol & Budding, 2012). While there are many advocates for using only rating scales to diagnose people with ADHD (Barkley, 2019), the heterogeneity of the disorder allows clinicians to identify specific deficits, subtypes, and provide appropriate recommendations (Koziol et al., 2015).

We now understand that the diagnostic catagory of ADHD involves several large-scale brain networks, and thus the functional neuroanatomy of ADHD is best understood within this context. For example, one child who appears *inattentive* may indeed have deficits with complex attention that warrant intervention with stimulant medication (along with other interventions), whereas another child, who has the same behavior profile of *inattentiveness*, may actually have deficits with cognitive proficiency (i.e., working memory and processing speed), which would require a different set of treatment recommendations (Koziol et al., 2013; Semrud-Clikeman & Teeter Ellison, 2009). To be clear, both approaches have value and provide unique contributions to conceptualizing concerns of the patient and guiding treatment (Koziol et al., 2015).

I really want to emphasize the interaction/influence between cognitive and emotional functioning manifesting in Lili's evaluation, as I think that is an important aspect that needs to be considered as interventions are implemented. That being said, emotional dysfunction is clearly the greater cause of functional impairment at this point, and while the specifics were not necessarily clear in a number of areas, I think it is more than safe to say that a **Mixed Anxiety Disorder** best characterizes Lili's current presentation. Her triggers are (at least) those of the Generalized and Social Anxiety Disorders with Test Anxiety and (again, at least) a Specific Phobia to driving. Manifestations of her anxiety include marked feelings of tension, apprehension, and nervousness that seem to be a persistent trait-like characteristic that reflects a dispositionally low threshold for the experience of events as dangerous/threatening – Lili clearly experiences a great deal of tension, has difficulty relaxing and is probably easily fatigued as a result of the high-perceived stress she is under. Further manifestations include autonomic nervous system-based physical symptoms, such as a racing heart, sweaty palms, rapid breathing, and dizziness, and it is not uncommon for patients with issues in this area to realize that what is happening is a psychological matter. Interestingly, the more routine physical complaints of somatization (headache, back problems, pain, and GI ailments) were not endorsed as much as I was expecting. While the thought disruptions were specifically correlated to test anxiety, I have to assume it goes further than that, and Lili frequently experiences floods of anxiousness (referred to as anxiety attacks) that are at least on the path towards, and probably often get to the point of, "full-blown" panic.There is also an aspect of **Depression** perhaps in response to the persistence of her anxieties over the years, but, at this point, her profile reflects a clinically significant depressive thought process that seems to go beyond simple negative affectivity as a direct reaction to the anxieties.While I did not have the same difficulty getting the specifics of Lili's cognitive profile from her in terms of *current functioning*, the level of acute anxiousness that she showed during the testing process does make it difficult to know what, if anything, would remain were her anxieties able to be magically factored out from the cognitive data. What I can say is that all three family members endorsed Lili's current cognitive dysfunction as clinically significant and much worse than in childhood (her mother did not even endorse cognitive dysfunction in childhood), but Lili did describe some behaviors sensitive to neurodevelopmental ADHD during that time period and it is within the realm of possibility that the two disorders present comorbidly.

That being said, *attentional capacity* (obtaining and maintaining attention) was shown to be *intact* on all but two scores, one of which was clearly an over-diligence issue while the other followed a pattern suggestive of non-neurological factors. In contrast, **executive control** skills were repeatedly shown to be an area of **deficiency** (which may be part of why Lili struggles to control her thoughts so much). Specifically, the data reflects a rather marked impulsivity problem along with milder "autopilot" tendencies, problematic shifting attention/mental control skills and what appears to be a deficiency with the mental manipulation aspect of working memory. Indeed, her higher order executive skills (mental organization in particular, but also planning, judgment, strategizing and the like) are also shown to be impaired, so the more appropriate diagnosis would be an **Executive Function Deficit** regardless of whether what was captured was simply the effect of her acute anxieties on her ability to utilize her executive skills on these tasks, or whether this is a primary common neurodevelopmental problem. While admittedly this is a bit of conjecture, my "gut reaction" to Lili's overall presentation says this is probably more the latter than the former, although certainly the severity would not be the same were she only dealing with either the emotional or cognitive problems alone, as we are really looking at a sizable "the whole is more than the sum of its parts" situation.

Clinical Psychology and the Biological Basis of Behavior

Until recently, much of the literature in behavioral sciences relied on anecdotal impressions—practitioners have unfortunately and inevitably relied on knowledge that has been gained through "*a mixture of truths, half-truths, and falsehoods*" (Meehl, 1997, p. 91). As a result, many practitioners have relied on **unscientific thinking** and the assumption that clinical experience alone is a valid source of knowledge and expertise in the field. Fortunately, there has been a shift in the field, and clinicians are now being trained in an era where scientific **research** informs clinical decision-making. Clinicians now rely on objective-knowledge from well-designed studies from both clinical psychology and neuropsychology and related fields to inform their day-to-day practice (Bowden, 2017).

Evidence-Based Practice

Evidence-Based Practice (EBP) is a frequently cited term in clinical psychology and mental health treatment in general, but what does it really mean and why is it so important? EBP refers to health service practice (including intervention choice and application) that is research-informed. Outcomes research in particular, has a recent history informing mental health practice as a type of applied research. This approach has continued to help develop a bridge between research and clinical practice in order to prove that treatments were effective (Kazdin, 2008, 2020). The push of the profession toward EBP came out of concerns about rising health care costs in the age of managed care, and also from a desire to police the public interest by monitoring protracted treatments in medicine, including specifically within mental health (Chelune, 2010).

EBP is defined by the APA as clinical treatment decisions made through the integration of client needs and characteristics, the best, clinically relevant research, and likely, costs of treatment (APA, 2005). EBP research uses measurement of events or specific intervention moments in treatment to assess impact on the patient (APA, 2005). When there is some structure or standardization to the intervention, this outcome data can be amassed from many patients to more reliably measure the efficacy of the treatment itself, while it can also be used by the individual provider to assess individual client improvement (Bower, 2003; Spring, 2007).

Evidence-Based Practice in Neuropsychology

EBP within a neuropsychological practice specifically, includes this core definition, but also considers the role of clinical neuropsychologist as diagnostician and thus focuses on accurate and useful assessment in order to provide high quality patient care (Bowden, 2017). Chelune (2010) proposed that a definition of **evidence-based practice** in clinical neuropsychology should integrate clinical experience and proficiency with the best available outcomes research – all being done within the context of the patient's unique characteristics and circumstances. As such, there is a reduced emphasis on *subjective* clinical opinion and taking reports at face value, but instead relying on a rigorous evidence-based (*objective*) approach. This requires the use of reliable, well-validated assessment measures. While entire books can be written on the topic of psychometrics and validity, for the purposes of this chapter, the reader needs to be aware of two concepts: (1) the diagnostic *sensitivity* of a test (the extent to which a test correctly identifies people with the condition), and (2) diagnostic *specificity* (the extent to which the test correctly identifies people without the condition (Bowden, 2017). The referral question underlying the collaborative relationship must be integrated into the picture as well. If the clinical neuropsychologist intends to follow the objectives of EBP, they must consider the referral question and the concerns of specific referral sources and decide how much assessment is necessary to appropriately achieve the specificity and accuracy of diagnosis. The clinician's expertise is counted on throughout the decision-making process, so that EBP is a **dynamic process** existing between researcher and clinician or data and clinical judgment (Kazdin, 2008, 2020). Simple data, familiar to the neuropsychologist and clinical psychologist, such as knowing **base rates** of different disorders, is crucial to clinical decision-making and can also make this practice simpler than first suggestion may imply (Chelune, 2010). It is important that all practitioners in applied settings adopt evidence-based practices, to be good consumers of research and to stay up-to-date with relevant research and practices within the field.

Prior to coming to my office, Lili sought consultation with a psychiatrist for her initial mental health consultation. From the point of view of her family, the purpose of the evaluation was to collect data, insights, and recommendations to be used in the treatment planning, particularly from what seemed to be anxiety-based emotional. From Lili's point of view, the purpose of the evaluation was to improve her productivity, as either cognitive or emotional dysfunction – or more likely a combination of the two – hindering her ability to complete tasks and various school-related requirements.Moving forward with planning the assessment battery and considering rating scales to administer, it was important to consider the perspective and concern of each individual involved in the case – and how they will ultimately play a role in the treatment process.

Evidence-Based Practices with Interventions in Neuropsychology

While neuropsychology has long used empirical research in its practices, it is only recently that the use of evidence-based practices has become more widespread (Chelune, 2010). It is certainly beyond the scope of this chapter to provide an exhaustive list of all possible diagnostic criteria and evidence-based interventions; graduate training does not equip us to walk away knowing every possible diagnostic classification. Rather, the purpose of graduate training in psychology is to equip us to know how to research and reference source material. What we hope to convey to those in training and even seasoned practitioners is that the goal of this or any one text is not to walk away with a simple decision-tree of diagnosis→intervention, but rather to be able to critically analyze case information, develop appropriate case conceptualizations based on integrated objective data, which, in turn, informs specified interventions and treatment recommendations.

Differential Diagnosis and Clinical Neuropsychology Interventions

In clinical neuropsychology, several considerations should be made once a differential diagnosis has been made. The clinician should consider if attempts should be made to remediate a deficit through intervention or provide accommodations, or some combination of the two. It is also the duty of the clinician to present recommendations that are appropriately linked to the identified area of need in the assessment (Riccio et al., 2010), which is frequently done through a feedback session and ideally, a treatment-planning meeting with multidisciplinary professionals. We would argue that the feedback session is a primary intervention of the clinical neuropsychologist, typically conducted with the patient and/or the patient's family following the evaluation and later, ideally, continued through consultation with other treating professionals, including the clinical psychologist. This provides an opportunity for psychoeducation about the specific strengths and weaknesses in their cognitive and psychological profile, and to engage in a conversation about the feasibility of interventions – this encompasses the patient's wishes, and availability of resources (e.g., time, financial, transportation, practicality). Gorske (2008) suggests it is most therapeutic to approach feedback as a dynamic discussion in order to keep the evaluation process relevant and responsive to the needs of the identified client and their supports. It is during this time that the neuropsychologist is able to fully explain the assessment results, frame them in a way that they are understood, and hear and consider multiple perspectives. If done well, the session can dissuade inaccurate perceptions, but can also guide a patient into considering psychotherapy as an option (Postal & Armstrong, 2013). Arming patients with accurate and useful information allows them to **advocate for their needs** and feel empowered to access new resources. This provides patients with hope that improvement is possible, which often requires taking ownership of one's recovery process and taking one strategy/intervention/step at a time (Nicholls, 2018). One can teach patients that they are *building a boat*, and to not get overwhelmed by looking at the entirety of the sea.

Neuropsychological Interventions with Children

For pediatric and adolescent evaluations, one commonly overlooked aspect is to involve the child in the evaluation process and the feedback session in particular. All too often, intake sessions, school meetings, and/or feedback sessions are done without the individual being evaluated having an understanding of why they are being evaluated or even told about the results. Many children and adolescents who qualify for additional services at school under **Special Education law**, such as an Individualized Education Plan (IEP; IDEA part of ADA 2004) or Section 504 Plan (Section 504 of the United States Rehabilitation Act, 1973), often do not even know such a plan exists—much less what curricular modifications or accommodations have been afforded to them (D'Amato et al., 2005). Thus, we implore all providers to **advocate** for involving the child or adolescent in feedback sessions and explaining results and recommendations in a developmentally appropriate way. Direct feedback has been shown in research to predict best outcomes and have positive therapeutic effects on clients (Gorske, 2008). Thus, feedback is seen as a *crucial intervention* before the actual treatment even begins.

Multistage Neuropsychological Assessment-Intervention Model

Semrud-Clikeman and Teeter Ellison (2009) developed the Multistage Neuropsychological Assessment-Intervention Model (MNM), connecting assessment and intervention. This model suggests that assessment and intervention do not exist as two distinct and separate phases, but rather present options for ongoing evaluation and remediation efforts – pinging back and forth, continually fine-tuning the rehabilitation process until support is no longer needed by the client. Thus, it seems that clinical and neuropsychologists working together to create an assessment battery that best captures the referral question allows for the combined effect of their expertise. Both the fields of clinical psychology and neuropsychology hold the view that in order to establish that a particular treatment works, it must demonstrate worthwhile clinical effects that are carefully controlled, can be replicated under observational studies, or single-case designs using multiple baselines (Strauss et al., 2006). It is no longer sufficient to use anecdotal information from a single case to support a claim that a treatment works. As such, in clinical or applied settings, in order to determine if a treatment has worked, it is common to monitor a patient over time and assess any changes in performance (hopefully improvement) on neuropsychological assessment measures. In this case, the traditional normative bases of the test are of limited application, and instead the clinician relies on intra-individual change. The concept of a *Reliable Change Index* or RCI provides an index of relative change and provides a metric for determining statistically significant change. Put simply, an RCI is like a repeated measures *t*-test for the individual. Many popular tests now have RCIs already provided within the manual and are listed on the protocol; however, the RCI can also be calculated by hand (Bowden, 2017).

Because many of the measures used by neuropsychologists are performance-based, they have the potential to be susceptible to learning effects or "practice effects" (Mitrushina et al., 2005), which is of great concern to practitioners who may need to do serial assessments. Some models of RCI have taken practice effects into account and attempt to mitigate their potential impact (Hinton-Bayre, 2012). It is important to keep in mind that while RCI represents a statistically significant change, it does not imply a *clinically meaningful* change. Instead, RCI is seen as the minimum qualification, or a precursor, to clinically meaningful change (Hinton-Bayre & Kwapil, 2017). We must always remember the complexity of this profession and the necessity to use all the tools we have at our disposal to inform and assess care.

In addition to assessment, feedback, and consultation, neuropsychologists can be the primary (or one of the primary) interventionists alongside clinical psychologists and other mental and general health professionals. Interventions can take place in a school, a hospital, a rehabilitation facility, a clinic, or an outpatient practice. Riccio et al. (2010) note "*most* neuropsychological interventions *are multidimensional and incorporate academic, behavioral, and psychotherapeutic techniques but also include motivational, metacognitive, medical, and classroom management techniques*." This alone highlights the necessity for multidisciplinary and integrative approach to treatment, including other mental health providers, medical professionals, teachers, and family. Terms, such as rehabilitation, remediation, accommodation, and of course, intervention and therapy, are primary terms associated with the brain-based interventions neuropsychologists employ and recommend. Knowledge of neurodevelopment and impact of brain dysfunction on typical functioning and adaptation allows the neuropsychologist to holistically incorporate knowledge about the client's dependency and ability levels, their preserved and impaired functions and levels of insight and metacognition to determine individualized plans for rehabilitation (Riccio et al., 2010). Just as importantly, ongoing strides by neuroscientists to understand brain plasticity is heavily influencing development of neuropsychological intervention.

Brain plasticity, or neuroplasticity, is the brain's ability to change in response to development, the environment (including learning and intervention), injury, or aging (Kleiner, 2018). Early understanding of brain development and structure has evolved significantly beyond the notion of strict localization for each function and skill performed by the brain. We now understand that function is not strictly localized and that in the case of acquired injury or loss of function of a particular structure or region of the brain, adjacent structures will compensate (Noggle et al., 2013). Thus, they note, "*the brain is malleable and capable of dynamic reorganization*" (p. 14) following an injury or other complications arising in development. Recovery from a brain injury illness-induced event is often thought to essentially consist of two-phases; acute recovery and long-term recovery. The first phase is often managed medically, with perhaps some neuropsychologically informed cautions for protection from further damage. The second phase, lasting much longer and needing to accommodate the client's life adaptation needs through a changing recovery landscape, is where neuropsychological cognitive rehabilitation in particular is useful. Thus, rehabilitation and neuropsychological intervention are highly influenced by this knowledge and the understanding of how the brain heals and adapts over time. This knowledge is not just helpful to a client who suffered from brain injury or is recovering from surgery to address a tumor or seizure, but beyond these typical areas are often seen as points of intervention for neuropsychology, as a larger world of potential impact.

Clinical Psychology and Multicultural Issues

With a focus on individual assessment data, functioning, and pathology, do neuropsychologists equally consider environmental impact on brain and behavior or is the focus primarily on the individual and what is biologically based? Lamberty and Nelson (2012) suggests it is vital to the work that clinicians consider environment and biological bases of behavior equally. Miller (2013) contends that "*neuropsychology has tended to underemphasize and underestimate the potential influence of cultural factors on valid assessment*" (p. 5). Two theorists, Vygotsky and Luria, centered their significant contributions to understanding cognitive development on culture and environment (Hunter & Donders, 2007). These theories are the bases for explaining typical cognitive development of all humans and describe that culture and environmental exposure are the media through which we develop. Assessment and intervention, including cognitive rehabilitation in neuropsychology, are all heavily influenced by these theories. The actual wiring and firing of neuronal networks are shaped by individual culture and environment as much as by the genetics or typical biological-developmental course shared among humans. Li (2003) proposed a model that incorporates the **dynamic interplay of culture and biology** across the lifespan. He described the reciprocal and dynamic process by which genetics and neuronal mechanisms interface with environment and culture to determine development based in concepts such as brain plasticity.

Multicultural Issues in Assessment

Historically, most clinical research and normative sampling were completed on individuals who are middle-class and Caucasians (Semrud-Clikeman & Teeter Ellison, 2009). Since many neuropsychological tests are not available in other languages, one common practice is to simply translate the test. This can be problematic for many reasons—this practice is often done without understanding the culture or the language in which the test will be used. As such, lower scores are often seen on assessment measures from members of ethnically and culturally diverse groups (D'Amato et al., 2005). A thorough evaluation should include questions examining language use of the patient and the family. This process is often overlooked or the assumption is made that English is a primary language. Record review, parent interview, including language or languages used at home, age of acquisition of each language, preferred spoken language, preferred language for reading, listening to music, etc., should be considered. It is important to note that frequency of use should not be an indicator of language proficiency. If language proficiency is a question, language proficiency measures in both languages should be incorporated into the assessment (D'Amato et al., 2005).

Earlier in this chapter, we highlighted the **evaluation** as the foundation of intervention, and the first intervention was described as the assessment process itself along with feedback to clients and others. Multiculturally competent practice is crucial to the success of these interventions. First, the assessment tools and the interpretation of the data they provide, must be understood in a cultural context, and the limitations of the instruments must be actively considered throughout. As Gorske (2008) and others have noted, dynamic and collaborative post-assessment feedback can be experienced as empowering and useful to the client, which is crucial to success of follow-up interventions and recommendations. Research specifically on competence in treating diverse populations has shown that cultural minority clients are more likely to drop out of treatment or not adhere to treatment recommendations at a higher rate due to frustrations of feeling misunderstood (Sue & Zane, 1987). We cannot impose our view of the problem or pathology on clients. This can be avoided by first understanding the client's conceptualization of the *problem*, including what they call it, when they feel it started, how they would know if it was gone, and how it impacts their lives. We might find evidence of other deficits, but if these deficits were not defined or do not fit into the problem picture from the client's point of view, we must consider that the "deficits" do not truly exist just because a finding does not match expectations set by the norms. In simple terms, do not look upon data or definitions of problems as *universal*, but rather always consider the *relative* impact on the individual. Miller (2013) suggested that neuropsychologists are not as aware generally of the impact of culture on patients' lives and experiences as clinical psychologists given the neuropsychologists' immersion in brain-behavior relationships and less on the dynamics of relations and social contexts.

Why Neuropsychological Interventions are Critical in Clinical Practice

The fields of clinical psychology and neuropsychology are often viewed as separate and distinct entities. However, we propose that the two fields should have a more synergistic relationship and approach to patient care. As stated previously, each field brings its own unique perspectives and contributions to approaching diagnosis and treatment, and by inviting collaboration, we can only improve our understanding of our patients, and ultimately treatment outcomes.

Communicating Assessment Results to Other Professionals

Neuropsychological assessment results to other professionals is done through a combination of the written report, interdisciplinary meetings, and direct consultations. Regardless of the method used, it is essential to effectively and efficiently communicate results to referral sources and other treating providers, which ultimately supports patient care (Postal & Armstrong, 2013). Thus, it is important to build and maintain collegial relationships with other colleagues that invite open dialogues about patients. One often overlooked aspect of the neuropsychologist's practice is the report. It is the document that

> *"formally presents the clinical neuropsychologist's integration and interpretation of all available information, along with a logical set of conclusions and recommendations. It is an important piece of feedback to the referring agent and the patient, and provides a permanent record of the service"* (Donders, 2016).

It is absolutely consequential to outcomes as it guides future treatment and serves as a "road map" to treatment providers. Thus, it is important to establish validity of the testing results as they are then used to guide in the treatment process. It is through this document that the neuropsychologist communicates all relevant findings and allows the treating provider to obtain a clear and thorough understanding of the patient in order to most accurately apply the most appropriate evidence-based interventions. Think of trying to navigate your way through the Grand Canyon without a tour guide – you might make your way through, but you may occasionally get lost, hit some dangerous terrain, or not find the most scenic areas. Navigating treatment without a report is similar to that of the clinician blindly meandering through treatment without really knowing where they are going.

An Integrated Approach to Diagnosis and Treatment

To highlight, one common area of treatment for both clinical psychologists and neuropsychologists is both acquired and genetic neurological disorders and conditions (e.g., traumatic brain injury, stroke, brain tumors, Parkinson's, dementia, substance use, infections). As mentioned previously, the brain is responsible for regulating emotional, cognitive, and physical functions and damage to any one domain can impact another. For example, if an individual were to suffer a TBI, there are common cognitive deficits that may result from that injury. However, often overlooked is the **emotional impact** of such an injury and the role of a psychotherapist is often underutilized in these cases because the physical and cognitive recovery is typically the forefront of intervention (Ruff & Chester, 2014).

In such cases, a clinical neuropsychologist may be utilized to provide a comprehensive picture of the patient's cognitive and emotional profile, which can then be used by a **multidisciplinary team** targeting identified areas for cognitive rehabilitation, as well as supporting the patient in adjustment and acceptance post-injury. A collaboration between the psychotherapist and the neuropsychologist would be of paramount importance, because the neuropsychological evaluation will help to identify deficits in cognitive process, which could inform the psychotherapist about modifications that may be necessary in treatment planning.

The role of the clinical neuropsychologist is intended to be ongoing wherein consultations with the psychotherapist and patient would occur, and may even provide follow-up assessment either following the provision of services. This way outcomes are measured and the patient is able to see a tangible record of their progress, which may also provide emotional reassurance and foster additional psychological healing. Additionally, if some deficits continue to be present, it allows the interventionist to "shore up" any treatments and specifically target anything that may need to be targeted.

As was mentioned at the outset of the chapter, Lili's case really exemplifies an integrated model for mental health case. She was referred back to her psychiatrist, and to answer her referral question the impression from the evaluation was that there is a frontally-mediated executive dyscontrol issue contributing to Lili's overall current presentation. However, her profile largely does not suggest actual problems with attention capacity itself, and even if the subtle indicated reflected a true deficit, she is likely experiencing too much anxiety for a stimulant to be of much benefit at this point. Instead, she would likely benefit from focused pharmacotherapies, such as SSRIs and an as needed benzodiazepine. Even more important than the pharmacotherapy, was the recommendation that Lili start psychotherapy. Cognitive Behavioral Therapy (CBT) holds the highest level of research support for the treatment of anxiety-related disorders – the combination of medication and psychotherapy is shown to have the greatest efficacy in treatment. Lili's treatment was also to involve heavy psychoeducation as she was not fully "on board" because of the perceived stigma and lack of awareness of her anxiety. In terms of neurointerventions, Lili was recommended for Executive Skills Training taking a "bottom up" approach to explicitly teach how to adjust and function with the higher order deficits seen in Lili's profile. Lili would also benefit from some EF-based cognitive rehabilitation training in tandem with the application, implementation, and maintenance portions of the training.

Given Lili's difficulties with school, she was encouraged to provide a copy of her neuropsychological report to the student services department on campus in order to be considered for accommodations moving forward. To highlight, some of the recommendations included an alternate test taking environment so that that her limited pool of cognitive resources can be devoted to test taking, extended time for test taking due to slower processing speed with greater cognitive demands, breaks when anxieties "flare up," and the ability to audiotape lectures and to be provided with a set of lecture notes ahead of time to help factor out the impact of inattention/working memory issues.

Evidence-Based Interventions in Clinical Neuropsychology and its Relationship to the Future

Unfortunately, the collegial and collaborative relationship described between clinical psychologists and clinical neuropsychologists is not commonly found. The typical model is that the two professions are seen and considered as separate and distinct entities. Moving forward, imagine a more **integrated model**, where psychologists are involved in interdisciplinary teams, with each provider contributing their expertise to the pool of knowledge about the patient. In this age of evidence-based practice, assessment techniques and intervention methods are becoming more refined such that patients are able to fully understand their neuropsychological profiles, engage in intervention options specifically targeting their deficits, and have treatment and diagnostic providers collaborating with one another on a continuing basis.

Ultimately, Lili did follow-up on her treatment recommendations. As anticipated, she had some initial issues with the stigma surrounding the idea of being in treatment. While away at school, she did not want to "be seen" at the college counseling center, so she ultimately chose to commute home to see a psychotherapist. In the same practice, she was able to see a neuropsychologist for executive skills training. By seeing both interventionists with different specialties, she was able to focus her treatment goals with each, while the interventionists were able to collaborate on her case. Each interventionist was able to address the psychoeducation component from a different lens, contributing to her understanding of her profile, the importance of treatment, and treatment goals.

Given Lili's hesitation to initiate pharmacotherapy and engage with school services, a component of Lili's intervention work involved psychoeducation centered specifically around the benefits of those and exploring her reluctance. I am happy to report that Lili did eventually follow up with her psychiatrist and was prescribed an SSRI and a prn benzodiazepine. She described how much better she felt on the medications as she really did not know a life without anxiety. As far as the school accommodations, Lili did eventually reach out to her professors and explain her situation and formally request accommodations. This allowed her to feel more comfortable with discussing herself, asking for help when she needed it, and ultimately be more successful in school.When Lili began interventions, she was finishing up her final year of undergraduate work. At the time of her evaluation, she was massively behind in most of her classwork, was unaware of most of her assignments, and even unsure if she would earn all of her credits in her final semester to graduate. Due to the collaborative response of multiple providers and a lot of hard work on Lili's part, she was able to graduate that final semester. She was accepted into graduate school and she decided to enroll. At present, she continues her work with each interventionist, has regular appointments with her psychiatrist, and actively uses her school accommodations.

Conclusions

In this era of rapidly evolving scientific knowledge, it is critical for all health service providers, including clinical neuropsychologists, to continue to develop increasingly advanced assessment techniques and evaluate the outcome of intervention methods. Having a **neurodevelopmental** perspective will provide a foundation for the clinician to fully understand **brain-behavior relationships** and convey results in a meaningful way. Increasing collaborative efforts between providers allows for the expertise of providers to be added to all aspects of patient care, which ultimately serves the *best* interest of the patient while also providing the *best* outcomes.

Discussion Questions:

1. How is neuropsychology different from clinical psychology?
2. Why is it important to understand premorbid functioning when conducting a clinical neuropsychological evaluation with someone who sustained a Traumatic Brain Injury?
3. Describe methods (I.e., hold tests) that are used to estimate a patient's premorbid functioning.
4. What multicultural issues must be considered when conducting a clinical neuropsychological evaluation?
5. Why are neuropsychological evidence-based interventions critical to effective clinical psychology practice?
6. What are the benefits of using an integrated model for the future when providing clinical neuropsychological services?

EPPP Sample Questions

1. How does integration of clinical psychology and clinical neuropsychology improve treatment outcomes for clients?
   a. It gives clients more services for the same cost
   b. The integration of these two areas is directly identified and instructed by Evidence Based Practice (EBP) guidelines such as the American Psychological Association policy
   c. It is an example of EBP recommendations to use a variety of techniques to guide assessment, treatment planning, and identification and tailoring of treatment strategies and modalities for patients
   d. It is not clear that integration does improve treatment outcomes

2. What form of data has clinical psychology often singularly relied upon in its history, which is no longer identified as best practice?
    a. Clinical judgment
    b. Empirical outcome data
    c. Data from multiple sources and multiple methods
    d. Qualitative research-based data
3. When considering cost in determining assessment plans and treatment options for clients, clinicians should:
    a. Not consider cost in making decisions about assessment or treatment
    b. Weigh all risks and benefits of recommended assessment or treatment plan
    c. Choose assessments and treatment plans prioritizing the need to reduce cost for clients
    d. Present options and then leave decision to client
4. The Halstead-Reitan Neuropsychological Battery was derived from:
    a. A process-based, qualitative approach
    b. Studies of patients with neurological impairments
    c. Very little research foundation
    d. A specific theory of cognitive processing
5. The purpose of a neuropsychological evaluation is to:
    a. Determine a cognitive pattern of strengths and weaknesses
    b. Assist in the treatment planning process and target specific interventions
    c. Diagnostic clarity
    d. All of the above

Answers: C, A, B, B, D

Proactive Readings

Transcending the Past

D'Amato, R. C., Fletcher-Janzen, E., & Reynolds, C. R. (2005). *Handbook of school neuropsychology*. John Wiley & Sons.

Kazdin, A. E. (2008). Evidence-based treatment and practice: New opportunities to bridge clinical research and practice, enhance the knowledge base, and improve patient care. *American Psychologist, 63*(3), 146–159.

Excelling in the Present

Hinton-Bayre, A. D. & Kwapil, K. (2017). Best practice approaches for evaluating significant change for individuals. In Bowden S. C. (Ed.), *Neuropsychological assessment in the age of evidence-based practice: Diagnostic and treatment evaluations.* Oxford University Press.

Koziol, L. F. & Budding, D., (2012). Requiem for a diagnosis: Attention-Deficit Hyperactivity Disorder. *Applied Neuropsychology: Child, 1*(1), 2–5. https://doi.org/10.1080/21622965.2012.665774

Transforming the Future

Nicholls, C. J. (2018). *Neurodevelopmental disorders in children and adolescents: A guide to evaluation and treatment.* Routledge.

Postal, K. & Armstrong, K. (2013). *Feedback that sticks: The art of effectively communicating neuropsychological assessment results.* Oxford University Press.

References

American Psychiatric Association. (2013). *Diagnostic and statistical manual of mental disorders* (5th ed.). Arlington, VA: American Psychiatric Association.

American Psychological Association. (2005). *Report of the 2005 presidential task force on evidence-based practice.* https://www.apa.org/practice/resources/evidence/evidence-based-report.pdf

American Psychological Association. (2017). *Standards of accreditation for health service psychology.* https://www.apa.org/ed/accreditation/about/policies/standards-of-accreditation.pdf

Barkley, R. (2019). Neuropsychological testing is not useful in the diagnosis of ADHD: Stop it (or prove it)! *The ADHD Report, 27*(2), 1–8. https://doi.org/10.1521/adhd.2019.27.2.1

Boone, K. B. (2013). *Clinical practice of forensic neuropsychology: An evidence-based approach.* The Guilford Press.

Bowden, S. C. (2017). *Neuropsychological assessment in the age of evidence-based practice: Diagnostic and treatment evaluations.* Oxford University Press.

Bower, J. (2003). Efficacy in evidence-based practice. *Clinical Psychology & Psychotherapy, 10,* 328–336. https://dx.doi.org/10.5688%2Fajpe807123

Chelune, G. (2010). Evidence-based research and practice in clinical neuropsychology. *The Clinical Neuropsychologist, 24*(3), 454–467. https://doi.org/10.1080/13854040802360574

D'Amato, R. C., Fletcher-Janzen, E., & Reynolds, C. R. (2005). *Handbook of school neuropsychology.* Wiley.

D'Amato, R. C., & Perfect, M. (2020). History of the future of proactive school psychology: Historical review at our 75th APA anniversary to transcend the past, excel in the present, and transform the future. *School Psychology, 35*(6), 375–384. https://doi.org/10.1037/spq0000420

Davis, A., Finch, W., Drapeau, C., Noggin, M., Moss, L. E., & Moore, B. (2016). Predicting verbal fluency using word reading: Implications for premorbid functioning. *Applied Neuropsychology. Adult, 23*(6), 403–410. https://doi.org/10.1080/23279095.2016.1163262

DeRight, J., & Carone, D. A. (2015). Assessment of effort in children: A systematic review. *Child Neuropsychology: A Journal on Normal and Abnormal Development in Childhood and Adolescence, 21*(1), 1–24. https://doi.org/10.1080/09297049.2013.864383

Donders, J. (2016). *Neuropsychological report writing: Evidence-based practice in neuropsychology*. Guilford Press.

Faust, D., Hart, K., & Guilmette, T. (1988). Pediatric malingering: The capacity of children to fake believable deficits on neuropsychological testing. *Journal of Consulting and Clinical Psychology, 56*(4), 578–578. https://psycnet.apa.org/doi/10.1037/0022-006X.56.4.578

Franzen, M., Burgess, E., & Smith-Seemiller, L. (1997). Methods of estimating premorbid functioning. *Archives of Clinical Neuropsychology, 12*(8), 711–738. https://doi.org/10.1016/S0887-6177(97)00046-2

Furr, R., & Bacharach, V. (2014). *Psychometrics: An introduction* (2nd ed.). Sage Publications, Inc..

Goodheart, C. (2011). Psychology practice: Design for tomorrow. *American Psychologist, 66*(5), 339–347. https://psycnet.apa.org/doi/10.1037/a0024222

Gorske, T. T. (2008). Therapeutic neuropsychological assessment: A humanistic model and case example. *Journal of Humanistic Psychology, 48*(3), 320–339. https://doi.org/10.1177%2F0022167807303735

Guilmette, T. J. (2013). The role of clinical judgment in symptom validity assessment. In D. Carone & S. H. Bush (Eds.), *Mild traumatic brain injury* (pp. 31–43). Springer.

Hannay, H. J., Bieliauskas, L., Crosson, B. A., Hammeke, T. A., Hamsher, K. d S., & Koffler, S. (1998). Proceedings of the Houston Conference on specialty education and training in clinical neuropsychology. *Archives of Clinical Neuropsychology, Special Issue, 13*, 157–250. https://doi.org/10.1093/arclin/13.2.157

Heilbronner, R. L., Sweet, J. J., Morgan, J. E., Larrabee, G. J., Millis, S. R., & Conference Participants. (2009). American Academy of Clinical Neuropsychology Consensus Conference statement on the neuropsychological assessment of effort, response bias, and malingering. *The Clinical Neuropsychologist, 23*, 1093–1129. https://doi.org/10.1080/13854040903155063

Hinton-Bayre, A. D. (2012). Choice of reliable change model can alter decisions regarding neuropsychological impairment after sports-related concussion. *Clinical Journal of Sport Medicine, 22*, 105–108. doi: 10.1097/JSM.0b013e318248a526

Hinton-Bayre, A. D., & Kwapil, K. (2017). Best practice approaches for evaluating significant change for individuals. In S. C. Bowden (Ed.), *Neuropsychological assessment in the age of evidence-based practice: Diagnostic and treatment evaluations*. Oxford University Press.

Hunter, S. J. & Donders, J. (2007). *Pediatric neuropsychological intervention: A critical review of science & practice*. Cambridge University Press.

Kazdin, A. E. (2008). Evidence-based treatment and practice: New opportunities to bridge clinical research and practice, enhance the knowledge base, and improve patient care. *The American Psychologist, 63*(3), 146–159. https://psycnet.apa.org/doi/10.1037/0003-066X.63.3.146

Kazdin, A. E. (2020). *Single-case research: Methods for clinical and applied settings* (3rd ed.). Oxford.

Kleiner, J. S. (2018). Brain plasticity. In J. S. Kreutzer, J. DeLuca, & B. Caplan (Eds.), *Encyclopedia of clinical neuropsychology*. Springer.

Kolb, B., & Whishaw, I. Q. (2009). *Fundamentals of human neuropsychology* (6th ed.). Worth Publishers.

Koziol, L., Barker, L., & Jansons, L. (2015). Attention and other constructs: Evolution or revolution? *Applied Neuropsychology: Child, 4*(2), 123–131. https://doi.org/10.1080/21622965.2015.1005482

Koziol, L. F., & Budding, D. (2012). Requiem for a diagnosis: Attention-Deficit Hyperactivity Disorder. *Applied Neuropsychology: Child, 1*(1), 2–5. https://doi.org/10.1080/21622965.2012.665774

Koziol, L. F., Budding, D. E., & Chidekel, D. (2013). *ADHD as a model of brain-behavior relationships*. Springer. https://doi.org/10.1007/978-1-4614-8382-3

Lamberty, G. J., & Nelson, N. W. (2012). *Specialty competencies in clinical neuropsychology*. Oxford University Press.

Lezak, M. D., Howieson, D. B., Bigler, E. D., & Tranel, D. (2012). *Neuropsychological assessment* (5th ed.). Oxford University Press.

Li, Shu-Chen. (2003). Biocultural orchestration of developmental plasticity across levels: The interplay of biology and culture in shaping the mind and behavior across the life span. *Psychological Bulletin. 129*(2), 171–94. https://doi.org/10.1037/0033-2909.129.2.171
Luria, A. R. (1973). *The working brain*. Basic Books.
Macniven, J. A. B. (Ed.). (2016). *Neuropsychological formulation: A clinical casebook*. Springer. https://doi.org/10.1007/978-3-319-18338-1
Meehl, P. (1997). Credentialed persons, credentialed knowledge. *Clinical Psychology: Science and Practice, 4*(2), 91–98. https://doi.org/10.1111/j.1468-2850.1997.tb00103.x
Meyers, J., Miller, R., Rohling, M., & Kalat, S. (2019). Premorbid estimates of neuropsychological functioning for diverse groups. *Applied Neuropsychology: Adult, 27*, 1–12. https://doi.org/10.1080/23279095.2018.1550412
Miller, D. C. (2013). *Best practices in school neuropsychology: Guidelines for effective practice, assessment, and evidence-based intervention*. Wiley.
Mitrushina, M., Boone, K. B., Razani, J., & D'Elia, L. F. (2005). *Handbook of normative data for neuropsychological assessment* (2nd ed.). Oxford University Press.
Nicholls, C. J. (2018). *Neurodevelopmental disorders in children and adolescents: A guide to evaluation and treatment*. Routledge.
Noggle, C., Dean, R., & Barisa, M. (Eds.). (2013). *Neuropsychological rehabilitation*. Springer.
Postal, K., & Armstrong, K. (2013). *Feedback that sticks: The art of effectively communicating neuropsychological assessment results*. Oxford University Press.
Price, C. J., & Mechelli, A. (2005). Reading and reading disturbance. *Current Opinion in Neurobiology, 12*, 231–238. https://doi.org/10.1016/j.conb.2005.03.003
Reitan, R. M., & Wolfson, D. (1993). *The Halstead-Reitan neuropsychological test battery: Theory and clinical interpretation* (2nd ed.). Neuropsychology Press.
Reynolds, C. R., & Fletcher-Janzen, E. (2009). *Handbook of clinical child neuropsychology*. Springer.
Riccio, C. A., Sullivan, J. R., & Cohen, M. J. (2010). *Neuropsychological assessment and intervention for childhood and adolescent disorders*. Wiley.
Ruff, R. M., & Chester, S. K. (2014). *Effective psychotherapy for individuals with brain injury*. Guilford.
Russell, E. W. (2012). *The scientific foundation of neuropsychological assessment: With applications to forensic evaluation*. Elsevier.
Semrud-Clikeman, M., & Teeter Ellison, P. A. (2009). *Child neuropsychology: Assessment and interventions for neurodevelopmental disorders* (2nd ed.). Springer.
Smith, B. (2015). New standards for psychology training. *Monitor on Psychology, 46*(5), 52–53.
Spring, B. (2007). Evidence-Based practice in clinical psychology: What it is, why it matters; what you need to know. *Journal of Clinical Psychology, 63*(7), 611–631. https://doi.org/10.1002/jclp.20373
Strauss, E., Shermann, E. M., & Spreen, O. (2006). *A compendium of neuropsychological tests: Administration, norms, and commentary* (3rd ed.). Oxford University Press.
Sue, S., & Zane, N. (1987). The role of culture and cultural techniques in psychotherapy: A critique and reformulation. *The American Psychologist, 42*(1), 37–45.
Watson, R. (1953). *A brief history of clinical psychology. Psychological Bulletin, 50*(5), 321–346. https://psycnet.apa.org/doi/10.1037/h0062847

Chapter 12
Neuropsychologically Driven Evidence-Based Interventions in Counseling Psychology

Kristin Perrone and Ashley Schoener

Learning Objectives

- To understand the history of neuropsychological interventions in counseling psychology.
- To identify ways that neuropsychological research can inform counseling psychology practice.
- To understand how the biological aspects of behavior are crucially important to counseling psychology practice.
- To increase awareness of multicultural factors salient to the practice of neuropsychologically informed counseling psychology practices.
- To consider future directions for the integration of neuropsychology and counseling psychology practice.

History of Neuropsychologically Driven Interventions in Counseling Psychology

The American Psychological Association (APA) was first established in 1892 by Dr. G. Stanley Hall to represent the newly emerging scientific discipline of psychology. There were 19 APA divisions established in 1944. The largest two divisions were Clinical Psychology and the Society for Counseling Psychology (SCP; previously known as Personal Guidance Psychology and the Division of Counseling and Guidance; Gelso, Williams, & Fretz, 2014). Counseling Psychology was distinguished from Clinical Psychology by the notion that counseling psychologists spent

K. Perrone (✉) · A. Schoener
Department of Counseling Psychology, Social Psychology, and Counseling, Ball State University, Muncie, IN, USA
e-mail: kperrone@bsu.edu

R. C. D'Amato et al. (eds.), *Understanding the Biological Basis of Behavior*,
https://doi.org/10.1007/978-3-030-59162-5_12

more time promoting growth and development of individuals who were already within the normal range of functioning whereas clinical psychologists spent more time working with clients who were below the normal range of functioning or who had more severe clinical concerns (Hahn, 1955). This difference has become less prominent as the fields have evolved and converged over time. Historically, clinical psychologists were more likely than counseling psychologists to work in hospital settings (e.g., traditional clinical psychology positions working with individuals who required residential or long-term care). Over the past several decades, counseling psychologists have increasingly worked in hospital settings with a wide range of clients as part of interprofessional behavioral health medical teams. With this greater integration into the health care system, the scope of practice for counseling psychologists began to shift from a vocational focus to a more holistic health focus including psychological, physical, and spiritual well-being (Heppner et al., 2000).

Research describing the relationship between neuropsychology and counseling psychology can be found beginning in the 1980s and corresponding with the advent of managed care and the trend for counseling psychologists to increasingly identify with the title of health care provider (Heppner et al., 2000). Prior to that time, most neuropsychology research literature was housed within journals in the field of clinical psychology (Solomon et al., 1985). Nicholas and Stern (2011) discussed the history and scholarship of counseling health psychologists and noted that The Society of Counseling Psychology (APA Division 17) established a health psychology section in 1996, and the division's journal, *The Counseling Psychologist*, has published health psychology contributions regularly since 1985. Nicholas and Stern (2011) described the ways that counseling health psychologists have contributed to the overall field of health psychology in unique ways and have held true to the counseling psychology field's emphasis on prevention over remediation, on normative, developmental issues across the life span, and on multicultural competent provision of services to a diverse range of clients.

Over the years since the inception of counseling psychology, counseling psychologists have maintained their value of a strengths-based, growth-oriented, and holistic view of the client. For example, Lichtenberg et al. (2016) discussed traditions and core values of counseling psychologists and highlighted counseling psychologists' focus on client strengths, the emphasis on the collaborative relationship as crucial to therapeutic effectiveness, and the multicultural awareness and values. Packard (2009) described counseling psychology core values as including positive relationships, integration of science and practice, the focus on healthy life span development, a holistic view of the person within multiple contexts, and the celebration of diversity and inclusion.

When considering the application of neuropsychology to counseling psychology, it may be helpful to also consider the relevant intersection of the fields of rehabilitation psychology and counseling psychology. These two fields share a core value of emphasizing positive psychology (e.g., McMahon & Kim, 2016; Mills & Kreutzer, 2016; Uyanik et al., 2017), and both rehabilitation psychologists and counseling psychologists employ neuropsychologically driven interventions within the field of neuropsychological rehabilitation (Eslinger, 2002). Rehabilitation work focuses on a holistic manner of care in which behavioral, emotional, and cognitive difficulties are attended to for individuals with disabilities or brain injuries. This corresponds with the general purpose of neuropsychological interventions, which Eslinger described as the restoration of functioning through improvement of skills and compensatory training.

The value of a holistic and contextual view of clients translates into the scope of care for extending to the family system and support network of the individual who has sustained a brain injury or who is coping with a neurocognitive or neuropsychologically based disorder. For example, counseling and rehabilitation psychologists have collaborated on interdisciplinary applied research to examine the implications of the spouse taking on a caregiving role for individuals with chronic neurological conditions such as multiple sclerosis (Gordon & Perrone, 2004; Perrone et al., 2006). In a more recent example, Hess and Perrone-McGovern (2016) examined characteristics of romantic partnerships for persons who have sustained a traumatic brain injury and found that secure attachment within romantic relationships contributed significantly to health-related quality of life. They discussed ways to enhance neuropsychological rehabilitation counseling efforts by involving romantic partners in treatment for individuals with neuropsychological impairment.

Solomon et al. (1985) provided an introduction to research examining neuropsychology practice and research within the field of counseling psychology. At the time, neuropsychological assessment was a rapidly growing area within the broad field of psychology. However, it was not a common area of study for counseling psychology students with only 73% of training directors reporting the availability of a formal course in neuropsychology, and approximately half (58%) reported that students were only able to pursue a formal course in neuropsychology as an elective rather than a programmatic requirement. This was inconsistent with student and training director perceptions of neuropsychology as a professional asset and student reports of neuropsychology as a field of interest to them. Not surprisingly, further research evaluating the state of neuropsychology within the field of counseling psychology was conducted (Agresti, 1992; Corazzini, 1992; Larson & Agresti, 1992; McMahon & Shaw, 1996) as counseling psychologist practice and interest in neuropsychology continued to increase. Larson and Agresti (1992) reported an increase in the prevalence of counseling psychologists practicing neuropsychology, using neuropsychological interventions, and conducting neuropsychological research. This corresponded with an acknowledgment that counseling psychologists were working within settings previously associated with exclusively clinical psychologists (i.e., rehabilitation facilities, hospitals). In the most recent available research examining the use of neuropsychological assessments, counseling psychologists comprised only 11% of the participants. However, counseling psychologists were the second largest group behind clinical psychologists who comprised 62% of the participants (Rabin et al., 2005).

Multicultural Considerations for Neuropsychologically Driven Counseling Interventions

As noted, the field of counseling psychology places a value on diversity and culture (Packard, 2009). The field first developed a focus on individuals with disabilities and older adults in 1945 with an increased attention to ethnic minorities in the 1970s. Further, Division 17 began organizing committees to promote diverse cultural representation within the field (e.g., Committee on Lesbian and Gay concerns). The 1980s and 1990s included significant changes in the field marked by an increased attention to issues of diversity and the relationship between psychological and physiological factors of health (Heppner et al., 2000). This increased consideration for culture became evident as culture became a central component of research, influenced clinical practice, and became a fundamental facet of professional training.

Multicultural competence became a central component of counseling psychology training after Sue, Arredondo, and McDavis (1992) made a call to the profession proposing new competency standards specifically related to diversity and multiculturalism. This call was supported by demographic data revealing shifts to more diversity in the United States population and research showing the ethnocentric (i.e., based on one culture) nature of early psychological interventions. The shift in the demographic composition of the population reflected the need for an understanding of cultural factors because counseling psychologists would be working with more diverse populations as a result of the shift. Further, psychological interventions have been shown to be inherently based on western values, particularly those of middle-upper class, Christian individuals of European descent (Arnett, 2008). There is evidence that persons with minority identities face potential harm from interventions not consistent with their worldview and beliefs (Sue & Sue, 2012).

Minorities have been prominently shown to experience significant stress related to discrimination and prejudice they experience as a result of their identities. For example, there is extensive research showing that individuals with minority identities face additional systemic barriers (Sue & Sue, 2012) and experience disparate rates of cognitive, affective, and physical difficulties (Cargill & Stone, 2005). As such, this creates unique challenges to treatment that clinicians must understand in order to provide culturally appropriate treatment. Neuroscience has provided support for the effect of discrimination on individuals' functioning. Specifically, Ivey and Zalaquett (2011) described physiological effects of a stressful environment caused by discrimination and the way in which these effects can manifest in the form of impaired physical, psychological, and/ or social health.

Neuroscience has also provided a foundation upon which culturally appropriate treatments and practices can be developed. Gordon (2003) describes the collaborative efforts of a multidisciplinary international consortium to establish a database of quality-controlled neuroimaging information that will assist multiple disciplines to understand and describe the human brain across cultures (Brain Resource International Database; Gordon, 2003). This database includes electroencephalogram (EEG), Event Related Potential (ERP), functional magnetic resonance imaging (fMRI), and neuropsychological test batteries. Paul and colleagues (2007) examined cognitive performance (via neuropsychological battery) and electrophysiological indices of brain functioning for individuals in the United States, Europe, and Australia and found a high degree of similarity in the brain functioning of individuals in developed Western cultures. More research is needed to continue adding to this and similar databases, and the scope of the database should be widened to better represent a broader range of cultures and geographical areas.

All psychologists should abide by ethical guidelines that include a requirement for cultural competence and consideration of culture throughout the treatment process. However, there is an added level of technical and ethical complexity when considering the assessment and treatment of individuals with neuropsychological conditions across cultures (Brickman et al., 2006). For example, Evans et al. (2019) discussed challenges for Latinx immigrant parents in regard to understanding and knowing how to utilize results from neuropsychological testing for their children. They mention general language and literacy barriers as well as specific health literacy barriers related to medical and psychiatric treatment settings (e.g., immigration status and access to health care, cultural values from their country of origin that may not be consistent with United States health care practices particularly in regard to mental health treatment, socioeconomic status, and limitations in parental time and financial resources). Their recommendations for treatment providers include limiting technical language, providing concrete instructions and resources, and communication of respect for cultural factors.

There are further concerns of high false positives when using testing norms not appropriate for an individual's cultural background. Daugherty et al. (2017) found that 20% of participants received a misdiagnosis of a cognitive disorder when tests from the United States were used cross-culturally in Colombia, Morocco, and Spain. The differences in rates of misdiagnosis also varied across the different countries implying significant differences across nationality. With the high rate of demographic diversity in the United States, these limitations must be considered. While there have been cross-culturally adapted assessments (Nielsen et al., 2018), cross-cultural validation studies are somewhat rare. As such, counseling psychologists utilize a multicultural approach to the interpretation of results and application of findings in a way that is appropriate for each individual client. This can be implemented when counseling psychologists utilize assessment-based practices to inform their counseling practices through the obtainment of diagnostic (e.g., personality assessments) and neuropsychological data (e.g., intelligence tests). This is consistent with a call suggesting the field of neuropsychology should move toward an increased focus on diversity factors (Rivera Mindt et al., 2010).

Application of Research on the Biological Basis of Behavior to Counseling Psychology

Neuroscience is the direct study of the brain and nervous system, and this has been used to inform and support counseling interventions. Research has demonstrated a relationship between neurochemistry and behavior in which neurotransmitters impact individuals' behavior (Yanowitch & Coccaro, 2011), and individuals' experiences and behaviors impact neurotransmitter activity (Krach et al., 2010). This relationship is particularly important for counseling psychologists within the context of the dopaminergic reward system due to its close association with motivational behaviors. For example, psychotropic medications, such as selective serotonin reuptake inhibitors (SSRI), increase dopaminergic activity and have been shown to be associated with improved attention and executive functions (Herrera-Guzmán et al., 2010). Alternatively, positive social feedback or emotional interaction has been shown to facilitate dopaminergic activity (Krach et al., 2010). As such, counseling psychologists benefit from an understanding of brain chemistry because interventions can promote experiences that cause ideal neurochemistry.

Similarly, Kandel's (1998, 2000) seminal work on neuroplasticity (i.e., the adaptability of neuronal connections) elucidated relationships between social and cultural experiences and changes in neurological morphology. Kandel also described mechanisms through which biological changes can occur through psychotherapy intervention. Kandel (2000) described negative plasticity and positive plasticity as the inhibition of neuroplasticity and facilitation of neuroplasticity, respectively. Negative plasticity occurs as a result of habituation because synaptic transmissions decrease without novel stimuli. Meanwhile, positive plasticity occurs as a result of sensitization because synaptic transmissions are facilitated in response to novel stimuli. Positive plasticity is associated with neurogenesis (i.e., generation of new neurons) and synaptogenesis (i.e., generation of synapses), which are thought to be indicative of learning and increased cognitive ability.

Researchers have described psychosocial factors that contribute to positive or negative neuroplasticity (e.g., Clemenson et al., 2015; Duman et al., 2016; Goncalves & Perrone-McGovern, 2016). Factors such as emotional neglect, addiction, stress, and environmental impoverishment have been identified as contributing to negative plasticity while factors such as nurturing, healthy lifestyle, emotional regulation, and environmental enrichment have been identified as contributing to positive plasticity (Gonçalves & Perrone-McGovern, 2014). As Gonçalves and Perrone-McGovern (2014) noted, neuroplasticity is salient to the integration of neuroscience research into counseling practice because areas of the brain that are associated with cognitive functions such as memory, emotion, and executive functioning have been revealed to be flexible, and maladaptive functions or impaired functions have the potential for improvement and adaptability.

Gonçalves and Perrone-McGovern (2014) proposed a holistic developmental health approach for the integration of counseling psychology and neuroscience, as shown in Fig. 13.1, that describes a dynamic interplay between 4 factors:

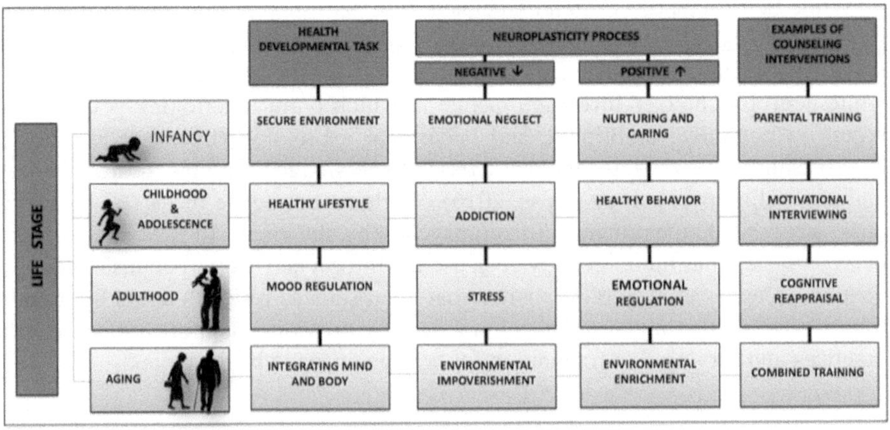

Fig. 13.1 Developmental health approach for the integration of counseling psychology and neuroscience. (Cited from Gonçalves & Perrone-McGovern, 2014)

Psychological Processes, Brain Networks, Developmental Tasks, and Interpersonal and Environmental Factors. Psychological processes include executive functioning (e.g., attention, inhibition), emotional expression and regulation, self-representations, and Theory of Mind (ToM), as well as cognitive and behavioral structuring and learning processes. These involved engaging the appropriate brain networks for attention, social cognition, motivation, and emotion regulation. Our conceptualization of developmental tasks is a holistic one that encompasses cognitive, social, identity, emotional, and vocational domains. Interpersonal and environmental factors can serve to promote neurodevelopment and neurogenesis (e.g., nurturing close relationships) or can be neurotoxic in nature (e.g., stress, emotional neglect). Counseling interventions (e.g., mindfulness, modeling of a positive attachment relationship via the therapeutic bond) can also serve as corrective or healing factors within this category.

Coutinho et al. (2014) noted as follows:

> The use of neuroimaging methods can help move counseling psychology from an evidence-based practice to a science-based practice by identifying the pathophysiological mechanisms of psychological disorders as well as specific processes responsible for change in psychotherapy... Similarly, psychotherapy research can move from an evidence-based toward a science-based paradigm by using neuroscience research to identify the active ingredients responsible for psychotherapeutic change. Neuroimaging can be an alternative way of assessing the effects of psychotherapy and testing its efficacy in promoting healthy brain functioning. (Coutinho et al., 2014, p. 331).

Neuroimaging research has been used to provide empirical evidence for the effectiveness of therapy (e.g., Linden, 2006) by demonstrating that psychotherapy is effective in changing neuronal activity associated with several psychological disorders, including anxiety and depressive disorders as well as post-traumatic stress (for a review, see Barsaglini et al., 2014).

While neuroscience is often associated with neuropsychology due to the focus on neurological processes and functioning, these are two differentiated field of study. Specifically, neuroscience is the broad study of the brain and nervous system while neuropsychology involves practice in which brain functioning is examined based on cognitive, emotional, and behavioral expression (Lezak et al., 2012). Neuroscience research has served as a base of knowledge for both neuropsychology and counseling psychology (Goss, 2016). While neuroscience research was previously attributed to the practice of neuropsychology, the broad study of the brain and nervous system has more recently been used to inform and support counseling interventions. Cappas et al. (2005) posited that neuroscience research could be used to improve psychotherapy and clinical practices by providing support for established practices and serving as a foundation for new practices to be developed.

Why Neuropsychologically Driven Evidence-Based Interventions Are Critical to Professional Practice for Counseling Psychologists

Affective disorders frequently include cognitive symptoms that would be categorized as neuropsychological deficits, such as attentional symptoms within diagnostic criteria for depressive disorders, anxiety disorders, psychotic disorders, and other mood disorders (APA, 2014). As such, neuroscience research has been used to provide support for counseling interventions that focus on improving cognitive symptoms. Neuroscience support for counseling interventions has become more prominent, and there is support for various interventions, including eye movement desensitization and reprocessing (Rousseau et al., 2019), cognitive-behavioral therapy (Makinson & Young, 2012), emotion-focused therapy (Greenman et al., 2017; Johnson et al., 2013), and mindfulness interventions (Johnstone et al., 2007).

Eye Movement Desensitization and Reprocessing (EMDR) Neuroscience research has provided empirical support for the effectiveness of EMDR treatment for post-traumatic stress disorder (PTSD). For example, Boukezzi et al. (2017) found that participants with PTSD who were treated with EMDR recovered from their symptoms (whereas participants undergoing supportive therapy remained symptomatic) and further discovered gray matter density enhancement of neural structures involved in emotion regulation for the group treated with EMDR. Guina and Guina (2018) described a case in which EMDR was used effectively to treat a patient with comorbid poststroke depression and expressive aphasia. Rousseau et al. (2019) used fMRI methods to study participants with PTSD who received EMDR treatment (vs. wait list control) and found significant connectivity and functional activity changes for the EMDR group indicated a significant improvement of fear-related symptoms.

Cognitive-Behavioral Therapy (CBT) Neuroscience research has demonstrated the effectiveness of cognitive-behavioral interventions on a variety of types of psychological distress, including panic disorder (Luekenet al., 2013); social anxiety disorder (Månsson et al., 2013); and psychosis (Kumari et al., 2011). Ochsner et al. (2002) used fMRI methods to study neural correlates of cognitive reappraisal and found that the use of the reappraisal strategies can modulate neural activity across multiple systems involved in emotion processing. Lueken et al. (2013) studied neural correlates of fear condition and extinction with fMRI prior to and following participant completion of a manualized CBT program for panic disorder with agoraphobia. Results of this study supported the effectiveness of exposure-based CBT for creating positive changes in neuroplasticity. Månsson et al. (2013) studied Internet-delivered cognitive behavior therapy (iCBT) for patients with social anxiety disorder and found that this treatment caused changes in the amygdala that are associated with a reduction in social anxiety symptoms. Further, Mason et al. (2016) studied the effectiveness of cognitive-behavioral therapy for psychosis (CBTp) using fMRI methodology to study threat processing and appraisal during a social threat condition pre-and post-intervention. They found that participants in the CBTp group showed an increase in connectivity between the dorsolateral prefrontal cortex and other prefrontal regions (i.e., dorsal anterior cingulate).

Emotionally Focused Therapy (EFT) for Couples Greenman et al. (2017) discuss social neuroscience research support for the EFT approach for couples, specifically regarding neurophysiological substrates of relationship distress and satisfaction, pair bonding, and emotional experiencing in couples. They assert that clients who have participated in EFT therapy can experience altered neural functioning that is consistent with the theory of relationship functioning and change. For example, Johnson et al. (2013) examined threat responses in female partners of heterosexual couples using fMRI scans before and after therapy. Female partners were primed with the threat that they would receive electric shock while either lying alone in the fMRI scanner, holding a stranger's hand, or holding their partner's hand. At the pre-therapy scans, areas of the brain involved in processing fear were illuminated across all three conditions. However, post-therapy scans indicated a difference in which female partners who had undergone EFT demonstrated an attenuated fear response when holding their partner's hand (but not in the condition while alone or holding a stranger's hand; Johnson et al., 2013). EFT therapy emphasizes the role of attachment styles and patterns in adulthood. Schore (2000, 2002) discussed how attachment styles are first developed through early childhood experiences which then influence neurobiology and emotion regulation processes. He emphasized the importance of understanding neural correlates of the relational processes in therapy and incorporating neuroscience into clinical models of therapy (Schore, 2014). Specifically, Schore described a "rupture and repair" pattern in which positive interpersonal interactions serve as healing and protective factors for children and their parents in times of interpersonal rupture (i.e., conflict). As such, certain behaviors (i.e., laughing) and emotional reactions (i.e., joy, excitement) are considered indicators of attachment style.

Mindfulness Interventions Mindfulness interventions have been shown to be associated with positive changes in various areas of functioning and have been found to cause neurological changes. Mindfulness is practice derived from Buddhist meditation that emphasizes active attention, awareness, and non-judgment (Van Dam et al., 2018). Kabat-Zinn was identified as the individual who first brought mindfulness into the psychotherapy world when he founded his Mindfulness-Based Stress Reduction (MBSR) approach in 1979 (Baker & Saari, 2018). Since then, mindfulness-based interventions have become more prominent within counseling psychology literature with other formalized treatments, such as the 12-week mindfulness cognitive-behavioral therapy (Schoenberg et al., 2014) and mindfulness inductions. Mindfulness inductions are one-time novel and brief mindfulness practices that involve no further explanation of mindfulness theory (Dickenson et al., 2012). These interventions have been investigated using neuroimaging research to understand the neurological mechanisms under which therapeutic changes occur.

Mindfulness interventions have been shown to be effective for difficulties related to emotional (Leyland et al., 2018), cognitive (Chiesa et al., 2011), and behavioral functioning (Heppner et al., 2008). Specifically, mindfulness interventions have been found to be related to structural changes as shown by research using magnetic resonance imaging (MRI) to explore the effect of mindfulness on cortical and subcortical density. Tang et al. (2015) reported findings that mindfulness interventions are associated with changes in density of white and gray matter, as well as changes in the volume of cerebral cortex and cerebellum.

Further, fMRI has allowed for researchers to find evidence of changes in activation and functional connectivity of multiple areas of the brain related to mindfulness (Tang et al., 2015). Various changes in connectivity between different brain regions have been revealed with Grant et al. (2010) and Northoff et al. (2006) showing meditators experiencing a change in connectivity between the dorsolateral prefrontal cortex (PFC) and parietal lobe. Finally, EEG research has shown that mindfulness is related to increases in alpha and theta band activity resulting in increased communication between particular structures in the brain (Lagopoulos et al., 2009). Specifically, research has shown that mindfulness causes changes in the P300 amplitude (Banquet & Lesévre, 1980), N2 amplitude (Johnstone et al., 2007), and late positive potential (LPP) amplitude (Schoenberg et al., 2014). While some of these findings vary, or appear undetailed, they suggest that more global neurological changes may result from mindfulness which is a critical finding. The aforementioned neurological changes have been thought to be responsible for some of the emotional, cognitive, and behavioral changes associated with mindfulness.

Future Directions for Neuropsychologically Driven Interventions in Counseling Psychology

In 2014, counseling psychologists and neuroscientists worked collaboratively on a special section of the *Journal of Counseling Psychology* to provide recommendations for future research and practice directions in this area (Coutinho et al., 2014; Fine & Sung, 2014; Gonçalves & Perrone-McGovern, 2014; Sampaio & Lifter,

2014; Simon-Dack & Marmarosh, 2014; Wright & Díaz, 2014). Since then, neuroscience has been used to explain the effect of physiological functioning on social, cognitive, and behavioral functioning (Goncalves & Perrone-McGovern, 2016). This basis has provided a foundation for further use of neuroscience in counseling practice. For example, this foundational knowledge can be provided to clients in the context of psychoeducation regarding their treatment, and neuroscience research can be used more prominently to validate practices as evidence-based treatments.

As we continue to validate treatment approaches in counseling psychology using neuropsychological methods, we must not forget to consider the role of culture in shaping how individuals may respond to treatments (Chiao, 2010). Individuals presented with the same stimuli may respond differently based on their history of cultural experiences and their worldview (Han et al., 2013). For example, Beblo et al. (2011) examined the effect of clinical, demographic, and neurobiological factors on neuropsychological testing results in order to help increase understanding of how culture, affective disorders, and neuropsychological functioning are interrelated. When designing future interventions, the role of specific Diagnostic and Statistical Manual of Mental Disorders-Fifth Edition (DSM-5; American Psychiatric Association, 2013) DSM-5 symptomology, such as that associated with major depressive disorder, bipolar disorder, and addiction, should be considered within the context of neuropsychological functioning (Gruber et al., 2007; Lee et al., 2014), as well as within the context of cultural considerations.

There has not been a review specifically examining the state of neuropsychological practice and training within the field of counseling psychology since the 1990s (Larson & Agresti, 1992; Ryan et al., 1999). As such, an updated review is recommended to gain a necessary understanding of the current state of neuropsychological practice within the field of counseling psychology and inform future directions for treatment of individuals with neurocognitive disorders.

In addition to developing interventions for individuals with neurocognitive disorders, future directions could also include the development of interventions for caregivers and family members of individuals with neurocognitive disorders (e.g., those who have suffered a stroke or traumatic brain injury, those with Alzheimer's Disease or other progressive conditions). For example, researchers have recently shown that patients with traumatic brain injury benefit from counseling focused on their caregiver (Wade et al., 2014) because caregiver efficiency was shown to increase.

Finally, future training in counseling psychology, including classes on psychopathology as well as other practice-based courses, could include a greater emphasis on neurocognitive disorders, and counseling psychologists are encouraged to pursue continuing education classes that will increase their knowledge and familiarity of various neurocognitive disorders and typical symptom presentations. For example, counseling psychologists may be familiar with and able to recognize neurocognitive disorders such as Alzheimer's Disease, but may be less likely to recognize neurocognitive disorders such as frontotemporal dementia that do not initially include marked memory difficulties but manifest in behavioral and personality changes.

Conclusions

The field of counseling psychology has experienced an ongoing evolution that both expanded counseling psychologists' range of practice and converged their work with that of clinical psychologists. Counseling psychologists have maintained their values of healthy life span development, a holistic view of the person, and the consideration of diversity while broadening their clinical work and research to include more physiological and neurological foci (Heppner et al., 2000). Counseling clinicians now work in hospital and medical settings while counseling researchers conduct neuroscience research that informs both counseling and neuropsychological practice (Kandel, 2000). This is all done through the multicultural lens that serves as a foundation for all counseling psychology practice (Packard, 2009).

Counseling psychologists utilize neuropsychological interventions in a variety of ways. Individuals with disabilities and neuropsychological impairment often experience psychological or emotional distress in addition to their disability or injury (Hess & Perrone-McGovern, 2016). As such, counseling psychologists must have knowledge of rehabilitation-based practice in which the focus of treatment is to improve emotional, cognitive, and behavioral functioning. Further, counseling psychologists also practice as neuropsychologists within interdisciplinary care teams and utilize assessments to inform counseling interventions. This integration of neuropsychological interventions and counseling is largely based on neuroscience research revealing a relationship between neurological functioning and an individual's emotional, cognitive, and behavioral functioning. Interventions can be developed based on research showing that the environment changes individuals' physiology; factors have been shown to have a positive or negative effect on individuals emotional and cognitive functioning based on the neurological effect they have (Goncalves & Perrone-McGovern, 2016).

Discussion Questions

1. What significant counseling psychology changes mark the evolution that led to the incorporation of neuropsychology and neuropsychological practices into counseling psychology practice?
2. What are some biological processes underlying behavior, and how do they influence the field of counseling psychology?
3. How is research used to incorporate neuropsychological practices into counseling psychology practice?
4. What are some strengths related to the incorporation of and use of neuropsychological practices within counseling psychology?
5. What are some challenges related to the incorporation of and use of neuropsychological practices within counseling psychology?

EPPP Sample Questions

1. During an intake for couples counseling, Mrs. Smith relates that her husband Mr. Smith, who is in his late 30's, has begun acting strangely. She reported that he has been exhibiting uncharacteristically impulsive, rude, and socially inappropriate behaviors, has made poor financial decisions, and appears to have difficulty respecting the personal boundaries of others. Mr. Smith seems to lack any awareness or insight of the changes in his personality. What might these symptoms suggest?
   (a) Frontotemporal Neurocognitive Disorder
   (b) Borderline Personality Disorder
   (c) Parkinson's Disease
   (d) ADHD
2. According to Allan Schore, __________ is a better indicator of attachment than anxiety in young children.
   (a) Joy and Laughter
   (b) Attention-Seeking
   (c) Emotion Regulation
   (d) Crying
3. Positive interpersonal experiences can cause the brain to release dopamine which helps:
   (a) Increase neuronal activity
   (b) Improve attention
   (c) Both a and b
   (d) None of the above
4. The individual who first brought mindfulness into the psychotherapy world when he founded Mindfulness-Based Stress Reduction (MBSR) was:
   (a) Kabat-Zinn
   (b) Wechsler
   (c) Stanley Hall
   (d) Kandel
5. __________ can be used to move counseling psychology from an evidence-based practice to a science-based practice by identifying the pathophysiological mechanisms of psychological disorders as well as processes responsible for change in psychotherapy.
   (a) Neuroimaging methods
   (b) Psychotherapy
   (c) Neuropsychology
   (d) Affective disorders

   Answers: A, A, C, A, A.

Proactive Readings

Transcending the Past

Larson, P. C., & Agresti, A. A. (1992). Counseling psychology and neuropsychology: An overview. *The Counseling Psychologist, 2*, 549–555.
Corazzini, J. G. (1992). To be a counseling psychologist or a counseling neuropsychologist. *The Counseling Psychologist, 20*, 640–644.

Excelling in the Present

Azouvi, P., Arnould, A., Dromer, E., & Vallat-Azouvi, C. (2017). Neuropsychology of traumatic brain injury: An expert overview. *Revue neurologique, 173*(7–8), 461–472.
Goncalves, O., & Perrone-McGovern, K.M. (2014). A neuroscience agenda for counseling psychology research. *Journal of Counseling Psychology, 61*, 507–512.
Coutinho, J., Perrone-McGovern, K.M., & Goncalves, O. (2017). The use of neuroimaging methodology in counseling psychology research: Promises, pitfalls and recommendations. *Canadian Journal of Counseling and Psychotherapy, 51,* 327–348.

Transforming the Future

Goncalves, O.F., & Perrone-McGovern, K.M. (2016). Translating neuroscience into counselling practice. *Canadian Journal of Counseling and Psychotherapy, 50,* 421–440.
Rivera Mindt, M., Byrd, D., Saez, P., & Manly, J. (2010). Increasing culturally competent neuropsychological services for ethnic minority populations: A call to action. *The Clinical Neuropsychologist, 24*(3), 429–453.
Taylor, J. M., Kolaski, A. Z., Wright, H., Hashtpari, H., & Neimeyer, G. J. (2019). Predicting the evolution of counseling psychology in the United States: Results from a Delphi poll of academic training directors. *Counselling Psychology Quarterly, 32*, 169–185.

References

Agresti, A. A. (1992). Integrating neuropsychological training into a counseling psychology curriculum. *The Counseling Psychologist, 20*(4), 605–619. https://doi.org.proxy.bsu.edu/10.1177/0011000092204004
American Psychiatric Association. (2013). *Diagnostic and Statistical Manual of Mental Disorders* (5th ed.). American Psychiatric Association.
American Psychological Association. (2014). *Graduate Study in Psychology*, 2014 edition.
Arnett, J. J. (2008). The neglected 95%: Why American psychology needs to become less American. *American Psychologist, 63*(7), 602. https://doi.org/10.1037/0003-066X.63.7.602
Baker, B. M., & Saari, A. (2018). 'The anatomy of our discontent': From braining the mind to mindfulness for teachers. *Discourse: Studies in the Cultural Politics of Education, 39*(2), 169–183. https://doi.org/10.1080/01596306.2018.1394425

Banquet, J. P., & Lesévre, N. (1980). Event-related potentials in altered states of consciousness. *Progress in Brain Research, 54*, 447–453. https://doi.org/10.1016/S0079-6123(08)61659-3
Barsaglini, A., Sartori, G., Benetti, S., Pettersson-Yeo, W., & Mechelli, A. (2014). The effects of psychotherapy on brain function: A systematic and critical review. *Progress in Neurobiology, 114*, 1–14. https://doi.org/10.1016/j.pneurobio.2013.10.006
Beblo, T., Sinnamon, G., & Baune, B. T. (2011). Specifying the neuropsychology of affective disorders: Clinical, demographic and neurobiological factors. *Neuropsychology Review, 21*(4), 337–359. https://doi.org/10.1007/s11065-011-9171-0
Brickman, A. M., Cabo, R., & Manly, J. J. (2006). Ethical issues in cross-cultural neuropsychology. *Applied Neuropsychology, 13*(2), 91–100. https://doi.org/10.1207/s15324826an1302_4
Boukezzi, S., El Khoury-Malhame, M., Auzias, G., Reynaud, E., Rousseau, P.-F., Richard, E., et al. (2017). Grey matter density changes of structures involved in posttraumatic stress disorder (PTSD) after recovery following eye movement desensitization and reprocessing (EMDR) therapy. *Psychiatry Research: Neuroimaging, 266*, 146–152. https://doi.org/10.1016/j.pscychresns.2017.06.009
Cappas, N. M., Andres-Hyman, R., & Davidson, L. (2005). What psychotherapists can begin to learn from neuroscience: Seven principles of a brain-based psychotherapy. *Psychotherapy: Theory, Research, Practice, Training, 42*(3), 374. https://doi.org/10.1037/0033-3204.42.3.374
Cargill, V. A., & Stone, V. E. (2005). HIV/AIDS: A minority health issue. *Medical Clinics, 89*(4), 895–912. https://doi.org/10.1016/j.mcna.2005.03.005
Chiesa, A., Calati, R., & Serretti, A. (2011). Does mindfulness training improve cognitive abilities? A systematic review of neuropsychological findings. *Clinical Psychology Review, 31*(3), 449–464. https://doi.org/10.1016/j.cpr.2010.11.003
Chiao, J. Y. (2010). At the frontier of cultural neuroscience: Introduction to the special issue. *Social Cognitive and Affective Neuroscience, 5*, 109–110. https://doi.org/10.1093/scan/nsq064
Clemenson, G. D., Deng, W., & Gage, F. H. (2015). Environmental enrichment and neurogenesis: From mice to humans. *Current Opinion in Behavioral Sciences, 4*, 56–62. https://doi.org/10.1016/j.cobeha.2015.02.005
Corazzini, J. G. (1992). To be a counseling psychologist or a counseling neuropsychologist. *The Counseling Psychologist, 20*(4), 640–644. https://doiorg.proxy.bsu.edu/10.1177/0011000092204008
Coutinho, J. F., Silva, P. O., & Decety, J. (2014). Neurosciences, empathy, and healthy interpersonal relationships: Recent findings and implications for counselling psychology. *Journal of Counselling Psychology, 61*(4), 541–548. https://doi.org/10.1037/cou0000021
Dickenson, J., Berkman, E. T., Arch, J., & Lieberman, M. D. (2012). Neural correlates of focused attention during a brief mindfulness induction. *Social Cognitive and Affective Neuroscience, 8*(1), 40–47. https://doi.org/10.1093/scan/nss030
Daugherty, J. C., Puente, A. E., Fasfous, A. F., Hidalgo-Ruzzante, N., & Pérez-Garcia, M. (2017). Diagnostic mistakes of culturally diverse individuals when using north American neuropsychological tests. *Applied Neuropsychology: Adult, 24*(1), 16–22. https://doi.org/10.1080/23279095.2015.1036992
Duman, R. S., Aghajanian, G. K., Sanacora, G., & Krystal, J. H. (2016). Synaptic plasticity and depression: New insights from stress and rapid-acting antidepressants. *Nature Medicine, 22*(3), 238. https://doi.org/10.1038/nm.4050
Eslinger, P. J. (Ed.). (2002). *Neuropsychological interventions: Clinical research and practice* (Vol. 494). Guilford Press.
Evans, C. L., Pulsifer, M. B., & Grieco, J. A. (2019). Communication of neuropsychological results to caregivers of Latino immigrant children. *Translational Issues in Psychological Science, 5*(1), 42–50. https://doi.org/10.1037/tps0000178
Fine, J. G., & Sung, C. (2014). Neuroscience of child and adolescent health development. *Journal of Counselling Psychology, 61*(4), 521–527. https://doi.org/10.1037/cou0000033
Gelso, C. J., Williams, E. N., & Fretz, B. R. (2014). *Counseling psychology* (3rd ed.). American Psychological Association.

Gonçalves, Ó. F., & Perrone-McGovern, K. M. (2014). A neuroscience agenda for counselling psychology research. *Journal of Counselling Psychology, 61*(4), 507–512. https://doi.org/10.1037/cou0000026

Goncalves, O. F., & Perrone-McGovern, K. M. (2016). Translating Neuroscience into Counselling Practice Transposition la neuroscience dans la pratique du counseling. *Canadian Journal of Counselling and Psychotherapy (Online), 50*(4), 421. https://doi.org/10.1177/0011000016650263

Gordon, E. (2003). Integrative Neuroscience. *Neuropsychopharmacology, 28*, 52–58. https://doi.org/10.1038/sj.npp.1300136

Gordon, P. G., & Perrone, K. M. (2004). When spouses become caregivers: Counseling implications for younger couples. *Journal of Rehabilitation, 70*, 27–32.

Greenman, P. S., Wiebe, S., & Johnson, S. M. (2017). Neurophysiological processes in couple relationships: Emotion, attachment bonds, and the brain. In J. Fitzgerald (Ed.), *Foundations for couples' therapy: Research for the real world* (pp. 291–301). Routledge/Taylor & Francis Group.

Goss, D. (2016). Integrating neuroscience into counseling psychology: A systematic review of current literature. *The Counseling Psychologist, 44*(6), 895–920. https://doi.org/10.1177/0011000016650263

Grant, J. A., Courtemanche, J., Duerden, E. G., Duncan, G. H., & Rainville, P. (2010). Cortical thickness and pain sensitivity in Zen meditators. *Emotion, 10*, 43–53. https://doi.org/10.1037/a0018334

Gruber, S. A., Silveri, M. M., & Yurgelun-Todd, D. A. (2007). Neuropsychological consequences of opiate use. *Neuropsychology Review, 17*(3), 299–315. https://doi.org/10.1007/s11065-007-9041-y

Guina, J., & Guina, C. (2018). Wants talk psychotherapy but cannot talk: EMDR for post-stroke depression with expressive aphasia. *Innovations in Clinical Neuroscience, 15*, 45–48.

Hahn, M. E. (1955). Counseling psychology. *American Psychologist, 10*(7), 279. https://doi.org/10.1037/h0043179

Han, S., Northoff, G., Vogeley, K., Wexler, B. E., Kitayama, S., & Varnum, M. E. (2013). A cultural neuroscience approach to the biosocial nature of the human brain. *Annual Review of Psychology, 64*, 335–359. https://doi.org/10.1146/annurev-psych-071112-054629

Heppner, P. P., Casas, J. M., Carter, J., & Stone, G. L. (2000). The maturation of counseling psychology: Multifaceted perspectives, 1978–1998. In *Handbook of counseling psychology* (Vol. 3, pp. 3–49).

Heppner, W. L., Kernis, M. H., Lakey, C. E., Campbell, W. K., Goldman, B. M., Davis, P. J., & Cascio, E. V. (2008). Mindfulness as a means of reducing aggressive behavior: Dispositional and situational evidence. *Aggressive Behavior, 34*(5), 486–496. https://doi.org/10.1002/ab.20258

Herrera-Guzmán, I., Herrera-Abarca, J. E., Gudayol-Ferré, E., Herrera-Guzmán, D., Gómez-Carbajal, L., Peña-Olvira, M., et al. (2010). Effects of selective serotonin reuptake and dual serotonergic–noradrenergic reuptake treatments on attention and executive functions in patients with major depressive disorder. *Psychiatry Research, 177*(3), 323–329. https://doi.org/10.1016/j.psychres.2010.03.006

Hess, R. A., & Perrone-McGovern, K. M. (2016). Quality of life for individuals with traumatic brain injury: The influence of attachment security and partner support. *Journal of Rehabilitation, 84*, 14–27.

Ivey, A. E., & Zalaquett, C. P. (2011). Neuroscience and counseling: Central issue for social justice leaders. *Journal for Social Action in Counseling & Psychology, 3*(1), 103–116. https://doi.org/10.33043/JSACP.3.1.103-116

Johnson, S. M., Burgess Moser, M., Beckes, L., Smith, A., Dalgleish, T., Halchuk, R., Hasselmo, K., Greenman, P. S., Merali, Z., & Coan, J. A. (2013). Soothing the threatened brain: Leveraging contact comfort with emotionally focused therapy. *PLoS One, 8*(11), e79314. https://doi.org/10.1371/journal.pone.0079314

Johnstone, S. J., Dimoska, A., Smith, J. L., Barry, R. J., Pleffer, C. B., Chiswick, D., & Clarke, A. R. (2007). The development of stop-signal and Go/Nogo response inhibition in children aged 7–12 years: Performance and event-related potential indices. *International Journal of Psychophysiology, 63*, 25–38. https://doi.org/10.1016/j.ijpsycho.2006.07.001

Kandel, E. R. (1998). A new intellectual framework for psychiatry. *American Journal of Psychiatry, 155*(4), 457–469. https://doi.org/10.1176/ajp.155.4.457

Kandel E. R. (2001). The molecular biology of memory storage: A dialog between genes and synapses. *Bioscience reports, 21*(5), 565–611. https://doi.org/10.1023/a:1014775008533

Krach, S., Paulus, F. M., Bodden, M., & Kircher, T. (2010). The rewarding nature of social interactions. *Frontiers in Behavioral Neuroscience, 4*, 22. https://doi.org/10.3389/fnbeh.2010.00022.

Kumari, V., Fannon, D., Peters, E. R., et al. (2011). Neural changes following cognitive behaviour therapy for psychosis: A longitudinal study. *Brain*, 2396–2407. https://doi.org/10.1093/brain/awr154

Larson, P. C., & Agresti, A. A. (1992). Counseling psychology and neuropsychology: An overview. *The Counseling Psychologist, 2*, 549–555. https://doi.org/10.1177/0011000092204001

Lee, R. S., Hermens, D. F., Scott, J., Redoblado-Hodge, M. A., Naismith, S. L., Lagopoulos, J., et al. (2014). A meta-analysis of neuropsychological functioning in first-episode bipolar disorders. *Journal of Psychiatric Research, 57*, 1–11. https://doi.org/10.1016/j.jpsychires.2014.06.019

Lezak, M. D., Howieson, D. B., Bigler, E. D., & Tranel, D. (2012). *Neuropsychological assessment* (5th ed.). Oxford.

Lichtenberg, J. W., Goodyear, R. K., Hutman, H., & Overland, E. A. (2016). Counselling psychology in the United States. *Counselling Psychology Quarterly, 29*, 216–224. https://doi.org/10.1080/09515070.2015.1127207

Lagopoulos, J., Xu, J., Rasmussen, I., Vik, A., Malhi, G. S., Eliassen, C. F., et al. (2009). Increased theta and alpha EEG activity during nondirective meditation. *The Journal of Alternative and Complementary Medicine, 15*(11), 1187–1192. https://doi.org/10.1089/acm.2009.0113

Leyland, A., Rowse, G., & Emerson, L. M. (2018). Experimental effects of mindfulness inductions on self-regulation: Systematic review and meta-analysis. *Emotion. 19*(1), 108–122. https://doi.org/10.1037/emo0000425

Linden, D. J. (2006). How psychotherapy changes the brain: The contribution of functional neuroimaging. *Molecular Psychiatry, 11*(6), 528–538. https://doi.org/10.1038/sj.mp.4001816

Lueken, U., Straube, B., Konrad, C., et al. (2013). Neural substrates of treatment response to cognitive-behavioral therapy in panic disorder with agoraphobia. *American Journal of Psychiatry, 170*, 1345–1355. https://doi.org/10.1176/appi.ajp.2013.12111484

Makinson, R. A., & Young, J. S. (2012). Cognitive behavioral therapy and the treatment of posttraumatic stress disorder: Where counseling and neuroscience meet. *Journal of Counseling & Development, 90*(2), 131–140. https://doi.org/10.1111/j.1556-6676.2012.00017.x

Månsson, K. N., Carlbring, P., Frick, A., et al. (2013). Altered neural correlates of affective processing after internet-delivered cognitive behavior therapy for social anxiety disorder. *Psychiatry Resident, 214*, 229–237. https://doi.org/10.1016/j.pscychresns.2013.08.012

Mason, L., Peters, E. R., Dima, D., Williams, S. C., & Kumari, V. (2016). Cognitive behavioral therapy normalizes functional connectivity for social threat in psychosis. *Schizophrenia Bulletin, 42*(3), 684–692. https://doi.org/10.1093/schbul/sbv153

McMahon, B. T., & Shaw, L. R. (1996). Neuropsychology and rehabilitation counseling: Bridging the gap. In R. J. Sbordone & C. J. Long (Eds.), *Ecological validity of neuropsychological testing* (pp. 369–386). Gr Press/St Lucie Press, Inc.

McMahon, B. T., & Kim, J. H. (2016). Foreword to special topic section on the interface of positive psychology with rehabilitation research and practice. *Journal of Occupational Rehabilitation, 26*(1), 1–3. https://doi.org/10.1007/s10926-015-9621-2.

Mills, A. L., & Kreutzer, J. S. (2016). Theoretical applications of positive psychology to vocational rehabilitation after traumatic brain injury. *Journal of Occupational Rehabilitation, 26*(1), 20–31. https://doi.org/10.1007/s10926-015-9608-z.

Nicholas, D. R., & Stern, M. (2011). Counseling psychology in clinical health psychology: The impact of specialty perspective. *Professional Psychology: Research and Practice, 42*, 331–337. https://doi.org/10.1037/a0024197

Nielsen, T. R., Segers, K., Vanderaspoilden, V., Bekkhus-Wetterberg, P., Minthon, L., Pissiota, A., et al. (2018). Performance of middle-aged and elderly European minority and majority populations on a cross-cultural neuropsychological test battery (CNTB). *The Clinical Neuropsychologist, 32*(8), 1411–1430. https://doi.org/10.1080/13854046.2018.1430256

Northoff, G., Heinzel, A., de Greck, M., Bermpohl, F., Dobrowolny, H., & Panksepp, J. (2006). Self-referential processing in our brain – A meta-analysis of imaging studies on the self. *NeuroImage, 31*, 440–457. https://doi.org/10.1016/j.neuroimage.2005.12.002

Ochsner, K. N., Bunge, S. A., Gross, J. J., & Gabrieli, J. D. (2002). Rethinking feelings: An FMRI study of the cognitive regulation of emotion. *Journal of Cognitive Neuroscience, 14*, 93–1229. https://doi.org/10.1162/089892902760807212

Packard, T. (2009). The 2008 Leona Tyler award address: Core values that distinguish counseling psychology: Personal and professional perspectives. *The Counseling Psychologist, 37*(4), 610–624. https://doi.org/10.1177/0011000009333986

Paul, R. H., Gunstad, J., Cooper, N., Williams, L. M., Clark, C. R., Cohen, R. A., ... & Gordon, E. (2007). Cross-cultural assessment of neuropsychological performance and electrical brain function measures: additional validation of an international brain database. *International Journal of Neuroscience, 117*(4), 549–568. https://doi.org/10.1080/00207450600773665

Perrone, K. M., Gordon, P. A., & Tschopp, M. K. (2006). Caregiver marital satisfaction when a spouse has multiple sclerosis. *Journal of Applied Rehabilitation Counseling, 37*, 26–32.

Rabin, L. A., Barr, W. B., & Burton, L. A. (2005). Assessment practices of clinical neuropsychologists in the United States and Canada: A survey of INS, NAN, and APA division 40 members. *Archives of Clinical Neuropsychology, 20*, 33–65. https://doi.org/10.1016/j.acn.2004.02.005.

Rivera Mindt, M., Byrd, D., Saez, P., & Manly, J. (2010). Increasing culturally competent neuropsychological services for ethnic minority populations: A call to action. *The Clinical Neuropsychologist, 24*(3), 429–453. https://doi.org/10.1080/13854040903058960

Rousseau, P. F., Khoury-Mahlhame, M. E., Reynaud, E., Boukezzi, A. C., Zendjidjiian, X., Guon, V., Samuleian, J. C., Guei, E., Chaminade, T., & Khalfa, S. (2019). Fear extinction learning improvement in PTSD after EMDR therapy: An fMRI study. *European Journal of Psychotraumatology, 10*(1), 1568132. https://doi.org/10.1080/20008198.2019.1568132

Ryan, J. J., Lopez, S. J., & Lichtenberg, J. W. (1999). Neuropsychological training in APA-accredited counseling psychology programs. *The Counseling Psychologist, 27*(3), 435–442. https://doi.org/10.1177/0011000099273007

Sampaio, A., & Lifter, K. (2014). Neurosciences of infant mental health development: Recent findings and implications for counselling psychology. *Journal of Counselling Psychology, 61*(4), 513–520. https://doi.org/10.1037/cou0000035

Schoenberg, P. L., Hepark, S., Kan, C. C., Barendregt, H. P., Buitelaar, J. K., & Speckens, A. E. (2014). Effects of mindfulness-based cognitive therapy on neurophysiological correlates of performance monitoring in adult attention-deficit/hyperactivity disorder. *Clinical Neurophysiology, 125*(7), 1407–1416. https://doi.org/10.1016/j.clinph.2013.11.031

Schore, A. N. (2014). The right brain is dominant in psychotherapy. *Psychotherapy, 51*(3), 388–397. https://doi.org/10.1037/a0037083.

Schore, A. N. (2002). Advances in neuropsychoanalysis, attachment theory, and trauma research: Implications for self-psychology. *Psychoanalytic Inquiry, 22*(3), 433–484. https://doi.org/10.1080/07351692209348996.

Schore, A. N. (2000). Attachment and the regulation of the right brain. *Attachment & Human Development, 2*(1), 23–47. https://doi.org/10.1080/146167300361309.

Simon-Dack, S. L., & Marmarosh, C. L. (2014). Neurosciences and adult health behaviors: Recent findings and implications for counselling psychology. *Journal of Counselling Psychology, 61*(4), 528–533. https://doi.org/10.1037/cou0000020

Solomon, G. S., Hale-Fiske, R., McCaffrey, R. J., & Isaac, W. (1985). Neuropsychological assessment training in APA-approved counseling psychology programs. *Professional Psychology: Research and Practice, 16*(1), 22–25. https://doi-org.proxy.bsu.edu/10.1037/0735-7028.16.1.22

Sue, D. W., Arredondo, P., & McDavis, R. J. (1992). Multicultural counseling competencies and standards: A call to the profession. *Journal of Multicultural Counseling and Development, 20*(2), 64–88. https://doi.org/10.1002/j.2161-1912.1992.tb00563.x

Sue, D. W., & Sue, D. (2012). *Counseling the culturally diverse: Theory and practice* (6m ed.). Wiley.

Tang, Y. Y., Hölzel, B. K., & Posner, M. I. (2015). The neuroscience of mindfulness meditation. *Nature Reviews Neuroscience, 16*(4), 213-225. https://doi.org/10.1038/nrn3916

Uyanik, H., Shogren, K. A., & Blanck, P. (2017). Supported decision-making: Implications from positive psychology for assessment and intervention in rehabilitation and employment. *Journal of Occupational Rehabilitation, 27*, 498–506. https://doi.org/10.1007/s10926-017-9740-z

Van Dam, N. T., van Vugt, M. K., Vago, D. R., Schmalzl, L., Saron, C. D., Olendzki, A., et al. (2018). Mind the hype: A critical evaluation and prescriptive agenda for research on mindfulness and meditation. *Perspectives on Psychological Science, 13*(1), 36–61. https://doi.org/10.1177/1745691617709589

Wade, S. L., Karver, C. L., Taylor, H. G., Cassedy, A., Stancin, T., Kirkwood, M. W., & Brown, T. M. (2014). Counselor-assisted problem solving improves caregiver efficacy following adolescent brain injury. *Rehabilitation Psychology, 59*(1), 1. https://doi.org/10.1037/a0034911

Wright, S. L., & Díaz, F. (2014). Neuroscience research on aging and implications for counseling psychology. *Journal of Counseling Psychology, 61*(4), 534–540. https://doi.org/10.1037/cou0000024

Yanowitch, R., & Coccaro, E. F. (2011). The neurochemistry of human aggression. In *Advances in genetics* (Vol. 75, pp. 151–169). Academic Press.

Chapter 13
Neuropsychologically Driven Evidence-Based Interventions in School Psychology

Scott L. Decker, Christopher Anzalone, Rachel M. Bridges, and Jessica C. Luedke

Learning Objectives

- To understand why neuropsychological approaches to test interpretation are important in the school context.
- To understand how neuropsychological assessment interpretation differs from standard assessment interpretation.
- To understand the importance of cognitive-based interventions to remediate academic deficits.
- To describe the Cognitive Attribute Matrix (CAM) for studying test responses.
- To describe the steps for using a neuropsychological approach for school-based assessment administration and interpretation and be able to apply these steps to a case example.

Neuropsychology in the School

Neuropsychology is an interdisciplinary approach involving neuroscience, cognitive neuroscience, genetics, learning, and behavioral measurement for the purpose of understanding behavior within an applied context. The origins of this inquiry date back to the nineteenth century (Catani & Ffytche, 2005; Hallahan & Mercer, 2001) and were primarily formed through observations of behavioral deficits as a result of brain injury (i.e., acquired dyslexia) associated with damage to the left angular gyrus (Hallahan & Mercer, 2001; Pickle, 1998; Shaywitz, 2003).

School neuropsychology has emerged as an interdisciplinary approach to apply neuropsychology for educational applications in a school context (Dean et al., 2003; Decker, 2008; Miller, 2007, 2010). Although relevant to numerous educational

S. L. Decker (✉) · C. Anzalone · R. M. Bridges · J. C. Luedke
Department of Psychology, University of South Carolina, Columbia, SC, USA
e-mail: sdecker@mailbox.sc.edu

R. C. D'Amato et al. (eds.), *Understanding the Biological Basis of Behavior*,
https://doi.org/10.1007/978-3-030-59162-5_13

domains, neuropsychology has arguably had the biggest influence on disability evaluations of children for special education. Namely, neuropsychological approaches have shaped (1) the development of most cognitive test batteries and (2) the constructs used to describe behavior, both of which are employed by school psychologists.

Despite its direct relevance for understanding children with neurodevelopmental disabilities, neuropsychological research and training have been highly under-represented in school psychology (Decker, 2008). Theoretical bias, lack of training, and misconceptions of neuropsychology all serve as barriers; however, a self-imposed obstacle for the growth of neuropsychology within school psychology has been the lack of simplified models of brain functioning that provide clear guidance for educational evaluations and interventions. Neuropsychological interpretation of test scores, as well as patterns of test scores, requires a process of clinical judgment that imposes "meaning" on test results. In turn, this application of meaning involves a substantial knowledge base of neuropsychology. Identification of "meaningful" patterns in test data, however, appears subjective to non-neuropsychologists. Additionally, the interpretive aspect of neuropsychology is a frequent criticism by school psychologists since it seemingly involves a high degree of inference.

The current chapter introduces a new method for implementing neuropsychological test interpretation that is more explicit and objective than clinical judgment alone and provides direct guidance for intervention approaches. First, neuropsychological interpretation is redefined as a form of pattern detection of behaviors consistent with theoretical neurocognitive models. Next, a neurocognitive pattern analysis procedure is defined for use with standard cognitive tests based on identifying common cognitive deficits across a multi-test cognitive battery. Detection of specific neurocognitive patterns of deficits increases intervention precision and thus intervention outcome success. Finally, a theoretical model for linking neurocognitive research to applied diagnostic testing in schools is provided in addition to case examples from school-based evaluations to demonstrate the application of the suggested approach.

Neuropsychological Approaches to Evidence-Based Assessment and Intervention

A neuropsychological framework for explaining learning and attention problems within a school environment has both diagnostic and remedial value. Within schools, children who struggle to learn at an appropriate developmental level become a concern to caregivers (adults and teachers), who seek an explanation for the problem. School faculty use data to quantify and identify the learning problem and apply interventions to remediate the problem. Most intervention and remedial attempts assume a causal connection between the intervention and the underlying problem; however, there is a lack of theoretical models to guide the selection of interventions that match the underlying cause, which is problematic for schools. Misattributing the causality of learning problems may delay appropriate treatment, waste time, effort, and resources and potentially further exacerbate the underlying learning problem.

The term data-based decision-making has become a popular principle for guiding educational assessment activities; however, data, by itself, are limited in utility. Equally important is the significance given to data and what it represents or "means." Effective decision-making with data requires an interpretive scheme that provides some underlying organization to raw data for making core diagnostic decisions. For example, the number of words read per minute will provide a numeric value (i.e., raw data). However, these raw data provide little value for answering core diagnostic questions such as "is the child significantly delayed in reading?" "does the child have a disability?" or "does the child need resources provided by special education?" Standard scores, frequently used in practice, provide a refinement of raw scores by controlling for age/developmental expectations, which provide a basic scheme for interpreting significance.

Similarly, neuropsychology is a framework for interpreting raw data (behavioral observations) in reference to brain functioning. The inherent value of a neuropsychological approach is in its ability to provide accurate inferences of behavior by understanding neurocognitive correlates of behaviors. Neuroscientific research is useful for neuropsychology to the extent it provides further clarification of cognition as instantiated by brain functioning and elucidates the distinction between typical and atypical patterns of behavior.

Neuropsychological approaches differ from standard assessment approaches using the general intelligence quotient (IQ) by explaining test performance as a product of information processing of the brain, as opposed to statistical composites from psychometrics. For example, overall IQ score, often derived from various measures of cognition, is psychometrically deduced (typically by factor analysis) based on statistical associations to form composite scores and given a label ("IQ"). This label is then used to explain the behavior that the measure is recording. Thus, an IQ score is both the result and the cause of behavior, which is circular in reasoning. In contrast, neuropsychological theories involve specific aspects of brain functioning (e.g., language, object recognition, memory, attention, etc.) and then explain test scores from these brain functions.

Similarly, Response-To-Intervention (RTI) approaches place greater emphasis on environmental or contextual factors as causes of behavior. Instructional and environmental parameters are manipulated (duration, frequency, stimulus exposure, etc.) to change behavior. While context is important, it cannot fully explain individual differences in learning outcomes for all children. Behavioral approaches provide limited guidance for understanding children with persistent learning problems due to intrinsic factors (i.e., cognition and the brain).

The benefit of a neuropsychological interpretative schema is in providing a framework for understanding the potential role of internal information processing capacities for causing learning problems. Neuropsychology provides a road map for understanding potential cognitive causes of behavior and is a required, not optional, step for understanding the cause of learning problems in children. Brain function is complex, and diagnostic evaluations need not search for cellular explanations in applied settings. Nonetheless, a "map" of cognition is needed and neuropsychology provides a theoretical collection of cognitive constructs based on neuroscientific studies of the brain.

Neuropsychological Interpretive Schemas and Case Conceptualization

While the need for a neuropsychological schema of cognition is clear, applying these concepts within schools to inform diagnosis and intervention involves the difficult task of interpreting assessment data. Interpreting test data to identify core neurocognitive deficits is difficult for two primary reasons: (1) each test measures a variety of neurocognitive processes and, (2) two individuals could each receive a low score on the same test for different reasons. The process of identifying neuropsychological causes of learning problems and ultimately using the underlying causes to inform intervention involve three important assumptions. First, behavioral responses to tasks (i.e., items on a test) are caused/influenced by a multidimensional sequence of neurological activity that as a whole represents the information processing elements referred to as cognition. Second, the sequential neurological processes generally involve perceptual (input), information processing (processing), and behavioral responses (output). Finally, inter- and intraindividual variation in cognition as inferred from responses to cognitive tasks results from variation in neurological activity. Understanding variation in cognition as a result of variation in the neurological sequences of brain activity requires explicit linking of task attributes (i.e., input, processing, output) to responses involved in cognitive tasks.

Identification of core neurocognitive problems that may manifest across a variety of tests is important for intervention planning. As a general rule, greater specification of a problem provides a more targeted approach for fixing the problem. The term ***intervention precision*** is used here to refer to the beneficiary aspects of assessment for providing more specific descriptions of learning problems that lead to more targeted interventions. Consequently, cognitive-based intervention outcomes will be enhanced through greater specification of cognition, not less.

The remedial benefits of specifying subcomponents as targets for intervention have been empirically demonstrated. For example, children with dyslexia were historically given visual therapies until the role of phonological processing was identified as a core process in reading decoding. Interventions targeting phonological processing have clearly demonstrated efficacy in helping children with dyslexia (Lyon, 1996; Peterson & Pennington, 2015; Shaywitz & Shaywitz, 2005). However, reading is multidimensional and deficits in other cognitive processes can result in reading problems (Paulesu et al., 2014). To name a few, reading problems can result from cognitive problems including language, phonology, rapid lexical retrieval, or working memory. It is evident that a child with learning problems due to language deficits, which is one of the most researched neurocognitive functions, would most appropriately be served with language interventions (as opposed to interventions for working memory). Improvement in understanding the specific problem (i.e., case conceptualization) leads to a narrowing of potential intervention options, otherwise known as intervention precision. Intervention precision results in tangible benefits in time and resources by not only encouraging the selection of the best intervention but also lowering the probability of considering inappropriate interventions, which may include instructional modification.

Although identifying the underlying neurocognitive problem improves intervention success, there is no standard and objective method for identifying common cognitive deficits across various diagnostic tests. Moreover, tests provide a hierarchy of scores (i.e., composite scores [overall reading] and individual scores [basic reading; reading comprehension]), yielding multiple levels of interpretation. The significance of a test score may change at these different levels. For example, a low score in reading would suggest a need for more reading instruction. Broken down further, a low score in basic reading with a low score in phonological processing would suggest a need for specific instruction in phonological processing; however; average basic reading and phonological processing scores but low scores in reading comprehension and working memory would suggest yet another direction for intervention.

Interpretation of multiple test scores often involves conditional influences, meaning the interpretation of one test may influence the interpretation of another test. For example, very low scores on a language test may lead to a conceptualization of language problems. Yet, very low scores on measures of language as well as all other cognitive measures may lead to a conceptualization of generally low cognitive ability. Henceforth, the term "pattern" is used to describe test interpretative situations in which a battery of tests is administered and test scores from one test may influence interpretation from other tests. Detection of these patterns will be discussed at length in the following section.

Neurocognitive Pattern Analysis

The primary benefit of neuropsychological testing is to detect core neurocognitive deficits by identifying patterns in behavioral performance. Consistent with historic approaches to neuropsychology, in neuroscience, brain functioning was deduced based on patterns of behavioral deficits in individuals with localized brain injuries. As a simplified example, lateralized brain injury can produce specific behavioral deficits isolated to one side of the body. Left-side brain injuries may result in sensory or motor impairment on the right side of the body (hemiparesis/paralysis). Because areas of the brain involved with language expression (Broca region) and right side of body motor movement are in close proximity, right-side motor deficits were often accompanied by language expression difficulties (Broca's Aphasia).

Observing the co-occurring patterns of behavioral deficits provided a direct association with impaired brain regions.

Brain imaging research has also distinguished unique patterns of brain activation for different tasks intended to measure different cognitive abilities. For example, the neurological basis of perceptual functions (occipital-vision, superior temporal-auditory, parietal-tactile) and motor movement (vocal or hand) are well-validated and highly predictive of brain region activation during task engagement. However, there are intermediary neurocognitive processes that occur in between perceptual and motor functions. Additionally, the neurocognitive influences are not in unity, meaning there is not a single process or brain region, in response to cognitive task challenges.

Consequently, linking neurocognitive influences to test scores requires decomposing potential influences into a sequence of perceptual, processing, and motor responses. Here, processing speed tests, a component of many cognitive batteries, will be used as an example. Measures of processing speed typically involve the rapid processing of simple visual tasks. Two important cognitive components on these tasks are *visual sequential processing* (scanning visual elements in a sequential order) and *cognitive efficiency* (speed in item completion). Neuroscientific research has revealed that visual processing involves the occipital region of the brain. The neurocognitive correlates of processing speed in the current example, and neuroscientific research on brain functioning at large, can be decomposed to provide the neurocognitive processes involved in tests used for school-based evaluations.

Cognitive Attribute Matrix: Decomposition of Neurocognitive Test Response Processes

As previously reviewed, tests that measure cognition elicit numerous neurological processes. Decomposition of specific test items into the corresponding neurocognitive elements facilitates a neuropsychological interpretation of test scores. An understanding of neurocognitive theories is critical for the ability to decompose items based on the specific neurocognitive processes needed to complete them. Generally, specification of the cognitive elements in test items as identified within a sequential process is the first step, which is common to all neurocognitive models of cognition. Moreover, the sequential process is part of each item on tests involving perceptual encoding, information processing, and behavioral response output.

Specification of the information processing stages for cognitive tasks is needed for each test, which can be listed in a matrix (henceforth referred to as the Cognitive Attribute Matrix [CAM]). The CAM provides explicit labels of the theoretical perceptual encoding (input), cognitive processing (processing), and behavioral response (output) elements of a given task. As a general procedure, the CAM should be determined prior to testing, not after, to prevent confirmation bias in hypothesis testing.

That is, specific items on tests are reviewed and cognitive processes, as well as input and output processes, are identified a priori. Cognitive task components should be guided by research as well as the clinician's judgment. While clinical judgment provides a subjective element, the clinician's input is an inevitable component of diagnostic decision-making. Explicating judgment in the cognitive task matrix, thus, reduces the subjectivity inherent in clinical judgment.

The CAM provides a basis for linking neuropsychological theories, which can provide data-based evidence with testable hypotheses, to applied practice. Theoretical models of the cognitive components of basic academic learning provide an essential "map" for guiding diagnostic evaluations. Furthermore, they provide a means for understanding the significance of score variations as linked to the "cognitive components" in cognitive tests. Table 13.1 provides a list of general cognitive components for input, processing, and output that might be included and represented in most cognitive test batteries. Note, visual icons are used to represent each cognitive component, academic ability (for achievement measures), and input modality which, as demonstrated later, has a functional purpose for facilitating identification of potential common cognitive, achievement, and/or perceptual deficits across different tests.

The Utility of Theoretical Neurocognitive Models

While understanding the neurocognitive basis of specific tests is important, it is insufficient for diagnostic testing. In addition to specification of cognitive components involved in a test, a theoretical model is needed for describing the sequential cognitive processes involved in specific skills and abilities. For example, reading involves known cognitive functions (phonological processing; working memory). Additionally, numerous studies of brain activity have found a predictable series of neurological activity associated with word reading.

Figure 13.1 provides a simplified theoretical model of basic reading (see Berninger & Richards, 2002 for more complex models in reading and other academic areas). Reading at the word-level starts with visual processing. Initial visual processing occurs in the occipital lobe of the brain, which receives projections from the optic nerve; thus, —predictably— initial visual processing in word reading begins in the occipital lobe. Visual sequential processing of letters involves ocular control as well as rapid perceptual scanning. Phonological awareness refers to the degree in which a child is aware of differential sound elements that compose words as orally spoken. Phonology involves the rapid associative learning of phonological sounds to specific letters and graphemes. When retrieved, phonological associations of graphemes match the auditory pattern of a known word within the child's vocabulary and semantic retrieval processes are activated that involve word meaning associations. Word reading measures require a child to accurately and fluently read (oral expression). A child may correctly read a word without knowing its meaning, indicating sufficient ortho-phonology associations and insufficient semantic activation.

Table 13.1 Cognitive attribute matrix

Processing	Description	Symbol
Visual	Involves the physical and mental abilities required to sense and interpret physical objects from the environment	
Auditory	Involves the physical and mental abilities required to sense and interpret sounds from the environment	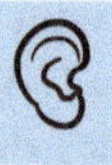
Tactile	Involves the physical and mental abilities required to sense and interpret the presence of objects touching one's body	
	Modality: Cognitive Abilities	
Attention	The ability to direct one's cognitive resources toward specific environmental stimuli	
Reasoning	The ability to direct one's cognitive resources in a logical way in order to form a judgment or conclusion	
Memory	The ability of one's cognitive systems to store and retrieve information	
Working Memory	The ability of one's cognitive systems to store and process information currently in use	
Visual-Spatial	The ability of one's cognitive systems to mentally manipulate 2-D and 3-D figures	
Processing Speed	The time it takes one's cognitive systems to perform mental tasks	
Phonological Processing	The ability of one's cognitive systems to parse and integrate subcomponents of written or spoken word sounds	
	Modality: Academic Skills	
Word Reading	The skills of one to fluently read written or printed material aloud	
Reading Comprehension	The skills of one to read and interpret strings of test or passages of text	
Written Language	The skills of one to fluently compose syntactically, structurally, and grammatically correct written sentences	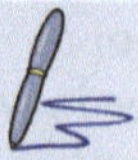
Calculation	The skills of one to compute mathematical questions and problems	
Applied Calculation	The skills of one to apply calculation skills toward orally presented problems	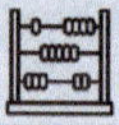

Table 13.1 (continued)

Output (Response)		
Point	Client is instructed to respond to the prompt(s) by pointing to their answer(s)	
Pencil	Client is instructed to mark or write their answer(s) with a pencil	
Voice	Client is instructed to respond to the prompt(s) or question(s) orally	
General Motor	Client is instructed to respond by manipulating physical objects or moving in a particular way	

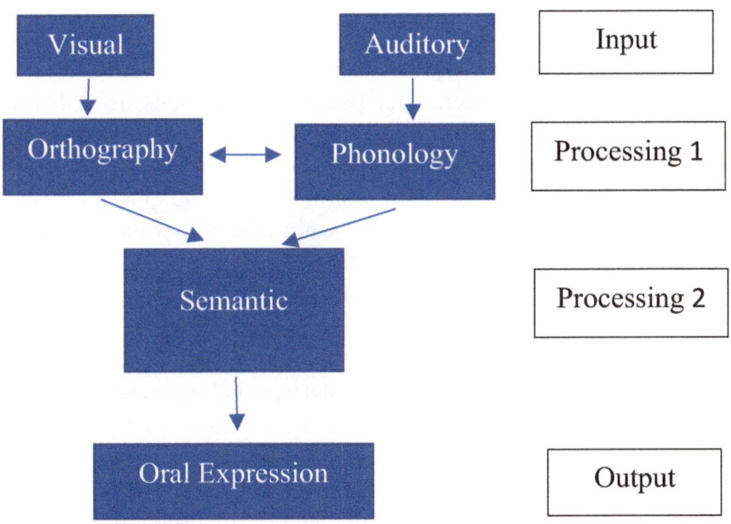

Fig. 13.1 Simplified cognitive model of reading

Simply asking a child to define the word helps distinguish this difference. Text comprehension, which goes beyond basic reading, involves additional cognitive components including syntax for comprehending sentence structure and working memory for creating a model of meaning from text. Note, while phonology has become a known component of reading and a hallmark deficit of dyslexia, it is rarely acknowledged that phonology is a cognitive process that mediates word decoding. Additionally, it is rare that phonology is understood within a cognitive model of processing.

The purpose of applying theoretical models of skills related to academics, such as the example provided above, to the neurocognitive components of tests is to inform diagnosis. Namely, within public schools there are specific eligibility categories through which a child can receive special education services. Since these categories are not labeled with neurocognitive components, a theoretical model describing the involvement these components have in different aspects of education is necessary. Moreover, neurocognitive models of academic skills provide a link between neurocognitive pattern analysis and school psychology. The following section will integrate the previously discussed steps into a user-friendly approach for applying neuropsychology into schools.

Data Organization for Identifying Common Neurocognitive Deficits in Multidimensional Cognitive Tests: Matrix, Model, & Match

One commonality across most approaches for diagnostic identification of children with disabilities is finding evidence for performance deficits using some form of measurement. General approaches using a pattern of strengths and weaknesses in performance focus on broad constructs or clusters (Alfonso et al., 2005; Flanagan & Harrison, 2012; Hale et al., 2008). The use of these broad clusters as the basis of weaknesses presumes the various measures within the cluster measure a single cognitive process, which is inconsistent with the neurocognitive assumptions presented in this chapter. Consequently, the approach advocated here is to allow the data to speak for themselves—low scores are simply low scores and the simplest method for identifying core deficits is to evaluate the commonality across these low scores.

Generally, assessment consists of administering a battery of tests measuring multiple dimensions of behavioral functioning (e.g., cognition, achievement, socio-emotional), which are administered for a specific purpose inherent in the referral or clinical description. Patterns of deficits are evaluated to determine the degree to which they match patterns expected for the underlying problem, often a disability condition. As a procedural description for implementing the approach outlined in this chapter, the following steps are provided:

1. Complete Cognitive Attribute ***Matrix (CAM)*** for all tests used in assessment. While clinical judgment is needed, guidance from test documentation and literature reviews is required for supporting evidence.
2. Select a Cognitive ***Model(s)*** for understanding potential cognitive mediators of learning as reflected in the referral question.
3. Sort scores in CAM from high to low.
4. Define Strength and Weakness based on level of performance (e.g., Strength >115, Weakness <85).
5. Identify cognitive deficits common across all weaknesses.
6. ***Match*** common cognitive processes specified by CAM on tasks determined to be a weakness to an appropriate intervention.

The *Matrix, Model, and Match* approach is provided for describing the procedural elements inherent in all clinical neuropsychological evaluations. It is important to note the degree of accuracy in specifying a Matrix or in outlining a Model is a matter of empirical evaluation and applied utility. Nonetheless, these steps are provided as an attempt to explicate the processes of clinical judgment that differentiate neuropsychological evaluations from standard evaluations.

Applications in Applied Practice

To provide concrete examples of employing the approach outlined in the current chapter, case studies are provided in various disability conditions. Tables 13.2, 13.3, and 13.4 present examples of cases in which the principles of the *Matrix, Model, and Match* practice were implemented. Each case presents a student with at least one cognitive deficiency that is consistent with a learning deficit (e.g., ADHD) that is often encountered by practicing school psychologists. To reiterate, by arranging the data in this way, the evaluator is better able to pinpoint the area of cognition that is deficient for each particular student and can thus formulate an intervention targeted to combat each weakness.

Learning Disability in Reading To expand upon the previous example of cognitive reading models, an example of a student identified as having a specific learning disability in reading will be discussed. Table 13.2 displays a matrix of data accumulated from multiple test batteries (i.e., NEPSY, WISC, WJ-ACH, WJ-OL, GORT) given to one student aggregated into a comprehensive display. In this dataset, based on the icons we can easily see that Phonological Processing is a common component among all of this student's lowest standard scores while all other icons (input modalities and output modalities) show no particular pattern and cannot be generalized to any range of results. As more test batteries are implemented to evaluate a particular construct (in this case reading), the pattern of results should grow increasingly distinct which serves to further support or refute various (or conflicting) hypotheses.

As illustrated in the organized data table, reading tests are highly represented as a weakness. Additionally, phonological processing and language measures are in the impaired range. Visual-Spatial and non-verbal reasoning measures are highly represented as personal strengths. Thus, the table demonstrates a clear trend of reading-based deficits concurrent with language-based measures, particularly in phonological processing. This pattern is implicated in most theoretical models of reading disabilities. Again, the table clearly points the direction of interventions toward the use of phonological processing and language-based approaches.

Learning Disability in Math versus Processing Speed Deficit Like all specific learning disabilities (SLD), children with math learning disabilities (i.e., dyscalculia) have core cognitive deficits that are direct causes of unexpected learning prob-

Table 13.2 Learning disability in reading

Score	Test	Input	Process1	Process2	Output
110	WISC Picture Concepts	Visual	Fluid Reasoning	Abstract Reasoning	Oral/Motor
105	WISC Block Design	Visual	Visual-Spatial Ability	Visual Spatial Fluency	Motor
105	WISC Matrix Reasoning	Visual	Pattern Recognition	Numerical Reasoning	Motor
105	WISC Symbol Search	Visual	Visual Processing Fluency	Graphomotor Speed	Motor
105	NEPSY Design Copying	Visual	Visual-Spatial Ability	Visual Attention	Motor
102	WJ-Ach Calculations	Visual	Mathematical Facts	Numerical Reasoning	Motor
100	WISC Similarities	Auditory	Verbal Reasoning	Concept Formation	Oral
100	WISC Comprehension	Auditory	Verbal Reasoning	Concept Formation	Oral
100	WISC Coding	Visual	Graphomotor Speed	Visual Processing Fluency	Motor
100	NEPSY Visuomotor Precision	Visual	Graphomotor Speed	Graphomotor Precision	Motor
100	NEPSY Mem Faces	Visual	Face Recognition	Visual Memory	Motor
99	WJ-Ach Math Fluency	Visual	Numerical Processing Fluency	Mathematical Memory Retrieval	Motor
95	WISC Vocabulary	Auditory	Oral Language	Language Retrieval	Oral
95	WISC Letter-Number Seq	Auditory	Working Memory	Verbal Attention	Oral
95	NEPSY Narrative Memory	Auditory	Verbal Memory	Verbal Attention	Oral
85	WISC Digit Span	Auditory	Auditory Working Memory	Auditory Attention	Oral
83	WJ-Ach Writing Fluency	Visual	Written Language	Graphomotor Speed	Motor
82	WJ-Ach Writing Samp	Visual	Written Language	Verbal Working Memory	Motor
79	WJ-Ach Spelling	Visual	Phono-Grapheme Ability	Verbal Memory	Motor
76	WJ-Ach Read Fluency	Visual	Word Recognition	Verbal Processing Fluency	Motor
75	WJ Pass Comp	Visual	Word Recognition	Verbal Working Memory	Oral
75	NEPSY Mem Names	Auditory	Language Processing	Verbal Working Memory	Oral
75	GORT Fluency	Visual	Rapid Word Reading	Verbal Processing Fluency	Oral
70	WJ Letter-Word ID	Visual	Verbal Comprehension	Verbal Reasoning	Motor
70	NEPSY Phono Processing	Auditory	Phoneme Awareness	Verbal Reasoning	oral
70	GORT Comp	Visual	Reading	Verbal Working Memory	Oral
60	WJ-Ach Word Attack	Visual	Phonological processing	Verbal Reasoning	Oral

Table 13.3 Processing speed deficit

Score	Test	Input	Process 1	Process 2	output
101	WJ-Cog Verbal Comp	Visual	Oral Language	Language Retrieval	Oral
100	WJ-Ach Calculation	Visual	Mathematical Facts	Numerical Reasoning	Motor
99	WJ-Ach Sound Blending	Auditory	Oral Language	Language Retrieval	Oral
94	WJ-Cog Spatial Relations	Visual	Visual-Spatial	Reasoning	Oral
89	WJ-Cog Concept Formation	Visual	Pattern Recognition	Reasoning	Motor
83	WJ-Cog Numbers Reversed	Auditory	Numerical Working Memory	Numeric Processing	Oral
83	WJ-Ach Applied Problems	Auditory	Numeric Reasoning	Numerical Working Memory	Oral
81	WJ-Cog Rapid Picture Naming	Visual	Verbal Processing Fluency	Language Retrieval	Oral
78	WJ-Ach Math Fluency	Visual	Numerical Processing Fluency	Mathematic Memory Retrieval	Motor
75	WJ-Cog Visual Matching	Visual	Visual Processing Fluency	Pattern Recognition	Motor

lems (Ardila & Rosselli, 2002; Ashkenazi et al., 2013; Decker & Roberts, 2015; Dehaene et al., 2004). Number sense, magnitude estimation, fact retrieval, and working memory deficits have all been identified as important constructs contributing to math SLD (Geary et al., 2012; Geary et al., 2012).

Identifying the cognitive deficits inherent in all SLD has been a major challenge (Geary, 2013). The neurocognitive procedure outlined in this chapter was implemented on a case study of a child identified as having math SLD. Table 13.3 displays a table of data accumulated from one student labeled with the CAM previously presented. The child's lowest Standard Scores in cognitive and achievement tests all involve visual processing. However, there are numerous tests that are not in the impaired range that also involve visual processing. Thus, visual-based perceptual deficits can be ruled out as a source of the learning problem. Similarly, graphomotor or tests involving holding a pencil are a deficit for 2 out of 3 tests. However, there is at least one test in the non-impaired range involving graphomotor output, which reduces the likelihood of it being the source of the problem. In contrast, tests involving processing speed in different perceptual modalities are in the impaired range and none are in the non-impaired range. The processing speed deficits involve math fluency but also language measures. Indeed, the child, who was identified in schools

Table 13.4 ADHD

Score	Test	Input	Process 1	Process 2	output
115	WJ-OL Rapid Pict Naming	Visual	Verbal Fluency	Verbal Memory	Oral
111	WJ-Cog Num Series	Visual	Numerical Reasoning	Numerical Working Memory	Motor
110	WJ-Cog Oral Vocab	Visual	Verbal Reasoning	Verbal Memory	Oral
109	WJ-Cog Verbal Attention	Auditory	Verbal Working Memory	Verbal Attention	Oral
108	WJ-Cog Visualization	Visual	Visual Working Memory	Visual Spatial Perception	Oral
105	WJ-Ach Letter-Word ID	Visual	Verbal Comprehension	Verbal Reasoning	Motor
99	WJ-Cog Numbers Reversed	Auditory	Numeric Working Memory	Numerical Attention	Oral
93	WJ-Cog Story Recall	Auditory	Verbal Comprehension	Verbal Working Memory	Oral
93	WJ-Cog Phono Processing	Auditory	Phoneme Awareness	Verbal Fluency	Oral
90	WJ-Ach Calculation	Visual	Mathematical Facts	Numerical Reasoning	Motor
81	WJ-Cog Pair Cancellation	Visual	Visual Attention	Visual Processing Fluency	Motor
72	WJ-Cog Letter-Pattern Matching	Visual	Visual Attention	Orthographic Processing Fluency	Motor

as having a SLD in the area of Math, performed in the normal range for math calculation. Thus, as evidenced by the arranged data in Table 13.3, the core underlying problem is best described by processing speed, as opposed to SLD math, and the best intervention approach is to remediate or accommodate processing speed deficits.

Attention Deficit Hyperactivity Disorder (ADHD) Current definitions describe ADHD as a *neuro*developmental disorder (American Psychiatric Association, 2013; Barkley, 2015), indicating continued recognition that underlying deficits within the central nervous system generates impairments observed in behavioral functioning. Models have long suggested that the fundamental neural deficits of individuals afflicted with ADHD reside within the improper functioning of the frontal lobe. Specifically, fronto-striatal and frontoparietal networks, which support a range of executive processes, are frequently found to be loci of dysfunction in ADHD (Barkley, 1997; Castellanos & Tannock, 2002). Consistently, a pattern of hypoactivity in frontal regions with altered patterns of activity in anterior cingulate, dorsolateral prefrontal, and ventrolateral prefrontal cortices, as well as related parietal, striatal, and cerebellar regions, has been found through reviews of PET, SPECT, fMRI, EEG, and cognitive paradigms studying inhibitory control, selective attention, working memory, and vigilance (Bush et al., 2005).

Like Tables 13.2 and 13.3, Table 13.4 organizes the data from the test batteries in a congruent fashion; however, this case exemplifies a student with ADHD. When arranged using this method, the evaluator can see a significant drop in scores for two subtests in particular. The subtests with the lowest standard scores are seen to have two cognitive processes in common: Attention and Processing Speed. To rule out any competing hypotheses, we follow the same procedures outlined in the previous example.

The underactivity in the aforementioned brain regions associated with ADHD results in various deficits, but can be summarized broadly as deficits in attention and efficient cognitive processing, congruent with the results suggested by the data obtained by from the case displayed in Table 13.4. Non-pharmacologic interventions for ADHD exist and are growing in popularity as the field of psychology continues to advance. Current interventions that include behavioral modification have shown to be somewhat effective for treating location-specific symptoms, but are most often less pronounced than those obtained with psychostimulant medication (Kutcher et al., 2004). In this particular case, visual attention is an ideal target for intervention.

Traumatic Brain Injury (TBI) Despite the large evidence-base linking TBI symptomology to underlying neural changes, limitations such as large costs and lack of resources result in a lack of consistent and repeated usage of neuroimaging techniques (Rapp et al., 2015). Additionally, the wide variety in symptoms and the variability in severity render it difficult to pinpoint specific changes in the brain in connection with definitive symptoms and outcomes. Furthermore, TBIs often complicate previous diagnoses and medical issues (Leddy et al., 2012). As such, interventions for individuals with TBI are typically symptom specific and considerate of other comorbidities.

More contemporary research on TBI has long been associated with general impairments including physical, emotional, behavioral, and cognitive changes (Alexander, 1995; Belanger et al., 2005; Langlois et al., 2006). Although symptoms may vary on a case-by-case basis, common symptoms include headaches, fatigue, decreased self-regulation, depression, reduced processing speed, and working memory deficits (Frencham et al., 2005; Kaldoja & Kolk, 2012; Holland et al., , 2015; Levin et al., 2004; Paniak et al., 2002). Recently, working memory and visuomotor speed have been linked to various TBI outcomes through neuroimaging techniques (i.e., CT, fNIRS, DRI, fMRI, and EEG; Kontos et al., 2014; Kumar et al., , 2009, 2013; Levin et al., 2008; Wilde et al., 2011; Wozniak et al., 2007).

Table 13.5 displays data obtained from a student who had experienced a recent TBI. When examining this table for patterns, the examiner can see a general trend in the cognitive processes used for the tests with the lowest standard scores. Moreover, these data suggest that the student has deficits in Processing Speed as well as in Attention. Although symptoms may vary on a case-by-case basis, the deficits suggested by this dataset do align with certain symptoms that are typically seen in patients with TBI, as described above. While the cognitive and achievement tests implemented in this case are not sensitive to all possible symptoms of TBI (and more measures would be necessary to confirm a diagnosis), the deficits displayed in these data are consistent with what one would expect a patient with a TBI to display based on the measures administered.

Table 13.5 TBI

Score	Test	Input	Process 1	Process 2	output
134	WJ-Cog Number Series	Visual	Numerical Reasoning	Numerical Working Memory	Motor
130	WJ-Ach Applied Problems	Auditory	Numerical Reasoning	Numerical Working Memory	Oral
124	WJ-Ach Calculation	Visual	Mathematical Facts	Numerical Reasoning	Motor
118	WJ-Cog Verbal Attention	Auditory	Verbal Working Memory	Verbal Attention	Oral
117	WJ-Cog Visualization	Visual	Visual Working Memory	Visual Spatial Perception	Oral
111	WJ-Cog Concept formation	Visual	Pattern Recognition	Reasoning	Motor
110	WJ-Cog Story Recall	Auditory	Verbal Comprehension	Verbal Working Memory	Oral
107	WJ-Ach Letter-Word ID	Visual	Verbal Comprehension	Verbal Reasoning	Motor
92	WJ-Cog Pair Cancellation	Visual	Visual Processing Fluency	Visual Attention	Motor
88	WJ-Ach Math Fluency	Visual	Numerical Processing Fluency	Mathematic Memory Retrieval	Motor
82	WJ-Cog Letter-Pattern Matching	Visual	Orthographic Processing Fluency	Visual Attention	Motor
73	WJ-Cog Phono Processing	Auditory	Verbal Fluency	Phoneme Awareness	Oral
68	WJ-Cog Numbers Reversed	Auditory	Numeric Working Memory	Numerical Attention	Oral

Conclusions

The future of education at large is in cognition. Traditional educational models focused on rote memorization, in part, because education was viewed as a process of developing representations of facts and information in memory. Technologically based information retrieval systems (i.e., computers) have all but replaced this need, and the development of rote memory skills is decreasing in importance. In contrast, flexible cognitive processes that (1) are integrated and (2) facilitate rapid behavioral adaptation to changing environmental conditions will likely increase as a focus of education. With this change, the emphasis of general schooling and intervention techniques must be on building and remediating deficits associated with cognitive processes.

Thus, neuropsychology has a strong future in schools, with its foothold in diagnostic evaluations and selecting appropriate interventions to help children with cognitive disabilities. While neuropsychological research has historically demonstrated importance in describing disorders of learning and attention, several barriers have prevented a seamless integration within the school system. The current chapter described a model to be employed by school psychologists in order to better inform psychoeducational assessments and associated interventions.

Here, the ***Matrix, Model, Match*** system is described as a solution for applying complex neurocognitive theories to education. School psychologists are provided a step-by-step process for determining sequential cognitive components within tests and test items; finding patterns of weakness among multiple tests; applying a theoretical cognitive model to match weaknesses with referral questions and eligibility categories; and ultimately use the sum of this information to guide intervention selection.

The model presented in this chapter is a significant departure from standard methods of test interpretation in school psychology. Currently, factor analytic approaches are frequently used to define test constructs based on factor loadings for specific tests. While factor analyses provide suggestive evidence for understanding the underlying cognitive processes in a test, factor groupings are solely based on statistical probabilities. Factor results must be supplemented with the theoretical model of specific test's constructs—decomposing the neurocognitive components of tests provides such a means.

In part, the factor analytic groupings of contemporary measures directly reflect general components of cognitive tests. For example, *Ga* and *Gv* factors in the Cattell-Horn-Carroll (CHC) model of intelligence directly reflect perceptual modalities (auditory and visual, respectively). Other factors such as *Gf* (Fluid Intelligence) and *Gc* (Crystallized Intelligence) are less direct because the terminology (fluid and crystallized) is from a theoretical background reflecting a metaphorical description of cognition rather than a neurocognitive basis.

Neurocognitive theory provides a more concrete and experimentally testable approach to understanding the neurocognitive process in specific tests. Additionally, it provides a means of understanding cross-factor loadings by clarifying shared or common cognitive processes.

While this chapter provides a rationale and basic overview for applying the ***Matrix, Model, Match*** system, a comprehensive outline of all cognitive deficits and theoretical explanations is beyond the current scope. Future works may look to provide more in-depth exploration of using this method in meeting requirements for specific eligibility categories (e.g., SLD in reading), interpreting more complex CAMs, identifying individuals with multiple disabilities, and determining if interventions match an underlying deficit. Nonetheless, school psychologists are encouraged to employ this technique, either formally or informally, within their current practices to better inform the link between assessment and intervention.

Discussion Questions:

1. What are some barriers to implementing neuropsychology when serving children and adolescents?
2. How does the practice of school psychology differ from that of clinical neuropsychology?
3. Describe Response to Intervention (RTI) and benefits of using such a system in schools.
4. Describe the Cognitive Attribute Matrix (MAX) and its relation to clinical neuropsychology.
5. What is the Matrix, Model, Match System and how can it be implemented?
6. How does the Matrix, Model, Match System apply to evidence-based practice in neuropsychology?

EPPP Sample Questions

1. Neuropsychological approaches to assessment are different from standard approaches to assessment in that neuropsychological approaches:

   A. Evaluate specific aspects of brain functioning to explain test scores from these brain functions
   B. Place greater emphasis on environmental or contextual factors as causes of behavior
   C. Can only be used for understanding learning disabilities
   D. Inform assessment but not interventions for neurocognitive disorders

2. Which of the following underlying cognitive processing deficits may contribute to academic reading difficulties?

   A. Phonological awareness
   B. Working Memory
   C. Processing Speed
   D. All the above deficits may contribute to reading difficulties

3. The *Matrix, Model, Match* system is a solution for applying complex neurocognitive theories to:

   A. Education
   B. Psychology
   C. Teaching
   D. Counseling

4. More contemporary research on TBI has long been associated with general impairments including physical, emotional, behavioral, and _______ changes.

   A. Academic
   B. Social
   C. Oral
   D. Cognitive

5. *Intervention precision* refers to the beneficiary aspects of assessment for providing more specific descriptions of learning problems that lead to __________.

   A. Private counseling sessions
   B. Academic instruction
   C. Targeted interventions
   D. Teletherapy

   Answers: A, D, A, D, C.

Proactive Readings

Transcending the Past

Gaddes, W. H., & Edgell, D. (1994). *Learning disabilities and brain function: A neuropsychological approach* (3rd ed.). Springer-Verlag.

Reynolds, C. R., & Gutkin, T. B. (1999). *The handbook of school psychology*. John Wiley & Sons Inc.

Excelling in the Present

D'Amato, R. C., Fletcher-Janzen, E., & Reynolds, C. R. (Eds.). (2010). *Handbook of School Neuropsychology*. John Wiley & Sons.

Hale, J. B., & Fiorello, C. A. (2017). *School neuropsychology: A practitioner's handbook*. Guilford .

Decker, S. L. (2008). School neuropsychology consultation in neurodevelopmental disorders. *Psychology in the Schools*, *45*(9), 799–811.

Transforming the Future

Traughber, M. C., & D'Amato, R. C. (2005). Integrating evidence-based neuropsychological services into school settings: Issues and challenges for the future. In R. C. D'Amato, E. Fletcher-Janzen, & C. R. Reynolds (Eds.), *Handbook of school neuropsychology* (pp. 827–857). Wiley.

Witsken, D., Stoeckel, A., & D'Amato, R. C. (2008). Leading educational change using a neuropsychological response-to-intervention approach: Linking our past, present, and future. *Psychology in the Schools*, *45*(9), 781–798.

References

Alexander, M. P. (1995). Mild traumatic brain injury: Pathophysiology, natural history, and clinical management. *Neurology. 45(7)*, 1253-1260 https://doi.org/10.1212/WNL.45.7.1253

Alfonso, V. C., Flanagan, D. P., & Radwan, S. (2005). The impact of the Cattell-Horn-Carroll theory on test development and interpretation of cognitive and academic abilities. In *Contemporary intellectual assessment: Theories, tests, and issues* (2nd ed., pp. 185–202). The Guilford Press.

American Psychiatric Association. (2013). *Diagnostic and statistical manual of mental disorders* (5th ed.). https://doi.org/10.1176/appi.books.9780890425596

Ardila, A., & Rosselli, M. (2002). Acalculia and dyscalculia. *Neuropsychology Review, 12*(4), 179–231. doi: 10.1023/a:1021343508573

Ashkenazi, S., Black, J. M., Abrams, D. A., Hoeft, F., & Menon, V. (2013). Neurobiological underv549–569. https://doi.org/10.1177/0022219413483174

Barkley, R. A. (1997). Behavioral inhibition, sustained attention, and executive functions: Constructing a unifying theory of ADHD. *Psychological Bulletin, 121*(1), 65. https://doi.org/10.1037/0033-2909.121.1.65

Barkley, R. A. (2015). Etiologies of ADHD. In R. A. Barkley (Eds.), *Attention Deficit Hyperactivity Disorder: A Handbook for Diagnosis and Treatment* (pp. 356–390). The Guilford Press.

Belanger, H. G., Curtiss, G., Demery, J. A., Lebowitz, B. K., & Vanderploeg, R. D. (2005). Factors moderating neuropsychological outcomes following mild traumatic brain injury: A meta-analysis. *Journal of the International Neuropsychological Society, 11*(3), 215–227. doi: 10.1017/S1355617705050277

Berninger, V. W., & Richards, T. L. (2002). *Brain literacy for educators and psychologists*. Academic Press.

Bush, G., Valera, E. M., & Seidman, L. J. (2005). Functional neuroimaging of Attention-Deficit/Hyperactivity Disorder: A review and suggested future directions. *Biological Psychiatry, 57*(11), 1273–1284. https://doi.org/10.1016/j.biopsych.2005.01.034

Castellanos, F. X., & Tannock, R. (2002). Neuroscience of Attention-Deficit/Hyperactivity Disorder: The search for endophenotypes. *Nature Reviews Neuroscience, 3*(8), 617. doi: 10.1038/nrn896

Catani, M., & Ffytche, D. H. (2005). The rises and falls of disconnection syndromes. *Brain, 128*(10), 2224–2239. https://doi.org/10.1093/brain/awh622

Dean, R. S., Woodcock, R. W., Decker, S. L., & Schrank, F. A. (2003). A cognitive neuropsychology assessment system. In F. Schrank & D. Flanagan (Eds.), *WJ III clinical use and interpretation* (pp. 345–376). Academic Press.

Decker, S. L. (2008). School neuropsychology consultation in neurodevelopmental disorders. *Psychology in the Schools, 45*(9), 799–811. https://doi.org/10.1002/pits.20327

Decker, S. L., & Roberts, A. M. (2015). Specific cognitive predictors of early math problem solving. *Psychology in the Schools, 52*(5), 477–488. https://doi.org/10.1002/pits.21837

Dehaene, S., Molko, N., Cohen, L., & Wilson, A. J. (2004). Arithmetic and the brain. *Current Opinion in Neurobiology, 14*(2), 218–224. https://doi.org/10.1016/j.conb.2004.03.008

Flanagan, D. P., & Harrison, P. L. (2012). *Contemporary intellectual assessment: Theories, tests, and issues*. Guilford Press.

Frencham, K. A., Fox, A. M., & Mayberry, M. T. (2005). Neuropsychological studies of mild traumatic brain injury: A meta-analytic review of research since 1995. *Journal of Clinical and Experimental Neuropsychology, 27*, 334–351. https://doi.org/10.1080/13803390490520328

Geary, D. C., Hoard, M. K., & Bailey, D. H. (2012a). Fact retrieval deficits in low achieving children and children with mathematical learning disability. *Journal of Learning Disabilities, 45*(4), 291–307. https://doi.org/10.1177%2F0022219410392046

Geary, D. C., Hoard, M. K., Nugent, L., & Bailey, D. H. (2012b). Mathematical cognition deficits in children with learning disabilities and persistent low achievement: A five-year prospective study. *Journal of Educational Psychology, 104*(1), 206-223. https://doi.org/10.1037/a0025398

Geary, D. C. (2013). Early foundations for mathematics learning and their relations to learning disabilities. *Current directions in psychological science, 22*(1), 23–27. https://doi.org/10.1177%2F0963721412469398

Hale, J. B., Flanagan, D. P., & Naglieri, J. (2008). Alternative research-based methods for IDEA 2004 identification of children with specific learning disabilities. *Communiqué, 36*(8).

Hallahan, D. P., & Mercer, C. D. (2001). LD: Historical perspectives. *Learning disability summit, United States Department of Education*, Washington, DC.

Holland, A., Hernandez, A., & Stavinoha, P. (2015). Neurological and neuropsychiatric disorders: traumatic brain injury B-78. Cognitive and social/emotional functioning following pediatric TBI: a five-year longitudinal study. *Archives of Clinical Neuropsychology, 30*(6), 551–552. https://doi.org/10.1093/arclin/acv047.173

Kaldoja, M. L., & Kolk, A. (2012). Social-emotional behaviour in infants and toddlers with mild traumatic brain injury. *Brain Injury, 26*(7–8), 1005–1013. https://doi.org/10.3109/02699052.2012.660516

Kontos, A. P., Huppert, T. J., Beluk, N. H., Elbin, R. J., Henry, L. C., French, J., ... & Collins, M. W. (2014). Brain activation during neurocognitive testing using functional near-infrared spectroscopy in patients following concussion compared to healthy controls. *Brain Imaging and Behavior, 8*(4), 621–634. https://doi.org/10.1007/s11682-014-9289-9

Kumar, S., Rao, S. L., Chandramouli, B. A., & Pillai, S. V. (2009). Reduction of functional brain connectivity in mild traumatic brain injury during working memory. *Journal of Neurotrauma, 26*(5), 665–675. https://doi.org/10.1089/neu.2008.0644

Kumar, S., Rao, S. L., Chandramouli, B. A., & Pillai, S. (2013). Reduced contribution of executive functions in impaired working memory performance in mild traumatic brain injury patients. *Clinical Neurology and Neurosurgery, 115*(8), 1326–1332. https://doi.org/10.1016/j.clineuro.2012.12.038

Kutcher, S., Aman, M., Brooks, S. J., Buitelaar, J., van Daalen, E., Fegert, J., … Kusumakar, V. (2004). International consensus statement on Attention-Deficit/Hyperactivity Disorder (ADHD) and disruptive behaviour disorders (DBDs): Clinical implications and treatment practice suggestions. *European Neuropsychopharmacology, 14*(1), 11–28. https://doi.org/10.1016/s0924-977x(03)00045-2

Langlois, J. A., Rutland-Brown, W., & Wald, M. M. (2006). The epidemiology and impact of traumatic brain injury: a brief overview. *The Journal of Head Trauma Rehabilitation, 21*(5), 375–378. doi: 10.1097/00001199-200609000-00001

Leddy, J. J., Sandhu, H., Sodhi, V., Baker, J. G., & Willer, B. (2012). Rehabilitation of concussion and post-concussion syndrome. *Sports Health, 4*(2), 147–154. https://dx.doi.org/10.1177%2F1941738111433673

Levin, H. S., Hanten, G., Zhang, L., Swank, P. R., Ewing-Cobbs, L., Dennis, M., ... & Hunter, J. V. (2004). Changes in working memory after traumatic brain injury in children. *Neuropsychology, 18*(2), 240. https://psycnet.apa.org/doi/10.1037/0894-4105.18.2.240

Levin, H. S., Wilde, E. A., Chu, Z., Yallampalli, R., Hanten, G. R., Li, X., ... & Hunter, J. V. (2008). Diffusion tensor imaging in relation to cognitive and functional outcome of traumatic brain injury in children. *The Journal of Head Trauma Rehabilitation, 23*(4), 197. https://dx.doi.org/10.1097%2F01.HTR.0000327252.54128.7c

Lyon, G. R. (1996). Learning disabilities. *The Future of Children, 6*(1) 54–76.

Miller, D. C. (2007). *Essentials of school neuropsychological assessment*. Wiley.

Miller, D. C. (Ed.). (2010). B*est practices in school neuropsychology: Guidelines for effective practice, assessment, and evidence-based intervention*. Wiley.

Paulesu, E., Danelli, L., & Berlingeri, M. (2014). Reading the dyslexic brain: Multiple dysfunctional routes revealed by a new meta-analysis of PET and fMRI activation studies. *Frontiers in Human Neuroscience, 8*, 830. https://dx.doi.org/10.3389%2Ffnhum.2014.00830

Paniak, C., Reynolds, S., Phillips, K., Toller-Lobe, G., Melnyk, A., & Nagy, J. (2002). Patient complaints within 1 month of mild traumatic brain injury: A controlled study. *Archives of Clinical Neuropsychology, 17*(4), 319–334. https://doi.org/10.1016/S0887-6177(01)00115-9

Peterson, R. L., & Pennington, B. F. (2015). Developmental dyslexia. *Annual Review of Clinical Psychology, 11*, 283–307. https://doi.org/10.1146/annurev-clinpsy-032814-112842

Pickle, J. M. (1998). Historical trends in biological and medical investigations of reading disabilities: 1850–1915. *Journal of Learning Disabilities, 31*(6), 625–635. https://doi.org/10.1177%2F002221949803100614

Rapp, P. E., Keyser, D. O., Albano, A., Hernandez, R., Gibson, D. B., Zambon, R. A., ... & Nichols, A. S. (2015). Traumatic brain injury detection using electrophysiological methods. *Frontiers in Human Neuroscience, 9*, 11. https://doi.org/10.3389/fnhum.2015.00011

Shaywitz, S. E. (2003). *Overcoming dyslexia: A new and complete science-based program for reading problems at any level.* Alfred A. Knopf.

Shaywitz, S. E., & Shaywitz, B. A. (2005). Dyslexia (specific reading disability). *Biological Psychiatry, 57*(11), 1301–1309. https://doi.org/10.1016/j.biopsych.2005.01.043

Wilde, E. A., Newsome, M. R., Bigler, E. D., Pertab, J., Merkley, T. L., Hanten, G., ... & Hunter, J. V. (2011). Brain imaging correlates of verbal working memory in children following traumatic brain injury. *International Journal of Psychophysiology, 82*(1), 86–96. https://doi.org/10.1016/j.ijpsycho.2011.04.006

Wozniak, J. R., Krach, L., Ward, E., Mueller, B. A., Muetzel, R., Schnoebelen, S., ... & Lim, K. O. (2007). Neurocognitive and neuroimaging correlates of pediatric traumatic brain injury: A diffusion tensor imaging (DTI) study. *Archives of Clinical Neuropsychology, 22*(5), 555–568. https://doi.org/10.1016/j.acn.2007.03.004

Chapter 14
Proactive and Transformational Directions: What We Need to Learn About Our Biological Basis of Behavior for Clinical Practice

Andrew S. Davis, Bethany M. Schwandt, Elizabeth M. Power, and Rik Carl D'Amato

Learning Objectives

- To understand the importance of the biological basis of behavior to applied clinical practice.
- To understand the importance of neurodevelopment to applied clinical practice.
- To understand the importance of prenatal development to the lifespan.
- To understand the importance of the prodromal stage of psychiatric disorders.
- To understand the importance of a systems level of intervention.
- To understand the importance of incorporating neurodiversity and culture in applied clinical practice.

Neurobiological science is advancing so fast that we must embrace and learn from these advances in an effort to keep practice current (D'Amato & Perfect, 2020; Davis, 2011). Although this text was designed primarily for graduate students, beginning practitioners, and/or individuals who wish to consider practice from a neuropsychological perspective, the advanced expertise of the chapter authors renders this text useful for currently practicing clinical neuropsychologists as well. The future of applied neuropsychology will rest on the integration of neurobiologically driven, brain-focused, evidence-based interventions to serve all clients (Power & D'Amato, 2018) as well as the incorporation of biomarkers for

---

A. S. Davis (✉) · B. M. Schwandt
Department of Educational Psychology, Ball State University, Muncie, IN, USA
e-mail: davis@bsu.edu

E. M. Power
Department of School Psychology, The College of Saint Rose, Albany, NY, USA

R. C. D'Amato
Department of School Psychology, The Chicago School of Professional Psychology & Presence Learning, Chicago, IL and New York, NY, USA

R. C. D'Amato et al. (eds.), *Understanding the Biological Basis of Behavior*,
https://doi.org/10.1007/978-3-030-59162-5_14

interventional diagnostics. Each of the chapters has been carefully selected to ensure wide coverage of topical issues germane to the field. This final chapter provides an overview of the reasons it is important to consider the biological basis of behavior in clinical practice as well as discussion of some future directions as well as briefly considering a few additional topics.

Overview of the Importance of the Biological Basis of Behavior

Graduate students and practitioners who embark upon the advanced study of psychology may be somewhat surprised to discover how much emphasis is placed on the biological basis of behavior. Indeed, the list of topics in a graduate class focused on the biological basis of behavior may feel quite overwhelming given the seemingly medical nature and complicated feeling related to many of of the terms (Davis, 2011). A practitioner or student may look at this list and wonder why they need to understand this information and how it relates to clients as they provide therapy, consultation, or implement interventions. The answer lies at the heart of the rationale for this book, which is that all observable human behavior involves the central nervous system. Conversely, central nervous system damage will be reflected in changes in human behavior and/or alter a client's developmental trajectory. At times, an insult to the central nervous system may be minimal, not appear on conventional neuroimaging techniques, and may result in mild behavior change that is only detectable via objective standardized assessment instruments (D'Amato et al., 2005; Davis, 2011). Additionally, the identification of biomarkers that underlie psychiatric conditions is likely to continue which will shift the focus in the future away from diagnostic services toward measurement of strengths and weaknesses for the determination of a client's functional capacity. As such, uninitiated psychologists who lack understanding of the neurobiological foundation of client functioning will quickly find that a thorough understanding of the brain–behavior relationship is integral to understanding their clients' healthy *and* dysfunctional behavior (Casaletto & Heaton, 2017). Furthermore, awareness of the connection between physiological functioning and its effect on neurological status will help clinicians learn how their patients' health status is required to understand pathological behavior. For example, changes in a client's glycemic control, sleep, endocrine functioning, and blood pressure could all be indicators of neurological dysfunction as well as alter neurological functioning, thus affecting behavior. In essence, understanding a patient's medical status will facilitate the assessment for intervention process and provide evidence for hypotheses regarding the etiology of the behavioral concern that underlies the referral questions.

History of Health Service Psychology

More than a decade ago, William Wundt argued that a new discipline of study was needed which would fall *between* philosophy and physiology/biology (D'Amato et al., 2011). In fact, Wundt was invited to join the departments of philosophy and physiology, but he did not believe either of these disciplines *in isolation* focused on what was needed to empirically understand human behavior. Wundt's novel proposed integrative discipline was developed in the area which we now call *psychology*. In fact, Wundt continued across his life to serve as a productive scholar, and he completed 22 seminal books including *human physiology* (4 editions), *physiology psychology* (6 editions), *systems of philosophy* (4 editions), *logic* (4 editions), *cultural psychology*, *outline of psychology* (14 editions), and *ethics* (3 editions). Many of these works are related to what we currently label experimental psychology, but this area certainly forms the foundation of understanding our brain–behavior relationships (Mandler, 2011). Some of his books were lengthy sporting up to 800 pages in length. Given his voluminous work, and the fact that all were initially published in German, some of his work continues to be inaccessible without knowledge of the German language. However, some of his books are available in English online (Wundt, 1897, Mandler, 2011).

Witmer, frequently called the father of clinical and school psychology, ventured to Europe to complete his doctorate with Wundt at his new psychology laboratory. After graduation, Witmer returned to the University of Pennsylvania to start the first applied psychology training clinic (D'Amato & Perfect, 2020; D'Amato et al., 2011). This is not surprising since Witmer had previously reported work with school children that was bewildering because they demonstrated distinctive difficulties and when he searched the literature to discover how to intervene with them Witmer found no published answers (D'Amato et al., 2005). Thus, Witmer began a quest to discover how to best serve these children. This foundation may explain why he completed his doctorate, accepted a university position, and began working with children with reported difficulties in a psychology clinic.

In 1892, the American Psychological Association (APA) was founded to promote the new psychology in America (APA, 2020). At an early APA convention, Witmer advocated for the training of specialized professionals who could offer comprehensive psychological services to a variety of clients in numerous settings working with a multidisciplinary team (Witmer, 1907, 1911). These integrated psychological services were viewed as being provided to normal and abnormal children, in a psychological training clinic (including school/hospital settings), covering the areas of education and medicine, with a goal of training students for a **new psychological profession** (D'Amato & Dean, 1989/2017; Witmer, 1896, 1897). The APA (1947) accepted this vision and has continued to represent both clinically-focused and research psychologists who have been trained at the doctoral level. However, even at that time APA was extremely focused on what we call experimental psychology and accordingly Witmer's recommendation for a new focus was not enthusiastically received (Collins, 1931). However, after much discussion, APA advocated for generic *clinical* psychological standards for both training programs and state licensure (APA, 2011, 2012). Clinical, counseling, and school psychology all followed this path. First, clinical psychology was accredited by the APA with school and counseling psychology both following this same course (Altmaier, 2014). Based on the medical model, all specialties in psychology complete predoctoral training and then have available numerous postdoctoral specialization options (American Psychological Association, 2017a, 2017b). More recently, all psychology specialties have been designated as *Health Service Psychologists* with a definition that integrates science and practice to improve individuals in society and the world (Hennington et al., 2020). Health service psychologists emphasize providing evidence-based services for health promotion, prevention, consultation, assessment, and treatment of health-related disorders. Psychologists who follow this sequence are eligible for licensure as generic doctoral-level psychologists (American Psychological Association, 2011, 2017a, 2017b).

Clinical Training and the American Psychological Association

To become a clinical neuropsychologist, one must first obtain a doctoral degree in clinical psychology. While not mandated in every state licensure law, some state laws require that doctoral programs be accredited by the APA (APA, 2011). APA is considered the most elite accreditation for clinical, counseling, and school psychology programs since it requires a consistent level of high quality in education and training (APA, 2012; D'Amato et al., 2011). APA also accredits internships in clinical psychology, counseling psychology, school psychology, and a combination of these areas, in addition to postdoctoral residencies. APA standards for accreditation assist in measuring student learning outcomes and the incorporation of competency-based measures that assist with evaluating program success (Henington et al., 2020). Furthermore, in July 2018, APA appointed a task force to study and implement accreditation for master's programs (APA, 2017a, 2017b; Mills, 2018). The decision came after much debate within the association and the field about the role of masters—trained individuals who may be able to reach underserved populations in society. It is imperative that clinical neuropsychologists stay abreast of the literature as this relatively new field continues to develop; for example, the American Academy of Clinical Neuropsychology recently released a statement on labeling test scores (Guilmette et al., 2020).

Neuropsychology at the Systems Level

As has been demonstrated across this volume, clinical neuropsychology can be applied at the *primary*, *secondary*, and *tertiary* system levels to improve the functioning of individuals in society (D'Amato et al., 2005). This approach can be applied to any sector of society including business, education, health services, government, and more. One of the primary avenues used to facilitate societal change and improve the well-being of others is offering psychological services through multiple levels. The public schools are offered as an example of how these levels can be applied to practice. Primary, secondary, and tertiary levels are provided which show how each systems-level can be affected via neuropsychological interventions. At the *primary level* services are offered that are preventative in nature, and consist primarily of evidence-based programs and interventions for all individuals (Kratochwill & Stoiber, 2002). At the *secondary level*, services are offered to target smaller groups of individuals who are identified as at-risk. Tertiary interventions offer the most intensive level of neuropsychological intervention. A theoretically focused, brain-based, instructional intervention model built around *neurodevelopment* and *neurocognitive processing* makes clear practical and conceptual sense and will improve the outcomes of individuals.

At the **primary level**, specialized neuropsychological screening could be offered at the preschool level to evaluate children with special needs. The overall curriculum should focus on neuropsychological student strengths, teach positive health beliefs, and talk about good brain health (Maykel & Bray, 2020). For example, adages like *eat well, your brain can tell* should be taught in each classroom, and health issues like getting enough sleep and teaching how to decrease stress should be covered. **Basic brain health**, such as wearing helmets in sports and biking should also be discussed. Teaching children how to pay attention and remain on task for a given amount of time should also be discussed. Since the general education curriculum covers all grade levels, discussion of different types of brain injury and abuse (e.g., alcohol, drug use) should also be covered at higher grade levels. It is important to remember that a variety of sports have been shown to cause brain injuries. Knowledge of this has led to sports officials working with clinical neuropsychologists to conduct baseline testing to determine brain functioning in both pre- and post-injuries (Anunciação & Portugal, 2020; Bajaj, 2020; Tamura et al., 2020). Finally, scientific advances, psychopharmacology, and degenerative brain disorders should also be reviewed.

Individuals who did not respond to primary level interventions are often moved to the **secondary level**, where they typically receive targeted interventions based on their specific needs. These secondary interventions are often delivered to individuals in small groups with those who also present as at-risk for certain difficulties. For example, children who are experiencing grief as a result of a recent death in the family may be referred to a grief group. Children with social skills deficits will benefit from a small group targeting issues, such as initiating conversations and communicating with friends. Academic interventions can also be offered using a neuropsychological perspective, and this is often part of exceptional student service interventions (Power & D'Amato, 2018).

After receiving primary and secondary level school services, some students are not able to make suitable educational or behavioral progress and receive **tertiary interventions**. For those students who have difficulty making progress within the traditional curriculum, specialized educational and neuropsychological evaluations are conducted to determine the presence of student disabilities. Human neurodevelopmental knowledge can be organized to help us understand the unique abilities and disabilities of each child and determine which type of psychological or educational program can help them develop to their fullest potential. Tertiary interventions can be offered via focused unique special education programs that meet student needs. Public schools generally have specially trained teachers who work in exceptional educational settings. Another example would be a targeted curriculum delivered in a one-on-setting for a child with a traumatic background (Van der Kolk, 2014). Only when we early on meet the needs of diverse children using our neurodevelopmental knowledge of how the brain learns and how children develop will we be able to claim success in the educational enterprise.

Linking Neurodevelopment to Patient Functioning

The process of neurodevelopment (i.e., development of the central nervous system) is a lifelong process that starts with incredibly rapid growth during the prenatal period with changes in the central nervous system continuing throughout the lifespan. The entire process of neurodevelopment and development, in general, is a critical area that all practitioners must understand. Accordingly, for a more comprehensive understanding of this area, readers should consult Chaps. 2 and 4 of this book. The author of Chap. 2 presents information on typical neurodevelopment, whereas the authors of Chap. 4 discuss atypical neurodevelopment. Readers who want to learn more about this are directed to resources related to functional neuroanatomy, such as the circuits involved in cells and synapses in pediatric populations (Bishop, 2011). More information on functional neuroanatomy can be found in Chap. 3 of this book. This section focuses on the prenatal period given that rapid changes during this time can have a lifelong effect on neuropsychological functioning. Indeed, the intrauterine period presents many opportunities for complications and some of those will be reviewed here with an emphasis on how it could affect behavior and functional outcomes. Readers who are considering working with adults and have less interest in pediatric neuropsychology are encouraged to consider that disruption of the typical neurodevelopmental trajectory can have a lifelong effect and not knowing the patient's history could lead to improper attribution of maladaptive behavior which could have obvious effects on treatment and estimation of prognosis.

One of the first developmental stages the embryo goes through is the formation of the neural tube which goes on to form the central nervous system. The neural tube has openings at both ends which close during typical development. When problems with the neural tube are present, a group of conditions arises called neural tube defects (NTD). Incomplete closure of the anterior and posterior neuropores (openings at the ends of the neural tube) can result in NTDs such as spina bifida and anencephaly. Spina Bifida has the potential to continue to affect neurodevelopment throughout the lifespan including lower cognitive functioning and impaired motor quality (Vinck et al., 2009). Deficits in motor functioning have been linked to a host of negative outcomes including trouble with academic achievement including reading, writing, and math (Suggate et al, 2019; Cameron et al., 2016), and social interactions (MacDonald et al., 2017).

Although there are a large number of other prenatal complications that can affect neurodevelopment, an important example is periventricular leukomalacia (PVL), a condition that occurs when the white matter around the ventricles begins to soften affecting areas of functioning such as motor, cognition, social, behavioral, and adaptive functioning (Choi et al., 2015). This condition can be observed in children born to term as well as those born preterm (Lasry et al., 2010); however, being born preterm can be a strong predictor of cerebral palsy in children with PVL (Krageloh-Mann & Horber, 2007). Cerebral palsy (CP) is the most common physical disability in childhood and is an umbrella term used for varying physical disabilities. Gosling (2017) reported on advancements in neuroimaging and neurological profiles of children with CP and stressed the heterogeneity of this group, as well as the importance of understanding the continued advances being made in neuroimaging, associations between brain and behavior, and individualized neuropsychological profiles. Outcomes among children with CP will be most beneficial when a holistic approach is incorporated and individualized interventions are implemented.

Early Biological Evidence of Psychiatric Problems

Virtually every individual with a medical condition, including psychiatric and neurological disorders, benefit from early identification and intervention. This can be difficult with psychiatric disorders as they may lack easily identifiable hard signs or biomarkers and thus diagnosis may be based on the clinician's observations, or report of the patient's behaviors. This can render psychiatric disorders more difficult to diagnose than other medical conditions and delayed, or incorrect, identification can result in behavioral problems taking root. As research related to psychiatric conditions becomes more extensive, early neurological markers can provide information related to the progression from prodromal states to clinical diagnoses (Davis, 2011; Lezak et al., 2012). Thus, recognizing the prodromal state may enable the clinician to implement interventions to either slow down, stop, or ameliorate the clinical effects of the condition. The prodrome of conditions like schizophrenia can be particularly important for future development of prophylactic measures. Identifying risk factors and early biological markers related to individuals with conduct disorder (CD) and/or with autism spectrum disorder (ASD) is another area of particular interest for early intervention to ensure adequate services and supports for families impacted by these conditions.

The overwhelming majority of information related to the neurobiology of schizophrenia involves the abnormalities in dopamine signaling systems and recent literature has discussed dopamine in prodromal schizophrenia (Petty et al., 2019). The *Diagnostic and Statistical Manual of Mental Disorders* (DSM-5; American Psychiatric Association, 2013) indicated symptoms of this condition may include delusions, hallucinations, disorganized speech, grossly disorganized or catatonic behavior or negative symptoms such as diminished emotional expression. Less understood are ways to identify early risk factors that begin to emerge as symptoms of the disease before they manifest as a clinically significant, debilitating condition. Yung et al. (2006) explored ways to assess at-risk psychopathology through the Comprehensive Assessment of At-Risk Mental States (CAARMS; Young, 2005) and reported a significant relationship between high scores on this measure among the ultra-high risk (UHR) group with later onset of psychotic disorder. Differing clinical presentation of symptoms among those considered to be UHR clients (i.e., delusions, hallucinations, or psychotic symptoms experienced for as little as a day) was further explored to better understand transition rates. Differences in attenuated symptoms among different cohorts were shown to contribute to the transition rate into psychotic disorders; however, these findings could not fully explain the decline, and therefore a holistic approach to assessing risk for future psychosis is encouraged (Hartmann et al., 2016; Maykel & Bray, 2020). Because of the differences among observable symptoms in UHR individuals, it is also important to consider neurotransmitter systems and neuroanatomical correlates that may help explain elevated risk for developing psychosis. Allen et al. (2012) explored this by comparing UHR individuals who developed psychosis and those who did not use functional magnetic resonance imaging (fMRI). They reported that those UHR individuals that went on to develop psychosis had increased activation and dysfunction between prefrontal and subcortical connections. Furthermore, assessing early biological evidence and risk for later psychosis, a combination of symptom onset, variability among symptom presentation, and neuroanatomical correlates should all be considered.

Incorporating Psychiatric Functioning to Neuropsychological Assessment

Psychiatric functioning can be defined a number of ways and is often confused with psychological functioning. Psychological functioning is somewhat of an amorphous term as a collection of "psychological disorders" has not been codified since psychologists use the same diagnostic classifications system as do psychiatrists, the DSM-5 (American Psychiatric Association, 2013). For the purpose of neuropsychological assessment, psychiatric functioning could be considered the behavioral, psychosocial, cognitive, and emotional effects of mental illness or disease. Another way to conceptualize psychiatric disorders during the process of neuropsychological assessment is their role in the presentation of behavioral disturbance that can present with a neurological etiology. This concept of psychogenic (i.e., of psychiatric origin) and neurogenic (i.e., neurological in origin) is a complicated one and the determination of neurogenic vs. psychogenic as an explanation for a patient's behavior is a key role in the process of neuropsychological assessment (see

Lezak et al., 2012). Determining the etiology of the patient's behavioral presentation (psychiatric vs. neurological) is essential when attempting to find the correct treatment/intervention as well as establishing a prognosis. There are several reasons why this determination is complicated, including that many psychiatric disorders present with motor, sensory, and cognitive features which could also have a neurogenic explanation. Thus, it is critical for neuropsychologists to understand the effects that psychiatric disorders have on behaviors that appear to be neurological in origin. The classic example of this is a Conversion Disorder (APA, 2015) in which a patient presents with sensory and/or motor disturbance in which the origin of the disturbance is psychogenic but appears neurogenic.

The Critical Understanding of Biological Basis of Behavior

As mentioned previously, the authors have advocated that all psychologists be trained in basic clinical neuropsychology. By studying brain–behavior relations, psychologists are afforded the opportunity to choose better assessments, which leads to a deeper understanding of unique client needs, which then drives appropriate evidence-based intervention selections (Riccio & Schwartz, 2020). For better or for worse, as frequently discussed across this text (see Chaps. 1 and 9), all psychologists **must choose** some type of model or paradigm in which to conceptualize, diagnose, and treat clients. Clinical neuropsychology has its roots in neurology and psychiatry. Neurology refers to the assessment and rehabilitation of abnormalities of the nervous systems. Psychiatry refers to the study of mental illness and abnormal behavior. The authors advocate that in regard to understanding the etiology of behavioral problems, environmental and organic factors **must** be viewed on an **interactive continuum**. With this spectrum in mind, practitioners can choose comprehensive assessments to answer more than yes/no questions regarding client functioning, neuropsychological integrity, and/or neurodiversity.

Both quantitative and qualitative assessments assist in understanding an individual's neuropsychological strengths and weaknesses. A qualitative approach allows clinical neuropsychologists to collect data that cannot be easily measured, such as projective assessments. While numerical data are not always produced, this approach focuses on the distinctiveness and uniqueness of the client. A quantitative approach focuses on hypothesis-testing and data collection. These assessments offer many data collection tools, including norm-referenced tests. It is not only essential to use various methods of assessment, but it is equally as important to consider a client's systems, contexts, settings, and sources, including multicultural factors. Neuropsychologists, similar to all health care providers, need to be vigilant about crosscultural considerations, and accordingly need to make appropriate interculturally-focused recommendations (Nastasi et al., 2020; Power & D'Amato, 2018). Clearly, a neurodevelopmental focus must be the foundation of our practice and understanding of clients.

Societal Changes That Impact Quality Clinical Practices and the Future

This chapter concludes with a discussion of areas that should affect quality neuropsychological services which merge from previous issues to create future service needs. Initially, multicultural factors will be discussed followed by the consideration of teleservices, remote training, and medical issues that drive societal changes.

Multicultural Factors in Clinical Neuropsychology

The important concept of adopting a multicultural approach to neuropsychological assessment is integrated throughout this text. Indeed, it is impossible to consider any approach to clinical neuropsychological assessment without a thorough understanding of an individual's cultural background, including their race and ethnicity (Howell, 2008). The experiences that a person has throughout their life may or not encapsulate the learning opportunities that are valued or measured by cognitive, particularly intelligence, tests. Failure to consider this can result in a misattribution of a low test score to ability instead of a lack of exposure to the information. Cultural differences may also be present in the patient's approach to test taking (APA, 2017a, 2017b). For example, stereotype threat, defined by Steele and Aronson (1995) "*is being at risk of confirming, as self-characteristic, a negative stereotype about one's group*" (p. 797). Thames et al. (2013) examined this effect by comparing the performance of African-American and Caucasian adults on neuropsychological testing under a series of conditions. Participants were randomly assigned to an examiner of the same or different race. They found that the African-American participants in the stereotype threat condition exhibited lower global performance than the African-American participants in the nonstereotype threat condition. Additionally, feelings of discrimination were associated with worst performance on memory tests when African-Americans were tested by an examiner of a different race. In essence, it is critical that neuropsychologists understand the research in this area before both administering and interpreting tests to *any* patient, not just those who the examiner may perceive as different from them (Nastasi et al., 2020).

An area that is not well-researched in clinical neuropsychology is working with individuals who identify as LGBTQ+ (lesbian, gay, bisexual, transgender, and queer/ questioning, with + meaning inclusion/acceptance of all). There is no reason to suspect that these individuals are biologically predisposed to neurocognitive or psychiatric difficulties rather they may be in conflict with society based upon their sexual orientation or gender identification. This conflict may manifest in marginalization, stigma, and discrimination that can indeed have a profound effect on social, physical, and emotional functioning; given the relationship between psychiatric distress and cognitive functioning neuropsychologists should be aware of the deleterious effects of these concerns. For example, Kosciw et al. (2018) reported the results of a nationwide survey of LGBTQ+ youth and they found a number of troubling findings including that LGBTQ students often experience a hostile school environment; some of their findings included a number of students feeling unsafe because of their sexual orientation (59.5%), gender expression (44.6%), and gender (35.0%). A high number (34.8%) of students missed school because they had been threatened and 70.5% avoided school and extracurricular activities due to feeling unsafe. Large numbers of students heard anti-LGBTQ+ remarks and were distressed by these comments. There was a significant number of students (87.3%) who reported harassment and assault based on factors including sexual orientation and gender expression. The authors also reported concerning discriminatory actions by schools.

Feeling unsafe, experiencing violence, being harassed, discriminated against, and falling behind academically places children at risk of developing psychiatric concerns. Related, the lifetime prevalence of suicide attempts for individuals who are transgender has been found to be 41% (Haas et al., 2014), and the rates of gay, lesbian, and bisexual students both considering (42.8% vs. 14.8%) and attempting suicide (29.4% vs. 6.4%) was higher when compared to heterosexual students (Kann et al., 2016). Discrimination, marginalization, stigma, and bullying are significant concerns for any group, but especially LGBTQ+ individuals who already have risk factors for numerous health problems. This includes transgender youth being found to have up to four times higher rates of substance abuse compared to their nontransgender peers (Day et al., 2017). Additionally, LGBTQ+ adolescents are almost three times more likely to report sexual abuse than sexual nonminority adolescents (Friedman et al., 2011). These statistics are particularly troubling as there seems to be a dearth of awareness about the high levels of discrimination and other risk factors LGBTQ+ individuals experience. Fear of being stigmatized, marginalized, and discriminated against appears common in the LGBTQ+ community when interacting with the health care system. For example, individuals who identify as transgender may worry about seeking medical assistance for fear of being judged by their healthcare providers. Clearly, education is needed for health care providers who work with LGBTQ+ individuals. All psychologists are also ethically tasked with advocating for disadvantaged members of our society and are encouraged to become aware of relevant federal and state laws while working to overturn discrimination.

Use of Telehealth and Telepsychology Practices

Telehealth refers to the provision of medical/health services using technology in lieu of, or in addition to, traditional face-to-face methods (Henington et al., 2020) and has been an area of increased focus given the effects of COVID-19. Telepsychology is the provision of mental health services using technology, such as videoconferencing, use of evaluation applications, and consultation via email (APA, 2013). Telepsychology may include working in real time (via webcams or phone) or in a delayed fashion, such as through consultation via email. Telepsychology is becoming increasingly popular due to limited access to specialists and mental health services in remote geographic areas, lack of availability of psychologists with disability intervention training, and few mental health practitioners who speak clients' native languages (Luiselli & Fischer, 2016).

Another approach to technology related to teletherapy is the provision of psychological services directly to clients using advanced technologies. This could relate to training patients' brains using neurofeedback, controlling stress using heart rate monitors, and computer games that teach advanced learning skills and organization. In fact, some video games have been used to develop social skills and team-building that includes community development. Many of these activities are used to integrate the mind with the body (Maykel & Bray, 2020). When all these psychological approaches are integrated with current technology, a new milieu of services is created (Cummings, 2011).

One way that telehealth can be demonstrated is through the provision of educational and psychological services in a medical setting. This type of integrated educational services can be utilized to meet the needs of hospitalized students (Fischer & Bloomfield, 2019). Numerous authors have demonstrated how children with significant medical impairments, who may be hospitalized for long-periods of time, can be directly connected to their classroom using technology which young students may call *robot* teachers (Fischer et al., 2019a; Fischer et al., 2019b). This type of system allows the student to observe what is happening in their classrooms as well as show how they are responding to such activities. The student can raise their hand which immediately does the same on the robot in the classroom. Essentially, the student can be a valued member of their classroom in real time. Before the use of this technology, the child would not have been able to have connected with their class (in real time) and would have used a hospital-based or homebound teacher. The benefits for children in the regular education classroom are also increased because of their knowledge of hospital logistics and relationships with students who have medical needs (Cummings, 2011). There are long-term benefits for all children when they are exposed to the provision of healthcare, including career choices to enter the medical field, additional empathy for those with medical needs, and comfort when family members, such as a grandparent, may be hospitalized (Casaletto & Heaton, 2017).

Teletherapy in Training

While many psychological services can be offered using various technologies from remote locations, such as work at home, the same is true for school psychological training. Lahman et al. (2006) offered an Education Specialist (Ed.S.) school psychology training program to students at remote locations in rural areas of Colorado at the University of Northern Colorado. In fact, some of the remote locations were accessible by passes that could close consistently during winter. Called the Giving Rural Areas Access to School Psychology (GRAASP), this grant-funded program offered training to Ed.S. level students in every year of the program. While some materials were emailed to students, many materials and tests were mailed back-and-forth. For example, each remote location had a diagnostic assessment library and the grant paid for materials, such as test kits to be ordered for each location. Teaching was completed via video instruction and many professors who have never taught online learned how to use this system. At the completion of the program a comprehensive qualitative evaluation was completed and students were interviewed which generated 100 single-spaced pages of data from students. This program evaluation led to a publication in the School Psychology International journal (see Lahman et al., 2006).

Teletherapy in Practice

Obviously, the educational and psychological benefits of such a system are far reaching especially given the coronavirus disease pandemic (COVID-19). While the practice of telehealth has existed for some time, it became an increased area of focus for all healthcare providers following the onset of COVID-19 (CDC, 2020). To meet the needs of clients, health-service providers were forced to learn how to provide psychological supports remotely. These health-service providers included school-based professionals, who in some states needed to navigate the legalities of offering telehealth support for the first time. For example, many school psychologists were required to conduct psychoeducation assessments via teleconference due to special education evaluation timelines. Some school districts based their psychoeducation evaluations on rating scales which have been normed with the use of online administration, which is considered an ethical practice—while others tried to individually administer assessments that may not have been normed for telehealth use. This forced many practitioners to evaluate if psychometrically normed instruments could be used in a remote setting without violating professional ethical guidelines. If it were not for the existence of our advanced technology, many individuals in need of mental health support would have struggled even more than they did. The COVID-19 pandemic greatly impacted how providers were able to treat clients and forced system-level consideration regarding the efficacy and ethics of neuropsychological assessment.

Conclusions

Historically, psychology began with the idea that a new discipline was needed to understand the complexity of humans and being able to help them progress through life difficulties. Innovators in **clinical neuropsychology** focused on helping us to understand and integratethe biological basis of behavior. Without considering the biological basis of behavior, it is difficult to understand and intervene with a patient's problems when attempting to offer appropriate evidence-based interventions.

Initially, psychological practice was offered as a general approach which ultimately was divided into multiple discipline areas including clinical psychology, counseling psychology, and school psychology. Seventy-five years ago, APA developed divisions along these same lines resulting in a variety of psychological specializations and interests. Currently, research continues to support biogenetic markers and neurodevelopmental stages which correspond to brain development and neuropsychological services. With advances being made in regard to neuroplasticity, as well as early interventions that may mitigate the adverse effects of brain trauma, there is a shift away from definitive prognoses following neurological insults. For example, we have a better understanding of prodromal stages of epilepsy, where we are better able to predict pre-seizure activity which can lead to better prevention for patients who are epileptic (Boerwinkle et al., 2019). Clinical neuropsychology was built from an understanding of basic neuroscientific research.

Clinical neuropsychologists are trained to practice with patients **across the lifespan**, from patients who are **in-utero** to **geriatric** developmental stages. A comprehensive understanding of neurological development includesserving individuals with degenerative and psychiatric disorders and their families. A neuropsychological approach should start as an initial course in a student's first year of training and continue as part of their elective courses in theory, application, and service. This approach could continue in practicum and predoctoral research leading to a predoctoral internship. Advanced training could culminate in a two-year postdoctoral specialization. Given recent neuroscientific advances, **clinical neuropsyhcology** has become one of, if not the most popular area of training and post-doctoral study in psychology.

Another way to conceptualize neuropsychological practice pertains to **primary**, **secondary**, and **tertiary neuropsychological interventions**. Primary interventions may include a community-wide intervention, such as the governmental *stay-at-home* orders during the COVID-19 pandemic. Secondary interventions may include the provision of a *support group* in public schools for students with social skills deficits. Tertiary interventions are targeted supports which may include a pragmatic *language intervention* for a child diagnosed with an Autism spectrum disorder. This model represents a significant shift away from use of the medical model, or treating one patient at a time, and demonstrates the need for multitiered interventions focused on individual *and* community health.

Our perspectives have changed as we now understand it is necessary to view individuals from multiple perspectives, which includes consideration of their culture, families, peers, and society (D'Amato & Perfect, 2020). The neuropsychological approach is the most comprehensive approach of any psychological paradigm because it considers the **neurogenetic underpinnings of the brain** which demonstrate the uniqueness of each individual and their family. With this as a foundation, clients are viewed using a **multicultural lens**, focusing on neurodiversity, and offering unique interventions and recommendations tailored to their specific neuropsychological needs. Clinical neuropsychology should no longer be viewed as a wave of the future. But instead, medical advances, such as neuroimaging have shown the brain to be the foundation of psychological practice. Any psychological services provided that do not stem from an understanding of the **biological basis of behavior** will leave health service psychologists with a lack of intricate knowledge that is required for quality service provision. In order to be **successful health service psychologists**, it is essential to use **evidence-based interventions** that are developed from a **neuroscientific foundation**.

Discussion Questions:

1. How should the history of health service psychology inform our clinical neuropsychology practice today?
2. What are the benefits of conceptualizing neuropsychological interventions using a multi-system level approach?
3. Why should we consider psychiatric functioning when conducting clinical neuropsychological evaluations?
4. Why might neurodiverse individuals be hesitant to work with health care providers, such as clinical neuropsychologists?
5. How has telepsychology improved our ability to offer medical/health services to individuals across the world?
6. Why is it critical to build from a neuroscientific basis when understanding, conceptualizing, and providing psychological services?
7. How will you incorporate neuropsychological principles into your practice?

EPPP Sample Questions

(1) Which of the following is likely not an indicator of neurological dysfunction which in turn could alter behavior?

a. Endocrine functioning
b. Hair loss
c. Sleep
d. Blood pressure

(2) LGBTQ + individuals have been found to be at risk for:

a. Higher rates of feeling unsafe in schools
b. Increased cardiovascular problems
c. Increased rates of substance abuse
d. All of the above

(3) Whether you like it or not, the behaviors you choose to focus on creates the psychological paradigm you practice. An individual practicing neuropsychology should focus on which of the following:

a. Only observable behaviors
b. Behaviors internal to the individual (e.g., cognitions)
c. Abnormalities of the nervous system
d. All of the above

(4) At which systemic levels can neuropsychology be applied?

a. Primary, secondary, and tertiary
b. Primary, secondary, and microsystemic
c. Environmental, organic, and neurological
d. First, second, and third levels

(5) Which forms of teletherapy are used in clinical practice?

a. Providing a remote counseling session using a webcam
b. Instructing a client to use biofeedback
c. Consultation through email
d. All of the above

Answers: B, D, D, A, D

Proactive Readings

Transcending the Past

D'Amato, R. C., Zafiris, C., McConnell, E., & Dean, R. S. (2011). The history of school psychology: Understanding the past to not repeat it. In M. Bray & T. Kehl (Eds.), Oxford handbook of school psychology (pp. 9–60). Oxford.

Excelling in the Present

American Psychological Association (2015). Guidelines for psychological practice with transgender and gender nonconforming people. *American Psychologist, 70*(9), 832–864. doi:10.1037/a0039906.

Power, E., & D'Amato, R. C. (2018). Should our future include the integration of evidence-based neuropsychological services into school settings? In D. P. Flanagan & E. M. McDonough (Eds.), *Contemporary intellectual assessment: Theories, tests, and issues* (4th ed., pp. 1017–1045). Guilford.

Transforming the Future

Casaletto, K. B., & Heaton, R. K. (2017). Neuropsychological assessment: Past and future. Journal of the International Neuropsychological Society, 23(9–10), 778–790. https://www.ncbi.nlm.nih.gov/pmc/articles/PMC6296381/

Bajaj, M. K. (2020). Neuropsychological assessment. In M. K. Bajaj (Ed.) *Examining biological foundations of human behavior* (pp. 213–225). IGI Global. DOI: 10.4018/978-1-7998-2860-0.ch012

References

Allen, P., Luigjes, J., Howes, O. D., Egerton, A., Hirao, K., Valli, I., Kambeitz, J., Fusar-Poli, P., Broome, M., & McGuire, P. (2012). Transition to psychosis associated with prefrontal and subcortical dysfunction in ultra high-risk individuals. *Schizophrenia Bulletin, 38*(6), 1268–1276. https://doi.org/10.1093/schbul/sbr194

Altmaier, E. M. (2014). Accreditation of education and training programs. In W. B. Johnson & N. J. Kaslow (Eds.), *The Oxford handbook of education and training in professional psychology*. Oxford University Press.

American Psychological Association. (1947). Committee on Training in Clinical Psychology. Recommended graduate training program in clinical psychology. *American Psychologist,* 2(12), 539–558. https://doi.org/10.1037/h0058236

American Psychiatric Association. (2013). *Diagnostic and statistical manual of mental disorders–fifth edition*. American Psychiatric Association.

American Psychological Association. (2011). Model act for state licensure of psychologists. *American Psychologist, 66*(3), 214–226. https://doi.org/10.1037/a0022655

American Psychological Association. (2013). *Guidelines for the practice of telepsychology*. https://www.apa.org/practice/guidelines/telepsychology

American Psychological Association. (2015). Guidelines for psychological practice with transgender and gender nonconforming people. *American Psychologist, 70*(9), 832–864. https://doi.org/10.1037/a0039906

American Psychological Association. (2017a). *Multicultural guidelines: An ecological approach to context, identity, and intersectionality*. http://www.apa.org/about/policy/multicultural-guidelines.pdf

American Psychological Association. (2017b). *Proceedings of the summit on master's training in psychological practice* [Report]. https://www.apa.org/pi/mfp/masters-summit/training-proceedings.pdf

American Psychological Association. (2020). *APA History*. https://www.apa.org/about/apa/archives/apa-history

American Psychological Association, Health Service Psychology Education Collaborative. (2012). *A blueprint for health service psychology education and training*. https://www.ncbi.nlm.nih.gov/pubmed/23915400

American Psychological Association, Task Force on Gender Identity and Gender Variance. (2009). *Report of the task force on gender identity and gender variance*. https://www.apa.org/pi/lgbt/resources/policy/gender-identity-report.pdf

Anunciação, L., & Portugal, A. C. (2020). A case study on strengthening the link between psychometrics, assessment, and intervention in Autism Spectrum Disorder (ASD). In *Special education design and development tools for school rehabilitation professionals* (pp. 154–171). IGI Global.

Bajaj, M. K. (2020). Neuropsychological assessment. In M. K. Bajaj (Ed.) *Examining biological foundations of human behavior* (pp. 213–225). IGI Global. DOI: 10.4018/978-1-7998-2860-0.ch012

Bishop, D. L. (2011). Cells, synapses, and circuits. In A. Davis (Ed.), *Handbook of pediatric neuropsychology* (pp. 89–99). Springer.

Boerwinkle, V. L., Cediel, E. G., Mirea, L., Williams, K., Kerrigan, J. F., Lam, S., … Curry, D. J. (2019). Network-targeted approach and postoperative resting-state functional magnetic resonance imaging are associated with seizure outcome. *Annals of Neurology, 86*(3), 344–356. https://doi.org/10.1002/ana.25547

Cameron, C. E., Cottone, E. A., Murrah, W. M., & Grissmer, D. W. (2016). How are motor skills linked to children's school performance and academic achievement? *Child Development Perspectives, 10*(2), 93–98. https://doi.org/10.1111/cdep.12168

Casaletto, K. B., & Heaton, R. K. (2017). Neuropsychological assessment: Past and future. *Journal of the International Neuropsychological Society, 23*(9–10), 778–790. https://www.ncbi.nlm.nih.gov/pmc/articles/PMC6296381/

Centers for Disease and Control and Prevention. (2020). *Coronavirus (COVID-19)*. https://www.cdc.gov/coronavirus/2019-ncov/index.html

Choi, J. Y., Rha, D., & Park, E. S. (2015). The effects of the severity of periventricular leukomalacia on the neuropsychological outcomes of preterm children. *Journal of Child Neurology, 31*(5), 603–612. https://doi.org/10.1177/0883073815604229

Collins, J. (1931). Lightner Witmer: A biographical sketch. In R. S. Brotemarkle (Ed.), *Clinical psychology: Studies in honor of Lightner Witmer to commemorate the thirty-fifth anniversary of the founding of the first psychological clinic* (pp. 3–9). University of Pennsylvania Press.

Cummings, J. A. (2011). Technology in the practice of school psychology: The future is past tense. In M. Bray & T. Kehl (Eds.), *Oxford handbook of school psychology* (pp. 831–859). Oxford University Press.

D'Amato, R. C., & Dean, R. S. (Eds.). (1989/2017). *The school psychologist in nontraditional settings: Integrating clients, services, and settings*. Routledge.

D'Amato, R. C., Fletcher-Janzen, E., & Reynolds, C. R. (Eds.). (2005). *Handbook of school neuropsychology*. Wiley.

D'Amato, R. C., & Perfect, M. (2020). History of the future of proactive school psychology: Understanding the past and transforming the future. In M. Perfect & R. C. D'Amato's History of the future of proactive school psychology (Special Issue). *School Psychology, 35(6), 375-384. https://doi.org/10.1037/spq0000420*

D'Amato, R. C., Zafiris, C., McConnell, E., & Dean, R. S. (2011). The history of school psychology: Understanding the past to not repeat it. In M. Bray & T. Kehl (Eds.), *Oxford handbook of school psychology* (pp. 9–60). Oxford University Press.

Davis, A. S. (Ed.). (2011). *Handbook of pediatric neuropsychology*. Springer.

Day, J. K., Fish, J. N., Perez-Brumer, A., Hatzenbuehler, M. L., & Russell, S. T. (2017). Transgender youth substance use disparities: Results from a population based sample. *Journal of Adolescent Health, 61*(6), 729–735. https://doi.org/10.1016/j.jadohealth.2017.06.024

Fisher, C. B., Fried, A. L., Desmond, M., Macapagal, K., & Mustanski, B. (2018). Perceived barriers to HIV prevention services for transgender youth. *LGBT Health, 5*(6), 350–358. https://doi.org/10.1089/lgbt.2017.0098

Fischer, A. J., & Bloomfield, B. (2019). Using technology to maximize engagement and outcomes in family-school partnerships. In S. A. Garbacz (Ed.), *Implementing family-school partnerships: Student success in school psychology research and practice*. Routledge.

Fischer, A. J., Clark, R., & Lehman, E. (2019). Telepresence robotics and consultation. In A. J. Fischer, T. Collins, E. Dart, & K. Radley (Eds.), *Technology applications in school psychology consultation, supervision, and training*. Routledge.

Fischer, A. J., Collins, T., Dart, E. H., & Radley, K. (Eds.). (2019). *Technology applications in school psychology consultation, supervision, and training*. Routledge.

Friedman, M. S., Marshal, M. P., Guadamuz, T. E., Wei, C., Wong, C. F., Saewyc, E., & Stall, R. (2011). A meta-analysis of disparities in childhood sexual abuse, parental physical abuse, and peer victimization among sexual minority and sexual nonminority individuals. *American Journal of Public Health, 101*(8), 1481–1494. https://doi.org/10.2105/AJPH.2009.190009

Gosling, A. S. (2017). Recent advances in the neuroimaging and neuropsychology of cerebral palsy. *Applied Neuropsychology Child, 6*(1), 55–63. https://doi.org/10.1080/21622965.2015.1074914

Guilmette, T. J., Sweet, J. J., Hebben, N., Koltai, D., Mahone, E. M., Spiegler, B. J., Stucky, K. Westerveld, M., & Conference Participants (2020). American Academy of Clinical Neuropsychology consensus conference statement on uniform labeling of performance test scores. *The Clinical Neuropsychologist, 34*(3), 437–453, https://doi.org/10.1080/13854046.2020.1722244

Haas, A. P., Rodgers, P. L., & Herman, J. L. (2014). *Suicide attempts among transgender and gender non-conforming adults: Findings of the national transgender discrimination survey.* https://williamsinstitute.law.ucla.edu/wp-content/uploads/AFSP-Williams-Suicide-Report-Final.pdf

Hartmann, J. A., Yuen, H. P., McGorry, P. D., Yung, A. R., Lin, A., Wood, S. J., Lavoie, S., & Nelson, B. (2016). Declining transition rates to psychotic disorder in "ultra-high risk" clients: Investigation of a dilution effect. *Schizophrenia Research, 170*(1), 130–136. https://doi.org/10.1016/j.schres.2015.11.026

Henington, C., Carlson, C., & DeMers, S. T. (2020). School psychology training within a competency framework: Transcending the past, present, and future. In M. Perfect & R. C. D'Amato's History of the future of proactive school psychology (Special Issue). *School Psychology.* https://doi.org/10.1037/spq0000422

Howell, E. (2008). Children's mental health care: Differences by race/ethnicity in urban/ruralareas. *Journal of Health Care for the Poor and Underserved, 19*(1), 237–247. https://doi.org/10.1353/hpu.2008.0008

Kann, L., Olsen, E. O., McManus, T., Harris, W. A., Shanklin, S. L., Flint, K. H., … Zaza, S. (2016). Sexual identity, sex of sexual contacts, and health-related behaviors among students in grades 9-12 - United States and selected sites, 2015. *MMWR Surveillance Summaries, 65*(9), 1–202. https://doi.org/10.15585/mmwr.ss6509a1

Kosciw, J. G., Greytak, E. A., Zongrone, A. D., Clark, C. M., & Truong, N. L. (2018). *The 2017 National School Climate Survey: The experiences of lesbian, gay, bisexual, transgender, and queer youth in our nation's schools*. GLSEN.

Krageloh-Mann, I., & Horber, V. (2007). The role of magnetic resonance imaging in elucidating the pathogenesis of cerebral palsy: A systematic review. *Developmental Medical Child Neurology, 49*, 144–151. https://doi.org/10.1111/j.1469-8749.2007.00144.x

Kratochwill, T. R., & Stoiber, K. C. (2002). Evidence based interventions in school psychology: Conceptual foundations of the procedural and coding manual of Division 16 and the Society for the Study of School Psychology Task Force. *School Psychology Quarterly, 17*(4), 341–389. https://psycnet.apa.org/doi/10.1521/scpq.17.4.341.20872

Lahman, M. K., D'Amato, R. C., Stecker, S., & McGrain, E. (2006). Addressing the shortage of rural school psychologists via technology. *School Psychology International, 27*, 439–461. https://doi.org/10.1177/0143034306070429

Lasry, O., Shevell, M. I., & Dagenais, L. (2010). Cross-sectional comparison of periventricular leukomalacia in preterm and term children. *Neurology, 74*, 1386–1391. https://doi.org/10.1212/wnl.0b013e3181dad62d

Lezak, M. D., Howieson, D. B., Bigler, E. D., & Tranel (2012). *Neuropsychological Assessment-Fifth Edition*. Oxford.

Luiselli, J. K., & Fischer, A. J. (2016). *Computer-assisted and web-based innovations in psychology, special education, and health*. Elsevier Science.

MacDonald, M., Ross, S., McIntyre, L. L., & Tepfer, A. (2017). Relations of Early Motor Skills on Age and Socialization, Communication, and Daily Living in Young Children With Developmental Disabilities. *Adapted Physical Activity Quarterly, 34*(2),179–194. https://doi.org/10.1123/apaq.2015-0091

Mandler, G. (2011). *A history of modern experimental psychology: From James and Wundt to cognitive science.* MIT press

Maykel, C., & Bray, M. (2020). *Promoting mind–body health in schools: Interventions for mental health professionals*. American Psychological Association.

Mills, K. (2018, July). *APA appoints task force to study accrediting master's programs.* American Psychological Association. https://www.apa.org/news/press/releases/2018/07/accrediting-masters-programs

Nastasi, B. K., Chittooran, M. R. M., Arora, P., & Song, S. (2020). Infusing global and intercultural perspectives to transform school psychology and school psychologists. *School Psychology, 35*(6), 440. http://dx.doi.org/10.1037/spq0000403

Petty, A., Cui, X., Tesiram, Y., Kirik, D., Howes, O., & Eyles, D. (2019). Enhanced Dopamine in Prodromal Schizophrenia (EDiPS): A new animal model of relevance to schizophrenia. *NPJ Schizophrenia, 5*(1), 6.

Power, E., & D'Amato, R. C. (2018). Should our future include the integration of evidence-based neuropsychological services into school settings? In D. P. Flanagan & E. M. McDonough (Eds.), *Contemporary intellectual assessment: Theories, tests, and issues* (4th ed., pp. 1017–1045). Guilford.

Riccio, C. A., & Schwartz, J. (2020). Neuropsychological impact on mental health and associated treatments for children with chronic illness. In C. Maykel & M. A. Bray (Eds.), Applying psychology in the schools. Promoting mind–body health in schools: Interventions for mental health professionals (p. 61–76). *American Psychological Association.* https://doi.org/10.1037/0000157-005

Steele, C., & Aronson, J. (1995). Stereotype threat and the intellectual test-performance of African Americans. *Journal of Personality and Social Psychology, 69*(5), 797–811. https://doi.org/10.1037//0022-3514.69.5.797

Suggate, S., Pufke, E., & Stoeger, H. (2019). Children's fine motor skills in kindergarten predict reading in grade 1. *Early Childhood Research Quarterly, 47*, 248–258. https://doi.org/10.1016/j.ecresq.2018.12.015

Tamura, K., Furutani, T., Oshiro, R., Oba, Y., Ling, A., & Murata, N. (2020). Concussion recovery timeline of high school athletes using a stepwise return-to-play protocol: Age and sex effects. *Journal of Athletic Training, 55*(1), 6–10. https://doi.org/10.4085/1062-6050-452-18

Thames, A. D., Hinkin, C. H., Byrd, D. A., Bilder, R. M., Duff, K. J., Rivera Mindt, M., Arentoft, A., & Streiff, V. (2013). Effects of stereotype threat, perceived discrimination, and examiner race on neuropsychological performance: Simple as Black and White? *Journal of the International Neuropsychological Society, 19*(5), 583–593. https://doi.org/10.1017/S1355617713000076

Van der Kolk, B. (2014). *The body keeps the score: Brain, mind, and body in the healing of trauma.* Penguin Books.

Vinck, A., Nijhuis-van der Sanden, M. W., Roeleveld, N. J., Mullaart, R. A., Rotteveel, J. J., & Maassen, B. A. (2009). Motor profile and cognitive functioning in children with spina bifida. *European Journal of Paediatric Neurology, 14*, 86–92. https://doi.org/10.1016/j.ejpn.2009.01.003

Witmer, L. (1896). Practical work in psychology. *Pediatrics, 2*, 462–471.

Witmer, L. (1897). The organization of practical work in psychology. *Psychological Review, 4*, 116–117.

Witmer, L. (1907). Clinical psychology. *The Psychological Clinic, 1*, 1–9.

Witmer, L. (1911). *The special class for backward children.* Philadelphia, PA: Psychological Clinic.

Wu, L., Sell, R. L., Roth, A. M., & Welles, S. L. (2018). Mental health disorders mediate association of sexual minority identity with cardiovascular disease. *Preventive Medicine, 108*, 123–128. https://doi.org/10.1016/j.ypmed.2018.01.003

Wundt, W. M. (1897/2020). *Outlines of psychology.* Translated by C. H Judd. Retrieved from Classics in the history of psychology (C. D. Green), York University. http://psychclassics.yorku.ca/Wundt/Outlines/index.htm

Yung, A. R., Stanford, C., Cosgrave, E., Killackey, E., Phillips, L., Nelson, B., & McGorry, P. D. (2006). Testing the Ultra High Risk (prodromal) criteria for the prediction of psychosis in a clinical sample of young people. *Schizophrenia Research, 84*(1), 57–66. https://doi.org/10.1016/j.schres.2006.03.014

Appendices

Appendix A: Sample Adult Neuropsychological Questionnaire

Rik Carl D'Amato, Elizabeth M. Power, and Michael J. Tincup

R. C. D'Amato et al. (eds.), *Understanding the Biological Basis of Behavior*,
https://doi.org/10.1007/978-3-030-59162-5

TheChicagoSchool of Professional Psychology

NEUROPSYCHOLOGICAL INTERVIEW QUESTIONNAIRE

Adult Version

Rik Carl D'Amato, Elizabeth M. Power, and Michael J. Tincup

Instructions

The following questionnaire is designed to help you describe your behaviors, thoughts, relationships, and health history. In some instances, you may have difficulty responding to particular questions. If such is the case, write in "DK" for don't know or "RNA" for rather not answer. It is our hope to better understand you through the information you provide. Therefore, try your best to answer as many questions as possible. If a response requires more space than provided, continue on the reverse side of that page. When finished, kindly bring this completed questionnaire to the initial interview.

DEMOGRAPHICS

Name: ____

Last First Middle

Current Gender Identity: ____________ **Sex Assigned at Birth:** ____________

Home Address: ____

Street City & State Zip Code

Date of Birth: ________ **Age:** ________ **Telephone:** ____________

Employer: ____________ **Position:** ____________

Please *circle* your highest level of education:

8th grade High School Undergraduate Graduate Other: ___________

Neuropsychological Interview Questionnaire - Adult
Page - 2
BEHAVIORS AND THOUGHTS

***Circle* any of the following behaviors that apply to you:**

Overeat	Suicidal attempts	Can't keep a job
Take drugs	Compulsions	Insomnia
Vomiting	Smoke	Take too many risks
Avoidance	Withdrawal	Lazy
Drink to excess	Nervous tics/habits	Eating problems
Work too hard	Concentration difficulties	Aggressive
Procrastination	Sleep disturbance	Excessive crying
Impulsive	Phobias	Anxiety
Social anxiety	Friendship difficulties	Work distress

*** Please note that the information requested herein is confidential. Any public or private use of the data obtained within this questionnaire is protected under the laws of psychologist/client privilege. In certain cases, however, some or all information provided may be used anonymously for research and/or training purposes.**

Are there any specific behaviors, actions or habits that you would like to change?

____
____
____
____

What are some special talents or skills that make you feel proud?

____
____
____

How do you spend your free time?

____
____
____

I picture myself: (*circle* any that apply to you)

being in control	losing control	not coping
being talked about	being followed	succeeding
hurting myself	failing	hurting others
being laughed at	being trapped	being promiscuous
being assertive	being self-confident	managing food appropriately
working out consistently	drug free	Others:

What picture comes into your mind most often (can be separate from above)?

____
____
____

Neuropsychological Interview Questionnaire - Adult
Page - 3

Describe a very pleasant image, mental picture, or fantasy:

____

____

____

Describe a very unpleasant image, mental picture, or fantasy:

____

____

____

Describe your image of a completely "safe place":

____

____

____

How often do you have nightmares? Circle the best option.

Never Rarely Sometimes Often Always

Circle **each of the words that you might use to describe yourself:**

intelligent	confident	worthwhile	ambitious	sensitive	loyal	trustworthy
regretful	worthless	crazy	evil	useless	considerate	deviant
unattractive	unlovable	inadequate	ugly	stupid	naïve	honest
incompetent	conflicted	forgetful	attractive	indecisive	suicidal	humorous
anxious	happy	lovable	decisive	hard-working	attractive	agreeable

What do you consider to be your most irrational thought or idea?

____

____

____

Check the boxes **that most accurately reflect your opinion(s):**

- ❒ I should not make mistakes
- ❒ I should be good at everything I do
- ❒ I should not disclose personal information
- ❒ I am a victim of circumstances
- ❒ My life is controlled by outside forces
- ❒ Other people are happier than I am
- ❒ It is very important to please other people
- ❒ I disagree with my assigned gender
- ❒ I value my cultural and racial identity
- ❒ I am bothered by thoughts that occur repeatedly
- ❒ When I do not know something, I should pretend that I do
- ❒ I'm struggling with my sexual orientation
- ❒ It is important to not take risks and be safe
- ❒ I don't deserve to be happy
- ❒ If I ignore my problems, they will disappear
- ❒ It is my responsibility to make others happy
- ❒ I should strive for perfection
- ❒ I am always responsible for my own action
- ❒ Basically, there are two ways of doing things - the right way and the wrong way
- ❒ I get along with others who are different from me

Please complete the following sentences:

I am a person who: ______________________________

All my life: ______________________________

Ever since I was a child: ______________________________

It's hard for me to admit: ______________________________

One of the things I can't forgive is: ______________________________

The bad thing about growing up is: ______________________________

One of the ways I can help myself but don't is: ______________________________

Neuropsychological Interview Questionnaire - Adult
Page - 5
RELATIONSHIPS

Family:

Who did you primarily live with when growing up? Describe your relationships (e.g., father, mother's girlfriend, grandparent).

____
____
____
____

Give a description of your parent/guardian/caregiver's personality and their attitude towards you (past & present)?

____
____
____

What types of discipline strategies did your parent/guardian/caregiver use when you were a child?

____
____
____
____

Describe your home environment while growing up (e.g., relationship with parents/guardians, siblings, relationships amongst members of household).

____
____
____
____

Were you able to talk openly with your parents/guardians/caregivers (e.g., sex, relationships, etc.)? Explain.

____
____
____
____

Did your parents/guardians/caregivers understand you when you were growing up? Explain.

____
____
____
____

Did you feel loved and respected by your parents/guardians/caregivers? Explain.

____
____
____
____

Neuropsychological Interview Questionnaire - Adult
Page - 6

Did you ever experience a divorce of your parents/caregivers/guardians? If yes, explain your reaction. *Write N/A if not applicable.*

____
____
____
____

At this point in time, who are the most important people in your life? Describe your relationships.

____
____
____
____

Friends:

Do you make friends easily? Explain.

____
____
____
____

Do your friendships tend to last? Explain.

____
____
____
____

Describe a relationship that gives you joy:

____
____
____
____

Describe a relationship that gives you grief:

____
____
____
____

When in social situations, to what degree do you generally feel comfortable? (*circle* one):

Very comfortable   Relatively comfortable   Relatively uncomfortable   Very anxious

Neuropsychological Interview Questionnaire - Adult
Page - 7

In general, do you express your feelings, opinions, and wishes to others in an open, appropriate manner? Explain.

Describe situations or individuals with whom you have trouble asserting yourself:

Do you have one or more friends with whom you feel comfortable sharing your most private feelings? Explain.

Intimate Relationships:

List the significant relationships you had prior to age 18:

If you have been divorced or experienced a breakup with a long-term partner, what was the reason for the divorce/breakup? *Write N/A if not applicable.*

If you have ever been widowed, what was the history of your relationship? *Write N/A if not applicable.*

Did your parents/caregivers/guardians ever attempt to influence your sexual orientation/partner preference? If so, explain. *Write N/A if not applicable.*

Current Spouse/Partner (skip this section if not applicable):

Current spouse/partner's name: ______________________________

Neuropsychological Interview Questionnaire - Adult
Page - 8

How long did you know your partner before you began dating or (if married) your spouse before engagement? ____________

How long have you been together/dating (if any separations, please explain)?

____
____
____

How old is your partner/spouse? ________

What is your partner/spouse's education level (e.g., completed high school, college, etc.)?

____

What is your partner/spouse's occupation? ______________________________

Briefly describe your partner/spouse's personality:

____
____

In what areas are you compatible/incompatible?

____
____
____

Is your present sex life satisfactory? If not, please explain:

____
____
____

If applicable, how do you get along with your in-laws/partner's parents/caregivers?

____
____
____

Do you have children? If so, give names, ages, gender identification, and any special needs associated with your children (e.g., learning disability):

____
____
____
____

Other Relationships:

Are there any problems in your relationships within the workplace? If so, please explain:

____
____

Neuropsychological Interview Questionnaire - Adult
Page - 9

Please complete the following:

One of the ways people hurt me is ______

I could shock you by ______

A parent should ______

A partner/spouse should ______

A true friend should ______

HEALTH HISTORY

Do you have any current concerns about your physical health? If so please specify:

______

Please list any medications that you are currently taking or have taken in the past 6 months (including aspirin, birth control pills, or any medications that were prescribed or taken over the counter):

______

Describe your eating habits (e.g., eat three meals a day, snack throughout day, binging/purging):

______

Do you exercise regularly? If so, what type and how often:

______

Place a *number after* any of the following that apply to you:

(0 = Never, 1 = Rarely, 2 = Frequently, 3 = Daily)

Neuropsychological Interview Questionnaire - Adult
Page - 10

Alcohol ( )	Cocaine ( )	Stimulants ( )	Blood Pressure ( )
Heart Problems ( )	Nausea ( )	Vomiting ( )	Insomnia ( )
Hallucinogens ( )	Diarrhea ( )	Constipation ( )	Allergies ( )
Marijuana ( )	Painkillers ( )	Tranquilizers ( )	Coffee ( )
Cigarettes ( )	Narcotics ( )	Sedatives ( )	Aspirin ( )
Headaches ( )	Backaches ( )	Fitful Sleep ( )	Poor Appetite ( )

***Circle* any of the following that apply to you or members of your family:**

Thyroid disease	Kidney disease	Asthma	Neurological disease
Gastrointestinal disease	Infectious diseases	Diabetes	Cancer
Prostate problems	Glaucoma	Epilepsy	Cardiac concerns
Depression	Anxiety	Stroke	High cholesterol
High blood pressure	Alcohol/Drug dependence	Migraines	Other: ____________

Have you ever had any head injuries or loss of consciousness? If so, please give details:

____

____

____

____

Please describe any surgery you have had (give dates):

____

____

____

____

Please describe any accidents or injuries you have suffered (give dates):

____

____

____

____

______________________ ______________

Client's Signature Today's Date

______________________ ______________

Psychologist's Signature Today's Date

Neuropsychological Interview Questionnaire - Adult
Page - 11

Revised March 1995 - MJT
Revised February 2005 - RCD
Revised November 2010 - RCD
Revised March 2015 - RCD
Revised May 2020 - RCD

Appendix B: Sample Neuropsychological Evaluation, Age 9

Report by: Amanda Skierkiewicz

NEUROPSYCHOLOGIAL SERVICES CENTER
1221 Lake Shore Drive, Chicago, IL

NEUROPSYCHOLOGICAL EVALUATION

CONFIDENTIAL

This report is for professional use only.
It is not to be released without permission by the person evaluated, or that person's legal guardian.

Patient's Name: Adam Ruben	**Date of Birth:** 01-01-2011
Psychologist: Amanda Skierkiewicz, Ed.D., NCSP	**Age:** 9
Pediatrician: Dr. Sherman	**Grade:** 2nd
Length of Consult: 1 Unit	**Date of Consult:**
Length of Testing: 16 Units	**Date of Testing:**
Length of Follow up:1 Unit	**Date of Follow up:**

REASON FOR REFERRAL

Adam is a 9-year-old, ambidextrous (though he slightly favors his right) male who was seen for a neuropsychological evaluation in my office. Adam was diagnosed with Autism Spectrum Disorder through an evaluation at St. John's Hospital just shy of his 3rd birthday. Ms. Ruben mother has actively pursued interventions since that evaluation, including Applied Behavior Analysis, Occupational Therapy, speech/language therapy and Adam is serviced under an Indvidualized Service Plan (ISP) at his private school. Current data will be used in updating the plan for Adam moving forward.

BACKGROUND INFORMATION

Developmental History:

Adam is the result of a full-term spontaneous vaginal delivery weighing 7 pounds, 15 ounces. No aids were required in the extraction. At birth, there was no jaundice, respiratory problems, or protracted hospital stay. Adam is the elder of two with no reported miscarriages. His mother did not report the use of any alcohol, tobacco, recreational or prescription medications during the pregnancy, and had no other medical, physical, or emotional problems while he was in utero.

Early temperament was described as easy. Adam was formula-fed and had some initial difficulties with vomiting and reflux. His mother did not know that at the time he was having a reaction to dairy. At the age of 4 and onward, Adam has been dairy and gluten-free. Despite the issues with dairy, Adam had no initial difficulties with weight gain.

Developmental milestones were on time for motor and language. His mother described a regression in language wherein Adam actually lost words until approximately age 4. His mother brought up some concerns to Adam's pediatrician who suggested an evaluation and subsequently began occupational therapy and speech/language therapy. Adam was toilet-trained by age 5 but he continues to experience nocturnal enuresis nightly.

Family History:

Family medical history is largely unremarkable for close relatives and unknown in his father. Family psychiatric history is remarkable for anxiety and OCD in his mother and substance use in his maternal grandfather. Medical and psychological history is unremarkable so far in his younger brother (age <12 months).

Medical History:

Adam's medical history is remarkable for chronic ear infections in early childhood, which were treated through the use of antibiotics. He has not had tubes placed and the ear infections largely seem to have resolved. He does have issues with snoring and frequently breathes through his mouth. He has no known allergies and does not take any current medications, over-the-counter or otherwise. Adam was also born with ankyloglossia (tongue-tied) and his mother is looking into having Adam see a sleep therapist. Hearing and vision are reportedly normal. Currently, there is no reported onset or maintenance insomnia, and no other parasomnias or dyssomnias.

Educational History:

Academically, Adam is enrolled in the 2nd grade and in a private school. Last year he had an initial evaluation and was found eligible for special education services under the designation of Autism. His mother provided me with his eligibility documentation and current ISP (dated 3-21-2019) to which I refer the reader for additional detail. To highlight, Adam's reading was average in terms of sight word reading, reading fluency, and decoding, though reading comprehension was below average. His math computation and math fluency were both within normal limits, though math concepts fell in the mildly impaired range. Written expression also fell within the mildly impaired range. An evaluation of his speech and language skills indicated deficits with his receptive and expressive language abilities. His motor coordination and writing speed were also deficient relative to his peers.

According to Adam's ISP, his current classroom accommodations include visual supports, proximity to teacher or adult, repeated/rephrased directions, increased time to process directions (simple one-step concrete verbal directions paired with verbal cues), and ask student to rephrase directions to check for understanding. He is also provided with noise-reducing headphones, decreased auditory and visual stimuli in his work area, decreased visual stimuli on worksheets and materials, movement breaks, alternative seating, support to plan his thoughts for writing, warnings prior to transitions, visual schedule, incomplete work folder, extra time, gaining his attention prior to giving directions, and repetition of directions. He currently receives 30 minutes of speech/language services per week.

His mother reported that Adam has been reading since he was 3 years old and does well with recalling details. He has an interest in science and history and prefers informational books over fiction. He does have some resistance to writing-based tasks.

Behavioral/Psychological History:

Following concerns with Adam's development, Adam's mother had an evaluation completed through St. John's Hospital when Adam was just shy of 3 years old and I refer the reader to that evaluation (dated 01-09-2014) at which point Adam was diagnosed with autism spectrum disorder and delays with expressive and receptive language were noted. Since that evaluation, Adam has actively participated in interventions, including speech/language therapy, occupational therapy, and ABA therapy. He also receives social work services at school. At present, Adam is working on conversation starters, greetings, entering play situations, following multistep directions, and increasing his attention span. His mother noted that she has seen some generalization of these skills into other areas.

EVALUATION PROCEDURES

Memory Validity Profile (MVP)
Wechsler Intelligence Scale for Children, Fifth Edition (WISC-V)
Woodcock-Johnson Tests of Achievement, Fourth Edition (WJ-IV)
Behavior Assessment System for Children, Third Edition (BASC-3) Parent Rating Scales
Multidimensional Anxiety Scale for Children, Second Edition (MASC-2) Parent Report
Conners Continuous Performance Test , Third Edition (CPT-3)
Test of Everyday Attention for Children (TEA-Ch)
Social Communication Questionnaire (SCQ)
Autism Spectrum Rating Scales (ASRS)
NEPSY Neurodevelopmental Inventory, Second Edition (NEPSY-II)

Affect Recognition
Comprehensive Assessment of Spoken Language, Second Edition (CASL-2)

Nonliteral Language
Pragmatic Language

Clinical Assessment of Pragmatics (CAPs)
Autism Diagnostic Observation Schedule, Second Edition (ADOS-2) 2 Module 3

OBSERVATIONS and VALIDITY

Validity:

Performance validity was assessed using the Memory Validity Profile (MVP), which is a standardized measure designed specifically for children and adolescents. Adam performed perfectly on the Visual items, but did make three errors on the Verbal items. His MVP Total score is certainly still valid, although I offer that even one error is worth remarking upon given the incredible ease and simplicity of this task. Still, he performed within normal limits on the embedded measures, with the exception of a conservative skew to his CPT-3 response style, though he certainly still made a number of responses for the CPT-3 itself to be considered valid. Adam's Reliable Digit Span score of 7 is above the required cut-off. Overall, I would say that basic effort is supported and that there is no evidence of active feigning.

Behavioral Observations:

Adam was a willing participant in the evaluation process. He worked diligently and certainly seemingly to the best of his ability. He was very talkative, though many of his comments were tangential in nature. He did require fairly consistent redirection throughout, frequently gave impulsive answers, and often walked about the room touching all items within reach.

Adam seemed to have some difficulty understanding some of the directions, so extra efforts were made to ensure he understood the tasks before starting, above and beyond the standard instructions, but without spoiling the tasks/"giving him an edge." Tests were most often attempted to be administered following standardization procedures as strictly as possible, and then modifications were made as needed based on how he handled that, with every effort made to keep the scores reflective of his current functioning as possible. For example, while alternative methods of getting Adam to understand instructions were utilized, if these explanations being given to Adam would actually spoil the results (such as overexplaining to the point that Adam no longer had to "figure it out"), the task was discontinued. I offer the comprehension issue as a minor caveat, though I intend to be as descriptive as possible as to any modifications that were made during the testing period. Regardless, I understand that Adam's presentation was reflective of his current day-to-day, I offer the following as a good representation of his functioning, although cross domain and secondary influences certainly need to be considered as possible sources of underrepresentation of his potential.

EVALUATION RESULTS

Intellectual reasoning and cognitive proficiency skills were assessed using the WISC-V. Adam achieved a Full Scale IQ score of 81 (10%), which falls in the low average range. There was some variability among his individual index scores, though a reader can better understand his abilities by consideration of the individual index scores. On those, he achieved a Verbal Comprehension Index score of 98

(45%), which is average. Visuospatial analytical and integration skills were assessed using the Visual Spatial Index, and his score of 84 (14%) fell in the low average range. His novel problem solving skills, as measured by the Fluid Reasoning Index, came in at an 82 (12%), which is low average. Within the latter two indices, Adam did seem to have some early errors and some impulsive responding, so it is certainly possible that there is some slight underrepresentation of his abilities. He performed consistently within all three indices.

Cognitive Proficiency: As to the indices of cognitive proficiency, his Working Memory Index came in at a 94 (34%), which is average. There was a 20 point discrepancy between his average performance on the subtest utilizing visual stimuli presented "all at once" (Picture Span=105, 63%) relative to his low average performance on the subtest utilizing auditory stimuli presented individually (Digit Span=85, 16%). Adam's Processing Speed Index came in at a 63 (1%), which falls in the moderately impaired range. He was frequently talking and had to be redirected back to the task at hand, so that score is likely reflective of secondary influences. He did perform consistently within the index, though I did have him complete the supplemental Cancellation subtest and that score came in at the cut-off for impairment (SS=80, 9%). What was more compelling was Adam's performance between the two trials within the task. On the first 45 minute trial, Adam's performance was solidly average (SS=95, 37%). On the second, he appeared less engaged and needed more frequent prompting to continue working and his performance fell within the impaired range (SS=70, 2%). Thus, I suspect speed of information processing itself may be intact, though secondary influences of engagement/attention are certainly going to have an impact from a functional standpoint.

Achievement:

Academic achievement was assessed in this case using the WJ-IV. Adam's Broad Reading score came in at a 91 (28%), which does fall in the average range and is largely consistent with expectations based on his VCI. His reading included a Letter-Word Identification score of 109 (73%), which is average and reflects his "sight word bank" and the application of phonics. He achieved a Passage Comprehension score of 93 (32%), which falls in the average range. His Sentence Reading Fluency score of 80 (9%) falls at the cut-off for impairment. During feedback, his mother indicated that measures of oral reading fluency have not indicated this to be an area of concern, so again, we may be dealing with a cross domain influence of attention/engagement, as the Sentence Reading Fluency task is three minutes long.

Adam's Broad Mathematics came in at a 70 (2%), which falls in the moderately impaired range and is below age, grade and IQ expectations based on his fluid reasoning. He had difficulty on the most complex task that is heavily mediated by quantitative concepts (Applied Problems=67, 2%). This was below expectations based on his Figure Weights performance (SS=80, 9%). On Calculation, wherein math formulas were laid out for him to complete on a worksheet, Adam performed in the mildly impaired range (SS=73, 3%). His Math Facts Fluency score was also problematic and in the mildly impaired range (SS=73, 3%).

Emotional/Behavioral Functioning:

I began the assessment of emotional and behavioral functioning by having Mrs. Ruben complete the BASC-3. All validity scale scores were within normal limits. Consistent with the referral concern, she elevated the probability scales for both Autism (68T) and ADHD (64T). The primary issues were seen on the scales related to odd or unusual behaviors (79T) and impulsive and hyperactive behaviors (74T), and executive dysfunction (70T). She also elevated for some concerns related to anxiety (65T), some sadness (61T), attention problems (61T), some irritability (61T), some immaturity/underdeveloped social skills (69T), some difficulties with emotional regulation (65T), and difficulties recovering from stress and adversity (31T). Adam can also have difficulty adjusting to changes in his routine (36T), making decisions (36T), and effectively communicating (34T).

As anxiety is not a unitary construct, I also had Adam's mother complete the MASC-2 for additional detail. The validity scale was within normal limits (consistency). Overall, the Total score was within normal limits (54T). She did endorse some rigidity commonly seen in the ASDs. She also sees some physical manifestations (61T), which are primarily related to agitation/restlessness (63T).

Complex Attention:

Complex attention and broader executive functioning skills were assessed using multiple objective measures in this case. I began with the CPT-3, which includes embedded PVTs, and while Adam made a valid number of responses overall, he skewed more towards a conservative type of responding focused on avoiding errors over speed (69T) rather than balancing the two as instructed. A conservative response style at this level would be associated with a slight increase in omission errors, a slight decrease in commission errors, and a slower speed of responding. His rate of omission errors is elevated at over 2 SDs, which is past the point where this would not be elevated were a conservative response style factored out. His rate of commission errors was within normal limits, so at worst this would increase a bit. The measure of his response speed was "atypically slow" (82T), so if affected that would skew closer to normal limits.

In addition to the 2 SD elevation for omission errors, four of the six measures of focused attention were impaired, including the two most important measures for focused attention itself, namely inconsistency, which was elevated at 4 SDs and at the ceiling of the test (90T) and Variability of attention (77T). Certainly, Adam has difficulty with focused attention. As to impulsivity, his rate of impulsive errors were within normal limits (48T), though it is really his rate of perseverative errors that was more compelling (78T), which can be thought of as "going on autopilot" or "acting without thinking." As to the measure of attention over time, focus was not great from the outset and Adam did have to be redirected back to the task at hand rather consistently. It was during this task that he did become upset and did attempt to close the computer and asked for the computer to be turned off. There was a spiked mark in omission errors between the second and third blocks (6% vs. 23%).

There was also impairment on the primary measure of vigilance (65T), which for the unfamiliar reader refers to "the *brain* becoming less responsive as the *brain* becomes understimulated." Overall, Adam's performance is associated with a "very high likelihood" of having a disorder characterized by attention deficits.

I also had Adam complete the TEA-Ch, which is another measure of complex attention skills, but assesses those individually rather than all at once. He continued to have difficulty. On the basic task of visual focused attention, he performed in the moderately impaired range (SS=60, <1%) and barely identified more than half of the targets (SS=75, 5%). Not only does that reflect poor attention to detail and consistently evidence impaired focus, it also exemplifies a poor balance of speed and accuracy and ineffective strategizing. Plus, his score was impaired on the basic task of auditory focused attention (SS=60, <1%). I really cannot overstate how simple this task really is – all he had to do was count tones up to 15 (the trick is there are gaps between the stimuli that serve as a "press" for inattentive types of lose focus, which is exactly what happened). I want to be clear that Adam understood the instructions, was providing sensible answers and chose intact skills elsewhere (such as the WMI) to indicate this was not an instance of invalidation. On top of that, when his attention was divided between the visual and auditory stimuli, Adam's score was severely impaired (SS=55, <1%), which is a decrement score that is calculated from Adam's own baseline (i.e., that initial impairment was essentially "reset" for this calculation and he still had this level of difficulty). He also had incredible difficulty when his attention was divided between two noncompeting sets of auditory stimuli (SS=60, <1%), although that is not a decrement score so it is difficult to say how much additional difficulty he had with the added demands. Finally, on the follow-up response inhibition task, Adam scored in the moderately impaired range (SS=60, <1%), which suggests there is some impulsivity in his profile which may have been "hidden" by a conservative response style. Overall, the objective data in this case shows a clear and prominent deficiency with complex attention skills.

Social Cognition:

Absolutely, direct assessment for developmental social disorders was included in this case as well. I began with the SCQ, which checks for early developmental indicators of the ASDs and other disorders of social cognition. Adam was scored at an 11, which is a bit below the cut-off (cut-off=15), but certainly above what would be expected in the non-ASD, neurotypical population. I also had Mrs. Ruben complete the ASRS, which is updated to the current DSM-5 nomenclature for the ASDs. She produced a Total score of 58T, which is just below the cut-off. She did rate Adam within normal limits for both criterion A (52T) and criterion B (56T). On the treatment scales, her concerns were primarily for atypical language (68T) and issues with attention (63T). During feedback, we discussed that her current ratings are likely reflective of improvement seen due to intervention and not necessarily full resolution of symptoms.

Nonverbal communication perception was assessed using Affect Recognition subtest from the NEPSY-II and Adam's score of 110 (75%) was high average. For the unfamiliar reader, this task does involve more "basic" emotions of happy, sad, disgusted, angry and fear. It is not uncommon for kids with ASDs who have been through intervention to be able to "logirhythming" static images and be able to perform well on basic affect recognition tasks.

To that end, I had Adam complete the Clinical Assessment of Pragmatics (CAPs), which assesses Adam's use of pragmatic communication skills, including the use of social language and nonverbal cues. This measure utilizes short (15 second) video clips depicting social interactions. His performance on the Paralinguistic Index fell in the mildly impaired range (SS=74, 4%), which measures his use of nonverbal communication, such as prosody, gestures, and facial expressions. Within the index, his performance on Paralinguistic Decoding (SS=75, 5%) fell in the mildly impaired range. That task measured his ability to read microexpressions and nonverbal language. Affective Expression, which is a measure of his ability to use non-instrumental communication that involves appropriately expressing polite refusal or regret, supporting peers, giving compliments, using humor or expressing empathy, gratitude, and encouragement fell in the mildly impaired range (SS=70, 2%). Finally, his performance was severely impaired with his ability to use various nonverbal cues, such as facial expressions, tone of voice, inflections, and prosody, gestures, and overall body language to express various communicative intents (paralinguistic signals=55, <1%).

I also assessed social language skills directly using the CASL-2. Adam performed at the cut-off for impairment on Nonliteral Language (SS=81, 10%), which measures figurative language and associated aspects of supralinguistic language. His performance on the Pragmatic Language subtest, wherein Adam had to identify and describe socially appropriate behaviors in general everyday situations fell in the mildly impaired range (SS=77, 6%). This is also below expectations based on his VCI. Known ASD populations are known to perform 1 SD or more below their VCI and Adam's performance was about 1.5 SDs below his VCI.

Finally, Adam completed the ADOS-2 (Module 3) which is comprised of interview questions and other opportunities for social interaction with embedded and intentional "presses" to elicit certain reactions/responses. From that, a scoring rubric is applied to his interactions with the examiner, which serves to identify social deficits found in ASDs. His overall Comparison score was a 10, which falls well above the cut-off for autism "proper" and is considered a "high" likelihood of autism spectrum-related symptoms.

While Adam willingly engaged, his responses to questions were often lacking in detail and he often required heavy prompting in order to provide detail to questions. His use of eye contact was minimal in order to appropriately regulate the interaction and he used very few instrumental or descriptive gestures during the interaction. His responses to questions about social relationships and emotions had a very "scripted" quality to them. For example, when asked to describe what he feels like when he's happy, he responded "when my face is smiling" and when asked how does it feel when he is frightened or anxious, he responded "my mouth is open wide like a circle." Similarly, when he was asked how he feels when he is sad, Adam responded "water is coming out of your eyes and your face is looking down." In terms of friendships, he did mention a couple of friends and that they like to play at his birthday party. When asked what being a friend means to him, he replied "by being nice and responsible to them." However, when asked how being a friend is different from someone whom you just go to school with, Adam replied "I don't know what this means." This question was rephrased and repeated in several ways and he did not understand the concept of the question. Overall, I am seeing consistent evidence of deficits in social cognition with ASDs.

IMPRESSIONS

I have already had the opportunity to discuss these results with Adam's mother directly during our feedback appointment. Consistent with the previous findings, my overall impression is that Adam's current profile continues to be best characterized as an **Autism Spectrum Disorder** (ICD-10=F84.0). His history is evidenced to include numerous unique developmental indicators of ASDs, as well as behavioral indicators on the subjective ratings are also consistently indicative of ASDs. Finally, the objective data consistently evidenced impaired deficits in social cognition and understanding pragmatics. From a severity level, I would place Adam at a **Level 1** (requiring support) for both social communication and restrictive, repetitive behaviors and severity specifiers. As to the specifiers, Adam is also presenting without "accompanying intellectual impairment" and without "accompanying language impairment," which is a positive finding.

I do have consistent evidence of a common comorbidity of **Attention Deficit Hyperactivity Disorder** (ICD-10=F90.2), which was consistently evidenced in the objective and subjective data. Given the shared symptoms, as well as the vast majority of the ASD population also presenting with deficits of ADHD, I discussed with Adam's mother how this is really best conceptualized as a shared neurodevelopmental condition rather than two separate problems, although the characterization offered by an ASD diagnosis does not technically include those of ADHD, hence the separate coding. As to Adam's specific profile, there are marked deficits with focused attention, sustained attention, divided attention, vigilance, impulsivity, as well as "autopilot tendencies." From a cognitive standpoint, I suspect that processing speed itself is intact, though secondary influences of issues of engagement and so forth have led to a repeated pattern of difficulty on tasks that were either designed to measure processing speed or susceptible to the secondary influence of speed.

In regard to his academic skills, Adam presents with some form of **Mathematics Disorder** (ICD-10=F81.2) with impairment of number sense, memorization of number facts, accurate calculation, and accurate math reasoning. Again, it is certainly possible that some of Adam's scores were susceptible to the cross domain/ secondary influences associated with poor attention, though math was consistently problematic. Regardless, interventions targeting this area are certainly appropriate.

RECOMMENDATIONS

1. I encouraged that a copy of this report be provided to Adam's pediatrician, Dr. Sherman – a release has not yet been signed, otherwise I would send this over to him directly. I want to make Dr. Sherman aware that the objective data indeed indicates that a trial of stimulant medication is both appropriate and likely to be beneficial. It is my understanding that his mother would prefer to table this for now, but I still wanted to make sure the recommendation was included. Of course, I ultimately defer the decision-making to Dr. Sherman's discretion, and if I could be of any additional assistance, I would be happy to make myself available.
   a. Mrs. Ruben noted that bedwetting continues to be an issue, and I wanted to make Dr. Sherman aware of this. While I am aware that there are medications such as imipramine that can be used to treat, I recommended that his mother consider the alarm bell and pad as a method of behavioral intervention. The research has repeatedly supported this system as the most effective without the same risk of rebound/relapse once discontinued as seen in medications. There are a number of different products on the market which the family could consider.
2. As requested, I will be providing a copy of this report to Adam's treatment providers at **ABA SERVICES** so that the findings can be disseminated and implemented into his treatment plan. Absolutely, he is appropriate for continuing with interventions focused on improving behavior, willingness, as well as abstraction and reasoning, in addition to the social/pragmatic language difficulties that are going to be key to addressing many of the problematic aspects of Adam's current profile. Not only is the use of therapy following applied behavior analysis well supported in the treatment of ASD populations, but in Adam's case I certainly recommend continuing with this service. Of course, I trust the specifics of treatment planning to his providers, and if it could be of benefit, I can certainly make myself available for any additional consult. As always, I appreciate the opportunity to participate in the care of your patients.
3. I discussed with Mrs. Ruben how there are essentially three interventions that hold Level 1 ("Best") research support according to the American Academy of Pediatrics for the use in the treatment of ADHD, the first being the aforementioned stimulant medication. The second is behavioral interventions with parent training, which is currently being provided through ABA therapy. The third is neurofeedback (neurofeedbackdefined.com), which is a service provided in my office and something I certainly think Adam could benefit from. If the family were interested, I would be happy to set them up.
4. While Adam's insufficient math skills are likely a secondary problem, the reality is that we are seeing some deficiencies with his math/calculation abilities. Thus, it may make sense to pursue some sort of intervention. It may be as simple as having the "neighborhood" or some sort of non-specialty tutor spend some time with Adam in a 1-1 scenario to get him some re-exposure, though it can be

argued that a specialist would be able to more efficiently (and effectively) address the problem. If Adam's mother were interested, I would be happy to provide some referrals.

5. Continuing to re-evaluate Adam's presentation is not only appropriate, but really a necessity given the amount of cross domain influence between skill areas, as improvement in one area would likely lead to a good deal of improvement elsewhere, creating a "snowball effect" of improvements on top of gains made via continued interventions. Of course, I would be happy to continue to provide those services for Adam, though I would be happy to consult with another provider if preferred. This is important to do regularly, as I do not want to miss capturing an important baseline.
6. I also encourage Adam's mother to provide a copy of this report to his school district so the results can be incorporated into their plan for him. I did review a copy of Adam's current IEP (detailed above) and it is my understanding that he is already provided with environmental supports and accommodations, as well as speech/language therapy and social work services through the school. If it would be of benefit to his education team, I would be happy to discuss the specifics of his case or provide specific recommendations.

Ultimately, I would be happy to stay actively involved in Adam's case as he moves forward. I typically see the family for a follow-up session in about a month so that I can address any additional questions and aid in the implementation of treatment interventions. From there, we can follow up at regular intervals or on an as-needed basis, depending on the needs of the family and the treatment team. At those times, I would be interested in his level of improvement, and if there are any lingering or newly emerging symptoms, additional recommendations could be made.

Amanda Skierkiewicz, Ed.D., NCSP

Amanda Skierkiewicz, Ed.D., NCSP
Clinical Neuropsychologist
Licensed School Psychologist
IL License # 071-009993
IEIN #959665

ALS/jnd (dictated but not read for expediency)

Appendix C: Sample Neuropsychological Evaluation, Age 12

Report by Cortney Bindrich

O'Rourke Psychology Group

123 Adams St, Chicago, IL

Neuropsychological Evaluation

CONFIDENTIAL

Name: Jacob Germaine	**Dates of Evaluation:** April 2019
Birthdate: Jan 1, 2006	**Age:** 12 years, 7 months
Referred by: Parents	

Reason for Referral: Mr. and Mrs. Germaine requested a comprehensive evaluation to clarify his cognitive and adaptive profile due to the auto-immune disease he acquired around two years of age. He has received special education support throughout his academic career. Jacob's parents sought to better understand his current cognitive and adaptive functioning strengths and weaknesses to identify the most appropriate placement and services for him in his new district.

Background Information: Jacob's history is documented in his chart and has been reviewed by the examiners. The following brief information is particularly relevant for the present evaluation.

Jacob recently completed the 7th grade at Blue River in Blue River, Wisconsin. Prior to attending Blue River, he attended school in the Green Meadow School District. Jacob currently receives formalized accommodations, direct instruction, and specialized services via an Individualized Education Plan (IEP) under the classification of multiple disabilities. His current academic placement is within the regular education program with special education instruction and/or related services provided for 21%-60% of his school day out side of the general education classroom. Jacob independently navigates through his school building with a wheelchair. He receives a full-day one-on-one aide, as well as speech and language therapy (360 minutes per month), an assistive technology communication device, and occupational therapy (120 minutes a month direct and consult). For more details related to Jacob's specific accommodations, modifications, and goals, please refer to his most recent IEP.

Jacob's fall 2018 NWEA MAP test for math revealed his performance at the 1st percentile. His STAR math scores placed him within the "urgent intervention" range. The STAR report indicated that he requires reminders at the start of a math problem solving activity, such as what application to use (e.g., multiplication, division, addition, or subtraction). Once Jacob has a review of the skill, he is able to input mixed problems into the calculator and solve the problem. He apparently benefits from step by step cues for multi-step problem solving.

Jacob's fall 2018 MAP test for reading indicated a performance at the 1st percentile. The Read 180 program, which assessed his ability to comprehend text, measured his reading at the "beginning reader" level. The school district further indicated that Jacob is currently unable to decode words fluently with accuracy above the kindergarten grade level, and he requires support in phonemic awareness and letter-sound correspondence.

At this time, the Blue River school district is proposing to move Jacob to their Modified Learning Program (MLP), which is a more restrictive educational environment outside of his home school. The school reports that his current placement is not appropriate for him, and that he is not comprehending and making meaning with the curriculum presented; even with significant modifications. Mr. and Mrs. Germaine are in disagreement with the school and the change in placement, and they have retained an educational attorney as they pursue due process.

Jacob was born full-term as a healthy twin, with no complications related to pregnancy, labor, or delivery. He reportedly achieved his developmental milestones within the normal range. At age 2, he contracted hand, foot, and mouth disease from his daycare. Jacob became increasingly ill after a few days, and his parents took him to Children's Memorial Hospital where he continued to decline. He was placed in the ICU at Children's for about a month, where he was subsequently diagnosed with a rare auto-immune disease. Jacob's parents reported skill regression during this time, and he eventually lost the functional use of his legs.

Jacob lives with his parents, twin brother, and younger brother (age 9) in Blue River, Wisconsin. His mother obtained a doctorate degree in education and currently stays at home to care for the family. Jacob's father is employed as an attorney. His parents describe him as a very happy boy that gets along well with his peers. Jacob is a characterized as a sweetheart who enjoys computers, music, swimming, cartoons, and horseback riding.

Classroom Observation: Jacob was observed on May 21, 2019 during a portion of his general education social studies class and in a smaller, co-taught English class. His behavior and level of engagement was described as 'typical'. Jacob received the assistance of an aide throughout the observation.

Jacob and two peers worked with his aide in a group apart from the rest of the general education students. He was provided with a modified assignment which reduced the amount of reading and responses required to complete the task, but which included the same conceptual demand. Although the teacher checked in briefly with the group of students and aide, the teacher did not directly interact with Jacob.

During the task, Jacob displayed a tendency to focus on his assistive communication device, which he used appropriately but also appeared to distract him from the written assignments. For example, due to the noisy nature of the large classroom (i.e., over 25 students), he had difficulty hearing the device, requiring him to hold it close to his ear. Jacob received frequent redirection from his aide back to the task, and he was repeatedly reminded to cite evidence from the text in his written responses. Concerns were noted with his comprehension of task demands and the necessary curriculum vocabulary to complete the task. Jacob communicated with his aide in mostly phrase speech.

At the end of the class period, Jacob had not completed the assignment. He did follow explicit two-step directions to pack up his materials and transition early to the next class before the passing period. Jacob displayed a bright affect and happily greeted teachers in the hallway, giving each a high-five as he passed.

Next, Jacob transitioned to his English classroom, a co-taught class with nine students. He followed verbal prompts to open his laptop and begin writing in his assignment notebook. Jacob received an accommodation of repeated prompting and a visual cue. He frequently subvocalized as he copied "no homework" into his agenda.

Students completed a persuasive writing task in which they wrote a paragraph to present an argument and read them aloud to the class. Jacob's aide provided visual prompts from a keychain for quiet mouth, still hands, and listening ears. He held his finger to his lips to demonstrate his understanding of her redirection. Jacob covered his ears when his peers clapped for each other, requiring reassurance from his aide when he anticipated future clapping.

Jacob completed a modified version of the assignment in which he wrote a sentence, using a word bank. He was asked to write the sentence by hand into a graphic organizer rather than using his laptop and the Co:Writer program. Jacob attempted to use both the laptop and his assistive communication device several times during the class, but he was redirected back to the paper and pencil task each time. He showed decreased frustration tolerance by saying "no" when asked to write words, engaging in repetitive scripted speech, and banging his hand on the table. Jacob did not provide a verbal response when asked what was wrong.

Overall, concerns were noted with several aspects of Jacob's academic functioning during the observation. Although he was provided with numerous accommodations and modified assignments, it was unclear if the degree of modification met his needs and academic comprehension level. Jacob followed two to three-step directions for basic needs and organization. However, he showed decreased understanding of the curriculum vocabulary necessary for comprehension of the core concepts.

Although Jacob participated in classrooms with typical peers, he did not have any direct interactions with peers. He typically communicated in phrase speech with his aide only. Jacob attempted several times to use his communication device and technology but was redirected.

Testing Observations: Jacob presented as a happy and pleasant boy. He demonstrated limited speech, but maintained typical eye-contact with the examiner for the majority of the evaluation.

Jacob also exhibited a limited range of emotional expression; however, he demonstrated a positive demeanor. While he appeared relaxed throughout the evaluation, he exhibited variable cooperation. Jacob further revealed mild distractibility during tasks, but was easily redirected.

Due to Jacob's limited speech, non-verbal measures of cognitive functioning were administered in addition to the adaptive functioning and language evaluations. Based on his mild distractibility concerns, the current assessment is considered a baseline sample of his current functioning.

Tests Administered: For a complete list of tests administered, the reader is referred to the attached *Summary of Scores* report.

Summary of Findings by Domain:
Intellectual Functioning: On the Wechsler Nonverbal Scale of Ability (WNV), Jacob's overall cognitive performance fell well below the average range. He demonstrated a personal strength on a measure of untimed pattern reasoning, and his understanding and sequencing of social vignettes revealed a personal weakness.

Jacob demonstrated variable performance on the Comprehensive Test of Nonverbal Intelligence (CTONI) revealing normative weaknesses and normative strengths. He revealed significant strengths on the geometric scale, which asked him to accurately identify pictures or shapes (from multiple choice options) belonging to specific categories. Jacob's performances on these assessments fell within the low average to high average range. Areas of weakness for him included accurately identifying which picture or shape would come next in a sequence.

Attention: On behavioral checklists, Jacob's parents denied symptoms of inattention and hyperactivity/impulsivity across all domains.

Jacob demonstrated average ability to focus his attention and visually discriminate between targets and not targets. While he identified an adequate number of targets, the time that he required to complete the task fell well below his same age peers.

Visual-Motor and Visual-Perception: Jacob is right-hand dominant. When administered a visual-motor integration task, his performance placed him well below the average range compared to same age peers. Jacob's visual perception and eye tracking also measured in the well below average range. He revealed low average speeded motor coordination, demonstrating the ability to adequately hold a pencil and draw geometric shapes and line with some guidance.

Language: Jacob's language comprehension and production skills fell in the well below average range. He exhibited difficulty comprehending verbal directions containing various linguistic concepts, including coordination, inclusion/exclusion, temporal relation/order, and quantitative concepts. Jacob's attention to language decreased when following two-level and three-level directions. He has acquired understanding of several basic concepts including attribution (cold, dry, slow), direction/location/position (inside, up, first, bottom), number/quantity (empty, many), and same. Jacob identified 56/108 drawings on a multiple-choice receptive vocabulary task assessing single word knowledge, and 41/52 drawings on an expressive vocabulary naming task, indicating substantial deficits in single word vocabulary.

Jacob's expressive oral language skills generally appeared commensurate with his language comprehension skills. This indicates that he was able to comment, request, direct, and name pictures/objects. Jacob frequently repeated the word or last word produced by the examiner. The oral language produced was reduced in terms of length; as he generally produced two- to four-word utterances. Grammatic errors occurred in spontaneous language consistent with Jacob's performance on standardized testing. He used personal pronouns (he, she, me), plural (-s), and present progressive (-ing). Jacob reportedly uses a touch talker to augment his expressive communication, though the communication device was not available during the current assessment.

Articulation: Jacob's overall speech intelligibility was judged to be fair at the single word level and mildly reduced at multi-word levels with known context. He produced several phonological processes including vowelization ("appo"/apple), stopping/stridency deletion ("lunt"/lunch), cluster reduction ("cacuh"/cactus), and cluster substitution ("airpwane"/airplane).

Academic Screener:

Reading: Jacob was able to accurately identify specific letters of the alphabet, both lowercase and uppercase, as well as independently read several words in isolation. Words that were more difficult for him to read included *morning, could, garden, point,* and *special*. Jacob's performance on this task fell approximately around the 1st grade level. On a curriculum-based measure, his reading fluency fell at the 13th percentile (23 cwpm). He demonstrated difficulty inferencing details from sentences he read aloud on a comprehension measure, indicating skills at approximately the kindergarten level.

Math: Untimed, Jacob completed several addition and subtraction calculation problems. He accurately solved *2+2, 6+1, 1-0,* and *9-0*. Jacob would often switch subtraction for addition, or vice versa, and solve problems incorrectly (e.g., *9+2=7, 12+4=12)*. His overall calculation and applied math solving abilities are additionally estimated to be around the kindergarten level.

Adaptive Functioning: Mrs. Germaine completed the Vineland Adaptive Behavior Scales-3rd Edition: Comprehensive Interview to assess Jacob's current level of adaptive functioning. The Vineland-3 is a commonly used and well-validated measure of the activities of daily living skills of an individual assessing three domains of adaptive functioning: communication, daily living skills, and socialization. Overall, Jacob reportedly shows low functioning (ABC SS = 55, <1st percentile).

Communication: Jacob reportedly evidences low ability to adequately communicate across settings. He displays difficulty with receptive language, including understanding 'why' questions, multistep (e.g., three or more actions) instructions, and recalling instructions after a delay of up to an hour. Jacob utilizes both spoken language and gestures to communicate; however, he exhibits weak ability to ask 'wh' questions, maintain correct, age appropriate grammar conventions, and create complex sentences by linking ideas (e.g., She ordered pizza *because* she was hungry). Jacob reportedly demonstrates limited independent understanding and use of written language. He struggles with interpreting visual, graphic information, reads well below grade level, and cannot generate spontaneous written communication, and is limited to copying pre-selected text.

Daily Living Skills: Jacob's mother indicated that he shows low, inconsistent ability to perform daily caretaking tasks, due in part to his physical impairments, but also due to lack of exposure and practice. He displayed limited, moderately low personal care skills, including weak understanding of making healthy food choices, and the health benefits of exercise. Jacob reportedly evidences a strength in his adequate ability to help with domestic tasks in the home. He continues to need support and guidance for tasks such as ironing, consistently securing the house with locked doors and alarms, and completing his laundry. Jacob displays low skill with navigating his community independently. He evidences limited utilization of social media and online communication and research tools, weak consistency with using calendars and clocks, and limited independent ability to maintain his money and make purchases.

Socialization: Jacob is reported to display overall low socializations skills across settings. He shows low interpersonal relating skills, with deficits in reciprocal conversation, ability to maintain close friendships, and inconsistent responding to the social advances of others. Jacob evidences moderately low ability to guide his leisure activities. He shows weak skill in planning outings with peers and needs prompts to adhere to rules for games and activities for others. Jacob's mother indicated that he demonstrates moderately low coping skills. Although generally easy going, he struggles to control his reactions when his feelings are hurt, and does not always understand accidental slights, resulting in strong frustration.

Overall, Jacob is reported to evidence low adaptive behavior skills, with many areas of strength and continuing improvement in areas of present weakness.

Social/Emotional Functioning: Jacob revealed below average ability to accurately identify the emotions of others. On behavioral rating scales, Jacob's parents denied significant concerns across all domains. There are no social emotional concerns at this time.

Clinical Impressions: Jacob's parents requested a comprehensive evaluation to clarify his cognitive and adaptive profile due to the auto-immune disease he acquired around two years of age. He has received special education support throughout his academic career. Jacob's parents sought to better understand his current cognitive and adaptive functioning strengths and weaknesses to identify the most appropriate placement and services for him in his new district.

Present findings indicate that, due to his previous medical condition, Jacob's overall cognitive abilities fall within the low to impaired range ($<1^{st}$ to 3rd percentile). His visual discrimination, ability to follow rote and discrete directions, fine motor coordination, and aspects of non-verbal reasoning indicate relative strengths.

Jacob's mother additionally endorsed adaptive functioning below that of his same age peers. At this time, Jacob cannot independently complete scholastic assignments from beginning to end, or consistently communicate through oral means, which are skills that can contribute to his quality of life. Due to the fact that Jacob has a neurotypically developing twin sibling, and his parents reported typical development before the acquisition of the disease, he currently meets criteria for **Major Neurocognitive Disorder Due to Another Medical Condition (ICD-10: F02.80)**.

Jacob displayed a relative strength in his social interest in peers. He greatly benefits from the use of cueing, context, repetition, and adherence to routines when required to learn and recall information at home and in the community.

Jacob presents as a happy and affable young boy. He responded well to redirection and thrives with direct interaction from his family and teachers. Jacob significantly benefits from the support he receives from his parents and educators.

Recommendations:

1. It is recommended that Jacob's educational placement be specific to his needs and integrate developmental therapies, including speech/language and occupational therapy. It should additionally fully integrate assistive technology to support his communication and development. Several accommodations are offered:

   - Provide extra time (up to triple time) for Jacob to complete tasks.
   - Instructions should be brief, clear, concise, and specific.
   - Continue providing Jacob with a one-on-one aide in the classroom throughout the day.
   - The staff working with Jacob requires more instruction and understanding of his assistive communication device, as well as how to appropriately integrate it into his daily activities. It appeared that Jacob was motivated to use the device, however, there was an apparent breakdown between how he was utilizing the device and how adults around him were receiving the information.
   - Allow Jacob to use his assistive technology device, or a keyboard, for writing assignments. Due to his slowed writing abilities, he should not be required to write by hand for lengthy writing assignments.
   - Provide single-step directions paired with a visual prompt.
   - Break down tasks and decrease work load as needed. Allow Jacob to only complete part of assignments if he has demonstrated mastery.
   - Provide a high level of visual cues and manipulatives to facilitate Jacob's learning. Jacob needs 'up-front' structure such as a template or visual model to demonstrate how to complete a task, and needs to reference this as he works.
   - Provide a predictable routine and schedule. Jacob will respond best to consistent, clearly defined expectations and consequences.
   - Provide Jacob opportunities for pre-exposure to new topics. Provide opportunities for repeated practice of concepts. Limit the number of new concepts introduced at once.
   - During class discussions, create opportunities for him to demonstrate success.
   - Visual sequence strips could be used within activities to teach Jacob what to do next. For example, if engaged in an activity that requires multiple steps, Jacob could have a strip on his desk that has representative pictures for each step in the task.
   - Assist organization by setting up a system for him to follow. Color-coding is a visually obvious system to use. For example, science materials would be blue – blue spiral notebook, blue folder, and blue book cover. These items could be placed in a basket with colored hanging files in his locker. When he needs his science things, he reaches for the blue items in the blue hanging file.

- Establish a simple positive reinforcement plan for initiating and completing independent tasks in the classroom. Similarly, create opportunities for Jacob to experience success or share his knowledge, as this will provide structure or a format to engage with peers in a positive manner.
- Allow Jacob "thinking time". That is, when asking questions, insert a waiting time of up to 60 seconds before allowing him to respond.

2. Jacob learns at a high level when provided meaningful context. His parents might expose him to real-life situations to provide a sense of the setting and to connect new information to his meaningful experience. He would benefit from watching educational television programming, such as Discovery Channel and National Geographic. Jacob's parents should continue to expose him to museums, plays, and concerts to further develop his knowledge base and give him opportunities to experience new information through a multi-sensory, high context format.

3. Several parent resources are recommended:

   a. Different Learners: Identifying, Preventing, and Treating Your Child's Learning Problems by Jane Healy, Ph.D.
   b. www.kidshealth.org contains articles and information for parents and children (as well as teens) on health, behavior, and development.
   c. www.pacer.org, the Parent Advocacy Coalition for Educational Rights, provides support and guidance for children and teens, as well as transitioning adults, about insurance, care plans, as well as transition to adult care.
   d. Everyday Skills is an app that provides self-directed learning sessions for 40 important skills for living independently and accessing the community. Includes community skills, personal skills, and transition and transportation skills.

Thank you very much for allowing us to participate in Jacob's care. If you have any further questions, please do not hesitate to contact us.

Cortney Bindrich, Ed.D.
Pediatric Neuropsychologist
Licensed Clinical & School Psychologist
IL License#: 071009776

Courtney Everette, M.S.
Neuropsychological Examiner
Autism Specialist

Lauren Roberts, M.A.
Assistant Director of Clinical Services

IL Type 73 License #2451317

Wechsler Nonverbal Scale of Ability (WNV)

	T-Score	
Matrices	26	
Coding	17	
Spatial Span	24	
Picture Arrangement	22	
	SS	%ile
FULL SCALE IQ	46	<1

Comprehensive Test of Nonverbal Intelligence - 2nd Edition (CTONI-2)

	Scaled	%ile
Pictorial Analogies	4	2
Geometric Analogies	4	2
Pictorial Categories	7	16
Geometric Categories	13	84
Pictorial Sequences	3	1
Geometric Sequences	5	5
COMPOSITES	SS	%ile
Pictorial Scale	65	1
Geometric Scale	83	13
Full Scale	71	3

Woodcock Johnson Tests of Achievement - 4th Edition (WJ-IV)

	SS	%ile
Letter-Word Identification	<40	<1
Sentence Read. Fluency	<40	<1
Passage Comprehension	<40	<1
Calculation	<40	<1
Applied Problems	<40	<1
Spelling	<40	<1
COMPOSITES	-	-
Brief Achievement	<40	<1
Reading	<40	<1
Broad Reading	<40	<1
Mathematics	<40	<1
Academic Skills	<40	<1

Peabody Picture Vocabulary Test - 4th Edition (PPVT-4)

	SS	%ile
Quotient	28	<1

Expressive Vocabulary Test - 2nd Edition (EVT-2)

	SS	%ile
Quotient	28	<1

Beery Developmental Test of Visual Motor Integration - 6th Edition (VMI-6)

	SS	%ile
Visual Motor Integration	<45	<1
Visual Perception	<45	<1
Motor Coordination	77	7

Hale-Denckla Cancellation Test (HDCT)

	Raw	Z
Correct	27	-.14

Time	354	-23.30

NEPSY - 2nd Edition

	Scaled	%ile
Affect Recognition Total	4	2

Clinical Evaluation of Language Fundamentals - 5th Edition (CELF-5)

Ages 9-21

	Scaled	%ile
Word Classes	1	<1
Following Directions	1	<1
Formulated Sentences	1	<1
Recalling Sentences	1	<1
Und Spoken Paragraph	1	<1
Word Definitions	1	<1
Sentence Assembly	1	<1
Semantic Relationships	1	<1
Composites	SS	%ile
Core Language	<40	<1
Receptive Language	45	<1
Expressive Language	45	<1
Language Content	45	<1
Language Memory	45	<1

ADHD Rating Scale - 5

	Symptoms Endorsed	
	Mother	Father
Inattention	0/9	0/9
Hyperactivity/Impulsivity	0/9	0/9

Child Behavior Checklist for Ages 6-18 (CBCL)

	T-Scores	
	Mother	Father
Anxiety/Depression	50	50
Withdrawal/Depression	57	60
Somatic Complaints	54	50
Social Problems	58	54
Thought Problems	51	51
Attention	52	52
Rule-Breaking	50	50
Aggression	50	50

Vineland Adaptive Behavior Scales – 3rd Edition

*V-Scale M=15, SD=3

	V-Scaled	SS	%ile	AE	Adaptive Level
COMMUNICATION		48	<1	-	
Receptive	7	-	-	3:0	Low
Expressive	1	-	-	2:2	Low
Written	9	-	-	7:0	Low
DAILY LIVING SKILLS		57	<1	-	
Personal	12	-	-	8:4	M Low
Domestic	15	-	-	12:9	Ade
Community	7	-	-	6:1	Low
SOCIALIZATION		55	<1	-	
Interpersonal Relationships	6	-	-	2:8	Low
Play and Leisure Time	12	-	-	7:1	M Low
Coping Skills	11	-	-	5:10	M Low

Test Interpretation: *All test scores were converted to standardized scores based on norms for age, with the exception of some academic measures, which compare to grade. Standard scores have an average range of 90-110, while scaled scores have an average range of 8 to*

Appendix D: Sample Neuropsychological Evaluation, Age 22

Report by: Walter R. Schamber, Stephanie Forness, and Rik Carl D'Amato

UNIVERSITY *of*
NORTHERN COLORADO

COLLEGE OF EDUCATION AND BEHAVIORAL SCIENCES
NEUROPSYCHOLOGY LABORATORY
DIVISION OF PROFESSIONAL PSYCHOLOGY

CONFIDENTIAL
NEUROPSYCHOLOGICAL EVALUATION

Name:	Ms. Garnet Fuman
Date of Birth:	1
Chronological Age:	22 years
Handedness:	Right
Occupation:	CSU College Student
School:	
Date of Report:	

Reason for Referral

Ms. Fuman was referred for a neuropsychological evaluation at the recommendation of Dr. Johnson, Ms. Fuman's psychiatrist. The evaluation was requested by Ms. Fuman to examine whether she might have a learning disability. Ms. Fuman wanted to receive greater clarification about her academic struggles, and receive suggestions on how she may improve her academic performance.

Evaluation Procedures

Clinical Interview
D'Amato Pre-Interview Questionnaire
The Wechsler Adult Intelligence Scale – Third Edition (WAIS-III)
The Woodcock-Johnson III Tests of Achievement (WJ-III Achievement)
The Wechsler Memory Scale – Third Edition (WMS-III)
The Halstead-Reitan Neuropsychological Test Battery

Category Test
Tactual Performance Test
Speech-Sounds Perception Test
Seashore Rhythm Test
Aphasia Screening Test
Reitan-Klove Sensory-Perception Examination
Trail Making Test A & B
Strength of Grip
Finger Tapping

The Minnesota Multiphasic Personality Inventory – 2 (MMPI-2)
The Substance Abuse Subtle Screening Inventory (SASSI)
The Beck Depression Inventory – 2 (BDI-II)
The Rorschach Test

Clinical Interview

Ms. Fuman is a 22 year-old single female of Latvian decent who is a full-time college student at Colorado State University (CSU), pursuing a degree in Computer Technology. Ms. Fuman also works in the CSU computer lab. Ms. Fuman stated that she would like to pursue a career related to animals. Ms. Fuman has no children and has never been married.

Ms. Fuman presently lives alone with her dog, two cats, and several other pets. Ms. Fuman has been on her own since graduating high school. Ms. Fuman reported that she has contact with her family consisting of one sister, who is a 28-year old school teacher in Redshoe, CO, and her father. Ms. Fuman reported that her mother passed away in 2010 from brain tumors. Ms. Fuman stated that she got along very well with her mother and sister and that they were all very close. She reported that her father was bossy and could be verbally and physically abusive. Ms. Fuman also stated that her father often drank too much alcohol, was very scattered and disorganized, had poor budgeting skills, and was never happy for her and her achievements. Ms. Fuman reported that she believes her father suffered from an Attention Deficit Hyperactivity Disorder (ADHD).

Ms. Fuman was diagnosed with Attention Deficit Hyperactivity Disorder (ADHD) and Obsessive Compulsive Disorder (OCD) in the spring of 2014, and later by Dr. Johnson in January of 2015. Ms. Fuman stated that she was prescribed and is presently taking Concerta (18 mg daily), and Paxil (10 mg daily). She has also tried Ritalin, Wellbutrin, Aderal, and Resperidol. Ms. Fuman reported that she finds it difficult to complete one task, especially homework, because she is often distracted and moves from task to task. Furthermore, she stated that she often repeats words, phrases, and/or songs over and over in her head throughout the day that can cause some frustration. During the interview, Ms. Fuman reported that there was a *red* song repeating in her head. She stated that the compulsion for her to check doors, windows, and her pets is persistent.

Ms. Fuman indicated that she was born through a C-section and weighed 5 lbs. but was not sure if she was considered premature. She stated that to the best of her knowledge she met all developmental milestones at a normal rate. She indicated that she had three ear infections as a child with high temperatures but that she assumed she had no long-term effects. Ms. Fuman recalled several scenarios when possible head injuries could have occurred. She stated that when she was in middle school she hyperventilated until she passed out, used marijuana daily in high school, and continues to use marijuana roughly 20 times a year. Also, she has tried LSD about 10 times in her life, methamphetamines 20 times, and mushrooms and opium about 2 to 3 time each. When 18 years old, Ms. Fuman reported that she got into a car accident while on LSD, alcohol, and marijuana. She stated that she hit a telephone pole with her car and broke the windshield with her head, which caused a severe bump, loss of consciousness, and loss of memory of the accident itself. Because of the accident, Ms. Fuman stated that her father made her leave his home and live on her own. Ms. Fuman reported that in April of 2008 she was skateboarding on a half-pipe and hit her head on the railing. She received emergency room services for amnesia and a severe headache, but never lost consciousness. She believes that a CAT Scan returned a report of no evidence of brain damage.

Ms. Fuman reported that when she was 21 she believes she was given Roehipnal, the "date rape drug," and possibly taken advantage of by a former male friend, but she is unable to remember much of the incident; during this episode, she also consumed four Long Island Ice Teas. Ms. Fuman reported that she continues to abuse alcohol one time a month, and has some flashbacks from drug use around once every three months. As reported, in Ms. Fuman's family there is a history of ADHD, Alcoholism, OCD, and suicide, with her father's brother committing suicide by stepping in front of a truck.

Academically, Ms. Fuman has few problems and stated that she mostly gets A's and B's in classes. She indicated that she utilizes the CSU Disability Resource Office (DRO) for her disabilities. The DRO provides Support Group services and organizational techniques, but Ms. Fuman reported that she would like to improve her study skills, and her ability to focus and concentrate. Ms. Fuman also stated that she feels her short-term memory functions may have decreased with time. She stated that she is generally poor in math and spelling. Ms. Fuman indicated that she spent six days in inpatient and six weeks as an outpatient with Red Valley Psychiatric Services. Furthermore, she reported that she was arrested once for marijuana and drug paraphernalia, and had to complete court ordered community service.

Ms. Fuman's occupational history indicated that she has worked since she was 10-years-old, originally helping her father at his business. She also worked as a waitress in Denver, and at McDonalds for four years. In Ms. Fuman's free time, she stated she spends time with her sister, and has two close friends that she can rely on. She also spends roughly every other weekend with her significant partner, a female friend named Ms. Rida River. She also enjoys activities with her dog, hiking (including a trip to Mexico), camping, and other outdoor activities.

Behavioral Observations

Ms. Fuman arrived on time for the majority of the evaluations sessions and was cooperative throughout the assessment period. She was seen for 13 sessions lasting from 1 to 2 hours each given her significant attention difficulties. Ms. Fuman was appropriately dressed at all sessions. She appeared conscientious and was not easily frustrated. Ms. Fuman was extremely friendly, talkative, and open during evaluation sessions. She volunteered background information and medical history information when appropriate.

Ms. Fuman appeared eager to please and seemed to put forth the effort needed to complete the tasks required. She was pleasant throughout the evaluation session and seemed to enjoy the process. Ms. Fuman worked diligently on tasks but often took an excessive amount of time to complete assessments when not given a time limit. Ms. Fuman also appeared confident in her abilities and never became overwhelmed by tasks asked of her. She presented with a high-pitched voice and behaved much younger than her chronological age would suggest. The current evaluation appears to be a good estimate of Ms. Fuman's neuropsychological skills and abilities.

Evaluation Results and Interpretation

The Wechsler Adult Intelligence Scale – Third Edition (WAIS-III)

The WAIS-III is a general measure of cognitive ability. Information is provided regarding verbal and nonverbal skills through subtests requiring specific abilities. Verbal skills are demonstrated through tasks such as defining words, explaining how two words are alike, computing math problems, and knowledge of general information. Nonverbal skills are assessed through assembling puzzles, putting pictures in sequential order to tell a logical story, identify missing pieces in a picture, and copying a design with blocks. Responses to items on the WAIS-III are reported as scaled scores, which on average, fall between 8 and 12. Average IQ scores are defined between 90 and 109.

WAIS-III Subtest

Subtest	Scaled Score	Classification
Verbal Subtests		
Vocabulary	14	Above Average
Similarities	13	Above Average
Arithmetic	12	Average

Subtest	Scaled Score	Classification
Digit Span	13	Above Average
Information	14	Above Average
Comprehension	11	Average
Letter-Number-Sequencing	13	Above Average
Performance Subtests		
Picture Completion	6	Below Average
Digit Symbol-Coding	11	Average
Block Design	12	Average
Matrix Reasoning	14	Above Average
Picture Arrangement	12	Average
Symbol Search	10	Average
Object Assembly	15	Above Average

(The average range on subtest scaled scores is 8-12.)

WAIS-III Composite Scores

	Standard Score	Percentile Rank	95% Confidence Level	Classification
Verbal	117	87	112-121	Above Average
Performance	105	63	98-111	Average
Full Scale	112	79	108-116	Above Average

(The average range of standard scores is 90-109.)

Ms. Fuman's scores placed her in Average range of intelligence when compared to individuals similar to her in the general population. These scores indicate that Ms. Fuman has good scholastic aptitude and is ready to master a college curriculum. It appears that Ms. Fuman's verbal and nonverbal abilities have some discrepancy between the two abilities, but is not statistically significant, with a range of 12 points (VIQ=117, PIQ=105). This particular occurrence of verbal skills being greater than performance is present in 17.7% of the general population. This means that she appears to have greater intelligence for tasks that require the use of words to complete problems, than for tasks that require visual recognition of patterns, or replicating a pattern of symbols.

On the verbal portion of the test, Ms. Fuman's scores were in the High Average range. The vocabulary subtest looked at her ability to define words, which requires several skills including knowledge and memory. On this subtest, Ms. Fuman performed in the High Average range. Similarities requires Ms. Fuman to explain how two words are alike, this task requires skills such as verbal comprehension and abstract and concrete reasoning abilities; she scored in the High Average range on this subtest. The arithmetic subtest asked Ms. Fuman to complete mathematics problems orally, which requires numerical reasoning skills, and concentration; she performed in the Average range. The digit span subtest asked Ms. Fuman to repeat numbers backwards and forwards that the examiner reads, which requires memory and attention abilities; she scored in the High Average range. The information subtest asked her to answer questions about common knowledge; this task includes skills such as fund of information, and long-term memory. Ms. Fuman scored in the High Average range for this subtest. The comprehension subtest is a task that requires her to answer questions about a wide range of social situations and problems; she scored in the Average range, demonstrating logical reasoning and long-term memory. The final subtest was letter-number sequencing, which asked her to repeat letters and numbers in a correct sequence that the examiner read aloud. This task demonstrated Ms. Fuman's High Average skills in memory, and flexibility of thought.

On the performance portion of the test, Ms. Fuman's score were in the Average range of functioning. The digit symbol-coding subtest asked her to replicate symbols that correspond with numbers, and requires skills such as visual-motor dexterity, and speed of mental operation. Ms. Fuman scored in the Average range of functioning on this task. On the block design subtest, Ms. Fuman had to replicate a specific design from a picture; she performed in the Average range of functioning, demonstrating her adequate skills in the areas of visual processing, and visual-motor coordination. Matrix reasoning is a subtest that asked Ms. Fuman to display the skills of perceptual organization and classification abilities by completing missing parts of a matrix; she scored in the High Average range.

The picture arrangement subtest asked Ms. Fuman to arrange a series of pictures in a logical, and sequential order. Her performance on this task demonstrated her Average abilities in the areas of nonverbal reasoning, and perceptual organization. On the symbol search task, Ms. Fuman demonstrated her Average abilities on a short-term visual memory task, and a psychomotor speed task, indicated by her ability to determine if one of two symbols were replicated in a group of symbols. The final performance subtest was object assembly, which asked Ms. Fuman to complete puzzles; she performed in the High Average range, displaying her spatial abilities and her visual processing.

Ms. Fuman displayed one weakness, as compared to her scores in other areas on the WAIS-III. The weakness was on picture completion, a task that required her to identify what part of an object or person is missing in a picture. She may display weaknesses in perceptual organization, the ability to differentiate essential from nonessential items, visual recognition of objects, concentration, and alertness to detail.

The Woodcock-Johnson - III Tests of Achievement (WJ-III Achievement)

The WJ-III is a general measure of academic achievement in relation to Ms. Fuman's peers in the general population. Information is provided regarding reading, mathematics, and written abilities.

WJ-III Tests of Achievement Subtest

(Norms based on age 22.)

Scale	Standard Score	Percentile Rank	68% Confidence Level	Classification
Oral Language	97	43	93-102	Average
Total Achievement	119	90	117-121	Above Average
Broad Reading	117	88	115-120	Above Average
Broad Math	107	68	104-109	Average
Broad Written Language	130	98	126-135	Very Superior
Math Calculation Skills	108	71	105-112	Average
Written Expression	140	99.6	134-146	Very Superior
Academic Skills	108	71	108-112	Average
Academic Fluency	122	93	121-124	Very Superior
Academic Applications	114	83	110-118	Above Average

(The average range on subtest standard scores is 85-110.)

WJ-III Composite Scores

Standard and Extended Batteries of Form A

Scale	Standard Score	Percentile Rank	68% Confidence Level	Classification
Letter-Word Identification	102	57	98-107	Average
Reading Fluency	117	88	116-119	Above Average
Story Recall	100	50	94-106	Average

Scale	Standard Score	Percentile Rank	68% Confidence Level	Classification
Understanding Directions	97	42	93-101	Average
Calculation	104	59	100-108	Average
Math Fluency	111	78	110-113	Above Average
Spelling	112	80	108-117	Above Average
Writing Fluency	135	99	131-140	Very Superior
Passage Comprehension	118	88	112-124	Above Average
Applied Problems	104	60	100-108	Average
Writing Samples	126	96	114-138	Very Superior
Handwriting	104	61	96-112	Average

(The average range on composite standard scores is 85-110.)

When compared to other individuals her age, Ms. Fuman's letter-word identification skills were in the Average range as reflected by a score of 102. She has an adequate ability to read many phonetically regular and irregular words, and has good word attack strategies, especially with both vowel and consonant blends in the medial position. Ms. Fuman obtained a passage comprehension standard score of 118, which is in the High Average range. She tends to read quickly and is able to understand the general concepts of a passage, even though the passage may contain unfamiliar words and information. Ms. Fuman's reading fluency was in the High Average range, displaying her ability to read quickly and consistently. Ms. Fuman obtained a Broad Reading score of 117, which is in the High Average range of reading skills.

Ms. Fuman was able to demonstrate Average math calculation skills. She was able to calculate a variety of math problems ranging from basic arithmetic to advanced algebra. On applied mathematical problems, Ms. Fuman obtained a score of 104, indicating that she is able to comprehend and utilize essential information provided in a verbal format to provide an accurate answer. Ms. Fuman's score for a timed basic arithmetic subtest, math fluency, was in the High Average range; she was able to compute basic math problems quickly and without having to self-correct. Her overall Broad Math standard score was 107, in the Average range of math skills.

Ms. Fuman's written expression skills were in the Very Superior range as reflected by a score of 140. This score indicates her advanced abilities to write sentences with great depth and breadth of information and vocabulary used. Ms. Fuman's timed writing fluency score was in the High Average range of functioning, indicating that she is able to join concepts into complete and organized written statements. Her writing sample score was in the Very Superior range, as reflected by a score of 126, indicating that she used advanced sentence content, and superior elaboration of ideas. Overall, Ms. Fuman's Broad Written Language skills were in the Very Superior range with a score of 130. She displayed advanced skills in writing proficiency, vocabulary, elaboration of ideas, and expressive skills.

All of Ms. Fuman's achievement scores were well within the Average to Very Superior range of functioning. Her Broad Written Language score were statistically significantly higher than her Broad Math and Oral Language skills. This indicates a relative strength as well as high motivation and interest in written language over other subjects. Her strengths appear to be in ability to elaborate in writing samples, vocabulary, speed in writing, and ability to be expressive with words. All of the addressed scores indicate that Ms. Fuman appears to be able to meet or surpass the challenges offered in a college curriculum.

The Wechsler Memory Scale – Third Edition (WMS-III)

The WMS-III is an individually administered battery of learning, memory, and working memory measures. The WMS-III focuses on immediate, delayed, and working memory. Each of these domains is tested in two modalities, auditory, and visual. A half-hour delayed recall of both verbal and visual material is reported. Each category is reported so average scores are defined between 90 and 109.

WMS-III Subtest

Subtest	Scaled Score
Logical Memory I	10
Faces I	11
Verbal Paired Associates I	13
Family Pictures I	11
Letter-Number Sequencing	13
Spatial Span	15
Logical Memory II	10
Faces II	11
Verbal Paired Associates II	12
Family Pictures II	11
Auditory Recognition	14

(The average range on subtest scaled score is 8-12.)

WMS-III Composite Scores

Scale	Standard Score	Percentile Rank	95% Confidence Level	Classification
Auditory Immediate	108	70	100-115	Average
Visual Immediate	106	66	95-115	Average
Immediate Memory	108	70	99-115	Average
Auditory Delayed	105	63	95-114	Average
Visual Delayed	106	66	95-115	Average
Auditory Rec. Delayed	120	91	104-126	Very Superior
General Memory	111	77	102-118	Above Average
Working Memory	124	95	111-130	Very Superior

Overall, Ms. Fuman's memory abilities appear to be in the Average to Very Superior range. Her memory capacities appear to be in the same range as her cognitive and achievement abilities.

The auditory immediate score represents Ms. Fuman's ability to remember information immediately after it has been presented to her in an oral fashion. She scored in the Average range on this test. Academically, this represents her adequate ability to retain lecture material in her memory long enough to make note of the information. The visual immediate score represents her ability to remember information immediately after it has been visually displayed. She scored in the Average range on this task, indicating that Ms. Fuman performs similar to peers when viewing written information from a chalkboard and remembering it long enough to write it down. The immediate memory score represents her ability to remember visual and auditory information immediately after it is presented. She scored in the Average range on this scale, indicating that she can remember this type of information equal to her peers.

The auditory delayed score represents Ms. Fuman's ability to remember orally presented information after 25-30 minutes of delay. She scored in the Average range on this task, indicating that she has adequate abilities in this domain. The visual delayed score represents Ms. Fuman's ability to remember visually represented information after 25-30 minutes delay. She scored in the Average range on this scale. These scores would represent skills similar to last minute "cramming" for a test or recalling information to give a presentation. The auditory recognition delayed score represents Ms. Fuman's ability to remember auditory information after 25-30 minutes delay, via recognition. She obtained a score within the Very Superior range of functioning, indicating that on this specific task she would perform as well or better that 91 out of 100 of her peers.

The general memory score represents Ms. Fuman's overall delayed memory ability. She scored in the High Average range on this scale. This would represent activities such as remembering information for a test or remembering appointments.

The working memory score represents Ms. Fuman's ability to remember and manipulate visually and orally presented information in short-term memory storage. She scored in the Very Superior range on this scale, indicating that she would perform as well or better than 95 out of 100 of her peers. This score represents abilities such as retaining and computing math problems internally, and the ability to manipulate (mentally) puzzle pieces to identify if they would fit.

A statistically significant difference was observed between Ms. Fuman's immediate memory and her working memory. This difference indicates that she has a greater capacity to manipulate information in her short-term memory than she must recall both visual and auditory information after immediate exposure to the stimuli. It is important to note that both scores are Average and Very Superior, but Ms. Fuman performs differently on these tasks in a relative, or ipsative, comparison.

The Halstead-Reitan Neuropsychological Test Battery

The Category Test

The Category Test evaluates complex concept formation, abstraction, integration, and ability to profit from reinforcement. It also measures visual acuity, attention, and concentration. The test requires the client to select numbers corresponding to a visual presentation, with immediate feedback provided. Ms. Fuman's score fell within the **Average range** of functioning (24 errors).

The Tactual Performance Test (TPT)

The TPT is a form-board that requires the blindfolded client to place blocks in appropriate slots. The TPT measures tactual discrimination, upper extremity motor coordination, manual dexterity, ability to visualize spatial configurations, learning in new situations, kinesthesis, incidental memory, and spatial memory. It also measures tactual-motor integration. With her dominant hand, she received a score in the **Average range** of functioning. With her non-dominant hand, she received a score that indicated **mild impairment** of functioning. With both hands together, she received a score in the **Average range** of functioning. Ms. Fuman's score on the memory section of this test also fell in the **Average range** of functioning. Her score on the localization aspect of the test, which assesses spatial memory and the ability to visualize spatial configurations, indicated **mild to moderate impairment** of functioning.

The Speech-Sounds Perception Test (SSPT)

The SSPT measures verbal auditory discrimination, perception and differentiation of rhythmic sequences, auditory-visual integration, and phonetic skills. It also measures auditory acuity, language, and attention in auditory context. A tape of nonsense words is presented to the client, who selects the appropriate written response from alternatives offered for each item. Ms. Fuman's score on this test fell within the **Average range**.

The Seashore Rhythm Test (SRT)

The SRT measures nonverbal auditory discrimination and auditory perception. It measures attention in auditory context and concentration. It also measures language, spelling, reading, writing, and nonverbal functioning. Performance can be indicative of education level, occupation, or concentration. On this test, the client identifies as same or different 30 pairs of musical beats or patterns. This is a concentration-and-attention-related task dependent on right and left hemisphere functioning. Ms. Fuman's score was within the **Average range** of functioning.

The Aphasia Screening Test (AST)

The AST measures wide band language and nonverbal functions. It surveys aphasic and related deficits: dysgraphia, dyscalculia, dysnomia, and construction apraxia. Items on this test require naming, copying, spelling, reading, and writing. Ms. Fuman followed instruction on this test very literally. She made a very detailed picture of the key and drew the square and cross very precisely. She made no errors on this test, however, and her score was within the **Average range**.

Finger Oscillation Test (FOT)

The FOT measures finger motor speed, dexterity, and distractibility. Comparison of the tapping speeds of the dominant and nondominant hands allows for localization. Fuman's score for her dominant hand was within the **Average range** and her score for her nondominant hand was within **the mild to moderate range** of impairment, with a significant difference between her dominant and nondominant hands.

The Trail Making Test A & Test B

The Trail Making A test measures motor speed, visual scanning, and visual-motor integration. It also measures immediate recognition of the symbolic significance of numbers, the ability to scan continuously, visual acuity, attention, and concentration. Ms. Fuman's score on this test was within the **Average range**.

The Trail Making B test measures the same concepts that the Trail Making A test measures, as well as mental flexibility and the integration of alphabetic and numeric systems. Ms. Fuman's score on this test was within the **Average range**.

Grip Strength Test (GST)

The GST measures motor strength in the client's upper extremities. Trials are performed with each hand, beginning with the preferred hand and alternating to the non-preferred hand. Ms. Fuman's scores for her dominant hand on this test suggested adequate upper motor strength and fell in the **Average range** of functioning. Her score on her nondominant hand on this test, however, suggested **mild to moderate impairment** with a significant difference between dominant and nondominant hands.

Bilateral Sensory Stimulation Tests

The bilateral sensory stimulation tests are designed to determine the accuracy with which the client can perceive bilateral simultaneous sensory stimulation in three areas: tactile, auditory and visual. Ms. Fuman's scores were within the **Average range** for tactile stimulation, within the **Average range** for auditory stimulation, and within the **Average range** for visual stimulation.

Impairment Index

The Impairment Index is the proportion of an individual's test scores, which are in the range characteristic of brain-damaged subjects. Ms. Fuman's score showed indicated ***no impairment*** on any of the seven tests used to compute the Impairment Index. Her overall score was within the **Average range**.

General Neuropsychological Deficit Scale (NDS)

The NDS is a summary score for assessing cerebral involvement and yields equivalent scores that reflect impaired functions of the cerebral hemispheres on a balanced scale. Ms. Fuman's NDS score places her in the **Average range** in terms of the adequacy of her neuropsychological functions.

The Minnesota Multiphasic Personality Inventory – 2 (MMPI-2)

The MMPI-2 is a self-report inventory in which questions are rated true or false. Scales reveal a picture of an individual's behaviors, traits, level of adjustment toward the world, and characteristic beliefs.

There are scales on the MMPI-2 that assess the respondent's honesty and their attempt to present themselves in a favorable or unfavorable light. Ms. Fuman's responses indicated an individual that may exaggerate symptoms or problems as a plea for help, and may be experiencing clearly psychotic symptoms and behaviors. These responses indicate that the results of the MMPI-2 should be interpreted with caution because they may not accurately represent Ms. Fuman's personality.

Individuals who respond in a fashion similar to Ms. Fuman may report moderate tension and anxiety, and may have physical complaints, including headaches and gastrointestinal discomfort, but their problems do not seem to be acute or incapacitating. Individuals who respond similarly to Ms. Fuman report that most of their difficulties stem from deep, chronic feelings of hostility towards family members. These individuals do not express their feelings directly, and much of the time they may not even recognize their feelings of hostility. When they become aware of their anger they try to justify it in terms of the behaviors of others. In general, individuals with response patterns mirroring that of Ms. Fuman tend to be defiant, uncooperative, and hard to get along with. They may express mild suspiciousness and resentment about others, and they are very self-centered and narcissistic. They may deny serious psychological problems and express a very naïve, Pollyannaish attitude toward the world.

Ms. Fuman reportedly perceives herself as a college student who procrastinates, feels anxious and worried, has somatic complaints during times of increased stress, feels ineffectual in school, has pessimistic views about academic activities, and feels that life is a strain much of the time. Ms. Fuman responded similarly to individuals who scored high on the Post-Traumatic Stress Disorder Scale (t score = 68). She may display intense emotional distress, symptoms of anxiety and sleep disturbance, guilt and depression, unwanted and disturbing thoughts, loss of emotional and cognitive control, and a feeling of being misunderstood and mistreated.

Ms. Fuman displayed elevated scores on the MacAndrew Alcoholism Scale-Revised and the Addictions Potential Scale. This indicates that Ms. Fuman may be abusing alcohol and/or other substances, and may have the personality component that increases her potential to abuse alcohol or other substances. It should be noted that individuals who previously abused substances but no longer do so may still obtain high scores on these two scales.

The Substance Abuse Subtle Screening Inventory (SASSI)

The SASSI is an assessment that is used to identify individuals who have high probability of having a substance abuse disorder. Ms. Fuman's responses indicated that she had a high probability of a substance dependence disorder. Ms. Fuman's responses were scored using the entire life scale and may have scored items that occurred in the past. Ms. Fuman stated chronic and severe past drug use, with recent use of marijuana and alcohol. Also, Ms. Fuman was prescribed medications for ADHD and OCD, and may have responded positive to items that related to illicit drug use.

The Beck Depression Inventory – 2 (BDI-II)

The BDI-II is a self-report inventory in which questions are rated on severity of depressive symptoms. Questions reveal a picture of an individual level of negative feelings for themselves within the last two weeks.

Ms. Fuman scored in the mild range for negative feelings and depressive symptoms. Ms. Fuman reported not enjoying things as much as she use to, feeling guilty, being overly critical of her faults, and being excessively agitated or restless and having to always be engaged in some activity. She also reported having trouble making decisions, sleeping less, craving food all of the time, poor concentration, and becoming easily fatigued. These responses indicate that Ms. Fuman appears to be experiencing a mild level of depression.

The Rorschach Test

The Rorschach is a measure of an individual's personality based on their responses to inkblots. Ms. Fuman gave an unusually large number of responses to the test (86), and her responses were often of extremely small details. Therefore, this record appears to be an accurate reflection of Ms. Fuman's personality. Several times during the inquiry phase of the test, she stated that her responses were meant to be two separate responses. These responses were then separated into two, and two inquires were done. At times, however, the responses were so superimposed on each other that it was impossible to separate them, and they were scored as one response. There were several responses in which she mentioned objects that were not part of what she perceived in the inkblot. For example, one response to card five was "a bridge between two mountains." During the inquiry, she clarified that the inkblot looked like the bridge and she indicated that the mountains were situated at the edges of the card. Another unusual response included using the white space of the blot to describe a "shadow". Responses including morbid imagery included words such as "tattered", "eroded", and "getting rusty." All of the images in these responses included inanimate objects.

It needs to be noted that Ms. Fuman shows many characteristics, as reported on the Rorschach, commonly observed in people who subsequently commit suicide. The possibility of suicidal tendencies and preoccupations should be evaluated carefully, and those responsible for her care should be alerted to the potential suicide risk. Ms. Fuman's protocol contains many features that are commonly found in persons with schizophrenia disorders, and among these features are some serious problems in thinking. She appears to be experiencing a substantial amount of intrusive ideation over which she has little control, involves an awareness of needs that are not being met and/or is worrisome about not being able to prevent other people or events from determining her destiny. These feeling may impair Ms. Fuman's ability to concentrate. She may also act highly inflexible and closed-minded, with a poor ability to change her opinions, and seldom entertains the possibility of modifying her perspectives on herself or events in her life.

Ms. Fuman appears to be a person confused about her emotions, and has evidence of a significant affective disturbance that is likely associated with either Major Depressive Disorder or a chronic disposition to becoming depressed. Ms. Fuman indicated that she maybe experiencing considerable emotional stress that is interfering with her pleasure in life and making her susceptible to becoming anxious and depressed. However, Ms. Fuman appears to be as willing as most people to process emotional stimulation when confronted, and appears open to assistance. She may compare herself to others and perceive them as more able, attractive, talented, and generally worth more than herself. It appears that Ms. Fuman may ruminate about aspects of herself or her actions that she regards as undesirable. She indicated statements that she may be unusually preoccupied with and/or concerned with her body and bodily functions, and views her body as damaged or dysfunctional.

Ms. Fuman presented as needing more closeness with others than she is presently receiving. As a consequence, she may feel lonely, emotionally deprived, and interpersonally needy. Because of her tendency toward dependency in relationships, she may be vulnerable to exploitation or manipulation by people who she reaches out to in times of her neediness. She sincerely pays attention to what others say and do, and shows a greater interest in others. Ms. Fuman appears more strongly committed than most to being agreeable and working to establish harmonious relationships with others.

Evaluation Summary

Ms. Fuman's evaluation was completed to address concerns about a possible learning disability and to clarify academic concerns. Ms. Fuman's scores suggest that she has above average cognitive abilities, with her verbal and nonverbal abilities being relatively equally well developed. Ms. Fuman's demonstrated cognitive strengths in verbal tasks that required recall and depth of vocabulary, differentiation of words, and general verbal information. On an achievement measure, Ms. Fuman's scores were in the average to very superior range. Ms. Fuman's highest scores were in written expression, writing fluency, and broad written language. Ms. Fuman's strengths are in verbal and writing tasks, and she is performing well above what her cognitive scores would indicate her potential to be; it appears from the assessment that Ms. Fuman does not have a learning disability at this time.

Ms. Fuman completed an assessment of her memory skills, which was a concern in relation to academic abilities. Ms. Fuman's memory skills were in the average to very superior range. She demonstrated strengths in her working memory, and in delayed auditory recognition. Ms. Fuman appears to have Very Superior abilities to remember and manipulate visually and orally presented information in short-term memory storage, and to remember orally presented information after 25 to 30 minutes of delay.

Ms. Fuman's scores on the Halstead-Reitan battery indicate that overall, she is functioning in the average range. Her scores do not indicate brain damage or cerebral impairment. Her scores do reflect, however, that performing motor tasks using her nondominant hand is a relative weakness and that performing motor tasks using her dominant hand is a relative strength. The ability to visualize spatial configurations also may be a weakness. Auditory discrimination and perception appears to be a strength of Ms. Fuman's.

Emotionally, Ms. Fuman appears to be experiencing significant symptoms of depression and anxiety. She may feel overwhelmed and nervous. The feelings that Ms. Fuman's is experiencing appear to stem from hostility directed at a family member, most likely her father. She appears to be suffering from a significant loss in her life; likely, she has not fully grieved the death of her mother, with whom she reportedly was extremely close. Assessment measures indicate that Ms. Fuman may be abusing alcohol and/or other substances, and/or may have the personality component that increases her potential to abuse alcohol or other substances. It is also noteworthy that individuals who previously abused substances, but no longer do so, may still obtain high scores on substance abuse scales. Ms. Fuman reported a history of drug abuse, and she reports that she still uses drugs from time to time.

Ms. Fuman showed many characteristics commonly observed in people who subsequently commit suicide. The possibility of suicidal tendencies and preoccupations should be evaluated carefully, and those responsible for her care should be alerted to the potential suicide risk. Ms. Fuman appeared to demonstrate serious impairment of her reality abilities with possible frequent failing to anticipate the consequence of her actions, and to misconstrue appropriate boundaries with others.

Ms. Fuman indicated that she may be experiencing considerable emotional stress that is interfering with her pleasure in life and making her susceptible to anxiety and depression. She also exhibited statements indicating that she does not have well defined coping strategies.

Ms. Fuman appears to be very competent cognitively and academically, and psychiatric issues appear to dominate her profile. If these psychological issues are explored and given the proper attention, she may be able to work through her unhappiness, grief, thought difficulties, and drug use.

Diagnostic Impressions

Axis I: 300.3 Obsessive Compulsive Disorder Attention-Deficit/Hyperactivity Disorder 304.8 Polysubstance Dependence in Remission

Rule Out: 297.1 Delusional Disorder Unspecified Type
Rule Out: 300.4 Dysthymic Disorder

Axis II: 71.09 No Diagnosis on Axis II

Axis III: None

Axis IV: Problems Related to Primary Family: Relationship with Father

Axis V: GAF Score=68

Evaluation Recommendations

Based on the results of Ms. Fuman's neuropsychological evaluation, the following recommendations are offered to Ms. Fuman's for her consideration:

1. Ms. Fuman should attend individual counseling to discuss her symptoms of depression and grieve over the loss of her mother. She is encouraged to complete an analysis of her primary relationships, review her drug use, and monitor her level of suicidal tendencies.
2. Ms. Fuman may want to utilize services available at her present university or college to help relieve anxiety stemming from assignments and tests. Organizational skills, study skills, and support groups may reduce some of Ms. Fuman's feelings of nervousness. Ms. Fuman would appear to be a good candidate for group activities and a university social-support group.
3. Ms. Fuman should share this report with her psychiatrist, support staff at her university or college, and all pertinent professionals that could help her succeed in academia and in her life. Ms. Fuman has indicated a number of areas that she would like to improve.

4. Ms. Fuman may want to consider reviewing her medications with her psychiatrist in order to decrease her current psychological symptoms. She may be able to fine more relief from her psychiatric difficulties.

5. Ms. Fuman may want to work with her counselor or psychologist to implement positive self-talk, which could help her cope with self-critical thoughts and remain positive about who she is. Positive self-talk may make her feel more confident and comfortable in social situations, confident about herself, less anxious of what others are think of her, and more secure about her behaviors.

6. Ms. Fuman may want to learn relaxation techniques, such as deep breathing, deep muscle relaxation training, guided imagery relaxation training or self-hypnosis. This may help her reduce some of her physical symptoms that have developed due to anxiety, as well as give her an additional technique to supplement medications.

7. Developing an exercise regime is recommended to Ms. Fuman after discussion with her primary care physician. Exercise has been proven to help individuals cope with depression, anxiety, and ADHD, as well as improving general health and body image. Ms. Fuman should select an activity that she enjoys and can practice on a regular basis.

8. Ms. Fuman should develop a study schedule where she sets aside 2 to 5 hours each weeknight to studying, with as few distractions as possible, and at regular times. Ms. Fuman can implement 10-minute breaks for every 50 minutes she studies, to promote more time on task. Ms. Fuman may want to review study techniques with members of her university support service staff.

9. Ms. Fuman may want to become involved in social activities through her school, church, or community; to increase her social experiences, gain greater confidence in her social skills, and build confidence in how she is perceived by others. She should consider joining clubs that interest her such as hiking associations.

10. Ms. Fuman may want to consider participating in study groups at the CSU DRO. Groups could help her academically as well as socially so that she receives modeling of how other students interact together and in a school environment. Such activities may help her reduce her feelings of depression and social isolation.

Walter R. Schamber, Ph.D.
Neuropsychology Fellow

Stephanie Forness, Psy.D.
Neuropsychology Fellow

Rik Carl D'Amato, Ph.D.
Neuropsychology Laboratory Director
Licensed School Psychologist
APA Fellow in Clinical Neuropsychology and School Psychology

Appendix E: Sample Neuropsychological Evaluation, Age 28

Report by: Amanda Skierkiewicz

NEUROPSYCHOLOGIAL SERVICES CENTER
1221 Lake Shore Drive, Chicago, IL

NEUROPSYCHOLOGICAL EVALUATION

CONFIDENTIAL

This report is for professional use only.
It is not to be released without permission by the person evaluated, or that person's legal guardian.

Patient's Name: Arleen Tallman
Psychologist: Amanda Skierkiewicz, Ed.D., NCSP
PCP:
GYN:
Length of Consult: 1 Unit
Length of Testing: 16 Units
Length of Follow up: 1 Unit

Date of Birth:01-01-1991
Age: 28
Education: Bachelor Degree
Counselor: Dr. Blue
Date of Consult:
Date of Testing:
Date of Follow up:

REASON FOR REFERRAL

Arleen Tallman is a 28-year-old, right-handed female who was seen for a neuropsychological evaluation in my office. While she has not previously been formally diagnosed, Arleen describes a history of depressive symptoms, including hopelessness, as well as some anxiety, distractibility, difficulty completing projects, and periods of what she called "euphoria." Arleen recently began seeing my colleague, Dr. Blue, who referred Arleen for the following evaluation to assess for a differential diagnosis and to assist in the treatment planning process.

BACKGROUND INFORMATION

Birth and Developmental History:

Arleen was able to report that she was the result of a full-term delivery weighing approximately 8 pounds. At birth, she was slightly jaundiced, which was easily resolved. She is the oldest of three siblings. She is not aware of any alcohol, tobacco, recreational or prescription medication use during the pregnancy, and had no other medical, physical, or emotional problems while she was in utero. Arleen is not aware of any developmental milestones. She does not recall any therapies for developmental purposes, including speech/language, occupational, or physical therapy.

Family History:

Family medical history is remarkable for type 2 diabetes in her father and cardiovascular issues in her paternal grandmother. Family psychiatric history is remarkable for recent Bipolar diagnosis in her father.

Medical History:

Arleen's medical history is largely unremarkable. She has some environmental allergies for which she takes an occasional OTC antihistamine. Hearing is reportedly normal and she has a slight astigmatism, though she is not prescribed corrective lenses. Currently, there is no reported maintenance or onset insomnias and no other dyssomnias or parasomnias. She reports no head injuries, seizures, or overnight hospitalizations and has had no other injuries or illnesses that could have complicated her cognitive functioning.

Academic History:

Academically, Arleen reported that she had a "good experience" throughout her schooling and typically earned a B/C average throughout her courses. She attended a four-year university and earned a Bachelor's Degree in Studio Art. She noted that while she was "proficient," she was more interested in English and the arts. She described some difficulties in her courses with management of homework and poor motivation to complete some of her assignments.

Behavioral/Psychological History:

While Arleen does not have a history of psychiatric or psychotherapeutic interventions, she describes some long-standing symptoms. Beginning in high school, she started noticing some "sporadic bursts" of energy and situations where she would become very excitable. During college, she started to experience some depressive symptoms. At which point, she would often ignore some of her work and become distracted. During college she started to notice symptoms of depression, including periods of sadness, hopelessness, anxiety, feelings of guilt, irritability, and increased time alone. She described how these symptoms will "wax and wane" for her and during times when she is feeling good, she feels motivated to complete projects, make lists, and prioritize. Arleen recently began seeing my colleague, Dr. Blue, who suggested Arleen come in for an evaluation to assess for a differential diagnosis and help in the treatment planning process.

EVALUATION PROCEDURES

Green's Medical Symptom Validity Test (MSVT)
Wechsler Adult Intelligence Scale– IV (WAIS-IV)
Woodcock-Johnson Tests of Achievement – III (WJ-III)
Fluency subtests
Conners Continuous Performance Test – 3 (CPT-3)
Delis-Kaplan Executive Function System (D-KEFS), Color Word Interference Test, Tower Test, and Verbal Fluency Test

Repeatable Battery for the Assessment of Neuropsychological Status (RBANS)
Wisconsin Card Sorting Test
Structured Interview for Mania

Rating Scales:
Barkley Adult ADHD Rating Scales - IV (BAARS-IV) Self Report
Barkley Adult ADHD Rating Scales - IV (BAARS-IV) Other Report
Behavior Rating Inventory of Executive Functioning - 2 (BRIEF-2) Self Report
Behavior Rating Inventory of Executive Functioning - 2 (BRIEF-2) Other Report
Personality Assessment Inventory (PAI)
General Behavior Inventory (GBI)
Axis II Personality Checklist (A-II)

OBSERVATIONS and VALIDITY

Validity:
Performance validity was assessed using the MSVT. Arleen performed perfectly on all basic effort measures as well as the easier memory portion, while performing well within normal limits and consistent with known credible effort populations on the relatively more difficult memory portion. She also passed all embedded validity checks, with the exception of a slightly liberal skew to her CPT-3 response style, although that did not appear to have much effect on her results and she certainly made a number of responses for the CPT-3 itself to be considered valid. Overall, I would say basic effort is well supported and that there is no evidence of active feigning.

Behavioral Observations:
Arleen was a willing participant in the evaluation process. She worked diligently and seemingly to the best of her ability. Testing was completed across two days due to the length of the battery. Arleen reported having gotten a good night's sleep and eating breakfast prior to each testing day. She was friendly and affable throughout and was open and forthcoming about her current presentation and experiences. There were numerous indicators of strong effort – she wanted to continue working even when time ran out, responded appropriately to all instructions, asked for clarification of instructions when she was unsure, put in extended effort on items that were difficult for her, remained engaged throughout, and even verbalized a desire to do well. That, in addition to her valid performance on the MSVT and embedded PVTs suggests the following to be a good representation of Arleen's current cognitive functioning. Symptom validity regarding emotional functioning will be discussed below.

EVALUATION RESULTS

Intellectual reasoning and cognitive proficiency skills were assessed using the WAIS-IV. Arleen achieved a Full Scale IQ score of 124 which falls in the superior range. She performed well across the indices with no single subtest score falling below the average range. Still, a reader can better understand her abilities by consideration of the individual indices.

On those, she achieved a Verbal Comprehension Index score of 130, which falls in the very superior range. Within the index, there was a 20 point discrepancy between Arleen's performance on the task mediated by exposure/retention and on the task mediated by fund of language (Vocabulary=135; Similarities=115), although even the lower score still falls in the high average range. On the third subtest, which is primarily mediated by crystallized knowledge/acquisition of facts, her performance continued to be superior (Information=125). Her nonverbal skills, as measured by the Perceptual Reasoning Index, were just as strong (SS=127, superior). Within the index, she performed better on the visuospatial tasks (Block Design=125; Visual Puzzles=130,) relative to the fluid reasoning task (Matrix Reasoning=115), though again even the lower score is still within the high average range.

Cognitive Proficiency: Turning to cognitive proficiency, Arleen's performance on the Processing Speed Index (111) was high average. She performed equivalently within the index. Her Working Memory Index score fell in the average range at a 102. There was a 1 SD discrepancy within the index as she scored better on the subtest more mediated by mental manipulation relative to span (Arithmetic=110; Digit Span=95). While the latter index still falls within the average range, it certainly represents an interpersonal weakness within Arleen's own profile.

Seeing that, I went ahead and calculated two additional indices. A General Ability Index (GAI) was calculated to provide a better representation of Arleen's intellectual reasoning skills, and that score came in at a 132, which is superior. We generally refer to score above 130 as "Gifted." I also calculated a Cognitive Proficiency Index (CPI), to provide a better representation of Arleen's ability to bring her intellectual skills to bear on various tasks. That came in at a 106, which is average. While that is within normal limits relative to the general population, that is nearly 2 SDs below Arleen's own potential. I offer this finding as quite enlightening to this case, as comparing the two providers a good understanding of some of Arleen's frustrations thus far.

To assess cognitive proficiency more broadly, I also had Arleen complete the academic fluency tasks from the WJ-III. Her overall index came in at a 111, which is high average and equivalent to her PSI. Her performances on the Reading and Writing tasks were consistent and followed expectations based on the pattern of her intellectual abilities (SS=112). Math was a little weaker at a 92, though still fell within normal limits. She made one error on this test.

To that end, I had Arleen complete the PASAT, which serves as a "challenge test" by placing a high demand on multiple frontal/executively mediated skills simultaneously, tapping both the short term and mental manipulation aspects of working memory, processing speed, and complex attention skills. Her performance on the initial rate of stimuli presentation was solidly average and consistent with baseline expectations (SS=107). On the second rate of stimuli presentation, her score dropped by nearly 1 standard deviation (SS=94), though that score is still within normal limits (WNL). This finding does suggest that the fall-off is actually more in processing speed than mental manipulation, though this is really less about a particular area of skill deficiency and more about a limitation of cognitive resources.

Executive Functions:

Complex attention and executive functioning were assessed using a series of measures in this case, and I began by having Arleen and her fiancée each complete the BAARS-IV. She endorsed experiencing inattention and impulsivity more than other adults around her age (89%; 81%). She also reported a significant degree of symptoms related to a sluggish cognitive tempo (96%). She endorsed hyperactivity to fall WNL (51-75%). In considering her experiences during childhood, Alreen indicated experiencing typical levels of inattention as well as hyperactivity/impulsivity (51-75%; 51-75%). Arleen's fiancée endorsed seeing similar current symptoms as Arleen's ratings as he endorsed inattention, impulsivity, and symptoms of a sluggish cognitive tempo (98%; 94%; 94%), and does not see symptoms of hyperactivity (51-75%). I then had Arleen and her fiancée each complete the BRIEF to capture a broader picture of Arleen's executive functioning. All validity scale scores fell WNL. Both raters elevated the Global Executive Composite (64T, 73T) indicating overall difficulties with executive functioning. Both Arleen and her fiancée gave similar ratings on the Behavior Regulation Index (66T; 68T), including on the subscales indicating difficulty with resisting impulses and the ability to stop her behavior at the appropriate time (60T; 63T) and difficulty regulating and modulating her emotions (78T; 69T) while her fiancée also sees difficulties with tolerating change, problem solving flexibly, switching her attention, and changing focus from one mindset/topic to another (69T).

The Metacognition Index was also elevated for both raters (61T; 74T), though Arleen's fiancée's ratings did indicate a higher level of severity. Within the index, both raters indicated difficulties with Arleen's ability to get going on tasks, activities, and implement problem solving approaches (69T; 65T) and set goals, develop appropriate sequential steps, as well as organizing information (61T; 75T). Arleen's fiancée also sees some indication of difficulty with holding information in mind, encoding information, or generating goals, plans or steps to achieve goals (77T) and her ability to monitor her own performances for accuracy/completion (73T).

Complex Attention:

Complex attention was assessed through objective measures as well. I began with the CPT-3. While Arleen did have a valid performance on the standalone PVT used in this case, and she made a valid number of responses on the CPT-3 to be considered valid overall, there is a second embedded PVT on this test that shows that Arleen's approach to the task skewed more towards the "liberal" end of the spectrum (38T), rather than correctly balancing the two as instructed. This response style is associated with faster reaction times, and increase of commission (impulsive) errors, and a decrease of omission (inattentive) errors, which can end up skewing the results on the primary measures of those. This is a mild skew and Arleen really performed well overall, so I will present the data as is. All six measures of focused attention were within normal limits, and even a little better than the general population on inconsistency (36T). While she responded "a little fast" (42T), impulsivity was really not an issue as far as impulsive errors (58T) or perseverative errors (48T). Arleen also performed well on the measures of attentional capacity wherein vigilance (46T) and sustained attention (43T) were not an issue at all.

Additional measures of executive control were administered from the D-KEFS. On the Color-Word Interference Test, Arleen performed well and consistent with expectations on the Inhibition Condition (SS=115, 84%, high average) without making any errors (SS=110, 75%, high average). Her completion time was near equivalent when a shifting component was added (SS=110, 75%, high average), and again she made no errors (SS=110, 75%, high average). I also added the Verbal Fluency Test. Her scores were strong on the more frontally mediated Letter Fluency task (SS=110, 75%, high average), as well as the more temporally mediated Category Fluency task (SS=105, 63%). When a shifting component was added, she continued to perform well (SS=125, 95%) with her score even falling in the superior range. Thus, complex attention and executive control are consistently evidenced to be intact.

Higher order executive functions were assessed using the Tower Test, which involves skills of planning, judgment and mental organization. Arleen's Total Achievement score came in as superior (SS=125, 95%), which reflects intact efficiency for solving problems and making decisions. As to her efficiency, Arleen had no difficulty initiating (SS=105, 63%, average), maintained an average pace as she completed the task (SS=105, 63%), was accurate in her moves (SS=105, 63%, average) without impulsively violating the rules (SS=100, 50%).

The Wisconsin Card Sort Test (WCST) was administered to assess conceptual reasoning and problem solving with incorporation of corrective feedback to inhibit perseverative responding. Arleen completed all six categories, though it took her 20 trials to complete the first category (2-5%). Overall, her rate of Perseverative Errors and Perseverative Responses were solidly WNL (SS=96, 39%; 94, 34%), suggesting that Arleen does indeed benefit from feedback. Thus, from a cognitive standpoint, executive functions are also shown to be intact.

Memory:

I screened memory using the Repeatable Battery for the Assessment of Neuropsychological Status (RBANS). Arleen's immediate memory came in at an 87 (19%), which falls within the low average range. This is comprised of two verbal tasks, wherein there was a 2 SD difference between her performance on the rote (SS=105, 63%) relative to the contextual (SS=75, 5%). In going over these results during feedback, Arleen did say that she had "checked out" during the contextual portion and really did not feel that it was an accurate reflection of her abilities. Her Delayed Memory Index score came in at a 97 (42%) which is average. Her recall of the rote task continued to be average (51-75%) and despite initial issues on the contextual task, Arleen did retain that information following a delay (90, 25%). She also had perfect recognition on the rote task (51-75%). Thus, formal memory appears intact.

Psychological Functioning:

I had Arleen complete the Personality Assessment Inventory (PAI) to broadly assess psychological functioning. While all of the validity scale scores were technically WNL, there were subtle indicators of some, be overly confident and have little recognition of her own personal limitations (72T), and have low frustration tolerance (60T). As to the subscales that make up the Borderline Features, she endorsed Identity Problems (71T) beyond what would be expected during adulthood, a tendency to act impulsively without much consideration for consequences (72T), a propensity for rapid and extreme mood swings (63T), and some problematic/chaotic relationships (68T). Other areas of elevation included some somatic manifestations (Physical Complaints; 70T), some unconventional/unusual ideas (63T), and difficulties with concentration and decision-making (73T). As to the treatment scales, positively, she endorsed being interested in and motivated to participate in treatment, as well as a positive attitude toward the possibility of personal change and the importance of personal responsibility. Further, no indication of suicidal ideation or issues with anger management were endorsed.

As Bipolar Disorder was part of the differential, I had Arleen complete the General Behavior Inventory (GBI) to assess symptoms associated with Bipolar Disorders in greater detail. Arleen's endorsements resulted in an "Extremely High" (17.1%) probability of having a Bipolar Spectrum Disorder. I also performed a structured interview to assess for features of mania, and the results provided additional clarity. Arleen endorsed all nine symptoms sensitive to mania (increased energy, pressured speech, irritability, grandiosity, racing thoughts, decreased need for sleep, elation and euphoria, poor judgment, and distractibility). She further endorsed four of the five symptoms identified as having the highest level of specificity to mania, including elation and euphoria, decreased need for sleep, racing thoughts, and mood lability. Greater clarity came from discussing these results during the feedback session with Arleen, wherein she provided additional detail, as well as cited some of her experiences. She described her elated mood as "feeling like a drug" and in the moment she feels like she can complete all of her projects and wants to tackle the world and feels very creative. Once this feeling wears off, she feels a "crash" and feelings of depression set in. While much of what Arleen described certainly met some of the criteria, her experiences seemed to be more reflective of hypomanic states.

Based on the results of the PAI, and some lingering diagnostic questions, I had Arleen complete a broad-based inventory of Axis II symptoms (A-II Checklist). She endorsed a broad range of symptoms/features consistent with a number of personality disorders, which is unsurprising as there tends to be a great deal of overlap in symptoms between personality disorders, especially those within a specific "cluster." While she did endorse some traits associated with "Cluster B" disorders, much of what she endorsed has a high level of overlap with mood disorders. In fact, more than half of the symptoms she endorsed could be attributed to a mood presentation. Within this "Cluster," her highest endorsements were for Borderline and Histrionic traits. Overall, while Arleen is endorsing some level of problematic personality traits, this does not seem to fit neatly into any specific diagnosis within the personality disorders.

IMPRESSIONS

I have already had the opportunity to discuss these findings with Arleen directly during a feedback session, and I also was able to consult with her psychotherapist, Dr. Blue, regarding the details of the case. From a cognitive standpoint, a good deal of those findings were positive, as the majority of Arleen's profile came in WNL. Frontally-mediated abilities such as attentional capacity and control, as well as higher order executive functions were all intact. At worst, she showed an intrapersonal weakness with working memory, though again even that was within normal limits.

As to Arleen's psychological profile, she consistently endorsed a profile marked by distinct affective instability and impulsive behaviors – core diagnostic features of both bipolar disorder and borderline personality disorder. While there is limited literature examining the differential between bipolar type 2 and borderline personality disorder, those with bipolar tend to evolve between euthymia and depressed and elated moods for several days, with longer and more persistent episodes of depressive morbidity, while those with borderline tend to experience more frequent negative affectivity that takes longer to abate and creates more distress, have greater fluctuations of hostility and anger, positive affects do not tend to last for periods of days, though shifts tend to be more rapid and cyclical, and affects tend to oscillate between euthymia, negativity, or dysphoria. In discussing this differential with Arleen during feedback, she said that she tends to be a "fairly restrained person" and has periods of days where she will feel "wonderful or great." She did not feel that the hostile reactivity was part of her day-to-day and she did not feel some of the "extreme" shifts that may be part of a BPD. Thus, I am seeing Arleen's current presentation as more consistent with a **Bipolar II Disorder** (ICD-10=F31.81) as there is indication of mood lability and affective instability. Given that Arleen's descriptions seem to fit more with hypomanic episodes (periods that are less severe than a full manic episode), along with depressive episodes, a diagnosis of Bipolar II was made. To that end, based on the results of the current neuropsychological evaluation, I offer the following:

RECOMMENDATIONS

1. I encouraged that a copy of this report be provided to Arleen's PCP a release has not yet been signed, otherwise I would send this over to her directly. I want to make Dr. Gupta aware that I am not seeing objective evidence of deficits in attentional capacity, so I would not expect stimulants to be beneficial in this case. Instead, I am seeing episodes of hypomania and depression consistent with Bipolar II. During feedback, we discussed pharmacological interventions and that the usual target is mood with the impact of restoring euthymia from a depressive or euphoric state. Positive outcomes on affective stability are associated with mood stabilizers and antipsychotic drugs – with antipsychotics seemingly more beneficial than mood stabilizers on affective stability, with mood stabilizers more effective for mood improvement. Of course, I ultimately defer the medical decision-making to Arleen's primary care provider, and if I could be of any additional assistance, I would be happy to make myself available.
    a. If it would be preferred, I could also provide a referral to psychiatry.
2. I will be providing a copy of this report directly to Arleen's counselor, Dr. Blue, so that the findings can be utilized in the treatment planning process. I also have already had the opportunity to discuss these findings with her directly, and I think there is a lot that can be done with Dr. Blue. Certainly, continuing with psychotherapy is appropriate for addressing Arleen's affective instability and mood lability that led to the initial referral from Dr. Blue. I want to emphasize that psychotherapeutic intervention for bipolar disorders can optimize stability and psychosocial functioning by targeting important therapeutic areas that medication alone cannot address, including support, acceptance of the diagnosis, improving understanding/psychoeducation, optimizing medication adherence, managing interpersonal and other types of stress, and identifying and responding to early signs of mood and episode relapse. Suggested objectives of treatment are to encourage Arleen to discuss relevant issues that may operate as both risk and protective factors for relapse, to explore aspects and effects of the bipolar, and attempt to solve crucial personal, work-related, social and other problems that she may be facing. Most forms of CBT are applicable here and have been shown to have a credible record of success in treating these types of problems/conditions. Of course, I would be more than happy to make myself available for further direct consult in the future, and I appreciate the opportunity to participate in the care of your patients.
    a. During feedback, Arleen mentioned wanting to explore different career options and have some career counseling both into her current work.
3. I also discussed **neurofeedback** (neurofeedbackdefined.com) as an adjunct to her other as a potential intervention that would be appropriate in this case. Certainly, she would benefit from a protocol targeting affective instabilities and mood labilities. If she were interested, I would be happy to set her up.

Ultimately, I would be happy to stay actively involved in Arleen's case as she moves forward. I typically see the patient for a follow-up session in about a month so that I can address any additional questions and aid in the implementation of treatment interventions. From there, we can follow up at regular intervals or on an as-needed basis, depending on the needs of the patient and the treatment team. At those times, I would be interested in her level of improvement, and if there are any lingering or newly emerging symptoms, additional recommendations could be made.

Amanda Skierkiewicz, Ed.D., NCSP
Clinical Neuropsychologist
Licensed School Psychologist
IL License # 071-009993
IEIN #959665

ALS/jnd (dictated but not read for expediency)

Appendix F: Sample Neuropsychological Evaluation Age 38

Report by: Erica McConnell, Christina Zafiris, and Rik Carl D'Amato

UNIVERSITY OF
NORTHERN COLORADO

NEUROPSYCHOLOGICAL LABORATORY
PSYCHOLOGICAL SERVICES CLINIC

CONFIDENTIAL NEUROPSYCHOLOGICAL EVALUATION

NAME:	Mr. Steve Smith
ADDRESS:	1234 Red Rock Lake #12, Rifle, CO
HANDEDNESS:	Right
OCCUPATION:	Full-time college student
DATE OF BIRTH:	3-23-00
TEST DATES:	2-3-00, 2-4-00, 2-3-00, 2-7-00, 2-11-00
CURRENT AGE:	38 years

REASON FOR REFERRAL

Mr. Steve Smith's evaluation was completed to address concerns regarding his college academic progress. Mr. Smith's advisor referred him to the University of Northern Neuropsychological Laboratory due to concerns regarding how much time Steve was studying for his classes relative to the grades he was earning, according to Mr. Smith. Specifically, Mr. Smith indicated that he had failed classes including basic mathematics, basic algebra, and English. He reported that he has had to repeat several classes that he has failed. His adviser believes Steve may have learning or emotional disabilities. Mr. Smith also expressed concerns about test anxiety. He also indicated working hard and yet he was not able to pass these required classes.

EVALUATION PROCEDURES

Clinical Interview using the Neuropsychology Adult Questionnaire
Wechsler Adult Intelligence Scale-Third Edition (WAIS-III)
The Halstead-Reitan Neuropsychological Test Battery

The Category Test
The Tactual Performance Test
The Speech-Sounds Perception Test
The Seashore Rhythm Test
The Finger Oscillation Test
Aphasia Screening Test
Sensory-Perceptual Examination
The Trails A & B Tests
The Strength of Grip Test

Woodcock Johnson Tests of Achievement-Revised (WJ-R)
Nelson-Denny Reading Test
Wechsler Memory Scale-Third Edition (WMS-III)
Minnesota Multiphasic Personality Inventory (MMPI-2)
The Rorschach Projective Test

BACKGROUND INFORMATION

Mr. Smith, a 38-year old single male, is a full-time college student. He is pursuing a degree in Computer Information Systems, as well as certification in Local Area Networking. He eventually hopes to obtain a position as a web page developer or a position in which he provides technical support. Mr. Smith stated that he has never been married, and that he has a son, age 4, who lives with him.

Mr. Smith reported that he lived with his parents and his sister while growing up. He described his relationship with his father as distant, indicating that they participated in activities together such as hunting, but that he and his father never talked a lot. He indicated that the nature of his relationship with his mother was much the same, and that he felt that his parents, who are currently married, are not happy. Mr. Smith indicated that he felt loved by his parents, but not respected. He explained that he and his sister have led very different lives, and that his sister is currently a school principal. Mr. Smith revealed that he was close to his sister while growing up and that they got along well in childhood; however, they are very distant now and rarely talk.

Mr. Smith indicated that to the best of his knowledge, he did not have any difficulty accomplishing developmental milestones within a normal age range. He recalled no health problems while growing up. Mr. Smith reported his first brain injury that he was knocked unconscious for a few moments at about age 5 when he fell while jumping from a high fence to a swing set. He indicated that he received no medical treatment for this incident.

Regarding academic history, Mr. Smith stated that he dropped out of school at the age of 16, and began doing construction work. He reported that writing has always given him trouble, and that he reads very slowly. Mr. Smith reported that he earned his GED, and also completed an apprenticeship in welding. He stated that he was employed in commercial construction for 20 years prior to pursuing an Associate's degree in Computer Information Systems 3. Mr. Smith explained that computer advances in commercial construction stimulated his interest in the computer field. He reported that he has failed classes in basic mathematics, basic algebra, and English while pursuing his degree. He specifically cited difficulties in writing essays, reading very slowly, and difficulty with basic math skills.

Mr. Smith confided that he is at risk of losing his financial aid due to his low-grade point average. He stated that he has received regular tutoring throughout his matriculation at college. Mr. Smith expressed great frustration regarding his academic situation because the tutoring, along with several hours per day of independent studying, have resulted in little academic progress.

Regarding health history, Mr. Smith reported that he had a life-threatening accident approximately 8 years ago while he was employed as a construction worker. He explained that a ladder fell on him, knocking him backwards off a house and onto a sawhorse. He had an extended period of hospitalization but refused back surgery. This resulted in five years of physical therapy for serious back problems. He also reported that his knee was rebuilt due to a football accident, and that he has a pin in his elbow as a result of a serious martial arts injury. Steve reported at one time he enjoyed intense physical workouts which keep him fit and in shape.

Mr. Smith indicated that he smoked dope and experimented with other drugs in high school but that he no longer engages in recreational drug use. He also explained that he has lost the ability to hear high frequency sounds, and he attributes this to his gun hobby, which he has had since the age of 12. He owned his first gun at age 13 and regularly hunted with his father as well as other friends. Steve won some marksmanship awards during his teen years. Mr. Smith also stated that he has had a high pitched ringing in both ears for a long time and he wonders if this is related to his disregard for ear protect when shooting.

Mr. Smith stated that he has been exposed to many different chemicals throughout his 20 years in commercial construction. These included glues, solvents, asbestos, paints, attic insulation, and asphalt when roofing. Initially, this physical work created an interest in Martial Arts with some of his construction buddies. He initially committed to this lifestyle and Steve won some competitive state Karate awards. At age 22 Steve was offered a contract for male modeling which he did not purse. He views this as one of his greatest mistakes. Mr. Smith gave up these activities because his team/coach complained about his drinking and he was unwilling to stop.

Mr. Smith stated that he likes to live on the edge and to that end was involved for many years in competitive motorcycle racing. During this time, Steve lost consciousness approximately five times while involved in motorcycle wrecks. He stated that during some of these episodes he lost consciousness for "only" short periods of time. Steve indicated that each time he felt he suffered significant brain damage although he never sought medical attention. After these numerous serious accidents he *worried for his life* and consequently Mr. Smith stated that he no longer races bikes given that he now has a son.

Mr. Smith also revealed that he received a near-lethal strike from a rattlesnake while hunting in the Colorado mountains approximately 12-years ago. He described this incident as very serious, because he received anti-venom for approximately six months and reportedly, he almost died but made what the Flight-for-Life workers called an *unbelievable* return from near death. Mr. Smith indicated that his hand where he received the strike continues to get cold and numb at times.

Mr. Smith confided that he was severely depressed for approximately one year following the construction accident which seriously injured his back. He stated that he took antidepressants for approximately one year, and attributed his depression to being unable to work due to injuries. Mr. Smith also revealed that he drank a lot during a custody battle with the mother of his child, in which he received sole custody of his son. He stated that he was "drunk six days a week" and that this lasted for approximately one year. Mr. Smith stated that he currently has no driver's license, as it was suspended for seven years due to various DUI charges. This prompted Steve to join AA and he has been alcohol-free for three years.

Mr. Smith also indicated problems with insomnia, and stated that sometimes he sleeps only 4 to 5 hours a night, and has difficulty getting to sleep. Mr. Smith consistently stated that he has low self-esteem. When given a list of words and asked to describe himself, Mr. Smith circled several words, including useless, worthless, inadequate, and stupid. Mr. Smith denied any suicidal ideation or thoughts of hurting others. It is significant that Mr. Smith reported that he has steadily lost weight in the past few years, and Steve voiced concerns about malnutrition due to financial concerns.

Regarding social relationships, Mr. Smith described himself as antisocial and cold. He explained that he has become antisocial because he no longer trusts people. He stated that he no longer approaches people for friendship, and that he has great difficulty talking to people in social situations. He indicated that relatives and friends would describe him as cold and distant. Mr. Smith specifically stated that this is one area of his life which he would like to change, and Steve wants to learn "how to talk to people." While Steve reported he is often approached by women, he indicated several failed relationships which he believes were short lived based on his commitment issues. He would like to change this part of his life.

Mr. Smith stated that his hobbies include watching sports and playing video games. He explained that he used to enjoy outdoor activities like hunting, playing sports, camping, and hunting, however, he no longer has the time or the resources to engage in these activities. He described himself as very mechanically adept, and explained that he likes working with his hands, specifically construction work, and working on motorcycles and cars. Steve also enjoys helping others when he can.

BEHAVIORAL OBSERVATIONS

Mr. Smith was seen on five occasions. He arrived on time and was appropriately dressed for each session, which lasted three to four hours. He appeared tall and physically attractive but was distant. Mr. Smith seemed to put forth his best effort on each task. Even when faced with tasks that were difficult for him, Mr. Smith was persistent and tried to complete all items. Mr. Smith did have difficulty on one task, in which he was asked to write a sentence about a given topic. He tried for several minutes to think of a sentence to complete this task, however, he indicated that he had gone blank, and could not complete this task.

It was noted that Mr. Smith became defensive during the clinical interview, particularly when asked questions regarding personal relationships and other information related to learning and his neuropsychological status. He appeared to be somewhat agitated, and asked the examiner why this information was important. Steve stated that many of these issues were subjects he did not discuss with anyone.

Mr. Smith listened to directions carefully, appeared to figure out how to complete tasks quickly, and was persistent in completing every task. He appeared truthful and seemed committed to completing all related activities. He was obviously dedicated to completing this evaluation. These results appear to be an accurate estimate of Mr. Smith's current level of neuropsychological functioning.

EVALUATION RESULTS

The Wechsler Adult Intelligence Scale-Third Edition (WAIS-III)

The WAIS-III is a general measure of cognitive ability. Information is provided regarding verbal and nonverbal skills through subtests measuring specific abilities. Responses to items on the WAIS-III are reported as scaled scores which, on average, fall between 7 and 13. Average cognitive scores are defined as falling between 90 and 110.

Verbal Scale	Score	Performance Scale	Scores
Information	9	Picture Completion	
Digit Span	8	Picture Arrangement	10
Vocabulary	11	Block Design	10
Arithmetic	10	Symbol Search	8
Comprehension	9	Digit Symbol	6
Letter-Number		Matrix Reasoning	11
Sequencing	9		
Similarities	11		

WAIS-III			
Index Areas	Standard Scores	Percentile Ranks	Descriptions
Verbal	97	27	Average
Performance	91	37	Average
Full Scale	95	37	Average
Verbal Comprehension	101	53	Average
Perceptual Organization	95	37	Average
Working Memory	94	34	Average
Processing Speed	84	14	Low Average

Mr. Smith's scores place him in the low average to average range of intelligence. It appears that Mr. Smith's nonverbal and verbal abilities are equally well-developed. Mr. Smith demonstrated no relative strengths or weaknesses on either the verbal or nonverbal scales, however he did exhibit a deficit in his ability to process information quickly. This may be related to some of his difficulties completing assignments rapidly.

Woodcock-Johnson Tests of Achievement-Revised (WJ-R)

The WJ-R is a comprehensive test of academic achievement. Basic areas such as mathematics; reading, and writing are assessed. Average Standard Scores on this measure range from 85 to 110.

Areas	Scores	Percentiles	Ranges
Letter-Word Identification	110	75	Avg
Passage Comprehension	98	43	Avg
Calculation	97	43	Avg
Applied Problems	89	24	Low Avg
Dictation	78	07	Low
Writing Samples	92	30	Avg
Proofing	77	06	Low
Writing Fluency	75	05	Low
Standard Clusters			
Broad Reading	104	61	Avg
Broad Mathematics	93	32	Avg
Broad Written Language	80	09	Low
Supplemental Clusters			
Basic Writing Skills	78	07	Low
Written Expression	80	09	Low Avg

Mr. Smith's academic scores varied greatly, ranging from Average to Low. Overall, his broad reading and mathematics skills fell in the Average range. These scores are commensurate with his overall WAIS-III scores. Within the area of mathematics, Mr. Smith's skill in performing mathematical calculations involving addition, subtraction, multiplication, and division is better developed than his ability to use these skills to solve practical problems in mathematics. However, Mr. Smith's broad written language skills fell in *the* Low Average range, indicating that his broad reading and mathematical abilities are clearly better developed than his written language abilities.

In the area of written language, Mr. Smith's responses demonstrated quality of written expression and content. In contrast, his ability to provide written responses requiring knowledge of spelling, punctuation, capitalization, and word usage is not as welt developed as the content of his written expression. In addition, Mr. Smith's ability to identify mistakes in capitalization, word usage, or spelling, and to correct these mistakes is not as well developed as the quality of his written responses. It appears that the mechanics of writing, such as spelling and punctuation, give Mr. Smith difficulty, not the content of the written response. Also with regard to written language abilities, Mr. Smith's written responses were of better quality and quantity when he was allowed unlimited time to respond versus when he was required to respond under timed conditions. This may be related to his speed of cognitive processing when he is required to produce written material.

The Nelson-Denny Reading Test

The Nelson-Denny Reading Test provides an assessment of student ability in three areas of reading: vocabulary, reading comprehension, and reading rate. This measure focuses on reading within a set time-period. Average standard scores ranges fall from the 25th to the 75th percentiles.

Subtests	Percentile Ranks
Vocabulary	52
Comprehension	01
Reading Rate	01

Wechsler Memory Scale-Third Edition (WMS-III)

The WMS-III is an individually administered battery of learning, memory, and working memory measures. The WMS-III focuses on immediate, delayed, and working memory. Each of these domains is tested in two modalities, auditory and visual. A half hour delayed recall of both verbal and visual material is reported.

Each category is reported so average scores are defined between 90 and 110.

Index	Index Score	Percentiles
Auditory Immediate	114	82
Visual Immediate	109	73
Immediate Memory	114	82
Auditory Delayed	114	82
Visual Delayed	100	50
Auditory Recognition Delayed	110	75
General Memory	109	73
Working Memory	111	77

Overall, Mr. Smith's memory abilities appear to be better developed than his cognitive abilities. All of Mr. Smith's scores fell in the Average or High Average range, with his General Memory abilities falling in the Average range. His visual and auditory memory abilities are equally well-developed when he is required to remember information immediately after it is presented. However, Mr. Smith's ability to remember orally presented information after a delay is better developed than his ability to remember visually presented information after a delay. This may have implications for his learning style.

The Halstead-Reitan Neuropsychological Test Battery (HRNB)

The Category Test:

The category test is a measure of abstract reasoning; concept formation, and problem solving. The test requires the client to select numbers corresponding to a visual presentation, with immediate feedback provided. Mr. Smith's score fell within the average range of functioning.

The Tactual Performance Test (TPT):

The TPT is a formboard that requires a blindfolded patient to place blocks in appropriate slots. This test provides information on tactual discrimination, sensory integration, and spatial memory. Mr. Smith received a score in the average range on all timed elements of the test. He performed in, the average range on the memory and location elements of the test.

***The Speech-Sounds Perception Test* (SSPT):**

The SSPT is a measure of verbal-auditory discrimination, integration, and attention. A tape of nonsense words is presented to the patient, who selects the appropriate written response from alternatives offered for each item. Mr. Smith's score on this instrument fell in the average range. This is interesting given that the test must be completed rapidly and no extra time is offered to process responses. One the test begins it continues until it ends.

***The Seashore-Rhythm Test* (SRT):**

The SRT is a measure of nonverbal auditory discrimination, auditory perception, attention and concentration. On this test,the client identifies pairs of 30 different musical beats or patterns as being the same or different. Mr. Smith received a score which fell in the mildly/moderately impaired range. His ability to process nonverbal information rapidly or in a timed fashion seems impaired and this may relate to his problems following directions especially if they related to nonverbal sounds especially if the task may be impacted by anxiety.

***The Finger Oscillation Test or Tapping Test* (FOT):**

The FOT is a measure of fine motor speed and manual dexterity. A comparison of the tapping speeds of the dominant and the non-dominant hand are often an indication of the functioning of the left and right hemispheres. Mr. Smith's scores on this measure fell in the average range for his right hand (dominant) and in the mildly/moderately impaired range with his left hand (non-dominant).

***Aphasia Screening Test* (AST):**

The AST is considered a broad band measure of both language and nonverbal functions, with items requiring naming, copying, spelling, reading, and writing. Mr. Smith experienced some difficulty copying geometric shapes and pictures, and performed in the moderately impaired range.

***The Sensory-Perceptual Examination* (SPE):**

The SPE is a measure of tactile, auditory, and visual modalities. The patient is asked to respond to stimuli such as light finger snapping next to the ears, light touches on the hands and face, and movement of the examiner's fingers in peripheral fields of vision. Mr. Smith's scores on this measure fell in the average range of functioning for visual perception. His scores fell in the mildly/moderately impaired range for both tactile and auditory perception, since he demonstrated a deficit with his left tactile ability and left hearing ability.

The Trail Making A & B:

Trail Making A and B are measures of visual-motor integration and mental flexibility. Mr. Smith completed Trails A and Trails B in times which suggest average perceptual and problem solving abilities, as well as motor speed and coordination.

The Strength of Grip Test (SGT):

This test measures motor strength in the client's upper extremities. Trials are performed with each hand, beginning with the preferred hand and alternating to the nonpreferred hand. Mr. Smith scored in the average range with his dominant hand and in the average range with his non-dominant hand, although his non-dominant hand was significantly weaker than his dominant hand. These scores should be considered in light of his injuries and rattlesnake bite.

The Halstead-Reitan Impairment Index

Overall, Mr. Smith received a 0.1 Impairment Index on the Halstead-Reitan. This impairment score means that Mr. Smith scored in the Normal range on 90% of the Halstead-Reitan tests. The impairment index is a measure of the consistency of brain functioning.

The Halstead-Reitan General Neuropsychological Deficit Scale

On the General Neuropsychological Deficit Scale (GNDS), Mr. Smith scored in the average range. The GNDS measures the level of functioning on the tests and is more comprehensive than the Impairment Index. The Left NDS and Right NDS are scores that compare the functioning of the left and right hemispheres. Mr. Smith exhibited a significant deficiency of functioning of his right hemisphere when compared to functioning of his left hemisphere. Overall, Mr. Smith's performance indicated that he appeared to have normal functioning in all areas except for an impaired ability on measures of auditory and tactile sensory perception, and fine motor functioning with the left side manifesting his deficiencies.

The Minnesota Multiphasic Personality Inventory (MMPI-2)

The MMPI-2 is a self-report inventory in which questions are rated as true or false. Scales reveal a picture of an patient's behaviors, traits, level of adjustment, attitude toward the world, and characteristic beliefs. This is a widely-used personality measure which provides significant information concerning psychiatric related personality issues.

Mr. Smith's profile should be interpreted with caution due to questionable validity. It appears that he took a defensive approach to the inventory, which indicated that he tried to present himself in an overly positive light by attempting to create an unrealistically favorable view of their moral character and psychological adjustment. Patients with such profiles tend to be unwilling to admit even minor flaws and claim adherence to excessively high moral standards. This measure did offer insight and information concerning Mr. Smith's feelings and daily functioning.

Individuals with similar profiles to Mr. Smith's appear to be both anxious and depressed. Of concern was Mr. Smith's elevated depression scale score. Mr. Smith reported feeling unhappy, uninterested in daily activities, useless at times, and he indicated feeling that life is not worthwhile. Steve also indicated that he has had periods when he could not get going, that he has difficulty in starting to do things, and that his life is a strain. Patients with responses similar to Mr. Smith's tend to report feeling inadequate and like a failure at school or on the job. In addition, individuals with a response patterns similar to Mr. Smith's may have problems coping with everyday life, and may fear losing control of their thoughts. His feelings of hopelessness may be related to his repeated school failure as well as a significant learning disorder.

Mr. Smith endorsed items indicating that his sleep is fitful and disturbed, and that he often goes to sleep with thoughts bothering him, suggesting that he may be experiencing periods of worry and anxiety at this time. Individuals with responses similar to Mr. Smith's seem to lack self-confidence, feel that life is empty, may be apathetic, and are prone to worrying. Moreover, patients with responses like Mr. Smith's are often viewed by others as introverted, reclusive, and aloof; they tend to maintain psychological distance and avoid interpersonal involvement.

Mr. Smith indicated feeling confused and misunderstood. Individuals with Mr. Smith's response pattern view their home situation as unpleasant, and lacking in love, support, and understanding. They tend to view their family as critical and controlling. Patients with responses like Mr. Smith's reported feeling alienated, isolated, and estranged from others. Steve also reported feeling lonely, unhappy, and uninvolved. Mr. Smith tends to blame others for his problems and reported finding life uninteresting and unrewarding. He also indicated feeling regret and remorse over his past actions. Mr. Smith may resent authority and reported that he has had trouble with the law. He reported definite opinions about right and wrong and Steve tends to stand up for his beliefs. Similar individuals also may report a history of behavior problems in school.

Mr. Smith endorsed items suggesting that someone has it in for him and that he believes he is a condemned person. Patients with Mr. Smith's response pattern report that they have feelings of being unfairly blamed or punished. Steve reported feeling suspicious, distrusting others, and tending to blame others for his problems. He may tend to be hypersensitive and overly responsive to the reactions of others, and may be hostile, resentful, and argumentative. Steve looks for risk and excitement in his life although it may have negative implications.

The Rorschach Projective Test

The Rorschach is a measurement of an individual's personality based. on their responses to inkblots. Mr. Smith completed the Rorschach with 25 responses, therefore this record is likely to be valid.

Mr. Smith appears to have insufficient resources to deal with the frustrations of everyday living and is most likely experiencing distress that extends beyond transient or situational difficulties. Mr. Smith's responses indicated that his preferred coping style is most likely extratensive and may be pervasive throughout all problem solving or coping activities. His responses were significant on the Coping Deficiency Index indicating that in coping with stressful situations and general life conditions, he may act impulsively or with anger. He may also be prone to withdraw from emotional or complex situations.

Mr. Smith's unique responses indicated perceptual distortions, problems with reality testing, and an over-commitment to individuality. His responses indicated that his ideation may be rigid and he is probably resistant to change. Steve may have difficulty in organizing his thought processes and he probably makes guesses based on minimal information rather than pursuing greater understanding. Mr. Smith's responses implied that he may lack control of his responses to emotional situations, and may have a personality style that makes it difficult to handle anger.

Mr. Smith indicated significant depression suggesting that he is experiencing low self-esteem, poor relationships with others, and that he feels he is in persistent distress. His responses also indicated that he may have a lack of interest in others or problems with his identity and self-image. Mr. Smith may have little need to interact with others, because he has abandoned his need for closeness and dependency. He also may be withdrawn from most if not all his relationships.

EVALUATION SUMMARY

Mr. Smith's evaluation was completed to address concerns regarding his academic difficulties, possible learning and/or emotional disabilities and test anxiety. Mr. Smith demonstrated a history suggesting significant brain trauma both from internal and external forces. This included repeated drug abuse, interpersonal difficulties, and emotional/communicative problems. His interest areas such as motorcycle racing, and mountain hunting, coupled with his employment injuries, frequent crashes, and accidents all seem to have led to his current academic problems. Given a review of his history, including accidents and relationships, it is easy to see why he may feel distrusting, disconnected, and angry. However, Steve would also like to have a positive relationship with his son and be a better father.

Mr. Smith's social-emotional, financial, and family stressors have also contributed to his psychological and physical difficulties. Other medical and neurological issues considered with his difficulty sleeping and his reported lack of food, considered considering his family obligations and responsibilities such as caring for his son, all add to his level of disfunction and create additional obstacles. Mr. Smith would like to improve many of these issues and he seems to be making psychological progress when his history is considered. His psychological evaluation indicated long-term emotional distress, difficulty coping, and life-long problems with others,

Mr. Smith's scores suggested that he has average cognitive abilities, with his verbal and nonverbal abilities being equally well-developed. Mr. Smith demonstrated a deficit in his ability to process information quickly. On achievement measures, Mr. Smith's scores ranged from average to low on measures of mathematics, reading, and writing achievement. Mr. Smith's broad reading skins and broad mathematics skills fell in the average range, and were commensurate with his cognitive processing scores. However, his broad written language abilities fell in the low average range. Mr. Smith's written responses demonstrated quality of content, however it seemed that it was the mechanics of writing, such as spelling, punctuation, and capitalization, that gave him great difficulty.

Of particular interest was the significant discrepancy between Mr. Smith's intellectual/verbal score and his score on the following academic measure that evaluated his basic writing skills, his broad written language, and written expression skills. This suggests a Learning Disorder in the area of written expression. The discrepancy was based on Mr. Smith's verbal score because he demonstrated neuropsychological processing deficits that seemed to impact his performance scores.

Mr. Smith exhibited a significant deficiency of functioning of his right hemisphere when compared to functioning of his left hemisphere. Overall, Mr. Smith's performance indicated that he appeared to have normal functioning in most areas with the exception of an impaired ability on measures of auditory and tactile-sensory perception, and fine motor functioning with his left hemisphere manifesting his deficiencies.

Erica McConnell, Ph.D.
Neuropsychology Fellow

Christina Zafiris, Ph.D.
Neuropsychology Fellow

Rik Carl D'Amato, Ph.D.
Neuropsychology Laboratory Director
Licensed School Psychologist
APA Fellow in Clinical Neuropsychology and School Psychology

RECOMMENDATIONS FOR THIS EVALUATION ARE LEFT FOR THE STUDENT TO COMPLETE AS A PROJECT FOR THIS APPENDIX.

Index

R. C. D'Amato et al. (eds.), *Understanding the Biological Basis of Behavior*,
https://doi.org/10.1007/978-3-030-59162-5

W